PENGUIN BOOKS
WORLD CLASS IN INDIA

Born in India, educated in the US and currently living in Europe, SUMANTRA GHOSHAL is a teacher, author and consultant in the field of international management. He is also founding dean of the Indian School of Business in Hyderabad. He has published eight books, over forty-five articles and several award-winning case studies. *Managing across Borders: The Transnational Solution*, co-authored with Christopher A. Bartlett, has been listed as one of the fifty most influential management books.

Author of the best-sellers *Business Maharajas* and *Business Legends*, GITA PIRAMAL is one of India's foremost business writers. A former freelance journalist with a Ph.D. in business history, Gita has been writing and commenting on Indian business for over twenty years for leading publications such as UK's *Financial Times* and India's *Economic Times*. She is now the managing editor of *The Smart Manager*, India's first world-class management magazine.

Educated in India and America, SUDEEP BUDHIRAJA is a career banker having spent eighteen years with Citibank N.A. As a member of the bank's international staff he has held challenging assignments in five countries across a range of areas including treasury, commercial banking, private banking, investment management and transaction banking. A visiting Research Fellow at the London Business School from 1997 to 1999, he worked with Sumantra Ghoshal on his India project, developing various case studies, which are included in this book.

Praise for the book

'The book fills a very vital gap-cum-need of having comprehensive cases on Indian companies. I would definitely like to use the cases in my corporate strategy classes...a commendable effort on the part of the authors.'

—Dr Sharad Sarin, Faculty, XLRI Jamshedpur

'The book meets a long-standing felt need of management education in India... *World Class in India* is a well-structured book... All the cases are exhaustive and complete. These provide a lot of learning for the students and practitioners of management. Diversity of content is a major feature of this book...this casebook would never get dated. Almost all cases have been provided with appendices giving relevant data, financial details and other information which help the understanding and analysis of the case material... Academic fraternity in general will benefit from the book. The book would provide an excellent platform to begin with for serious researchers and case writers... The book has promise of a "must read" for all students of management and deserves unconditional endorsement from the academic fraternity.'

—Dr H.H. Mankad, Director, Narsee Monjee Institute of Management Studies, Mumbai

'The book itself is world class and has come in handy to teach management students industry-based case studies…it will serve as a handbook for classroom discussion. I find it will be useful for general management and perspective management papers for all MBA courses.'

—Dr Bala Krishnamoorthy, Faculty, Jamnalal Bajaj Institute of Management Studies, Mumbai

'*World Class in India* is a well-written collection of in-depth case studies… The book is a welcome addition to the existing literature dealing with case studies useful for both practising managers and academics engaged in teaching and research and moulding future professionals in the area…it presents a comprehensive, coordinated, cohesive and accurate exposition of twenty world-class companies in India… I recommend this book for serious reading and study by all those who do management courses in leading business schools.'

—Dr P. Sudarsanan Pillai, Director, School of Management Studies, Cochin University of Science and Technology, Kochi

'(*World Class in India*) does try to address a gap that exists in management education in India—the absence of well-researched cases in the Indian context. The cases are quite well developed and written. They cover a broad spectrum of organizations in India so [they] can be a good resource for cases.'

—Dr Abhoy K. Ojha, Associate Professor, Indian Institute of Management Bangalore

WORLD CLASS IN INDIA

A Casebook of Companies in Transformation

Sumantra Ghoshal
Gita Piramal
Sudeep Budhiraja

PENGUIN BOOKS

PENGUIN BOOKS
Published by the Penguin Group
Penguin Books India Pvt Ltd, 11 Community Centre, Panchsheel Park, New Delhi 110 017, India
Penguin Group (USA) Inc., 375 Hudson Street, New York, New York 10014, USA
Penguin Group (Canada), 90 Eglinton Avenue East, Suite 700, Toronto, Ontario, M4P 2Y3, Canada (a division of Pearson Penguin Canada Inc.)
Penguin Books Ltd, 80 Strand, London WC2R 0RL, England
Penguin Ireland, 25 St Stephen's Green, Dublin 2, Ireland (a division of Penguin Books Ltd)
Penguin Group (Australia), 250 Camberwell Road, Camberwell, Victoria 3124, Australia (a division of Pearson Australia Group Pty Ltd)
Penguin Group (NZ), cnr Airborne and Rosedale Road, Albany, Auckland 1310, New Zealand (a division of Pearson New Zealand Ltd)
Penguin Group (South Africa) (Pty) Ltd, 24 Sturdee Avenue, Rosebank, Johannesburg 2196, South Africa

Penguin Books Ltd, Registered Offices: 80 Strand, London WC2R 0RL, England

First published by Penguin Books India 2001

10 9 8 7 6 5

Grateful acknowledgement is made to the following for permission to reproduce the following material:
Cosmode and Dharni P. Sinha for case 15;
Indian Institute of Management, Bangalore, and J. Ramachandran for cases 3 and 5;
Indian Institute of Management, Calcutta, and Sushil Khanna for case 4;
International Institute for Management Development for case 9;
Jay Anand for case 14;
London Business School and Arvind Sahay for case 8;
London Business School for cases 1, 2, 6, 7, 12, 13, 16, 18, 19 and 20;
London Business School and Donald Sull for case 11;
School of International Business, University of New South Wales, and Pradeep Kanta Ray for cases 10 and 17.

For sale in India only

Typeset in Sabon by Mantra Virtual Services, New Delhi
Printed by Saurabh Printers Pvt. Ltd, New Delhi

For Raj

CONTENTS

ACKNOWLEDGEMENTS

Operating out of a small windowless cubicle, Mohan Keyyath is an MBA with a gold medal. He is also secretary to Rahul Bajaj, chairman of Bajaj Auto. On 9 January 1998, Rahul handed Mohan a letter with the terse instruction to look after the matter. The matter in question was a request from Sumantra to write a case study on Bajaj Auto. This simple letter created hours of work for Mohan as he tracked the travel schedules of some thirty busy people and co-ordinated their programmes so that they could be simultaneously available at Bajaj Auto's bustling Akurdi plant for two-and-a-half days of intensive interviewing. And for almost three years after that, requests for odd little bits of information kept popping up, stretching Mohan's patience to the limit. Over at Reliance, P.P. Venkatesh played a similar role. As did Phiroza David and Arnaz Bhiwandiwala at Hindustan Lever. And all the other secretaries working in the two dozen or so companies covered in *World Class in India*.

We would like to thank the CEOs, managers and staff of the companies who made this work possible. They willingly gave their time, and more importantly, honestly and generously shared their knowledge. This book is in your hands because thirty researchers painstakingly interviewed over 350 managers possessing a cumulative minimum of 4,500 years' worth of hands-on experience in Indian industry. It is not possible here to thank every manager individually, but we would like them to know that had it not been for their insights and invaluable contribution, neither this volume nor the companion book, *Managing Radical Change*, could have been written.

Generally cases such as these, on average, take a minimum of 200 man hours to write—and this is not counting thinking time. The researchers who participated in this study are mentioned both on the contents page as well as on the opening page of each case, and we would like to take this opportunity not only to thank them but also acknowledge the tremendous hard work they put in. However, this is just half the account. In most cases, the case-writing process was funded by the business schools where the researchers teach. Not only did these eight schools enable the research process, they also freely and promptly donated us the copyrights necessary to publish the cases in this book. These were wonderfully munificent gestures, especially on the part of the Aditya V. Birla India Centre at the London Business School.

The story of this book would not be complete without the efforts of a few others. It fell to the unenviable lot of Gita's secretaries, Sindhu Sabale and Marie Pinto in Mumbai, and Sumantra's secretary, Sharon Wilson in London, to convert reams of notes and data into impeccable computerised text. They not only cheerfully accepted this onerous burden, but often went to extraordinary lengths to track and correct small details. Over at Penguin, a small army led by Krishan Chopra worked overtime to bring out this volume.

All of us involved in this project underestimated the effort this volume would require. For example, more than ten ways of writing a date had to be made uniform so that you, dear reader, would not get distracted from the main facts of the case. Arguments flew back and forth across the world—from Delhi to Sydney, Mumbai to Ohio and London to Calcutta—as we tried to simplify the tables, charts, graphs and figures. This book is a first rate example of virtual e-working and e-collaboration. Hundreds of people were involved, all of whom had difficult schedules, all of whom were on the move constantly. Yet email kept us together, as well as the desire to contribute to this project.

Compiling this volume was a rewarding and enriching experience. We hope you enjoy reading it as much as we have putting it together.

April 2001 Sumantra Ghoshal
Mumbai Gita Piramal
Sudeep Budhiraja

BECAUSE COURAGE CANNOT BE TAUGHT

In his autobiography, Nelson Mandela recalls his dismay when he boarded an airplane and found that the pilot was African. With shock, he realised that his reaction was exactly what he had been fighting against all his life. Mandela was discussing racism, but the same psychology surfaces in commerce. There are many in the economically developed parts of the world who expect companies from developing countries like India to be inferior not only in their products and services but also in their overall managerial sophistication. Unfortunately, Indian managers often share that perception. It is this psychological barrier that is perhaps the biggest stumbling block, preventing Indian companies from starting on the transformational journey to becoming world class in their strategies, organisation and management.

The primary purpose of *World Class in India* is to help both practising managers and management students in India overcome this psychological barrier. Indian companies can be world class. Some already are. This book of cases identifies and tells the tale of a few that are and others who are striving to become world class. Undoubtedly, there are many more Indian companies that could have been included in the list. If some companies could do it, others can too.

The French writer Antoine de Saint-Exupéry created a striking metaphor: 'If you want to build a ship, don't drum up men to go to the forest to gather wood, saw it, and nail the planks together. Instead, teach them the desire for the sea.' That is what Indian managers will need to become world class—not just concepts, tools and prescriptions, but the desire for excellence; the desire to be the best.

But how do you develop a desire for the sea? By seeing it. By experiencing it. By developing a passion for it.

Professor Chris Christensen, one of Harvard's most celebrated teachers, defended the case method in a lovely little piece titled 'Because Wisdom Cannot be Taught'. Researchers and teachers tend to tell and write what they know—to point out what, to their thinking and analysis, are the right things to do. They feel they have the right answers, and they attempt to give these to others, thus avoiding the need for those others to work things out for themselves. The accompanying book, *Managing Radical Change*, provides the concepts, frameworks and suggestions on what Indian companies need to do to become world class, based on our research in several Indian companies. The purpose of this book is to expose readers not to the processed and digested analysis, but to the raw data. It is stories that have historically triggered the human imagination and shaped people's aspirations. Here are the actual stories.

Taking Christensen's ideas one step further, if wisdom cannot be taught, courage certainly cannot, either. That is the rationale for this book, which tells the tales without interpretation or analysis: to allow the readers to create their own interpretations and take from each story whatever appeals most to them. If the lives of seafarers can create a desire for the sea, then the tales of world-class companies can create the courage to start on the journey to excellence.

Our hope in writing this casebook is to appeal to two audiences: MBA students and reflective managers. For MBA students, these reasonably detailed and current cases on some of India's most admired companies can enrich their courses and class discussions. Given the paucity of Indian case examples, many MBA instructors are forced to use old cases of foreign companies. While this handful of cases will by no means solve the problem, we hope that this book will at least make a small contribution in making some MBA classes more relevant to the Indian corporate context. Perhaps these cases can be used in an elective course on 'Managing Radical Change'. Alternatively, they can be used in existing courses on strategy, organisational behaviour or change management. Irrespective of whether the cases are formally used within any particular course, MBA students can benefit from them by relating them to class discussions and using them to understand, elaborate or challenge existing conceptual frameworks. Above all, we hope that the cases will give them inspiration and courage to become active change agents themselves in their professional careers.

For practising managers, the stories may serve as mirrors in which they can see their own situations reflected, or discover useful ideas and actions that can help address their own opportunities and challenges.

The case studies in *World Class in India* are divided into four sections: The Challenge of Change, Building the Future, Revitalising People, Organisations and Relationships, and Transforming Leadership Philosophy. Some users of this book may like to read the cases in the order in which they appear. The order is not entirely arbitrary; it is shaped by the conceptual structure of *Managing Radical Change*. Others may read the stories in a different order, focussing first on those whose situations are of greater interest or direct relevance. For both groups of readers, a quick summary of each case is provided to serve as a map.

The Challenge of Change

Almost every company in India is struggling with this issue: what to change, and how to change. Consulting companies are enjoying a boom period helping companies find solutions. Academic seminars on this topic are proliferating. Every airport bookshop is bursting with guru-speak. Generally they advocate similar actions: take the lead, shape a shared vision, mobilise commitment, create an action plan, monitor performance. We all know the formula. But why is something which is so easy to see, so hard to do? That too when the stakes are so high, when it is known that if companies don't take up the challenge of change, they will fall by the wayside?

As India moves away from a seller's market to a buyer's one, the need to woo customers is gradually seeping into India's corporate sector, driving companies to reassess the way they operate. Slipping market share is the challenge examined in the first two case studies and how two very different companies responded is recounted in 'The Transformation of a Giant' (Case 1) and 'Levers for Change' (Case 2). In the case of Bajaj Auto, its rival was Hero Honda, a joint venture between two world class companies—one Indian and the other Japanese. In the case of Hindustan Lever, competition emerged from Nirma—a local company in the so-called 'unorganised' sector. In both cases, the new kids on the block opened up untapped consumer segments.

The two giants countered with very dissimilar strategies. Bajaj Auto looked internally and fixed itself. In some ways, the story of Bajaj Auto is about the failure of success. The company was so successful that its formula had become ossified. The market was moving towards motorcycles but Bajaj Auto continued making its value-for-money scooters. The two-wheeler giant recast its manufacturing, supply chain management, marketing, distribution and after-sales service while maintaining its cost leadership and improving quality. Hindustan Lever set up a completely new operation—Operation Sting. It established a new company with a new team and a new brand.

'Coping with Uncertainty' (Case 3) reflects the dilemmas confronting Indian companies which began with the opening up of the economy to the winds of competition in the mid-1980s. When the government first proposed liberalising the insurance sector, employees of the Life Insurance Corporation heard the news with disbelief—and then reacted with the aplomb of the Bombay Club! At the end of a day's hunger strike, the head of its employee association insisted that 'insurance companies should be given a chance to see how well they can perform freed of controls before the opening up of the sector was contemplated'. This was in 1996. Till 2000, the proposed liberalisation had not come into force, but aware of the need to change, LIC employees for the first time introduced concrete proposals to improve customer service in their charter of demands to the LIC top management.

In an attempt to become world class, exiting a company or a division, be it through closure or selling out, is not an option for many. Certainly not for Tube Investments. 'Repositioning in a Liberalising Economy' (Case 4) examines the effect of a double-whammy on the company. It had just made some large investments in its business when a substantial devaluation of the Chinese currency led to decline in export prices. One manager summed up the situation as: 'TI's overall strategy, its positioning, its marketing capabilities, and its ability to match costs and productivity levels of competitors and in some cases its ability to deliver quality products were perhaps as much to blame for the poor performance.'

'Changing Times' (Case 5) also examines the effects of competitive shock on the key players in the Indian watch industry: HMT, Titan, Timex and Allwyn. In 1995, the over three-decade-old industry was in the midst of a major turmoil. Even as Indian companies were gearing up to combat multinational players from Switzerland, Japan and China, they were trying desperately to hold their ground against smuggled watches. For HMT, the undisputed government-run industry leader for almost two decades, this period was particularly painful. Even as it launched new products, introduced new marketing strategies and generally tried to restructure and reinvent itself, it came under flak from its own union, who held the top management 'solely responsible for the downfall of HMT'. The Indian watch industry case describes the various initiatives and different approaches taken by managers of the four companies.

Building the Future

Beyond courage, vision has an equally significant role to play. Simplistically put, vision is the ability to manage the present from the future. World class companies are world class because they not only see the big picture but can also manage numerous small details. History and context matter, so there is no universal formula. Yet there is one common thread. In order to win, companies must win at three very different stages of competition: the competition for markets, the competition for competencies and the competition for dreams.

The battle for markets, normally referred to as competitive strategy, is the kind of competition that Michael Porter wrote about and with which many Indian managers are by now familiar. It starts with a structural analysis of the industry, based on detailed evaluation of the relative powers of suppliers and customers and of the barriers to entry and substitution, to diagnose the dynamics of profitability and to identify the different strategic segments. This analysis, together with an evaluation of key success factors in each segment and the key strengths and intentions of competitors, leads to a choice of both strategic positioning and competitive posture. The key weapons in this competition for existing markets include market share, scale, a sustainable low cost position, the ability to differentiate, pre-emption strategies and so on. To achieve the overall competitive strategy, there is a need to co-align functional strategies: a low cost strategy, for example, requires a very different approach to manufacturing, marketing and financing than a strategy primarily focussed on differentiation.

Up to the mid-1980s, the Porter concept of competitive strategy dominated corporate thinking, particularly in the West. But soon thereafter, its limitations became apparent. Success could be explained on the grounds of cost leadership, but what became harder to explain was from where this cost leadership came. Why could their competitors not do what they did? A much more compelling argument was soon offered by C.K. Prahalad and Gary Hamel. Collectively, they made the case for a very different kind of competition: the competition for resources and capabilities.

While Porter's view of competitive strategy focussed on the external world—of industry structure and the strategy of competitors—Prahalad and Hamel focussed on the internal world of a company's strategic architecture consisting of all its resources and competencies. At the heart of this new view of strategy lay a profoundly different conceptualisation of what constituted a company. In Porter's view of strategy, a company was a portfolio of products and businesses. Prahalad and Hamel saw a company as a portfolio of resources and competencies.

Strategy, then, was not just about finding the best market position. It was about a deep analysis of what a company's competencies really were, and then a creative process of finding external opportunities into which those competencies could be parlayed into competitive advantage. In that process, a static view of competitive positioning also gave way to a more dynamic and evolutionary view of strategy based on two iterative processes. The first process was to continuously look for growth by identifying new market opportunities into which the company's existing resources and competencies could be exploited. The second process was to continuously improve on the strategic architecture, both by strengthening existing competencies and also by developing or acquiring new ones.

But this explanation too begs a question: where was the energy coming from? That question leads to the third stage of competition: the competition for dreams. This is where the power of corporate ambition and human will combine with a vision of future markets to create the exciting sense of purpose that energises the whole strategic process.

Some managers and strategy analysts make the mistake of thinking about the three stages of competition in either/or terms. The notion of core competencies and strategic architecture is seen as a replacement for the old and outdated concepts of competitive strategy. A far more appropriate approach is to think of them as the layers of an iceberg.

The concepts of competitive strategy remain as valid today as they were when Michael Porter wrote his famous book in 1980. Careful analysis of cost structures and of customer needs remain vital to arrive at cost leadership or differentiation to win in the market. But they form the visible tip of the iceberg. Competitive strategy is supported by the bulk of the strategic architecture that lies submersed under water—deeply embedded within the company, invisible to the outside observer. And, at the very base of the iceberg lies the vision, the ambition, the dream.

This may be so in the West, but what about India? Leaf through the case studies on Reliance Industries and Ranbaxy Laboratories. In both you will see a similar pattern. In 'Growth As a Way of Life' (Case 6), read how Dhirubhai Ambani's clear articulation of his dream was matched by Reliance's cost leadership in its main businesses and outstanding competencies in areas as diverse as project management and the mobilisation of low cost finance. In 'From Vision to Action' (Case 7), Dr Parvinder Singh talks about his dream of building a 'research-based, international company', an objective whose success was by no means guaranteed. Achieving this dream would require that Ranbaxy undertake a major transformation. The Indian government's introduction of the Process Patent Act in 1970 offered opportunities to all Indian pharmaceutical companies, but few made the kind of human and financial investments in building R&D competencies that Ranbaxy made. Twenty years later, Ranbaxy was able to leverage its learning to carve a niche for itself in international markets.

Just courage, an overall vision and a coherent plan are not good enough to create a sustainable growth process. To shape and manage the future, a company also needs the ability to effectively act on the vision and implement the plan. Here focus needs to be concentrated internally on the content and the process. To manage sustainable growth, a company needs to create an effective alignment between three key elements: its value-creation logic, its organising principles and its people processes.

In *Managing Radical Change*, we discussed the value-creation process at Thermax, where innovation in technology drove growth. At Bajaj Auto, the value-creation logic lay in giving customers 'the best value for money'. In this book, the story of NIIT provides an example of how the company managed the present from the future in each of its three businesses by completely aligning its value-creation logic, its organising principles and its people processes.

In computer education, NIIT is not only the market leader but enjoys phenomenal brand recall. 'New Opportunities in a Globalising Economy' (Case 8) describes how it was able to achieve this through a clear customer focus which meant offering quality products and services. This in turn was ensured through continuous monitoring of performance measurements, both internally and of its thousands of franchisees in India and elsewhere. At the frontline level, the process allowed firm control of quality but enough flexibility to spot dissatisfaction among customers. In a fast-moving industry, NIIT could not afford to be too early or late. There have been cases where a product has been launched too early in the market and has lost. The market has to be prepared to accept the product. Therefore, the technology identification and deployment process has to be tailored for each market and its stage of evolution. NIIT was able to do that because of its people processes.

'Profiting from R&D' (Case 9) is another story of an organisation which is paying close attention to building the future. After taking over as director general, R.A. Mashelkar started questioning the role of the Council for Scientific and Industrial Research (CSIR). Its value-creation logic at the time of its establishment was explicit, but the environment had changed. 'We had survived all these years because industry was not doing any R&D. Yet, R&D should be an industrial responsibility. Would CSIR then be needed and relevant by 2020?' he asked. This debate generated a new vision for CSIR, from which flowed new organising principles based on the logic that CSIR now had to position itself as an 'International Chemical Laboratory Ltd'. Therefore, CSIR would move away from a government-style culture to a corporate one, learn to network with foreign companies and researchers, and build an ambition to export rather than import technology. Researchers and managers were encouraged to work differently and it was hoped that the government would allow them to join company boards as directors. Underpinning the fuzziness were sharply defined goals, both financial and operational.

Sam Pitroda, an NRI telecom guru, once said, 'Technology is a passport respected anywhere in the world'. Another company which understood the importance of technology as a value creator is BPL. The key components inside a television set are virtually the same, whatever the brand. Yet BPL successfully differentiated itself from its competitors using the technology plank. In 'Global Competition and Guerilla Warfare on Local Territory' (Case 10), we see how the company created a powerful brand and a sense of pride among its employees and managers, and built up market share despite intense local and multinational competition by reverse and value-engineering techniques.

CSIR, NIIT, Ranbaxy, Reliance and BPL are primarily stories about organic growth. In the cases on Ispat International and Nicholas Piramal we discuss two companies which have grown through the acquisition route.

Mergers and acquisitions are heady adrenalin pursuits, but pre-acquisition euphoria quickly evaporates once the challenging post-acquisition integration process pulls up at management's doorstep. 'Spinning Steel into Gold' (Case 11) focusses on the three phases a company needs to go through after being taken over: the cleaning up and building up of the foundation, its strategic and organisational revitalisation, and finally the integration of people and operations with the rest of the group. Almost every company which Lakshmi Niwas Mittal, the founder of the Ispat International group, bought was engaged in steel-making using DRI technology. The post-integration process, therefore, concentrated on operations such as plant improvements and better marketing, and leveraging the learnings of the other plants.

The second case study on managing acquisitive expansion, 'Integrating Diversity' (Case 12), takes the story a step further. Three pharmaceutical companies with three very different products and cultures were merged to build one strong company. At Ispat International, each acquisition took place in a different country and so retained some part of its individual identity, particularly as the existing managements were largely kept intact. At Nicholas Piramal, the three companies were welded together. Managers were the same but they no longer worked alongside their mates, in their usual office or plant, but within a completely new infrastructure and to a new vision statement.

Acquisitions, organic growth and strategic alliances provide the three major means for business expansion. They are not mutually exclusive. And if the process leads to diversification, it must be matched with improvements in management capabilities: the building of entrepreneurial, empowered businesses; the cross-sharing of resources and knowledge; and the presence of a dynamic corporate engine. 'Balancing the Future' (Case 13) highlights the importance of these capabilities. Today, Wipro is better known for its software business, but the Bangalore-based company is composed of no less than eight distinct businesses, each operating independently yet held together by a clearly articulated code of behaviour—the Wipro Beliefs—which govern the behaviour of the company and its managers. Integration through shared beliefs and leadership values was reinforced through transparency of annual plans and specific goals at all divisions, locations and levels. As Azim Premji, its chairman, said, 'This reduces dependence on control mechanism, improves individual commitment to goals and adoption of sound methods.'

Having secured leadership in their domestic markets, most companies start looking outwards in their quest for growth. Globalisation is the current buzzword in India and many companies are building strategies for the future around either exports to capture international markets or international acquisitions to establish a local presence in other countries. Some, like Studds Accessories, believed that the easiest shortcut to globalisation was through a joint venture with the international leader in the same business activity. 'Pangs of Globalisation' (Case 14) describes the risks in this strategy. Studds was a successful Indian helmet manufacturer with a 36 per cent market share and also exported 20 per cent of its production. Nolan was an Italian firm and one of the world's top ten helmet manufacturers. Keen to globalise and confident that it was a low cost producer capable of manufacturing to international standards, Studds faced two main disadvantages: it did not have an advertising budget to build an international brand, nor it did have the distribution channels for its ambitions. Meanwhile, Nolan had its own objectives for entering into the joint venture, objectives which were quite different from Studds. In a very short time, the joint venture floundered on misunderstandings and was severed by both parties.

The Studds story begs several questions. Many Indian companies aspire to globalise their companies. But without powerful brands or proprietary technology, how realistic are these aspirations? Given their relatively small size in typically stable and mature industries, can they ever develop strong profitable positions in international markets? More generally, in a world of competitive consolidation and market globalisation, how can small companies—particularly from non-OECD countries like India—compete against the established and increasingly concentrated global giants? One part of the answer lies in revitalising what one already has.

Revitalising People, Organisations and Relationships

Success depends on people's ability to change. World class companies and their managers are able to continuously learn from experiences. Infosys recruits people on learnability. 'We define learnability as the ability to derive generic conclusions from specific instances and apply them to new problems. This is the key to our adaptability and a critical competitive advantage in our business', says K. Dinesh, a founder-director. Companies which cannot turn in mid-flight find it hard to survive in the market. Yet, renewing businesses requires that people change their behaviours and attitudes. But can you teach old dogs new tricks? Resolution of the dilemma lies in changing the workplace rather than people. By changing the smell of the place. HDFC did it rather well. It took ordinary people, created a workplace where they could deliver—and they did. Ditto at Infosys.

Changing behavioural context in a PSU is a far more challenging assignment than in the private sector. Typically, apart from normal business constraints, PSU managers have to additionally deal with stiffer government controls, large and unwieldy operations, wary unions and bleeding bottom lines. When J. Mehra took over as CMD at Rashtriya Ispat Nigam, an organisational survey found people at every level so demoralised that neither managers nor workers believed the plant was viable. Yet, a year later, 'we were flooded with suggestions . . . suddenly the ideas came thick and fast. RINL emerged as an entity that was much larger than the Visakhapatnam Steel Plant', recalled a consultant bemusedly. 'Steely Challenges' (Case 15) tries to understand how a mind-set change was created in this problem-riddled PSU, not by changing people, but by changing the smell of the place, by shaping an environment where line managers and workers felt free enough to give their insights and opinions to senior managers and consultants.

It is this energy which Hindustan Lever is trying to capture through Project Millennium, discussed in 'The Spirit of Entrepreneurship in the Big–Small Company' (Case 16). The company is a juggernaut. Cash rich and investor savvy, it is India's largest consumer products company with eighteen businesses, twenty-eight factories, 110 brands, employing 36,000 people and dealing with 2,000 suppliers and associates. When a company is so big and so successful, why should it change? A world class organisation by any standard, why should it tinker with a formula which clearly works brilliantly? But as Keki Dadiseth, its chairman between 1996 and 2000, pointed out, changes are continuously taking place in the economy, markets and the competitive environment.

In order to keep growing, Hindustan Lever had to address issues such as 'How can we retain the aggressiveness and agility of a smaller company as we get much larger?' or 'How should Hindustan Lever re-connect with the consumer so as to be absolutely sure we are delivering what the consumer expects?' To meet its stretch goals and the aspirations of its managers, Hindustan Lever started by analysing its external position in the market and its internal hierarchies. The company was convinced it had to free the entrepreneurial hostages within itself.

Freeing the entrepreneurial hostages inside the recruits he hired for C-DoT was not Sam Pitroda's stated agenda but success very much depended in meeting this challenge. C-DoT was founded with the objective of discovering a cost-efficient way to manufacture telephone exchanges. As we see in 'Switching on the Telecom Revolution in India' (Case 17), C-DoT was a wildly ambitious project, and perhaps the organisation's greatest success lay in the way it energised so many managers and engineers by simply changing the smell of the place where they worked.

Born of very different parents, Hindustan Lever and C-DoT are at two ends of the managerial spectrum. However, a mere belief that motivated people makes the difference between growth and stagnation will no longer be enough. In the New Economy, to build a truly entrepreneurial organisation, management will have to take on new roles and tasks.

In traditional organisations, top-level managers, sitting at the apex of the corporate hierarchy, act as the company's grand strategists and resource allocators. They think up the strategy and then drive it down the organisation through their control over the resource allocation process. The frontline managers in the operating units of the company play the role of operational implementers. Their key task is to implement the strategy that comes down to them from the top. Senior managers, located between the top and the frontline, play the role of administrative controllers, ensuring that the demands of checks and balances are effectively met in the vertical processes of information and resource flows.

In contrast, in a world class entrepreneurial organisation, the roles of these managers are very different. Frontline managers, heading small, disaggregated and interdependent units focussed on specific opportunities, are the company's entrepreneurs. They are the builders of the company's businesses and they drive the company's performance by continuously strengthening those businesses. Like coaches who leverage the strengths of individual players to build a winning team, senior level managers link these separate businesses into a coherent, winning company. Their value addition lies in creating the strategic and organisational framework within which the diverse capabilities of the frontline units can be integrated across businesses, functions and geographic regions. Top management infuses the company with an energising purpose to develop it as an enduring institution that can outlive its existing operations, opportunities and executives. Like social leaders, they can create the challenge and commitment necessary to drive change so that the company can continuously renew itself.

Implicit in these new entrepreneurial organisations is the concept of shared destiny as distinct from power relationships. Around the world, the power-based relationship was the dominant choice till the recent past. Strategy was framed in power terms—to decrease the power of customers and suppliers, as Michael Porter asserted—and profits were the outcome of market power. So companies bought out their competitors, to create monopoly power. Employees formed militant unions, to enhance their bargaining power. And customers bought from many sources so as to retain their purchasing power.

But around the world, this situation is changing. While efficient in the short term, power-based relationships deny themselves the benefits of those ideas and fall behind in the innovation game. Motivated, committed employees drive the process of continuous improvement in quality and operations. Companies that subdue employees with power sacrifice those benefits. Recognising these costs, companies around the world are moving towards what we call the shared destiny model, not in a spirit of altruism or generosity but simply as a business need for ensuring superior performance.

In India, a country that can be described as a low-trust society, there are many who doubt the value of the shared destiny model. Yet, several world class companies in India have been quick to spot its benefits and have reaped rich financial rewards. Reliance's attitude to its shareholders, HDFC's willingness to create competition for itself, and the transparency of information at Infosys are some examples. 'I never wanted to march alone', Brijmohan Lall Munjal, chairman of Hero Honda, once remarked. 'A Web of Relationships' (Case 18) provides a detailed illustration of a highly successful company where the shared destiny concept is a core corporate philosophy, applied to joint venture partners, customers, dealers, vendors, employees and indeed members of the Munjal family.

Transforming Leadership Philosophy

For managers who have grown up in the old economy, obsessed as they are with the 'real world' and focussed on pragmatism and actions, coming to grips with soft concepts such as 'a shared destiny' is difficult. That is why the most important challenge is also the most abstract: the need to change their basic management philosophy; to move beyond the doctrine of strategy-structure-systems to one of purpose-process-people.

The great power—and fatal flaw—of the former doctrine lay in its core objective: to create a management system that would minimise a company's reliance on the idiosyncrasies of individuals. If, from the top, the strategy could be clearly defined and communicated, if a clear structure could be established so that everyone knew who reported to them and who they reported to, and if clear systems could be developed for managing the flows of capital, information and other resources, then complex organisations could be run with people as replaceable parts. And indeed this is exactly what happened in large Indian companies, both in the private and public sectors.

Since the 1990s, however, the Indian economy has undergone some profound changes that have undermined the foundations of this strategy-structure-systems doctrine. Overcapacity and intense competition are the norm in most businesses. The line separating businesses have blurred as technologies and markets have converged, creating new growth opportunities at the intersection of traditional industries. And ideas and knowledge have increasingly replaced capital as the scarce resource and the key to competitive advantage. In the new economy, companies have to move to a new leadership philosophy.

In this, our last section, we discuss two very special companies—HDFC and Infosys. They are special because they instinctively understood this leadership philosophy. 'The Extraordinary–Ordinary Company' (Case 19) and 'Going Global' (Case 20) look at how instead of being designers of strategy, people like H.T. Parekh and N.R. Narayana Murthy took on the role of establishing a sense of purpose within the company, defined in terms of how the company will create value for its constituents, and strategy emerged within their organisations from the energy and alignment created by that sense of purpose.

At both companies, there was a focus on building core organisational processes that would support the entrepreneurship of frontline managers, integrate the resources and knowledge across the frontline units to develop new capabilities, and create the stretch and sense of challenge that would drive the company into continuously striving for renewal through new value creation. Parekh and Murthy built systems, but they also took on the role of being developers of people, creating a context in which each individual in the company could become the best he or she could be. In essence, they replaced the three S's of strategy-structure-systems with the three P's of purpose-process-people both as the philosophical core of the company and as the anchors for their own roles and tasks within the organisation.

In *Managing Radical Change*, we described companies who have walked away alive and kicking from 'valley of death' situations. The differentiating factor is a belief that becoming world class is possible. This is the fundamental premise behind this book—to make managers believe, really believe, that becoming world class in India is possible. Not only for large established firms but also for small firms. In a deregulated, competitive economy driven by the cruel logic of markets, a company that fails to change fast enough can and will die—as is already happening to many of India's great old companies. At the same time, in this deregulated market economy, a determined management can transform a company much more quickly and much more effectively than was possible in the past.

Dr Parvinder Singh once said, 'Ranbaxy cannot change India. Instead what it can do is create a pocket of excellence. Ranbaxy must be an island within India.' We hope that there will soon be a large enough number of people who share this philosophy to change India.

Part 1
The Challenge of Change

BAJAJ AUTO LIMITED: TRANSFORMATION OF A GIANT

To replace a legend is never easy; to replace a legend when the legacy needs a major overhaul is even more difficult. And that was the challenge facing Rajiv Bajaj in 1998 in the process of gradually taking over the leadership responsibilities at Bajaj Auto from his father, Rahul Bajaj.

With its large sales turnover (Rs 39 bn in FY99), wide product sweep and high profitability, cash rich Bajaj Auto dominated the Indian market for two- and three- wheeler vehicles. In 1998, Bajaj Auto was ranked India's fifth most valuable company.[1] Internationally, it was the world's largest scooter producer and the fourth largest two-wheeler manufacturer, behind Japan's Honda, Yamaha and Suzuki. The company's builder Rahul Bajaj enjoyed the reputation

This case was written by Sudeep Budhiraja, Research Fellow at the London Business School, Gita Piramal, business historian and Sumantra Ghoshal, Robert P. Baumann Professor of Strategic Leadership at the London Business School. The authors are grateful to Bajaj Auto Ltd for their help and support in writing the case and the Aditya V. Birla India Centre at the London Business School. This case was first registered by the London Business School in 1999.

1. *Business Today*, 'The BT 500', 7 September 1998.

of being one of India's most admired business leaders. Much more than a mere industrialist, however, he was a national celebrity—an outspoken iconoclast who was regularly in the news not only as a spokesman for Indian industry in general, but also for his often forward thinking and blunt views on a variety of social and economic issues that affected the country.

Rahul Bajaj had inherited a young company in a protected market and overseen its growth over a period of forty years into a large and profitable company. In the mid-1980s, however, the environment changed as the government liberalised the two-wheeler industry, permitting global giants to set up shop in India. Bajaj Auto's market share initially rose steadily, despite competition, to 49.3 per cent in 1994 but gradually declined thereafter to about 40 per cent by 1998. In response to this erosion of market share, the company was changing its focus on a standardised product to a wide range of models and variants designed to appeal to a broad cross-section of the market. It had recognised its problems on product, both in terms of features and in terms of the quality expectations of an increasingly demanding customer. Both of these were being addressed and the company was in the process of recasting itself.

A Bajaj had always been at the helm of affairs at Bajaj Auto. Rahul had carried the torch for 35 years. Those who knew him well, knew the company meant everything to him. But he felt it was now time to hand over the baton. Rahul was clear that his elder son was the person who should be groomed as his successor.

Rajiv had studied mechanical engineering and graduated at the top of his class. Besides, he had grown up in the Bajaj Auto Colony, having lived there ever since he was born. He was young, bright and hungry; everything that Rahul had been when he had stepped up to the plate in 1968. Rajiv came aboard as a general manager with responsibility for new product development and progressed quickly to become vice president–products (in charge of product and manufacturing engineering and marketing functions). Rahul remained the 'Boss' as Chairman and Managing Director. But everyone was quite clear in 1998 that Rajiv was the de facto Chief Operating Officer. His management team consisted of experienced stalwarts who had typically been with the company for decades tempered with some new young faces chosen for their specialist skills. His younger brother Sanjiv Bajaj was a general manager in the finance and materials areas and had been an understudy to the CFO since he had returned with an MBA from Harvard (see Appendix 1).

When Rajiv took on the responsibility of spearheading the company's products and market thrusts in 1996 at the age of 32, he found he had inherited a lumbering giant. His priorities thus included accessing new technologies, introducing new models, making a strong presence in the rapidly growing motorcycle market, creating a marketing culture, revamping manufacturing practices, focussing on quality, improving the supply chain and helping the new managers integrate into a conservative corporate culture. Being methodical by nature, Rajiv started working on all these issues one by one. He saw the major challenges facing the company as:

- Share of Customer's Mind: 'This is linked to innovation, but not necessarily technical innovation. Customer maturity has changed dramatically in a very short period of time. Me-too products don't work.'
- Product Differentiation: 'We have to develop product development skills. Product differentiation has become more important, particularly where everyone has access to similar technology.'
- Customer Satisfaction: 'Everything that was OK in the past is not OK today. We have to change everything to ensure customer satisfaction.'
- Customer Retention: 'For motorcycles, Hero Honda is the best brand, but it has only 52 per cent customer retention.'
- Cost: 'We have to manage the cost structure during the transition.'

When asked about his ambitions for the company, Rajiv said, 'My limited ambition is to complete the transition (to a new Bajaj Auto).' In order to fulfil this ambition, however, some key issues and questions needed to be addressed.

Issues and Questions

1. What are the primary strengths and weaknesses of Bajaj Auto? Is the company working on the right priorities? What, if anything, is it missing?
2. How important is global leadership? Does Bajaj Auto's mission statement need updating?
3. Would it be better to effect changes in one area at a time, or to do what Rahul and Rajiv have done by working on several areas simultaneously?
4. What is the future of Bajaj Auto?

The Bajaj Group

The Bajaj name is synonymous with the freedom struggle in India. Jamnalal Bajaj, a businessman from the very traditional Marwari community, accepted Mahatma Gandhi as his leader and spent most of his time assisting Gandhi and the Congress Party towards achieving India's independence from the British. His loyalty and commitment were exemplary and Gandhi once wrote to another prominent follower, Ghanshyam Das Birla, '. . . there was no work in which I did not receive Jamnalal's fullest co-operation in body, mind and wealth'. This partially explains why Mohandas Karamchand Gandhi—the Father of the Nation—often referred to Jamnalal as his fifth son.

Jamnalal rose to become the treasurer of the Congress Party and stayed in this position until his demise in 1942. His employees and other family members, including his older son, Kamalnayan, managed the family business of cotton ginning and pressing as well as indigenous banking. At the time of his demise, the business had expanded into the sugar industry and responsibility for managing it shifted to Kamalnayan, assisted by his younger brother Ramakrishna (see family tree). These were turbulent times with the end of the Second World War and the preparations for Indian independence in 1947. The Bajaj group reacted to the opportunities made available by the market and expanded the family business into the manufacture of scooters, three-wheelers, sugar, casting steel and other products, electrical lamps, etc., by the 1960s.

In 1999, Bajaj Auto was the largest company in the Bajaj group. Comprising twenty-six companies, the group's major manufacturing activities, apart from two- and three-wheelers, were special steels, consumer electricals and sugar. Group sales in FY99 were Rs 62 bn. Transactions between group companies were conducted on an arm's length basis. However, overall strategic planning for group companies was done in discussion within the Bajaj family and informal contacts between the top management of the various companies were common.

Bajaj Auto

Bajaj Auto Ltd was incorporated on 29 November 1945 as a trading company and began the import of two- and three-wheelers from Italy's Piaggio & Co in 1948. In 1959, the Indian government granted Bajaj Auto a licence to manufacture scooters and motorised three-wheeled vehicles. In 1960 it entered into a technical collaboration with Piaggio under which it obtained the right to manufacture and market Piaggio's Vespa brand scooters and three-wheelers in India. The first batch of scooters was assembled in a brick-and-tin shed in Kurla, Bombay. Bajaj Auto's first full-fledged manufacturing facility at Akurdi, 160 km away, was inaugurated in 1960–61. That year, 3995 scooters rolled out of the plant.

Bajaj Family Tree

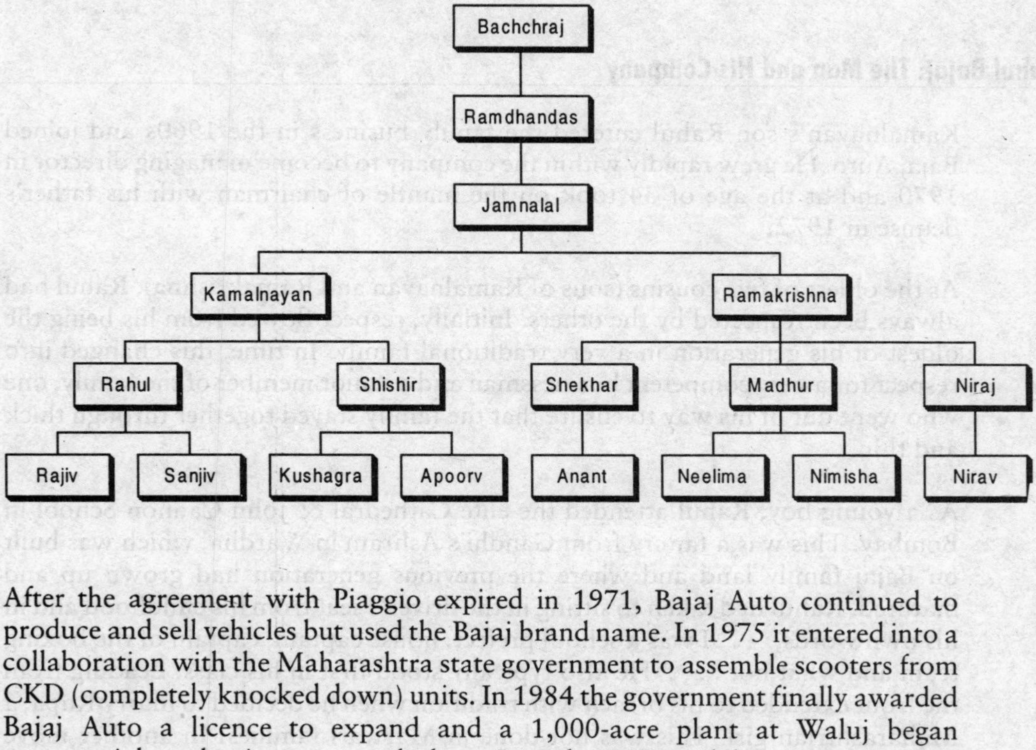

After the agreement with Piaggio expired in 1971, Bajaj Auto continued to produce and sell vehicles but used the Bajaj brand name. In 1975 it entered into a collaboration with the Maharashtra state government to assemble scooters from CKD (completely knocked down) units. In 1984 the government finally awarded Bajaj Auto a licence to expand and a 1,000-acre plant at Waluj began commercial production ten months later. In early 1998 work began on a Rs 3.15 bn plant on a 200-acre plot at Chakan near Pune, which was scheduled to go on-stream by mid-1999. Bajaj Auto's 1.9 million vehicles per year capacity was expected to touch 2.5 million by 2000. Production at Chakan would increase in phased slabs of 200,000 units according to market needs. The company proposed to spend another Rs 3.65 bn between 1997 and 2000 on improving the older plants. A broad financial summary of Bajaj Auto is provided in Appendix 2.

For the first twenty years of its history, with its products in great demand, Bajaj Auto did not feel the need to introduce any new products but merely tinkered with the old Vespa design. Bajaj Auto produced its first motorcycle in 1981. In 1986, it began making a Japanese-designed motorcycle in technical collaboration with Kawasaki Heavy Industries. The Bajaj Sunny, a scooterette, was introduced in 1990.

Rahul Bajaj: The Man and His Company

Kamalnayan's son Rahul entered the family business in the 1960s and joined Bajaj Auto. He grew rapidly within the company to become managing director in 1970 and at the age of 34 took on the mantle of chairman with his father's demise in 1972.

As the oldest of five cousins (sons of Kamalnayan and Ramakrishna), Rahul had always been respected by the others. Initially, respect flowed from his being the oldest of his generation in a very traditional family. In time, this changed into respect for a very competent businessman and a senior member of the family, one who went out of his way to ensure that the family stayed together through thick and thin.

As a young boy, Rahul attended the elite Cathedral & John Cannon School in Bombay. This was a far cry from Gandhi's Ashram in Wardha, which was built on Bajaj family land and where the previous generation had grown up and matured. Rahul had taken to sitting in the driver's seat from his childhood and in his own words, '. . . I was a school prefect, house captain, captain of the boxing team and what not . . . .' He also typically stood first in his class. Leading from the front extended to his breach with tradition when he decided to marry Rupa, a Maharashtrian girl. This was not done in Marwari families! In another move atypical of the scions of major Indian business families at that time, he also attended Harvard Business School to pick up an MBA degree (class of 1964).

Within a few years of their marriage, Rahul and Rupa decided to live within the factory colony. They could have lived in Pune and Rahul could have driven out to the factory and back. But no, Rahul had to be in the middle of it all. In fact, until the new office building was constructed, Rahul's office was inside the factory with his windows overlooking every key activity. For over twenty-five years, Rahul was personally in control of every crucial area of the company. He knew the financials inside out and was always aware of the daily production figures. Low cost was his mantra and cost control his passion. As Tarun Das, director general of the Confederation of Indian Industry, once said, only partly in jest, ' . . . even though Bajaj Auto was highly professional, one could not spend Rs 5 without Rahul's permission.'

When Rahul took over responsibility for the company in 1968 (even before he became MD in 1970), India and its Congress government were preoccupied with socialist objectives. The country was run based on a five-year forward planning process and nothing could be manufactured without a licence from the government. And woe betide the manufacturer who violated the conditions of his licence by producing above the licensed capacity, even if by improving productivity and utilization of existing equipment. This frustrated Rahul immensely and he was amazed that he was not allowed to produce more in an environment where there was a ten-year waiting period for a Bajaj scooter. Reflecting on that period, Rahul once said, 'My blood used to boil. The country needed two-wheelers. There was a ten-year delivery period for Bajaj scooters. And, I was not allowed to expand. What kind of socialism is that?'

The Bajaj family had played an important role in the freedom struggle and built considerable goodwill among the ranks of the political leadership of the 1940s. This reduced over time and then basically ended when Rahul's father Kamalnayan sided against Indira Gandhi during the Congress Party's split in 1969. Rahul's views on political access were:

> My family never had the kind of contacts you are talking about. We were very much in the freedom struggle, but we never used contacts for our business purposes. Maybe some others have . . . .
>
> Even if giving money could have bought any licences, I can categorically say we did not give any minister or any senior bureaucrat a single penny to get a licence.
>
> I know how difficult it can get to chase someone in Delhi for a license. Then some fool delays the whole project by procrastinating, because he wants something for himself . . . but thank goodness I was never actually penalised though I was quoted often enough for saying

> that I was ready to go to jail for excess production just as both my parents had for the freedom struggle.

Despite the frustrations of managing in the 'Licence Raj', Rahul and Bajaj Auto had done well. Production and turnover rose from 21,000 units and Rs 72 mn in 1968 to 510,000 units and Rs 5528 mn in 1988. This was accomplished through a commitment to providing a standardised product to the consumer at a price that allowed a healthy margin. The Bajaj scooter's popularity allowed the company to create capacity based upon assured demand and long production runs which, along with a constant focus on costs, earned high profits for the company.

The Failure of Success

The environment changed in the mid-1980s when Japanese manufacturers started nosing around India looking for possible partners. The Honda Motor Company set up Kinetic Honda with the Firodias to manufacture scooters, and Hero Honda with the Munjal family to manufacture motorcycles. Around the same time, Suzuki partnered with the TVS Group to set up TVS-Suzuki, Yamaha with Escorts to make motorcycles and Piaggio with the Singhanias in LML to make scooters.

Capacity constraints held back the new entrants for a while but by 1990 the newcomers had established themselves and were ready to ramp up production and take on Bajaj Auto. They had access to new technologies and up-to-date models courtesy their foreign partners. Bajaj Auto on the other hand had limited R&D and no partners to access for new models or technologies. The company had spent its time focussing on continuous reduction of production costs, but this was no longer going to be enough. With the passage of time, competition became intense and the market was flooded with increasing numbers of models and variants. This contributed to a declining market share for Bajaj Auto in the key scooter and three-wheeler segments right through to the late 1990s.

In May 1998, after announcing the 1997–98 results for Bajaj Auto, Rahul was at the receiving end of a number of questions from a panel of business journalists. These were some of his responses:

On the large cash reserves of the company: 'I'll keep the money with the company, in case of an emergency . . . . I have given enough to my shareholders in the past. I am not in the business for charity . . . . Can you name four companies who have gone in for acquisitions and are doing well. I can name many more who are down in the dumps . . . . We are a focussed company.'

On the loss of market share over the years: 'If the competition starts from a zero base, they are bound to get some market share . . . . Live and let live, that's my philosophy . . . .'

Bajaj Auto's Market Share

	FY99	*FY98*	*FY97*	*FY96*	*FY95*	*FY94*	*FY93*	*FY92*	*FY91*	*FY90*	*FY89*	*FY88*
All segs.	38.9	40.5	44.5	46.0	48.6	49.3	49.0	47.9	45.3	43.8	39.9	36.9
Scooter	64.8	64.5	69.1	70.45	71.71	74.87	75.86	76.33	71.90	73.03	73.00	73.00
M'bike	26.9	27.8	31.1	29.47	30.53	28.38	28.99	26.94	26.23	21.15	21.00	20.50
Moped	6.4	7.1	9.4	11.06	14.13	14.93	14.74	8.47	0.51	0.00	0.00	0.00
3-wheeler	83.6	82.1	84.4	87.12	94.12	96.29	91.28	87.24	88.73	88.86	89.00	87.00

Source: AIAM; Company annual reports.

In 1998, Bajaj Auto dominated the Indian two- and three-wheeler markets. None of its competitors came close to matching its top line or bottom line. The six players listed in the table below controlled around 90 per cent of the two-wheeler market. Because of its large volumes, the smallest drop in Bajaj Auto's market share benefited other players lavishly. A 10 per cent drop in Bajaj Auto's scooter sales in 1991–92, for example, translated into an 8 per cent growth for TVS-Suzuki's two-wheeler sales and 14 per cent for Kinetic Honda scooter sales in a year when the overall scooter segment grew by 0.8 per cent.

Leading Two- and Three-Wheeler Companies in India, FY98

	Sales (Volume)	*Sale (Rs Mn)*	*PAT (Rs Mn)*
Bajaj Auto	1333798	35132	4626
Escorts	191868	12830*	1298*
Hero Honda	407546	11607	766
TVS-Suzuki	576392	10399	688
LML	308456	7538	203
Kinetic Honda	113762	3582	22

*Combined balance sheet.

Source: Company reports, AIAM.

Despite its overwhelming numbers, Bajaj Auto's share of the Indian two- and three-wheeler market saw significant swings. The sharpest nick was in 1985 when market share dropped to 33 per cent. Bajaj Auto climbed up the edge of the saw by adding capacity at the Waluj plant and pepping up manufacturing efficiencies at its Akurdi plant; introducing a couple of products described as 'old wine in a not-so-new bottle'; and applying a sharper focus on marketing and distribution. Market share in 1994 peaked at 49.3 per cent of a much larger pie. (By this time, several new entrants—including most of the biggest names in the international two-wheeler business—had set up their manufacturing facilities in India.) There was no time to pop champagne corks, however, for in 1998 once again Bajaj Auto saw its market share drop—from 44.5 per cent in FY97 to 40.5 per cent in FY98 and 38.9 per cent in FY99.

In 1998, Bajaj Auto appeared to be more or less back to its 1989 position. Or was it? The environment in 1998 was far more complicated than in 1989.

- Global players had grasped the nuances of the Indian market and were well entrenched. Honda was gearing up to contest Bajaj Auto's dominance of the scooter segment and in the fast growing motorcycle segment it had established a clear leadership with its partner, the Hero group. Piaggio, through Greaves, was nibbling away at the three-wheeler market—Bajaj Auto's cash cow. TVS–Suzuki had established a lead in the moped segment.
- Intense competition had fragmented the Indian two-wheeler market into many segments. It was no longer neatly divided into scooters, mopeds and motorcycles. Apart from hybrids such as step-thrus and scooterettes, the features and prices of scooters, motorcycles and mopeds frequently overlapped.

For the managers at Bajaj Auto, these two factors combined to pose a perplexing question: What products should it make in the next round of capacity expansion if it was to remain India's leading two- and three-wheeler company?

On the surface, Bajaj Auto appeared to be continuing its struggle to maintain market share. Beneath the surface, some serious changes were occurring.

Rahul's older son Rajiv studied manufacturing engineering at Pune's College of Engineering, standing first in his class. He was then sent off to Warwick in the UK to study engineering before returning to the company in 1991 with responsibility for setting up and managing a new product development group. His designation was general manager. His father's brief was clear: Bajaj Auto had to have a product portfolio to suit every need. His only caveat, 'If your customer wants stainless steel, don't give him platinum.'

The team began its mission by scouting the world for technology boutiques. Over a dozen agreements were signed over the next few years. For example, Bajaj Auto tied-up with Austria's AVL to improve vehicle emission and fuel economy and to develop a direct fuel injection system for two-stroke engines. Collaboration deals were struck with Australia's Orbital Engine Company for combustion systems, with Italy's Cagiva Motor Company for scooters and USA's Unique Mobility for pollution-free electric powered scooters. The majority of the key tie-ups were with Japanese firms: Toyko R&D for scooterettes and mopeds, Kawasaki Heavy Industries for motorcycles, and Kubota for diesel engines for three-wheelers. At the Auto Fair in Delhi in January 1998, Bajaj Auto proudly announced that seventeen new models would hit the Indian market within the next twenty-four months.

R&D Expenditure of Major Indian Two-wheeler Companies, FY98

	Rs Mn	*% of Net Sales*
Bajaj Auto	241.3	0.9
TVS-Suzuki	154.5	1.5
Hero Honda	32.8	0.3
Kinetic Honda	6.8	0.2

Source: Company reports.

The new products marked Bajaj Auto's successful attempts to widen its customer base and also a new emphasis on improving the insides of its machines. In the first twenty years of its existence, Bajaj Auto had stubbornly refused to upgrade its models: the Chetak—which had provided and continued to provide 60 per cent of Bajaj Auto's scooter sales—didn't even have an electric ignition but had to be kick-started. At the same time, its two-stroke engine had an emission performance that, while acceptable in the Indian context, would be seen as highly polluting according to international standards. (However, by the late

1990s, India had set emission norms for two-wheelers which were tighter than in many other countries.)

Little could be done about the old two-stroke engines but the new products dispelled this passé image. According to Rajiv Bajaj, the new models were designed with three challenges in mind: the consumer, the environment and the competition—in that order. 'The consumer is increasingly demanding a vehicle which can provide him with pride and joy along with the comforts of easy riding, fuel efficiency and power.'

The Classic SL and Bravo scooters, therefore, provided superior styling backed by improved suspension and braking systems. The Spirit, aimed at the urban teenager, was the first two-speed scooterette in the market with greater fuel efficiency and more power than a variomatic. The Legend, a 150cc scooter, showed that Bajaj Auto had finally managed to develop a four-stroke engine in-house that was fuel-efficient and could meet emission norms set for the year 2000. This allowed it to catch up with Honda, whose worldwide success was rooted in its classic four-stroke engine.

The new models acted like adrenaline shots. The company claimed that Bajaj technology in the 50cc to 150cc two-wheeler category for petrol engines, geared and ungeared transmission, and monocoque and tubular structures could 'compete with the best in the world'. There was now a feeling that the company had been liberated. 'Some call us weak because in the absence of a joint venture, we do not have access to a transnational's technology,' said Rahul Bajaj. 'I believe it is a strength since it has given us freedom of action. Freedom to shop for technology. Freedom to become an independent multinational.'

Manufacturing and Supply Chain Management

Manufacturing

In FY98, Bajaj Auto produced over 4,400 vehicles a day in two shifts, six days a week, in spotlessly clean plants. Sixty-five per cent of these were scooters. Going by the current inter-segment shifts, the scooter segment's contribution in 2003 was likely to be much smaller. Trends in India had begun to mirror international ones. Bajaj Auto had been the last to enter the motorcycle race. Now its antennae were more sensitive to the winds of change. 'We are not a scooter company, we make products that sell', said Rajiv Bajaj. 'When the market wanted scooters, we made scooters. When the market wants motorcycles, we will make motorcycles. Our production facilities are flexible.'

Bajaj Auto's Sales FY98

	Units	*% of Industry Total*
Scooters	776676	64.5
Motorcycles	313068	27.8
Mopeds	51938	7.1
3-wheelers	192116	82.1
Total	1333798	40.5

Source: Bajaj Auto

To lend speed and agility to its large and expanding manufacturing operation, Bajaj Auto instituted a participative and '*unambiguous bottom-up approach*', in the words of one of its managers. On the shop floor, workmen and section managers were grouped into cells. These cell members were guided by a principle dubbed 'visual self-management of quality and productivity for continuous improvement'. It was an elaborate name for a simple system. There were ten charts (V1-V10), each for every aspect of cell working from man–machine balancing and material handling to preventive maintenance and process control. To ensure that all departments had access to the right information at the right time and at the required point, a Digital Equipment Alpha 8400 host computer linked 400 concurrent users at the three plants as well as suppliers, dealers and overseas distributors.

Gearing up production from twelve models in 1993 to twenty-nine by 1999 was a challenge and the man in the hot seat was Arvind Gupta (52), head of manufacturing engineering, who joined Bajaj Auto in 1991 from Telco. 'As it is a matter of survival, we will cajole, compromise and coax to get there,' said the pragmatist.

His immediate headache was tooling. Bajaj Auto needed 700–800 new tools according to a specific delivery schedule to manufacture the new models but no company in India had the design facilities to make them except Telco. Suppliers also needed help with their tooling—and depended on Bajaj Auto to provide it. 'We were doing 80 per cent of this new tooling ourselves. It was a tremendous workload but there was no option. Keeping know-how in control was also a problem. But we have to find a way out of this problem. We can't be bottlenecked', declared Gupta.

Bajaj Auto's solution was multi-pronged. Some of the tooling was farmed out. Designers were asked to go back to their drawing boards and come up with manufacturing processes that called for less tooling. Manpower expansion and new CAD computers led to a 30 per cent improvement in tool design productivity. Bajaj Auto had never spent so much on tooling. 'In the past, the high cost of tooling just would not have been accepted,' noted one manager.

Considerations of feasibility and cost counter-balanced the need for speed. Traditionally Bajaj Auto's greatest competitive advantage had been its cost structure and as the new lines came up, managers kept a tight rein on the purchase of new machines. Gupta explained, 'The new products will be competitively priced because we have been very cost effective in our equipment buying. Overall, we've paid less because we've bought from different manufacturers. We can do this because we have a strong integrating facility in comparison to others. Others may have an advantage over project time but then we are building in expertise through the integration process. However, we still have to source critical and key machines from outside and that is a problem. Yes, this strategy may cost the company more in the long run in terms of time—we could have handed it over as a turnkey job—but the transition might have been difficult and the costs would have been very different.'

Gupta acknowledged, however, that target dates were trailing. 'What should have been done in 1996 was being done in 1998. According to international standards, companies bring out a model in four years. Some companies are excellent and can bring out a new model in two-and-a-half years. For the Beta 3, it took us close to five years. And there were bugs in the product. There were failures in product testing and we need to spend time on reducing the cycle time.' No one in Bajaj Auto, and the marketing department especially, wanted a repeat of the mid-1990s, when the company had prematurely launched the Stride and the SX Endura which later had to be phased out.

For the product development process, Bajaj Auto had borrowed the platform concept from Chrysler. Bajaj Auto's six platforms were composed of engineers from product engineering, manufacturing engineering, component development, product management and quality assurance. Simultaneous and concurrent engineering concepts were extensively applied. The brainstorming sessions often included first tier suppliers *before* a concept was finalised.

Supply Chain

About 60 per cent by value of a Bajaj vehicle was outsourced. Virtually no components were imported and 70 per cent of Bajaj Auto's requirements were sourced from within the state of Maharashtra. Twenty per cent of its requirements were single-sourced and most components were procured from three or less vendors. Many suppliers were either completely or largely dedicated to Bajaj Auto. Compared to its competitors, Bajaj Auto's dependence on vendors was relatively low: over 90 per cent of Hero Honda's components, for example, were outsourced.

However, Bajaj Auto's growth was significantly constrained by the time required by its vendors to absorb technology or achieve significant expansions in their plants. This was partly because of Bajaj Auto's large volumes but was equally an intrinsic element of the Indian auto ancillary industry. Once a new component was designed by a two- and three-wheeler manufacturer, the vendor required anything from fifteen days for a simple part to about a year for sub-assemblies like brakes and transmission before commercial production could start. Further, many vendors were small-scale operations and family-owned, which often restricted large and fast capacity expansion due to funds constraints. And most vendors usually supplied to only one company and expanded according to the requirement of that company. In such a situation, they tended not to build surplus capacity.

Given these difficulties, Bajaj Auto had got used to depending on itself—an attitude which made for some significant benefits. Its relatively high level of backward integration allowed it to keep raw material costs below the industry average. The company bought raw materials in bulk for itself and for some of its vendors. This ensured quality components at low costs. For most two-wheeler companies, material costs accounted for about 70 per cent of operating income. In Bajaj Auto's case, it was 57 per cent in FY98—the lowest in the industry.

At the same time, the level of outsourcing had begun to creep upwards. According to Arvind Gupta, 'We used to take 1.9 mandays to make a scooter. Now because of outsourcing, it's come down to between 1.4 and 1.5 mandays. Of this reduction, 40 per cent is from offloading and 60 per cent from productivity increases.'

To improve quality, Bajaj Auto also began actively assisting its suppliers in finalising joint ventures with counterparts in Japan, Italy, Taiwan and Spain. Managers felt that this had led to a string of useful associations in crucial areas such as die casting, polymer moulding, ride control systems and auto electricals. 'We need to build a world-class supplier base if we want world-class vehicles,' said Rahul Bajaj.

Changes in Bajaj Auto's vendor policies were not always favourably received. During the 1991–93 recession, Bajaj Auto had extracted several concessions from its vendors, especially those supplying forgings. From the mid-1990s Bajaj Auto began to trim the number of vendors. For example, the Akurdi press shop used to have twenty-eight suppliers. This was streamlined to seven in 1998 and would be five by 2005. 'Fewer suppliers means their volumes increase and set-up time reduces', explained Ranjit Gupta (56), vice president, materials, who has been with the company since 1988 and was previously a general manager at Maruti Udyog. 'Lower set-up times mean more uninterrupted work and less quality problems.' But to get Bajaj Auto's volume business, vendors had to accept wafer-thin margins.

Maintaining Cost Leadership

Even as Bajaj Auto revved up the growth path, the company introduced specific programmes in its manufacturing operations to glean cost efficiencies. Every task in the company was evaluated on the basis of three parameters: time, quality and cost. Specific norms were set for each parameter and had to be met. Managers had to target and tackle inefficiencies in each area so that overall costs stayed in check.

'Given the strong presence of all the two-wheeler majors of the world in India, all employees, workmen and managers alike, recognised and understood that low cost mass manufacturing was a competitive tool,' said S. Ravikumar (41), senior manager, business development, who joined Bajaj Auto in 1984 after being a financial accountant at Enfield India. The 1991–93 recession further hammered in the message.

Manpower productivity in terms of number of vehicles per man year improved by 88 per cent in the decade 1988–98. Five thousand workers disappeared from the payroll. The remaining 17,000 worked a lot harder. 'Ideally there should be 9,000', said one manager. 'Fewer people made an important difference in cost and quality. The factory was a neater, cleaner and safer working environment.'

In June 1998, Bajaj Auto signed a three-and-a-half-year agreement with the Shiv Sena-controlled Bharatiya Kamgar Sena Union whereby the 6,100 permanent workers at the Akurdi plant would get an extra Rs 2,000 per month. The hike would increase labour cost by Rs 146.4 mn per year. Bajaj Auto also agreed to make a one-time payment of Rs 23,800 per worker based on his attendance between April 1997 and May 1998, which would cost an additional Rs 145 mn. In return it got a 8 to 10 per cent productivity increase, a commitment by workers to follow the cell manufacturing system and work 440 minutes per shift. In India, most agreements were negotiated for three-year periods. The Waluj agreement was due in February 2000.

The management accepted, however, that processes could be stretched only up to a limit, especially with a wider product range. Production of the Chetak was so fine-tuned after thirty years that the forty workers on its assembly didn't have more than 2 seconds free between one activity and the next. For the Classic SL, the time management was 95 per cent. But there would be no opportunity to improve on that 95 per cent performance because of changes in the product.

Plain vanilla cost cutting was only one of the many ways Bajaj Auto used to recover lost ground. Most of the other initiatives gave the phrase 'working smarter' an entirely new dimension. Lower costs were designed into new models. Extra features which actually increased costs by Rs 100 were added to models where designers felt that customers would willingly pay Rs 1,000 for them. In all these examples, the pay-off was higher profitability.

> 'In the future, cost has to be looked at in a different way,' said Rajiv Bajaj. 'The wrong way was to tell people that we were cutting costs. People want to come to work eager to work. But if in a meeting I say that today I want to talk about cost cutting, I am sure they will do their best but they will not be motivated. I will be talking in isolation. This is especially true in an owner-managed company. Inevitably there was a feeling among executives that the benefit of cost cutting will go into the owner's pocket. Managers and workers also see cost cutting as a way to rip them off and to make them work harder. Outside the company, among vendors and customers, the moment you talk of cost cutting, people think that the product's quality has gone down. Here in Bajaj Auto we feel that cost cutting is all about improving quality at lower cost. That's how profitability improves. That's how customers keep coming back.'

Managers took a back-to-basics approach to the relationship between cost, market price and profit margin. Bajaj Auto's accountants were told to forget the good old days when the company had monopolised the market. The starting point was now the market, what other companies were doing, and the prices at which they offered their products. Subtracting a predetermined profit margin from this, the residual was the cost at which the product had to be produced.

The net result was the cheapest scooter—at Rs 21,617—that money could buy. In India, Bajaj Auto's most expensive scooter cost less to make than LML's cheapest models. In the UK, a Bajaj Chetak was available for £1,189 vis-à-vis £1,880 for a Piaggio TS and £2,245 for Honda Bali.[2] And even at that price, Bajaj Auto's profits were the highest in the business.

Net Profit Margin FY98

Bajaj Auto	*Hero Honda*	*Escorts*	*TVS-Suzuki*	*LML*	*Kinetic Honda*
13.4%	12.7%	10.1%	6.6%	2.7%	0.6%

Net profit margin = Net profit as % to sales.
Source: *Business Today*, 7 September 1998.

Some concern had begun to build up, however, about how long the company would be able to maintain this cost structure. According to Rajiv Bajaj's calculations, Bajaj Auto would in the future need to spend considerably more on product development and manufacturing processes if its products were to match customers' expectations. More money needed to be spent on branding and market research, more money on hardware, more money on people. In 1997 Bajaj Auto recruited its first head of HRD (as opposed to personnel). Manpower in manufacturing engineering had gone up from sixty to 100. Almost forty 'bright stars' had been inducted into middle management in the past two years. Salaries were going up. As Rajiv Bajaj pointed out, 'If we want to do all this, it totally upsets the cost structure, and when the cost structure changes, the key is to manage change.'

Distribution and After Sales Service

As Bajaj Auto's volumes and market share climbed from 0.52 million and 36.9 per cent in FY88 to 1.33 million and 40.5 per cent in FY98, the company

2. *Scootering International*, September 1997.

virtually doubled its dealer network. In 1998, there were 380 dealers, 1,200 sales and service outlets (known as SSOs), 1,800 service points (SPs) and 18,000 non-exclusive local mechanic panel members. As two- and three-wheelers had a long running life, it was essential to have a wide network of service stations, as also to ensure easy availability of low priced genuine spares.

Dealers formed an important link between manufacturers and customers. They were a valuable source of information on customer preferences. They provided geographic penetration in rural, semi-rural and urban areas. They arranged credit finance for their clients, especially in areas where the auto finance companies did not have a presence. Roughly 700 dealers industry-wide accounted for 80 per cent of auto sales.

Dealer and Servicing Network of Two-wheeler Manufacturers

	Dealers	*Service Centres*
Bajaj Auto	380	1200
TVS-Suzuki	300	500
LML	380	820
Hero Honda	350	160

Source: Merrill Lynch.

Responsibility was clearly defined. Each 'Command Area', which was geographically determined, had a dealer under the supervision of Bajaj Auto's sales and service officers. Dealers had to ensure that the SSOs and SPs within their jurisdiction consistently improved their levels of sales and customer service. Roughly 6,000 mechanics a year, identified via dealers, were trained annually at Bajaj Auto's main training centres in Delhi, Bangalore, Calcutta and Pune and at mini training centres established at about 100 dealerships. In 1991 Bajaj Auto reorganised its distribution pattern by establishing nine depots. The introduction of depots significantly reduced the dealers' working capital requirements by reducing the average time taken to deliver vehicles.

Sales to dealers were usually made on a cash basis. However, during certain times of the year such as Diwali when demand was particularly strong, Bajaj Auto provided credit to certain dealers on a short-term basis at commercial rates of interest. It did not offer discounts or any other form of preferential pricing to any of its dealers on vehicle sales.

In 1997, Bajaj Auto kicked off a number of marketing initiatives. These included a corporate identity and dealer development programme, standardisation and modernisation of dealer networks, assisting dealers to maximise returns through better selling tactics and improved after-sales efficiency. The new theme was 'sales through service'. Dealer conferences were organised to exchange ideas on successful selling strategies and identify areas of improvement.

Earlier, after-sales was treated as a cost centre. In 1998 it was turned around into a profit centre. Bajaj Auto began working with dealers to modernise their workshops in order to increase productivity and reduce service time. The company believed that this would encourage customers to come to authorised workshops and service centres, where they were ensured good service and genuine spare parts, instead of going to small unlicensed mechanics. In its bid to extend its channels, Bajaj Auto roped in select mechanics and trained them as panel members for direct approach to customers.

Bajaj Auto's extensive servicing network and spare parts delivery system was an important competitive advantage. Any Bajaj model could be serviced and repaired quickly virtually anywhere in India. Customers could access spare parts quickly and easily through an extensive network of vehicle dealers, service dealers, Hamara Bajaj Retail Shoppes and consignee agents. Orders were immediately serviced through three warehouses. There was also a 'Fast Track' which executed urgent orders within 24 hours. Such services were particularly attractive to middle-class customers and those wanting 'safe' options.

The Market and Marketing

1982: My marketing department? I don't require it, I have a dispatch department. I don't have to go from house to house to sell.

—Rahul Bajaj, *Society*

1997: Whatever product or service a company offers, it must meet the customer's wants in the most satisfactory manner. That should be the aim of the company.

—Rahul Bajaj, *Business Today*

The company's products had always been well received. In 1980, the pending booking for Bajaj scooters stood at 1,123,731, equivalent to about thirteen times the company's annual output. A decade later, this figure had climbed to 2,133,943. By 1997 a customer could buy a Bajaj scooter off the shelf. The waiting list evaporated partly because of a sharp increase in production. In 1980, Bajaj Auto produced 88,651 two-wheelers, mostly scooters. In 1990, it made 731,523. By 1997, Bajaj Auto's product range had expanded and it doubled production to 1,439,174 scooters, motorcycles, scooterettes and three-wheelers.

The narrowing gap between supply and demand didn't fully explain Rahul Bajaj's U-turn over a fifteen-year period as reflected in the quotes above. Competition was the driver of change. It ruthlessly transformed the rules of the game. The scooter king's attitude towards marketing reversed after global competitors, notably Honda and Suzuki, set up shop in India and challenged Bajaj Auto's hegemony. The Indian auto giant's advertising reflected the change. The punch line 'You Just Can't Beat a Bajaj' started rapping a gentler ditty, '*Hamara* ('our') Bajaj'.

As Bajaj Auto's share of the Rs 8.6 bn Indian two- and three-wheeler market skidded, two issues stood out:

- In the Indian situation, could Bajaj Auto become world class, and how could this transformation take place?
- Could—or should—Bajaj Auto make a bid to recover its earlier awesome market share?

The two issues were intricately linked. Within India, given increasing competition, inevitably success on the second issue depended on the first. And unless Bajaj Auto could successfully compete with world-class players in India, it would not be able to make much headway against the same players in international markets. In any case, becoming world class was perhaps the last mountain left for Rahul Bajaj personally and Bajaj Auto, the company, to climb.

Clearly, major structural changes had taken place in demand. Rural markets had surged to roughly equal urban ones; there was an upward movement to more premium products. Younger people preferred motorcycles, and these were also popular in rural areas because of their large wheel diameter and consequent stability on rough roads. Mopeds were positioned at the lower end of the customer base where a high degree of importance was given to low price and fuel efficiency. Traditionally scooters were used as family vehicles by the middle class who could not afford a car. While this continued to hold true, scooter demand was softening, 'possibly because of the lack of new models . . .', felt Madhur Bajaj, Bajaj Auto's president.

Between 1992–98, to cater to these changes, all two-wheeler manufacturers had expanded their product range. The market was full of hybrids such as the step-thru (a cross between a scooter and a motorcycle) and the scooterette (a hybrid between a moped and a scooter). At the same time, price differentials had also become blurred. By 1998 there was a scooter more expensive than a motorcycle, and a moped or a scooterette more expensive than a scooter. The consumers decided how much they wanted to pay and which features they wanted and a product was available in that range.

Indian Demand Growth Rate 2000E

Segment	*Scooter*	*Motorcycle*	*Mopeds/Scooterettes*	*3-wheelers*
Projected	8%	25%	13%	25%

Source: Industry forecasts.

Annual Motorcycle Growth Rates (%)

FY92	*FY93*	*FY94*	*FY95*	*FY96*	*FY97*	*FY98*	*FY99*	*FY2000E*
-9	-12	24	39	24	21	16.5	24.7	25

Source: DBS Securities, Bajaj Auto.

Annual Scooter Growth Rates (%)

FY92	*FY93*	*FY94*	*FY95*	*FY96*	*FY97*	*FY98*	*FY99*	*FY2000E*
-15.4	-8.1	17	24	15.3	4.6	-4.5	3.3	8

Source: Bajaj Auto.

By 1998, Bajaj Auto had stepped up motorcycle production, introduced new scooters, step-thrus and scooterettes. But what of the future? As Rahul Bajaj mused, 'Cost leadership and customisation were two contrary things. But that is where manufacturing technology counts: even if you are producing slightly different versions for different segments of the market, you can derive economies of scale.'

Expected Capacity Expansion to 2000

	Moped/Scooterettes		*Scooters*		*M'cycles*		*3-Wheelers*	
	FY98	*FY00*	*FY98*	*FY00*	*FY98*	*FY00*	*FY98*	*FY00*
Bajaj	135000	135000	1050000	1320000	525000	840000	225000	270000
TVS-Suzuki	300000	300000	80000	260000	240000	400000	–	–
Hero Honda	500000	700000	–	–	–	–	–	–
Kinetic Honda	–	–	175000	175000	–	–	–	–
Escorts Yamaha	12000	12000	–	–	210000	450000	–	–
LML	–	–	400000	600000	–	??	–	–
Kinetic Engg.	150000	150000	12000	12000	–	??	–	–
Hero Motors	150000	150000	–	–	–	–	–	–
Enfield	–	–	–	–	25000	25000	–	–
Greaves	–	–	–	–	–	–	??	??

Figures in units. ?? = unknown.
Source: Industry estimates.

There was no debate about the attractiveness of the market. According to Crisil, penetration rates in India were much lower than in other developing countries: 26 per 1,000 households for motorcycles, 51 for scooters and 30 for mopeds in 1997. Overall, the two- and three-wheeler industry was expected to grow at an average of 16 per cent per annum for the period 1995–2000. Against this, a sudden jump in petrol prices could lead to a postponement of the decision to buy a two-wheeler. And the two- and three-wheeler market was vulnerable to economic cycles as it was closely linked to the economy, which in turn was closely linked to the monsoon.

Historically, Bajaj Auto had depended on the middle class who appreciated its products' well-earned reputation for ruggedness, reliability and long life. The Indian army used 4S Champion motorcycles on the Siachen glacier, the highest battlefield in the world. It wasn't unusual for a Bajaj scooter to be used for ten to fifteen years by one owner, only to be sold off and used again for an equally long period. True, studies showed that the middle class was growing but data was sketchy. More people were brand conscious, but what did the Bajaj brand stand for in the eyes of Generation Next?

Future product development in two-wheelers had to be geared towards three categories of users:

1. The entry level product, i.e., when someone gets off his own two feet or a bicycle on to a two-wheeler.

2. The low-to middle-income group who wants a value-for-money product.
3. Premium end of the market.

Rajiv Bajaj was clear that the value-for-money and premium segments were the segments where Bajaj Auto should concentrate, where volumes and profits would lie. 'Entry level price is getting redefined with vehicle regulations and this, which also has a good share of the pie, will also be addressed.' At the same time, 'I feel the term "premium" is a misnomer. It's like calling the Zen or Esteem a premium car. That's the way it was positioned in India but all over the world, it's a small, economy car', he stressed.

Profits were carefully squirrelled away at Bajaj Auto and not deployed in diversification as other Indian companies tended to do. Instead the company quietly played the inter-corporate loan market and the stock exchange with remarkable dexterity and subtlety. It took pride that 'its ability to make money was matched by its capacity to make that money multiply'. A company brochure claimed: 'It is difficult not to envy Bajaj's near-zero debt status, restricted interest costs, top quality current asset management, Rs 15 bn cash reserve chest and above all, its EBDIT to turnover ratio of over 23 per cent.' *Asia Money* promptly rated Bajaj Auto as one of Asia's best managed companies, and *Asia Inc* ranked it 20th among 'Asia's Most Competitive Companies'.

The rosy figures masked one crucial fact. Bajaj Auto enjoyed the best profits in the business but as market share dipped, so did profitability. From 1997 onwards, the company deliberately used its financial muscle to shore up market shares. A brake was applied to retail prices. Funds were lent at subsidised rates to Bajaj Auto Finance Ltd, a sister concern, for its consumer finance schemes. In FY98, on sales of Rs 35,132 bn, the share of other income in pre-tax profits was 51.6 per cent. Net profit rose 5.4 per cent but other income rose 19.8 per cent.

Meanwhile domestic competition was hotting up. A bull run followed the 1991–93 recession. Between 1993-96, CAGR for the scooter segment was 20 per cent, for motorcycles 31 per cent, mopeds 21 per cent and three-wheelers 38 per cent. Yet Bajaj Auto's growth rate was nothing to write home about. In FY96, when the industry grew at 21.5 per cent, Bajaj Auto grew at 15 per cent. And in FY97, when it was 13 per cent, that of Bajaj Auto was 10 per cent.

The dispatch days were gone. It was no longer 'you can have any model you like, as long as it is a Chetak'. It was no longer even a question of pushing sales but real marketing, requiring focussed positioning strategies, and clear definition of product attributes. The penalty for failed product launches had risen with so many quality bikes in the market.

Until the new products could enter the market (1998–99), Bajaj Auto used its financial clout to shore up its falling market shares. In July 1997 it launched an attractive finance scheme at a flat 9 per cent rate, which was at least 1 to 2 per cent lower than that offered by banks and much cheaper than certain other schemes. These were offered through its sister concern, Bajaj Auto Finance Ltd, and its network of twenty-six branches. Bajaj Auto lent the latter subsidised funds. Hero Honda jumped onto the bandwagon but offered finance at 12 per cent flat. Countrywide offered at 16 per cent flat. Customers also found the Bajaj Auto offer the easiest in terms of down payment and faster processing.

Had the scheme not been introduced, sales would have fallen even more than they did. Between April and July 1997, for example, Bajaj Auto's sales dropped 20 per cent even as Hero Honda gained 9 per cent in motorcycles, LML 7 per cent in scooters and TVS-Suzuki 5 per cent in mopeds and 3 per cent in motorcycles. The picture in August was much better. Sales were up by 14 per cent, with 60,500 scooters sold as against 53,000 in June 1997. Bajaj Auto stopped short of cross-subsidising models to win back further market share. All models were profitable even though the degree varied. Even the entry-level models such as the 'Sunny' made a 12.5 per cent profit before advertising costs.

Even as the finance guys held the fort, marketing got into the act. R.L. Ravichandran, marketing head at TVS-Suzuki, who had been credited for its jump in market share by 11 per cent in 1993, was invited to join Bajaj Auto.

To create more customer pull, advertising budgets were beefed up. On paper, selling expenses as a percentage of net sales barely grew—from 4.26 per cent in 1995 to 5.86 per cent in 1998. But as net sales grew by about 50 per cent during that period, the absolute spend increased by over 100 per cent in these three years. The tune changed in time with the beat.

In the 1980s, the ad line was 'You Just Can't Beat a Bajaj'; in the mid-1990s, it was 'Hamara Bajaj'. Towards the late 1990s, Bajaj motorcycles claimed to be 'Unshakeable'.

The theme came straight out of Rajiv Bajaj's experience. 'Consumers want something spicy more frequently. What made a terrific impact on me was when I heard a consumer say, "Yes, the Bajaj scooter is the cheapest, but that's what it deserves to be"', recalled Rajiv Bajaj. 'We have to understand the customer's mindset. This is directly linked to innovation. Not necessarily technology innovation. In the 1990s, globally the technology behind most two-wheelers is the same. What two-wheelers could not give in forty years, cars have done in just a few. Secondly, we have to be more innovative. The Bajaj Auto mindset was that once we introduced a product, people would buy in volume. Thirdly, we have lost a perspective on what constitutes value and cost. When people see a Rs 20,000 price tag, they no longer say "Oh wow, Rs 20,000!" We need real value.'

Quality Issues

Quality standards had also slipped. The quality of outside components was poor but demanding quality from vendors was easier because Bajaj Auto could reject the batch. Vendors might not be interested in improving quality but would respond because they wanted the business. The trickier issue was how to improve quality in-house.

This meant going back to manufacturing engineering. A quick analysis revealed that some complaints were due to shop floor habits but others were design-related. In October 1997, a task force was formed with new recruits attached to each GM at the works but reporting to Arvind Gupta. Complaints could mean a process redesign, a tooling modification or the reconditioning/replacement of a machine. This took between four to six weeks, sometimes eight to fourteen weeks. Earlier, there used to be a long waiting time for a problem to get attention. Now if there was a hot issue, it took a week; a less important issue could take up to six months, but all issues had to be corrected.

Public perception being what it is, the good news was taking its time trickling through to consumers. In 1998, there was a waiting list for Hero Honda motorcycles, not for Bajaj motorcycles or scooters for that matter.

Challenges of the Future

Overall, the economies of scale that Bajaj Auto enjoyed, its high profits and ability to manufacture a low cost product should have been the perfect vehicle on which to challenge world markets. Ironically, the cost efficiency of the Indian operation made Bajaj Auto reluctant to step outside India. 'Scale has made us extremely cost competitive in the market place. Size has also allowed us to offer a full range of products and bolstered our financial strength. But no market can provide me the volumes I can command in India. You need not have manufacturing facilities all over the world to be globally competitive. Hence cost does not compel me to move my manufacturing out,' said Rahul Bajaj. But by not stepping into the outside world, was Bajaj Auto's vision getting partially blinkered?

Bajaj Auto's Corporate Mission

As an organisation competing on a global basis, we focus our resources on continuously enhancing customer satisfaction with our products and services.

Under Rahul Bajaj, the company had evolved an extremely successful strategy based on cost leadership and product robustness. But the pieces of this strategy—high volumes, few product varieties, investment in production and distribution only after demand was in place, and conservative financial policies—were tightly knit together. A small change in any part of the picture—such as more product varieties—would necessarily impact the tight fit, and maybe unravel the strategy. Rajiv Bajaj was willing to take a chance. Convinced that the way forward was to offer the customer more than he or she was getting so far, Rajiv Bajaj asked, 'Had the rear view mirror become the windshield?'

The huge changes inside Bajaj Auto mirrored the equally significant changes occuring in the two-wheeler industry worldwide. Globally, two-wheeler production had shifted from the developed western economies to Asian countries. In 1993, Asian countries (including Japan) accounted for 65 per cent of the world's two-wheeler production. In the decade 1983–93, two-wheeler production in Japan and western Europe declined by 6 per cent and 8.5 per cent (compounded annually) respectively. In contrast, Asia (excluding Japan) grew at 13.5 per cent. India was the second largest market for two-wheelers in the world (after China). In 1994, India accounted for 12 per cent of the world's two-wheeler production.

Almost from the day he joined Bajaj Auto, Rahul Bajaj had dreamt of making his company the world's leading manufacturer of two-wheelers. This was when Bajaj Auto had only one product, that too a Piaggio look alike, and there was a local ten-year waiting list. Yet, in every interview he gave, Rahul would talk about exports, about the need to become world class in manufacturing, how the company must raise its quality standards, etc.

Asked once to spell out what he meant by 'world class', Rahul replied, 'The day 20 per cent of my production is exported, I will say I am world class.' To achieve this level of exports needed a combination of further price reduction, a better finish, a wider range, greater technological development and a distribution network in major markets. This was in 1989. By 1998, Bajaj Auto appeared to have progressed towards these objectives.

It had gained considerable experience of international markets, even if the 20 per cent target had not quite been achieved. The company was the lowest cost producer of scooters in the world. Aesthetics had become as familiar a buzzword as value-for-money on the shop floor. The product range had widened. And most important, Bajaj Auto had vaulted a major technology hurdle: it had learnt how to make the more fuel-efficient and environmentally friendlier four-stroke engine. As Rajiv Bajaj said, '. . . there was an internal "feel good" factor today which was missing in the recent past.'

A somewhat simplistic attitude to exports led to exports being 1 per cent of total sales in FY90 and over 4.5 per cent in FY98 (Rs 1,408 mn). Bajaj Auto claimed it had captured 65 per cent of Colombia's scooter market, 30 per cent of Uruguay's motorcycle market and 95 per cent of Bangladesh's three-wheeler market. However, as Rahul Bajaj candidly admitted, 'There's not much point in saying that we have a major presence internationally when we export 40,000 vehicles to fifty countries and of these 30,000 go to just five countries.' If Bajaj Auto wanted to be a truly global company, it had to make a greater impact across more markets.

Despite the impressive progress and cost leadership, the grail to world leadership seemed as distant as before. The company had scaled a steep learning curve but the gap between Bajaj Auto and a company such as Honda, for example, seemed as wide as ever. Bajaj Auto's record in accessing international markets was patchy. It had been able to develop a four-stroke geared scooter—a world first—but was struggling to routinely develop brand new products from scratch in-house. Why? In its attempts to become world class, what had Bajaj Auto learnt and what did it still need to learn?

APPENDIX 1

Organisation Chart

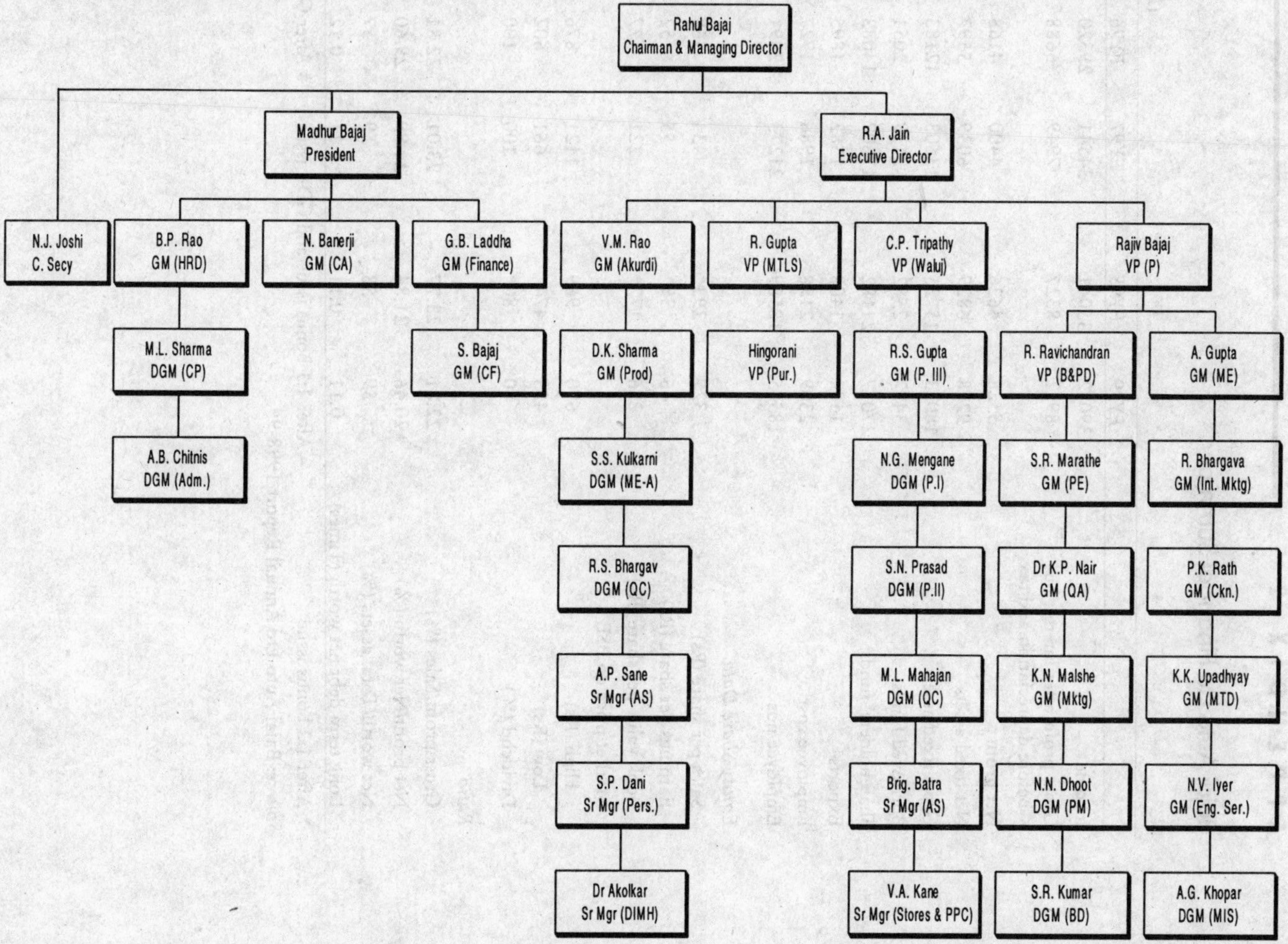
Rahul Bajaj
Chairman & Managing Director
Madhur Bajaj
President
R.A. Jain
Executive Director
N.J. Joshi
C. Secy
B.P. Rao
GM (HRD)
N. Banerji
GM (CA)
G.B. Laddha
GM (Finance)
V.M. Rao
GM (Akurdi)
R. Gupta
VP (MTLS)
C.P. Tripathy
VP (Waluj)
Rajiv Bajaj
VP (P)
M.L. Sharma
DGM (CP)
S. Bajaj
GM (CF)
D.K. Sharma
GM (Prod)
Hingorani
VP (Pur.)
R.S. Gupta
GM (P. III)
R. Ravichandran
VP (B&PD)
A. Gupta
GM (ME)
A.B. Chitnis
DGM (Adm.)
S.S. Kulkarni
DGM (ME-A)
N.G. Mengane
DGM (P.I)
S.R. Marathe
GM (PE)
R. Bhargava
GM (Int. Mktg)
R.S. Bhargav
DGM (QC)
S.N. Prasad
DGM (P.II)
Dr K.P. Nair
GM (QA)
P.K. Rath
GM (Ckn.)
A.P. Sane
Sr Mgr (AS)
M.L. Mahajan
DGM (QC)
K.N. Malshe
GM (Mktg)
K.K. Upadhyay
GM (MTD)
S.P. Dani
Sr Mgr (Pers.)
Brig. Batra
Sr Mgr (AS)
N.N. Dhoot
DGM (PM)
N.V. Iyer
GM (Eng. Ser.)
Dr Akolkar
Sr Mgr (DIMH)
V.A. Kane
Sr Mgr (Stores & PPC)
S.R. Kumar
DGM (BD)
A.G. Khopar
DGM (MIS)

APPENDIX 2

Bajaj Auto Ltd Financial Summary

(*Rs million*)

	FY99	*FY98*	*FY97*	*FY96*	*FY95*
Income	39072	35041	34541	29320	22871
Gross profit after interest but before depreciation and tax	8912	8327	7949	6688	5074
Net profit	5528	4626	4400	4168	3096
Net fixed assets	9218	6829	6039	5597	3346
Gross fixed assets	18023	15725	13603	12183	9220
Borrowed funds	3497	2582	2139	2051	2007
Shareholders' funds	27017	21182	17607	14083	10710
Exports	1584	1408	1582	1895	1302
Employee cost	2309	2198	1986	1727	1279
Employee nos	18585	18589	21273	22891	19400
Equity Share Data					
Sales per share (Rs)	327	293*	434	368	297~#
Earnings per share (Rs)	46	39*	55	52	40~#
Book value per share (Rs)	226	177*	221	177	135~
Market price on BSE					
High (Rs)	690	969	1121	876	1475
Low (Rs)	483	474*	661	602	590~
Dividend (%)	80	80*	100	100	80*
Ratio					
Gross profit/Sales (%)	22.81	23.77	23.01	22.81	22.18
Net profit/Net worth (%)	20.46	21.84	24.99	29.60	28.90
Net worth/Total assets (%)	59	58	59	57	57
Long term debt net worth (Times)	0.11	0.11	0.11	0.12	0.14

* After 1:2 bonus issue   ~ After 1:1 bonus issue and GDR issue   # After GDR issue

Source: Bajaj Auto Ltd Annual Report 1998-99.

CASE 2

HINDUSTAN LEVER LIMITED: LEVERS FOR CHANGE

For Hindustan Lever Limited (HLL), the Indian subsidiary of Unilever and one of the largest private sector companies in the country, 1991 was an excellent year (see Appendix 1). Revenues had increased by 22 per cent to Rs 17.75 bn while profit before tax had grown by 24 per cent to Rs 1.38 bn (in 1991 $ 1 million was roughly equal to Rs 30 mn). In the year-ending meeting of the management committee, therefore, the mood was one of quiet celebration. As S.M. Datta, the chairman of HLL, pointed out, there was enough cheer to pass around for all the divisions had performed well. For particular mention, however, he singled out the detergents group which had achieved record growth in volume during that year. He formally recorded his satisfaction with their performance, acknowledged the high state of alertness and motivation that he perceived

This case was written by Charlotte Butler, Research Associate, under the supervision and guidance of Sumantra Ghoshal, Robert P. Baumann Professor of Strategic Leadership at the London Business School. The section on India's fabric wash market draws on the work of Professor Sushil Vachani reported in his book *Multinationals in India*, Oxford and IBH Publishing Company, New Delhi, 1991. The authors are grateful to Hindustan Lever Ltd for their help and support in writing the case. The case was first registered by the London Business School in 2000.

among all the managers, and thanked everyone for their efforts. He then gestured to an empty chair. Sitting in that chair and deserving a special vote of thanks for helping the company develop its agility and competitiveness, he said, should be Karsanbhai Patel, the owner-director of Nirma chemical works, HLL's arch rival in the detergents business.

Everyone present knew exactly what he meant. None more so than S. Sen, ex-marketing director of HLL. Sen's thoughts drifted back to 1977, when he had stood in front of a small store in a remote village near Ghaziabad in North India and watched the shopkeeper serve a small boy with a plastic bag of Nirma detergent powder from a large gunny sack that was almost empty. It was the culmination of an official tour of the state, during which he had been haunted by the ubiquitous presence of this yellow detergent. In growing disbelief, he had calculated the Nirma sales figures he was gradually accumulating. Suddenly the sharp realisation had hit him. His company was fast losing a war they did not even know they were fighting.

During the 1980s Nirma had gone on to become the biggest detergent brand in India and then one of the biggest in the world, swamping Surf and threatening HLL's dominance in other sectors of the fabric wash market. By the time HLL fully recognized the danger Nirma represented and began to fight back, it had almost become too late.

Nirma's dramatic rise was the major lever for change within HLL. To create an adequate response, HLL had been forced to jettison some long cherished assumptions about both the detergent industry and the company's conventional business practices and, instead, adopt an entirely new way of operating.

HLL rose to the challenge, revolutionising its processes and systems to enter the low cost segments of the detergent market and arrest the growth of Nirma. This new-found flexibility and changed mindset had subsequently enabled HLL to overcome a threat from P&G in the concentrate detergent market.

But though the battles with Nirma and P&G had been temporarily won, it was at best only a truce. As Datta went on to exhort his assembled troops, HLL could not afford to rest on its laurels. In 1991, the detergent market was growing fast at about 20 per cent a year. With a push, HLL reckoned it could double its volume by 1995. However, that push would take place in a new, unknown environment created by government moves to deregulate India's markets. This new situation, promising not only increased competition but also unprecedented growth opportunities, represented yet another lever for change at HLL. The issue for the management committee was how best to prepare the company for the very different conditions it would face in the 1990s. What should be the next stage in the company's evolution to ensure its future as a major player on the Indian industrial scene?

Hindustan Lever Limited (HLL) was founded in 1956 by the merger of three companies—Hindustan Vanaspati Manufacturing Company (HVM), Lever Brothers India Limited and United Traders Limited. Established in 1931, HVM was Unilever's first Indian subsidiary, producing vanaspati, a granular edible oil. Lever Brothers, founded in 1933, manufactured soaps and a range of toilet preparations. It dominated India's soap and detergent industry from its inception and played a major role in popularising the use of these products throughout the country. The third subsidiary, United Traders Limited, was formed in 1935 to look after Unilever's personal products business which ranged from toothpastes to hair oils.

Since the 1960s, HLL had diversified into chemicals to participate in what government industrial policy designated as the core sector. This was now a strong and growing part of the business. HLL produced industrial phosphates, fertiliser, fluid cracking catalysts (for oil refineries) and functionalised bio-polymers (for paper, textile and food processing industries). It also developed a host of hybrid seeds, high yielding virus-free crop varieties and a chemical to improve photosynthetic efficiency in plants. The Hindustan Lever Research Centre, founded in 1967, was the biggest in India's private sector. In 1991, the company's businesses were divisionalised into Chemicals, Detergents, Agriproducts, Personal Products and Exports. These were supported by central services such as R&D, Finance, Personnel and Legal and Secretarial (see Appendix 2).

Until the 1992 policy changes, HLL's 51 per cent foreign shareholding meant that under the 1973 Foreign Exchange Regulation Act (FERA) it was required to export at least 10 per cent of sales, and over the years HLL had become one of India's biggest foreign exchange earners. By 1991, its exports had risen to a record Rs 2.02 bn, contrasting with the Rs 80 mn earned in 1972. More than two-thirds of these exports were value-added consumer products such as footwear, carpets and leather goods, as well as its brand of basmati rice and vanaspati.

In 1991, HLL had thirty manufacturing units in nine states and one union territory. Fifteen of these factories were in what the government designated as backward areas. Through its country-wide manufacturing and distribution activities, HLL directly employed over 10,000 people and through linkage with numerous ancillaries generated indirect employment for about 230,000 others.

HLL and Unilever

HLL formed part of Unilever's group of seven companies in India, the others being the food and tea companies Lipton and Brooke Bond, the personal products companies Pond's and Quest, and tea estates in Assam and South India. Unilever had a long and highly respected presence in the country—the first crates of Sunlight soap were unloaded in Calcutta in 1888—and the next four decades saw the introduction of its international brands of soaps, detergents and personal products as well as expansion into foods and beverages. The group had always been one of the top ten private sector companies in India. In 1990, the combined turnover of Unilever's Indian operations exceeded Rs 29 bn. In 1991, it aimed for Rs 35 bn, which would make it the third largest business group in the country.

The Anglo-Dutch multinational, Unilever, was one of the world's largest producers of branded consumer goods. Its products were manufactured in seventy-five countries and sold through subsidiaries operating in Europe, North America, Asia, Africa and Latin America. Consistently profitable since its foundation in the nineteenth century, Unilever's main strengths were size and geographical spread. Despite the continued recession in its two most important markets—Europe and the US—in 1991 it had a turnover of £23,163 million, a 2 per cent increase over the previous year (see Appendix 3).

Its major worldwide businesses were food and drinks (50 per cent of turnover in 1991), detergents, toilet preparations and other household products. In each country, Unilever's products usually comprised a mix of internationally known brands and a number of local brands. Until the late 1980s, HLL's product profile was somewhat different from that of its parent company. In 1981, 39 per cent of its sales came from soaps and 24 per cent from detergents. In 1983, HLL sold its foods business to Lipton India, a fellow Unilever subsidiary.

HLL's chairman and senior managers were appointed by Unilever and annual budgets, including sales and marketing plans, had to be approved by the head office. Unilever contributed centrally-held marketing expertise to help subsidiaries adapt and launch its international brands. It shared information and understanding of international marketing developments and provided multinational linkages. The subsidiaries also benefited from access to Unilever R&D and technology.

Unilever has always operated on the principle of 'think globally, act locally' and its decentralised approach to managing subsidiaries gave them a great deal of autonomy in taking decisions on a local level. In HLL's case, this tendency was reinforced by the company's reputation for successful innovation and effective local management. HLL's R&D centre in Bombay specialised in detergents for developing countries and its products were shared with other Unilever subsidiaries. HLL's managers assisted with the launch of detergents in Indonesia and Colombia.

Its belief in local autonomy made Unilever an early exponent of training and promoting local management to succeed Europeans. Unilever's Indian subsidiaries were far ahead of other foreign companies in this, the first Indian managers being appointed in the 1930s. Unilever later set up a Management Trainee Scheme in India to select 'young, bright locals' from the universities and attract them into the Unilever fold. For ambitious young Indians joining HLL was a guaranteed start to a successful career as a professional manager.

By 1955, 65 per cent of HLL's managerial cadre were Indians. The first Indian director was appointed in 1951 and the first Indian chairman a decade later. By then, 93 per cent of HLL's managers were Indians.

Within Unilever, all nationalities had equal opportunity and Indian managers contributed significantly to the running of Unilever business worldwide. In 1991, forty Indian managers were serving in Unilever headquarters, research establishments or companies abroad, half in senior positions. An ex-HLL chairman, T. Thomas, was on the main Unilever board between 1978 and 1989 and in 1991, his successor, Ashok Ganguly, was also made a member of the board as director for research and engineering in Unilever. HLL was very proud of its contribution to Unilever's acknowledged management strength.

HLL's managers were also very proud of their contribution to India's development. Unilever's reputation for moulding highly trained managers put HLL at the vanguard of the professional management movement in India. This brought it to the attention of the government, with whom it built up a strong relationship. The high standing enjoyed by HLL managers could be measured by the way the company regularly supplied people to lead private and public sector companies and government bodies in India.

Unilever took pains to transmit its culture throughout its global reach, aiming to build common values and ways of thinking among all its managers. This culture was transmitted via training programmes and, for promising managers, through time spent at the head office in London. There, they made useful contacts and learned the special language in which Unilever managers from all over the world communicated with each other. Unilever attributes, according to Dr Ganguly, included honesty and integrity, and 'a strong regard for meritocracy that valued talent and a respect for managers who displayed a genuine concern for others'.

The Unilever culture was readily absorbed and implemented by the strong cadre of managers created at HLL.

> Ganguly observed, 'I could never describe the culture except to state that HLL was able to attract a group of ordinary people and enable them to perform extraordinarily'. Each HLL employee was, he said, 'the product of a scrupulous meritocracy that sought excellence, calibre and potential.'

Consequently, in HLL, generations served Unilever with pride, secure in the knowledge that the company's reputation for producing effective managers automatically conferred respect from outsiders. To have the right to wear the HLL tie spoke for itself—they were an elite.

The Fabric Wash Market in India

With a population of over 800 million people, India represented one of the largest fabric wash markets in the world. Traditionally, clothes were washed by hand, using hard, yellow bars of laundry soap which accounted for over 95 per cent of the market up to the early 1970s. In the two decades since then, the sales of non-soap detergent (NSD) had soared, largely through expansion of the market but also through substitution for soap bars which, though cheaper, also tended to be less effective. The government, too, had encouraged the growth of the NSD market to curb the use of edible oil used in the manufacture of soap.

Large firms, for example, were not allowed to use edible oil for soap manufacture and, therefore, had an incentive to switch to producing detergents. Thus, to the original washing soap market, two new segments were added: NSD powders and NSD bars (see Appendix 4).

Laundry Soap

The highly fragmented laundry soap market was dominated by low-priced products made by small-scale local manufacturers in different parts of the country. In 1991, the ten largest competitors in this segment collectively accounted for less than 5 per cent of the national demand. HLL's flag carrier in this segment was the primrose yellow Sunlight soap, manufactured since 1934 at the company's Sewri factory near Bombay. At a quarter of the price of toilet soaps like Lux, Sunlight was sold for both personal and clothes-washing use. The only other branded product of any significance was the Tata Oil Mills Company's (TOMCO) Tata 501.

In the detergents business, there were neither any special regulatory constraints nor was the basic technology difficult to come by. The manufacturing processes for both NSD powders and NSD bars were common up to the point where the detergent slurry was prepared. While bars were then made by compressing and shaping the slurry, for powders the slurry was atomised in hot air spray towers to produce detergent beads. The key challenge in the manufacturing process lay in producing a consistent-quality product over large volumes and long time periods.

Detergent Powder

The first companies to begin manufacturing detergent in India were a local private sector firm, Swastik, and HLL. In 1956–57, Swastik produced a powder called Det while HLL test marketed Surf, a blue powder, between 1956 and 1958 and began manufacturing it in 1959. Det, a white powder, was successful in eastern India while Surf quickly became the national market leader with dominant positions in the West, North and South.

HLL worked hard to expand the detergent market by familiarising potential users; salesmen toured the villages in vans and, 'like high priests', preached to villagers about the usefulness and importance of Surf in daily life and its comparative advantages over other soaps: 'Surf has more lather and is more soapy than any other soap'. HLL also ran advertisements showing how clothes could be washed by soaking them in a bucket containing detergent dissolved in the water.

Between 1960 and 1965, the total volume of detergent manufactured in India grew from 1,600 to 8,000 tons. HLL held unchallenged sway over this market with a share of almost 70 per cent to Swastik's 25 per cent. Then, in 1966, another manufacturer, the Tata Oil Mills Company (TOMCO) entered the market with its powder, Magic. That year, the total manufacture of detergent, all of which was powder, was around 11,000 tons and these three were established as the main players, with HLL far out in front with a market share of 67 per cent against Swastik's 20 per cent and TOMCO's 7 per cent. In 1973, TOMCO introduced a low-price detergent called Tata's Tej and in 1976–77, an economy detergent powder called OK.

That same year saw the world-wide rise in the price of crude oil. This increased the raw material cost of detergent and, consequently, the selling price shot up. HLL's Surf, for example, doubled in price between 1974 and 1975. This created an opportunity for local producers of crude detergents—low-price, low-quality products based on cheap raw materials—to increase their market share.

After 1974, therefore, a host of new competitors diversified from laundry soaps into detergent powders to challenge the hegemony of HLL, Swastik and TOMCO. MSIL/Karnataka Soaps, a state-owned enterprise that had produced soap since the First World War, launched a powder called Point in 1975. Godrej, a local private sector company that had produced soap for a number of years, launched a powder called Key in 1977 and Detergents India Limited (DIL), another state-owned enterprise, launched a powder, Sixer, in 1978. Surf, however, continued to lead in both volume and value, commanding a premium of almost 40 per cent over the medium priced powders such as Key, Tej and Point.

Detergent Bars

Meanwhile, TOMCO and HLL had expanded the market further by introducing detergent cakes and bars into India. In 1968, TOMCO converted one of its washing soaps, Bonus, into a detergent cake and in reply HLL launched Rin a year later. In 1971, Swastik introduced a cake called Det. By 1975, the cake segment had caught up with the powder segment in terms of volume and by 1977 was slightly ahead of it.

Again, the three main players were followed by smaller competitors. MSIL and Godrej both launched detergent bars in 1979 and DIL, which had entered the market with a detergent cake called Regal in 1977, launched a new brand called

Chek in the form of both powder and cake in 1980. Meanwhile, the bigger players had also produced new offerings. TOMCO's blue detergent bar, 501, appeared in 1976–77 and in 1980–81 it launched a higher quality detergent cake called Dubble. Swastik, in the meantime, had been enjoying success with a detergent bar, Super 777, forcing HLL to reply with its Wheel bar in 1977. By 1979, Wheel had significantly reduced Super 777's share.

Price categories in the quality bars and cakes segment were comparable to those of the powder segment. Rin and Det were priced about 10 per cent below the highest priced powders like Surf. In the medium price category, brands like HLL's Wheel, Swastik's Super 777 and TOMCO's Bonus were almost 50 per cent cheaper than the price of the premium bars and 20 per cent lower than the price of the medium priced powders. Some small-scale local producers manufactured small quantities of detergent bars using very crude methods and these were priced substantially lower that the quality products from the established companies.

Despite all these efforts, penetration of the market was slow. One estimate put the size of the Indian yellow soap market at over 800,000 tons while total detergent sales in 1981 were estimated to be around 200,000 tons. In developed countries, by comparison, detergent penetration at this time was 90 per cent. By 1989, the NSD (bars and powders) share had grown to 55 per cent as against 45 per cent for laundry soap.

This then was the almost feudal structure of the industry that had developed by the 1970s. Competition there was, but it was not marked by the degree of aggression seen in western markets. At the top, HLL presided majestically over what was known as the organized sector—the premium detergent powder and bar markets. By this time, HLL knew its nearest rivals well and felt secure in the knowledge that with the range of international brands in the repertoire of its parent company at its disposal it would largely be able to dictate the market's future development. HLL's managers had made the rules of the game, they were its most professional players; it was a game they took for granted they would win.

Just below the big three players, the middle-sized companies competed with each other in a similar familiar pattern. Way beneath the heights and the notice of HLL and the other sophisticated, high quality manufacturers scrambled a shoal of local, 'cottage sector' firms producing a few hundred tons of cheap, poor quality powder sold loose in plastic bags. This was referred to as the unorganised sector.

However, in the mid-1970s the eruption of one such small 'cottage' firm into this industry with its packets of yellow powder shook the fabric of this well ordered hierarchy and, in particular, altered the competitive destiny of HLL.

The Nirma Assault

Nirma was the single-handed creation of an ambitious entrepreneur, Karsan K. Patel. An ex-lab assistant, in 1969 he decided to set up a business making and selling laundry soaps and detergent powders. Right from the start, Patel was totally committed to making his brand the biggest in the world. While in 1969 such an idea would undoubtedly have provoked helpless laughter among HLL's managers, the serious Patel would have remained unmoved and undeterred. His belief in his basic business principle—develop a good product and there will be a market for it—was absolute.

Production of the brand which, within just over a decade would indeed become one of the largest in the world, began in December 1969 in a small shed in Saraspur, a suburb of Ahmedabad in the state of Gujarat. Ahmedabad was then a big soap market with bars, cubes and chips stocked in almost all of the city's 2000 retail outlets and with over 200 large and small soap manufacturers. The laundry soap he began producing quickly became overshadowed by the detergent powder which Patel himself hand-mixed in batches and packed into polythene bags which he then stapled. This product he called Nirma after his younger daughter, Niru. To sell it, he loaded several gunny bags of the powder sachets on his bicycle and began a house-to-house round of the city. Working in this way, he produced 200 kg a day. His company was registered as Nirma Chemical Works.

During the next decade, Patel barely diverged from this simple approach to production, packaging and promotion, pricing and distribution. Though refined and enlarged, the formula remained essentially the same. Patel did not follow a fixed set of business rules, but built an operation that was easily adapted to changing market circumstances. As a modus operandi, it defied all the existing business logic of the large producers.

The Product

According to HLL's carefully developed lore, 'a well formulated detergent was a composite of several carefully selected ingredients such as AD (Active

Detergent), builder, buffer, anti-redisposition agent, etc., each one performing a special function'. Not only were the types of ingredients used important, but the levels were also critical 'to deliver good performance, and these levels must be fixed with a detailed knowledge of wash habits'.

Nirma powder conformed to none of HLL's carefully developed formulae. It contained no ingredient to improve the whiteness of the fabric and the level of AD was half that of Surf. Nirma had no perceptible perfume and clothes washed in it were harsher to the touch. Tested on guinea pigs, it proved to cause 'scaliness, crackling, leather skin and epidermal breakdown' and, according to HLL researchers, had the potential to cause blisters on the hands and skin irritancy among those using it for long periods.

Nirma was inferior to Surf and other premium powders on every single characteristic normally measured. And yet, despite the undeniable superiority of the HLL product, by 1977 Nirma was selling a little under a third the volume of Surf.

Production Method

From the early start of mixing the powder in his shed, Patel remained a small-scale producer. In Gujarat, soda ash and other raw materials were easily obtainable and Patel bought supplies locally using cash discounts. A key process—the sulphonation of linear alkyl benzene (LAB)—was contracted out to another small-scale operator in Ahmedabad.

The ingredients were then simply dumped on the floor and mixed by hand. Patel thus derived all the cost benefit of using no electricity and until 1985, Nirma enjoyed the 15 per cent excise benefit granted to small-scale producers not using any power. After 1985, when the change in rules removed this benefit, Patel began mechanised mixing for part of his production.

As sales increased, he began to employ people to do the mixing and opened up two further production facilities at Rakhial (1973) and Vatwa GIDC (1976), and then added four further sheds at Ramol. The powder was manually packed into polythene bags and stapled together. To avoid chemical reactions, the workers were changed every three months. Production was continuous from 8 a.m. to 6 p.m., with no interruption for Sundays or holidays.

In India, minimum wage rules laid down for urban and rural labour did not apply to small firms. The Nirma workforce consisted of contract workers, hired by job contractors and paid Rs 85 per ton for mixing the raw material which was then prepared in sacks of 1000 bags of 1 kg each by job labourers. One person could pack 300 kg of powder a day, so 3,500 people were required to pack 1,000 tons a day.

The labourers were paid on the basis of work done. In 1989, labour costs for Nirma's 8,000 workers were estimated at between Rs 15-25 per person day. Compared to this, HLL's labour costs (semi-skilled) were approximately Rs 30-40 per man day. This structure kept Nirma's production costs as low as Rs 100 per ton. Further, the manual production process kept investment in plant and machinery also very low, at about Rs 200 per ton, as opposed to about Rs 4,000 per ton for HLL's more capital-intensive production system.

Contracting out played a large part in keeping Nirma's overheads low. Besides the production of some raw materials, labour and distribution, major tasks like selling, accounting, and technical/production capabilities were also contracted out. This gave Patel the flexibility to adapt his operation when necessary and take advantage of downturns to negotiate cheaper rates.

As the operation grew, Patel took his relatives into a partnership. Registered in 1972, this partnership was dissolved in 1985 when Nirma reverted to a one-man show. Mr Patel maintained control over the overall administration, production and final decision making, as well as the critical decision areas of dealing with dealers and raw material buying. Of the 250 people employed by Nirma, 200 were clerical staff. His headquarters remained in Ahmedabad and one other operational office was opened in Bombay.

Distribution

Nirma had no field force or sales organisation of its own. Sales were generated purely through promotion. Once demand had outgrown personal deliveries by Patel on his bicycle, vans and later trucks were used to distribute Nirma. With transport, Nirma operated on the philosophy of obtaining the lowest cost at any point in time. Patel negotiated a daily price basis with the truck suppliers, so gaining significant cost advantages when market prices were low.

Slowly, sales were extended first to retail outlets within Ahmedabad and later to surrounding districts and towns. Stockists were then appointed to sell Nirma to shopkeepers. Initially, these stockists were all family members or close business associates, but as Nirma began to be sold in other states, people from outside the family were introduced into the system. Later, district level agents were appointed to distribute Nirma to the stockists, with state level agents for East and South India.

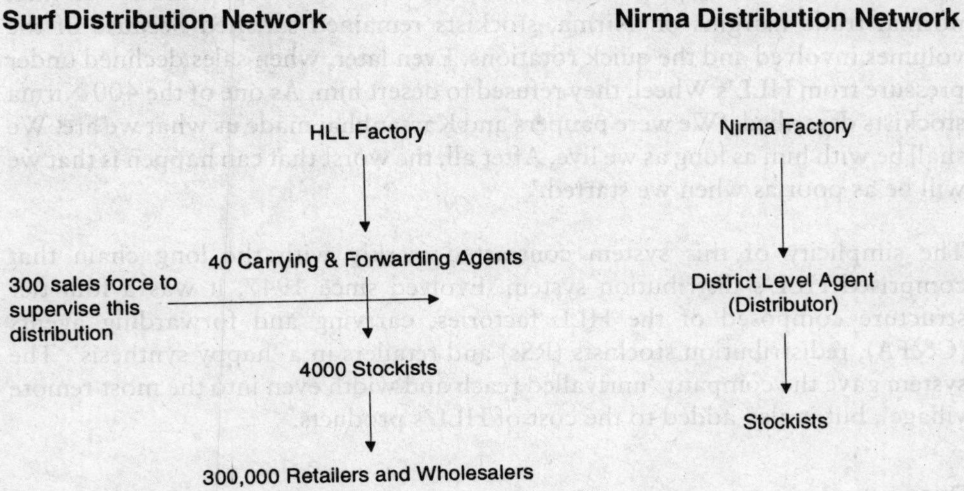

To avoid central sales tax (CST) charges in other states, the stockists were appointed as commission agents. To qualify as a Nirma stockist, minimum sales of 80-100 tons per month was demanded. Each agent received supplies at a predetermined rate: for example, if he was selling 100 tons per month, then every third day a truck would deliver 10 tons. No cancellation of orders was allowed. If additional stocks were needed, Nirma Chemical Works had to be notified well in advance.

The system ran on advance payment by demand draft. If demand drafts for payment were not received by the 30th of the month, stockists paid a 15 paise per bag interest charge. A deposit of 10p per bag was collected on all Nirma sales. Billing was on the basis of ex-factory prices and expenses on transport, octroi, handling and delivery were borne by the stockists. The stockists also funded promotional expenditure up to 50 per cent.

Shops received deliveries of Nirma from the stockist by van. The regularity of these deliveries varied from a week to thirty days. Only in the large towns was there a set schedule.

Nirma distributors displayed intense loyalty to Patel. Despite the lower than normal trade margins on Nirma, stockists remained satisfied because of the volumes involved and the quick rotations. Even later, when sales declined under pressure from HLL's Wheel, they refused to desert him. As one of the 400 Nirma stockists described, 'We were paupers and Karsanbhai made us what we are. We shall be with him as long as we live. After all, the worst that can happen is that we will be as poor as when we started.'

The simplicity of this system contrasted starkly with the long chain that comprised HLL's distribution system. Evolved since 1947, it was a four-tier structure composed of the HLL factories, carrying and forwarding agents (C&FA), redistribution stockists (RSs) and retailers in a 'happy synthesis'. The system gave the company 'unrivalled reach and width even into the most remote village', but it also added to the cost of HLL's products.

Price

The consequence of this low cost operation was Nirma's greatest strength—its price. In 1977, at a third of the price of Surf at Rs 4.35 per kg, Nirma was priced substantially lower than any of the quality detergents.

Over the years, Patel's strategy was to maintain this low unit price. From a low base, it was increased by only 40 per cent in seven years. Only after 1985 did the need to pay excise tax lead to a 15 per cent increase.

Packaging and Advertising

Nirma was sold in polybags, in contrast to Surf, which was sold in cartons, manufactured at 50 per cent more cost. A gunny bag with polyliner was used for outer packaging. From the start, Nirma had its own packaging material unit (again small scale) and printing press, further reducing costs.

Surf : Nirma Market Share

Year	*Market Share (Vol.)*	
	Surf	*Nirma*
1975	40.8	–
1976	38.2	–
1977	30.6	11.9
1978	26.3	11.7
1979	24.7	21.3
1980	21.8	31.00
1981	19.4	33.2
1982	15.2	43.2
1983	11.5	51.5
1984	9.4	57.3
1985	8.4	58.1
1986	8.4	59.1
1987	7.4	61.6
1988	6.7	59.5
1989	6.7	54.6

Surf : Nirma Price Ratio

Year	*Price (Rs per kg)*		*Price Ratio*
	Surf	*Nirma*	
1975	10.65	–	–
1976	10.15	–	–
1977	12.80	4.35	2.94
1978	12.25	4.75	2.58
1979	11.95	4.45	2.69
1980	18.50	6.00	3.08
1981	20.20	6.25	3.23
1982	21.05	6.00	3.51
1983	20.90	6.25	3.34
1984	22.20	6.80	3.26
1985	23.15	7.20	3.22
1986	23.70	8.00	2.96
1987	27.10	8.50	3.19
1988	28.70	9.00	3.19
1989	30.00	9.25	3.24

In the early years, the Nirma packet featured a lady washing a garment. In this, it was indistinguishable from scores of other cottage sector products. From 1973, however, Patel broke new ground by featuring his daughter on the pack and from then on, adopted an increasingly innovative approach to sales.

His first marketing efforts were directed towards gaining trade acceptance. Young women were hired to visit retail shops in Ahmedabad asking for Nirma. The effect was immediate as retailers accepted stocks of Nirma to fulfil the perceived demand. A providential shortage of soda ash, used by many Indian women for their bulk wash, further aided Patel by encouraging consumers to switch to Nirma, which contained 65 per cent soda ash.

Advertising and promoting Nirma was the one area where Patel spared no expense. In 1974 and 1976, he announced prize draws offering winners sums of Rs 30,000 and Rs 50,000 respectively, enormous sums by Indian standards. Held in the Ahmedabad Town Hall, they were a great success and by the third draw in 1982, increased sales had boosted the prize money to a stunning Rs 2.2 mn. In 1980, the year of the Moscow Olympics, the Nirma calendar was launched, followed by Nirma plastic shop boards. Nirma was the only Indian advertiser at the Olympics apart from the State Bank of India.

Over the next few years, advertising expenditure grew from Rs 2 mn in 1980 to Rs 4.5 mn in 1983 and to an estimated Rs 20 mn (2 per cent of net sales value) in 1985. However, sharing the Nirma brand name across different products did give tremendous synergy in advertising.

It was widely rumoured that Patel had hired a leading Indian marketing consultant to design his campaigns. Neither in town nor countryside could people escape Nirma—the name appeared in urban stores, in village shops and in advertisements everywhere, on passing vans and in the newspapers. Hoardings blazoned Nirma's message, a film was a great success, and the catchy jingle that punctuated every programme on the radio—'Nirma washes clothes white as milk'—invaded the minds of Indian housewives and children. With the expansion of commercial TV from about 1977 onwards, Nirma's advertising spread and its budget grew by leaps and bounds. For Patel, it was money well spent.

Among consumers, Nirma went from nowhere to having the highest top-of-the-mind recall (55 per cent) and the highest unaided recall (69 per cent) of all soap powders in 1986. It had an awareness level of over 90 per cent. Its uniqueness rating rose from 53 per cent in 1982 to 82 per cent in 1984. Strongly entrenched in the daily wear/household linen wash area, Nirma was seen as a powerful detergent able to remove stubborn dirt, economical in use and good value for money. Its use extended across all income and age groups, though Nirma was more popular among younger housewives (the older ones were more inclined to use Surf) and blue/white collar workers. Middle and upper income groups still largely stuck to Surf.

> In a neat irony which HLL managers would later recognise to their chagrin, Patel succeeded for the same reason as Lord Lever and his original Sunlight—he offered 'value for money for a well differentiated brand which was well distributed and supported'.

Nirma's Growth

Sales of Nirma grew steadily as Patel slowly but methodically extended his operation—first to three and then eight surrounding districts of Ahmedabad, then to the whole state of Gujarat, next to adjoining states, and finally to the whole of northern and western India. By 1977, Nirma was the second largest volume seller in the country with a market share of 12 per cent to Surf's 30.6 per cent.

This was the year that Sen first became aware of the brand's impact on the market. Curious to know more, he wrote to HLL's branch manager in Ahmedabad asking for information on a brand called Nirma. The branch manager replied dismissively, 'You don't expect me to know about every junk product coming out of Ahmedabad'.

But Sen wanted to meet this small-scale manufacturer who advertised regularly in the local press and had built up a distribution system covering a 100-mile radius. He went to Ahmedabad himself to try and meet Patel. A meeting was held of the small-scale manufacturers, who were honoured to be noticed by one of the big chiefs of HLL. Patel did not attend. Deciding that the mountain should go to Mohammed, Sen went to the Nirma office and sent in his card. The message came back, 'Patel is not willing to see you.'

Sen played his last card. He asked for a glass of water and this ploy finally got him into the presence of Nirma's creator. Asked why he had refused to meet him, Patel's reply took Sen's breath away. 'You are selling detergents. I am selling detergents. We are competing. I don't want to talk. Soon, you see, I will be bigger than Surf. I will be Number 1 in India. After that, I will be Number 1 in the world.'

Between 1977 and 1985 Nirma sales grew at a compound rate of 49 per cent as it extended throughout India. By 1980, Nirma was outselling Surf by three to one. Between 1983 and 1984, Nirma spread further into southern and then eastern India and as a consequence, by 1985 at 200,000 tons a year, Nirma had a market share of 58 per cent to Surf's 8.4 per cent and was one of the largest selling detergent powder brands in the world (see table on p. 46). In India, it had a market share of over 50 per cent in all zones except East India. With its geographical expansion complete, growth in the next years was expected to slow to the same rate as the total market, 13 per cent.

By 1986, the Nirma Group had six companies, four with factory licences and two without, plus two ancillary units manufacturing polybags and copper stapler pins. Patel was also constructing a giant manufacturing unit on a 24-acre plot near Ahmedabad. Because it was to be sited in a backward area, the factory would benefit from a five-year tax holiday. By then, production was at 800 tons per day and the company became liable for excise duty. The company was also becoming vertically integrated, producing chemicals and using its own fleet of eighty trucks for raw material deliveries. This helped Nirma maintain its cost advantage. By 1992, Nirma had sales of 333,000 tons a year and a 55 per cent market share.

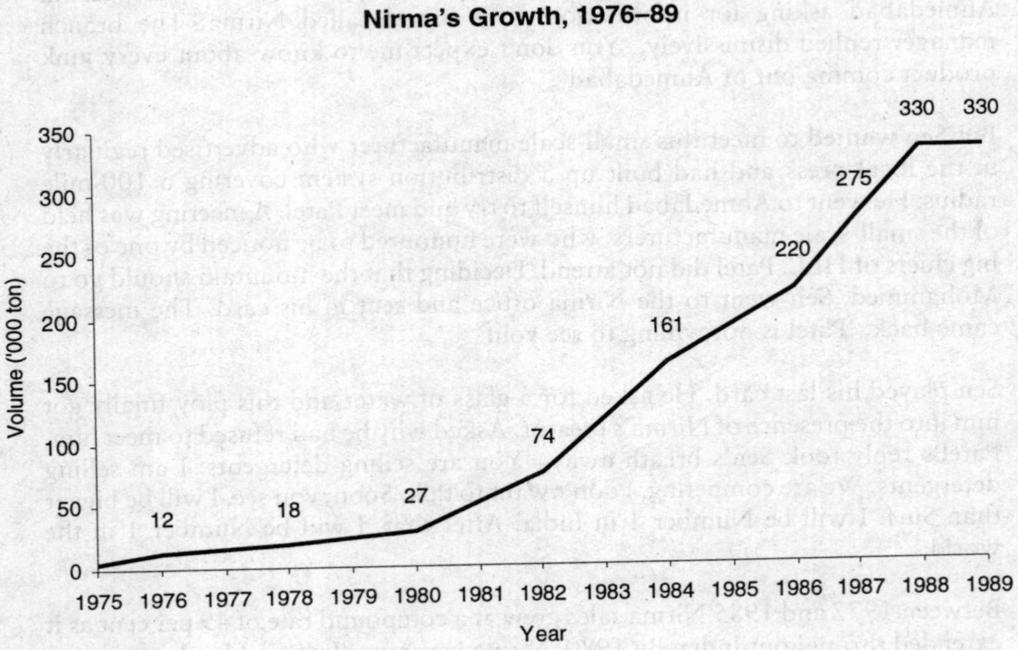

Other Products

In 1970, Patel introduced a second washing powder, Milan. Sales of Milan were at first restricted, but in 1986 sales were extended into all parts of Gujarat. Though virtually the same formula as Nirma, Milan was sold at a lower price, so acting as a protective barrier for Nirma against other, lower priced cottage-sector powders.

In 1977-79, Patel went on to launch a Nirma detergent bar. This was blue in colour and 150 g in weight. In May 1986, a newer version was tested in the market. This cake was manufactured by three third-party manufacturers based in Ahmedabad.

With the resources and distribution network built up over the years, Patel also planned to attack the premium market of Surf with Super Nirma, a blue powder, to be marketed at a premium of Re 1 per kg over the original Nirma powder. After that, he would enter into the toothpaste and toilet soap market. Indian consumers would thus be offered the whole Nirma range of toothpaste, soap, detergent bar and powder.

The Effect of Nirma

Nirma's greatest success was in converting the unorganised laundry soap market in urban areas and also, more importantly, in rural India, to detergent powders. At price parity with cheaper laundry soaps, Nirma powder provided a product that was better than any soap and excellent value for money. For the consumers, this meant an upgrade in terms of wash quality and a lower cost per wash. Against the Nirma advertising onslaught, local soap producers were unable to offer any resistance and were decimated.

For a long while HLL and its fellow high quality manufacturers failed to offer any significant competition to Nirma. Myopically focussed on their premium brands, which were more or less unaffected in terms of volume by Nirma's growth, all seemed as usual to them. Indeed, HLL's competitive benchmarking against products in the organized sector it considered its home ground showed that Surf was still the leading brand and growing, whilst its bar, Rin, was 'going through the roof at 20 per cent yearly growth'. The gulf between Surf's sales of 20,000 tons and Nirma's 200,000 was not remarked on. Between 1979 and 1984 HLL did look at the Nirma product but concluded that 'in the end, we can't make this product. It is so different in terms of quality, unit cost, etc.' In any case, HLL's freedom to respond was limited by the production capacity constraints of its licence. Until 1984, the company depended over 60 per cent on a single location, the Sewri factory in Bombay, which was then experiencing productivity and industrial relations problems. The manufacturing capacity of HLL's other factory at Garden Reach was taken up by production of Surf and Rin. According to Mr Sen, HLL's mistake was that 'we did not see him as he saw us . . . . We did not try to understand his business system.' Neither did HLL consider the housewife's view of Nirma.

By 1984, however, the situation had become very different. With Nirma, Patel had unlocked a huge mountain of opportunity. The detergent powder market had expanded to ten times that of Surf, which was losing ground as a number of consumers who used to buy brands in the two higher priced categories of powder shifted to buying the low priced Nirma.

Between 1980 and 1985, Surf's volume stagnated and its market share dropped. Now HLL's market research showed that premium Surf and the low price Nirma were perceived by consumers as sharing a high degree of commonality. Nirma was seen as having roughly the same value for money as Surf and both Nirma and Surf as having higher value for money than other brands. Unable to increase price, HLL had to put a lot of support below the line just to keep volume up, thereby eroding Surf's profitability.

SURF : NIRMA
General Association by Paired Attributes

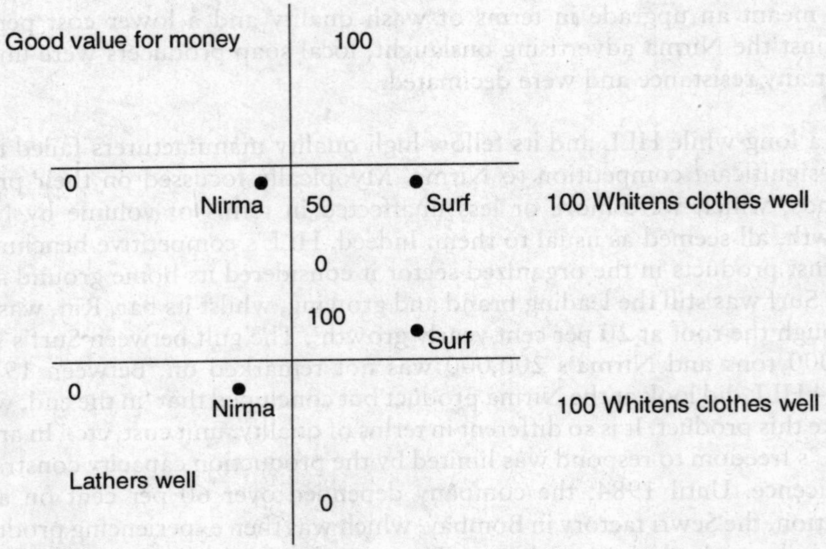

The coup de grâce was delivered by the news in 1986 that Nirma was testing its detergent bar—a direct challenge to Rin, the market leader and HLL's most profitable brand. When the Nirma bar was launched and 'we lost consumers and profits to him', the alarm bells Sen had first heard in 1977 finally rang throughout the HLL organisation. Belatedly, the giant stirred and realized a dangerous competitor was about. Rumours that Patel was then set to test a toilet soap spurred HLL into a stop-Nirma campaign—codenamed STING—Strategy To Inhibit Nirma Growth. The company was determined to fight back.

HLL Fights Back

HLL's reaction to Nirma comprised several stages.

Its first response was to begin selling Surf in polybags rather than the more expensive cartons. This move met with a lot of opposition at first as the carton represented the high ground of quality, which HLL was giving up. But the change enabled HLL to reduce costs and offer better value. In addition, Surf's formula was slightly improved, thereby reducing costs, and discounts were offered to reduce the price.

Another change was in the advertising approach. Surf's established campaign used the slogan 'Surf washes whiter' and the advertisements showed a small boy getting his clothes dirty and then the clothes being cleaned by Surf. In 1985, advertisers created a character called Lalitaji, 'a very sensible housewife acutely aware that good value was a combination of quality and price'. The first commercial, which showed Lalitaji buying a more expensive tomato because it was good value for money, was overlaid by the voice of God. His message was that though Surf might be three times more expensive than Nirma, measured on cost per wash, Surf was only one-and-a-half times dearer. This was because, vis-à-vis Nirma, the same washing load required only half the quantity of Surf.

These measures proved effective in shoring up Surf. Between 1985 and 1991 it grew from 30,000 to 42,000 tons, adding both share and profitability.

Another action was to launch a powder called Sunlight. This was positioned to match Nirma directly on price and was white to appeal to the predilection in East India for colour care. Launched first in Calcutta in 1985, Sunlight sold well in East and South India, areas where Nirma was weak, and by 1992, was as profitable as Surf.

HLL then turned to its most urgent concern—the severe competitive threat to Rin posed by the Nirma detergent bar, then being tested by Patel as a consumer promotion on purchase of two packs of Nirma washing powder. Similar in pack design to Rin, the blue Nirma bar got instant sampling in almost every household using Nirma powder. The differences between the two bars were slight—the rate of wear of the Nirma bar was high but its surface was harder and dryer. Nirma's aggressive advertising campaign played up the fact that the quality of this bar was almost as good as Rin. It was then put on sale at Rs 1.50 for a 150 g cake, a third of the price of Rin. Within eighteen months, Nirma bar sales had reached

100,000 tons. By 1989, it had a market share of almost 40 per cent and had taken 10,000 tons directly from Rin. This time, Patel was moving very fast indeed.

1988 was 'a traumatic year' for HLL. The threat to Rin was the last straw that galvanised the company into thinking about new ways of proceeding. This move took place in the context of the liberalisation policies adopted by Rajiv Gandhi's government after 1984. The first forty years of post-independent India had been characterised by a highly interventionist economic policy and growth had been a slow 3 to 3.5 per cent per annum. From the mid-1980s on, through a process of slow economic reform such as the opening up of licensing capacity, India's industrial structure began to change, stimulating growth, investment and consumer spending but also intensifying competition.

The result was a changing pattern of consumption towards services and household goods and away from staples such as food and basic clothing. It also meant the emergence of a growing base of urban consumers, a 'middle class' whose numbers were estimated to have grown from 10 million out of 350 million in 1947 to 170 million out of 840 million by 1991. This middle class began to pursue a more luxurious lifestyle, which demanded access to a growing range of consumer goods.

Deregulation removed many of the external restraints, such as restriction on output volume, that had hampered HLL in the past. But to take full advantage of the opportunities now available, HLL's management concluded that perhaps it should first undertake a thorough internal review. Nirma had challenged all the values and norms developed over decades, and perhaps it was time for HLL to adopt a different mindset and business approach. As a result, the company radically altered its thinking about quality, financial management, production methods and so on, in order to implement STING.

As part of the STING campaign, a 'competitor's meeting' was held every Monday at 9.30 am. Led by the then chairman, Ganguly, and attended by all the senior managers, it tried to frame a response to Nirma. The first hurdle was the product itself. A common complaint about Nirma was that persistent use caused blisters on the skin and, in the long run, damaged clothes by weakening the fabric. Accordingly, HLL's R&D team were given the task of producing a low-cost powder that gave a better performance in terms of whiteness, but without the side effect of itching and wear and tear caused by Nirma's high soda ash content.

> As summarised by Datta, the philosophy behind the new product was straightforward: 'When it was clear to us that consumers wanted a low priced product, we got down to doing something about it. The point was that economy price should not be equated with low quality.' If it could come up with a better quality product at the right price, HLL knew it would be a winner.

HLL's R&D laboratory had already begun work on a new NSD powder in 1984 and consumer research on alternate formulations of the new product had been carried out in 1985. In 1986, the mix development was completed and the as-yet-unnamed new powder was ready to enter production. In 1977, HLL had launched a green detergent bar, Wheel, to counter the growth of Swastik's Super 777. Wheel had only been launched in three states as, at the time, HLL preferred to retain capacity for its premium products. In 1986, the brand name was resurrected for the new detergent powder.

Production Method

Another part of STING was a task force to evaluate alternative ways of marketing the new product. At first, Wheel was made in HLL's factory as usual and sold at 20 per cent less. However, the work of the task force shortly resulted in the setting up of Wheel Business Systems. This new system took advantage of the altered political climate and was designed to duplicate as far as possible the low-cost Patel operation, but with the value-added gloss conferred by HLL's strengths in management and organisational reach.

One of Nirma's key advantages had been easy access to raw materials. On the basis of an optimisation model matching raw material availability and sales potential throughout the country, HLL selected certain regions where new plants could be set up to maximum advantage. As a result, towns were chosen in the states of Gujarat, Rajasthan, Uttar Pradesh, Punjab and Pondicherry for the location of new units.

In these towns HLL set up AFACON manufacturing units or third party production. Five existing suppliers and agents were asked to set up plants for the production of Wheel powder according to a blueprint drawn up by HLL. The units were given conversion contracts. Raw materials were made available by HLL and the contractors hired their own labour. Working on a just-in-time basis kept working capital very low. AFACON manufacture enabled HLL to start up new units much faster and gave it greater flexibility to increase or decrease production.

These semi-automated units replicated the small scale manufacturing units and cost advantages, especially labour costs, enjoyed by Patel. In early 1988, Wheel's costs were approximately 15 per cent higher than Nirma's. However, by 1989, a cost effectiveness programme had resulted in a similar cost structure (see Appendix 5).

Later, HLL set up Stepan Chemicals in Punjab as a wholly-owned subsidiary of HLL, which eventually took over all marketing and distribution activity for Wheel. Its turnover was kept separate from that of HLL and so did not increase HLL's export commitment under FERA. This also avoided potential labour problems as Stepan was not obliged to take on permanent employees. Stepan thus gained even more importance as a separate, low cost company.

By 1991, HLL had fifteen manufacturing installations, as opposed to only three in the early 1980s.

Distribution

To distribute the product to its 300,000 units, HLL initially used its existing system which the company considered one of its greatest strengths. From its factories, stocks went to the forty-strong carrying and forwarding agents (C&FAs). The C&FAs supplied the 4,000 redistribution stockists (RSs) who in turn supplied HLL's 300,000 retailers throughout the country. The stockists were also aided by a company sales force.

Between 1976 and 1991, the RSs had considerably strengthened their presence in rural areas. From having about forty rural vans, by 1990 they ran about 1,200 Indirect Coverage (IC) and Operation Harvest Vans. HLL ensured its stockists made good profits and, consequently, they stayed loyal for generations. With this structure, HLL was able to distribute throughout the country in over 3,200 towns and almost 60,000 villages, ensuring all shops a regular service. However, this structure was expensive and so in 1990 distribution too was given to Stepan Chemicals who evolved a simpler system. Again in a manner close to Patel's for Nirma, supplies of Wheel were sent directly to the stockists, bypassing the C&FAs.

Advertising

HLL stepped up its advertising for Wheel, spending the same sum of Rs 50-60 mn per year that Mr Patel was investing in Nirma. The advertising strategy was to 'create dissonance among Nirma users on safety, and provide reasons to switch to Wheel'. Thus, the campaigns emphasised that Wheel provided extra power, extra lather and was 'safe on hands and clothes'.

After a successful test market in 1987, Wheel powder finally went on sale in strong Nirma markets in 1988, priced at Rs 5.50 as against Rs 5.25 for Nirma. Sales quickly grew to 100,000 tons, half that of Nirma. By 1989, Wheel had grown swiftly to become the second largest brand in India and by 1990, was larger than any other Unilever brand in the world.

In 1987, HLL had lost the leadership of the fabric wash market to Nirma. By 1990, it had regained that lead in value though not in volume. Wheel had succeeded in inhibiting Nirma's growth and for the first time since its launch, Nirma's market share started to decline.

The self-audit and the consequent restructuring of its operations also helped HLL react to Nirma's threat in the NSD bar segment swiftly and efficiently. Rin was improved and relaunched in 1989. The advertising countered the Nirma message; Rin gave a cheaper wash with more lather. Rin had dropped from 79,000 to 69,000 tons, but by 1991 it was back to annual sales of 84,000 tons. The Wheel bar was also relaunched. The price was kept similar to that of Nirma and by 1991 the Wheel bar was selling about 100,000 tons, about half that of the Nirma bar, and HLL was again ahead in terms of value, if not in volume (see Appendix 6).

Bolstered by this success, HLL then turned to deal with an attack on its flagship brand in the laundry soap segment, Sunlight, whose volume and market share had been dropping under attacks from lowcost producers. The high excise levy kept Sunlight's cost higher than those of players like Tata, who were not liable for the levy. By 1991, Sunlight had dropped from sales of 30,000 tons to 6,000 and had less than 7 per cent of the market. Unless it acted quickly, HLL knew it would be out of the market altogether. It also realised that despite all the activity in the powder segments and against all expectations, laundry soap still enjoyed 45 per cent share of the fabric wash market and was not going out of fashion.

Helped by a technological breakthrough, HLL relaunched Sunlight at a much lower cost. Where the old Sunlight had been sold in 150 g packets at Rs 16 per kg, the new product was sold in 200 g packets at the same price. As a result, sales went up from 7,000 to 15,000 tons a year in 1992 and HLL set a target of 30,000 tons by 1994. Plans were also afoot to launch a Premium Sunlight, a high quality product.

However, HLL could not afford to relax. Yet another threat had appeared in the form of Procter and Gamble (P&G) India, a competitor with the same global backing and access to high technology, marketing experience and a range of international brands as itself. HLL had recently opened up the concentrated detergent sector of the market in India. Now, P&G was about to enter that sector with its own powerful offering, Ariel. HLL's ability to beat off this challenge would be a real test of the effectiveness of its changed mindset.

A Changed Mindset

In 1989–90 P&G had a turnover of Rs 99.5 mn in India, 13 per cent of which came from exports. P&G had not hitherto been active in the detergent market. However, in 1988, it had acquired Richardson Vicks in the US and with it, Richardson Hindustan, an established company in India with a strong marketing and distribution infrastructure for branded consumer products. HLL had been expecting an invasion of the detergent market by P&G ever since news of the takeover had broken. P&G's target was expected to be the top end of the organized detergent sector.

In November 1990, backed by heavy investment in advertising, P&G test marketed its product, Ariel Microsystem. It was a powder which used their most advanced and proprietary enzyme-based technology and was superior to Surf. It was priced at Rs 32 per 500 gm compared with Surf's Rs 15.80 and Rs 17.50 for Surf concentrate (and Rs 4.90 for Nirma).

P&G positioned its product on more value for money as well. A 500 g pack of Ariel would last for a month's normal washing, it claimed, and would eventually work out as cheap as Nirma, for according to P&G: 'It's not HLL or Surf, Nirma is our competition'.

In urban areas where the growing middle class was found, HLL knew that this message would hold great appeal. HLL managers travelled to the test market in Visakhapatnam in Andhra Pradesh and, by the end of January 1991, knew that

P&G's product represented a serious threat to them, squeezing them from the top just as Nirma had squeezed them from the bottom.

HLL had been the first to open up the concentrate sector in India by launching Rin Powder as a concentrate in some areas of the country. For housewives, it was positioned as a superior product at no extra cost. The advertising message was that a spoonful of Rin equalled three spoonsfull of Nirma. However, Rin could not deliver the quality of the P&G product.

HLL's parent company, Unilever, did of course have an enzyme-based technology and HLL's management had repeatedly discussed whether or not to launch an 'ultra' product in India. But the proposal had been rejected on the grounds that Indian consumers would not pay for the advanced technology of latest western products.

However, faced by the reality of Ariel's market presence, HLL's view changed and in contrast to P&G's cautious progress, it moved fast. First, advertising for Surf was stepped up throughout the test province, Andhra Pradesh, and prices were cut. Second, the national roll out of Rin concentrate powder was expedited to capture the concentrate image.

In February 1991, the company also set to work to develop their own 'ultra' product based on indigenous technology that was cost effective. The product was on the market by 1 September and was on sale nationally by February 1992.

To achieve this, HLL compressed its conventional method for the development and launch of a new product. Instead of its traditional step-by-step approach which meant waiting for results before proceeding with the next stage, HLL carried out every stage in parallel (see Appendix 7). While the product was being developed in the laboratory, work on the packaging and perfume was simultaneously carried out. While the product was being test marketed, the production went ahead with capacity creation. The effect was to cut the lead time from two years to four months.

The result was a triumph for the company. HLL was able to limit the progress of Ariel. By 1992, of the 11 per cent national market captured by concentrated detergents, 7 per cent belonged to HLL (3 per cent Rin concentrate and 4 per cent Surf Ultra) and 4 per cent to P&G. HLL's total value share of the fabric wash market had risen from 39 to 42 per cent. In a pre-emptive move, HLL launched an elaborate segmentation and positioning exercise. The different segments for each of its product categories were analysed one by one, and if a vacuum was found anywhere, a special project was initiated to create and launch a product to fill that gap. The objective was to avoid any loose brick in HLL's defensive wall against P&G. In this, Unilever's world-wide intelligence of P&G products was of great assistance. The emphasis was on competitive pricing, made possible by the company's new methods and cost reductions down the line.

In 1991 the detergent market was growing fast at about 20 per cent, especially in the rural areas, which by then accounted for nearly half the total demand for many of the business key segments. HLL anticipated that with a push it could double its volume by 1995. The movement to liberalise the markets, it expected, would give both growth opportunities and more aggressive competition.

In the period between 1988 and 1992, HLL had broadened its strategic approach and dramatically changed its management processes. It had understood what competition could do and learnt that no competitor could be left unchallenged. Their confidence restored, hungry and ambitious HLL managers were ready to face anything and anyone.

HLL's watchword for the future would be 'edge'—competitive edge through marketing edge, distribution edge and technology edge.

HLL chairman S. Datta had had a dream for HLL. With Wheel, he explained, the company had successfully moved into the popular segment of the detergent market. In his dream, HLL went on to become the lowest cost and highest quality producer in a variety of products, both within HLL's existing categories and in new areas, to reposition itself at the frontier of the emerging consumer markets in India. In that process, it would also open up new opportunities for Unilever world-wide, as similar consumer markets emerged in other developing countries. But, he added, 'If we come up with a new vision, we must review our structures and procedures to match that new vision. If our current ways of working impede our ambition, we must change these ways of working.'

He then provided his managers with their next challenge. 'Even the existing middle-class consumers we serve in India represent about 4 per cent of the total world-wide market served by Unilever. We should therefore be contributing 4 per cent of Unilever's world-wide revenues. We are actually generating 2 per cent. The challenge is not just holding share. The challenge is dramatic improvement to double our revenues to fill this gap. Twenty per cent per annum growth will not get us there. We need a quantum leap, not just incremental improvement. How must we make this leap to fill this gap?'

APPENDIX 1

Hindustan Lever Limited: Ten-Year Record

(Rs lakhs)*

	1982	*1983*	*1984*	*1985*	*1986*	*1987*	*1988*	*1989*	*1990*	*1991*
Fixed assets	8202	8114	8432	9472	10828	12556	14747	17126	18770	20113
Net current assets	8585	8530	11023	12956	11983	17879	17603	18545	22674	25471
Total capital employed	16787	16644	19455	22428	22811	30435	32350	35671	41444	45584
Shareholders' funds	11498	11333	12425	14281	16522	18349	20607	22852	25538	29110
Sales (with excise)	52623	58240	63424	72586	84459	95331	102106	121642	146027	177529
Profit for the year before taxation	4455	4222	4401	5556	6507	7829	7938	8961	11074	13770
Profit available for distribution	2331	1913	2128	2551	3429	3775	5264	6015	7403	10000
Retained earnings for the year	1602	863	1008	1151	1843	1442	2278	2749	3483	4610
Dividends	729	1050	1120	1400	1586	2333	2986	3266	3920	5390
Dividends (%)	25.0	22.5	24.0	30.0	34.0	25.0	32.0	35.0	42.0	38.5
Bonus issue		3:5				1:1			1:2	
No. of shareholders	91594	93694	98313	104780	111849	119912	129010	127761	129505	136404

* 100 lakhs = 1 crore.
1 crore = 10 million.

APPENDIX 3

Unilever Financial Highlights, 1991

(Year ended 31 December 1991)

	1991	*1990*	*% Increase*
Results (£ million)			
Turnover	23163	22734	2
Operating profit	1990	2051	(3)
Profit on ordinary activities before taxation	1792	1782	
Net profit on ordinary activities	1152	1112	4
Extraordinary items	1	(195)	–
Net profit after extraordinary items	1153	917	26
Key ratios			
Operating margin (%)	8.6	9.0	–
Profit after taxation as a percentage of turnover (%)	5.2	5.1	–
Return on capital employed (%)	16.4	17.3	–
Net gearing (%)	27.9	36.7	–
Net interest cover (times)	7.5	6.4	–
Combined earnings per share on ordinary activities			
Guilders per 11.4 of ordinary capital	13.55	12.86	5
Pence per 5p of ordinary capital	61.62	59.52	4
Ordinary dividends			
Guilders per 11.4 of ordinary capital	5.56	5.27	5
Pence per 5p of ordinary capital	18.94	18.16	4
Combined earnings per share after extraordinary items			
Guilders per 11.4 of ordinary capital	13.57	10.60	28
Pence per 5p of ordinary capital	61.67	49.04	16

Turnover by Operation, 1991
(£ million)

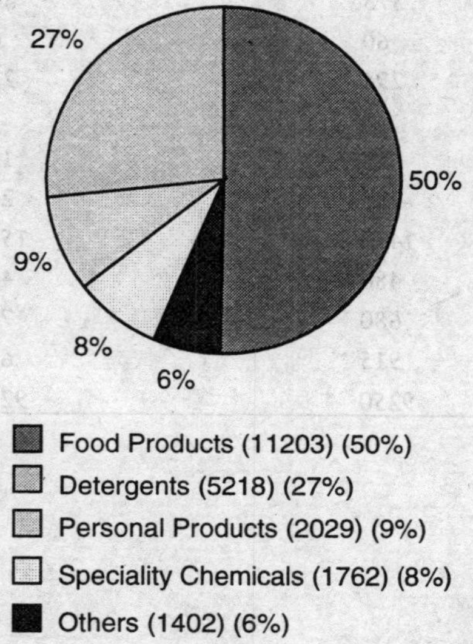

Turnover by Geographical Area, 1991
(£ million)

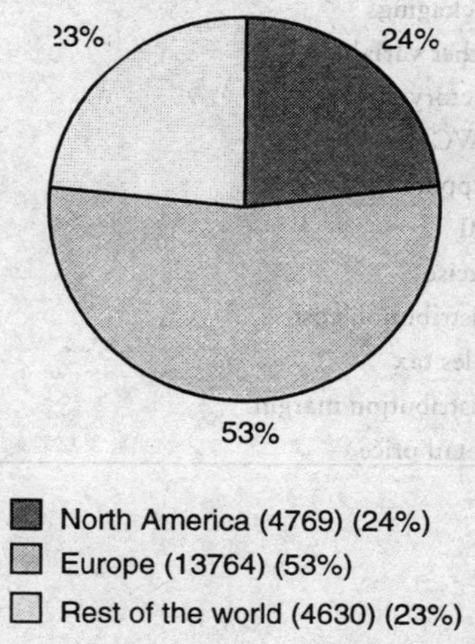

APPENDIX 4

Fabric Wash Market

	1970	1975	1980	1985	1986	1987	1988	1989
Volume (000 T)								
NSD powders	26	49	122	360	440	500	555	610
NSD bars	4	44	123	200	240	295	360	430
Laundry soap	656	660	825	898	907	875	867	957
Total	686	753	1070	1458	1587	1670	1782	1897
Share (%)								
NSD powders	3.8	6.5	11.4	24.7	27.7	29.9	31.1	32.2
NSD bars	0.6	5.8	11.5	13.7	15.1	17.7	20.2	22.7
Laundry soap	95.6	87.6	77.1	61.6	57.2	52.4	48.7	45.2
Total	100	100	100	100	100	100	100	100
Growth (% p.a.)	1975:75		1975:80		1980:85		1985:89	–
NSD powders	13.5		20		24.2		14.1	–
NSD bars	61.5		22.8		10.2		21.1	–
Laundry soap	0.1		4.6		1.7		-1.2	–
Total	1.9		7.3		6.4		6.8	–

APPENDIX 5

Wheel : Nirma Cost Structure

Costs (Rs per ton)	*Wheel*	*Nirma*
Raw materials	4605	4730
Packaging	575	500
Other variables	60	60
Factory directs	295	225
CWC	30	–
Support	425	150
PBI	-285	210
Excise	1470	1545
Distribution cost	480	480
Sales tax	680	700
Distribution margin	915	650
Retail price	9250	9250

APPENDIX 6

HLL : Nirma Market Shares

	1987	1988	1989	1990
NSD Powders				
Volume (%)				
HLL	11	14	21	24
Nirma	62	59	54	50
Value (%)				
HLL	25	26	33	35
Nirma	52	50	46	42
NSD Bars				
Volume (%)				
HLL	25	28	28	–
Nirma	42	40	39	–
Value (%)				
HLL	39	42	40	–
Nirma	33	32	32	–

APPENDIX 7

HLL Development Process

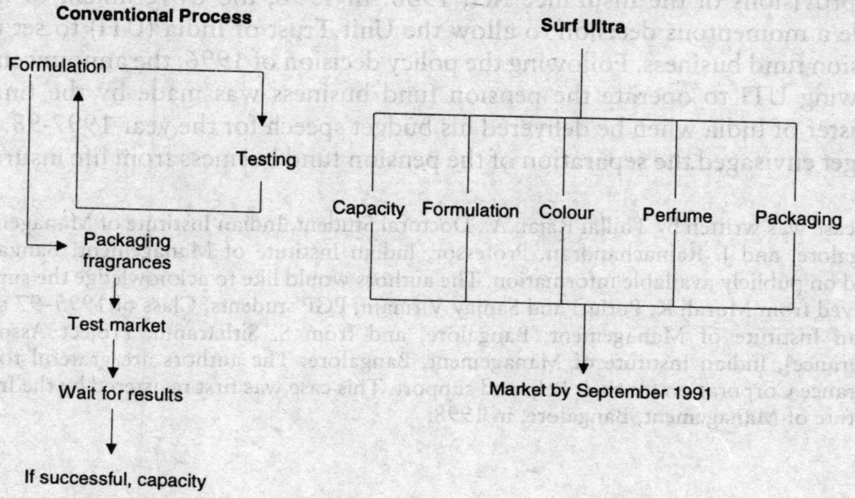

CASE 3

LIFE INSURANCE CORPORATION OF INDIA: COPING WITH UNCERTAINTY

The year 1996 was a significant one for the pension fund business in India. Till then, by virtue of Section 30 of the LIC Act, 1956, only the Life Insurance Corporation (LIC) was authorised to transact life insurance business and the pension business was treated as a part of the life insurance business according to the provisions of the Insurance Act, 1938. In 1996, the Government of India made a momentous decision to allow the Unit Trust of India (UTI) to set up a pension fund business. Following the policy decision of 1996, the announcement allowing UTI to operate the pension fund business was made by the finance minister of India when he delivered his budget speech for the year 1997-98. The budget envisaged the separation of the pension fund business from life insurance

The case was written by Thillai Rajan A., Doctoral Student, Indian Institute of Management, Bangalore, and J. Ramachandran, Professor, Indian Institute of Management, Bangalore, based on publicly available information. The authors would like to acknowledge the support received from Murali K. Potluri and Sanjay Virmani, PGP students, Class of 1995–97 at the Indian Institute of Management, Bangalore, and from S. Sitharamu, Project Associate (Insurance), Indian Institute of Management, Bangalore. The authors are grateful to Life Insurance Corporation for their help and support. This case was first registered by the Indian Institute of Management, Bangalore, in 1998.

business and allowed UTI to operate a full-fledged pension fund which would compete with LIC's pension schemes. Simultaneously, the government also granted permission to LIC to set up and promote joint ventures in the pension business.

Opening up of the pension business for competition was just a forerunner to opening up of the entire insurance sector. The insurance sector encompasses general and life insurance, and the pension fund business. The insurance sector reform envisaged opening up of the insurance sector to private players which had till now been the monopoly of public sector corporations. Since the liberalisation exercise in 1991, the Government of India had taken a number of initiatives in the financial sector. New policies were formulated covering the banking system and the capital markets with the objective of creating a more efficient and competitive financial system. Insurance was an important part of the overall financial system and reforms were considered necessary in the insurance sector too. Therefore, under the chairmanship of the former governor of the Reserve Bank of India, R.N. Malhotra, the Government of India appointed a committee for suggesting suitable reforms in the insurance sector.

Important recommendations of the committee were:

- The private sector be allowed to enter the insurance business, though no single company will be allowed to transact both life and general insurance business.
- The new entrants would have to write a specified portion of their business in rural areas.
- The minimum paid-up capital of a new entrant would be Rs 1 bn. However, a lower capital requirement can be prescribed for state-level co-operative institutions taking up life insurance business.
- Foreign insurance companies would be permitted to enter on a selective basis and would be required to float an Indian company for the purpose, preferably as a joint venture with an Indian partner.
- Regulatory environment in the post-deregulation insurance industry will look as follows:
- The office of the Controller of Insurance will be given its full functions as stipulated under the original Insurance Act.
- The legislation and government notification exempting LIC from several provisions of the Insurance Act will be withdrawn.

With the opening up of the insurance sector LIC would lose its monopoly status to conduct life insurance business in the country. Further, to ensure a level playing field for the private players the government may also withdraw some of the special privileges of LIC which it enjoyed because of its public corporation status. Given the huge size and relatively smaller penetration of the insurance concept, foreign insurance companies were viewing the Indian market as an attractive proposition. Many had expressed interest in entering the insurance business in India and had formed joint ventures with Indian entities to start the insurance business as soon as the sector was fully opened up (see Appendix 1 for a list of joint ventures in the life insurance business with brief descriptions of the foreign joint venture partners).

The coming years were also significant for LIC as there was vast potential for greater growth in the life insurance business. The Malhotra Committee examined the adequacy of the present structure of LIC to meet the future challenges. The committee found that: (a) handling of the business at branch level was already facing difficulties; (b) there was substantial customer dissatisfaction on the policy servicing front; (c) delegation of authority to zonal and divisional offices and the system of supervision and control were inadequate; (d) lines of communication within the organisation had lengthened greatly; (e) due to hierarchical functioning at the central office and the zonal office, decision-making had slowed down and this had led to poor response to customer needs and market situations. In this context, there was a strong view that the existing structure of LIC and the way it was functioning did not provide sufficient assurance that the organisation could handle efficiently the vast potential in the growth of business.

G. Krishnamurthy, chairman of LIC, was deeply engrossed in these issues. How should LIC deal with the pension fund business and handle the competition from new entrants? Though LIC still enjoyed monopoly status in the life insurance business, this privileged position would not exist for long. The insurance sector reform envisaged the gradual opening up of the life insurance business to private sector participants. What should be LIC's strategies in the new scenario? What were the changes required in the organisational structure and processes of LIC?

Genesis of LIC

Life Insurance Corporation (LIC) was formed in September 1956 by an Act of parliament, viz., LIC Act, 1956 with a capital contribution of Rs 50 mn from the

Government of India and had the sole mandate for conducting life insurance business in India. Before the formation of LIC, there were 154 Indian insurers, sixteen non-Indian insurers and seventy-five provident societies who were carrying on life insurance business in India. The business was then confined mainly to the cities and better-off segments of society. In order to promote the concept of life insurance even in rural India and to regulate the operation of the sector, the management of life insurance business of 245 Indian and foreign insurers and provident societies then operating in India was taken over by the central government and then nationalised on 1 September 1956.

The objective behind the nationalisation and government control of the life insurance sector was to safeguard the interest of the policyholders against the embezzlement or misuse of funds by the insurers. The state ownership of the Corporation was supposed to create a sense of confidence in the minds of the people regarding the safety of their funds which they invest in insurance. Section 37 of the Life Insurance Corporation Act, 1956 says that '. . . the sums assured by all policies issued by the corporation including any bonuses declared in respect thereof and subject to the provisions contained in Section 14 (relating to powers of the corporation to modify contracts of life insurance in certain cases), the amounts assured by all policies issued by any insurer, the liabilities under which had vested in the corporation under this Act, and all bonuses declared in respect thereof, whether before or after the appointed day, shall be guaranteed as to payments in cash by the Union government.'

Indeed when the Malhotra Committee had suggested that the capital base of LIC be hiked to a minimum of Rs 2 bn from the present capital base of Rs 50 mn, the finance ministry held the view that the hike was not necessary as long as government guarantees were available on the payment of claims.

Growth of LIC

LIC had come a long way since its nationalisation in 1956. Over forty years later, in 1997, LIC had grown from Rs 3.28 bn of new business in 1957 to Rs 518.15 bn with rural India accounting for around 40 per cent of the business. In 1997 LIC had spread to the farthest corners of the country with an extensive network of over 550,000 agents, 2,024 branches, 1,363 centres, 100 divisions, seven zones, besides the corporate office. LIC had branch offices in the UK, Mauritius and Fiji. In the UK, LIC had a working arrangement with Sun Life, one of the

Objectives of LIC

- To spread life insurance much more widely and in particular to the rural areas, and to the socially and economically backward classes with a view to reaching all insurable persons in the country and providing them, at a reasonable cost, adequate financial cover against death.

- To maximise mobilisation of people's savings by making insurance-linked savings adequately attractive.

- To bear in mind, in the investment of funds, the primary obligation to its policy holders, whose money it holds in trust, without losing sight of the interest of the community as a whole: the funds to be deployed to the best advantage of the investors as well as the community as a whole, keeping in view national priorities and obligations of attractive return.

- To conduct business with utmost economy and with the full realisation that the money belongs to the policyholders.

- To act as trustees of the insured public in their individual and collective capacities.

- To meet the various life insurance needs of the community that would arise in the changing social and economic environment.

- To involve all people working in the Corporation to the best of their capability in furthering the interest of the insured public by providing efficient service with courtesy.

- To promote amongst all agents and employees of the Corporation a sense of participation, pride and job satisfaction through discharge of their duties with dedication towards achievement of corporate objectives.

leading life insurance companies of that country. The total employee strength in all LIC offices by the end of 1995-96 was 125,736.

LIC: Growth of Rural Business

	1990–91	*1991–92*	*1992–93*	*1993–94*	*1994–95*	*1995–96*
No. of policies (mn)	3.675	4.127	4.439	4.856	4.902	5.257
Sum assured (Rs bn)	102.94	124.39	140.85	166.80	215.71	212.63
Growth rate						
Policies (%)	20.6	12.3	7.6	9.4	1.0	7.2
Sum assured (%)	27.3	20.8	13.2	18.4	29.3	-1.4
Share of the rural new business in total new business						
Policies (%)	42.5	44.7	44.6	45.3	45.1	47.7
Sum assured (%)	36.6	38.8	39.2	39.9	39.1	41.0

LIC: Milestones on the Move

	1957	*1965*	*1975*	*1985*	*1995*
No. of new policies (mn)	0.942	1.444	1.8	2.705	10.88
Sum assured in new business[1] (Rs bn)	3.37	7.01	17.72	53.98	554.72
Life fund[2] (Rs bn)	4.1	9.01	30.33	111.91	59.978
Business in force[3]					
No. of policies (mn)	5.686	10.862	18.820	26.531	65.930
Sum assured (Rs bn)	14.74	38.86	118.52	339.50	2156.45
Total premium income (Rs bn)	0.88	1.62	5.11	15.59	115.27
Overall expense ratio (%)	27.3	27.55	30.48	24.68	21.39

1. New business denotes the total life insurance business written during the financial year.
2. Life fund is the sum total of premiums received to date and interest earnings less expenses of management and claims. It is out of this fund that future policy claims are paid.
3. Business in force is sum assured under policies in force at the end of a financial year.

In keeping with its mandate, LIC had contributed significantly to the growth of the Indian economy over the years. LIC had invested Rs 1866.9 bn to upgrade the quality of life in areas of housing, electrification, transport, water supply and sewerage. LIC had pioneered some of the world's largest social welfare schemes by providing insurance cover to a group of 12 million landless agricultural labourers and 13.3 million beneficiaries under various government assistance schemes, besides providing social security to over 4 million members of weaker sections. Over the years, LIC had diversified into related businesses by creating various subsidiary companies.

Subsidiaries of LIC

LIC Mutual Fund and Jeevan Bima Sahayog Asset Management Company

In 1988, a mutual fund subsidiary was set up named LIC Mutual Fund (LICMF). The subsidiary was created with the view that it would provide opportunity to savers across the country to participate in the capital market and enjoy security, yield and growth on their investments. The objective was to tap the vast potential of semi-urban and rural areas where LIC already had a strong presence.

During the year 1995-96, when the mutual fund industry as a whole experienced depressed market conditions, LICMF mobilised Rs 1,170 mn under 35,000 applications through various schemes. The cumulative mobilisation of funds till then had been Rs 18.1 bn under 1.38 million applications. During the year, seven area offices of the subsidiary were also opened in Mumbai, New Delhi, Calcutta, Chennai, Bangalore, Kanpur and Indore for closer liaising with the investors. In order to strengthen the market network, chief agents were also appointed at six places—Pune, Ernakulam, Hyderabad, Chandigarh, Raipur and Varanasi. The total number of agents (including brokers and institutional agents) in the marketing set-up of LICMF during the year 1995-96 was 62,753.

LIC Housing Finance Limited

In 1989 a separate subsidiary called LIC Housing Finance Limited (LICHFL) was set up to cater to housing finance needs. The main objective of the subsidiary was to provide long-term finance for purchase and construction of houses to individuals and groups of individuals in order that LIC could play a more meaningful role in the critical area of housing. This decision was to aid and augment the macro-level national efforts to mitigate the hardships of the people, particularly in providing shelter to the homeless. Various products were designed like 'Own Your Home Scheme' and 'Bima Niwas Yojana' which covered financing individuals for construction or purchase of a house or flat.

In 1997, the company had a total number of sixty-seven area and unit offices plus six regional offices, making LIC the housing finance institution with the widest marketing network in the country. As on 31 March 1996, the outstanding loan portfolio of the company was Rs 21.34 bn as against Rs 16.72 bn in the previous year, registering a growth rate of 27.6 per cent. The net profit of the company for the year 1995-96 was Rs 516.6 mn and the company declared a divided of 18 per cent, as against 16 per cent the previous year.

International Business Subsidiaries of LIC

An overseas subsidiary of the corporation, LIC (International) E.C., was established in Manama, Bahrain, in 1989 in collaboration with International Agencies Company Limited, Bahrain, to cater to the needs of Gulf-based NRIs. In 1997, it was operating in the kingdom of Saudi Arabia too with centres at Riyadh, Jeddah and Alchobar. It had also extended its operations to Kuwait through an agreement with Warba Insurance, in which the Kuwaiti government had a major shareholding. During the year ending 31 December 1995, LIC (International) issued 6,118 policies for a sum assured equivalent to Bahrain Dinar 15.3 mn. The total policies issued since the inception of the company were 21,574 for a sum assured of Bahrain Dinar 55.95 mn. The year 1996 also witnessed a growth in premium of 22 per cent.

In Kenya, it had a joint venture, viz. KenIndia Assurance Company Limited, in collaboration with General Insurance Corporation of India and its four subsidiaries and others. By 1997, KenIndia was the biggest general insurer and largest life insurer in Kenya, where international giants like AIG and Royal also operate.

Products of LIC

LIC basically had two broad products—assurances and annuities—targeted at both individual and group segments. Assurance plans were basically targeted at those who wanted to provide a safety net to their dependents. These were insurance products which facilitated the dependents of the insured to maintain their standard of living in the event of the untimely death of the insured, i.e., they were products which primarily covered the 'risk of death'. Annuity plans took care of the needs of the pensioner and provided regular payments for life after a specified age, i.e., basically they covered the 'risk of longevity'. Appendices 2, 3 and 4 give the performance of individual insurance business, group superannuation schemes and individual pension schemes respectively.

The basic assurance and annuity plans were tailored with various modifications with respect to the timing and method of premium payments to suit the different needs of the various segments of policyholders. These plans catered to all categories of people and to their diverse needs. Investment plans with LIC offered various advantages like tax exemption to the investors, e.g., the maturity amount was exempt from income tax in the year of receipt.

Pension Fund Business in India

The concept of pension was to provide a regular income to a person when he/she retired which would take care of normal expenditure. There are basically three kinds of retirement benefits, viz., provident fund, gratuity and superannuation. Retirement benefits like provident fund and gratuity are paid in lump sum when the employee retires. These are often spent quickly if not invested prudently. Superannuation schemes provide an annuity during the lifetime of the ex-employee after retirement. The concept of a superannuation scheme is of recent origin. In western countries it appeared on the insurance map towards the beginning of this century and since then its growth has been phenomenal. Life insurance companies have specialised in this branch of business and business worth several thousand million is underwritten every year.

In India, under the LIC Act, only LIC was authorised to transact life insurance business and the pension business was treated as a part of life insurance business according to the provisions of the Insurance Act, 1938. There were broadly two kinds of pension schemes offered by LIC—the group superannuation schemes which were provided by the employers for employees and the individual annuities which were targeted at self-employed professionals, businessmen and employees who did not otherwise enjoy pension benefits.

Under the present guidelines of group superannuation schemes, organisations that had arrangements for payment of pension to their employees had to set up an irrevocable trust fund and the trustees of the fund had either of two options: (1) accumulate the periodic contributions into the trust fund and purchase an appropriate life annuity from LIC as and when an employee retires, or (2) purchase a group pension policy from LIC and pay appropriate contributions from time to time. The LIC would arrange for the pension as and when the contingency arose. In the first case, during the service period of an employee, the funds pertaining to his/her pension were administered by a trust set up by the employer. In the second case, the funds pertaining to the scheme were fully under the control of LIC.

Policies Offered by LIC

Name of Policy	*Scheme*
For children	
Jeevan Sukanya	An ideal scheme for the girl child between 1 and 12 years of age.
Jeevan Balya	Provides for a monthly income to the child up to age 21 in case of the unfortunate death of the parent.
Jeevan Kishor	An exclusive plan for children. Risk cover commences from the age of 7.
Jeevan Chhaya	An ideal policy to make provisions for a child's higher education.
For couples	
Jeevan Sarita	A joint-life last survivor annuity-cum-assurance policy for husband and wife.
Jeevan Saathi	A joint-life insurance plan for couples. Sum assured payable on first death and again on the death of the survivor.
Multiple cover policies	
Jeevan Mitra	An endowment assurance policy with additional insurance cover.
Jeevan Griha	Double and triple cover plans. Ideal for covering housing loans fully.
Jeevan Surabhi	An excellent plan featuring increased life insurance cover with lump sum payments at short intervals.
Basic insurance plans	
Whole Life Policy	Low-cost assurance plan. Provides for a fixed sum of money to the nominee on insured's death.
Endowment Assurance	Serves the dual purpose of family protection and old age provision.
Bima Sandesh	A low premium term assurance plan with return of premiums on survival.
Policies for special needs	
Money Back Policy	Provides for lump sum payments at periodic intervals, risk cover and old age protection.
Bhavishya Jeevan	A special endowment plan with profits for professionals who have very high earnings for a limited span of time.
New Jana Raksh	Provides farmers and industrial workers a three-year grace period in case of non-payment of premium.

LIC also offered various individual annuity plans, viz. immediate annuity, deferred annuity, Jeevan Akshay, Jeevan Dhara and Jeevan Suraksha. Jeevan Suraksha was a new deferred annuity type of personal pension plan introduced in 1996, targeted at the unorganised sector. Organised sector employees could also avail themselves of the scheme to supplement their post-retirement income. Under the scheme, the purchaser had the option to choose alternative pension arrangements depending on individual needs.

Even though in the normal course the pension business had been the monopoly business of LIC, several organisations had been exempted by the government and were allowed to manage pension funds and make payments to their employees independently. Such pension schemes were available to employees of the central government, state government, State Bank of India, Reserve Bank of India and other public sector banks. Recently, a few organisations came out with savings-type retirement benefit plans. The Unit Trust of India's (UTI) retirement benefit scheme at present has about 80,000 subscribers with a corpus size of Rs 800 mn (see Appendix 5). During 1995-96, on account of high interest rates, the UTI scheme yielded a return of around 16 per cent while in the LIC group superannuation funds, the LIC provided an income between 11.75 and 12.8 per cent. The first private sector asset management company-managed superannuation fund—Kothari Pioneer Pension Plan—on the lines of the UTI retirement benefit plan was also launched. Other private sector mutual funds are planning similar pension funds.

The Malhotra Committee report on the insurance sector recommended that pension funds needed to be encouraged as a sizeable portion of the population was not covered by any retirement benefit scheme. This was much more relevant for a country like India where the population was not covered under any social security net. Further, mobilisation of pension funds would help in funding long gestation infrastructure projects. The expert group constituted by the Ministry of Finance, Government of India, for 'commercialisation' of infrastructure projects had estimated that the total infrastructure investment in India would be about $ 115-130 bn over the next five years. For funding infrastructure projects, the expert group recommended the introduction of appropriate reforms in provident, pension and insurance funds so that the private sector could have access to these funds for infrastructure development.

Performance of LIC

India had an estimated middle class of 250-300 million people who could afford to buy life insurance, disability insurance and pension plan products. The insurance market in India was estimated at Rs 159 bn with a growth rate of 17 per cent when compared to the negative growth rates in some developed countries like the US, the UK as well as Japan. The projected premium income could be as high as Rs 225 bn by 2003, from around Rs 70 bn in 1995-96. In spite of these favourable market conditions, in the financial year 1995-96, LIC recorded a negative growth rate of more than -15 per cent, missing its target of total assurance amount sold by about 60 per cent. And, after almost four decades of near monopolistic existence, it covered 23 per cent of the insurable population, which included working men between twenty and sixty. Furthermore, the rate of return for LIC policyholders worked out to just a meagre 8 per cent on average.

These trends were even more disturbing because of the fact that LIC, in addition to being a near monopoly, also enjoyed considerable protection from the government. On policies sold, buyers enjoyed a tax rebate of 20 per cent, creating an added attraction for its products. Besides, LIC's income tax liability on the profits from its core businesses had been pegged at a meagre 12 per cent ever since its inception, compared to the corporate tax rate of 40 per cent which even other PSUs were subject to.

LIC: Analysis of Income

(Rs million)

	1991–92	*1992–93*	*1993–94*	*1994–95*	*1995–96*
First year premium (%)	14.19	13.67	12.8	11.57	10.79
Renewal premium (%)	48.03	50.25	49.87	50.67	48.85
Single premium and consideration for annuities	2.88	1.31	1.33	1.44	4.68
Income from investments	33.43	33.96	35.01	35	34.99
Miscellaneous	1.47	0.81	0.99	1.32	0.69

Returns to Policyholders: Rates of Bonus Declared since 1957
(Rs per 1000 sum assured per annum)

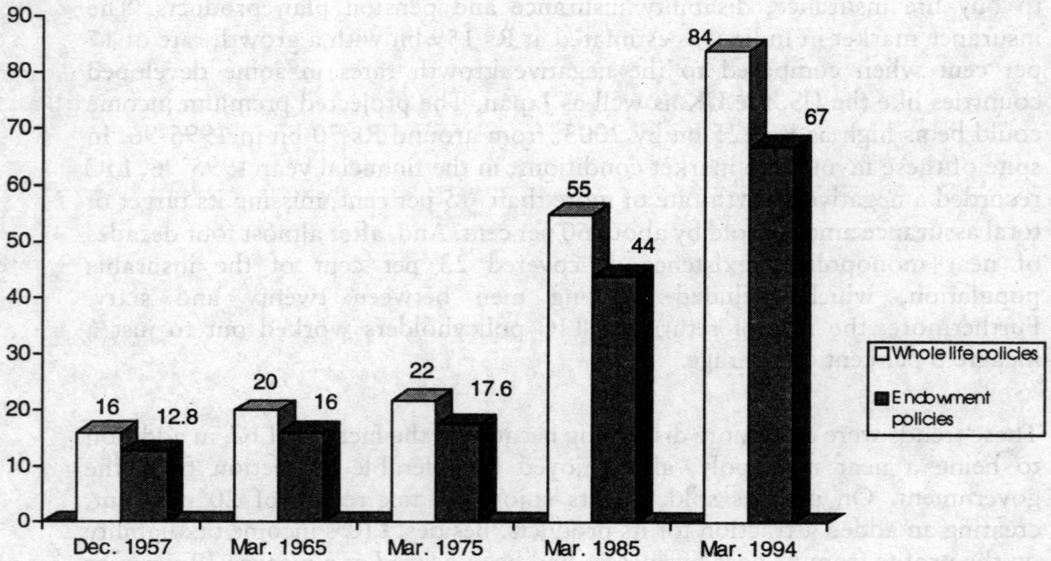

At the behest of the Malhotra Committee, MARG conducted a market survey among both users and non-users of life insurance to assess their perceptions of LIC and to find out satisfaction levels with LIC among users. The results showed that the awareness level of various 'plans' of LIC was quite limited even among policyholders. The main reasons behind purchasing insurance cover were mentioned as savings for the future by 67 per cent respondents, 45 per cent said they wanted to provide risk cover for family in case of death, and only 19 per cent mentioned tax benefits as a motivating factor. Seventy-five per cent of the individual respondents felt that the claims were settled satisfactorily and 67 per cent felt that the settlements were really fast. The survey also brought out that the average time taken to settle a claim was eighty-seven days; about 64 per cent of the individual respondents rated the quality of overall service to be excellent or good and only 3 per cent rated it as poor or very poor.

LIC: Claims Settlement Ratio

	1991–92	*1992–93*	*1993–94*	*1994–95*	*1995–96*
Claims intimated (in mn)	2.496	3.011	3.46	4.061	4.19
Amount (Rs bn)	24.22	35.80	38.45	46.66	53.53
Claims outstanding at the end of year					
Number (%)	3.25	3.09	3.05	3.47	3.86
Amount (%)	5.5	5.27	4.86	5.26	5.99
Amount (Rs mn)	1249.8	1515.2	1715	2262.3	2887

The responses of corporate policyholders were less favourable to LIC than those of individual policyholders as regards the quality of overall service. Though a majority of the corporate clients also viewed LIC employees to be courteous and efficient, a third of them felt that they were not efficient. Sixty per cent of LIC's corporate customers felt that LIC was innovative and developed schemes to suit their organisation's needs and 92 per cent of the corporate subscribers said they were satisfied with the yield.

A large majority of individual respondents complained that they did not get the policy documents for a long time after application, that they did not get premium/default notices in time and that premium receipts and policy documents had a lot of mistakes. There was a feeling that LIC took a long time to send payment on maturity and changes in policy were not incorporated quickly. The general consensus was that though LIC offered a range of policies suited to various people, the premia were too high.

The survey also showed that LIC had achieved several of the objectives of nationalisation. It had spread the insurance culture fairly widely, mobilised large savings for national development and financed socially important sectors like housing, electricity, water supply and sewerage. It had also acquired considerable financial strength and gained the confidence of the insuring public and had built up a large and talented pool of insurance professionals. At the same time, several negative perceptions and constraints were mentioned. The vast marketing and services network of LIC was inadequately responsive to customer needs; insurance awareness was low among the general public; marketing of life insurance with reference to customer needs was not adequate; term assurance plans were not being encouraged and unit linked assurance was not available; and returns from life insurance were significantly lower compared to other saving instruments due to excessive government directed investments of LIC funds.

Opening Up of the Insurance Sector

When questioned about the opening up of the insurance sector to private insurance firms, half the individual respondents did not favour the prospect of private life insurance companies for fear that private insurers might not be safe. On the other hand, 72 per cent of corporate respondents favoured private sector entry in the area of life insurance, 60 per cent of them preferred a mix of public and private life insurance companies, with only 9 per cent favouring 'only private sector'. Though there were fears among respondents that money with private insurers might not be safe, payment might not be guaranteed on death or maturity and tax benefits might not be available, the major advantages of privatisation were perceived to be more efficient and better service, more innovative schemes and timely payment of claims.

Nevertheless, the reaction to the opening up of the insurance sector was met with predictable opposition from employees. On 27 November 1996, when the government placed the reforms bill in parliament, the employees of LIC went on a one-day hunger strike.

> N.M. Sundaram, General Secretary, All India Insurance Employees Association (AIIEA), orchestrating the opinion of the members said: 'The insurance companies should be given a chance to see how well they can perform freed of controls, before opening up of the sector is contemplated.'

The move also did not go well with the leftist political parties. Gurdas Dasgupta, Communist Party of India (CPI) MP, announced that:

> If the government introduced the bill for privatisation, the employees would intensify their struggle. If foreign firms were allowed to enter the insurance sector, a substantial part of the profit would be taken out of the country. Nowhere in capitalist countries was a foreign firm allowed to enter the insurance sector. The entry of foreign and Indian private companies would lead to unhealthy competition and gross malpractices

and if the worldwide experience is any guide, no regulatory authority would be able to check it.

Simultaneously, going by the trends in other sectors, employees had begun to soften their stand towards collective bargaining.

> The employees said: 'We are willing to identify them [our faults], improve services, meet target requirements, introduce new products. We are willing to underwrite an MoU between the corporation and the government for performance guarantee if autonomy is granted and opening up deferred.'

Employees, for the first time, introduced concrete proposals to improve customer service in their charter of demands to LIC. In terms of the latest charter of demands presented to LIC by the All India LIC Employees Federation (AILEF), the employees called for extending the service hours for customers to twelve hours on every working day and for the introduction of two shifts with shorter working hours. The Federation also called for special services to certain categories of policyholders. The Federation, in a release to its employees, said, 'The charter of demands has been prepared after taking into account an altogether new situation emerging in the process of globalisation, liberalisation and jerky switchover to a free market economy along with the new ongoing revolution in information technology.'

Organisational Set-up of LIC

Organisation Structure

The organisational structure of LIC was a four-tier structure with the central office at the top. Zonal offices assisted the central office in matters of development, planning and review of business and supervision of divisional offices within their jurisdiction. The divisional office was concerned with all activities of the insurer from procurement of new business to the settlement of claims. Under each divisional office there were branch offices, sub-offices and development centres, all of which maintained direct administrative and operational control over procurement and servicing of the business.

LIC: Organisation Structure

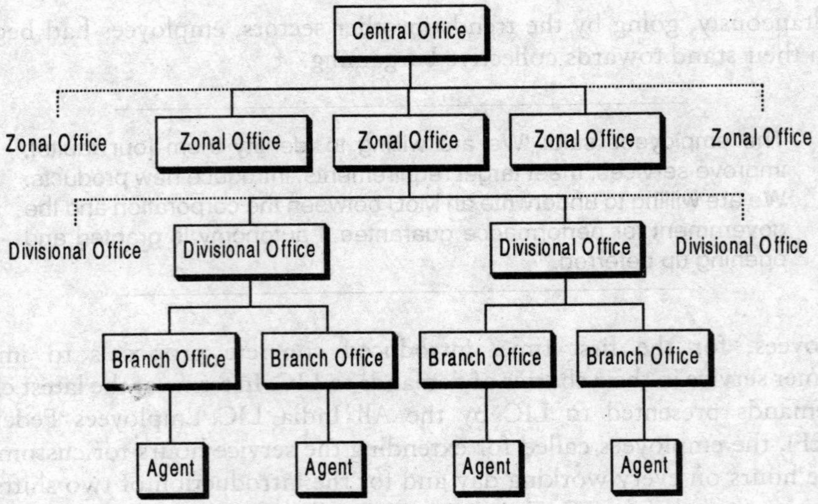

The Central Office

The Corporation maintained a central office in Mumbai which performed three functions: (1) Setting policy directions which included not only broad strategy guidelines but also certain executive level aspects like investment policy, underwriting standards and premium rates; (2) Co-ordinating and maintaining control over the activities of the various lower level units like zonal offices, which involved standardisation of procedures and forms, inspection and internal auditing of the various offices, etc; and (3) Formulation and underwriting of large proposals which were beyond the limits of the operating divisional office, submission of statutory returns to the government, and drawing up of prospectus.

The central office was divided into various functional departments, viz., marketing, actuarial, investment, long-range planning, management services, engineering services, estate and office services, personnel and industrial relations, finance and accounts, legal and housing finance schemes, group schemes, and inspection and audit. Each department was headed by a committee which had specific responsibilities for that function. The various committees were co-ordinated and supervised by an executive management committee, which also had the role of providing the direction to the business of the Corporation. The chairman of the Corporation was the chairman of all these committees. He made the various general policy decisions with the help of the executive committee. The executive committee was guided by 'such directions, in matters of policy involving public interest, as the Central government may give it in writing' under Section 21 of the LIC Act.

Zonal Offices

There were seven zonal offices in Mumbai, Chennai, Delhi, Calcutta, Hyderabad, Kanpur and Bhopal. The zonal office controlled the entire field staff working in the zone and also planned for the business development of the whole zone. They also advised the central office on personnel and legal matters, management of buildings belonging to the Corporation, purchase of stationery, printing of literature, etc. Accounts of the zone were compiled by them and general guidance to divisional offices in the matter of accounting principles and procedures was also provided. Besides, investigation of all doubtful claims arising in the zone was managed by the zonal manager. The zonal office was divided into various functional departments like marketing, actuarial, personnel and HR, finance and accounts, legal, management services, and estates and office services.

Divisional Offices

There were 100 divisional offices with definite territorial jurisdictions and they were concerned with the development of new business in their respective areas as well as the complete servicing of the insurance policies already sold. The office was divided into five main departments which were:

- New Business Department, which handled all new proposals for life insurance from the stage of proposal till the issue of the policy.
- Accounts Department, which handled all accounting work including control of branch accounts, maintenance of bank accounts and accounting of premium collection and other receipts, and all payments.
- Policyholders' Servicing Department, which handled all policy servicing from the stage of issue of the policy till settlement of the claim.
- Development Department, which handled all work in connection with field organisation including maintenance of business statistics, appointment of agents and field officers.
- Personnel and Establishment Department, which handled all staff matters including maintenance of salary and leave records, inward mail and dispatch work, supply of stationery, etc.

Branch Offices

There were 2,024 branch offices and 1,363 centres all over the country. The main departments of a branch were new business development, policyholder's servicing, accounts and establishment. The responsibilities of the branch office were related to registration and scrutiny of new proposals, collection of premium against new proposals and issue of receipts, correspondence with the prospects and agents in connection with new proposals, settlement of commission on first premium instalment and payment of medical fees to doctors, collection of premiums under policies, supervision of the working of agents and field officers attached to the branch, development of new business, and disbursement of loans on policies serviced by the branch.

LIC: Branch Office Structure

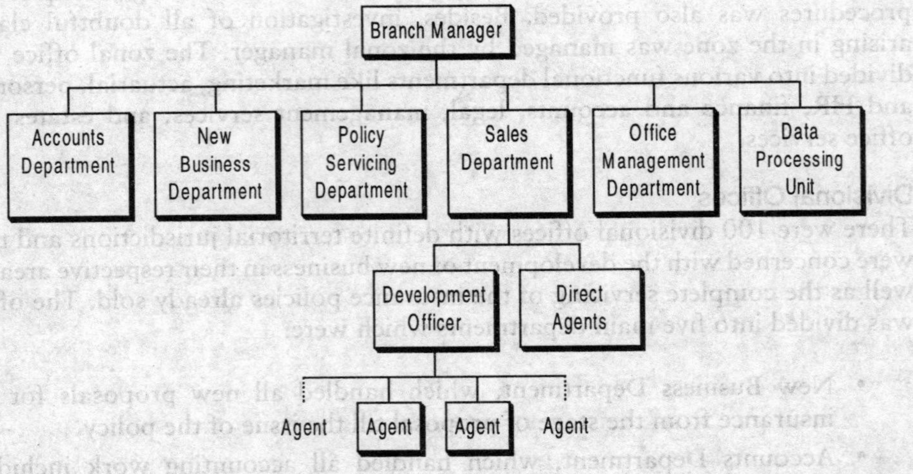

Field Organisation

LIC employed a large number of insurance agents for selling the polices. The agents constituted an important part in the organisation chain as they were primarily responsible for bringing in new business for individual policies. These agents, not being employees of the Corporation, were paid a commission on the premiums received on policies sold by them. They were the lowest operational units in implementing the business of the organisation and performed various field-level functions including selling policies to the prospects, completion of underwriting and keeping in touch with policyholders to ensure regular payment of premiums.

The agents were trained and supervised by development officers, who were full-time employees of the Corporation. These development officers assisted their agents in matters connected with procurement of new business and other relevant functions. They also recruited new agents in order to develop a stable agency force, kept the agents motivated and were hence responsible for enhancing policy servicing quality. While these development officers were paid a fixed salary, the agents were paid on a commission basis, the rates varying according to the plan and terms of the policies sold. Agents were also eligible for bonus commission depending on the volume of new business they introduced. An assistant branch manager (sales) normally supervised development officers and looked after the sales section at a branch office.

The selection of agents and their training was loosely administered and the turnover of these agents was very high. Agents were also not exclusive to LIC as many of them functioned as agents for other corporations like UTI as well. The average performance of an agent during 1995–96 stood at Rs 1,008,286 sum assured. In order to recognise agents who performed consistently year after year, clubs of four levels were designated. The four levels of clubs were chairman's club, zonal managers' club, divisional managers' club and branch managers' club. Club members enjoyed certain privileges and were vested with authority for attesting certain documents, etc. Development officers were recruited from amongst agents, LIC staff and open market candidates on the basis of written tests and interviews and were trained for nine months.

The MARG survey indicated that though the agents and development officers were perceived to be very helpful and knowledgeable at the initial stage of selling a policy, the enthusiasm wore off once the policy was bought. It was felt that development officers concentrated on their incentives and neglected the training of agents and the building up of an efficient agency organisation. This indifferent attitude by the sales agents and development officers resulted in significant lapses of policies without acquiring paid-up value (see Appendix 6). More than 25 per cent of sold policies lapsed within the first three years of their issue without acquiring their paid-up value.

Percentage of Net Lapses to Mean Life Insurance Business Force

Year	*Percentage*
1991–92	6.1
1992–93	5.9
1993–94	6.3
1994–95	6.1
1995–96	6.4

Net Lapse Ratio

Year of New Business	*Net Lapse Ratio at Mean Duration*				
	0	*1*	*2*	*3*	*Total*
1991–92	0.9	14.5	8.9	3.5	27.8
1992–93	1.0	15.6	8.9	3.8	29.3
1993–94	0.6	17.0	8.5		
1994–95	0.6	17.0			
1995–96	0.9				

Organisational Practices

LIC being a government organisation was subject to stiff and long-drawn monitoring mechanisms. The MARG survey also showed that the LIC management was perceived as top-heavy and excessively hierarchical, especially at the central and zonal offices. The supervision and control functions in the organisation had also considerably weakened. LIC was overstaffed, work culture within the organisation was unsatisfactory and trade unionism had contributed to the growth of restrictive practices.

Bureaucratic rigidity and inflexibility had resulted in creating low responsiveness to customer needs, poor service quality in terms of operational efficiency and flexibility, quality of delivery and price of products. This was evident in the high premiums that were being charged by LIC. Monthly cost of funding a life policy was 1.85 per 1000 for covering a man of age thirty, while no major UK insurer charged more than 1.45, and the premium could be as low as 1.08. Life insurance premiums were higher in India compared with international price levels because LIC assumed a lower level of life expectancy based on pre-1975 data. However, mortality had fallen sharply since then as improvement of health services and nutrition levels had resulted in an increase in life expectancy.

Investment Practices

Investment operations were incidental and yet crucial to the business of insurance. Insurers were required to generate reserves for claims that might arise and over a period a large corpus of funds had been built up. Insurance companies need to invest these funds judiciously with the combined objectives of liquidity, maximisation of yield and safety. Returns on investments from life insurance funds influence premium rates and bonuses to a large extent. Like banks, insurance companies are entrusted with public money. But unlike depositors, policyholders stand to lose the potential value of the policy, a sum far greater than what they have invested. In the public interest, investment of insurance funds is regulated in many countries.

Investment made by LIC is governed by Section 27-A of the Insurance Act. The investment management committee advised LIC towards implementation of this framework, the various guidelines of which were quite specific and explicit to the extent of being rigid. As per Section 27-A, LIC should at all times keep invested 75 per cent out of the accretion to the 'controlled fund' in accordance with the following:

- In central government marketable securities being not less then 20 per cent.
- In loans to National Housing Bank, including (a) above, being not less than 25 per cent.
- In state government securities including government guaranteed marketable securities, inclusive of (b) above, being not less than 50 per cent.
- In socially oriented sectors including the public sector, the cooperative sector, house building by policyholders, own your home schemes, inclusive of (c) above, being not less than 75 per cent.

The remaining 25 per cent of the accretion may be used by LIC for purposes such as investment in the private corporate sector, loans to policyholders and construction and acquisition of immovable property under the guidance of its investment committee.

LIC invested in the shares and bonds of all-India and state-level industrial financing institutions. The total subscriptions to these issues and bonds aggregated to Rs 20.44 bn in March 1993 compared to Rs 46 mn in 1956–57. This represented 5 per cent of the life fund. These increases were actually due to planned economic development efforts in the economy involving the setting up of a number of special purpose government-sponsored financial institutions to which LIC was directed to contribute its funds.

LIC also sanctioned direct term loans to private corporates. This constituted 3.3 per cent of the life fund in 1993. LIC also financed private projects by directly subscribing to their shares and debentures. This share had been decreasing steadily over the years. As a percentage of the life fund, LIC's securities portfolio declined from 14 per cent at the end of 1956-57 to around 8 per cent in 1993. Another aspect of this part of LIC's investments was the business of underwriting capital issues. The vast funds available with it enabled it to underwrite issues on a fairly massive scale, something which prevents smaller companies entering this arena. In the post-1990 period, however, merchant banks, brokers, etc., had replaced LIC as the major players in this sphere and its share had substantially declined. LIC now had more or less withdrawn from the securities market.

Investments by LIC

(as on 31 March 1996)

Areas	*Rs (in billion)*	*% of Total*
Government securities	377.57	55.3
Loans to National Housing Bank	9.05	1.33
Special deposit with Government of India	19.70	2.89
Debentures	52.00	7.62
Preferences shares	0.16	0.02
Equity shares	41.14	6.02
Loans for housing	60.03	8.79
Loans to state electricity boards	42.35	6.20
Loans for water supply and sewerage	13.15	1.93
Loans to state road transport corporations	2.21	0.32
Loans on policies	22.78	3.34
Loans on house, property and land	4.72	0.69
Loans to companies	31.18	4.57
Others	6.71	0.98
Grand total	682.76	100.00

LIC had been very conservative in managing its equity portfolio. Relative to its holdings of company shares, it tended to book rather small profits.

LIC: Investment in Equity Shares

(Rs billion)

	1990–91	*1991–92*	*1992–93*
Book value of equity shares at the end of the year	7.24	9.94	14.61
Market value of equity shares at the end of the year	37.18	126.11	69.53
Capital gains realised	0.51	0.49	0.46

Share prices in stock markets fluctuate and it is possible to improve profits through efficient and timely market operations. Though the objectives of safety of investments and mobilisation of resources for the public sector are important, the extent of directed investments of insurance funds, mostly at below market rates of interest, limits the scope for exploiting more lucrative investment opportunities and reduces benefits to the insured either by keeping premium on the higher side or by lesser bonuses on 'with profit' life policies.

Coping with Uncertainty

The insurance reform bill was introduced in parliament in 1997. Though the motion was defeated, the chairman of LIC, G. K. Krishnamurthy, thought that it was just a question of time before it was introduced again. He estimated that insurance sector reforms would be a reality in the next twelve to fifteen months. In the meanwhile, Krishnamurthy was discussing with various foreign partners the possibility of a joint venture in the life insurance and pension business. He was wondering whether he should form a joint venture with any of the partners.

The major challenge before LIC was to reorient the organisation to the new business scenario. Krishnamurthy was in the process of identifying the changes required in the organisational structure and processes which could make LIC more competitive. He was also wondering whether he should embark on the organisation transformation process on his own or whether he should seek the help of international consultants.

APPENDIX 1

Joint Ventures Interested in Entering the Life Insurance Market

Foreign Partner	*Indian Partner*
Allianz, Germany	Alpic Finance
CIGNA International, USA	Ranbaxy
Commercial Union, UK	Hindustan Times
General Accident Fire & Life, UK	Bombay Dyeing
Legal and General Insurance, UK	S.K. Modi group
Prudential Insurance, USA	ICICI
Rothschild Insurance, UK	Godrej group
Royal and Sun Insurance, UK	DCM Shriram
Standard Life, UK	HDFC
Zurich Insurance, Switzerland	C.K. Birla group

Zurich Insurance Group

Zurich Insurance Group provided insurance and financial service worldwide. The Swiss company, which was founded in 1872, operated in about fifty countries. Its products and services included non-life and life insurance, reinsurance, and investment management for customers in the personal, commercial and corporate market segments.

CIGNA International

CIGNA was a leading provider of health care, insurance and financial services throughout the United States and around the world, with assets of approximately $104 bn and over 48,000 people dedicated to helping 12 million people stay healthy, 6 million people save for retirement, and 21,000 companies provide valuable benefits for their employees. CIGNA ranked among the largest investor-owned insurance organisations in the United States, with shareholders' equity of $7.2 bn. It was also one of the largest US-based insurers active in international markets, as measured by international revenues of $3.1 bn in 1996.

Commercial Union

Commercial Union was one of the world's leading insurance companies, providing a comprehensive service to customers for all forms of general insurance and life assurance business, with operations in over fifty countries. The worldwide group had assets of over £55 bn, with a further £12 bn under management. The group had a market capitalisation of about £4.5 bn. Commercial Union was the largest composite insurance company in the UK. And had a total premium income of £2.1 bn. It employed some 8,000 people to service the needs of about 4.5 million customers ranging from private individuals to the largest multinational companies. Commercial Union was the fifth largest investment house in the UK and conducted more business in continental Europe than all the other UK insurance companies put together.

Prudential

Prudential was the largest US life insurer, with $178.6 bn of statutory assets and $169.2 bn of statutory liabilities as on 31 December 1996. It served nearly 50 million people worldwide. Prudential was a diversified financial services company meeting the needs of both retail and institutional clients. It offered a variety of products and services including insurance, investment management, annuities, securities, mutual funds, health care management, employee benefits and administration, real estate brokerage and relocation services, and banking.

Standard Life

Standard Life was one of the world's leading life assurance companies. It offered a wide range of life assurance, pension and investment products and services. Standard Life UK was based in Edinburgh. It employed over 6,000 people in the UK, managing assets of £50 bn worldwide.

APPENDIX 2

New Business: Individual Insurance (Excluding Annuities)

Year	New Business in India			New Business out of India			Total New Business		
	No. of Policies	Sum Assured (Rs bn)	Annual Premium Receivable (Rs bn)	No. of Policies	Sum Assured (Rs bn)	Annual Premium Receivable (Rs mn)	No. of Policies	Sum Assured (Rs bn)	Annual Premium Receivable (Rs bn)
1991–92	9238264	320.64	17.90	9596	1.31	81.9	9247860	321.96	17.98
1992–93	9957848	359.56	20.37	10271	1.59	99.8	9968119	361.15	20.47
1993–94	10725633	418.13	25.08	12976	1.99	121.3	10738009	420.12	25.19
1994–95	10874682	552.28	25.34	13304	2.40	149.3	10887986	554.69	25.49
1995–96	11020825	518.15	28.14	13345	2.56	156.3	11034170	520.71	28.29

Business in Force: Individual Insurance (Excluding Annuities)

Year	In India			Out of India			Total		
	No. of Policies (in mn)	Sum Assured and Bonuses (Rs bn)	Premium Income (Rs bn)	No. of Policies (in mn)	Sum Assured and Bonuses (Rs bn)	Premium Income (Rs mn)	No. of Policies (in mn)	Sum Assured and Bonuses (Rs bn)	Premium Income (Rs bn)
1991–92	50.86	1459.29	59.46	0.063	7.48	348.0	50.93	1466.77	59.81
1992–93	56.61	1772.68	71.46	0.067	8.52	395.1	56.68	1781.20	71.86
1993–94	60.80	2076.01	87.58	0.073	10.18	461.9	60.87	2086.19	88.04
1994–95	64.55	2533.33	103.85	0.077	12.39	573.4	65.53	2545.72	104.42
1995–96	70.88	2943.36	120.94	0.082	14.22	654.1	70.96	2957.58	121.59

APPENDIX 3

New Business: Progress Under Group Superannuation Schemes

Year	New Schemes			Renewal of Existing Schemes				Total Annuity per Annum (Rs mn)
				New Members		Existing Members		
	No. of Schemes	No. of Members	Annuity per Annum (Rs mn)	Number	Annuity per Annum (Rs mn)	Number	Increase in Annuity per Annum (Rs mn)	
1991–92	306	15028	67.8	7559	34.2	215263	21.0	123.0
1992–93	249	28411	91.0	6298	30.1	234662	23.1	144.2
1993–94	273	31695	116.5	10487	38.5	271480	26.7	181.7
1994–95	328	31299	148.5	9407	44.6	313662	49.3	242.4
1995–96	353	75692	493.4	12384	45.2	330906	54.7	593.3

Business in Force: Group Insurance and Superannuation Schemes

Year	Group Insurance Schemes			Group Superannuation Schemes			Total
	No. of Schemes	No. of Members (in mn)	Sum Assured and Bonuses (Rs bn)	No. of Schemes	No. of Members (in mn)	Amount of Annuities per Annum (Rs bn)	Premium Income (Rs bn)
1991–92	54704	18.953	329.73	2806	0.254	3.02	6.81
1992–93	59128	21.254	430.86	3040	0.269	3.59	7.26
1993–94	64426	22.731	467.42	3314	0.314	4.04	8.73
1994–95	71726	24.188	510.34	3642	0.354	4.28	10.34
1995–96	72592	24.649	646.51	3977	0.419	4.83	19.79

APPENDIX 4

Individual Pension Schemes

	1995–96	1994–95	1993–94	1992–93	1991–92	1990-91
New business						
Sum assured (Rs mn)	108.0	96.2	96.5	168.6	1655.0	1927.5
No. of policies	11000	11000	9000	15000	153000	157000
Annual premium (Rs mn)	18.3	34.9	35.2	66.2	616	NA
Business in force						
Sum assured (Rs bn)	4.98	4.92	4.93	5.93	8.29	7.15
No. of policies	458000	461000	465000	506000	696000	564000

APPENDIX 5

Unit Trust of India

Unit Trust of India (UTI) was established as a Trust by the Government of India in February 1964 under terms of the UTI Act 1963. It was an associate institute of the Reserve Bank of India (RBI) till February 1976 when it was made an associate institute of the Industrial Development Bank of India (IDBI). UTI has borrowing powers from these parent institutions. It provides attractive investment opportunities through issue of units and shares under various schemes. The initial capital contributed by RBI, LIC, State Bank of India (SBI) and other banks, borrowings from RBI/IDBI and other banks, and the unit capital were the major sources of its funds. The funds so mobilised were invested largely in corporate securities with a view to earning maximum return to the primary investor, keeping in view the element of safety. Consequent upon amendment to the UTI Act in April 1986, UTI was allowed to grant term loans, rediscount bills, undertake equipment leasing and hire-purchase financing, provide housing and construction finance, provide merchant banking and portfolio management services, and set up overseas or 'off-shore' funds.

UTI became a household name, providing unitholders a safe avenue for investment in a wide variety of funds at attractive returns. It has evolved into a Trust with:

- A portfolio of Rs 570 bn under management.
- An array of sixty-six saving schemes catering to a broad cross-section of investors.
- An investor base of 48 million unitholding accounts.
- A distribution network of agents, numbering nearly 96,000, along with 310 District Representatives spread all over the country.
- A network of forty-nine UTI branch offices and twenty-five franchise offices.
- A low cost of service, with gross (annual) cost of less than 0.8 per cent of investible funds as against 3 per cent permissible under the Securities Exchange Board of India (SEBI) regulations.

UTI adapted to changing financial conditions and new investor needs by expanding its product range and services to suit a broad spectrum of investment goals. Between 1990 and 1996 the number of schemes managed by UTI doubled from thirty to sixty-six, while the number of unitholding accounts jumped sevenfold, from 6.5 million to 48 million. The schemes run by UTI were:

- Unit Linked Insurance Plan for insurance cover at a minimal cost.
- Monthly income schemes to meet regular and recurring income needs of retired persons, women and persons looking for such income.
- Scheme to manage funds of religious and charitable institutions and trusts.
- Schemes to help meet the rising cost of education and career plans for children.
- Schemes that pay special attention to the girl child and women's needs.
- Schemes for providing medical insurance for the aged.
- Pension plan for senior citizens.

Fund Development

Fifty per cent of UTI's total investible funds had been invested in equity. It was the largest operator in the Indian equity market with total investments worth over Rs 280 bn at book value. Its various funds collectively held stocks in more than 1,500 Indian companies and accounted for over 8 per cent of the market capitalisation of all listed scrips on the Bombay Stock Exchange. Investment in debt instruments accounted for 35 per cent of the total investible funds. Credit market operations covered a range of instruments including publicly issued and privately placed debentures, bonds and medium-term notes. UTI was also one of the largest investors, among non-banking financial institutions, in the money market. About 15 per cent of the total investible funds of UTI was accounted for by government paper and call deposits.

UTI: Performance Indicators

Performance Indicators	*1991–92*	*1992–93*	*1993–94*	*1994–95*	*1995–96*
Wide variety of schemes					
Number of schemes/Plans introduced	18	21	18	19	21
Number of schemes/Plans in operation	43	51	54	59	66
Growing customer response					
Face value of units sold (Rs bn)	121.82	64.92	109.82	128.53	49.42
Sales to individuals, face value (Rs bn)	115.91	57.44	64.84	70.88	43.34
Infrastructure strength					
Number of offices	39	41	43	48	49
Number of employees	1920	2122	2286	2381	2441
Number of registrars	6	5	6	6	6
Number of agents ('000)	85	89	96	85	96
Financial strength					
Outstanding unit capital (Rs bn)	248.15	306.49	392.98	454.33	432.57
Total investible funds (Rs bn)	318.06	389.77	517.09	596.19	568.41
Appreciation in book value (%)	43.57	18.42	50.12	15.65	NA
Dividend rate under US-64 (%)	25	26	26	26	NA
Reserves and provisions (Rs bn)	51.33	70.08	98.73	110.94	NA
Gross income (Rs bn)	50.35	55.32	79.07	79.94	NA
Gross expenditure (Rs bn)	2.89	2.65	3.18	4.69	NA
Equity investments (Rs bn)	88.62	149.20	211.17	284.99	NA
Operating efficiency					
Investible funds per employee (Rs mn)	165.7	183.7	226.2	250.4	232.9
Sales per employee (Rs mn)	63.4	30.6	48	54	20.2
Accounts serviced per employee ('000)	12.29	14.18	16.62	20.9	19.66
Trust's net income per employee (Rs mn)	24.7	24.8	33.2	31.6	NA
Investible funds per account (Rs '000)	13477	12949	13611	11978	11842

NA = Not available.

APPENDIX 6

A Note on Policy Lapse, Paid-Up and Surrender Values

An insurance policyholder can at any time discontinue his contract with the insurance company by surrendering his or her policy or fail to pay the premium when due. When the policyholder stops payment of premiums within a specified number of years, then the policy is said to have lapsed without acquiring any paid-up value, in which case the policyholder would not get any compensation for the premiums paid.

If the policyholder wishes to discontinue his contract at a later stage then he or she can surrender the policy to receive a surrender value. During the early years of the policy, the surrender value is usually less than the full reserve.

A reserve can be defined as 'the difference, at any point in time, between the present value of future benefits and the present value of future net premiums'. At the start of the insurance policy, the two sides of the equation, viz., the present value of the benefits promised under the contract, and the other, the present value of the sum of money required to provide the benefits, are in balance. Once a premium has been paid, however, the situation has changed. The present value of future benefits is no longer equal to the present value of future net premiums. The former would have increased, since the benefits are nearer to maturity, while the latter has decreased, since less premiums remain to be paid. The difference is the reserve.

During the initial years of the policy, the surrender value of the policy would be less than full reserve because of the high proportion of initial expenses incurred by the insurance company, and to protect continuing policyholders from loss. The surrender value of the policy increases over the duration of the policy when it gradually equals reserves. The following table shows an extract from surrender value tables of the Life Insurance Corporation for endowment assurance.

Endowment Assurance
Surrender Value for Rs 100 Paid-Up Portion

Duration (Yrs)	5 years (Rs)	6 years (Rs)	7 years (Rs)	8 years (Rs)	9 years (Rs)	10 years (Rs)	15 years (Rs)	20 years (Rs)	25 years (Rs)	30 years (Rs)	40 years (Rs)
2	61.80	58.13	54.66	51.96	49.56	47.43	37.27	25.93	18.45	13.63	8.88
3	67.34	63.34	59.55	55.97	53.18	50.70	40.18	27.91	19.83	14.62	9.48
4	73.39	69.03	64.89	60.98	57.28	54.40	43.32	30.06	21.31	15.68	10.13
5	0.00	75.23	70.71	66.44	62.40	58.59	46.71	32.37	22.91	16.82	10.81
6	0.00	0.00	77.06	72.40	67.98	63.82	49.58	34.86	24.63	18.04	11.54
7	0.00	0.00	0.00	78.90	74.08	69.53	52.79	37.54	26.48	19.35	12.32
8	0.00	0.00	0.00	0.00	80.73	75.76	56.42	40.44	28.47	20.76	13.15
9	0.00	0.00	0.00	0.00	0.00	82.57	60.51	43.57	30.61	22.27	14.04
10	0.00	0.00	0.00	0.00	0.00	0.00	65.15	46.94	32.92	23.89	14.99
11	0.00	0.00	0.00	0.00	0.00	0.00	70.95	49.80	35.44	25.64	16.00
12	0.00	0.00	0.00	0.00	0.00	0.00	77.28	53.00	38.10	27.51	17.08
13	0.00	0.00	0.00	0.00	0.00	0.00	84.19	56.60	40.98	29.52	18.22
14	0.00	0.00	0.00	0.00	0.00	0.00	91.74	60.67	44.09	31.67	19.43
15	0.00	0.00	0.00	0.00	0.00	0.00	0.00	65.28	47.43	33.98	20.71
16	0.00	0.00	0.00	0.00	0.00	0.00	0.00	71.04	50.25	36.44	22.06
17	0.00	0.00	0.00	0.00	0.00	0.00	0.00	77.33	53.40	39.09	23.48
18	0.00	0.00	0.00	0.00	0.00	0.00	0.00	84.21	56.95	41.92	24.98
19	0.00	0.00	0.00	0.00	0.00	0.00	0.00	91.74	60.95	44.97	26.57
20	0.00	0.00	0.00	0.00	0.00	0.00	0.00	0.00	65.49	48.24	28.24
21	0.00	0.00	0.00	0.00	0.00	0.00	0.00	0.00	71.19	50.98	30.01
22	0.00	0.00	0.00	0.00	0.00	0.00	0.00	0.00	77.41	54.05	31.87
23	0.00	0.00	0.00	0.00	0.00	0.00	0.00	0.00	84.24	57.50	33.83
24	0.00	0.00	0.00	0.00	0.00	0.00	0.00	0.00	91.74	61.41	35.91
25	0.00	0.00	0.00	0.00	0.00	0.00	0.00	0.00	0.00	65.84	38.11
26	0.00	0.00	0.00	0.00	0.00	0.00	0.00	0.00	0.00	71.45	40.44
27	0.00	0.00	0.00	0.00	0.00	0.00	0.00	0.00	0.00	77.55	42.91
28	0.00	0.00	0.00	0.00	0.00	0.00	0.00	0.00	0.00	84.29	45.53
29	0.00	0.00	0.00	0.00	0.00	0.00	0.00	0.00	0.00	91.74	48.32
30	0.00	0.00	0.00	0.00	0.00	0.00	0.00	0.00	0.00	0.00	51.31
31	0.00	0.00	0.00	0.00	0.00	0.00	0.00	0.00	0.00	0.00	53.76
32	0.00	0.00	0.00	0.00	0.00	0.00	0.00	0.00	0.00	0.00	56.51
33	0.00	0.00	0.00	0.00	0.00	0.00	0.00	0.00	0.00	0.00	59.60
34	0.00	0.00	0.00	0.00	0.00	0.00	0.00	0.00	0.00	0.00	63.12
35	0.00	0.00	0.00	0.00	0.00	0.00	0.00	0.00	0.00	0.00	67.15
36	0.00	0.00	0.00	0.00	0.00	0.00	0.00	0.00	0.00	0.00	72.31
37	0.00	0.00	0.00	0.00	0.00	0.00	0.00	0.00	0.00	0.00	78.05
38	0.00	0.00	0.00	0.00	0.00	0.00	0.00	0.00	0.00	0.00	84.48
39	0.00	0.00	0.00	0.00	0.00	0.00	0.00	0.00	0.00	0.00	91.74
40	0.00	0.00	0.00	0.00	0.00	0.00	0.00	0.00	0.00	0.00	0.00

CASE 4

TUBE INVESTMENTS OF INDIA LIMITED: REPOSITIONING IN A LIBERALISING ECONOMY

Tube Investments achieved a remarkable turnaround in the year 1999–2000. From being a problem child of the Murugappa group two years ago, it turned in excellent financial results and gained a new position in the marketplace. Its turnover reached a new height of Rs 12.35 bn and profit before interest and tax (PBIT) touched Rs 1.04 bn. While its operating profitability went up to 9 per cent, profit after tax (PAT) improved by a whopping 56 per cent to Rs 330mn, which was also the highest in its long history. Return on capital employed (ROCE) rose to an all-time high of 32 per cent and the company recorded a positive economic value added (EVA) for the first time. This excellent performance made Tube Investments the most profitable company in the Murugappa group.

In addition to this significant growth in turnover and profits (see Appendices 1

This case was written by Sushil Khanna, Anindya Sen and Saugata Ray, Professors at Indian Institute of Management, Calcutta with assistance from Biswatosh Saha, doctoral candidate at the Institute. The authors are grateful to Tube Investments of India Ltd for their help and support. This case was first registered by the Indian Institute of Management, Calcutta, in 1998.

to 3 for a financial overview of the company), the market share of its two major divisions, namely bicycles and steel tubes, rose to new heights. In its bicycle business, Tube Investments (TI) regained the number two position in the industry with a 23 per cent market share after several decades and consolidated its leadership of the 'special' segment with a 47 per cent market share. Similarly, the Tube Division, already a market leader in India, recorded an impressive growth of 80 per cent in sales volume in 1999–2000 over the previous year, while in steel strips the company recorded 41 per cent growth. Its share price rose to a three-year- high of Rs 184 in October 1999, before settling down to the Rs 100–110 range in March 2000.

V.A. Raghu, the chief executive, was also promoted to the position of managing director, the first amongst the professional managers to hold that position. A veteran of several turnaround and corporate restructuring efforts, Raghu had been brought into the company in 1998 as the chief executive with a clear mandate of improving performance.

When Raghu joined TI, the company had not been performing well for the last couple of years. The company's return on investment (ROI) of 4 per cent in 1996–97 was far below market expectations. The return on shareholders' funds had fallen from a high of 13.9 per cent in 1992 to a low of 6.36 per cent in 1997. The capital market marked its share value down from a high of Rs 340 in February 1994 to an abysmal Rs 31.50 in February 1998. A slowdown in the economy had squeezed margins, while cheaper supply from neighbouring Asian countries armed with devalued currencies after the financial crisis had intensified competition both in the domestic as well as the export markets. Hence this rapid turnaround was a vindication of Raghu's belief that TI was a strong company with untapped potential.

'However, this marks only the beginning of a long-term revival, as the company must build a sustainable corporate and competitive advantage on the current foundation', felt Raghu. What was particularly worrying him was that the improved showing of TI failed to regain the confidence of the stock investors. Its position in the capital market was yet to improve much, as the market capitalisation recorded only Rs 2.48 bn against a book value of Rs 3.65 bn. This was despite the fact that TI had a favourable capital structure and a strong financial flexibility, being a member of the Murugappa group which earned an AA rating from CRISIL for its latest non-convertible debenture issue of Rs 200 mn. It was observed by analysts that the favourable factors were to a great extent offset by TI's presence in highly competitive and price sensitive industries resulting in consistently depressed operating margins for the company. There were other related concerns too. The company had set an ambitious target of Rs 20 bn turnover by 2005 AD and a profitability of 8-10 per cent on sales. To carry out some of the planned projects and embark on fresh investment necessary to achieve these targets, the company desperately needed additional funds from the market. Moreover, given that it had a liquid cash reserve of Rs 2.07 bn and promoters' holding only at 29.13 per cent of equity, some experts believed TI could become a target for a hostile takeover bid as well.

Brief History of Tube Investments of India

Tube Investment of India belonged to the Rs 33 bn Murugappa Group based in Chennai. It was engaged in the manufacturing of bicycles, steel tubes and strips, door frames for cars, shutter products, pollution control products, and light commercial vehicle products. Currently, Tube Investments consisted of three main divisions—the bicycle division, the tubes and strips division (engineering division), and the 'roll form' division. The first two divisions were the largest, contributing more than 80 per cent of the total revenue in 2000.

TI was incorporated as TI Cycles of India in collaboration with TI of UK as the major shareholder. The unit was the first cycle manufacturer in India. The foreign share holding had gradually declined to 4.04 per cent. In 1959, Tube Products of India (TPI) was merged with TI and TI Miller, a manufacturer of cycle accessories, was merged with the company in 1984. Historically, TI Cycles had been the largest integrated manufacturer of bicycles in India and was still a market leader in the category of special cycles. TI marketed its product under the popular 'BSA' and 'Hercules' brand names.

The company diversified into cycle and then auto/industrial chains in 1985 through a subsidiary, TI Diamond Chain, which was subsequently spun off as an independent company in 1995. In 1993, TI established an overseas subsidiary—Parry Overseas Ltd—incorporated in the Virgin Islands, to assist in its export thrust abroad. The Diamond Chain Company for all practical purposes functioned like another business division. Appendix 4 gives the new organisation chart of the company.

TI Cycles

The golden jubilee year of 1999–2000 was a landmark for TI Cycles. It achieved the highest growth in volume by any Indian bicycle company ever with 5.78 lakh units additional sales over the previous year. It also generated 32 per cent operating return on capital employed, making it one of the most profitable businesses in the Murugappa group portfolio. Though the cycle business still remained the major business of the company, its contribution to overall sales had gone down from 45 per cent in 1995 to 41 per cent in 2000.

The first three decades of TI Cycles were its golden period. There were times, like the 1971 Bangladesh war, when cycles were in acute short supply due to large-scale smuggling into Bangladesh and the marketing department was forced to act as a 'rationing' office. There was a large unsatisfied demand for cycles and consumers began to look for better value for their money. Hero Cycles Limited, a small manufacturer set up in 1956 by the late Dayanand Munjal in Ludhiana, grabbed this opportunity and aggressively captured a share of the hungry market. By the late 1970s Hero and Atlas emerged as major players in the industry. Avon emerged as the fourth largest player. Hero had an integrated operation with in-house rolling facilities for steel and manufacturing facilities for critical components such as freewheels. Hero moved on to become the market leader with a production expanding from sixty cycles a day in 1956 to 18,500 cycles a day in 2000. Hero Cycles was the world's largest producer of bicycles with an annual installed capacity of 5.8 million and about 50 per cent share of the Indian market.

Market Shares of Standard Bicycles

Firm	*1994–95*	*1995–96*	*1996–97*	*1997–98*	*1998–99*	*1999–2000*
Hero	47	48	51	53	50	48.6
Atlas	27	27	26	25	30.3	30
TI	12	12	12	11.7	11.2	13.5
Avon	14	13	11	10	8.4	7.9

The Indian Bicycle Industry

In India, bicycles were the second most widely owned durable product. There were no government regulations on assembly and manufacture of bicycles, though manufacture of certain components was reserved for small-scale industries. Despite rapid expansion, cycle penetration in India remained low. Ownership of eleven per 100 persons was far below that of developed countries such as France, Germany, the UK and Holland (one bicycle for every two to three persons). It was even less than half of the Chinese twenty-five per 100 persons. In 1998, with a total penetration of 45.50 per cent, about 80 million households owned at least one bicycle. More than 90 per cent of bicycle owners belonged to the low and low middle income households, where it was used essentially as a utility vehicle. About 43 per cent bicycle owners belonged to the upper and middle income groups, the rest being from the lower income group. Out of the total buyers, 70 per cent were from rural India.

Bicycle Ownership by Income in India, 1998

Income Group	*Urban*		*Rural*		*Total*	
	House-holds (in mn)	*Penetration (%)*	*House-holds (in mn)*	*Penetration (%)*	*House-holds (in mn)*	*Penetration (%)*
Lower (<Rs 2,000)	17.7	40.00	98.6	39.00	116.30	39.00
Middle (Rs 2,000-6,000)	24.6	57.00	25.8	60.00	50.40	59.00
Upper (>Rs 6,000)	5.40	54.00	3.00	60.00	8.40	56.00
Total	47.70	50.00	127.40	44.00	175.10	45.50

The market was expanding at 8 per cent per annum during the 1980s and early 1990s. In recent years, growth rates had declined sharply. Overall, in the last thirteen years, the market had grown at the rate of 4 per cent. With rising family incomes, Indian buyers graduated to mopeds, scooters and motorcycles. The bicycle industry was broadly divided into two categories—Standard and Specials. Further, Specials category consisted of four different segments, namely, SLR, Mountain bikes, Kids and Juveniles. Increasing urbanisation and rising incomes were expanding the market for Specials. The growth in demand for Standards, which constituted 71 per cent of the market, began to peter out by 1996. The growth of Standards over the last ten years stood at 21 per cent as against 83 per cent in Specials. The industry was plagued by overcapacity and low growth in demand. The three large players, namely Hero Cycles, Atlas Cycles and TI Cycles, dominated more than 90 per cent of the market.

Market for Bicycles in India

(Units in lakhs)

Year	*Demand*	*Standards*	*Specials*	*Capacity*
1994–95	86.6	69.1	17.5	114.5
1995–96	89.7	70.2	19.5	121.4
1996–97	87.8	66.5	21.3	131.0
1997–98	92.5	68.3	24.2	134.0
1998–99	99.7	73.4	26.3	137.0
1999–2000	108.0	77.0	31.0	137.0
2000–01	117.2	81.5	35.7	137.0
2001–02	123.5	84.3	39.1	137.0
2002–03	129.3	87.0	42.3	137.0

Income Projection for Households in India

(in millions)

	1994–95		*2001–2002*		*2006–2007*	
Income Group	*Rural*	*Urban*	*Rural*	*Urban*	*Rural*	*Urban*
Lower (<Rs 2,000)	71	15	49	7	34	2
Middle (Rs 2,000-6,000)	40	23	68	30	89	30
Upper (>Rs 6,000)	5	7	11	15	16	28
Total	116	45	128	52	139	60

Source: NCAER.

As more than 70 per cent of the market for cycles was for the Standards with little product differentiation, customer loyalty to brands was poor and the market was highly price sensitive. Operational efficiency and volumes were the key to profitability in the Standards segment. Thus, in this category, TI found itself at a significant competitive disadvantage vis-à-vis Hero. The market leader was the lowest cost and most profitable producer with an extensive dealer network and an excellent image in the trade. Hero cycles were sold at a discount of Rs 150 to the cheapest models of TI, a price/cost gap TI found hard to bridge. Dealers who assembled a cycle and sold a few accessories like saddle, lights, belts, chain-covers, etc., were in a position to influence the customer's choice. Unable to match Hero in the Standards segment, TI had diversified into the

Specials category. The key success factors in Specials were TI's superior and innovative product designs, new features and added benefits. The growth in the demand for Standards declined by 1995. The Specials category continued to grow, but was not large enough to provide succour to the players in the industry. With increasing competition, smaller manufacturers like Avon began to be edged out.

Trends in Bicycle Sales in India Across Segments

(Units in lakhs)

	1994–95	*1995–96*	*1996–97*	*1997–98*	*1998–99*	*1999–2000*
STDS	69.1	70.2	66.5	68.3	73.4	77.0
SLRS	5.0	4.9	4.8	4.8	5.1	6.0
Kids	3.2	3.7	3.8	4.3	5.5	6.0
MTBs	4.6	5.5	5.8	6.7	7.5	8.8
Juniors	4.7	5.4	6.2	6.8	8.7	10.3
Total	86.6	89.7	87.8	92.5	99.7	108.0
Specials	17.5	19.5	21.3	24.2	26.29	31.4

Hero consolidated its lead further by increasing its market share to 53 per cent in 1998. However, its penetration in southern and western India remained low, and during 1999–2000 its share declined to 48.6 per cent. The largest penetrated markets were the East and North (penetration between 60 and 70 per cent) and accounted for 57 per cent of the total market, leaving the remaining 43 per cent for South and West with much lower penetration levels (only 25 to 40 per cent). TI had been a marginal player in the North and East, both of which were important markets for Standards bicycles. A recent survey carried out among 14,000 people countrywide by IMRB showed that Hero's top-of-the-mind recall was the highest across all bicycle brands in all age groups.

Historically, TI's low penetration in the North and East was also a result of poor distribution network. In 1996, TI Cycles had only 405 dealers in the North compared to 1,210 for Hero. In 2000, Hero Cycles opened a call centre in Gurgaon in Haryana. This was the company's biggest call centre in the country, having a capacity of around 2,000 employees.

Regional Market Shares of Cycles, 2000

Firm	*North*		*East*		*West*		*South*	
	1996	*2000*	*1996*	*2000*	*1996*	*2000*	*1996*	*2000*
Hero	45	45	53	53	31	31	39	36
Atlas	24	24	7	7	36	36	18	17
TI	4	10	22	24	18	23	43	45

Source: TI Cycles.

'Despite our premium pricing, we should have done better but poor network and lack of local warehousing facilities had been a major handicap', said K.K. Paul, GM (marketing). TI's low market shares in the northern and eastern markets had a cascading effect even on its superior Specials models in these markets. Without significant volumes in Standards it became costlier to distribute the Specials models. In the last two years, TI was able to make some improvement in its position in the North and East, predominantly through higher sales in the Standards segment.

Market Shares of Specials Bicycles

Firm	*1996–97*	*1997–98*	*1998–99*	*1999–2000*
Hero	36.4	37.3	34.7	30.9
Atlas	14.6	13.8	13.5	12.7
TI	38.5	39.3	41.7	47
Avon	10.5	9.5	10.1	9.3

Source: TI Cycles.

Although market leader Hero had a strong presence in the Specials segment, it relied more heavily on standard products for achieving aggressive growth targets. Hero historically had remained a follower in product development. However, more recently, it was attempting to improve its position in Specials through innovative products. In 1999, it came up with Power Bike, a battery powered bicycle. Power Bike, weighing 38 kg and with a top speed of 20 km per hour, could run for 40 km after which the battery needed to be recharged. It had an all-India launch of another bicycle called Hero Neon in 2000. The cycle was made available in different colours and marketed abroad also. In order to boost sales, a football was being offered free with the purchase of every Hero Neon bicycle.

The other major competitor, Atlas Cycles, had been concentrating mainly on the Standards segment. However, the company had ambitious plans for the future to raise its net sales to Rs 5 bn by 2004. It had recently launched a number of sophisticated models such as mountain bikes, all-terrain bikes and exercisers. In 2000, it introduced a new bicycle, Atlas Macho Millennium. Targeted at youngsters and priced at Rs 1,900, the Macho had features like revo shift, Simono gears of Japan, a strong body and light weight. The company envisaged that the new launches of Specials would lead to a share of more than 30 per cent in total revenue. It had three units in Sonepat (Haryana), Sahibabad (U.P.) and Malanpur (Gwalior) and was planning to set up another unit in Maharashtra or Tamil Nadu. It was exporting about 10 per cent of the cycles to more than thirty-five countries in Africa and Europe. However, Atlas was financially weaker (return on capital employed being only 10 per cent against 22 per cent of TI and 29 per cent of Hero) compared to both Hero and TI.

TI Cycles' Early Responses to Competition

In the early 1990s, TI's cycle business came under severe strains, partly because of competition from other players in the domestic market, partly because of high demands on quality from foreign buyers and partly because they were operating in an industry that provided very low margins. Unable to compete in the Standards segment, it shifted focus to the Specials category where its superior design capabilities could be leveraged. However, TI's expectation that the Specials category would expand rapidly to constitute 40 per cent of the domestic market by the mid-1990s did not materialise. Standards remained the bread and butter of the industry. TI found it costly to market its more advanced models in the northern and western markets without significant volumes in Standards. Moreover, even in the Specials category, both Hero and Atlas had been nibbling away at its market share by launching products that imitated the design and features launched by TI. As the market for Specials was small, the overall impact on profitability of the new launches was marginal.

Despite substantial improvements in productivity and reduction in component costs, there was deterioration in the profitability of the cycle division. In 1994–95 and 1995–96 the division made small losses. Though there was some improvement in 1997–98, the profit before tax to capital employed was a meagre 11 per cent, half that notched up by Hero.

TI's Early Foray into the Global Market

Devaluation of the rupee made bicycle exports from India very attractive. When the European Union (EU) imposed anti-dumping duties on Chinese and Taiwanese bicycle exports in 1992, TI moved rapidly to grab the opportunity and began to export MTB bicycles, then in fashion in Europe. It set up an Export Oriented Unit (EOU) at Paruthipet (Madras) to manufacture frames. The business was good and during the first two years the unit exported about 240,000 frames each year. The Chennai plant was upgraded at a cost of Rs 100 mn to manufacture assembled bicycles or ready-to-assemble kits, with a capacity of 2,000 cycles per day. A new EOU was set up with a dedicated capacity of 3 lakh cycles per annum. By 1994, TI emerged as the largest exporter of bicycles from India.

However, the success of Indian firms in penetrating European markets prompted Europeans to build several non-tariff barriers, making it costly for Indian firms to ship assembled cycles to Europe. By 1997, the European bicycle boom had begun to peter out and demand for cycles had started going down at the rate of 4 per cent per annum. The sharp devaluation of the Chinese currency and partial roll-back of dumping duties made China an aggressive player in the global market. Indian exports declined to 383,000 cycles by 1996, and further came down to 328,000 in 1998. In contrast, Chinese and Taiwanese exports rose during 1996–98.

TI Cycles: Export of Products

Year	*Frames*	*Assembled CKD Cycles*	*Profit Before Tax (Rs lakhs)*
1992–93	237900	–	0.85
1993–94	138600	105726	35.00
1994–95	18500	186126	(122.00)
1995–96	26400	186703	(16.00)
1996–97	14500	140521	(79.00)
1997–98	Nil	89627	(268.00)
1998–99	10000	136000	–
1999–2000	45000	152000	–

Source: TI Cycles.

The EOU continued to make heavy losses and was liquidated in 1997. The export production was shifted to the main plant at Madras, integrating production for domestic and export markets to achieve economies of scale.

The erosion of the firm's profitability despite substantial investments pointed to several basic weaknesses in the company. Within the company, the cycle division's low profitability was largely attributed to its export losses. 'However, it would be incorrect to blame the recession and the export losses for the declining fortunes of TI', confided a senior manager. TI 's overall strategy, its positioning, its marketing capabilities, and its inability to match costs and productivity levels of competitors, besides, in some cases its inability to deliver quality products were perhaps as much to blame for the poor performance.

TI Cycles: Exports to Different Countries

(Numbers in lakhs)

Year	*France*	*Germany*	*UK*	*Scandinavia*	*Others*	*Total*
1992–93	1.08	0.00	0.05	0.00	0.15	1.28
1993–94	2.02	0.37	0.57	0.10	0.34	3.40
1994–95	1.40	0.58	0.70	0.34	0.54	3.56
1995–96	0.87	0.58	1.29	0.21	0.65	3.60
1996–97	0.09	0.37	0.45	0.20	1.89	3.00
1997–98	0.00	0.64	0.91	0.16	0.16	1.87
1998–99	0.10	0.34	0.91	0.00	0.11	1.46
1999-2000	0.15	0.66	0.71	0.00	0.09	1.61

Source: TI Cycles.

There was a silver lining as well, particularly in the area of a changing managerial mindset that the foray into the global markets brought about. International benchmarking and appreciation of the strengths of the Taiwanese and Chinese cycle industry laid the basis of renewed thrust on product development and productivity.

Embarking on a Turnaround in Cycles

Raghu, when assuming charge of turning around TI's deteriorating fortunes in early 1998, knew he had a formidable challenge on his hands. He felt that TI needed an organisational renewal with greater focus on costs and productivity, and new marketing and distribution strategies.

Imports into European Union (EU) from Selected Countries, 1992–94

(In units)

Country	*1992*	*1993*	*1994*
Taiwan	2308207	2272500	1724430
India	121290	373900	492730
Malaysia	344140	489700	415650
Thailand	521850	419100	343250
Poland	189900	173700	286200
Indonesia	359620	311200	266320
Czech Rep.	162720	244200	256960
South Korea	104390	189500	181900
USA	127920	117900	135850
Vietnam	92900	295300	101360
Slovenia	48975	101100	60970
Lithuania	NA	70900	56560
China	1681250	387900	50310
Others	224423	84100	84100
Total	6287585	5531000	4422080

It was clear that TI had always prided itself as an engineering and manufacturing company. It lacked a consumer and market orientation. It neither understood the importance of branding nor had it the capability to carry out brand marketing. The other challenge facing the company was to change its focus from cost control to regenerating growth. 'With low growth and stagnant market shares our efforts at productivity improvement and technological upgradation are rapidly eroded', said Raghu. And the growth has been constrained not only by market conditions but also by the inability to find creative solutions to its current positioning.

In the first instance, he insisted that TI Cycles break out of its traditional dependence on the South Indian market and provide focus on branding, distribution and outsourcing. The export market needed a different strategy and alliances with Chinese firms or import of accessories from places like Singapore might help raise margins.

In the medium term TI had set itself an ambitious target of becoming the number two bicycle manufacturer by 2000 with sales of 35 lakh bicycles in the domestic market, while at the same time achieving 40 per cent ROI. TI Cycles singled out a few areas of the value chain for special attention and thrust.

Since locational disadvantages made TI a marginal player in North and East India, the possibility of sourcing entire bicycles from a medium-sized manufacturer in the North was vigorously pursued. A team of young production engineers was detailed to study plants in the North.

The company tied up outsourcing arrangements with Avon Cycles in Punjab and Hamilton Cycles in Mumbai with a view to expanding its reach in the northern and western markets respectively. The alliance with Hamilton Cycles provided for supply of 50,000 bicycles per annum to be sold under TI brands in the western market. Under another agreement, Avon Cycles would supply 1.6 lakh Hercules brand bicycles to TI for the North Indian market. With these arrangements, TI reached a stage where its outsourcing was much higher than Hero and Atlas, who were more vertically integrated.

Marketing and Branding Strategy

Ram Kumar and his team in the cycles division identified marketing and distribution as the key elements of a turnaround and repositioning strategy. With cheaper and proximate source of supply (from Avon and Hamilton), they set about expanding their dealer network. In less than two years, the number of dealers in the North and the East rose by 60 per cent. Three large stock points were set up to feed this expanding network.

The company analysed that the number of households in the low income group—which constituted the largest section of the population and were the major buyers of Standards—were on the decline and would come down to about 18 per cent by 2006–07. A study conducted by the company also revealed noticeable shift in the profiles of consumers purchasing bicycles. Recent buyers were found to be younger, more affluent and more urban. The largest and fastest growing segment was constituted by students (36 per cent) in the age group of 10–25 years, followed by employed people (21 per cent) mainly in the middle and upper income groups. The ladies segment (11 per cent) that constituted a significant part of the student category was also showing steady growth. The farmers segment (13 per cent), predominantly above 25 years of age, was shrinking. It seemed that the majority (60 per cent) of the future buyers of bicycles would be below 25 years of age.

Based on these inputs, TI Cycles redefined the market into two broad segments—one that used bicycles as a functional product and the other which used it for fun, leisure, fitness, etc. By changing the segmentation variables from rural/urban or Standards/Specials to customer utility, TI could identify more segments that offered great opportunities for growth.

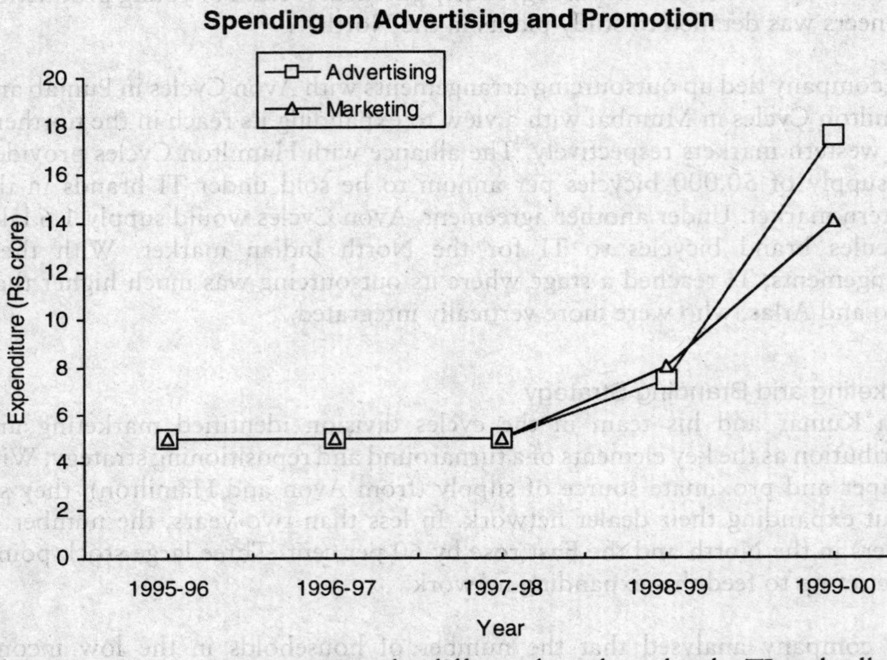

The next move was to reposition the different brands under the TI umbrella and strengthen them through higher spending on advertising and promotion. TI changed its branding strategy, making it more customer-centric as opposed to product-centric. The popular brands Hercules and BSA were repositioned targeting the consumers in these segments. While Hercules was positioned as a symbol of strength and ruggedness, BSA was positioned as a stylish, light and easy to ride bicycle. Within these two umbrella brands they introduced several sub-brands. Each model of Specials was given a distinctive brand name like 'Rockshock', 'Rambo' or 'Shakti'. Product development efforts were geared towards filling the void where customer needs existed without matched offerings. Unlike in the past when new product launches had never received adequate advertising support, a substantial promotional budget was allocated to make new launches a success. While pushing its popular brands, Hercules and BSA, the company also decided to keep the other brand 'Phillips' dormant for the time being.

Given that TI was dominating the Specials segment and offering differentiated products, a larger outlay on advertisement was expected. However, the company had always spent less on advertisement than its competitors. While in 1997 Hero Cycles spent about Rs 120 mn on a volume of 4,200,000, of which 3,400,000 were Standards, TI spent only Rs 40 mn on a total volume of 2,000,000 cycles. Further, unlike TI, all products from Hero were promoted under the mother brand of 'Hero'. No wonder Hero was rated as the most popular bicycle brand in India.

In 1998, TI increased its advertising outlay to Rs 60 mn. For a change, TI Cycles hired the services of cricket star Ajay Jadeja to promote the 'Top Gear' model. More than Rs 20 mn was spent on advertising the launch of 'Top Gear', of which only about 10 mn was spent on advertisements in the mass media. One company official said, 'Of all models, the launch of Top Gear has been supported most intensively.' The advertising and marketing outlays continued to increase. By 1999–2000, TI was spending close to Rs 170 mn on advertising and an additional Rs 140 mn on marketing, an increase of more than 350 per cent.

Product development: The export experience of TI Cycles had strengthened the product development capability in the company. Since they were supplying custom-made designs to their foreign customers, they had also acquired certain skills in designing new models. In 1998, the product development wing was reorganised and about 15–20 new models began to be introduced each year. As tool manufacturing and product development functions had been merged and the product development exercise was integrated with marketing, production and sourcing, the lead time for new product development was reduced substantially. The timing of new launches was now based on market seasonality and consumer buying behaviour. For example, new launches for kids were done during April–June, close to their holiday time.

In 1998, TI launched India's first geared bicycle under the brand name 'Hercules Top Gear'. It was also musing about developing some 'futuristic' models, like electric bikes. TI Cycles lined up a series of state-of-the-art geared bicycles to meet the growing demand in the segment, and stepped up production in the last two years. The company launched 10–12 new models in the last two years, progressively increasing the number of gears for more speed to meet the growing demand in the gear sector. It also launched a number of new models aimed at children in the 8–15 age group and at girls.

It launched special edition bikes including those for kids (3–4 years of age) and girls who belonged to the upmarket segments. This created a ripple in these markets. Popular models like 'Top Gear' (promoted by cricketer Ajay Jadeja through TV ad shots), 'Lady Bird' (for use by young girls and women) and 'Hercules MTB' (the mountain terrain bike) also featured in these special editions.

Around the same time it also launched a low priced AXN. This model was a modified version of the SLR with additional features like welded instead of brazed joints, thicker tyres, colourful appearance and special carrier targeting the MTB segment. Top Gear and AXN had been the most successful launches in the company's history. 'AXN is our most successful launch in terms of volume and Top Gear is our best launch in terms of value', said a visibly proud R.K. Bhat, general manager (product development and technology). By 1999, the company had more than fifty models targeting different groups of customers.

Competitive Performance of New Products during 1999–2000

(Numbers in '000s)

Segment	*TI*		*Hero*		*Atlas*	
	Volume	*% of Company's Segment Total*	*Volume*	*% of Company's Segment Total*	*Volume*	*% of Company's Segment Total*
SLR	16	3	780	10	12	2
MTBs	204	23	5	1	4	5
Juniors	33	4	4	1	33	4
Kids	99	17	90	15	10	2
Total	352	–	879	–	62	–
Contribution to total volume (%)		15		18		3

'Our product development and design capabilities, already superior to other Indian firms, have seen a qualitative improvement. Today we are capable of designing and manufacturing cycles with different materials, with features not yet popular in the Indian market and in the days to come should be able to differentiate our products from the poor imitators in the Indian market. We also expect more manufacturers in Europe and North America to abandon manufacturing and source from countries like India and China', said Ram Kumar.

TI came a close second to Hero in terms of new product introduction. Contribution of new launches to overall sales volume of the company had gone up steadily from 3 per cent to 15 per cent in the last three years.

Cycle Distribution Network

Given the wide spread of the market, distribution was a critical activity. Establishing relationships with dealers was crucial to achieving certain minimum volumes. The channel structure of bicycles in India is very skewed. While consumption is 65 per cent rural and only 35 per cent urban, 'distribution stops reaching beyond small towns with less than 20,000 population', observed Paul. There were about 3,500 dealers, mostly small and widely spread across the country, for all the manufacturers put together. TI now had 2,200 dealers, Hero had about 3,000 dealers and Atlas had about 3,500 dealers. They had an accent on distribution rather than marketing and sales and had little customer service orientation. However, these dealers directly contributed to only 16 per cent of industry volume. There were around 12,000 sub-dealers who catered to the rest of the market. They were fairly unorganised and not amenable to commercial discipline in terms of regularity of orders and collections, and perhaps too small in size to be handled by the manufacturers directly. These sub-dealers selling bicycles in the small towns and rural market were serviced by dealers.

Given the low density of customers in the rural market these sub-dealers were a necessary evil and likely to play a critical role in the future. In the small towns and rural market they wielded strong influence on the choice of brands. Before 1998 most of these sub-dealers, particularly those based in the North and East, had been selling very few TI bicycles. The company in the last two years targeted about 1,000 such sub-dealers from each region and offered attractive packages to them for promoting TI brands. Still a large number of outlets did not display TI's bicycles. 'To grow rapidly we have to reach out to the customers in the rural areas with 5,000 to 10,000 population. However, we are struggling to find an appropriate distribution structure that will give us this reach', lamented Paul.

Consumer satisfaction surveys had clearly pointed out that dissatisfaction had been prevailing among bicycle customers, particularly in the area of service. Bicycle manufacturers had historically neglected customer service, which forced customers to depend on roadside mechanics for servicing and repairs. Since 1998, TI started promoting 'Cyclinics' (cycle clinics) to repair and maintain bikes through a system of franchising. As mechanics found it difficult to repair geared bikes, it launched a region-wise programme to train cycle mechanics. This effort had preceded the launch of geared bicycles in the region to dispel customer concern regarding maintenance of geared bikes. By 2000 the company had over 500 authorised cycle service stations all over India. It also put up five warehouses spread across the country.

All these initiatives led to improved market share. In North India, TI increased its market share from an insignificant 4 per cent in 1996 to 10 per cent in 2000. In the West, its share rose by 5 per cent. All this made TI regain second position in the Indian market for cycles.

Reorganising exports: Decline in exports and an even sharper decline in export prices had persuaded management to shift the export production to the main plant at Avadi and close down the cycle EOU. After reaching its lowest ebb in 1998, exports were gradually picking up in the last two years. Learning from its earlier experience, the company was trading cautiously and rebuilding exports brick-by-brick. The company was concentrating on a limited number of customers. Major customers were Prophete of Germany, Universal, Tradewinds and Halfords of UK, and Citison of Sri Lanka. Faced with a non-tariff barrier on export of cycles to France, TI Cycles resumed exporting painted frames and forks while negotiating with authorities concerned on the issue of exporting bicycles. It bagged major orders from Decathlon of France, a leading distributor of cycles for painted frames and forks. As a business proposition, this system suited the company, since these components were made by TI itself and were not outsourced.

'We have not abandoned our export efforts and are waiting for improvement in the market conditions. Recently, Huffy, one of the largest bicycle manufacturers in the USA, shut down its plants and is sourcing from China as well as from us. We hope to overcome the entry barriers through better product development and sourcing components from China. In the long run our global competitiveness has to improve and that will provide valuable spin-offs in the domestic market', said an optimistic Paul. TI Cycles expected to increase exports through expanding product range with the existing customers and entering into new markets.

Supply Chain Management

In the early days, bicycle companies used to make most of the components in-house. The norms of the industry had changed subsequently, as parts manufacturers, capable of producing components at lower costs, were developed. The rise of North Indian cycle manufacturers like Hero led to the clustering of component manufacturers around Ludhiana, helping them outsource components locally. To enhance their productivity as well as profitability, TI cycles embarked on a re-engineering exercise. It redesigned the manufacturing system and started strategic sourcing to reduce costs. There was substantial reduction in manufacturing lead time (from six to three days) and in inventory, work-in-process, etc. The productivity per worker rose from a low of 1.85 cycles per man day in 1993–94 to 2.4 cycles per man day in 1998 and 2.85 cycles per man day in 2000.

To drive down the cost and be competitive to Hero, the entire supply chain of TI was revamped. Better productivity, lower component costs and saving of transportation costs collectively were expected to give TI a benefit of Rs 150 per cycle. The company also started sourcing a greater proportion of components from outside suppliers and made only the frame, mudguard, fork, and about 40 per cent of the rims in-house. Emphasis was given on developing closer relationships with vendors, most of whom were small-scale manufacturers of components. The company encouraged them to move up the value chain by supplying sub-assemblies and provided technical help to improve their quality. It started sourcing rims, chains, chain wheels, saddles, etc., from forty selected vendors. The company was also trying to improve the local vendor base and helping Ludhiana-based vendors set up manufacturing facilities in Chennai. However, they faced problems and some of them closed down the facilities as local labour laws did not provide the flexibility enjoyed by them in Ludhiana.

TI redesigned the complete supply chain and benchmarked itself on certain parameters like inventory turnover, manpower cost, cycle turnover per employee, etc. Inbound and outbound freight and labour costs were found to be quite high and these made the reduction of the Rs 150 gap with Hero impossible without a complete supply chain revamping. The other option of only redesigning the manufacturing process again could at best reduce the gap by Rs 60-70, not sufficient to achieve cost parity with Hero in Standards. In the last two years a rationalisation of manpower to bring down the size of the workforce from 2,000 to 1,400 and a new wage agreement pushed up the labour productivity by 20 per cent. The production system was also made increasingly leaner with inventory turnover improving rapidly. Total Quality Management initiatives were also taken up in the last two years at the plant at Chennai and capacity was also enhanced to 12,000 cycles per day. The western zone was chosen for a pilot project, where an assembly and painting unit is being established. Eventually, it will move assembly and painting facilities into every region.

A team of people from TI was working in tandem with a team of IT consultants under the banner of 'Project Vijay' to make a blueprint for this model and establish the pilot plant at a cost of Rs 90 mn at Nasik to cater to the western region. Almost all parts will be outsourced from the local auto parts suppliers of Mahindra and Mahindra. Nasik was the nodal point for the western zone and also had a strong base of highly skilled and technologically developed vendors affiliated to Mahindra who had a more cyclical business. With TI being their customer, these vendors would be able to produce a steady and almost ten times larger volume than Mahindra.

TI was also actively looking for global sourcing and placed evaluative orders for a couple of containers on a Chinese bicycle maker. 'Post WTO, if the import duty is brought down from the current level of 44 per cent to 20–30 per cent, global sourcing of components and even semi-knocked down bicycles may work out to be much cheaper', observed N. Shivkumar, general manager (materials). Extensive work was done to rationalise vendors, streamline vendor development system, and reduce inventory. Inventory levels were brought down to five days in 2000 from a level of fourteen days in 1997. However, it was much higher than the market leader Hero, which had an inventory of one day only.

Future Challenges for TI Cycles

With TI becoming aggressive in the North and East, the long-time bastion of Hero, a price war was likely, particularly in Standards. Moreover, like all Indian bicycle manufacturers, TI face the imminent threat of competition from Chinese imports even in the domestic market as soon as the government opens up the Indian market for bicycles under its commitment to WTO. Currently the tariff barrier was kept quite high at 45.6 per cent. Once the duty structure has been rationalised, Chinese bicycles will have a price advantage of 5 to 10 per cent. However, Om Prakash Munjal, CEO of Hero Cycles, played down the threat. 'We are fairly competitive compared to Chinese cycles . . . our biggest advantage is the availability of our spare parts all over the country at very reasonable prices. It will be impossible for any foreign player to match that advantage', he said.

TI management was less confident. 'We expect severe competition in kids' and geared bicycles as Chinese manufacturers enjoy about a 15-35 per cent cost advantage. However, we have superior quality and brand image. Also, distribution won't be easy for the Chinese. We are controlling the brand, market, and distribution—manufacturing is incidental to all these. The scope for added value in manufacturing will be much less compared to other areas. If we see Chinese bicycles are cheaper, we shall source from them and market under our brands', said a confident Paul.

TI planned to press all the levers of competitive advantage by cutting down cost, focussing on quality, innovative products and services, and expanding volume. Some of the possible moves being contemplated by the company were creating higher brand equity, market expansion through conversion of non-users, creating new categories of users, mass customisation of product offerings, being customer-centric and a service leader, breaking the price barrier at both ends, equalling home quality at par with exports, and coming up with new and unconventional distribution channels.

Engineering Division: Strips and Tubes

The tubes division of TI, known as Tubes Products of India (TPI), was engaged in the business of cold rolled steel strips and tubes. TPI had been set up in 1955 in collaboration with Tube Products (Oldbury) Ltd, UK, to produce Electric Resistant Welded (ERW) and Cold Drawn Welded (CDW) steel tubes. Though TPI had initially started its operation mainly to cater to the tubes needs of TI Cycles, subsequently through expansion of range of products and manufacturing facilities it started catering to a wide variety of industries. Its share in corporate revenue had gone up substantially from 28 per cent in 1998 to 34 per cent in 2000. The tubes division had integrated backward in 1957 and set up a narrow width cold rolling mill to manufacture cold rolled close annealed steel strips. The strips division, other than meeting the in-house demand of TI, catered to customers in automotive, auto ancillary, white goods, general engineering sectors, etc. TPI had currently three SBUs, namely, Strips, Tubes Home and Tubes Exports. During 1999–2000, it had a turnover of Rs 5.95 bn including supplies for in-house consumption of TI.

Tubes Division

TPI had over the years grown into a powerful manufacturer of quality tubes for the special and precision industries. It was also exporting tubes to Australia, Europe, USA and the Asia Pacific region. It commanded a formidable 85 per cent share in the CDW tubes market and around 45 per cent share in ERW tubes market in India. It was a market leader in automotive tubes (for propeller shaft, shock absorbers, etc.). TPI had three manufacturing facilities. The parent plant at Avadi, about 30 km from Chennai, produced a wide range of CDW and ERW tubes and steel strips. TPI established a new plant at Shirwal in Satara district in 1995–96 to cater to the growing market for special and precision tubes in western India, where several automobile manufacturers were setting up new plants. In 1999 it expanded its production base to the North by taking over the SSTL plant in Mohali in Punjab. Thus, currently the company had tube manufacturing facilities in the North, South, and West, with warehouses in Chennai, Hosur and Pune and branches in all major cities in India. It had also set up a 100 per cent Export Oriented Unit (EOU) in 1996 at Avadi at a cost of Rs 130 mn.

TPI had the capabilities to produce a wide range of ERW (in bright and semi-bright conditions) and CDW tubes. ERW tubes could be supplied in round, rectangular, square and elliptical shapes with diameters ranging from 15.88 to 114.30 mm, thickness ranging from 0.46 to 5.70 mm and length up to a maximum of 7 metres. CDW tubes were drawn from the ERW tubes and provided closer dimensional tolerances, better internal surface finish, greater strength, etc., with diameters ranging from 4.76 to 110.00 mm, thickness ranging from 0.81 to 6.00 mm and length up to a maximum of 14 metres. Tube production involved a series of operations such as slitting of steel strips to size, straightening of the cut strips, bending of the cut pieces into tubular form, welding of the bent joints, and cutting the tube to required length. The critical aspects of tube making were weld integrity, surface quality, finish, and tolerance and most rejections were due to weld failures. Wire drawing in draw benches and straightening were also critical operations to determine the quality of precision tubes.

TPI now had a total capacity of about 92,000 tons, of which 45,000 tons was in two plants near Madras, about 18,000 tons was at Pune and the rest, about 30,000 tons, at Mohali. TPI operated at about 95 per cent of its capacity and was the market leader in the auto and boiler tubes segment. Its customers included TELCO, Mujula Showa and global manufacturers like Delfi. Steel Authority of India Limited (SAIL) and Jindal Steel were main suppliers of hot and cold rolled coils. The latter was emerging as the chief source in recent years. During 1999–2000, the tubes division had a turnover of Rs 3 bn including supplies for the in-house consumption of TI. The division had a corporate mandate to reach to Rs 5.5 bn with a positive EVA by 2004.

Steel Tubes Industry

The steel tubes industry was broadly classified into two product segments—welded and seamless. There were several product categories within the welded tubes segments, such as Soaked Annealed and Welded (SAW) and Galvanised Annealed and Welded (GAW) pipes, standard tubes such as Black and Galvanised Iron (GI) pipes, and precision tubes. Most of the large tube manufacturers had a presence in multiple product segments. But TPI at present catered only to the precision steel tubes market. This product had few substitutes because of its greater strength, tolerance and finish and found wide applications in manufacturing of products such as cycles, furniture, boilers, heat exchangers, and automobiles and auto components. Within precision tubes, there were variations such as ERW, CEW and CDW. The precision tube manufacturers mainly belonged to the organised sector. Small manufacturers produced mainly cut tubes for the furniture market.

The main customers for precision tubes were manufacturers of automobiles (0.55 lakh tons), boiler and air heaters (0.20 lakh tons), bicycles (0.35 lakh tons), and furniture, oil and companies in general engineering industries (0.55 lakh tons). Except Godrej and Mark Auto, no other customer was integrated backward into tube mills. Customers preferred to transact directly with tube makers. The bulk of auto customers were concentrated in western and North India where Steel Tubes of India (STI), Tata Iron and Steel Company (TISCO) and Steel Strips and Tubes Ltd (SSTL) had locational advantages.

The installed capacity in India was about 4 lakh tons while the domestic demand was about 2.17 lakh tons in 1999–2000, leading to large underutilised capacity and severe price competition. Industry profitability was under pressure due to continuous rise in input costs such as steel, power, consumables, railway freight and wages, and sluggish demand. Due to overcapacity, competitors sometimes resorted to predatory pricing behaviour pushing down the profitability further. TPI's profitability (PBIT/Sales) steadily came down from 8.9 per cent in 1995–96 to 6.3 per cent in 1997–98 and STI's from 7.8 per cent to 5.9 per cent. According to industry analysts, no significant change in domestic demand in the industry was expected in the near future.

The industry had been de-licensed after economic liberalisation and any domestic or foreign player could enter the industry without any restriction. It was estimated that Rs 300 mn investment was required to build a new 15,000 tons precision tubes plant. The learning curve effect was significant in the industry as it would normally take two years to perfect ERW tube making and at least three years for CDW tube making. Imports had been insignificant at 10,000 to15,000 tons and mainly confined to project imports or to segments where domestic capacity was absent. International prices of tubes were much higher (estimated to be 10-30 per cent even if tariff rate was brought down to 20 per cent from the current level of 41 per cent) than domestic prices.

Market for Precision Steel Tubes in India

(Units in lakh tons)

Year	*Demand*	*Capacity*	*Production*	*Exports*	*Capacity Utilisation (%)*
1995–96	1.54	3.65	1.58	0.04	43
1996–97	1.84	3.80	1.82	0.06	48
1997–98	1.97	3.80	1.98	0.15	52
1998–99	2.00	3.93	2.07	0.20	53
1999–2000	2.17	4.00	2.32	0.35	58
2000–01*	2.32	4.00	2.45	0.40	61
2001–02*	2.50	4.00	2.55	0.45	64
2002–03*	2.70	4.00	2.80	0.50	70

* Projections.

The tubes industry became technologically more and more sophisticated as new automobile manufacturers had been demanding better quality products. The three large manufacturers enjoyed a wide product range and were able to meet customer's expectations. On the whole, Indian manufacturers were globally competitive and exported about 15,000 tons in 1997–98. Exports were rising and expected to touch the 40,000 ton mark in 2001. The global market for steel tubes was roughly valued at $17 billion and the major markets were USA, Germany, France, the UK, the Netherlands, China and Malaysia.

TPI's Early Evolution to Industry Leadership

The company had been the market leader in the auto and boiler tubes segment for quite some time. The tubes division attributed its market leadership to its technological competence and its ability to design and deliver products to meet the stringent standards demanded by new manufacturers entering the Indian automobile and boiler industries. Initially, it imported its tube mills from foreign suppliers. But subsequently, it had been able to reverse engineer and design the next generation mills in-house. Thus, in 1986, TPI imported a state-of-the-art tube mill from Italy. By 1992–93, when it embarked on the next expansion project (the Shirwal plant and the EOU), it could design the tube mills in-house and fabricate them locally at a much lower investment. It also introduced small design changes in the imported mills to increase their flexibility (the size ranges that could be handled) to suit Indian market conditions. In the early 1990s, it also designed in-house a draw-bench to manufacture the large dimension fork tubes used in motorcycles. Being a critical component, it had to be 100 per cent defect free and TPI could meet the stringent quality demands of motorcycle manufacturers and became the dominant producer in this product category.

In 1994, TPI bought an old plant from Mitsuba in Japan and moved it lock, stock and barrel to Madras. The plant was bought for a very low price of $1 million that instantly made TPI a low cost producer. 'It was an opportunity we were able to seize due to our superior capabilities that allowed us to upgrade, install and commission the plant', said Gopala Rathnam, general manager, strategic planning. TPI dismantled and imported the critical machinery (draw-benches and straightening machines) and installed it in the two plants at Shirwal and Ambattur. Small design changes were made, mainly in the electrical equipment, to adapt it to Indian voltage standards. Installation of this plant made TPI an internationally competitive producer of a wide range of tubes.

The Japanese experience also had useful spillovers for the company. Going through the process sheets at the Japanese plant-site, the engineers of TPI learnt of a new cold drawing process, called oil drawing. Oil drawing was started in the EOU, but some initial problems remained, mainly on account of the oil used. The oil was not available in India and foreign suppliers were unwilling to provide the oil unless the company made a long-term purchase commitment. TPI started using a local substitute, but it gave some quality problems in the form of oil stains on the surface. For the exacting foreign customer, that was unacceptable, as it would be a probable rust-prone area. TPI managers subsequently abandoned the idea of getting a local substitute. It finally settled for a supplier from Taiwan and a technological collaboration was being worked out for oil drawing and other processes. 'This is expected to improve not only CDW tube making but would have spillover effects in other areas of operation', observed Krishna Kumar, general manager (tubes).

Responses to Recession and Intensifying Competition

By 1996 all the new plants of TPI had been commissioned and substantial additions had taken place to its tubes capacity. This was when market conditions began to deteriorate. Both the tube products and steel strips markets were plagued by overcapacity. The tube division's profitability had been satisfactory till 1995–96. Despite overcapacity, industry margins had improved from 10 per cent in 1993–94 to 14.1 per cent by 1996. However, the recession in the auto industry and capital goods sectors from late 1996 eroded margins and profitability. The new mills took unusually long to stabilise and break into the market. It also led to a situation when the new plants at TPI were saddled with large idle capacities. The profit before tax (PBT) declined from a high of Rs 100 mn in 1995–96 to a meagre Rs 2.87 mn by 1997–98. Several tube manufacturers like TISCO, Steel Tubes and Kalyani Tubes had been reporting large losses. TISCO subsequently shut down its plant and entered into a strategic alliance with Kalyani Tubes at Pune to source its requirement.

As the industry was plagued by overcapacity and prolonged recession in the domestic auto sector, only a further shake-out in the industry could provide some succour. In 1998, TPI had embarked on a project called ELCOM, i.e., eliminate competition, to gain higher market share. Some merchant bankers had approached TI management to buy the STI plant at Dewas. However, as TPI was not utilising its own capacity fully, it was not very enthusiastic to add more assets unless the price was really attractive. Taking over just to shut the plant down seemed an expensive option. STI was desperate as it needed a steady positive cash flow from the tubes business to finance new ventures in textile and power. Ultimately, after protracted negotiations, an agreement was signed between TI and STI in 1999 by which the latter became a conversion agent to supply tubes to be sold under TPI's brand name. Subsequently, the company also acquired the 30,000 ton capacity tube manufacturing facilities at Mohali from Steel Strips & Tubes Ltd at a sum of Rs 400 mn. This deal was expected to help TPI gain in northern India where SSTL had been a dominant player, with Bhushan and Atma Steels having marginal presence. 'This acquisition and our alliance with STI has helped the company raise its market share in both the ERW and CDW tubes segments substantially. The move has not only widened the geographical spread of TPI's market, but also enabled us to have a stronger presence in the North', observed Krishna Kumar.

The company had been looking for other measures, such as improving productivity and concentrating on higher value added segments. Further, improving the quality of products, offering more stringent specifications to customers and tapping the export market were being planned. TPI had divided the products into three categories—base, key and leverage—and chalked out different strategies for each of them. In the base products the company was competing on cost advantage gained through cost reduction and productivity improvement efforts. In the key and leverage products it attempted to provide differentiated value proposition to customers with more value added products and services such as galvanised and colour-coated tubes. 'We are leveraging our distinctive competence in producing tubes with smaller diameter and thickness and operating with smaller batch sizes. We are able to supply small order sizes, much smaller than our competitors, and thus provide greater convenience and flexibility to customers. We are also providing wider choices in terms of diameters and thickness', observed Sehanobis, president of TPI. In CDW, TPI was providing three types of variations: a) standard tubes having different OD and ID, b) standard tubes having different OD and ID with special surface, and c) tubes made to order OD and wall thickness. The third type of tubes was the most difficult to make and commanded the largest margins.

However, there was a flip side to providing greater flexibility and choice to customers. The smaller lot size and orders for difficult sizes increased rejection rate and material wastage. Further, as the company did not have an activity-based costing system in place, these inefficiencies were not factored into the prices charged to specific customers and were passed on to all and sundry. 'In a way, we are going for a socialistic way of pricing whereas we should charge the right price to the right customer', observed one manager. It was also not clear whether this strategy, though improving the top line, had an adverse impact on the bottom line.

The company also stressed higher capacity utilisation, reduction of conversion cost through savings in raw material and energy cost and waste minimisation, and productivity improvement through manpower rationalisation. In the last two years it cut down workers by 186 and reduced the managerial staff by 35 per cent. Manpower productivity improved from 5 ton/month/man to 7.5 ton/month/man; some managers even felt 10 ton/month/man was an achievable target. Senior managers were sent to visit Japanese and Taiwanese plants to learn the latest methods of work organisation in a tube mill. They could then benchmark productivity with international standards and work towards achieving the same. For example, in 1986–87, each tube mill in the old plant was manned by about twenty-three people, which came down to fourteen in the new plant. This were further brought down to seven in 1999. The Japanese and Taiwanese, however, organised the production with only four people. The layout of the new plant was much better and the plant was adhering to higher standards of safety. Workers were given multi-disciplinary responsibilities and were being equipped with multiple skills. Employees at the plant had to interact with the customers regularly to understand their requirements and become more customer oriented. TPI managers were also trying to introduce these standards in their old plant.

Material yield improved from 84 per cent to 90 per cent in CDW, and 87.5 per cent in ERW, but was still far below the international standard of 95 per cent. Process lead time, which provided greater flexibility and responsiveness to cater to customers' requirement, was also brought down to one week. This was much lower than other domestic competitors, but compared unfavourably with the international level of ten hours. The company also focussed more on achieving higher contribution per unit sales rather than volume.

Tubes Division: Performance Highlights, Domestic

	1996–97	*1997–98*	*1998–99*	*1999–2000*
Sales (Rs crore)	232.52	266.65	313.39	488.83
PBT (Rs crore)	2.53	0.287	5.01	16.78
PBT/Sales (%)	1.1	0.1	1.6	3.4
ROCE (%)	11.5	10.1	12.2	16.5
ERW market share (%)	20	22	39	41
CDW market share (%)	48	54	73	90

All these measures brought about a turnaround in the division's performance as the return on net worth and return on capital improved from 4.75 per cent and 7.48 per cent in 1998 to 9.27 per cent and 11.59 per cent in 2000. It consolidated its market position as the dominant force with 85 per cent share in CDW and about 45 per cent share in ERW, leaving other competitors like TISCO, Bangalore-based Jemini, and Gwalior-based AVN Tubes way behind. However, Bhushan was fast emerging as a dangerous competitor with aggressive pricing strategy and improved supply chain management.

Thrust on Exports

Looking for exports, TPI found its costs to be high and productivity and quality poor. Better quality could help the company substantially improve its margins in the domestic market. The search for new international markets and the effort to establish itself as the major long-term supplier was held back by quality problems in the new plants as well as time needed to seed the markets and convince customers of its ability to deliver products. In their effort to penetrate the markets in the USA, Europe and Australia, TPI managers discovered that there were big hurdles for Indian products in those markets. In the early 1990s many Indian companies had gone to these markets, booked orders, dumped suspect quality products, and bagged the benefits of export promotions declared by the Indian government. They never bothered to come back and service the customers if the supply was defective. Even in those cases when buyers took them to international courts for arbitration, Indian manufacturers stayed away and did not make amends for poor quality supply. 'Quality perception is very critical in these markets for our products as they are precision tubes used in automobiles or boilers, and Indian manufacturers had destroyed that by their short-sighted opportunist behaviour', observed Shrikant, general manager (export division).

TPI was still grappling with its problems in stabilising the new plants. The new EOU plant had a 7,500 ton capacity with a new set of workers and an inexperienced management team. It initially failed to deliver international quality products and services to its highly demanding customers, damaging the image of TPI. In 1997, it had started shipping large quantities of tubes to the USA through barge and had a substantial cost advantage in spite of high freight costs (12-13 per cent of the landed cost). Subsequently, TPI's margin suffered when tube prices in the US market went down by 20 per cent because of greater domestic production as well as increased supply from neighbouring countries such as Mexico and Canada. TPI started supplying tubes to auto manufacturers such as Ford and other users directly and tried to boost the margin by eliminating trade commissions. 'However, we have to tread very cautiously on pricing our products, we cannot afford to attract attention as North American tube manufacturers have a strong lobby and they are highly vigilant on imports', observed Shrikant. The division was trying to find cheaper and faster shipping links to the auto industry around Detroit and in Europe.

The company was also targeting the Asia Pacific market. 'We have explored some markets such as Malaysia, Singapore, Thailand and Indonesia and found that barring Singapore, Malaysia is the most lucrative market where we are facing competition mainly from Taiwanese and South Korean manufacturers,' commented Shrikant. Customers in these markets demanded smaller quantity but provided higher contribution per ton as price realisation was higher and transportation cheaper. Here also TPI could use its competitive advantage to operate smaller batch sizes. Other markets such as China, Philippines and

Vietnam had an underdeveloped auto sector and demand for CDW tubes was low in these countries. Australia also remained a green territory for TPI, as it could not locate a very active representative who could promote its products aggressively against Japanese products marketed by companies like Marubeni. Because freight charges were quite high (25-30 per cent of sales price) for ERW tubes, it was promoting CDW tubes in all other markets except Sri Lanka where absence of any domestic ERW producer also yielded better margins.

The material yield at the EOU was 85-86 per cent lower than at the other tube plants of TPI. The yield was lower primarily because the product mixes of these plants were different. The EOU supplied tubes with exact length, outside diameter and wall thicknesses made to order. Utmost care was taken to ensure quality of welding and quality control checks were made for every welded joint. German experts were also brought to improve the 'fin' cutting operation, a prerequisite to CDW tube making. However, lack of bright annealing facility continued to put the company at a disadvantage, particularly in the developed market, as the current annealing facility left dark patches on the tubes and needed to be further cleaned by customers.

Though, as per the provision of the EOU, the company could sell 50 per cent of its volume in the domestic market, it was targeting exports for higher margins (around 15 per cent more). In the domestic market it was targeting strategic customers such as Anand-Gabriel and Hyundai who had principals or collaborators abroad. TPI wanted to develop long-term partnerships with these customers to penetrate their parents in the international market. Once it demonstrated its capability by adhering to cost, quality, delivery and other service parameters to the domestic outfits, the company fancied its chances of supplying the global operations of these customers.

The EOU simultaneously emphasised product development, particularly in three areas of application—cylinder bore tubes with very fine surface, hydraulic cylinders and tubular components. Though the domestic market for fine surfaced cylinder bore tubes was underdeveloped, there was high demand in the West. The company still needed substantial investment to launch these products.

Nonetheless, these measures had a positive impact on the performance of the EOU. It had been showing a steady improvement in the last three years. It made a loss of Rs 35 mn in 1998–99 and Rs 10 mn in 1999–2000, and expected to make modest profit in the current year.

Tubes Division: Financial Highlights, EOU

	1996–97	1997–98	1998–99	1999–2000
Sales (Rs crore)	5.83	18.69	20.10	27.36
PBT (Rs crore)	-2.69	-2.87	-3.23	-1.06
PBT/Sales (%)	-46.1	-15.4	-16.1	-3.9

Strips Division

'Things have really changed for the strips businesses in the last five to six years', observed Shivaprasad, general manager (technical services). Until 1995, TPI had a comfortable position in strips as most of the production had been used for captive consumption of the tubes division and other group companies. Due to strength and surface finish, cold rolled steel strip had advantage over hot rolled steel, aluminium or plastic. However, for thicker gauge strip and applications for which surface finish and other physical properties were not critical, HR might be preferred over CR. Therefore, the future of the business had a direct link with the evolution of auto, auto ancillaries, stamping, fine blanking, general engineering, white goods and bearing industries. Other than the auto sector, the industry provided very unattractive margins. The recession in the auto industry after 1997 had lowered growth expectations. The weakening of the rupee and the special import duty of 4 per cent imposed in the 1998 budget had provided some breather from imports, but devaluation in other Asian countries rapidly eroded the advantage.

Market for CR Steel Strips in India

(Units in lakh tons)

Year	Demand	Capacity	Production	Gap	Imports	Exports
1993–94	18.37	35.89	17.06	17.52	1.31	Negligible
1994–95	23.00	35.89	20.65	12.89	2.35	Negligible
1995–96	27.60	37.50	25.80	9.90	1.80	0.75
1996–97	30.38	36.00	28.38	5.62	2.00	1.20
1997–98	31.87	37.50	29.87	5.63	2.00	1.25
1998–99	38.65	37.50	36.15	(1.15)	2.50	1.50
1999–2000	53.00	41.00	41.00	12.00	4.00	2.00

Most manufacturers of steel strips were in the organised sector. The competitive situation had worsened after 1995 as seven to eight new players like Bhushan

Steel and Nippon Dendro entered the market with far superior technology, product mix and quality. As a result, TPI was pushed into being a regional player with about 3 per cent market share of the overall strips market in India and 8-10 per cent market share of the narrow and medium width segment.

Responding to Intensifying Competition in Strips

The strips division, although it had been profitable throughout, had suffered a nearly 20 per cent fall in turnover to Rs 1.17 bn in 1996–97. TPI managers realised that the unit had been caught in the narrow width segment where about fifty-one manufacturers were concentrated and margins were extremely poor. In contrast, there were only ten manufacturers in the wide width section with Bhushan Steel and TISCO as market leaders. None of the manufacturers were south of Andhra Pradesh and the company envisaged gains from its locational advantage in meeting its own and the auto industries' need for wide width strips in South India. TPI added a new medium width mill (>650 mm) in 1997 at a capital investment of Rs 500 mn. With this investment the unit now produced both narrow and medium width (up to 1050 mm) steel strips and had a 100,000 ton capacity. However, even the new plant was not as modernised as those of competitors like Bhushan and TISCO which had facilities like six angle draw-bench, electrostatic spraying, top-of-the-line controls and processors, and product quality was not as good.

The company was now concentrating on cost reduction. Raw material contributed 70 per cent of the unit cost. Thus, elimination of raw material wastage and edge damages had a marked influence on margins. Yield was improved to 91 per cent as compared to 85 per cent in 1997. Transportation cost was also a critical factor as the plant was located 400-500 miles away from most customers and also away from raw material suppliers such as SAIL.

The company began to offer value added products to customers. 'Ability to supply variety and small lots is our main source of competitive advantage. Customers come to us for narrow width as competitors cannot supply the same', observed A.V. Rao, general manager, strips. Some of the new products developed in TPI were high quality strips for auto bodies, electro galvanised strips for petrol tanks, and colour-coated strips for applications in the white goods industry.

Providing variety in width, thickness and chemical properties put high pressure on the shop floor, which had to be extremely flexible to meet the demand while simultaneously minimising rejects and material wastage. TPI also had locational advantage being the dominant player in the South, with the other regional competitor, Penner Steel, not doing well and on the verge of closure. It could respond to the demand of customers like Lucas TVS, Hyundai and Ford within one-and-a-half to two days. The other major national competitor, Bhushan, had plants only in the North. It was handicapped by the absence of local infrastructure to be as responsive to customers in the South. A substantial investment was required in developing a warehouse, cutting facilities, and sales and service staff which would reduce its ability to aggressively cut price and erode TPI's position.

During the last three years, the division had registered high growth and in 1999–2000 reached a turnover of Rs 1.95 bn and PBT of Rs 65.6 mn, up from Rs 6.73 mn in 1997–98. Profitability (PBT/Sales), however, remained very low, showing a marginal improvement to 3.4 per cent over the lowest ever figure of 0.5 per cent in 1997–98. With all the advantages, TPI realised only a 3-5 per cent higher price from its nearest competitors, even though it was a niche player in the South. Rao sounded unsure as he said, 'Perhaps customers are smart, they may be dumping orders on us, which are difficult and not high value added for us. Perhaps competitors are smarter not to accept these orders.'

Efforts were on to develop new markets, new applications, and producing more varieties along with concerted attempt at cost reduction. Most of its focus on value added products was in areas such as customised size in length, width and thickness and small order quantity. However, TPI seemed to lack the capability to produce high value added items such as copper coated strip, titanium rolled sheets and low thickness (below 4.9 mm) cold rolled sheets. Neither could it provide the super quality strip as produced by Bhushan that looked like zinc. The company did not have the facility to cater to customers like Suzuki, Daewoo and Hyundai who needed strip of width beyond 1,400 mm. Currently, most automakers were meeting their requirements through imports.

The future did not seem very rosy for this division, given the worsening market condition. TISCO has just commissioned its new cold rolling mill (CRM) in 2000 and would add to the supply. Rising freight costs and emergence of regional plants was intensifying regional competition. With China joining the WTO and removal of quota restrictions from early 2001, imports currently running at 2.5 lakh tons could easily double. The company expected to improve profitability in spite of recurring steel price increase through continuous focus on enhancing market share in the South, reducing in-house rejection, increase in equipment effectiveness through implementation of Total Productivity Management (TPM) and improving customer service.

Strips Division: Performance Highlights

	1996–97	*1997–98*	*1998–99*	*1999–2000*
Sales (Rs crore)	117.07	145.01	163.85	194.95
PBT (Rs crore)	4.66	0.673	3.03	6.56
PBT/Sales (%)	4.0	0.5	1.8	3.4
ROCE (%)	17.6	10.7	13.0	16.6
Market share (%)	14	4	6	7

Future Challenges for TI

In the last few years TI had emphasised value added products and cost reductions in all its businesses. The company was looking to exit from certain low volume and low profitable products and businesses. In the Roll Form Division, the company carried out a product profit portfolio analysis based on which it exited from certain products. It extended its product portfolio from cycles, chains, metal strips and tubes to making door panels for car manufacturers such as Maruti and Hyundai and decided to make other kinds of auto components as well.

To implement its growth strategies, it had gradually been moving from acquisitions to value added partnerships by using some of its competitors as conversion agents. Recent tie-ups with STI in tubes and Avon and Hamilton in cycles not only helped it reduce or eliminate competition but also gave it manufacturing presence in geographically dispersed locations. While on the one hand it gained greater penetration in markets where it had been a marginal player, on the other it improved its cost position by savings in raw material and transportation costs. In cycles, the company shifted its focus from manufacturing to brand development and laid greater emphasis on design, product development, supply chain management and advertisement. In all the divisions it initiated total quality movements. It was also carrying out competence mapping of managers for identification of a talent pool and upgrading managerial competencies through training interventions. New control systems and compensation and incentive schemes were worked out using techniques like balanced score cards.

As the newly appointed managing director, Raghu contemplated a new leadership position for TI in the Murugappa group. He wanted to launch the company on a rapid growth path, to start identifying fresh investment opportunities in new areas by capitalising on its engineering and manufacturing strengths. 'The biggest challenge to rapid growth is perhaps the mindset of the people . . . the culture changes have not fully penetrated all the businesses yet, people have to change their way of thinking', observed Raghu. There were also other areas of concern. The business units and divisions seemed to be insulated from each other. Learning and experiences were not transferred from one unit to the other. Even in the same business, interaction between domestic and export operations was limited to improvement in operational effectiveness, not in exchanging ideas or joint work on product and business development.

'The turnaround in the last two years came mainly through correcting weaknesses, improving efficiencies, and volume increases in the main businesses', observed Raghu. But was that enough to be a Rs 20 bn company by 2005 AD with profitability to be pushed up simultaneously from the current level of 5 per cent to 8-10 per cent? What additional measures should the company take to consolidate its position and gain sustainable competitive advantage in its existing businesses? Would the current businesses provide enough opportunities to double the corporate profitability while growing at the targeted pace? Should TI look for investment opportunities in new business areas? Should it explore hitherto uncharted territories in defence equipment and component manufacturing, exploiting its existing competencies in manufacturing of tubes, strips, chains and auto components? On what basis would it judge new business opportunities?

APPENDIX 1

Balance Sheet

(Rs crore)*

	Mar-97	Mar-98	Mar-99	Mar-00
Liabilities				
Net worth	333.16	343.58	343.21	364.95
Share capital	24.62	24.62	24.62	24.62
Reserves and surplus	308.54	318.96	318.59	340.33
Total borrowings	150.98	145.08	137.73	180.74
Bank: Short term	80.15	31.68	22.86	27.36
Bank: Long term	37.26	36.19	13.75	0
Financial institutions	0	0	4.17	3.39
Govt sales tax deferrals	0	0	1.5	3.68
Debentures bonds	26.05	35.49	32.92	69.48
Fixed deposits	2.93	4.4	2.69	2.94
Commercial paper	0	25	40	65
Other borrowings	4.59	12.32	19.84	8.89
Current liabilities and provisions	118.54	123.87	130	203
Current liabilities	111.77	117.55	114.11	175.87
Sundry creditors	104.61	111.53	73.78	119.76
Interest accrued due	7.09	5.94	3.8	4.13
Other current liabilities	0.07	0.08	36.53	51.98
Provisions	6.77	6.32	15.89	27.13
Tax provision	0	0	10.89	19.39
Dividend provision	6.77	4.92	3.69	6.16
Other provision	0	1.4	1.31	1.58
Total liabilities	602.68	612.53	610.94	748.69

* 1 crore = 10 million.

Appendix 1 contd . . .

	Mar-97	Mar-98	Mar-99	Mar-00
Assets				
Gross fixed assets	319.46	345.93	373.31	398.36
Land and building	50.9	62.21	73.32	77.89
Plant and machinery	202.26	241.02	287.55	304.64
Other fixed assets	5.96	7.32	7.43	9.15
Capital work-in-progress	60.34	35.38	5.01	6.68
Less: Cumulative depreciation	85.88	102.65	124.06	139.02
Net fixed assets	233.58	243.28	249.25	259.34
Investments	91.11	84.06	53.58	67.11
In group/associate companies	78.59	79.87	46.76	52.62
In mutual funds	1.87	0.37	0	8.05
Other investments	10.65	3.82	6.82	6.44
Inventories	100.05	105.51	86.2	121.55
Raw material and stores	79.58	75.19	51.65	71.55
Finished and semi-finished goods	20.47	30.32	34.48	50
Other stock	0	0	0.07	0
Receivables	157.88	158.12	188.89	265.82
Sundry debtors	98.36	125.7	134.46	205.12
Advances/loans to corporates	6.29	11.49	3.95	0.06
Deposits with govt/agencies	3.3	1.04	2.87	3.56
Advance payment of tax	0.88	0.53	12.65	26.43
Other receivables	49.05	19.36	34.96	30.65
Cash and bank balance	20.06	20.2	23.99	29.02
Intangible/misc. expenses	0	1.36	9.03	5.85
Total assets	602.68	612.53	610.94	748.69

APPENDIX 2

Sources and Uses of Funds

	Mar–96	Mar–97	Mar–98	Mar–99	Mar–00
Sources of funds					
Internal sources	38.68	25.24	26.01	13.62	40.05
Retained profits	27.87	14.82	9.24	-7.79	25.09
Depreciation	10.81	10.42	16.77	21.41	14.96
External sources	53.11	15.71	-0.57	-1.22	116.01
Capital markets	28.37	-0.74	10.91	-4.28	36.81
Fresh capital (excl. bonus issue)	1.79	0	0	0	0
Share premium	30.21	0	0	0	0
Debentures/bonds	-1.4	-1.4	9.44	-2.57	36.56
Fixed deposits	-2.23	0.66	1.47	-1.71	0.25
Borrowings	-1.41	37.22	-16.81	-3.07	6.2
Bank borrowings	3.47	36.8	-49.54	-31.26	-9.25
Short-term bank borrowings	26.05	33.23	-48.47	-8.82	4.5
Financial institutions	1.85	-4.17	0	4.17	-0.78
Loans from corporate bodies	0	0	0	0	0
Group/associate cos.	0	0	0	0	0
Other borrowings	-6.73	4.59	32.73	24.02	16.23
Current liabilities and provisions	26.15	-20.77	5.33	6.13	73
Sundry creditors	26.63	-22.75	6.92	-37.75	45.98
Uses of funds					
Gross fixed assets	75.44	58.04	26.65	27.63	25.22
Work-in-progress	39.44	8.07	-24.96	-30.37	1.67
Investments	39.21	-31.95	-7.05	-30.48	13.53
In group/associate companies	41.82	-2.99	1.28	-33.11	5.86
Current assets	-22.86	14.86	5.84	15.25	117.31
Inventories	10.88	-8.54	5.46	-19.31	35.35
Debtors	-3.42	9.6	27.34	8.76	70.66
Cash and bank balances	4.38	-0.52	0.14	3.79	5.03
Receivables	-28.36	15.11	-32.3	29.55	10.16
Loans/advances to corporates	-6.34	-0.79	5.2	-7.54	-3.89
Group/associate companies	-6.34	-0.79	5.2	-7.62	-3.87
Total sources/uses of funds	91.79	40.95	25.44	12.4	156.06

APPENDIX 3

Income and Expenditure Statement

	Mar-96	*Mar-97*	*Mar-98*	*Mar-99*	*Mar-00*
Income					
Sales	636.14	630.13	637.07	712.65	1022.61
Manufacturing	623.57	627.47	634.72	702.39	1002.89
Trading	7.14	0	0	0	0
Fiscal benefits	2.45	2.07	1.03	1.15	1.53
Internal transfers	0	0	0.86	0.58	0.89
Others	2.98	0.59	0.46	8.53	17.3
Other income	29.14	19.61	13.49	5.25	4.95
Change in stocks	-1.8	-0.29	9.85	4.16	15.52
Non-recurring income	0.58	2.02	0.45	8.94	4.15
Provisions written back	0	0	0	0.01	0
Others	0	0.75	0.15	0	0
Expenditure					
Raw materials, stores, etc.	421.97	407.24	419.37	462.28	634.32
Wages and salaries	42.34	47.08	46.52	58.31	68.14
Energy (Power and fuel)	18.78	19.54	24.68	14.29	16.13
Other manufacturing expenses	2.14	2.68	2.41	8.36	42.45
Indirect taxes	49.11	49.4	50.74	57.11	93.11
Repairs and maintenance	10.22	10.89	9.01	9.5	13.61
Selling and distribution expenses	33.58	31.44	30.09	37.53	65.92
Miscellaneous expenses	14.77	17.42	17.17	15.36	20.45
Non-recurring expenses	0	1.07	0.61	16.93	0.3
Less interest capitalised	0	0	0.53	0	0
PBDIT	71.15	64.71	60.26	51.33	92.8
Interest	25.57	24.4	23.07	21.95	21.88
Lease rent	0	0	0	0	0
PBDT	45.58	40.31	37.19	29.38	70.92
Depreciation	13.26	16.16	19.69	22.23	29.58
PBT	32.32	24.15	17.5	7.15	41.34
Tax provision	4.35	2.71	1.49	0.46	8.5
Corporate tax	4.3	2.66	1.43	0.42	8.5
Other direct taxes	0.05	0.05	0.06	0.04	0
PAT	27.97	21.44	16.01	6.69	32.84
Dividends	6.31	6.15	4.92	6.16	9.85
Retained earnings	21.66	14.67	10.6	-0.12	21.91

APPENDIX 4

Organisation Structure of Tube Investments, March 2000

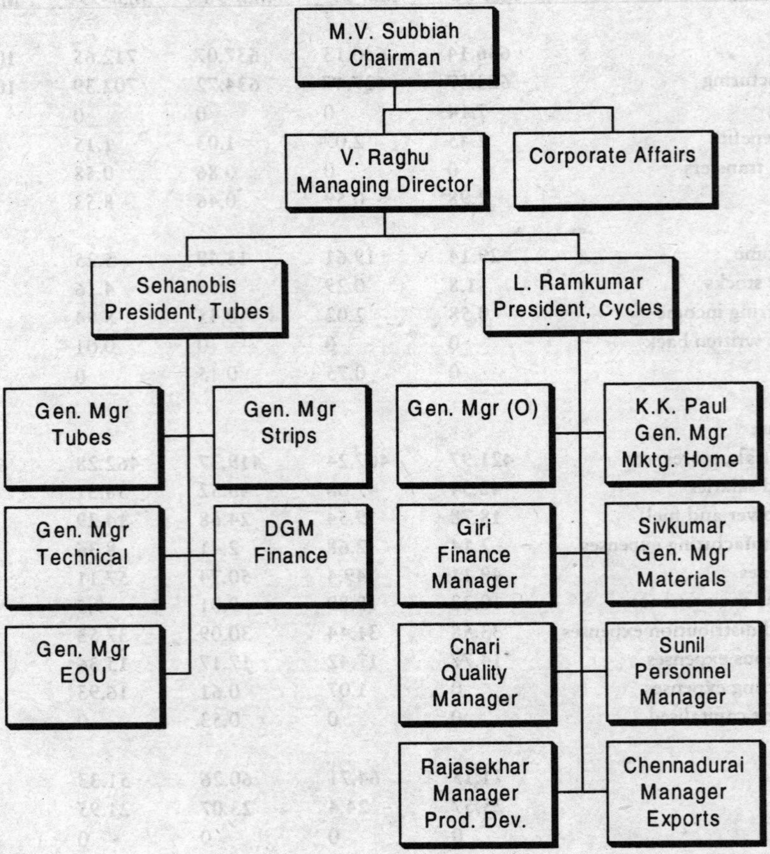

APPENDIX 5

Manufacturing System Redesign (MSR)

Bicycle Manufacturing Process at TI Cycles

The main components, which are manufactured in TI Cycles India, are:

- Frame
- Fork
- Mudguard
- Rim

Frame/Fork

The operations performed are manipulation and joining of tubes by metal joining processes like brazing (a metal joining process that uses brass as the joining medium) and welding (mainly CO_2 welding), machining of the fitment areas, surface treatment that includes phosphating and painting on electro-static spray booths and finally finishing operations like stickering, etc.

Mudguard

The operations performed are rolling and parting to size of the steel strip, press metal operations, surface treatment (phosphating), painting and finishing.

Rim

The operations are rolling and parting to size to give a definite profile to the strip, welding and press metal operations (to form the spoke and valve holes), and finally polishing and plating. Other components like crank, hubs and pedals, chain and chain-wheel are sourced from outside.

The Redesign Exercise

Starting from around mid-1995, TI Cycles of India implemented a thorough overhaul and redesign of their manufacturing system at Plant-1, which included a change in the layout of the factory. The exercise, involving an outlay of approximately Rs 180 mn, lasted for about two years and was done with the technical help/consultation from M/s Lucas Engineering & Services, who were having a JV with TVS, another business group based in Chennai.

The Earlier Plant Design

Before the redesigning was carried out, the layout of the plant was process based (see Figure 1). Shops were designed as process centres. There was a tube preparation shop, a brazing or welding shop, a painting and plating shop, an assembly shop and so on. Material moved through the various shops and the various stages of value addition were carried out on it. Each of the shops or the process centres handled all the models that the company made. Thus, the frames of all the models were made at one shop and the painting was done in one line in the painting shop. Production scheduling was done centrally and elaborate production plans were given to the different shops. Final assembly and dispatch for all the models were done at one place, which received the different components from the respective shops.

Figure1

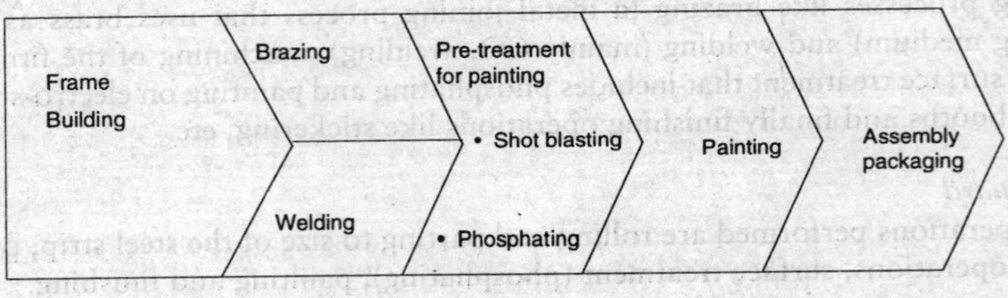

This system design became a drag when the number of models manufactured and marketed by the company increased phenomenally. In 1992–93, when MSR was first conceived, TI Cycles was manufacturing over 30 models for the domestic market and in addition was manufacturing for exports according to the specifications and designs provided by the overseas customers—making each batch of export orders, a different model in itself. So, all shops had a complex production schedule (prepared centrally) involving many different models, which required frequent change of tooling and set-ups. The greatest problem was in the final assembly shop where matching of the components (frames, forks, mudguard and rims) for the different models was a constraint. All this resulted in:

- Increase in work-in-process, inventory, manufacturing lead-time and problems in schedule adherence.
- Poor traceability and status verification of various orders.

The Redesigning

To overcome all these problems, an MSR project was conceived in 1992–93. The redesign involved a change in the plant layout and revamping of the planning and control function deployment, which resulted in a considerable decentralisation of operations. As a first step, all the different models were classified into four groups.

- Standards
- SLRs (Brazed specials)
- MTBs (Home welded)
- Export (Welded)

The grouping was made on the basis of similarity between models with respect to the features available, technology of metal joining (welding or brazing), number of colours used and chances of design changes. The manufacturing system was then redesigned to concentrate all the processes involved for one group of models (say SLR or MTB) in one shop, called a module. Thus, the redesigned plant had a Standard module, an SLR module, an MTB module and an Export module, each module carrying out all the value addition activities for that group of models. In addition, there was a rim module that made the rims for the other modules. Production planning and control was decentralised and each module (the module head) was given the responsibility for preparing the production schedules for its models. Each module was conceived as an 'ownership' centre responsible for outsourcing bought-out components, maintaining stores of raw materials and intermediates, planning of production schedules, manufacturing and assembly, before sending it in batches of 500 cycles to the despatch unit, from where all the models were centrally shipped out. This removed, to a large extent, the earlier problem of component/parts mismatch in the final assembly section. New material handling equipment was procured (fork-lift trucks and steel cages) to transport the assembled models in batches to the despatch module. The new plant layout and the arrangement of the manufacturing facilities within each module was designed to:

- Minimise the amount of material handling (in ton-kilometres).
- Cause minimum amount of disruption to existing production.
- Minimisation of new construction.
- Maximisation of old facilities.
- Minimisation of relocation of existing machinery.

However, some functions were centralised or 'shared' between the modules. These included activities like vendor development, price fixation for bought-out components, quality control and major maintenance works where centralisation gave economic benefits.

This whole process was completed in a period of two years with no loss in production during the transition period.

The project involved a total expenditure of Rs 180 mn, about 50 per cent of which was on account of increase in capacity. In the SLR, Home, Welded and Standard modules capacity was increased and a new export module was set up in 1995. New building construction, new equipment (painting plant, material handling equipment, etc.), took up about Rs 150 mn. This investment was funded from part of the proceeds of the GDR issue by Tube Investments. The expected payback period of the investment was calculated to be about 4.3 years.

Factory Layout Before MSR

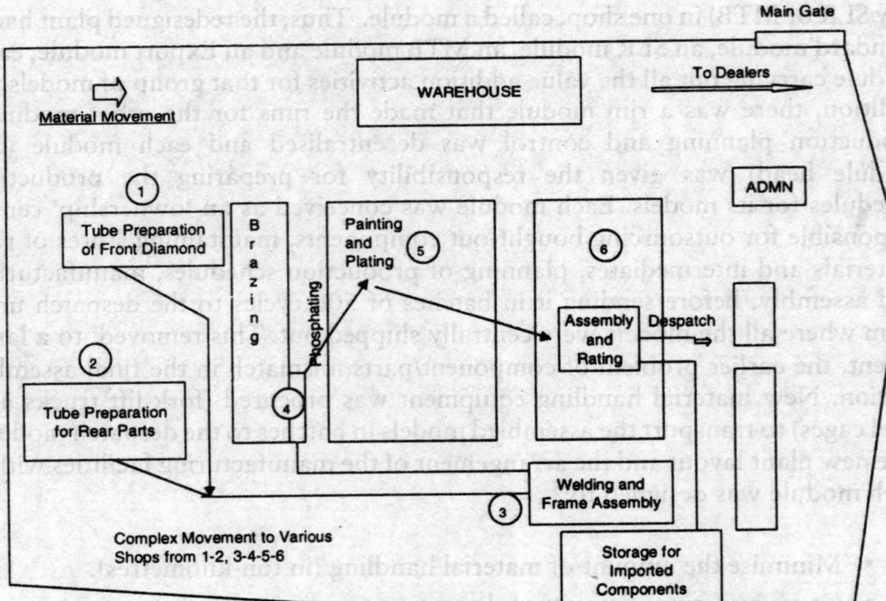

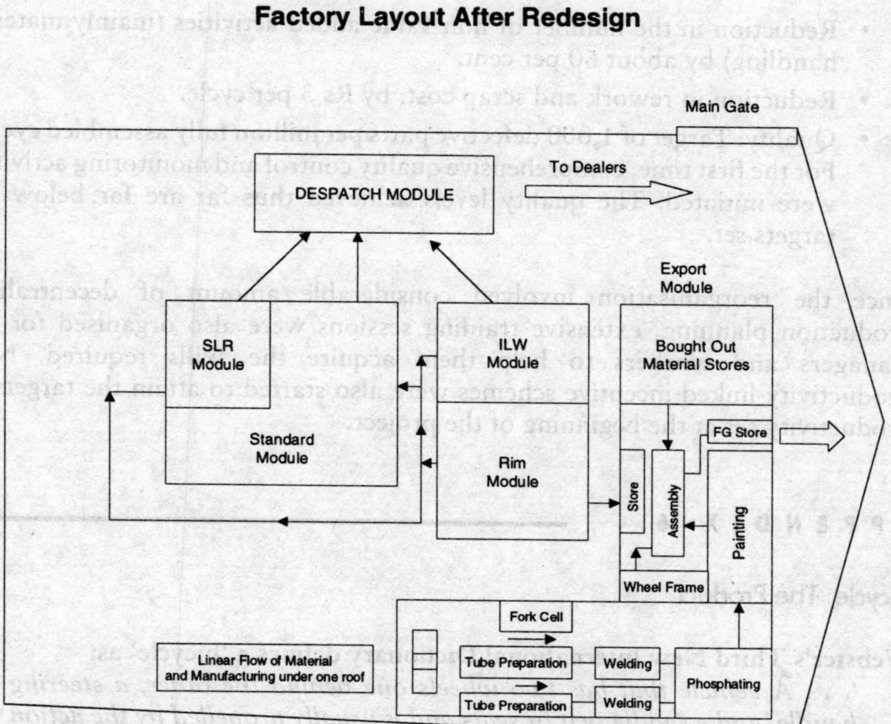

Benefits Expected from the MSR project:

- Decrease in inventory.
- Raw materials: from 19 to 13 days.
- Work-in-process: from 5 to 2 days.
- Finished goods: from 8 to 4 days.
- Reduction in manufacturing lead time: from 6 to 3 days.
- Improved schedule adherence.
- 100 per cent orders within seven days for the home market and thirty days for the export market.
- Improved productivity.
- Number of cycles produced per man per day: from 1 to 2.

- Reduction in the number of non-value added activities (mainly material handling) by about 60 per cent.
- Reduction in rework and scrap cost: by Rs 3 per cycle.
- Quality: Target of 1,000 defective parts per million fully assembled cycles. For the first time, comprehensive quality control and monitoring activities were initiated. The quality levels achieved thus far are far below the targets set.

Since the reorganisation involved considerable amount of decentralised production planning, extensive training sessions were also organised for the managers and workers to help them acquire the skills required. New productivity-linked incentive schemes were also started to attain the targets of productivity set at the beginning of the project.

APPENDIX 6

Bicycle: The Product

Webster's Third New International Dictionary defines a 'bicycle' as:

> '. . . *A vehicle that has two wheels one behind the other, a steering handle, and a saddle seat or seats and is usually propelled by the action of the rider's feet upon pedals.*'

A Short History of the Bicycle

Comte De Sivrac introduced the first known vehicle with two wheels in 1791, in the form of a wooden horse. This early bicyle was not very sophisticated! Despite that the velocifere (as it was called) became quite popular in the 1790s and gave people a newfound mobility.

In addition to mobility, the bicycle industry literally paved the way for the introduction of the automobile, in the form of concern for better roads, and the areas of technology the bicycle pioneered. Some of the early names in automotive development, like the Duryea brothers, Henry Ford and J.J. Dunlop, were just a few years earlier honing their technological and manufacturing skills on the bicycle.

The pioneers who popularised the bicycle used it for long distance fun-rides and had to brave unpaved roads and the incredulity of people they met on the way. In 1878 the first bicycle organisation of national scope was formed in England—the British Touring Club. America followed suit in 1880 with the creation of the League of American Wheelmen (LAW). By 1896 there were over 400 bicycle manufacturers in the US, and related industries—steel, wire, rubber, and leather—were booming as well. Between 1890 and 1896 over 100 million dollars were spent on bicycles. American production in 1897 was two million bicycles for a population of 65 million or one bike for every thirty people. The bicycle became a part of American life, an important means of mass public transport, and American life adapted to its use. Eugene Sloane asserts that 'the impact of the bicycle was almost as great, in fact, as the advent of the Model T Ford.'

With the coming of the automobile, however, the bicycle lost its pride of place as the private means of mass transport. Cycling on roads along with speeding cars became hazardous and a movement began to separate bicycles from the cars, trucks and buses out on the streets, in the interest of bicycle safety. Though by 1970 more than 175 American cities had special bikeways, the bicycle was definitely upstaged by the motorcar as the people's means of transport in the United States.

In the 1970s a new type of bicycle, based on the off-road motorcycle, became popular. These motocross bicycles were first designed for children, and they were designed to take the abuse they were bound to get when the kids took them out in the dirt. Motocross bicycle racing became another expensive sport for the middle class. Today there are a growing number of cyclists who have forsaken the paved roads for the firetrails, fields, and trails on their 'Mountain Bikes'. A whole new class of mountain bikes are becoming available that work incredibly well off-road. Bicycles have again been transformed into an entertainment product.

Product Categories

The different categories of bicycles are as follows:

- *Standards*: The Standards model is the most basic bike, with a fork, frame, mudguard, seats and the moving parts, that include crank and crank-wheel, chain, chain-wheel, pedals and the wheel. It has no special added features and is used as a utility product. Strength and sturdiness, as viewed by the consumer, is the most important functional aspect of these models. Brazing is used as the metal joining process in these models. The bikes come in single colours like green or black. This segment does not exist in the developed countries. In India, the consumer in this product segment is extremely price sensitive, prices of various manufacturers ranging from Rs 1,150 to 1,300 per set. Bicycle marketers refer to this category as a '*doodhwala*' (milkman's) bike.

- *SLR (Sports light roadster)*: These bikes are lighter, more fashionably designed and slightly higher priced than the standard bikes. Brazing is used as the metal joining process and these models are usually available in different colours.
- *MTB (Mountain terrain bikes)*: MTBs constitute the premium segment of the Indian market. The bikes are sturdy and fashionable, and come in combinations of resplendent colours. The frames are welded and are often designed to please. They also carry added-on features like shock absorbers (the Rock-Shock model of TI) and gears (Hercules Top Gear recently launched by TI). MTBs are supposed to give a smooth, effortless and comfortable ride on any type of terrain. Prices in India range from Rs 2,000 to about Rs 3,000 per set. In the USA, MTBs constitute the largest market segment and all MTBs, compulsorily have gears as an added feature (5 to 25 speeds).
- *Other categories*: Producers also make what they call *kids and juvenile bikes* aimed at children of different age groups. Those models are basically either like SLRs or MTBs and come as smaller versions suited for young kids. Recently, TI Cycles has launched a kids model whose external features are designed to resemble a motorbike, and is trying to promote it as a toy for kids.

In the United States, a number of other categories of bicycles with more advanced and specialized features are available. A very recent innovation has been the two-wheel drive bicycle models in which power from the pedals is transferred to both the front and the back wheel. The most common improvement in bicycle design is, however, on account of use of new materials. In India, all bicycles are made of mild steel materials (chrome or stainless steel). The new materials used in the advanced markets are aluminium, carbon fibres and titanium for making the bicycle frames and other parts like hubs. The new materials considerably increase the strength/weight ratio of the bicycles, but it comes at a price. Bicycles with titanium frames (the costliest), exotically designed, can cost as much as *US $ 3500,* while in USA the average retail price of a set is about US$ 112 (for bicycles sold through mass merchant stores) and US$

295 (for those sold through independent bicycle dealers). The bulk of the premium bikes are sold for US $ 500-1000. Indian manufacturers presently do not have the technological capability to engineer with any of these new materials.

In India, bicycle production and use expanded after independence and India's drive for industrialisation. Jawaharlal Nehru, India's first Prime Minister, wanted to take India from the 'bullock-cart' age to 'bicycle age'. Cycles soon acquired the status of an essential consumer durable, and along with the wristwatch, an essential part of a bride's dowry.

CASE 5

THE INDIAN WATCH INDUSTRY: CHANGING TIMES

In 1995, the three-decade-old Indian watch industry was in the midst of a major turmoil. Even as they were gearing themselves up to combat the imminent entry of multinational players in the Indian market, the domestic players were being engulfed by an ominous increase in smuggled watches—their age-old bète noire. Ironically, at a time when the domestic watch market was estimated to have grown by 8 per cent, the total sales of mechanical, digital and quartz watches of the four domestic watch majors—HMT, Titan, Timex and Allwyn—fell by nearly 18 per cent. As against an estimated sales of around 19 million, actual domestic production was of the order of 11 million.[1] As in the past, the gap was

This case was written by J. Ramachandran, Associate Professor of Strategy at the Indian Institute of Management, Bangalore, and C. Lavanya, PGP student, Class of 1995, based on publicly available information. The authors are grateful to HMT Ltd, Titan and Timex Ltd for their help and support and to Mrs Sonu Goyal for the research support received. This case was first registered by the Indian Institute of Management, Bangalore, in 1995.

1. NCAER survey. The survey also estimated ownership of quartz watches in the country, as of 1992–93, to be 59 million. Cumulative domestic quartz watch production until 1992–93 was around 15 million.

met by the 'smuggled' sector. The nature of smuggling in the 1990s, however, was different from the past. Bulk of the smuggling now was in the form of watch movements (the innards of a watch) as against the earlier unauthorised imports of fully assembled watches. The smuggled watch movements were being assembled locally and sold, typically, under leading international brand names.[2]

The past pleas of domestic manufacturers to the government to combat smuggling had little impact. Xerxes Desai, vice chairman and managing director of Titan, asserted: 'In the seven years that I have been associated with the watch industry in India, I have not been witness to any serious efforts on the part of the law enforcement agencies to curb the smuggling menace which is of enormous proportions and which has made India the laughing stock of the world.' Domestic manufacturers were particularly agitated over the government practice of auctioning in the local markets the watch movements seized, little as they were, by law enforcement agencies. They had recommended to the government that the seized goods be exported back to the manufacturer or sold legally in the world market or destroyed, but not auctioned within India itself. They contended that these watches and their movements were being purchased by Indian counterparts in the smuggling operation and used to create a legal front for a much larger operation. To drive home the point, Titan recently participated at a customs auction and acquired 10,000 Citizen watch movements. Desai then wrote a letter to Citizen, Japan, and offered to sell the movements back to Citizen at its purchase price of Rs 11.3 per movement.

According to Desai, the smuggling menace had the implicit backing of known international manufacturers. He said:

> It is a worldwide phenomenon and everybody is aware of it. The network is known to the key players. Manufacturers who are responsible for smuggling their products into India must be told in no uncertain terms that if they want to come into India and operate legally then they must first bring their illegal operations under control. Throwing open the market to foreign brands must be made conditional upon a reduction in smuggling.

Bulk of the smuggled watches, often of suspect quality, were sold at prices below Rs 500. Domestic majors could not compete against these watches because of

2. About 90 per cent of them were branded Citizen, the Japanese brand belonging to the world's largest manufacturer of watches, Citizen, Japan. According to K.S. Gergan, HMT's executive director (watches), a number of these watches were also being sold under the HMT brand name.

cost disadvantages. They were essentially operating in the Rs 500 to Rs 1,500 price segment and offered better quality products. This domain was now being threatened by global watch manufacturers, principally from Switzerland and Japan, who were seeking to enter the Indian market.

Thus, in 1995, the Indian watch industry was caught in a double bind. On the one hand it had to battle the 'illegal' competition from smuggled watches, implicitly supported by international manufacturers, while on the other it would soon have to contend with 'legal' competition from global players who were planning to enter India with their portfolio of well-known international brands and with significant scale and experience advantages.

The HMT Years

The Indian watch industry came into being in the 1960s when the Government of India took the momentous decision to set up the country's first watch factory. The task was assigned to HMT, as it had developed, in the seven years since its inception in 1953 as a manufacturer of machine tools, considerable skills in high precision technology.

HMT (formerly known as Hindustan Machine Tools Limited) had been set up with the objective of producing a limited range of machine tools of the value of Rs 50 mn per annum. The constantly growing demand for machine tools resulted in the company expanding its activities to later include small tools, cutting tools and CNC systems. Over the years, the company diversified its product range to include printing machines, agricultural machinery, dairy machinery, watches and electric lamps. The diversity in the company's portfolio also stemmed from the fact that the Government of India, influenced by the company's outstanding performance—Pandit Jawaharlal Nehru, India's first prime minister, had called it the 'jewel' among public sector undertakings—employed it as a vehicle for implementing policy initiatives.

Thus in 1961, HMT set up India's first-ever factory for manufacturing mechanical watches in Bangalore in technical collaboration with Citizen of Japan. From then on, for the next two-and-a-half decades, HMT dominated the Indian watch industry like a colossus. The HMT brand became synonymous with watches in the country, lending credence to the company's claim of being 'Timekeepers to the Nation'. The company acquired a formidable reputation for producing sturdy watches, which were of good quality and, more importantly, were highly reliable. HMT focussed on producing 'no frills but sensible' watches. And for a long time, every watch sold and the company was amongst the most profitable companies in India.

To cope with the burgeoning demand for watches, HMT set up a second watch manufacturing unit in Bangalore in 1972. Almost immediately thereafter it set up its third plant in Srinagar (Jammu and Kashmir), when the government reviewed its policy towards the watch industry and decided to enhance domestic capacity wth a view to counteract smuggling. In 1979, the company set up its fourth unit in Tumkur, at that time an industrially backward area, near Bangalore. The choice of location was influenced by the government's desire to develop yet another industrially backward area in the hilly area of Kumaon in Uttar Pradesh. Once again the location was influenced by the government's policy thrust of achieving balanced regional development.

Further, in keeping with government policy of encouraging small-scale units and increasing employment in these sectors, HMT set up fourteen ancillary units all across the country. These ancillary units were set up primarily to assemble watches from the components manufactured by the company. These ancillaries also served the objective of dispersing the watch making technology to all parts of the country.

Over the next three decades HMT produced over 80 million watches. It had started by producing just over 14,000 watches in 1961–62.

If You Have the Inclination, We Have the Time

To encourage watch ownership and to build equity for its brand, HMT advertised heavily. The company's advertising—with its memorable baseline 'If you have the inclination, we have the time'—firmly established the HMT brand. Even three decades later, the HMT brand was among the few Indian brands in the county which enjoyed considerable equity with the consumer.

The company kept in close touch with its consumers. It regularly carried out market research studies with a view to track buyer behaviour, ownership patterns and even psycho-graphics to understand demand patterns. The company used this knowledge to alter or modify its communication. For instance, observing the increase in the sales of watches during the wedding season, the company promoted watches to be given as gifts to newly-weds.

Similarly, when one of the studies conducted by the company revealed the average age of the first time buyer of watches to be 23, the company directed its efforts to reducing this age and bringing teenagers into its fold. It modified the communication package to show teenagers wearing watches in its advertisements. The company, however, did not introduce a separate model for teenagers, nor did it promote any of the models in its existing range as a watch for teenagers. Though the company produced a number of models (including a pocket watch which it introduced in the 1970s) for a variety of consumers (e.g., a Braille watch for the blind), its advertising, until the 1980s, promoted only the umbrella brand—HMT.[3]

Product development, for a very long time, was essentially a careful monitoring of the quality of watches produced by the company. The watches produced by the company were for the most part copies of foreign models. Executives in the product development department regularly visited the markets of Southeast Asia such as Hong Kong and Singapore and came back with designs which they thought would sell well in India. These designs were then duplicated by the company's factories and sold. These models were almost always the more sturdy, durable and utilitarian ones. If one wanted a more fancy watch, one had to depend on the generosity of one's relatives and friends returning from an overseas trip. Alternatively, one could buy it from the friendly neighbourhood smuggler!

Building the Channel

Though the demand for HMT's watches was very strong, the trade was never too happy with the company. HMT's problems with the trade began as far back as 1961. At first, retailers trading in watches were just not interested in HMT's home-grown product. The foreign watches that they were selling such as Favre-Leuba were doing well and they did not believe that an indigenous watch would do as well. HMT, therefore, decided to go it alone and began selling its watches through its thirteen offices which, until that time, were selling its machine tools all over the country.

The tide, however, turned with the imposition of restrictions on the import of watches. Retailers now found that they would have to cooperate with HMT if they wanted to be in the watch business at all. HMT continued to sell its watches only through its own offices, though it took advantage of the change and

3. Ironically, the company's rival Titan, successfully launched its pocket watches in the 1990s which apart from doing well in the marketplace, did wonders for Titan's brand image.

established service centre facilities with fifty key retailers across the country. However, in 1973, when the company introduced a new range of expensive watches (priced approximately at Rs 330 each), it felt the need to have more retail outlets stocking its watches. The company then selectively converted some of the outlets where it had established its service facilities into company authorised retail outlets. Over time, and in order to improve its reach, the company expanded the number of such retail outlets to over 250. These authorised outlets were serviced by the nearest sale offices of the company. Further, the growth of its watches led to the company expanding its service network. These numbered over 800 by the mid-1980s.

Despite the expansion of its retail network, HMT did not have a system of carrying out regular trade audits. As a consequence, some of the authorised retailers became de-facto wholesalers, even though the company had not authorised them to perform this role. The 'wholesale–retailers' found it advantageous to buy in bulk from the company and sell to other 'small' retailers at a premium as the demand for the company's watches was very high. Though the other 'small' retailers, in turn, recovered the premium from the consumers, they were a disgruntled lot for the few 'wholesale–retailers' were effectively controlling the watch market in the country.

If You Have the Inclination, We Have the Exact Time

Until 1980, HMT manufactured only mechanical watches. The explosive growth of quartz watches in the world market led HMT to include these in its product portfolio. The company launched its quartz range in 1981.[4] The company targeted the 'modern young man' and positioned its quartz watch as the 'space age' generation watch. The launch failed—the watch was neither affordable by the young, because of its high price, nor appealing to the middle-aged conservative person, who could afford it.

HMT then reoriented its strategy. It slashed the prices of quartz watches to the Rs 800 to 850 price range and relaunched the quartz range, with quartz technology as the USP. The ads talked about how different the watch looked at the back though it looked the same on the wrist. The communication focussed on the benefits of accuracy and convenience. In order to drive home the point the company also modified its signature tune to 'If you have the inclination, we have the time. The exact time'.

4. Initially, HMT sourced the innards of the watch—the quartz movement—from its collaborator, Citizen.

Consumer acceptance was still hard to come by. Most consumers did not find the chunky looking quartz watches sold by HMT to be superior to the cheaper mechanical watches. The equation worsened when they factored in the cost of replacing the then relatively high priced battery cells, which, in addition, were not easily available.

By 1984–85 HMT was selling only 200,000 quartz watches per annum. The company concluded that quartz watches would have only a limited demand in India and restricted the total installed capacity for these watches to 560,000 pieces per annum. It also virtually stopped advertising the quartz watch and went back to advertising all the watches under the umbrella brand name of HMT.

Despite the failure of its quartz range, HMT continued to dominate the Indian watch industry. This, however, did not imply that it did not confront competition. The company faced competition from three sources: the organised sector, the small sector and the 'invisible' sector (smuggled watches).

Competition from the Organised Sector

Hyderabad Allwyn Limited, a company owned by the government of Andhra Pradesh, was HMT's single largest competitor. At the time of its entry into the watch industry, Allwyn had a formidable presence in the bus body building and refrigerator industries. The company had a history of pioneering with its products. It was the first company to produce a double-decker bus in the country (1956) and was also the first to produce a refrigerator (1958).

Allwyn entered the watch industry in 1981. The company entered into a collaboration with Seiko, the Japanese major in the global watch industry, and set up a state-of-the-art facility to manufacture 2 million watches, both mechanical and quartz. Though it remained second to HMT in terms of overall market share, the company emerged as a leader in both the mechanical and automatic watch segments and, importantly, in the quartz segment.

Allwyn, despite its leadership of the quartz segment and the observed rapid displacement of mechanical watches with quartz watches in the global market place, did not discontinue the manufacture of mechanical watches as it did not wish to cause a drain on the country's foreign exchange resources (the manufacture of quartz watches, at that time, was highly import intensive). R.P. Agarwal, the then vice chairman and managing director of the company, had declared:

> A country must draw its own strategy by striking a balance between what is the latest in technology in the world and also what is for the good of its own economy. One need not imitate in toto what is the latest abroad. A balance in production between quartz and mechanical watches appears to be in the best interest of the country and Hyderabad Allwyn will sincerely follow this path.

The company's policy of striking a balance between global trends and domestic market needs resulted in the company pioneering the introduction of low priced polyamide ('plastic') watches in the country. The polyamide Swatch watches from Switzerland had met with phenomenal success the world over and to cash in on this phenomenon Allwyn launched its range of polyamide watches under the brand name Allwyn Trendy. Positioned as a watch for the young, Trendy was a runaway success. It captured the interest of the youth of the country and belied all apprehensions about the acceptance of 'plastic' watches by the Indian consumer. The company followed up the success of its initial range of Trendy watches by launching Trendy Co-ordinates, with which it pioneered the concept of 'co-ordinating' a watch with one's wardrobe, and once again met with success. Trendy's success, however, was a mixed blessing for the company. Its contribution in percentage terms to the bottom line of the company was very small and as R.S. Reddy, the then executive director (marketing), rued: 'It shifted the focus from our mechanical and quartz watches. When you introduce lesser priced watches, it eats into your market.'

Competition from the Small Sector

HMT also confronted competition from a number of small watch manufacturers. This included, Indo French Time (IFT) Industries Ltd, the first private sector watch making company in India. While the company started by making mechanical watches, marketed under the brand name Timestar, it launched its quartz range of watches almost immediately after its introduction by HMT in the country. Similarly, following the success of Allwyn Trendy, the company launched its polyamide range under the brand name TSWatch. The high profile foray into the 'plastic' watch segment was initially quite successful. However, the company lost momentum when it lost the battle in the course for brand infringement of the Swiss company, TS Watches, and remained a marginal player.

The other players in the small sector included Jayna Time Industries Pvt. Ltd, New Delhi, manufacturers of the Jayco brand of watches and Indo Swiss Time

(IST) Industries Ltd who, in addition to making the low-priced IST brand of mechanical and quartz watches in collaboration with Ronda SA of Switzerland, made stopwatches and were also suppliers of time-keeping mechanisms to the defence department.

Competition from the 'Invisible' Sector

Right through the history of the Indian watch industry, the demand for watches far outstripped supply from the small and the organised sector. The gap, estimated to be half of demand, was filled by watches smuggled into the country. Watches smuggled into the country were at the two polar ends of the price spectrum. The high-priced watches (over Rs 1,000) were essentially top international brands and were popular because of their attractive styling. At the lower end (below Rs 300), the watches were in great demand, despite the doubtful nature of their quality and reliability, because of their attractive pricing. Further, even the low-end watches came in attractive shapes, sizes and colours and offered the consumer a wide variety. The smuggled watches were also strongly patronised by the trade who, apart from being able to cater to the latent demand for these watches, also benefited greatly from the enormous freedom they possessed in pricing these watches.

Domestic manufacturers could not match the products, both in terms of styling (and the superior appeal of the international brands at the top end) and prices. Smuggled watches were cheaper as they escaped government restrictions like import and excise duties and sales and income taxes. Efforts of domestic manufacturers, which were rather half-hearted, to curb these unauthorised imports were to no avail. Smuggling flourished, aided partly by unrealistic government policy.

Government Policy

The government reserved the manufacture of appearance parts like straps and dials to the small-scale sector. With regard to case manufacturing too the policy favoured the small-scale sector. This affected the competitiveness of the Indian watch industry, especially at the top end, as the quality of supplies from the small-scale units was rather poor. For example, consumers routinely complained about the poor quality of the straps. Despite the claims of the watch industry association that manufacture of high quality straps required heavy investment (anywhere between Rs 50 mn and 100 mn for a 2 million metal straps facility) which was much beyond the scope of the small-scale sector, the government persisted with this policy, largely on ideological grounds.

In addition to favouring the small-scale sector for appearance parts, the government also imposed restrictions on sourcing of electronic circuit blocks (ECBs), a critical but low technology component required for the manufacture of electronic watches. The Chandigarh-based public sector undertaking Semiconductor Complex Limited (SCL) had a monopoly over the manufacture of ECBs in India. Watch manufacturers were not allowed to produce ECBs. The domestic requirement was in excess of what SCL could supply and the balance was being met through imports, which in turn had to be routed through SCL. Not only did SCL charge exorbitant prices—almost three times the international price—for the the ECBs, its supplies were highly erratic.

The government's policy towards the domestic manufacture of digital watches, which formed a substantial part of the watches which were smuggled, also shackled the domestic industry. While the manufacture of mechanical and quartz analog watches came under the purview of the industry ministry, the administrative ministry overseeing the manufacture of digital watches was the Department of Electronics (DoE). The DoE required Indian manufacturers to make their own LCDs (an essential component for the manufacture of digital watches) and place at the disposal of SCL adequate technical information which would enable SCL to manufacture integrated circuits (ICs). This put the watch industry in a double bind. In the case of LCDs, the technology available for the manufacture of high quality and reliable products was suited only for mass production in quantities far greater than could be absorbed by the Indian market. Moreover, the investment costs for setting up such a facility were very high. In the case of ICs, no party who had developed an IC was willing to place that information at the disposal of SCL even on the payment of a technology transfer fee. Thus, the development of a local digital watch industry got bogged down in the unrealistic expectations of DoE. And, meanwhile, the demand for digital watches was being met by smuggled watches.

Thus, until the mid-1980s, the Indian watch industry was predominantly producing mechanical watches, even though the world over, these watches had lost out to quartz analog and digital watches (see Appendices 1, 2 and 3).

The World Watch Industry [5]

Until 1970, Switzerland was the undisputed leader of the world watch industry with a 42 per cent volume share and a 78 per cent value share. Over the next twenty-five years, the world watch industry experienced radical changes. Innovation in production and marketing resulted in a great deal of volatility and the industry witnessed a period of rapid entry of new competitors and the departure of some established producers.

The Swiss conquered the world market with mechanical watches and had, over time, acquired a reputation for fine craftsmanship, elegance and style. Although quartz technology was first invented in Switzerland (a Swiss engineer, Max Hetzel, invented the first electronic watch in 1954), most of the watches manufactured by the Swiss were mechanical watches. Quartz crystal watches began appearing in the market place only in the 1960s. Digital watches first appeared in 1972. The Swiss ignored both the quartz and the digital technologies. This was largely due to:

1. The large installed base in the country for the manufacture of mechanical watches.
2. Fears about reduction in employment (a large number of people were employed in Swiss watchmaking firms as mechanical watch manufacture was manpower intensive.
3. The fragmented nature of the Swiss watch industry—a consequence of the then prevailing legal framework.

Traditionally the Swiss operated on a two-tier system—components manufacturing and assembly—and Swiss watch firms fell into one of three categories. First, there were a large number of 'one man-one boy' and other small enterprises which produced components or movements or put purchased parts into cases. Second were the well-established, privately-owned watchmakers who produced expensive, handmade watches. And finally, there was a group of companies which operated under the umbrella of either of the two giant organisations—ASSUAG and SSIH.[6] Swiss laws, until the deregulation of the industry in the 1970s, made it illegal to open, enlarge or transform any

5. This section draws on the article by William Taylor, 'Message and Muscle: An Interview with Swatch Titan Nicolas Hayek', *Harvard Business Review*, March–April, 1993.

6. Between them they controlled nearly a third of the Swiss production of watches and over 40 per cent of Swiss watch exports and they had some of the most well-known watch brands—Omega, Longines, Rado, Tissot, etc.— in their portfolio.

watchmaking facilities without government permission. Exports of components and movements were also illegal without permission, as was the export of watchmaking machinery. These regulations were instituted to protect the Swiss watch industry from foreign competition.

The Rise of Japan

While the Swiss ignored the quartz and digital technologies, the Japanese embraced them with great fervour and quickly carved out a strong position in the world watch industry. Quartz technology greatly simplified the manufacture of a watch. The quartz analog watch could be manufactured in an automated setting with semi-skilled labour.[7] The manufacture of a mechanical watch, on the other hand, required the employment of skilled labour. High-quality mechanical movements were made by hand which required a combination of semi-skilled and highly skilled workers. And mechanical watch assembly required highly skilled workers, especially at the final stages of production, as mechanical watch quality was dependent as much on the care taken in assembly as on the quality of the individual components.

Seiko was amongst the first to mass produce watches using the assembly line system of manufacturing. It began manufacturing quartz watches in 1969 and by the early 1980s had emerged as a global major. Mass production enabled Seiko and Citizen, the other Japanese major in the world watch industry, to price their watches significantly below the Swiss watches and cater to the mass market. The Japanese companies, however, did not rely only on price as a source of competitive advantage. Seiko, for example, created a strong brand image based on its quartz technology and accuracy. It annually spent over $50 million in advertising, mostly on television, to sell its quartz watches. Further, Seiko, contrary to the then prevailing practice, set up its own sales subsidiaries in all the major world markets. It also established service centres in these markets. This enabled the customer to bring in or mail a repair problem directly to the company, bypassing the retailer.

Sustained technological and product innovation enabled Japanese watchmakers to dominate the middle price segment of the world watch industry.[8] For example,

7. The manufacture of digital watches was even simpler. Unskilled labour could be used to assemble digital watches on automated assembly lines.
8. Their success was partly aided by the fact that the Japanese companies were protected from foreign competitors in the domestic market. Only expensive watches, about 5 per cent of the total units and 20 per cent of the total value of Japanese purchase, were imported.

designing electronic watches for women had initially created problems. To create models which fit a woman's smaller wrist required considerable miniaturisation of the movement and battery. Improvements in miniaturisation and advancement in large-scale integrated (LSI) circuits and battery technology provided manufacturers with greater design flexibility, which in turn enabled them to add special functions to watches without making them excessively bulky. Watches, then, began to take on the appearance of multifunction instruments. Casio, a Japanese calculator company, entered the watch industry in 1974 with digital watches. Its product line consisted of only digital watches, with many of them being multifunctional as stopwatches, timers and calculators. In fact the Casio brand was almost synonymous with multifunction watches on a worldwide basis. The company retailed its watches at the camera, calculator or stereo sections of departmental stores instead of retailing them at the conventional jewellery sections as it believed that the appeal of the digital watch was more technical than aesthetic.

Decline of the US Watch Industry

In the mid-1970s, the US was a key player in the world watch industry. Following the emergence of the electronic watch, a number of US electronic companies, mostly chip producers, entered the watch industry in the 1970s with digital watches. Most started as suppliers of watch movements and components integrated forward into production and assembly of complete watches. In the early days of the digital watch, demand far outstripped capacity. Nevertheless, electronic companies continually pushed prices down in a market share war which eventually destroyed their attempted entry into the watch business.

By the mid-1980s, the USA had all but disappeared as a significant manufacturer of watches, though it continued to be the world's largest market for watches. The onslaught of Japanese companies in the middle price segments and Hong Kong companies at the lower end took its toll. Only Timex, USA, the world's fourth largest producer of watches, which entered the watch industry in the late 1950s, continued to have a significant presence with a 30 per cent share of the US market. Most Timex watches were priced at the higher end of the low-price segment. The watches were mass produced and manufacturing was mechanised, simplified and standardised. When the company faced resistance from conventional jewellery stores because of its pricing strategy, which restricted the margins of retailers, it sold its watches through mass outlets such as drugstores, departmental stores, hardware stores and even cigar stands. Though Timex produced a large number of styles, it did not promote any single model or style. Much of the advertising (which was spent on television) promoted the durability of the product (the commercials typically showed the Timex watch functioning properly despite being put through a number of torture tests) through its now famous catchline 'Takes a licking but keeps on ticking'.[9]

The Emergence of Hong Kong

Hong Kong entered the world watch industry in a major way in 1976. It leveraged the low cost of wages in Hong Kong and quickly emerged as a major player in the global watch industry. Most watch production in Hong Kong was assembly. Hong Kong watch companies specialised in inexpensive electronic and mechanical watches. These companies opted to outsource the 'guts' of the watch, viz., movements, instead of manufacturing them, as building electronic movements required mastery over multiple technologies. Japan emerged as the biggest supplier of watch movements to the Hong Kong companies. As Hong Kong assembled hundreds of millions of cheap watches, Japan made investments to supply them with movements. The Japanese companies built big factories and slashed prices. The average prices of watch movements which earlier ranged from $8 to $20, dropped significantly to the $2 to $5 price range.

Ten major producers accounted for over 70 per cent of all watches sold from Hong Kong, though it was estimated that over 800 'loft workshops' also existed. Hong Kong manufacturers kept their design costs low by producing copies and near copies of watches displayed in trade fairs and jewellery stores. They also kept their marketing costs low as they did not sell the watches under the name of their own company or brand name. A number of the smaller companies also indulged in manufacturing counterfeit watches sold under Japanese or Swiss brand names.

By the mid-1980s, Hong Kong led the world in the manufacture of watches in terms of units while Switzerland continued to lead the world in terms of value, though its value share had halved from the 1970 level. Japan was the first runner-up in both cases.

9. For example, in one TV commercial, the Timex watch was tied to the hoof of a galloping horse and later shown performing as before.

Revitalisation of the Swiss Watch Industry

Faced with severe competition from Japan and Hong Kong, the Swiss watch industry spent much of the 1970s retreating. According to Nicolas Hayek, who masterminded the spectacular comeback of the Swiss watch industry in the second half of the 1980s, the world watch industry in the early 1980s looked like a three-layer wedding cake. Hayek said:

> Back then, the world market for watches was about 500 million units per year. The low end segment, the bottom layer of the cake, had watches with prices up to $75 or so. That layer represented 450 million units out of 500 million. The middle layer, with watches up to $400 or so, represented 42 million units. That left 8 million watches for the top layer, with prices from $400 into millions of dollars. The Swiss share of the bottom layer, 450 million watches, was zero. We had nothing left. Our share of the middle layer was about 3 per cent. Our share of the top layer was 97 per cent.

The resuscitation of the Swiss watch industry began with the merger of the two umbrella giant and insolvent watch manufacturers of Switzerland—ASSUAG and SSIH. The Swiss banks, majority shareholders in both, orchestrated the merger based on the recommendations of Hayek, who was then founder and CEO of a Zurich-based consulting firm. Soon thereafter, Hayek became the CEO of SMH—the merged entity—when, following differences with the banks over the future direction for SMH, he acquired the single largest stake in SMH. Over the next decade Hayek revitalised SMH and in the process put Switzerland back on the pinnacle of the world watch industry.

According to Hayek, the typical Swiss reaction to the invasion from the Far East in the 1970s was:

> Why should we compete with Japan and Hong Kong? They make junk, then they give it away. We have no margin there. Of course, as we retreated the Japanese moved up to the next layer of the cake. Then the retreat would start again. I decided that we could retreat no longer. We had to have a broad market presence. We needed at least one profitable, growing, global brand in every segment—including the low end . . . if we did not have a strong position in the low end, we could not control quality and costs in other segments. Hayek's decision to have a strong presence in the low price segment resulted in the enormously successful Swatch.

> Swatch is . . . really a triumph of imagination. If you combine powerful technology with fantasy, you create something very distinct . . . I understood that we were not just selling a consumer product, or even a branded product. We were selling an emotional product. You wear a watch on your wrist, right against your skin. You have it there for 12 hours a day, maybe 24 hours a day. It can be an important part of your self-image. It does not have to be a commodity. It shouldn't be a commodity. I knew that if we could add genuine emotion to the product, and attack the low end with a strong message, we could succeed.
>
> —Nicolas Hayek

The brash and playful Swatch (whose basic models retailed for $40) went on to become a cult product. Its success was attributed to its having turned the watch into a fashion statement. Hayek, however, contended that the Swatch made more than a fashion statement. According to him, Swatch was an emotional product. He said:

> We are not just offering people a style. We are offering them a message. This is an absolutely critical point. Fashion is about image. Emotional products are about message—a strong, exciting, distinct, authentic message that tells people who you are and why you do what you do. There are many elements that make up the Swatch message. High quality. Low Cost. Provocative. Joy of Life.

Franco Bosisio, the head of SMH Italy, added:

> . . . the appeal of Swatch rests on four pillars: design, communication in the widest sense, quality and price. Few people appreciate how and why price has been so important. Everywhere in the world, Swatch is sold at an affordable price . . . Despite our incredible success in the market . . . we have never raised the price of Swatch . . . Can you name another fashion product whose price has stayed exactly the same for ten years . . . Price becomes a mirror for the other attributes we try to communicate . . . A Swatch is not just affordable, it's approachable. Buying a Swatch is an easy decision to make, an easy decision to live with. It's provocative. But it doesn't make you think too much.

The success of Swatch set the stage for the spectacular comeback of the Swiss watch industry. Hayek said:

> Swatch . . . restored our credibility with the public. It has restored our credibility with the trade. The perception of Swiss watches today is so different from ten years ago . . . . We have re-established our technical superiority over the Japanese watchmakers . . . I really believe the phenomenal success of these $40 watches helps create the climate for selling $500 watches, or $5,000 watches, for that matter . . . . If we can build beautiful, high quality watches that sell for only $40, imagine what must be the quality and accuracy of watches that sell for $2,000!

By 1991, Swiss watch production was 15.9 per cent of global volume (up from 9.3 per cent level in 1983) and its value share had jumped to 52.8 per cent, up from 38.5 per cent in 1983. Brand image, aesthetics and craftsmanship became the new selling points for Swiss watches, especially the mechanical watches which dominated the high price end of the market.[10] Technology, which had given Japanese watch industry a leading edge, stopped being a major source of competitive advantage after the mid-1980s. Thus, in the 1990s, the Japanese watchmakers were left floundering in the middle with neither the brand image of a premium product nor the low price of the Hong Kong watches and more recently the even lower prices of Chinese watches.

The Indian Watch Industry: Titanic Changes

In many ways, developments in the Indian watch industry during the last ten years resemble the developments in the global watch industry, albeit with a time lag. The second foray of the Tata group, India's largest industrial house, into the watch industry radically changed the face of the Indian industry. Earlier, in the late 1970s, Tatas had acquired a 10 per cent stake in the Bangalore-based watch company, Hegde & Golay, with an intent to acquire a majority stake in it. This, however, failed to fructify. Xerxes Desai, the then CEO of Tata Press, a group company, who had spearheaded the Tata effort, said 'the affairs of Hegde & Golay were so messy that we got out of it'. The company, which even at the time of the takeover bid was floundering, eventually faded out of the watch market and closed down in the early 1980s.

10. Yet another noticeable trend in the late 1980s was the entry of fashion designers like Pierre Cardin, Cartier and Gucci into the watch industry. They began putting their names on watches, buying the 'guts' from others. They sought to carve out a share at the very-high-price end of the market. These watches were often specially designed for the customer and the face and the bracelet of the watch were typically set with precious stones.

In 1981, having been aware of the Tata group's desire to enter the watch industry, I.M. Mahadevan, chairman and managing director of TIDCO, invited the Tatas to team up with TIDCO. TIDCO was seeking an Indian partner to collaborate with.[11] It had already commenced negotiations with the French watch movement manufacturing company, France Ebauches, for accessing technology. The Tatas accepted the invitation. However, the government approval took three years to fructify. Xerxes Desai, who continued to spearhead the Tata effort, said: 'Our entry into watches was attempted to be blocked by various lobbies.—the anti-big business lobby, the smugglers lobby, Indian manufacturers like HMT, bureaucrats, etc. It was only after Rajiv Gandhi became prime minister that the situation changed and we were given the go-ahead.'

Titan, the Tata-TIDCO joint sector company, came into being in July 1984, with Desai at the helm. The company set up its corporate office in Bangalore, and located its 2 million watch manufacturing facility in Hosur, which was approximately 30 km away from Bangalore, in Tamil Nadu. According to Desai:

> The reason we chose Hosur was its proximity to Bangalore, the centre of HMT's watch operations. Based at Hosur it would be easier for us, we felt, to draw people out from HMT, particularly people with technical and managerial experience. To put it straight, we aimed to raid HMT and we did it. It turned out to be good for us and for them. HMT was grossly overstaffed and promotional avenues at the top were not many.

Titan opted to manufacture only quartz watches. According to Desai:

> Initially we thought of making both mechanical and quartz watches, but on second thoughts we chose to put everything into quartz. A sensible move, considering the huge investments required today to set up a mechanical watch plant. Also HMT had left the market wide open for new entrants. They were just making a handful of ordinary-looking quartz watches, which was what Citizen considered fit for India. We realised that HMT had neglected quartz and styling altogether. It had grossly underestimated the Indian consumer's desire to own a good-looking watch.

11. The Government of India as a part of its effort to step up watch production in the country had granted TIDCO the licence to manufacture watches. The other recipients were predominantly small-scale units.

Titan launched its quartz range in March 1987 with heavy advertising support. Titan positioned its quartz watch as an international watch from the Tata group. The first advertisement described the Titan quartz as 'The international watch you can pay for in rupees'. It followed this up with 'You don't need to pay in dollars, pounds or dirhams to buy a Titan watch' and 'To find watches like these, you don't have to go to Europe, Japan, America or a duty free shop'. The Titan campaign also stressed the watch as a gift item, with ads saying : 'The next time your husband wants to buy a saree, ask him for a Titan watch'.[12] The Titan campaign was an enormous success. It gave the company what K.S. Gergan, HMT's executive director (watches), described as 'a great deal of visibility'.

The thematic campaign was supported by full-page colour catalogue ads in newspapers and magazines which displayed Titan's wide range of watches. Ravi Kant, the then vice president (marketing), had said, 'My watches are my salesmen. You won't see skimpily dressed models or anything like that. The product is the model and our hero.'[13]

At the time of Titan's entry the consumer had a total of 400 models to choose from across various brands and companies. Titan entered with 200 models of its own and rapidly expanded its product range to over 850 models.[14] The company's product development cell, manned mainly by graphic designers, and headed by Desai (who also said that it was more enjoyable designing a watch than running a company!), devoted its time and efforts to thinking up ways to expand the market. Principally their focus was on (a) encouraging ownership of multiple watches; (b) preponement of the watch replacement decision; (c) preponement of the acquisition of the first watch, and (d) increasing the usership in low ownership segments like women.

The Retail Revolution

Titan opted to bypass the wholesale channel. It reached out to the retail channel directly.

12. Titan later wooed corporate houses to use the watch as a gift/reward/promotional item. It embossed the logo of the client company on such watches.
13. He later left Titan to join the troubled two-wheeler venture LML-Piaggio, and went on to successfully turn that company around.
14. To dispel consumer apprehension about the quartz battery cells, Titan made efforts to ensure that these were readily available and at a reasonable price.

> Bhaskar Bhat, Titan's vice president (marketing and sales) said: 'Before Titan, all watch manufacturers used to go through wholesalers, who naturally had a stranglehold on the distribution set-up. As a result, there was a high level of dissatisfaction among retailers. Also, the manufacturers tended to be out of touch with the retail point. It was not controlled distribution.'

Titan, while launching its watches, held a national launch conference, to which even the smallest retailer was invited. The Titan sales force was instructed to call on all retailers, regardless of whether or not they stocked the brand, and relentlessly sell the idea of Titan to them. Further, in order to maximise its reach, the company converted non-conventional outlets like jewellery stores, departmental stores and even auto dealers(!) into retail outlets for its brand.

Titan's innovations on the retailing front, however, did not end there. In December 1987, nine months after the launch, the company opened its own retail showroom. The showroom was a phenomenal success as it radically altered the consumer's in-shop experience. Following the success of its first showroom, Titan rapidly expanded its showroom network. By 1995, the company had over seventy showrooms (bulk of them franchised) in over fifty cities. Titan showrooms stocked Titan watches exclusively and the company paid the franchisees higher margins to compensate for opportunity losses.

Until the emergence of Titan showrooms, watch outlets in India had traditionally been dreary places, small and dark, usually located in the general market area of a town and one that a consumer could never casually walk into for a casual look. Titan showrooms changed all this. They were an easily recognisable landmark located in the most fashionable shopping centres. External show windows created the initial appeal to lure the consumer into the showroom. Research done by Titan while planning the showrooms had shown that a majority of people, on entering an unfamiliar environment, tended to walk closer to the left. So most of the showrooms had doors opening to the left. The customer walked past a long display stand of Titan watches—or, to use a Titan phrase, mood windows—and finally reached the sales counter, by which time hopefully his/her appetite for a Titan watch was strong enough for him/her to buy one happily and be proud of his/her purchase.

Titan showrooms had yet another beneficial spin-off. The success of the showrooms resulted in traditional watch dealers wanting to upgrade their properties. Titan then started a scheme of converting some of these outlets into Titan shops which would primarily be Titan dealers, though they would stock other brands.

Titan's efforts paid off handsomely. At the time of Titan's entry, Allwyn had a 54.55 per cent share of the quartz market while HMT had the rest. The company quickly displaced Allwyn as the market leader in quartz. Desai attributes the company's success to it having redefined the watch market. According to him: 'We saw the watch as something more than a time-keeping device. A watch has to fit your lifestyle, your mood and what you are wearing. Apart from that, a good watch brand must confer status. A Titan watch did all that.'

Integrating Backwards

At the time of receiving the approval for the manufacture of watches, Titan was not given permission to manufacture the other parts of a watch like cases, dials and straps. These were to be sourced locally. However, Titan's experience with domestic suppliers was largely unsatisfactory. According to Desai, the non-availability of appearance watch parts held up Titan's growth. To overcome this problem, the company embarked on a backward integration drive.

The company, after a delayed receipt of government's approval, set up an in-house case manufacturing facility with technical support from Citizen, Japan. To overcome its dependence on imports for step motors, the company set up an in-house facility to manufacture step motors. Titan also planned to set up its own case dial manufacturing facility. The company, however, shelved this project when a Bangalore-based unit, Kamla Dials, set up such a facility in March 1992 and whose output fulfilled all of its specifications.

Further, to ensure supply of high quality straps, Titan assisted Hirsch of Austria, a world leader in leather straps, to set up a leather strap manufacturing unit at Hosur. The unit began commercial production in late 1993 and Titan entered into a contract to buy the unit's entire production for a minimum period of three years. The company was also working on a project to set up a unit to produce quality folded sheet metal bracelets in association with a Japanese manufacturer.

Titan also became the first watch manufacturer to produce ECBs. The company set up a 5 million ECB facility at Goa jointly with the Economic Development Corporation of Goa. Titan Time Products Limited—the joint venture—commenced manufacture of ECBs in November 1992.

Expanding the Scale and Scope

Titan's response to its success was twofold. One was to expand its capacity of quartz from the initial 2 million to 4 million watches (in two stages), and the other was to expand the scope of its operations and achieve a wider market presence.[15] The strategy it followed was to move further upmarket with the Titan brand—it had started with the middle and the premium segments—and fill the vacuum that would result from its upgradation for good quality low to middle segment priced watches with another brand.

In 1990, the company tied up with Timex, USA, to cater to the low–middle segment. In fact, the company signed an MOU with Casio, Japan, in 1989 for this purpose, but it failed to fructify. Titan, meanwhile, launched its Aqura range of polyamide watches to have a presence in this segment. According to Desai, the Aqura experience gave the company the confidence to invest in Timex.

Timex, USA, had earlier entered into a tie-up with Jayna Times. The tie-up, however, was short-lived. Timex then scouted around for another Indian partner familiar with the domestic business environment. Its search coincided with Titan's search for an alternative to Casio. The two companies agreed, in October 1990, to set up a joint venture. Desai said: 'It was necessary to float another company as Titan was looking at the high range—above Rs 25,000—market of jewellery watches. It would not look good if that same company marketed watches that occupied the lower segment of the market.'

The joint venture—Timex Watches Limited (TWL)—was set up specifically to cater to the low–middle segment. According to R.J. Masilamani, managing director, TWL, the joint venture company was set up to basically target first-time users and to try and convert mechanical watch users to quartz.

> Desai explained: 'The Timex product range is a result of a carefully thought out strategy to address the untapped potential in the market and deliver quality products at affordable prices. The two product ranges (Titan and Timex) would complement each other, address different consumer segments and would not come into conflict. There would be a marginal overlap of price ranges but there would not be any wasteful competition.'

---

15. The company was in the third phase of expanding its capacity further to 5 million watches.

To eliminate 'wasteful' competition, Titan transferred its Aqura range to the new company. Desai said, 'The agreement between the two companies ensures that Titan keeps out of plastic watches while Timex keeps out of metal.' Further, under the agreement, Timex was to manufacture the watches and Titan was to market and distribute them.

Timex, which had its manufacturing facility at Noida, near Delhi, launched its watches in October 1992, with high decibel advertising which positioned the product as a solid watch with style. The campaign was woven around adventure sports like rafting and rock climbing and sought to leverage the Timex, USA, and Tata connections. The product range comprised over 200 styles in four distinct categories in terms of both price and styling. The Timex Lextra was at the bottom of the price range with fairly sober and conventional designs. The next category was Timex Aqura, priced higher than Lextra but with more youthful and trendy designs. The third category was the Timex Sports, a high-tech, rugged, multifunction category—branded Gimmix—that comprised colourful watches with whacky designs and was meant for children below 12 years of age. Later, in November 1993, soon after Timex USA launched its Indiglo range, which was based on what has been described as the most amazing technological innovation in watches since the quartz and which was rated by *Fortune* magazine as the 1993 Product of the Year, TWL launched it in the Indian market. The Indiglo range was priced at the premium end.

Timex met with quick success, partly due to its having piggybacked on Titan's established distribution network. During 1993–94, the first full year of operations, the company sold a million watches. The success, however, was partial. The company found that while its franchise among the owners of multiple watches was very strong, its performance was rather weak in the first-time owners and true replacers segments, who constituted over half the market. Mechanical watches continued to dominate the first, while the latter was dominated by other quartz watches, principally by Titan and HMT. Further, the company also found that while it had strong brand franchise among those below twenty years and those above forty years of age, its performance in the crucial twenty to forty age group—which constituted nearly two-thirds of the market—was rather poor. Similarly, the company's performance outside the metros and among the blue-collar segment was rather weak. Mechanical watches continued to dominate these two segments as well.

Timex realised its 'only plastic watches' strategy would not enable it to wrest the leadership of the mass market, which perceived metal to be more reliable than plastic. To overcome this disadvantage and to broaden its appeal to the mass market, the company, in October 1994, launched its metal range of watches branded Vista.[16] The Vista was launched with fifty-five different styles and in the Rs 475–950 price range. Though the lowest priced Vista was higher than HMT's bottom range of mechanical watches, the company expected its larger and more stylish range and quartz appeal would persuade the consumer to overlook the price differential.

The company also planned to widen the distribution network to tap the rural segments. Masilamani said, 'The urban segment will soon reach a saturation point and to stay ahead in the market, it will be essential to tap the smaller towns and the interior markets.'

Further, the Titan–Timex distribution network was being bifurcated into two distinct channels in order to achieve 'harder' push for the Timex range. Timex also planned to have separate Timex showrooms which would be different from Titan showrooms. These showrooms, in keeping with the company's brand image, were to be more trendy.

Going International

France Ebauches, from whom Titan had sourced its movement technology, had, at the time of entering into the technology arrangement, agreed to buy back a part of Titan's production of watch movements. Titan commenced export of movements in 1989. However, the company was keen on selling the value-added watch in the international market instead of selling the movements. This led the company to launch, in 1991, its watch range in the Middle East market. Despite stiff competition from the global majors, Titan, within a year of its launch, achieved sales of over 100,000 watches. The company's watches were available in the UAE, Bahrain, Qatar and Oman and the company was in the process of adding Kuwait and Saudi Arabia to this list. The company followed up on the Middle East effort by launching its watches in the UK market in 1993. Its intention was to gain first-hand experience of operating in Western markets.

The experience it gained from these overseas forays, coupled with its success in the domestic market, emboldened the company to push for what Desai described as the 'big opportunity'. According to Desai, 'The next professional challenge Titan had to face was to compete in the world market.'

16. Also, given the economics of its operations, Timex, to break even, needed to sell 1.5 million watches per annum.

The company decided against the 'soft option' of driving its internationalisation through private label exports. Desai said:

> It's not only a question of exporting. It's a question of finding the right product at the right price, to be sold at the right place. Competing with the best in the world, establishing your brand as an Indian brand, that's where the honour and glory lie. In private label export, you're building things for someone else's brand. There is no honour and glory in that! No ego satisfaction! You are a serf!

The company zeroed in on the European market to announce its arrival in the global arena. According to Desai, 'It had to be Europe. For watches, Europe is the testing ground.' The company then hired leading European designers, on a time-sharing contract, to design a distinctive watch collection to spearhead its entry into the world market. The company also set up a separate manufacturing facility (capacity 200,000) for manufacturing 'Eurowatches'.

Titan, after an extensive survey of the European market, found that accommodation of a new brand was a very big decision for a retail store because it had to displace some other. To address this problem, the company, in 1994, participated in the world-renowned Basle Fair—an annual event in which the world's biggest watch and jewellery manufacturers customarily participate. According to Desai, the rationale for participation was to seek out distributors and partners rather than selling what it had (the company had unveiled its Eurowatch range at the fair). Jacob Kurien, general manager (international operations), said: 'We were somewhat overwhelmed by the amount of interest in Titan and its plans. We have seen interest from major watch distributors and major companies, the kind we hoped to receive but did not expect.'

Soon thereafter, Titan inducted a French watch industry veteran and the man credited with establishing Seiko in Europe, Jacques Meyer, to the board of its London-headquartered overseas subsidiary, Titan International Marketing Limited.[17] Meyer, who had a wealth of distribution contacts throughout the Continent, was to spearhead Titan's operation of setting up distributors and retail outlets and position the watches, which were to be priced at between $75 and $750. According to Desai, 'Meyer sees in Titan what he saw in Seiko in the 1960s.'

17. Titan later set up yet another subsidiary—Titan Holdings BV—in the Netherlands. This subsidiary was to operate as a holding company and oversee its global operations.

The Jewellery Range

Very early in its drive for a global presence, Titan realised that its watches alone might not be able to prise open the global market. The company then sought to leverage India's traditional strength and global reputation in jewellery and diversified into manufacturing jewellery and jewellery watches. Its strategy was to lead with jewellery and follow it up with premier watches.

> Desai said: 'Jewellery gives us one foot in the door because Indian jewellery is a credible story in Europe. Given this splendid entry point, we knew watches could ride in next, despite the present domination of Switzerland and Japan. Of course, at one stage, we hope our watches will help sell our jewellery.'

The company started the manufacture of its jewellery and jewellery watches in 1994.[18] It launched these products—branded Tanishq—in the domestic market in late 1994. And the stage was set for launching Tanishq in the European market in 1995. The company had spectacular dreams for its jewellery range. Desai said:

> The world trade in finished diamonds alone is $40 bn and that's the price the jewellers pay. The retail prices are at heavy mark-ups. World consumption of gold is 2500 tonnes. Multiply that by $340 an ounce. Imagine the numbers if we can get even a small share of the business!

Desai, however, was cautious about success. He said, 'One may put everything right, but, after all, this is a consumer durable where there is always the element of the unpredictable.'

The Leader's Response

Titan's entry did not provoke an immediate response from HMT. Titan's entry was, in fact, welcomed by HMT. K.S. Gergan, HMT's executive director (watches), said: 'Titan's coming into the watch industry is a good move. They have a sense of purpose. Mechanical watches are still a lucrative segment for us. For Titan, it's a do-or-die situation—either sell quartz or wind up.'

18. To reflect the change, the company also changed its name to Titan Industries Limited.

The company believed the market was large enough for all manufacturers to sell their output in different segments of the market. The company did not perceive any need to reorient its marketing policy. Gergan said:

> The marketing policy of HMT is governed by the fact it is the largest manufacturer in the country, catering to a wide segment of consumers. We are looking at a market that consists of 800 million people and not only 150 million that everybody else is talking about. Further, in our assessment, the demand for mechanical watches will continue. There may be a slight decline but a fairly large segment of the rural and semi-urban markets still have a strong preference for these ranges of watches.

However, the rapid growth of Titan led HMT, in 1988, to (a) commission a market research study by IMRB, the country's leading market research agency and (b) bring the quartz watch, which it had almost completely sidelined by that time, back into its marketing agenda. Though the company added ana-digi watches to its portfolio, it continued to essentially compete with the four basic designs with which it had launched its quartz range in 1981.

The IMRD findings were revealing. One of the principal findings was that the awareness levels among consumers for HMT's quartz watches was very low! The finding prompted the company to substantially step up its advertising effort, albeit reluctantly. Gergan had said, 'I personally think we are all overdoing it. It does not fetch you much. The only gainers are the ad agencies.'

The findings of the study and the burgeoning growth of Titan's quartz range prompted the company to revamp its quartz portfolio. It recognised the importance of aesthetics in a watch and came out with a new range. In 1990, the company launched this new range of quartz 'dress' watches, assembled from original Citizen watch kits. The watches, branded HMT Elegance, were priced between Rs 1,600 and Rs 3,000. The company's strategy was to pre-emptively carve out a share at the top end of the market (Titan had no presence in this price segment at that time) while simultaneously upgrading its image. The high profile advertising support given to Elegance yielded results. According to Gergan, 'People started enquiring about our watches.'

HMT did not restrict its response to revamping its product portfolio. In fact, the Elegance launch highlighted the urgent need to revamp its distribution network. The company had encountered problems retailing its Elegance range. The 'elite watch' could not be sold through the usual HMT retailer, nor could it be sold through the branch office showroom. Neither provided the requisite 'ambience'. The company then embarked on setting up exclusive showrooms called Time Art—both its own and franchised. The company also increased the retailers' margins and wooed them with schemes like the 'sell-and-win-scheme', where winners were given free trips to Bangkok, Singapore and Hong Kong.

In 1991, the company set up, for the first time, a product development centre for watch design. M.R. Naidu, the then chairman of HMT, said:

> We recognise the emerging competition in quartz watches and a market that is becoming increasingly stratified. HMT, as the largest watch manufacturer in the country, is accepting this challenge by expanding its product range and enhancing the excellence and sophistication of its products.

If You Have the Inclination, We Have the Time. Plenty of Time

In 1991, the company launched its Astra and Pace range of watches. Both were mid-priced 'plastic' watches (price range Rs 350–700). While Pace was targeted at teenagers (and competed with Allwyn's Trendy and Titan's Aqura), the Astra was aimed at slightly older buyers and was positioned as a multifunctional watch. And in 1992 the company pre-empted Titan once again, by being the first to launch watches for children—branded Zap! The HMT advertisements now said, 'If you have the inclination, we have the time. Plenty of time', to highlight the choice the consumer could now get from the company.

All the new brands, whose launch was well supported by high advertising spends, met with great success. The company could not keep pace with the demand for these watches and consumers often went back without being able to buy these watches. The demand for these products had caught the company unawares. The company's limited capacity to manufacture quartz watches proved to be a constraint. The company then embarked on converting its Tumkur mechanical watch facility into a quartz one.[19]

19. To enhance capacity the company had even considered the takeover of Allwyn's watch unit in 1992. Allwyn, after suffering a severe setback in the late 1980s, largely due to internal strife, had virtually withdrawn from the market. The Andhra Pradesh government then sought to sell off the watch division and HMT had bid for it. The deal, however, fell through as HMT was not willing to buy Allwyn's watch unit lock, stock and barrel, because of the huge accumulated losses, high manpower surplus and piled up inventory. HMT then offered to provide managerial and administrative support and this was not acceptable to the government. After an extensive search over the next two years, the Andhra Pradesh government decided to sell the unit to the BPL group, a leading manufacturer of consumer electronics. The BPL group was yet to take over the reigns of

In 1993, HMT launched its Utsav and Roman range of watches. The Utsav range was launched as an answer to Titan's Raga and came in the form of bracelets, bangles and costume jewellery watches. The Roman, on the other hand, was targeted at the male segment. Targeting the male segment was a fallout of the findings of a market research study which revealed that the consumer perceived Titan as being slightly feminine. Further, the Roman watch was the first HMT watch which did not say that the watch was 'from HMT' on its face—a significant departure from the company's over-three-decade-old practice. The Roman received an excellent response from the consumer who was attracted by the macho, male image of the watch. However, once again, the consumer found that the Roman watch was not easily available. In addition to production lagging behind, poor availability was caused by disruptions in the company's distribution network. The company's decision, in September 1992, to bypass the resistance from the wholesale trade and switch over to Titan-style distribution through C&F agents met with fierce resistance from the wholesale trade, causing the disruption.

Despite these launches, the company continued to lose market share to Titan. According to M. Jagannath, HMT's former general manager (marketing):

> It's the price you pay for being the leader. In a way we created the competition to ourselves. HMT had to create an indigenous base and infrastructure for quartz watches in the country, which we did. But even as the company was concentrating on these, Titan built the awareness for quartz watches and its brands through high-profile advertising.

The price HMT paid was not confined to loss of market share. In 1992–93, the watch division slipped into the red (estimated loss of over Rs 100 mn) as watch sales declined from 6.7 million units in 1991–92 to 5.4 million units.[20] In 1993-94, the performance worsened. Watch sales declined to 4.5 million units and the division made losses estimated at Rs 600 mn, out of the total loss of over Rs 1,170 mn incurred by the whole company in that year. Importantly, for the first time in its over-three-decade-old history, the company was not the

the company, although, according to the MOU signed, it was to take over the management of the company with effect from October 1994. The BPL group had asked for certain concessions to be granted, including considerable interest waiver from financial institutions and sharing of the accumulated losses of Allwyn by the government, before taking over the ailing unit. The new party in power in Andhra Pradesh was yet to decide about granting the concessions sought by the BPL group.

20. Partly owing to disturbances in Jammu and Kashmir which resulted in the closure of its Srinagar plant.

undisputed leader of the Indian watch industry. The company had ceded market leadership in terms of value to Titan. The company, however, remained the leader in terms of volume.

This disastrous performance also caused a deterioration in the company's internal working environment. Accusations started flying thick and fast. The HMT Officers' Federation held the top management of the company 'to be solely responsible for the downfall of HMT'. And the workers' union appealed to the government to induct 'professionals into the top management to revive the sagging fortunes of the company'.

Restructuring

In order to revive itself HMT embarked on a restructuring exercise. The exercise was based on the report submitted to the company by the Japan International Cooperation Agency (JICA) jointly with the World Bank in 1992. The JICA report made an exhaustive SWOT analysis of each of HMT's divisions and outlined a short-term and a long-term strategy for the company. Gergan said: 'By rationalising product range, getting rid of sloppiness and acquiring a savvy image, JICA's targets of 12 million watches in 1996–97 and 17.5 million in 1999–2000 are achievable.'

The company restructured its various businesses into four distinct groups: capital goods (comprising machine tools, industrial machinery and the tractors division); engineering components (casting and forging and bearings); consumer goods (watches and lamps) and services (trading, software and technical consultancy). The plan was to spin off each of these four groups into subsidiaries so that they could eventually be converted into joint ventures with foreign companies.

> P.C. Neogy, chairman and managing director of the company, explained: 'I am seeking four things: global market, state-of-the-art technology, funds and informational technology architecture. Only an international partner can give us all four.'

Neogy was confident that HMT would regain its competitiveness and leadership. He said: 'It will require tremendous effort. But if all of us put our hearts and souls into the job, I am confident we can make it happen . . . . We will have to change the way we think and work; we're talking about a total cultural transformation.'

In May 1994, the watch division entered into an agreement with ISA Quartz of France, under which ISA would supply its latest watch modules, along with the necessary appearance parts such as dials and cases, to the company on a most favoured customer basis. HMT was to use these modules to cater to the high price segment of the market, where Titan had a much bigger presence. ISA was also to supply HMT with the tools and jigs required for assembly, provide training free of charge to HMT personnel and help HMT revamp its production. The agreement was to be a precursor to the formation of a joint venture with ISA.

In 1994–95, HMT released 200,000 watches which were assembled from the imported ISA modules into the market under existing brand names. Gergan, who continued to oversee the watch division as director of the consumer products group, said: 'We are at the first stage of our plans with ISA. The release of 200,000 watches is aimed at testing the waters. The next stage of our collaboration will be setting up of a joint venture with them to make modules.'

During the year, the company also test-marketed watches with dials imported from Fraporlux, France. Based on the market feedback, the company planned to enter into a technical tie-up with the company and invest in machinery to make the dials.

These efforts, however, could not arrest the decline in watch sales and the company ceded even its volume leadership to Titan. In 1994–95, Titan sold 3.2 million watches as against HMT's sales of 3 million.

Thus, for the first time since its inception in the 1960s, the domestic watch industry, at a time when it was gearing itself to meet the coming onslaught from multinational players, did not have HMT at its helm as the leader (see Appendices 4–10)

The MNC Challenge

In 1995, the threat to the domestic watch industry from multinational players was very real. According to Desai, vice chairman of both Titan and Timex:

> The threat to Indian brands will come from three different directions. At the very top end of the market, the threat will be from the Swiss. The second threat comes from the Japanese, i.e., Seiko, Citizen and Casio. And the third threat will be from what I call the unholy alliance between China, Hong Kong and the Middle East. It is essentially the Chinese products that are at the lower end. So I think the biggest threat will initially be from watches of Chinese origin.'

Numerous foreign brands—Rado, Omega, Longines, Citizen, Casio, etc.—had already started advertising in the country. The Swiss had gone one step ahead. With a view 'to pre-empt competition (i e., the Japanese) and stitch up deals before the rivals arrive', the Federation of the Swiss Watch industry organised an exhibition of Swiss watches in Bombay. The who's who of the Swiss industry—Blancpain, Cartier, Omega, Piaget, Rado, etc.—displayed their watches (they were not permitted to sell) in the exhibition held in mid-1994. The exhibition was a huge success as it attracted a large number of people. Francois Habersaat, President of the Federation of Swiss Watch Industry, said:

> We from the federation were here to smell the Indian market for our businessmen and I am quite amazed at the response. We have made some great contacts. I think India has a very large market waiting to be tapped.

Most foreign companies planning to enter India were unlikely to set up manufacturing facilities in India. They were likely to establish a presence only through assembly and distribution tie-ups.[21] The Swiss giant SMH had already initiated negotiations with Titan for marketing their products in India. Desai said:

> The only way they can get in is through our shops. We are willing to provide them a distribution channel, but on our terms. We want in exchange some fine watch movements that the Swiss have never given to foreigners.

Titan, even as it was negotiating with the Swiss, decided to spin off its Titan showrooms into a new retail chain under the name 'World Time'. Titan planned to promote the new retail chain in a big way. The company constituted a separate cell which was to operate as an independent profit centre, to look after the World Time retail chain.[22] The company also planned to rename the Titan shops as 'Prime Time' shops. Desai said:

21. Seiko was exploring the possibility of an equity stake in Allwyn.
22. Titan showrooms and Titan shops together accounted for over 30 per cent of the company's turnover.

> We are planning to rebrand and promote our retail chain, presently sharing the Titan brand name, as an independent entity next year. This will enable us to sell multiple brands without creating between brands at the retail point.

A marketing arrangement with some of the Swiss manufacturers, however, did not imply that Titan was not readying itself for battling the multinationals. As part of their strategy to combat competition from multinationals, both Titan and Timex planned to further strengthen their distribution network. Masilamani, managing director of Timex, said: 'The only possible way to outposition them (the new entrants) is to enter the interiors by building a strong distribution and retailing network.' To achieve this, according to him, Titan and Timex had plans to go into collaboration with a corporate giant which had a strong presence in the interior segment and a penetrative distribution network. 'It can be anyone, even Godrej', he said. Further, according to Desai:

> Titan is raising barriers to the entry of foreign competition in every possible way—by having a wide selection of products in terms of looks, functions and price and by giving very good value for money. We have not succumbed to the temptation of raising prices.[23]
>
> We kept the prices down and tried to do with lean margins. Then we developed a very strong brand equity, a strong retail presence and dealer loyalty. We also increased our advertising budget. Our ad budget for next year is slated to be around Rs 300 mn. Anyone wanting to enter India will have to do all these things to be able to make a dent. And, of course, we will definitely attack anyone entering the market.

Desai assessed the challenge posed by MNCs as a serious one, though, in his opinion, the Indian watch industry enjoyed a comparative advantage in the manufacture of quality watches. He said:

> The watch majors in India do not manufacture cheap or suspect quality products. This is our competency and we will have to build on this strength . . . The Indian watch industry would probably have to offer a greater variety in terms of looks and functions. It has to cater to both upmarket and downmarket segments. The bulk of the products today are in the Rs 500 to Rs 1,500 price range. The watch majors do not

23. Both Titan and Timex had slashed prices on a number of their models immediately after the grant of reliefs—primarily reduction in import duties of components—to the watch industry in the 1994–95 Union budget. Both the companies, unlike HMT, which had almost fully indigenised its watch manufacturing, benefited from the reduction in import duties.

offer much of a choice in the price segments below Rs 500 and above Rs 1,500.

Discussion Questions

- What was HMT's position at the time of Titan's entry? What entry barriers had HMT created?
- Why was Titan successful? What were Titan's strategies?
- Evaluate HMT's response.
- Why did the Swiss lose leadership of the global watch industry? How did they regain it?
- Assess the performance of Timex in the Indian market place?
- Should Titan be going global?
- Assess Titan's strategy to counter MNC competition.

APPENDIX 1

Mechanical Watch and Movements Exports as Percentage of Total Exported, 1960–84

	1960	1970	1975	1980	1982	1984
Switzerland	100.0	99.6	98.1	80.4	50.8	29.4
Japan	100.0	NA	NA	33.6	16.5	8.5
Hong Kong	–	NA	NA	28.7	15.1	7.6
France	100.0	94.4	98.2	75.5	60.7	45.1
West Germany	100.0	85.8	84.7	50.7	29.2	16.8

APPENDIX 2

World Watch Production, 1985–93

(in millions)

	1985	1986	1987	1988	1989	1990	1991	1992	1993
Quartz	173	200	227	302	345	400	472	NA	559
(%) of total	(37.20)	(35.84)	(38.80)	(46.25)	(50.36)	(50.00)	(57.63)		(59.47)
Digital	149	225	230	228	225	300	245	NA	254
(%) of total	(32.04)	(40.32)	(39.32)	(34.92)	(32.85)	(37.50)	(29.91)		(27.02)
Mechanical	143	133	128	123	115	100	102	NA	127
(%) of total	(30.75)	(23.84)	(21.88)	(18.84)	(16.79)	(12.50)	(12.45)		(13.51)
Total	465	558	585	653	685	800	819	NA	940
Growth		20.00	4.84	11.62	4.90	16.79	2.38	NA	–

APPENDIX 3

World Consumption of Watches in 1993

Region	*Consumption/1000 persons*
North America	725
Western Europe	590
Japan	415
China	065
India	012
World average	157

APPENDIX 4

HMT Watch Operations

Year	*Installed Capacity (Million)*	*Production (Million)*		*Sales (Million)*		*Total Sales Volume (Million)*	*Turnover (Rs crore)*	*Profit (Rs crore)*
		Mech.	*Quartz*	*Mech.*	*Quartz*			
1985–86	4.8	4.370	0.160	4.390	0.210	4.600	122.30	NA
1986–87	5.1	4.800	0.200	4.880	0.200	5.080	139.10	NA
1987–88	6.1	4.640	0.310	4.720	0.260	4.980	142.20	NA
1988–89	6.1	5.390	0.440	5.560	0.350	5.910	187.40	NA
1989–90	7.1	NA	NA	NA	NA	NA	NA	NA
1990–91	7.1	5.510	0.810	5.120	0.830	5.950	218.27	NA
1991–92	7.1	5.530	1.450	5.400	1.300	6.700	284.58	NA
1992–93	7.1	4.399	1.274	4.188	1.299	5.420	212.00	-10.00
1993–94	7.1	2.326	0.637	2.022*	0.611*	2.630*	99.93	-60.00
1994–95	7.1	2.249	0.601	2.502	0.519	3.020	NA	NA

* This figure does not include 'sales made to retailers'. Until the previous year, the company used to include even such sales—called Goods Held in Trust, even though the watches were lying with the company and were not yet paid for by the retailers—in its sales figures. In 1993–94, sales made to consumers from the retail counters were estimated to be 4.53 million watches—3.47 million mechanical watches and 1.06 million quartz watches.

APPENDIX 5

Allwyn Watch Operations

Year	*Installed Capacity (Million)*	*Production (Million)*	*Sales (Million)*	*Turnover (Rs crore)*	*Profit (Rs crore)*
1985–86	NA	NA	NA	NA	NA
1986–87	NA	NA	NA	NA	NA
1987–88	1.6	1.150	1.14	44.03	NA
1988–89	2.0	NA	1.35	NA	NA
1989–90	2.0	NA	NA	NA	NA
1990–91	2.0	0.834	NA	34.98	NA
1991–92	2.0	NA	NA	NA	NA
1992–93	2.0	NA	NA	NA	NA
1993–94	2.0	NA	NA	NA	NA
1994–95	2.0	NA	0.32	NA	NA

APPENDIX 6

Titan Watch Operations

Year	*Installed Capacity (Million)*	*Production (Million)*	*Sales Volume (Million)*	*Turnover (Rs crore)*	*Profit After Tax (Rs crore)*
1985–86	–	–	–	–	–
1986–87	2.0	0.08	0.05	02.40	-0.05
1887–88	2.0	0.39	0.34	16.80	0.26
1988–89	2.0	0.51	0.51	27.60	1.07
1989–90	2.5	1.35	1.30	70.00	4.33
1990–91	3.0	2.03	2.03	106.26	9.11
1991–92	3.0	2.26	2.24	155.50	11.10
1992–93	3.0	2.60	2.57	192.82	10.87
1993–94	3.0	2.92	2.78	228.81	19.09
1994–95 (Estimated)	4.0	3.35	3.20	300.00	NA

APPENDIX 7

Timex Watch Operations

Year	Installed Capacity (Million)	Production (Million)	Sales Volume (Million)	Turnover (Rs crore)	Profit After Tax (Rs crore)
1992–93	2.0	NA	0.4	NA	NA
1993–94	2.0	1.299	1.0	44.52	-0.84
1994–95	2.0	NA	NA	68.43	2.78

APPENDIX 8

Total Production in India

Year	Production (Million)	Growth
1985–86	6.50	–
1986–87	7.50	15.38
1987–88	9.00	20.00
1988–89	10.00	11.11
1989–90	11.70	17.00
1990–91	13.80	17.95
1991–92	12.60	-8.70
1992–93	11.30	-10.32
1993–94	9.80	-13.27
1994–95	10.50	7.14

APPENDIX 9

Estimated Market Shares

	1988-89	*1990-91*	*1993-94*
HMT	69.96	66.27	38.40
Titan	9.61	20.42	43.69
Allwyn	16.04	8.20	–
Timex	–	–	15.50
Others	4.39	5.11	02.41

APPENDIX 10

Estimated Advertising Expenditure

(Rs crore)*

Year	*HMT*	*Titan*	*Allwyn*	*Timex*
1989	1.58	1.87	1.53	–
1990	2.26	3.63	1.08	–
1991–92	8.75	9.52	1.24	–
1992–93	9.37	13.16	0.20	3.40
1993–94	9.56	16.06	NA	5.74
1994–95	2.29	20.00	NA	7.00

* 1 crore = 10 million.

Part 2
Building the Future

RELIANCE INDUSTRIES LIMITED: GROWTH AS A WAY OF LIFE

> We are happy to announce Dhirubhai Ambani as the Businessman of the Year 1993. As in past years, the selection was made by a panel of eminent and independent persons . . . The panel was unanimously of the view that due recognition must be given to the amazing rise of Dhirubhai from nowhere to the top of Indian industry . . . It is the fundamental impact that Dhirubhai Ambani has had on the Indian business scene that singled him out as the Businessman of the Year 1993.
>
> —*Business India*, 20 December 1993

This announcement, made in one of India's leading business journals, followed the emergence of Reliance Industries Limited (RIL) as India's No. 1 private

This case was written by Sumantra Ghoshal, Robert P. Baumann Professor of Strategic Leadership at the London Business School and J. Ramachandran, Professor of Management at the Indian Institute of Management, Bangalore. The authors are grateful to Reliance Industries Ltd for their help and support in writing the case and to the European Foundation for Management Development (EFMD) for funding the project, of which this case is a part. This case was first registered at the London Business School in 1999.

sector company, fulfilling a long cherished ambition of its founder chairman and managing director, Dhirajlal Hirachand Ambani—known and admired commonly throughout India as Dhirubhai. From an initial investment of a mere Rs 15,000 (less than $2000) in 1958 to start a trading house, followed by the setting up of his first tiny manufacturing facility in 1966, Dhirubhai has managed to build up a synthetic yarn, textiles and petrochemicals empire—one which had a market capitalisation in excess of Rs 80 bn (about $2.7 bn) in 1994 and was the only Indian entrant in *Business Week*'s listing of the fifty largest companies headquartered in developing countries. In India, Reliance was the foremost non-government company by almost every measure including revenues, profits, net worth and asset base. Between 1977, when RIL first went public, and March 1993, RIL's turnover has increased from Rs 1.2 bn to Rs 41.06 bn, operating profit from Rs 150 mn to Rs 8.81 bn, net profit from Rs 25 mn to Rs 3.22 bn, net worth from Rs 140 mn to Rs 26.13 bn and asset base from Rs 310 mn to Rs 46.41 bn (see Appendix 1 for financial summary). To fund this staggering growth RIL had mobilised over Rs 30 bn from the Indian public, increasing the number of its shareholders from 58,000 in 1977 to over 3.7 mn in 1993. An overwhelming majority of them held less than 100 shares and one of every four Indians who directly or indirectly owned company shares, owned shares in RIL.

This breathtaking growth rate of the past, however, would appear positively lethargic if the company managed to achieve its plans for the future. 'Growth has no limit in Reliance', according to Dhirubhai. 'I keep revising my vision. A vision has to be within reach, not in the air. It has to be achievable. I believe we can be a Rs 300 bn ($10 bn) company by the end of the century'. To achieve this ambition of another eight-fold growth in six years, the Reliance group was planning to invest over Rs 100 bn between 1994 and 1998 (see Appendix 2). Forty per cent of this investment was earmarked for expanding the polyester fibres and fibre intermediates businesses that would help the company emerge as the world's largest integrated producer of polyester. A bulk of the remaining 60 per cent was earmarked for setting up one of India's largest oil refineries—a logical next step in Reliance's relentless drive for vertical integration. Not included in the Rs 100 bn investment plan was the bid it had made in partnership with Enron, one of the world's fastest growing producers of crude oil and natural gas, for production of oil and gas in the offshore fields in India. By March 1994 the bid was successful, raising the company's growth prospects enormously as well as its investment requirements by another Rs 13 bn.

Amid all the external acclaim for its past accomplishments and the internal excitement of its future plans, the leadership team within the company was grappling in 1994 with a set of issues that would have a huge impact on the kind of company Reliance would be in the years to come.

1. First, there was a need to review the company's most fundamental strategic logic. The historical growth of RIL was built on a step-by-step process of backward integration from textiles and fibres to fibre intermediates and feedstocks and, finally, all the way to oil refining and exploration (see Appendix 3). The company took great pride in being the only large company in India to be totally focussed in a single vertical value chain.
   The radical changes in India's business environment raised the question: Should the company not think beyond this growth logic? With fast paced deregulation, a number of one-time opportunity windows were opening up in India in potentially giant sectors like telecom, power and insurance. Should the company use its proven competencies in mobilising large amounts of capital, in creating large new markets and in managing mega-projects to jump into these relatively unrelated businesses?
2. Inexorably linked with the question of future strategy was the issue of how the company should be organised and managed. Historically, Dhirubhai and his two sons, Mukesh and Anil Ambani, had been clearly and firmly the ultimate decision makers in the company. They were supported by a group of senior managers whose relative role and status within the company changed frequently within a loose organisational structure that was always in flux. With increasing size and complexity, this relatively ad-hoc but highly effective way of organising and managing the company might have reached its limits. The leadership team was reviewing various alternatives for its future organisation, almost all of which would require some significant changes in the internal roles and relationships within the senior management group and some 'adaptation' in the management style of the family members at the top of the hierarchy.
3. Finally, perhaps the biggest challenge for the company lay in the domain of people. It had so far managed the break-neck speed of growth by continuously bringing in talent from the outside. There was no time for consolidating the management team, for creating team spirit or for the systematic development of people from within. Having emerged as the largest company in India, there was a need to create a more organised process for nurturing and developing the company's

human resources, and this might require a far more radical change in the company's management style than any change in its strategy or formal structure.

The Growth History

A village school teacher's son, Dhirubhai had journeyed, at 17, to the West Asian port of Aden, in South Yemen, then a British colony, to 'earn his livelihood'. After working as a clerk for eight years with A. Beese & Co., a French firm that acted as agents for Shell Oil, he returned to India in 1959 after the change in the government there. He set up Reliance Commercial Corporation in Bombay with a total capital of Rs 15,000 and started operating from a shared office.[1] He exported ginger, cardamom, turmeric and other spices to the West Asian market where he had established links during his Aden stint. His most unusual export, however, was earth—a sheikh in Saudi Arabia was keen on cultivating a rose garden and needed a good soil mixture, and Dhirubhai supplied it!

He branched out to trading in fabrics and yarn in the early 1960s, following a heavy demand for rayon fabrics in India. He used the export replenishment license to import rayon into India and sold it at a premium in the local market. Later, when nylon started getting popular in India, he began exporting rayon fabrics from India and importing nylon in exchange. The healthy margins, ranging from 100 to 300 per cent, that import of nylon provided more than compensated for the loss he made on the export of rayon fabrics.

Finding good quality fabrics for export, however, was proving to be increasingly difficult. As a measure of backward integration, Dhirubhai started manufacturing operations in 1966. He imported four knitting machines involving an outlay of Rs 2.7 mn and started manufacturing fabrics for export at Naroda, Ahmedabad, 500 km north of Bombay. The then seventy-employee company, comprising primarily family members and friends who had been with him at Aden and who had since returned, achieved a turnover of Rs 9 mn and a profit of Rs 1.3 mn in 1967.

Towards the late 1960s, nylon, like rayon earlier, was losing ground to another man-made fibre—polyester. In 1971, to bring polyester into the country without

1. The name was subsequently changed to Reliance Textile Industries in the late 1960s and to Reliance Industries in the mid-1980s.

loss of foreign exchange, the Government of India announced a new scheme under which import of polyester was permitted against export of nylon fabrics. Already in a similar trade, RIL took maximum advantage of the scheme and at one stage accounted for nearly 60 per cent of the nylon fabrics exported from India. Its turnover and profits shot up from Rs 49.1 mn and Rs 3.9 mn in 1970 to Rs 689.8 mn and Rs 43.3 mn respectively in 1977 when Dhirubhai decided to take his company public.

Weaving the Future

The sustained growth in export turnover resulted in RIL expanding its manufacturing facilities. While it continued to import polyester yarn (for captive consumption and for local sales), it also used the import entitlements that were permitted against exports to import state-of-the-art technology. The machinery imports included both machinery for adding value to the imported yarn before selling it locally (in the yarn form) as well as machinery for fabric manufacture (weaving and fabric processing). RIL also set up a full-fledged textile design studio at Naroda to continuously come up with fresh design ideas. The *Japan Textile News* in 1977 commented, after inspecting its design studio facilities, 'Such a scene is hardly seen even in the highly advanced textile producing countries like Japan'. Earlier, in 1975, a technical team from the World Bank had inspected a number of textile mills in India and in its report had certified that only RIL's textile plant 'could be described as excellent by developed country standards'.

The focus on exports continued till the late 1970s when the government modified the scheme. RIL then shifted its attention to domestic markets and found itself well equipped to meet the burgeoning demand for polyester fabrics in India. The company used the experience gained from manufacturing high quality fabrics for the export market to attain leadership for its Vimal brand in the domestic market. Bulk of the domestic textile mills, who manufactured cotton fabrics, had not upgraded their technology, which enabled RIL to leverage its technological lead. Further, the company offered the entire range of fabrics—sarees, dress materials and suitings. At that time, most textile mills, save a few like Grasim (a key competitor owned by the Birla family), offered only one of the products.

Historically, the textile market in India has had a three-tier structure—manufacturer–wholesaler–retailer. The market was heavily controlled by the wholesale trade. Dissatisfied with the distribution structure, RIL opted to bypass the wholesale trade by opening retail showrooms—both its own and franchised—across the country. While RIL's competitor Bombay Dyeing had innovated this practice, it had done so on a relatively small scale. Reliance pursued this strategy on a grand scale. 'In fact, on a single day in 1980 we opened as many as 100 Vimal showrooms', said Mr K. Narayan, president of the textile division, who prior to joining RIL in the early 1970s, had been a professor of commerce in a local college. By 1980, Reliance fabrics were available all over India through over 20 company owned retail outlets, over a 1000 franchised outlets and over 20,000 regular retail stores.

RIL supported its entry into the domestic market with an advertising blitz that was unprecedented in India. Initially hoardings, radio and press and later television—when the television network was established in India—blazoned RIL's message: Only Vimal. Its jingle 'Only Vimal' and the baseline 'A woman expresses herself in many languages—Vimal is one of them' invaded the minds of Indian consumers. In addition to conventional media, the company held fashion shows across the country to support its brand.[2] Not only did RIL outspend its competition, its advertising budget was among the highest for all products promoted in India, a practice it has maintained since then.

By 1980 turnover jumped to Rs 2.1 bn and the company faced capacity constraints despite continuously upgrading technology and replacing the slower looms with faster ones at its weaving facility. It could not install additional looms because of government restrictions. The textile industry, like most other industries, was subject to licensing. Government policy favoured expansion in the small sector—the powerlooms—and sanction of additional loom capacity was hard to come by for larger companies.[3] To overcome this constraint, RIL started sourcing grey fabrics from the powerlooms located in nearby Surat (about 150 km from Ahmedabad and a major powerloom centre), processed them at its textile facility in Naroda, and sold them under its brand name. It also acquired a sick textile mill, by exchange of shares, at nearby Sidhpur (about 100 km north of Ahmedabad) to enhance its capacity. However, after initial efforts

2. Once again, RIL was not the innovator. This had been pioneered by a rival firm—Calico Mills.
3. Powerlooms were often one or two man operations. They typically sourced the yarn from outside and carried out only the weaving operation. They sold the woven grey (unfinished) fabric to process houses, which then completed the rest of the operations (processing/printing) and sold the finished fabric—often unbranded—to the wholesale trade (which invariably financed the whole operation). In contrast, large-scale 'composite' textile mills were fully integrated operations which carried out the entire set of activities in-house—from spinning the yarn to producing the finished fabric.

to modernise the dilapidated facilities, compounding the problem of surplus labour the unit had all along suffered from, the Sidhpur facility was spun off into a separate subsidiary.

Reliance quickly emerged as the largest producer of fabrics in India, a position it has maintained since then. It also continued to modernise its textile facility (see Appendix 4) at regular intervals and its Naroda complex, in 1994, was the largest textile plant in India.

The Next Step Backward

In 1981, RIL sought to further backward integrate its operations. Following rapid growth in the demand for polyester fabrics, domestic demand for Polyester Filament Yarn (PFY) had outstripped domestic supply, the shortfall being met by imports. RIL secured a license for manufacturing 10,000 MT of PFY and obtained technology from DuPont for setting up the facility. Beyond the straightforward opportunity for import substitution, Dhirubhai also saw the move as a way to improve his competitive position. As he later explained:

> I was a buyer of this product all over the world and I was observing what was going on—not only with the producers in India but also abroad. I went to a major company in the West and saw how inefficient they were . . . people were not working . . . were having long lunch hours. The bosses too were not committed . . . and the cost of all these inefficiencies were loaded on to the product and was being passed on to me. I knew that we could manage the business a lot better, make more money than them, and yet supply better and cheaper products to our mills.

For installing this facility, the company acquired a massive 300 acre plot of land in Patalganga, a sleepy village 71 km from Bombay on the banks of an even sleepier river. The total area was over 20 times larger than what was required for the PFY project.

In implementing this project, the company adopted three strategies that it has since repeated over and over to drive its phenomenal growth.

First, the size of Reliance's facility represented a major departure from the 'normal' Indian business practice of the time. Instead of creating a 'safe' capacity based on reasonable projection of demand, Dhirubhai applied for 'world scale' capacity that could meet the cost and quality standards on a global basis.

According to H.T. Parekh, the then head of ICICI Limited (India's premier corporate bank) who had sanctioned Reliance's first institutional loan, 'Dhirubhai always spoke of international standards and sizes. Initially, I admit that I had some doubts whether he would really be able to carry it through. But he has disproved me by his resourcefulness'. This commitment to creating world scale capacity, in turn, was based not only on Dhirubhai's ambition to 'do only extraordinary things', but also on a specific logic.

As described by S.P. Sapra, president of the Polyester Staple Fibre (PSF) business unit, who had joined RIL after a two-decade-long career with ICI India (the Indian subsidiary of ICI, UK, that had pioneered polyester manufacturing in India twenty years ahead of Reliance): 'The fundamental difference between Reliance's approach and that of other companies was that Dhirubhai saw things that were hidden to other companies. The user industry was held back by non-availability of supplies. Other companies would typically do a market survey that would show the current usage at, say, 2000 MT. They would project that usage into the future and arrive at a demand of, say, 5000 MT. They would then set up a 2000 or 3000 MT facility, depending on their projections of their market share.

Dhirubhai threw that incrementalist mind set away. He created capacity ahead of actual demand and on the basis of the latent demand. Then, he would go about systematically removing the barriers that were constraining the demand.'

At the time RIL set up its plant, filament yarn was reserved by the Government of India for use by small-scale weavers in the 'art-silk' industry; large textile companies could only use cotton. This was the key barrier to consumption. To stimulate demand, RIL launched a 'buy back' scheme whereby it sold its 'Recron' brand yarn to the small powerlooms who then sold the grey cloth back to the company for finishing and eventual sale under the Vimal brand name. 'We gave fantastic financial support to the little weavers', said Sapra. 'We gave them 90 days credit to create demand'. Once the positive loop of a supply-led demand creation process became fully operational, the company would revert to its tight asset management strategy. 'Today, 90 per cent of our sales is on cash basis. Whatever we ship today, payment is received by 2 p.m. tomorrow.'

The second element of the strategy was to purchase technology from the best foreign source rather than to create joint ventures. According to Sapra:

> Take Century Enka; everything needs Enka's approval. Enka is used to the low growth European environment. So they are incrementalist and cautious. They slow down the Birlas . . . . If Dhirubhai created an alliance with DuPont everyone in India would have said 'great, he has got DuPont in India'. But it would have slowed everything down.

The third element of the strategy was speed. 'Most traditional economic calculations are wrong because they do not take the cost of time into account', said Anil Ambani. 'Long before time based competition became a management hype, we did everything to compress time in both our projects and our operations.'

RIL had already built up a reputation for setting up projects quickly; it had, for instance, set up its worsted spinning plant within eight months of grant of the license. However, for the PFY plant it outdid even its collaborators by getting it ready in fourteen months—a feat DuPont, until then, had not managed to achieve anywhere else in the world. Instead of adopting the normal practice of linking the various pieces of the equipment through long arrays of pipes (typical for a continuous process plant) after receipt of the equipment, RIL laid scores of kilometres of pipes in readiness for the equipment to arrive and to be installed as soon as it landed.

By 1983, PFY displaced fabrics as the major revenue earner in RIL's portfolio, a position it has since maintained as the company has continuously modernised and expanded its PFY capacity (see Appendix 5). This would be another classic strategy the company would follow for all its businesses: not only would it enter the business with a large, world scale plant far higher in capacity than its domestic rivals, it would also continuously modernise and increase capacity to mop up all incremental market growth to build a position of absolute industry leadership. For managers used to the more staid approach of large Indian companies, this strategy took some getting used to. As described by K. Ramamurthy who joined Reliance from Chemplast:

> Initially I would go to them (Dhirubhai, Mukesh or Anil) with proposals that reflected my conservative market share objectives. And they would say 'think what a true world class operation must look like'. And my investment objectives would quadruple.

This continuing capacity growth allowed the company to emerge as the lowest cost polyester producer in the world. In 1994, its conversion cost was 18 cents per pound, as against the costs of 34, 29 and 23 cents per pound for West

European, North American and Far Eastern producers. But, beyond the cost advantage, capacity was also the company's key instrument for enhancing customer service.

> Said Sapra: 'Because of our capacity, we could diversify the range of yarns available locally by introducing several new products such as flat yarns, bright yarns and fancy yarns, which allowed our customers, in turn, to diversify their product range . . . . Also my biggest customer requires 500 MT per month. If my capacity was 2000 MT, I simply could not have given him the service I do. We took the fundamental decisions about capacity strategically, but the benefits came when we exploited the capacity operationally.'

Spiralling Growth

In 1984, RIL sought to further expand its polyester portfolio. It obtained the license for manufacturing 45,000 MT of Polyester Staple Fibre (PSF). The domestic manufacture of 37,000 MT was not adequate at that time to meet the demand and an estimated 10,000 MT of PSF was being imported. Both PFY and PSF were used for manufacturing fabrics and were largely substitutable.[4] The ruling PSF price was much lower (and has since continued to be lower) than that of PFY, largely due to the higher excise levy on PFY.

In addition to expanding its polyester portfolio, RIL sought to further backward integrate its operations. It obtained licenses to manufacture fibre intermediates—PTA and MEG. RIL had started manufacturing polyester from DMT—an alternate raw material for PTA. It, however, switched to importing PTA as it found it to be a more economic intermediate, though DMT was being manufactured locally by the public sector giant IPCL and further additions to DMT capacity were in the anvil.[5] Bombay Dyeing, RIL's competitor in the fabrics business, was in the process of setting up a DMT manufacturing facility, though it did not manufacture any polyester yarn.

4. PFY imparted better sheen (shine) and an apparent silky feel to the fabric and did not wrinkle as much as a PSF-based fabric did. PSF-based fabrics, on the other hand, provided greater comfort in wear (better breathability), especially in a tropical climate, to the consumer. They, however, were relatively more expensive to care for.
5. In the former process, DMT was combined, via a catalyst, with MEG to make polyester. The PTA route required less of MEG in the mix and also did not require the use of a catalyst.

Further, RIL obtained sanctions for capacities which were far in excess of its needs of these products for captive consumption.

RIL also sought to diversify its product portfolio. It obtained the license to manufacture 50000 m. tonnes of Linear Alkyl Benzene (LAB), an intermediate for production of detergents, the demand for which was burgeoning following the explosion of the detergents market triggered by the success of Nirma, a new low-cost brand.[6] 'Similarly, following the explosive growth in the colour TV market in India in the mid-1980s, it sought and received the clearance, in 1986, from the government to manufacture colour glass shells and colour picture tubes (see Appendix 6).

RIL, in keeping with its strategy of continuous investment in additional capacity, expanded its capacities in each of these businesses (see Appendix 7). In fact, in a number of cases it expanded the capacities even as it was installing the originally sanctioned smaller capacities. Further in each of these businesses, RIL achieved a level of capacity utilisation that was far higher than that of most competitors. 'With low utilisation, high capacity can be a millstone round your neck', said Sapra. For example, the demand for PSF remained sluggish throughout the second half of the 1980s. The domestic industry was plagued with surplus capacity when, in a period of eighteen months, the overall industry capacity went up from 40,000 MT to 250,000 MT because of expansion of capacities by existing players and entry of new players like Reliance. Realising that the domestic market could not absorb this volume, RIL turned to exports. It not only used its scale to advantage, it also upgraded its quality to export a major part of the output. It marketed the product both under its own brand name 'Recron' and through Du Pont who marketed the product worldwide under their own 'Dacron' label. For LAB, too, the company faced a similar situation of over capacity and responded by exporting nearly 25,000 MT of the product. To support such exports, the company set up Reliance Europe Limited, its own wholly-owned subsidiary in London. The improvement in quality necessary for export together with its experience with international customers, in turn, reinforced the company's competitive advantage at home.

Beyond export, the company also pursued an aggressive strategy of demand creation at home. It often set up special 'business development groups' to create

6. One other company—Tamilnadu Petro Products of the SPIC group (a large industrial house in South India)—was granted the licence to manufacture LAB of a similar capacity at the same time. This company too did not have any presence in the detergents business at that time. In the 1990s, one of the SPIC group companies entered the detergents market, following a tie-up with Henkel, Germany.

new investment opportunities that would use its own products as feedstock.[7] It provided such services free of cost to potential investors and also used its own network to help these investors secure both funding and distribution. As a result of such 'demand creation activities' at home and abroad, RIL could achieve 100 per cent capacity utilisation in PSF, for example, while most of its competitors struggled to achieve 50 per cent.

Financing the Growth

Reliance approached the investing public directly to finance its growth. Mobilising funds directly from the public was a departure from the prevailing practice among Indian businesses at that time. Most Indian businesses sought to finance their projects by mobilising funds—typically debt funds—from the state-owned public financial institutions. RIL preferred to raise capital directly from public as the funds mobilised from public financial institutions often had a rider attached to them: an option for the lending institution(s) to convert the debt into equity at a later date.

After the initial public offering of equity in 1977, RIL approached the public again in 1979, this time with an offer of a partially convertible debenture to finance setting up a worsted spinning plant which would enable its entry into the manufacture of worsted (wool-blend) fabrics. Though not an innovation, Standard Alkali having issued them earlier, RIL had a difficult time persuading the government (capital issues required government approval) of the attractiveness of convertible debentures as an investment proposition before receiving approval. RIL proved right in its assessment. The 1979 issue was oversubscribed six times. Since then RIL has employed this instrument with great success in mobilising funds from the public. And convertible debentures (both partially convertible and fully convertible) have become a major form for mobilising resources from the capital markets in India.

The appeal of this instrument to the 'small investor' at that time lay in the facts that:

1. The instrument yielded interest on the entire amount in the initial period (often linked to the gestation period of the project for which the funds were being mobilised) and thereafter on the non-convertible

7. In the late 1980s, RIL entered into a strategic alliance with Shri Mahila Udyog, a women's voluntary organisation which had scored great success with its Lijjat brand of papad and helped it launch a relatively low cost detergent named Sasa. The brand, however, failed to garner significant share.

portion. Despite a boom in the stock markets, following the forced dilution of equity of MNCs under the Foreign Exchange Regulation Act, equity offerings had not gained widespread public participation. The typical 'small' investor continued to prefer investing in safe return instruments like bank deposits. In such a scenario, an instrument which offered both interest and an opportunity to gain capital appreciation attracted support.

2. The conversion under the capital issue norms operational then (which were abolished only during the recent economic reforms of the 1990s) was carried out at a price which was far below the price of the equity quoted in the stock market, resulting in substantial capital appreciation on the investment.

The 1979 issue was quickly followed with issues of partially convertible debentures in 1980 (for modernising its textile facilities), 1981 (to finance its foray into the manufacture of PFY) and a record (then) Rs 500 mn offering in 1982 to further modernise its textile facilities. Two months prior to the 1982 offering, RIL's equity was subject to a severe bear hammering in the stock market and its share price nose dived. On a single day RIL's equity lost nearly 10 per cent of its value. Following this, Dhirubhai moved into the market reportedly on behalf of what later came to be referred to as 'Crocodiles and Fiascos'—the colourful names of non resident Indian investment companies registered in the Isle of Man—and bought up all the shares that were being sold and demanded delivery of the shares. The resultant panic buying by the bears (to cover their short sales) lead to an over-40 per cent rise in RIL's equity price. While the ownership of these controversial non resident Indian investment companies has never been firmly established, Dhirubhai became the small investor's stock market deity.

This image of Dhirubhai got further reinforced when in 1983 RIL, in an unprecedented move, offered to convert the non-convertible portion of the debentures issued between 1979 and 1982 into equity. It offered to exchange every Rs 100 of debt for 1.2 equity shares of Rs 10 face value. The offer met with an overwhelming response, for the Reliance share was being quoted at Rs 115 on the stock market, while the market value of every Rs 100 of debt was hovering around Rs 84. In a single stroke the company had not only eliminated the debt burden, it had also increased its future fund raising capacity significantly. Within a year of the extinguishment of the debt, RIL mobilised over Rs 3.5 bn of fresh funds from the markets: Rs 800 mn as partially convertible debentures (Series E) and Rs 2.7 bn as non-convertible debentures (Series F) to finance its growth (see

Appendix 8). The latter established yet another record. Not only was it, at that time, the largest ever issue in Indian capital market history, it met with over subscription despite being a non-convertible offer. Dhirubhai had once again demonstrated his capital raising legerdemain.

Yet another facet of RIL's growth history has been its tax planning. While its profits continued to grow, it had not paid a single rupee to the exchequer as corporate income tax. RIL's continuous investments in expansion/ modernisation of its facilities enabled it to set off the profits from operations against the tax credits it was allowed on investments made (investment allowance). In a bid to make companies like RIL, which came to be known as zero-tax companies, to pay taxes, the Government of India amended the laws to require companies to pay corporate income taxes on at least 30 per cent of their profits after depreciation but before seeking investment allowance and other tax benefits. RIL, however, continued to be a zero-tax company. It changed its accounting practice. Against the earlier practice of capitalising interest on long-term debt obtained for procuring fixed assets till the date of commissioning of the assets, it capitalised interest for the entire contracted period of such debt on the assumption that 'interest accrues at the time of availment of the loan till the date of repayment of the said loan, and all loans shall be repaid on due dates'.[8]

A Setback

In February 1986, Dhirubhai suffered a paralytic stoke. As a consequence his two sons, Stanford educated Mukesh and Wharton educated Anil, then in their late twenties, were catapulted into managing the company while their father recuperated. It was trial by fire for them.

All through its history RIL has rarely been far removed from controversy. Its critics contended that its ability to get licenses granted; obtain fast approvals for its resource mobilisation plans from the capital markets and capital goods imports, and get policies formulated which favoured it (or disadvantaged its competitors or both) were a consequence of the enormous political clout it wielded. In 1986, however, following the assassination of Prime Minister Indira Gandhi and the consequent change in the Indian government, the company found itself caught in a storm of controversies.

In June 1986, the government banned conversion of the the non-convertible portion of debentures into equity hours before RIL's board of directors was to

8. Annual Report, 1982, p. 23.

meet to recommend conversion of the non-convertible portion of its Series E and F into equity. The ban followed allegations in the press, principally in *The Indian Express*, one of India's leading newspapers. *The Indian Express*, which ran a series of exposes on RIL, alleged that state-owned banks had provided huge sums of money to investment companies belonging to the Ambanis in violation of prevailing lending norms, enabling these companies to acquire large quantities of Series E and F debentures months before the board meeting. Following the ban, RIL's share price crashed.

The Indian Express followed this with a report alleging that RIL had set up plants whose capacities were far in excess of its licensed capacity by smuggling them into the country. This eventually lead to a show cause notice from the Customs authorities alleging 'import and installation of additional machines/lines unauthorised' and also alleging 'misdeclaration of more than twice the declared capacity' and claiming alleged differential duty/penalty of Rs 1190 mn.[9] RIL, however, denied any wrong doing and contested the claim.[10]

In July 1986, the government abolished a customs levy (anti-dumping duty) imposed on the import of PFY around the time when RIL's PFY plant was being commissioned. The government action was triggered by the accusation that while publicly justified as protection to domestic producers from low cost imports, the duty actually enabled domestic producers—Reliance foremost among them—to generate windfall profits. As a result of this action, PFY prices dropped by 20 per cent in the domestic market.

The soap opera-like year ended with RIL's profits nose-diving from Rs 713 mn the year before to only Rs 141 mn. The same *Business India* that only two years ago had described Dhirubhai as 'a legend in his own lifetime', now proclaimed the 'end of a myth'.

The company fought back the only way it knew—by a direct appeal to India's investing public. In December 1986, following the ban on the conversion of the non-convertible portion of debentures into equity, it approached the capital

9. Annual Report, 1987–88, p. 21.
10. RIL was successful in its claim before the Collector of Customs. However, the customs department preferred an appeal with the Customs Tribunal. And RIL filed a writ petition in the Delhi High Court against the appeal. A similar allegation was made with regard to the import of its PTA plant in 1989–90. RIL received a show cause notice from the customs authorities in 1989–90 alleging import of a PTA plant of higher capacity and claimed a sum of Rs 1.7 bn as differential customs duty. RIL has disputed the demand.

market with a record Rs 5 bn offer of fully convertible debentures (Series G). The issue was labelled in one section of the press as a public referendum on Reliance. And the result of the referendum was an unblemished victory for the company: the offer was oversubscribed by over seven times, with an unprecedented number of 1.75 mn applications for allotment before the offer closing date. Despite all the allegations and setbacks, the company had retained the confidence of its shareholders.

The success of this offer, together with another round of changes in the government, began to turn the tide of the company's fortune from early 1987. A number of favourable government decisions followed: import of PSF was canalised through a state agency thus preventing direct import by end-users; a special customs levy of Rs 3 per kg on PTA (which Reliance was still importing) was abolished; RIL's Patalganga complex was granted the status of a refinery, thus it became entitled to a lower level of domestic excise duty for raw materials like Naphtha; and the company was permitted to prepone the conversion of the Series G debentures into equity, which resulted in an estimated saving of about Rs 330 mn in interest costs. RIL declared a hefty profit of Rs 800 mn in the next accounting year, which it had extended to eighteen months so as to synchronise the commissioning of the PTA and LAB projects with the accounting year and to 'reflect a consolidated position in respect of fixed assets, increase in equity capital with corresponding extinguishment of debt, and achieving the product range envisaged'.[11] It also changed its practice of accounting for depreciation. Without this change the reported net profits for the period would have been lower by at least Rs 245 mn.[12]

Reliance Petrochemicals Limited (RPL)

In 1983, after the Bhopal disaster had crippled Union Carbide's operations in India, Reliance made a bid to acquire Carbide's plastics operations. While that bid had to be aborted for regulatory delays, the company acquired a licence for producing high density Polyethylene (PE) and Polyvinyl Chloride (PVC) in 1985 (see Appendix 9). During 1987-88, RIL set up a separate subsidiary—RPL—and transferred the licences to this new company 'with a view to speedily implement the Letters of Intent/Industrial Licenses as also to effect better control and avail of fiscal benefits/incentives'.[13] All these plants would be set up at a new location in Hazira, in the state of Gujarat, about 230 km north of Bombay.

11. Annual Report, 1987–88, p. 4.
12. Annual Report, 1987–88, p. 21.
13. Annual Report, 1987–88, p. 6.

RPL, in 1988–89, issued fully convertible debentures for financing these projects and mobilised a record-breaking Rs 5.9 bn from the capital market. Its investor base of 2.3 mn investors was yet another record. Additionally, for the first time in the capital market history, a financial issue was marketed like a branded product. RPL branded the convertible debenture Khazana (meaning treasure).

Soon thereafter, the government announced a new policy which allowed lower licensed capacities granted earlier to be scaled up to new 'minimum economic capacities'. RPL opted to upgrade the capacities of the plants it was setting up to higher levels. This lead to modification in the implementation schedules. Importantly, it also lead to an upward revision in the projected investment outlays. The increased fund requirement was met by mobilising debt funds from state-owned financial institutions, who required RPL to prepone the conversion of part B of the convertible debentures issued to March 1991 (see Appendix 8). RPL opted to convert even part C of the debenture at the same time. Both the conversions were done at par, though, at the time of the issue, RPL had planned to convert them at a premium. As a result the equity base of RPL ballooned to over Rs 7 bn. Further, the delay in commissioning of the plants of enhanced capacities resulted in projects costs shooting up to over Rs 15 bn, up from Rs 7 bn estimated earlier. RPL not only had to service the huge equity base, it was also saddled with a debt of over Rs 8 bn.

Effective 1 March 1992, RPL was merged with RIL by an exchange of shares. Ten RPL shares were exchanged for one RIL share. The end result: an addition of Rs 750 mn to RIL's equity and an addition of Rs 6.7 bn to its reserves.

Larsen & Toubro (L&T)

RIL, in 1988, through an investment subsidiary, acquired significant stakes in L&T. Apart from being India's No.1 construction and process engineering company, L&T had a significant presence in the cement, shipping and electronics industries. At the time of the acquisition, the RIL group was L&T's largest customer and the two had had a long standing supplier–customer relationship. RIL acquired the stake with a view to exploit this 'synergy' and to form a 'strategic alliance'. The incumbent management did not have a controlling stake in L&T, which was described as a 'professionally managed' company. State-owned financial institutions were the largest shareholders in L&T—they had over 35 per cent stake in it. Following its investment in L&T equity, RIL through its subsidiary became the single largest shareholder of the company outside the state-owned financial institutions. Within six months Dhirubhai became chairman of the board of L&T. In the interregnum, three other RIL directors were inducted into the L&T board. RIL thus gained effective control over L&T.

The apparently smooth takeover of L&T soon ran into rough weather. The RIL subsidiary was accused of having employed surreptitious methods for acquiring a significant portion of the stakes it held in L&T. The leading financial institutions had sold a part of their stakes in L&T (amounting to about 7 per cent of L&T equity) to a newly set up investment subsidiary of a leading nationalised bank, apparently with a view to provide it with a jump start. This firm instead sold the stakes so acquired to the RIL subsidiary. It was later unravelled by *The Indian Express* that the entire operation was orchestrated to facilitate RIL to acquire significant stakes in L&T. Following this revelation, in a settlement of the issue, the RIL subsidiary returned the stakes it had so acquired to the financial institutions.

The controversy, however, did not end there. RIL was accused of using L&T to shore up its finances. In 1989, L&T made a record public offering of Rs 8.2 bn of convertible debentures.[14] RIL was accused of having mobilised the money to fund the cost overrun of its projects (about Rs 6 bn of the funds mobilised had been earmarked as suppliers credit from L&T to the RIL group). Following these accusations and a change in the government in 1990, the state-owned financial institutions sought the ouster of RIL directors from the L&T board. The issue was finally settled with Dhirubhai stepping down from the board. The number of RIL directors on the L&T board was also reduced to two. L&T reverted to its original status of operating as an 'independent professionally managed company'. However, RIL, through its investment subsidiary, continued to be the single largest non-institutional shareholder in L&T.

Backwards and Beyond

Between 1989 and 1992, RIL further backward integrated its operations. It set up facilities to manufacture LAB directly from kerosene with n-paraffin as intermediate raw material. It also commissioned the facilities for the manufacture of paraxylene (input material for manufacturing PTA). Both these facilities were set up at its Patalganga complex. At its Hazira complex, it commenced manufacturing MEG, PE and PVC.

14. The issue was oversubscribed and L&T's investor base crossed the 1 million mark—against an earlier base of less than 200,000—aided by the fact that RIL shareholders were given a preferential allotment in the issue.

In a further step to backward integrate its operations it obtained in 1988–89 (see Appendix 9) a licence for setting up an ethylene cracker complex at Hazira. The cracker complex would provide the ethylene required for the manufacture of PE, PVC and MEG. To fund this complex it mobilised over Rs 9 bn from the investing public and rolled over the Series F debentures which were due for redemption.

RIL was also in the process of setting up facilities for manufacturing ethylene di-chloride, a feed stock for manufacturing PVC. It also planned to build a world scale caustic soda chlorine facility. While the chlorine was to be fully used for meeting its own captive needs for the manufacture of ethylene di-chloride, caustic soda was to be sold in the local market.

In 1992, the company sponsored the creation of Reliance Polypropylene Ltd and Reliance Polyethylene Ltd, both joint ventures with C. Itochu, Japan, one of the largest trading houses in the world. These companies would manufacture 250,000 MT of polypropylene and 160,000 MT of polyethylene respectively at Hazira. They together mobilised over Rs 6 bn from the capital market in November 1992 to part finance the projects which were expected to go on stream by the end of 1994.

In its bid to emerge as a vertically integrated manufacturer, RIL secured, during 1991–92, a license to set up a 9 MT refinery (Appendix 9). It subsequently promoted a new company, Reliance Petroleum Limited, in which it had a 21 per cent stake, for setting up the refinery which would meet its feed stock requirements of naphtha for the manufacture of paraxylene (PX) and kerosene for the manufacture of LAB. The new company successfully approached the capital markets in September 1993, with a Rs 21 bn offering of convertible debentures, to part finance the Rs 51 bn refinery which was scheduled to go into commercial production by mid-1996. The new company entered into a marketing and distribution arrangement with the state-owned Bharat Petroleum Corporation Limited (BPCL), the third largest integrated refining and marketing oil company in India and the prinçipal supplier of naptha and keronsene to RIL, for marketing the products of the refinery. Under the terms of the agreement, BPCL would have exclusive rights to market the entire range of products of the refinery except that (1) RIL could sell petroleum products to large consumers through pipeline transfers, and (2) RIL and other RIL group companies would have the first option to obtain their requirements of feed stocks in bulk and through pipelines.

And to complete the vertical integration chain, RIL entered oil and gas exploration in 1994. It joined hands with Enron, USA, in an equal (50:50) partnership and bid for development of proven oil fields when this sector was opened up by the government for private sector participation. In early 1994, the RIL–Enron consortium was awarded the contract to develop three oil fields. Under the existing policy framework, however, the RIL–Enron consortium could not directly market the oil so produced. It was required to sell the entire output to the government.

In addition to vertically integrating its operations, RIL was also expanding its existing businesses, in each of which it had already achieved positions of absolute leadership in the domestic market (see Appendix 10). It was in the process of setting up a new polyester complex at Hazira, where it intended to manufacture 120,000 MT of PFY, 100,000 MT of PSF, 80000 MT of PET and 350,000 MT of PTA. 'This complex would be bigger than our own polyester complex at Patalganga. On completion, our total polyester capacity would be over 500,000 MT and that would make us the No.1 integrated producer in the world. Don't you think that would be a truly unique achievement for an Indian company?' said a jubilant Dhirubhai.

Managing the Organisation

The last lights to be switched off at RIL's corporate headquarters in Bombay, after they have typically put in a twelve hour day, are in the offices of Dhirubhai's two sons, Mukesh and Anil, who actively managed the company. 'Both of us work as a team. We revolve areas among ourselves, so that we are both well-rounded. Control of finance and people is the most important thing and this is where both of us work in the simple way of conferencing. What kind of training, what kind of people, our future, everything', said Mukesh.

Anil, who usually was also the first person to come in to work at RIL, said, 'One must not mistake entrepreneurs who actively manage the business as unprofessional. We are equipped with qualifications from leading educational institutions, and are building professional motivated teams to seize opportunities.'

At the same time, these two inheritors of Dhirubhai's mantle also claim to be different from the scions of other industrialist families in India. Asked to define how they thought of themselves, Mukesh explained:

> As two bright young Indians, without the historical baggage of saying we are a great big multinational company, or with a 100-year family history, we have a fire in our belly, *ki kuch karke dikhana hai* ('we have to achieve something'). That is what keeps us driving.

Dhirubhai himself does not put in such long hours in the office any more, having moved away from day-to-day operations to being the visionary and the strategist for the Group. Nevertheless, he continues to be passionately involved, with a single minded commitment to the institution he has built.

Dhirubhai said: 'I do not give and have never given attention to anything except Reliance. I have never been a director in any other company. I am not actively involved in any associations or in anything else. My whole thinking—100 per cent of my time from morning till evening—is about how to do better and better at Reliance. Business is my hobby. It is not a burden to me. I enjoy it enormously.'

What sustained this single minded commitment? K.K. Malhotra, the ex-managing director of Indian Oil Corporation (the largest government-owned company in India) who headed RIL's manufacturing operations, offered the following anecdote in explanation:

> One day, Dhirubhai and I were having lunch together at Patalganga. He ordered a soup and a papad. I ordered a one-egg omelette. Then he said 'this is all we need, right! This is all we can consume . . . but the excitement is to build . . . *us me nasha hai*' ('that is intoxicating').

'In Reliance, the family is clearly and firmly the ultimate decision makers', said Prafulla Gupta, a Harvard MBA who joined Reliance after working for almost twenty years around the world with Booz, Allen and Hamilton, the international strategy consultants. 'They have, both individually and collectively, shown a clear willingness to delegate—once there is satisfaction that an executive's judgement and ability to act are consistent with their own perspective and value system . . . We do not have formal delegation of authority in our company—nothing like in position X you may have a Y level of signing authority, etc. If there are two people at the same level one could have the authority to sign a cheque for an eight-digit figure and the other for trivial amounts. It varies with the role, and the confidence the person can evoke.'

It was often said in India that Ambani was an acronym for ambition and money. While the family members had both in ample measure (in 1994, for the first time, the family featured in Forbes' list of billionaires), they also have a third characteristic that has an enormous influence on their management style. They have an enormous appetite for information.

> According to Ramamurthy: 'They are enormously bold but their actions are influenced by their unmatched access to information. They would know what is happening in every single corridor of government ministries. They know about their customers. They know more about their competitors—even about day-to-day operations—than the top managers of those companies . . . they would know where money would flow . . . and it is not just about their immediate business. They suck up knowledge about everything, constantly. Their magic is not just ambition but ambition with information.'

Reporting directly to the family is a senior management team that consists of people with three very different kinds of background:

1. In the first group were a set of early business associates of Dhirubhai (including in some cases their kith and kin) who had historical links with him, personally, rather than with the company. They were the intermediaries in his financial operations, in his relationship with government functionaries and in de-bottlenecking his implementation plans. By 1994, their role within the company had diminished significantly though some of them still remained involved in a largely consulting capacity.
2. In the second group were a number of people whom Reliance had attracted away from very senior positions in India's largest companies. A majority of these managers came from large public sector corporations. As one of them explained: 'Most private sector CEOs have the view that public sector managers are useless bureaucrats rather than managers, incapable of taking decisions and only good at creating files that protected their own hides. Dhirubhai, on the other hand, had the vision to go in for mega projects. He recognised that in India only public sector companies had any experience of executing projects of the size he was contemplating. So, he hired the best people from these companies and made the best use of their skills and experience'. It was this group—most of whom who had either retired or were nearing

retirement in the jobs they held before joining Reliance—that served as professional implementers of Dhirubhai's vision over the 1970s and 1980s.

3. In the 1990s, however, a new and much younger group of managers were inducted at the senior level. Like Mukesh and Anil, this new group has typically been educated in the best technical and management schools in the USA and India and they often have considerable experience of working, typically abroad, with international suppliers and customers.

The relative roles and status of managers in the senior group is always in a flux. Similar to most family managed companies around the world, relations with family members in the top management often mean a lot more than formal titles or job descriptions. As described by V.V. Bhat, responsible for the human resource function at the group level, 'in RIL, authority, responsibility and power have to be taken. They are never given. No one has the time to give! We are too busy growing'.

Decision Making

At RIL, most decisions are verbal. Information came through paper but decisions are made by discussions and talking, typically over the telephone. 'Verbal decisions work because of the trust', said Sapra.

'Trust is not a function of being a blood relation of Ambanis. I am not and most of us in the senior management today are not. Trust is a function of my capacity to deliver. It, however, is a two way process. I know that if something goes wrong and my family is in trouble, the Ambanis would put the entire RIL corporate muscle behind them to support my family. And this is not restricted to the top. What they do at the top, I do to people down below. Often the issues are not big. For example, if a clerk's child is seriously sick, I send a car for him to use at that time. We practice this with our trade as well. I tell my trade-doing business with us is risk free. If you lose, come back to us.

If you make profits, it is yours. Textile is a trade driven product. Consumer acceptance is necessary but then trade must help too. Most traders are small entrepreneurs. Even if he is confident, he has a fear—what happens . . . . So when I specify targets to him he would do his damnedest to perform.'

—K. Narayan

Added Kamal Nanavaty, vice president (marketing, polymers), and a veteran of Indian Petrochemicals Limited (IPCL), the state-owned petrochemicals giant:

> Our style of decision making does not signal lack of planning or analysis. Even before I joined in April 1989, I was asked to prepare a blue print for the marketing organisation I was to set up. It was debated before approval. Once the plan was approved, I went ahead and set it up, making modifications along the way that were needed. I did it and informed them of it. I went to them with a problem only if I couldn't solve it. I did not have to seek sanctions again and again. That would cut down our speed. The marketing organisation, the down stream project feasibility reports, etc. were in place before the first granule came out.

Speed

At RIL there is a great emphasis on speed. 'We don't accept a barrier as a barrier', said Sapra. 'We deal with issues directly. We do not build defences for non-performance'. K. Narayan provided an example:

> In 1973, the rotary machine at Naroda broke down on a Friday evening. The import of the component to be replaced would have normally taken two to three months. So I went abroad the same night, bought the component and got it back on Sunday night and the plant was in production from Monday afternoon.

Perhaps the most dramatic illustration of Reliance's speed came when its huge Patalganga complex was flooded on the night of 24 July 1989 by flash floods from the nearby a river. Technical experts from DuPont flown in at considerable cost estimated a minimum period of ninety to hundred days before the complex could be operational again. Local newspaper reports, based on the opinion of India's best experts, were even less optimistic, predicting that some of the units would not be operational for at least five months. Reliance had the entire complex fully functional in twenty-one days.

The real secret to speed, according to Malhotra, lay in two things: careful planning to quantify tasks and then saturating the tasks with resources: 'Most companies do not quantify the tasks, do not quantify the resources required . . . anyone who says we will do this is twenty-four months has not done a proper estimation for only by accident can the real requirement match such a nice round number . . . we assess the requirement precisely. And then, once the plans are done, we saturate resources. We put in the largest amount of resource that the task can absorb, without people tripping over each other . . . . If I had all the time in the world, I would optimise. But given my opportunity cost of lost production, it almost does not matter how much it costs because, if I can get the production going earlier, I always come out ahead . . . only when you put the value of time in the equation do you get sound economics and then saturation almost always makes sense. And finally, we follow a dictum: co-ordinate horizontally, when in trouble go vertical. That dictum—both parts of it—are also vital for speed.'

K.K. Malhotra, chief of RIL's manufacturing operations, provides some details: 'Understand the scale of the havoc . . . . After the water receded, we had to remove 50,000 tons of garbage—silt, dead animals, floating junk—before we could get to the actual recovery work. All our sophisticated electronic and electrical equipment had been under water for hours . . .

We set up a control room to connect the site with the outside world. Then we took time to carefully look at the damage and quantify the work. Based on that quantification, we set up objectives for each plant as to when it would be on track.

Each day at 11 a.m. I would have a meeting for an hour to review . . . on the third day I asked the DuPont people, "what do you think?" We had planned to get our two huge compressors ready in fourteen days. They said, "Out of two, if you can get one ready in a month, you will be lucky." I phoned Mukesh that evening and said "I want these guys out of here. If they say this, it will percolate . . . it will break the will." We had the compressors one day ahead of schedule and the whole plant going a week ahead of plan.'

The Organisation Structure

With constant flux in both the status and role of senior managers, it is hard to draw a formal organisation structure of Reliance nor is one readily available inside the company. Historically, the company has been managed along functional lines. The company's focus on rapidly building and tightly managing its assets is supported by the professional excellence of a group of managers who have complete responsibility for specific functional areas like finance, manufacturing, planning, purchase and human resources on a group-wide basis. In the recent past, the revenue side has been strengthened by the creation of a set of business units with profit and loss responsibility for specific products such as PFY, PSF, PTA, LAB, fabrics, etc. While the different products are produced in common manufacturing sites that are managed by the manufacturing function, the business unit managers are expected to liaise with these site managers with regard to their own specific requirements. Individuals heading the different business units and functions typically carry the title of president or chief executive and each of them reports to the 'Ambanis'.

The result of such a structure is a high degree of ambiguity but also a high level of flexibility. People can be brought into the organisation from the outside quite easily; responsibilities can be adjusted without openly declaring winners and losers; and positions can be created and abolished overnight. Managers more often than not work on special projects that have little relationship with their formal position. Bhat, for example, was responsible for the polyester manufacturing operations at Patalganga over and above his group level human resource management role.

The Emerging Challenges

In 1994, India was in the midst of a radical change. Following the government's economic reform programme in India, petrochemicals was no longer a select preserve of a privileged few. Entry was made easy for both domestic and global companies. Protective import tariffs were reduced and were expected to be reduced even further over the next few years. While these very tangible changes in policy had direct effects on industry, perhaps their more significant influence was on the mind sets of managers in RIL's Indian and foreign competitors. As described by Sapra:

> By operating as if the environment was deregulated, we have a head start. But others are catching up. In the Indian side, the visibility and success of Reliance has made others develop the courage to think big. The Reliance formula is no longer a secret. Also, they will not have the impediments we had. They will be on tested grounds. More importantly, they will be able to benchmark themselves against us. At the same time, there is also a big change in the global companies. Earlier, they were not very interested in India—the country did not have credibility. Now they see India as a major growth opportunity. So, they will provide a driving force. They will push their technology . . . they will educate our domestic competitors.

Overall, the easing of entry barriers did not worry RIL too much. As argued by Anil Ambani. 'It would cost Shell $8 bn to replicate our position in India. Given their worldwide resource needs, they cannot commit that amount of money to one market.' The reduction in tariffs, however, had already led to increasing competitive pressures. 'The world is in a recession and the fear is that India may be exposing itself to recessionary competition and large-scale dumping', said Dhirubhai. 'At our stage of development, we cannot afford to do that.' Itself subject to an anti-dumping suit launched in 1993 by a European chemical company in Brussels, RIL had launched its own anti-dumping suit in India against Brazilian, Mexican and South Korean companies exporting petrochemicals to the Indian market.

While unleashing fiercer competition, the economic reform programme had also opened up new opportunities, not only in the refining and exploration of oil—which RIL had already taken actions to exploit—but also in a host of other areas. Prafulla Gupta described the power sector as an example:

> We have a terrifying deficit of the order of 50,000 MW. Recognising the need for massive investments to improve both the size and the quality of the power sector, the government has offered a very exciting scheme for attracting private companies. It will provide exchange rate protection, guarantee a 16 per cent return on equity . . . all calculated at a plant load factor significantly below what we believe to be achievable.
>
> We have the experience of running our own 100 MW captive power plants at Patalganga and Hazira. They are among the most sophisticated and best run power plants in the country—we routinely operate them at 95 per cent+ capacity. We can mobilise large amounts of capital and have a demonstrated competence in managing mega projects.
>
> At one level this is a no-brainer—we will get returns higher than our cost of capital and create a huge new growth opportunity. In fact, we have already bid for one facility each in Delhi and in Maharashtra for a total of 750 MW. But we also have to think of the opportunity cost, of the risk of oil price rise and so on.

Besides power, similar one-time opportunities were available in telecommunications, insurance, electronics and many other areas. In most cases, entry would become far more difficult and expensive at a later stage. Therefore a key decision within the leadership team of RIL focussed on whether the company should go beyond the fabric of the crude oil vertical chain that it had historically focussed on and which still offered almost unlimited opportunities for further growth. It was essential that any field the company entered must provide opportunities for the kind of Return on Assets and growth performance that Reliance had come to expect. The benefits of focus were obvious, yet to a group in a hurry and a management team accustomed to achieving the impossible, the new opportunities were almost too attractive to resist.

Inseparable from the debate on the company's business portfolio was its historical practice of avoiding joint ventures with foreign companies. It had already violated the dictum against JVs when it had entered into joint ventures with C. Itochu of Japan for manufacture of polymers and a 50:50 partnership with Enron for the oil and gas exploration project. As described by Akhil Gupta, the chief executive of this business, it was not easy to get the company used to the notion of a partnership: 'Our habit is that we are in control. There is a natural tendency to fall back on habit. The key challenge is to move from habit to reason—to be willing to do what adds the most value in a given situation.'

Prafulla Gupta provided a further elaboration of this issue:

> As recently as twenty-four months ago, if you were a company with a significant non-Indian share holding, you walked with a chain and ball around your neck . . . our business needed speed, so we avoided foreign equity. Now the playing field is level- it does not matter whether you have domestic or foreign equity. That is a big change.
>
> In the businesses we got into in the past, we had the necessary management capabilities and there was enough technical and operational skills within India that we could recruit.
>
> Now we are getting into oil field development and production. For these businesses, there are lots of technical capabilities in India but not enough management capability. At the same time these are \$100 mn to \$1 bn plays, and we must run these with absolutely world class competence. So, we have three choices. We can identify suitable people abroad and hire them and help them get used to working in India as quickly as possible. Alternatively, we can license or purchase the technology, as we did for polyester, and grow our competence as we go along. Or, we need to review our strategy with regard to alliances and be willing to get into more and more partnerships to quickly enter the new businesses.

The plethora of new opportunities, in turn, raised questions about RIL's classic organisation and management style. Historically, the different managers heading key functions came together only at the level of the family members at the apex of the company. While this structure worked well, it did so at the cost of a severe overloading at the top.

Another key constraint of the existing organisation was the lack of teamwork and cooperation within the senior management group heading the different businesses and functions. Given the diversity of their backgrounds, each of them had a different style and was the product of a different culture. The existing organisation provided little incentive for them to collaborate horizontally or to build a shared culture across the units they managed. Because of the lack of coherence and integration at the top, according to Sapra, sharing of learning and best practices within the company suffered. 'There are pockets of excellence, but we are not fully able to get the best out of every component. It is happening at least to some extent in the production and technical side, but less so in the business management side', said Sapra.

One of the options under consideration was to re-shape the company into a classic multi-divisional organisation, structured around sectors such as fibres (PSF and PFY), chemicals (LAB, caustic soda, etc.), polymers (PE, PVC), fibre intermediates (PX, PTA, MEG) and textiles, with each sector reporting to a group executive committee. With integrated business responsibility, the sector managers would be responsible for existing businesses, freeing up the top managers at the executive committee for only strategic and administrative oversight and for corporate entrepreneurship. Such a restructuring would call for a major readjustment of the roles and tasks of existing business and functional managers, together with substantial delegation of operating responsibility from the family to them.

Finally, the company was aware of a need to build norms and a better structured process for management development. Because of a historical reputation for being a 'sharp deal making company', it had limited success in recruiting talented graduates from Indian technical and managerial institutions. It also lacked any formal system for developing managers internally through on-going training and effective career path management. Employment at Reliance was largely a test by fire. A time had clearly come for building a better organised HR system.

Asked to comment on what would differentiate the future of Reliance from its past, Dhirubhai asserted: 'We have not grown fast enough . . . Reliance was slowed down by my stroke. But not any more . . . . Now, we will grow faster, much faster.'

As a part of this process, the company had begun to actively recruit graduates from IITs and IIMs—India's prestigious technical and management schools. The presence in the company of individuals like Mukesh and Anil as well as Akhil and Prafulla Gupta—all highly educated professionals with technical and management degrees from the most prestigious international institutes—was of considerable help in attracting such candidates. At the same time, following the withdrawal of government regulations on executive compensation, the company was in the process of rationalising management pay and perquisites. Plans were also afoot for creating a large and modern campus with the best possible facilities and faculty for internal management training.

The decisions and actions the company would take on these emerging issues of strategy, organisation and management development would decide whether, once again, he would confound the world by making his seemingly impossible prophecies come true.

APPENDIX 1

Financial Performance, 1983 to 1992-93

(Rs 10 million)

	1992-93	*1991-92*	*1990-91*	*1989-90*	*1988-89*	*1987-88*	*1986*	*1985*	*1984*	*1983*
Sales and earnings										
Sales	4105.50*	2953.21*	2098.34	1840.66	1112.45	1770.74	905.48	733.14	622.01	520.35
Other income	68.46	42.15	6.55	15.64	7.88	7.45	5.73	4.94	7.11	4.68
(A) Subtotal	413.96	2995.36	2104.89	1856.30	1120.33	1778.19	911.21	738.08	629.12	525.03
(B) Manufacturing and other expenses	2295.43	1765.56	1617.87	1432.10	862.58	1495.27	781.82	604.83	511.23	433.61
(C) Inter-divisional transfers	997.62	655.19	–	–	–	–	–	–	–	–
(D) Gross profit (A-B-C)	880.91	574.61	487.02	424.20	257.75	282.92	129.39	133.25	117.89	91.42
(E) Interest	279.35	218.65	187.05	171.73	91.58	110.74	54.24	24.45	22.61	21.52
(F) Depreciation	279.81	192.64	174.42	161.97	86.80	91.41	60.98	37.46	34.18	31.38
Subtotal	559.16	411.29	361.47	333.70	178.38	202.15	115.22	61.91	56.79	52.90
(G) Net profit [D-(E+F)]	321.75	163.62	125.55	90.50	79.37	80.77	14.17	71.34	61.10	38.52
What the company owned										
Fixed assets										
Gross block	4640.53	4314.33	2186.42	1998.79	1871.76	1862.66	1137.55	735.68	530.93	394.88
Less depreciation (cumulative)	1272.69	976.22	703.85	529.78	368.98	278.58	188.09	128.88	104.65	73.42
Net block	3367.84	3338.11	1482.57	1469.01	1502.78	1584.08	949.46	606.80	426.28	321.46
Investments	516.89	61.95	69.53	58.05	58.50	1.25	0.37	37.30	0.17	0.12
Current assets	2198.28	1480.15	1160.22	1026.26	849.46	607.83	1052.83	402.10	253.41	215.19
Total	6083.01	4880.21	2712.32	2553.32	2410.74	2193.16	2002.66	1046.20	661.86	536.77

Appendix 1 contd. . .

	1992-93	*1991-92*	*1990-91*	*1989-90*	*1988-89*	*1987-88*	*1986*	*1985*	*1984*	*1983*
What the company owed										
Long-term funds	2193.42	1794.15	708.96	595.89	579.44	609.82	546.12	515.16	276.96	239.99
Medium/Short-term funds	156.25	176.24	131.26	219.50	195.11	103.83	143.78	81.90	44.83	35.46
Current liabilities and provisions	1120.57	966.20	718.65	650.95	564.88	457.39	1001.23	138.02	93.68	131.44
Total	3470.24	2936.59	1558.87	1466.34	1339.43	1171.04	1691.13	735.08	415.47	406.89
Net worth of the company										
Equity share capital	245.48	227.08	152.12	152.12	152.11	152.10	51.61	51.61	46.18	36.15
Reference share capital	5.50	5.80	5.80	5.80	5.80	5.80	5.80	5.80	5.80	5.80
Reserves and surplus	2361.79	1710.74	995.53	929.06	913.40	864.22	254.12	253.71	194.41	87.93
Net worth	2612.77	1943.62	1153.45	1086.98	1071.31	1022.12	311.53	311.12	246.39	129.88
Earnings per equity share ** (Rs)	13.24	10.26	8.20	5.89	6.91	5.19	2.58	14.16	15.62	10.42
Cash earnings per equity share** (Rs)	24.79	22.42	19.66	16.54	14.52	11.21	14.39	21.69	24.47	19.10
Net worth per equity share (Rs)	106.21	85.34	75.44	71.07	70.05	66.82	59.24	59.16	52.10	34.32
Debt:Equity ratio	0.84:1	0.92:1	0.61:1	0.55:1	0.54:1	0.50:1	1.75:1	1.66:1	1.12:1	1.85:1
Number of investors (in lakhs)	37	38	24	26	31	31	18	17	15	3
Number of employees	11836	11935	11666	11355	10983	10697	9376	9066	8914	8440

* Includes inter-divisional transfers.

** Annualised and based on weighted average equity shares outstanding.

APPENDIX 2

Major New Investments: Total Estimated Outlay

Projects	*Location*	*Capacity (Tons per annum)*	*Estimated Outlay*
A. In Reliance Industries Limited (Estimated investment: Over Rs 50 bn)			
Ethylene Cracker	Hazira	750,000	
New Polyester Complex			
PFY	Hazira	120,000	
PSF		100,000	
PET		80,000	
PTA		350,000	
EO/EG		100,000	
Modernisation/Expansion			
PVC	Hazira	From 100,000 to 300,000	
PE	Hazira	From 160,000 to 200,000	
EO/EG	Hazira	From 100,000 to 130,000	
PTA	Patalganga	From 200,000 to 275,000	
PSF	Patalganga	From 60,000 to 80,000	
LAB	Patalganga	From 80,000 to 100,000	
POY/PFY	Patalganga	From 75,000 to 100,000	
Textiles	Naroda		
B. Others			
Reliance Petroleum Ltd: Refinery	Jamnagar	9,000,000	Rs 51.4 bn
Reliance Polypropylene*	Hazira	250,000	Rs 6.0 bn
Reliance Polyethylene*	Hazira	160,000	Rs 5.5 bn

* Both joint ventures with C. Itochu, Japan.

Note: This table does not include proposed investments in oil exploration–production (Reliance-Enron consortium).

Source: Chairman's statement, company reports and other published information.

APPENDIX 3

The Product Flow

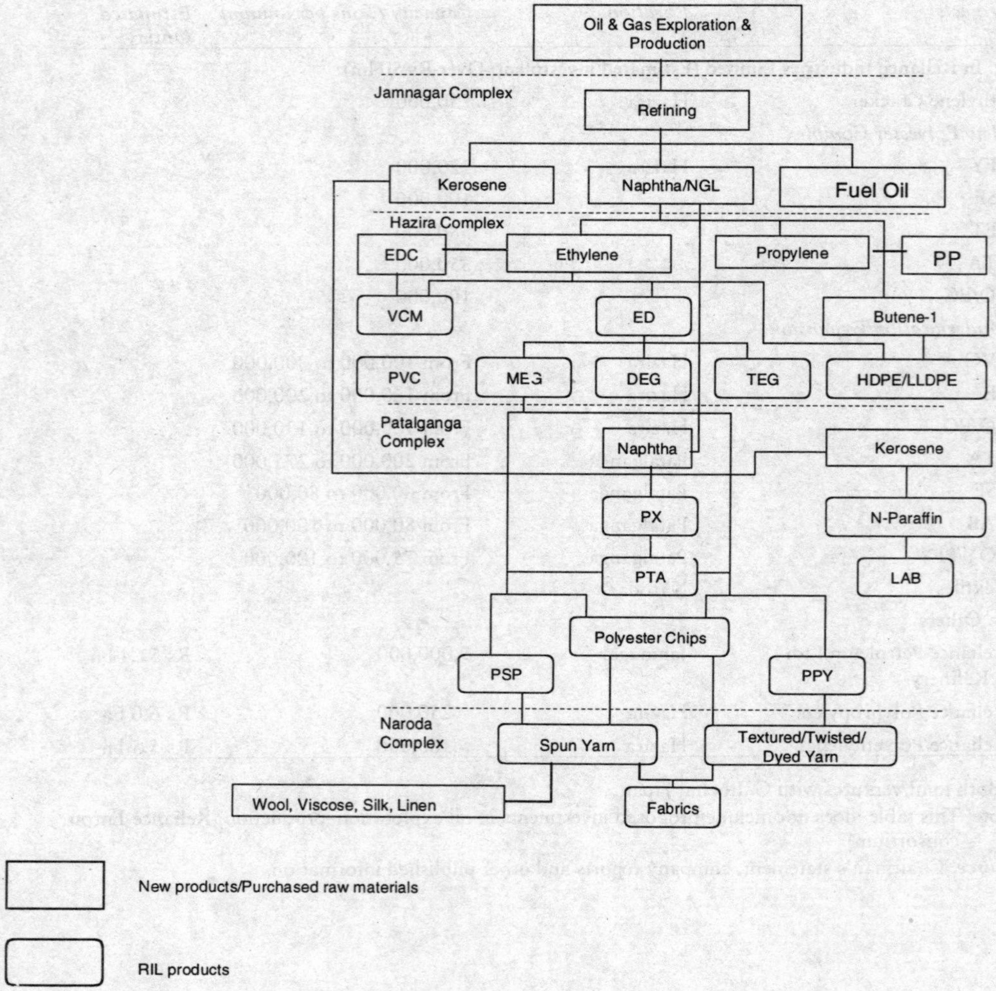

APPENDIX 4

Fabrics: Modernisation and Expansion

1982	Modernisation of the textile plant completed and balancing equipment installed. Installation of additional diesel generating sets for maintaining continuous production and to combat any power crisis undertaken.
1983	Additional modernisation of textile plant commenced. Replacement of existing shuttle looms with shuttle-less Waterjet and Sulzer Machines (state-of-the-art technology) undertaken. Other (balancing) investments to improve the quality and widen the product range also undertaken. An effluent treatment plant also set up—the first of its kind for the textile industry in the country.
1984	Modernisation of weaving and other facilities completed.
1985	Diesel generating capacity enhanced to 13 MW. Modernisation of knitting and yarn twisting facilities undertaken. On completion the twisting installation will be the largest in the world under one roof. The knitting facility will enable production of sophisticated furnishing fabrics.
1987–88	Furnishing fabrics launched.
1988–89	Modernisation programme completed. License capacity for manufacture of worsted spun increased from 12,500 spindles to 20,000 spindles.
1992–93	Industry de-licensed. Fresh capital outlay of Rs 1 bn planned.

Source: Annual reports and the director's report of the company for various years.

APPENDIX 5

Polyester Filament Yarn: Modernisation And Expansion

1982	Started commercial production on 1 November. Operations at full rated capacity of 10,000 MT.
1983	Installation of an additional 4th line for the production of flat finer denier yarn which enables manufacture of light-weight fabrics started. Additional investment in a waste recovery plant (to reclaim polymer waste and effect economies of production) and diesel generating sets as stand-by to meet power requirements.
1984	Additional line installation completed.
1985	Licence endorsed to a higher capacity—from 10,000 to 25,125 MT. Enhanced capacity implemented by the third quarter of 1985.
1989–90	Under the new policy of Minimum Economic Scale (MES) announced by the government licensed capacity for PFY increased to 32,300 MT. Further, as per the new broadbanding scheme announced, manufacture of PFY was feasible against licensed PSF capacity. Manufacture of polyester chips for sale was also feasible. Expansion of PFY capacity planned. Memorandum of Understanding signed with West Bengal Industrial Development Corporation (WBIDC) for setting up a joint sector project for the manufacture of 150,000 MT of PFY in West Bengal.
1990–1991	New joint sector company—Reliance Bengal Industries Ltd—formed. Steps undertaken to (i) transfer the LOI from WBIDC to the joint sector company and (ii) enhance capacity to 25,000 MT.
1992–93	Industry de-licensed. Efforts on to increase production by de-bottlenecking. Expansion plans were afoot to set up a 70,000 MT polyester plant at Hazira, Gujarat, based on DuPont technology currently in use at the Patalganga plant.

Source: Annual reports and the director's report of the company for various years.

APPENDIX 6

Other Projects Considered

Project	*1985*	*1986*	*1987*
Polyester industrial yarn	LoI received for manufacturing 2,000 MT. LoI includes manufacture of tyre cord.		
Spandex fibre/yarn	LoI received for manufacturing 300 MT. Licence surrendered.		
Electronics:			
Colour picture tubes and colour glass shells		Clearance obtained for manufacture of 0.5 m colour picture tubes and 1.5 m colour glass shells. Action initiated for identification of collaborators to implement the project.	
Acrylic fibre			LoI received for manufacture of 20,000 MT.

Source: Annual reports and the director's report for the company for various years.

APPENDIX 7

Modernisation and Expansion

A. PSF	
1984	Licence obtained for setting up a 45,000 MT manufacturing facility. Active implementation started. Commissioning expected within fifteen months of receipt of Letter of Intent (LoI) on 1 February 1985.
1986	45,000 MT plant commissioned in March 1986—fourteen months after receipt of LoI. Plant production and quality stabilised in the latter half after overcoming initial teething troubles.
1989–90	As per the MES policy, licensed capacity enhanced to 60,000 MT.
1992–93	Industry de-licensed. Strategic alliance with ICI. Additional capacity of 30,000 MT of PSF.
B.PTA	
1984	Government clearance obtained for setting up 75,000 MT manufacturing facility.
1985	Implementation of the 75,000 MT facility in progress. Expected completion by end of 1986.
1986	Requisite permissions received after unexpected delay. Expected completion of the enhanced facility for 100,000 MT (licence endorsed to this figure) by mid–1987.
1987–88	100,000 MT plant commissioned in early 1988.
1988–89	Application for setting up a 100 per cent export oriented unit (EOU) made.
1990–91	Under MES policy, licensed capacity increased to 200,000 MT. Expansion of PTA taken up. Government clearance for setting up a 200,000 MT 100 per cent EOU received.
1990–91	First stage of capacity expansion to 200,000 MT completed.
1991–92	Capacity expansion to 200,000 MT completed.
1992–93	Industry de-licensed. Full capacity utilisation. Plans afoot to set up a fresh 350,000 MT facility at Hazira, Gujarat. Proposal submitted to financial institutions for appraisal.
C. Paraxylene	
1988–89	Trial production commenced. Application for setting up a 100 per cent EOU made.
1988–89	Over 10,000 MT produced for sale. Government clearance for setting up a 270,000 MT 100 per cent EOU received.

Appendix 7 contd. . .

D. Mono Ethylene Glycol/Ethylene Oxide	
1984	Licence obtained for setting up a 40,000 MT facility.
1986	Land for setting up the project acquired at Hazira, Gujarat. Permission for enhancing capacity to 60,000 MT sought.
1987–88	Government clearance for enhanced capacity obtained.
1989–90	Under MES, capacity enhanced to 100,000 MT. A captive gas-based power plant and construction of jetty for transporting ethylene and other products being set up as they were found necessary. Commissioning rescheduled to the first quarter of 1991 from previous estimate of late 1990.
1991–92	100,000 MT facility commissioned.
1992–93	Capacity expansion planned to 130,000 MT through de-bottlenecking and expansion. Government clearance obtained for manufacture of 10,000 MT of ethylene oxide. Production already achieved.
E: LAB	
1984	Government clearance obtained for setting up a 50,000 MT manufacturing facility.
1986	Licence re-endorsed to 60,000 MT. Implementation delayed due to delay in receipt of requisite clearances. Expected completion by mid–1987.
1987–88	60,000 MT plant commissioned in the second quarter of 1988.
1989–90	Under MES policy, licensed capacity increased to 80,000 MT.
1992–93	Industry de-licensed. Capacity expansion to 80,000 MT completed. Capacity expansion to 100,000 MT planned.
F. LAB Front End: N-Paraffin	
1989–90	Until now N-Paraffin was raw material for manufacture of LAB and was being imported. Plans afoot to install machinery that would facilitate manufacture of LAB from kerosene with N-Paraffin as intermediate raw material.
1991–92	Facility for production of N-Paraffin from kerosene completed.

Source: Annual reports and the director's report of the company for various years.

APPENDIX 8

Major Financial Events Related to Capital Markets

Accounting Year	*Event*	*Amount (Rs million)*	*Remarks*
1983–84	1. Fund Mobilised: Partially Converible Debenture (Series E) of Rs 150 face value	800	Rs 50 converted into one share at a premium of Rs 40 for financing the modernisation programme at textiles and polyester filament yarn units.
	2. Extinguishment of Debt	723.2	Exchange ratio:issue 1.4 equity shares for every Rs 100 outstanding.
1984–85	1. Fund Mobilised: Non-convertible Debenture (Series F) of Rs 100	2700	To finance the PFY expansion, establishment of PSF and PTA facilities, and to augment long-term resources for meeting working capital requirements.
1985–86	1. Fund Mobilised: Fully Convertible Debenture (Series G) of Rs 145 face value	5000	Convertible into two equity shares to part finance the capital expenditure programme (PTA, MEG and HDPE projects) and to augment long-term resources for meeting working capital requirements.
1987–88	1. Fund Mobilised: Equity Shares Non-convertible Debentures of Rs 100 face value	1980	Issued at a premium of Rs 50 per share to part finance PTA, MEG and HDPE projects.
		800	To augment long-term resources.
1988–89	1. Funds Mobilised: Reliance Petrochemicals Limited—subsidiary company		To finance MEG, PVC and HDPE projects. In addition RIL has invested Rs 576 mn as equity and provided interest free non-refundable loan of Rs 500 mn to be converted into equity in October 1991.
	Fully Convertible Debenture of Rs 150 face value	5930.4	

Appendix 8 contd. . .

Accounting Year	*Event*	*Amount (Rs million)*	*Remarks*
1990–91	1. Funds Mobilised: Non-convertible Debenture of Rs 100 face value.	750	
	Reliance Petrochemicals Limited ceases to be a subsidiary company on early conversion of debentures into equity.	—	Conversion of Part B and Part C preponed. Conversion into equity at par.
1991–92	1. Funds Mobilised: Partly Convertible Debentures (Series H)	5469	Debentures Series H, J and K were issued to part finance the cracker project.
	Non-convertible Debentures (Series J) with a detachable warrant	1311	Rs 2280 mn worth of K series debentures devolved on the underwriters as they were not taken up.
	Non-convertible Debentures (Series K) of Rs 100 face value	2655	
	Roll Over Series F Debentures	—	Roll over made, inter alia, for financing the additional cost of arising out of enhancement in cracker complex capacity.
	Reliance Petrochemicals Limited merged with Reliance Industries Limited by exchange of equity. Exchange ratio of one RIL share for ten RPL shares.		Equity amounting to a total of Rs 749.4 mn issued to shareholders of RPL. Surplus of Rs 6744.7 credited to amalgamation reserve.
1992–93	1. Funds Mobilised: First-ever issue of GDR for US$ 150.42 mn	4624.8	Each GDR--two underlying equity shares of Rs 10 each of RIL. As a result the equity of RIL increased by Rs 184 mn. The rest being share premium.
	Reliance Polypropylene Limited and Reliance Polyethylene Limited identical issues	3250 3250	To part finance the polypropylene and polyethylene projects. Each comprising Rs 250 mn of equity at par and Rs 3000 mn of optionally fully convertible debenture.
1993–94	Reliance Petroleum Limited Triple Option Convertible Debentures (TOCD) of Rs 60 each with tradable warrants	21720	To part finance the refinery project. No interest would accrue on the TOCDs for the first five years from the date of allotment.

APPENDIX 9

Petrochemicals: History of Projects - The Last Ten Years

A. Plastics: Polyethylene/Polyvinyl Chloride

1983	Entered into an agreement with Union Carbide for the acquisition of their plastics and chemicals unit at Bombay which produced, among others ethylene, polyethylene, benzene, etc. Post-acquisition (which was expected to be completed by June 1984) additional investment planned to double the turnover of the unit from Rs 500 mn to Rs 1 bn.
1984	Union Carbide takeover delayed.
1985	On account of delays in obtaining various approvals for the takeover of Union Carbide, the acquisition proposal was called off. HDPE/PVC government clearance obtained. LoI for manufacture of 50,000 MT of HDPE and 100,000 MT of PVC received.
1986	Land acquired at Hazira, Gujarat, for setting up the plastics complex. Technology agreements signed. Recruitment of key personnel undertaken.
1987–88	LoI transferred to RPL.
1988–89	Under implementation by RPL. All the necessary steps for purchase, supply and import of equipment taken. Expected commissioning in second half of 1990 as per schedule.
1989–90	Under MES, capacity of HDPE enhanced to 100,000 MT. Mechanical completion of both PVC and HDPE plants by the first quarter of 1991.
1990–91	Under MES, capacity of HDPE further enhanced to 160,000 MT. Also, permission for manufacture of LLDPE along with HDPE under the same capacity received. No change in PVC manufacture.
1991–92	Construction of both 160,000 MT facility for manufacture of polyethylene HDPE/LLDPE and 100,000 MT PVC facility completed.
1992–93	Industries de-licensed. Trial production of polyethylene commenced. After initial start-up problems, PVC capacity utilisation of over 100 per cent achieved. Capacity expansion of polyethylene from 160,000 MT to 200,000 MT and PVC from 100,000 MT to 300,000 MT planned. In addition, joint ventures with C. Itochu of Japan for manufacture of 160,000 MT of polyethylene and 250,000 MT of polypropylene under implementation. Completion end 1994.

B. Ethylene Cracker

1988–89	LoI for manufacture of 320,000 MT of ethylene, 155,000 MT of propylene, 98,000 MT of butadiene and other C4s received.

Appendix 9 contd. . .

1990–91	Appraisal by financial institutions. Licence endorsed for higher capacities: ethylene to 400,000 MT, propylene to 195,000 MT, butadiene and other C4s to 120,000 MT.
1992–93	Licence further endorsed for higher capacities: ethylene to 750,000 MT and propylene to 365,000 MT. Permission also received to produce 235,000 MT of benzene, 197,000 MT of toluene and 100,000 MT of xylene. Majority of detailed engineering work completed. To be completed towards the end of 1995.
C. Refinery	
1991–92	Government clearance received for setting up a refinery of 9 MT per annum capacity grassroots refinery. Techno-economic feasibility under evaluation. Several international companies also approached for equity participation.
1992–93	A new company—Reliance Petroleum—formed for implementing the project. Project location site selection made. Project appraised by IDBI for techno-commercial feasibility. MOU signed with Bharat Petroleum for marketing the products. Trial runs and commercial production were expected by the second quarter of 1996.

Source: Annual reports and the director's report of the company for various years.

APPENDIX 10

Market Share of Key Products

Product	*Market Share (%)*	*Size vs. Next Competitor*
Purified terephthalic acid	65	3.3
Monoethylene glycol	56	5.0
Polyester filament yarn	49	3.5
Polyester staple fibre	31	3.9
Linear alkyl benzene	40	1.0
Polyvinyl chloride	37	2.1
Polyethylene	48	1.5
Fabrics	NA	Largest producer of fabrics in India

C A S E 7

RANBAXY LABORATORIES LIMITED: FROM VISION TO ACTION

> 'What differentiates an entrepreneur? To visualise a dream and go after it. At the end of the day, that's what you do in life. Either that dream can be so unreachable, so crazy that you never reach it—or that dream can have the inherent ability to be achieved.'

With these words, Dr Parvinder Singh, chairman of Ranbaxy Laboratories Ltd, described the ambitious targets he had set for the company his father had founded. In 1993 Ranbaxy had enunciated a long-term objective to become a research-based international pharmaceutical company. Two milestones were also defined. By 2003, the company aimed to achieve revenues of US$ 1 bn, as well as the development of a proprietary therapeutic molecule. These targets

This case was written by research associates Manisha Dahad, Neill Mooney, Asif Ahmed and Huma Varcie under the supervision of Sumantra Ghoshal, Robert P. Baumann Professor of Strategic Leadership at the London Business School. The authors are grateful to Ranbaxy Laboratories Ltd for their help and support. The case was first registered by the London Business School in 1999.

represented a significant stretch for a company that, in 1993, had revenues of US$ 85 mn and no appreciable basic research capability.

By most measures, Ranbaxy was a phenomenal success story. The company was the first Indian pharmaceutical company to look for an export market in the 1970s. By 1997, Ranbaxy had 16 per cent of the Indian pharmaceutical export market share and was ranked eleventh in *Business Week*'s list of fifty 'excellent' companies in Asia. It was also the first Indian company to achieve international acclaim for a world class technical capability in chemical process re-engineering. Ranbaxy was further recognised as one of the leading Indian investors in state-of-the-art pharmaceutical plant and R&D.

In 1989, the president of India acknowledged Ranbaxy's contribution to R&D by awarding it the national award for research. On four occasions the company had won the Indian Chamber of Commerce 'Trishul' award for export achievements. Ranbaxy had become a household name in India and international fund managers were increasingly taking notice of the activities of this small but fast-growing Indian company.

The considerable achievements of his company gave Dr Singh confidence that his dreams would become realities. However, success was by no means guaranteed. Achieving his dreams would require that Ranbaxy go through a major transformation. This transformation would be especially challenging as it would have to occur within the Indian context in an increasingly globalising and competitive industry. Dr Singh commented on the challenge that lay ahead: 'Ranbaxy cannot change India. Instead what it can do is create a pocket of excellence. Ranbaxy must be an island within India.'

History

Ranbaxy was founded in Amritsar in 1937 by Ranjit Singh and Dr Gurbax Singh, starting out as the Indian distributor of vitamins and anti-tuberculosis drugs for a Japanese pharmaceutical company. After the Second World War, Ranbaxy continued in its role as a distributor, and in 1951 took over the North Indian distribution for Lapetit, an Italian pharmaceutical company. A wealthy businessman, Bhai Mohan Singh, joined the company as a partner in 1952, bringing with him capital to fuel the company's continuing growth (see Appendix 1).

Protectionist government policies requiring the indigenous manufacture of essential drugs provided Ranbaxy with the opportunity to become involved for the first time in the manufacture of pharmaceuticals. With technological assistance from Lapetit, Ranbaxy established its first manufacturing plant in Okhla in 1961. By 1962, Ranbaxy had 200 employees, with seventy field staff selling products to retailers and doctors. In 1966, Ranbaxy's relationship with Lapetit faltered because of disagreements over the degree of value to be added in the Indian operations. Lapetit wanted to export completely packed products from Italy, whereas Ranbaxy was interested in importing bulk pharmaceuticals and moving formulation and packaging to India. As a result of this conflict, Lapetit pulled out of the partnership and Ranbaxy had to quickly replace Lapetit's brands with its own. Ranbaxy met this challenge, rapidly developing capabilities in chemical synthesis and marketing. By the end of 1969, all of Lapetit's brands had been replaced by Ranbaxy equivalents.

Ranbaxy's first real breakthrough came with Calmpose—a copy of Roche's patented Valium tranquilliser. Calmpose was launched in 1969—before Roche could establish a presence in the market. The Calmpose campaign was based on an excerpt from a famous Indian poem—'If the long sleep of death is certain, why am I denied sleep in this life'—and proved to be so successful that the posters became collector's items. Ranbaxy took further aggressive action to block Valium's entry, dropping Calmpose's price by 25 per cent and issuing credit notes for a similar discount on existing stocks. As a result of the success achieved with Calmpose, the company achieved a higher level of market recognition and subsequently found the introduction of new products easier. Ranbaxy achieved further successes with Roscillin, India's first ampicillin, and paracetamol.

In 1967, Dr Parvinder Singh, Bhai Mohan Singh's son, returned from Michigan after completing his PhD in pharmacology. He injected a new management style and a renewed focus on technology and quality. On one occasion, stock worth Rs 200,000 was discarded after failing to meet quality standards—an expensive decision for a company which had net profits of only Rs 1.8 mn in 1968. Ranbaxy also made efforts to deepen the company's pool of technological and managerial expertise, hiring staff who had previous experience abroad or with multinationals in India.

By 1971 Ranbaxy had gained a strong position in anti-infectives in the Indian market and expanded manufacturing capacity to keep pace with sales. The company financed its first bulk drugs facility at Mohali, India, with a public issue of equity in 1971 for Rs 17 mn which was oversubscribed sixteen times. A second multipurpose plant at Mohali was financed by another public issue for Rs 31 mn.

The period from 1970 to the late 1980s saw two major developments in the Indian pharmaceutical industry. The first of these was the introduction of the Process Patent Act in 1970, which required Indian companies to recognise international process patents. Crucially, the Act did not require recognition of product patents, granting Indian companies the licence to reproduce patented foreign drugs as long as they were produced in a novel way. Ranbaxy was well placed to capitalise on the opportunity this presented, having built a formidable chemical synthesis capability while reverse-engineering Lapetit's drug portfolio. In 1978 Ranbaxy became the first Indian pharmaceutical company to develop a novel process for the manufacture of the antibiotic doxycycline. This process was granted its own US patent in 1990. In 1985, Ranbaxy found a new way to manufacture ranitidine, the generic of Glaxo's Zantac anti-ulcerant—the world's best selling drug. Ranbaxy gained international recognition in 1992 with the development of a non-patent infringing process for the antibiotic cefaclor. This was remarkable, as the molecule was complex and Eli Lilly, the product originator, had protected it with twenty-two process patents.

The second piece of Indian legislation that had a profound effect on Ranbaxy's development was the Price Control Act of 1979. By capping prices for drugs sold in the domestic market the government severely restricted profit and growth opportunities for Indian pharmaceutical companies. This prompted Ranbaxy to look to export markets to realise its ambitious growth targets. At that time, this was a radical strategy for an Indian pharmaceutical company to pursue and Ranbaxy's competitors remained steadfastly focussed on the Indian market. The main force behind Ranbaxy's export drive was D.S. Brar, who joined the company as a business development manager in 1977. The result-oriented Brar was later to become the company's president and would play a key role in the further international expansion during the 1990s.

Ranbaxy initially targeted export markets in developing countries, focussing on the export of bulk pharmaceutical feedstocks and intermediaries manufactured at Mohali. The ten years from 1986 to 1996 saw exports increase dramatically, with an average annual growth rate of 34 per cent (Appendix 2). Major markets contributing to this growth were China, the UK, Italy, Russia, Ukraine and the USA. By the mid-1990s exports accounted for nearly half of Ranbaxy's turnover and, with total export revenues of $120 mn in 1996, the company accounted for almost 0.5 per cent of total Indian exports. Eighty-four per cent of the exports were still in bulk chemicals, the other 16 per cent in formulations. In addition to exporting bulk pharmaceuticals, Ranbaxy entered into a number of joint ventures with foreign partners with the objective of establishing a manufacturing and marketing presence abroad.

As Ranbaxy entered the 1990s, fundamental changes were taking place in many of the company's key markets. The core Indian market was moving towards full membership of the World Trade Organisation by 2005. This change would require Indian companies to fully comply with international patent legislation—including the recognition of product patents. The Indian economy was becoming increasingly integrated into the global economy and foreign investment was reaching record levels. In 1997, one Ranbaxy manager commented on this changing environment:

> Complying with WTO will cause strategic shifts in the industry. We will increasingly see a trend towards mergers, brand acquisitions, consolidation and the exit of many smaller companies. Cross-licensing from overseas and the entry of multinationals in the Indian market will also be widespread. In short, the next six or seven years will see the second birth of the Indian pharmaceutical market.

The Global Pharmaceutical Industry

The international companies with which Ranbaxy increasingly had to compete could be categorised into two groups, viz., manufacturers of either ethical or generic pharmaceuticals. The largest ethical companies engaged in new drug discovery programmes, in a business characterised by high investments in R&D and by high returns on a few blockbuster drugs. International patent law provided these innovators with protection from competition for a period of time over which they could recoup their investments in R&D. Upon patent expiry, generic pharmaceutical companies were allowed to introduce copies of ethical drugs, with a subsequent erosion of margins.

Ethical Manufacturers

Barriers to entry in the ethical pharmaceutical industry were high. R&D spending requirements and high marketing costs combined to make new product introduction very expensive. Ethical companies spent an average of US $ 300 mn bringing each new product to the market. The time required to realise positive returns on these significant investments was also very long, as new drugs were subject to very stringent regulatory controls. Despite these large investments and long payback periods, the major ethical pharmaceutical companies created significant value for their shareholders.

Value for Shareholders

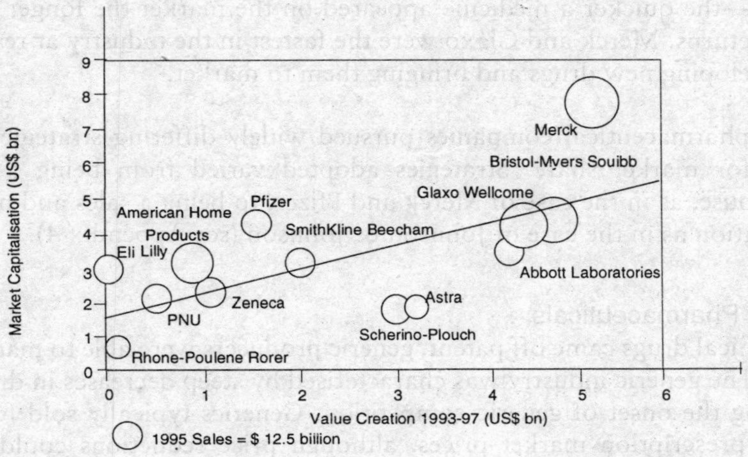

Pharmaceutical researchers described the traditional drug development process as 'molecular roulette'. Only one out of every 5,000 compounds discovered by researchers proved safe and effective enough to receive regulatory approval. In the 1990s, firms pioneered new approaches to improve the 'hit rates' on research. New research techniques such as combinatorial chemistry permitted the screening of many more compounds than conventional methods. These techniques allowed a greater number of chemicals to be tested and manufactured by a smaller number of highly skilled scientists.

The development life cycle of a drug could be as long as twelve years (see Appendix 3). In the US, the first two to four years were spent on pre-clinical testing, the next five to six years on human clinical testing and the last one to three years gaining regulatory approval from the FDA. Over 80 per cent of the total R&D cost of a successful new drug was typically spent in the three stages of clinical trials.

Patents were granted for a period of twenty years starting from the day a patent for a new molecule was filed with the Patent Technology Office. As it took about twelve years to bring a new product to market, this system typically left ethical pharmaceutical companies eight years, on average, to recoup their investments. A premium was therefore placed on bringing new drugs to market as rapidly as possible—the quicker a medicine appeared on the market the longer it had to realise returns. Merck and Glaxo were the fastest in the industry at researching and developing new drugs and bringing them to market.

Ethical pharmaceutical companies pursued widely differing strategies as they fought for market share. Strategies adopted varied from being a research powerhouse, as in the case of Merck and Pfizer, to being a sales and marketing organisation as in the case of Johnson & Johnson (see Appendix 4).

Generic Pharmaceuticals

Once ethical drugs came off patent, generic producers were able to manufacture copies. The generic industry was characterised by steep decreases in drug prices following the onset of generic competition. Generics typically sold for 30 per cent of prescription market prices, although price reductions could be even greater. Margins could sometimes be increased by marketing products in dosage forms and strengths different from those of the innovators' products.

Generic products were marketed either under a generic chemical name or under a generic company brand name. Generics of Glaxo's Zantac brand would, for example, be marketed as ranitidine (chemical name) or under the private brand of the generic manufacturer. Marketing requirements varied from country to country. India, Russia, Germany and China were branded generic markets. The US and UK were examples of non-branded generic markets which were more like pure commodity markets, characterised by a higher degree of price competition.

The US market for generics in 1995 was worth about US$ 7 bn. Although this accounted for 40 per cent by volume of the US pharmaceutical market, it only accounted for 11 per cent by value. It was projected that seventy-nine drugs would go off patent in the US in the 1996–2001 period, creating a potential market worth US$ 5 bn. This new market represented a window of opportunity for the world's generic manufacturers.

There was no standard business model for generic drug companies, each choosing to add value in a different way. Activities could range from bulk manufacture to formulating fully packaged dosage forms. There was an increasing trend for generic companies to perform R&D activities in the search for added value in formulations. A few companies even engaged in research for new therapeutic compounds.

Significant Launches Anticipated

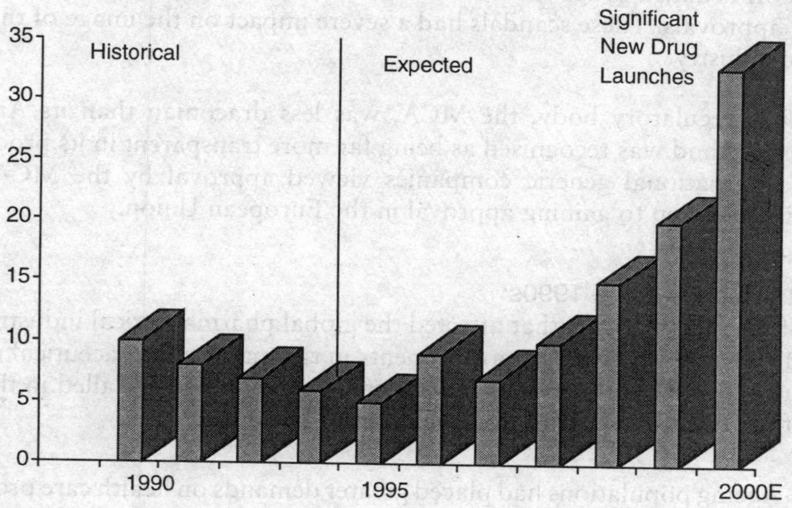

Generic firms had much lower profit margins—in the order of 10 per cent for bulk chemicals and 40 per cent for formulations—than their ethical counterparts. The world's major generic companies included Ivax, Teva and Novopharm. Generic companies followed a number of different strategies in their quest for margins and market share (see Appendix 5).

Although generic companies could capture market share in a number of ways, they all had to address the challenge of gaining regulatory approval in the markets they served. The US Food and Drug Administration (FDA) was widely recognised as being the most stringent regulatory body in the world. The FDA approval process required the submission of an Abbreviated New Drug Application (ANDA) to the authorities. ANDA submissions were expensive as they required the manufacture of a sizeable batch of the product. The batch had to pass stringent quality control tests and demonstrate 'bio-equivalence'. The demonstration of bio-equivalence involved matching drug concentration profiles in the bloodstream of volunteers with those of the innovator's product. The average time from filing an ANDA application to FDA approval was three years.

Regulatory approval for generics in the US market had become exceptionally stringent because of a highly publicised scandal in 1988–91. Investigations had revealed that a number of generic companies had submitted fraudulent data, passed off branded drugs for testing as their own and paid off FDA officials to obtain approvals. These scandals had a severe impact on the image of the entire generic industry.

The UK's regulatory body, the MCA, was less draconian than its American counterpart and was recognised as being far more transparent in its procedures. Many international generic companies viewed approval by the MCA as an essential first step to gaining approval in the European Union.

Industry Trends in the 1990s

One of the major drivers that affected the global pharmaceutical industry in the early 1990s was an effort by governments in the major pharmaceutical markets to reduce health care spending. Health care spending had spiralled in the latter half of the twentieth century for a number of reasons:

- Ageing populations had placed greater demands on health care providers.
- Consumers demanded more from their doctors and felt increasingly empowered to choose the 'best' care on entering rather than coming out of the consulting room.
- Public budgets for health care had decreased and insurers passed on ever larger premiums at the company level.

To combat the rising costs of health care, a number of schemes had been introduced by governments and insurance companies. In the US and other Western countries, Managed Care Organisations (MCOs) were established that integrated the financing and delivery of health care from the outset. Managed care involved a number of cost reduction methods—the two most common being bulk purchase of services and generic substitution.

The second factor that affected the global pharmaceutical industry was the ability of key players to greatly shorten the time required for the development of new drugs. This was a result of scientific innovations which increased the effectiveness of the drug discovery process.

As pharmaceutical companies reduced development times, regulators also reduced new drug approval times. During 1997, the FDA was expected to review 90 per cent of priority applications within six months of filing, compared with only 56 per cent of priority applications reviewed over a similar period in 1996. The combination of reduced drug development times and faster approval stimulated new drug discovery research programmes and was expected to contribute to a glut of new drug launches by the year 2000.

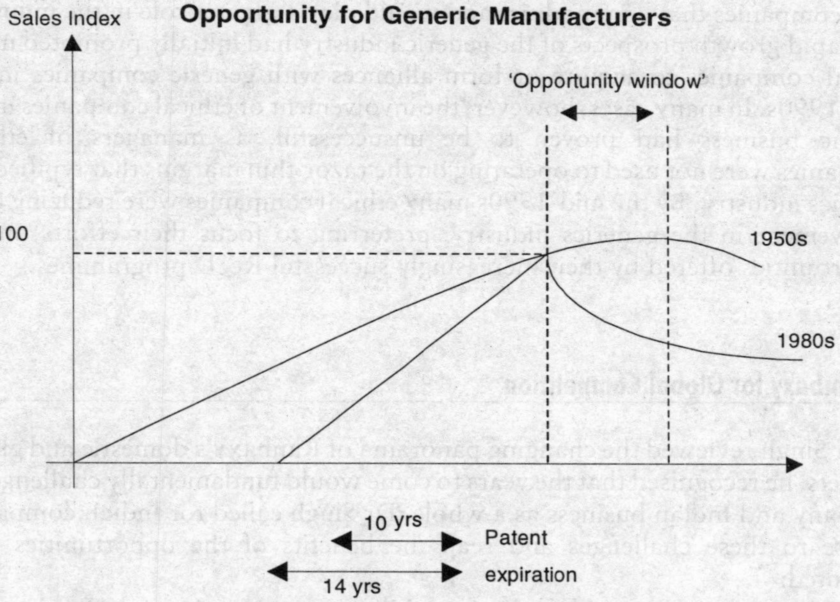

Changes were also underway in the FDA approval process for generic drugs. The FDA had traditionally phased in generic competition on expiry of the innovator's product patent, granting production rights to only a very few generic companies over an extended period of time. Increasingly, larger numbers of generic manufacturers had been given approval simultaneously. This development had the effect of greatly increasing the intensity of generic competition and consequently shortening the economic life cycles of branded drugs. The effects of this change were often dramatic: the price of Bristol Myers Squibb's hypertension drug Capoten fell by almost 90 per cent the day after its product patent expired.

Industry Response

The ethical pharmaceutical companies responded to the changing environment with a move towards 'big is beautiful'. Merger and acquisition activity resulted in the creation of still larger drug companies which could apply greater economies of scale both to their R&D costs as well as to their general operations. The financial depth of these organisations also gave them a greater ability to compete on price and resist competition.

Implicit in the move towards consolidation was the recognition on the part of drug companies that commoditisation would play a greater role in the industry. The rapid growth prospects of the generic industry had initially prompted many ethical companies to acquire or form alliances with generic companies in the early 1990s. In many cases, however, the involvement of ethical companies in the generic business had proven to be unsuccessful, as managers of ethical companies were not used to operating on the razor-thin margins that typified the generics industry. By the mid-1990s many ethical companies were reducing their involvement in the generics industry, preferring to focus their efforts on the opportunities offered by their increasingly successful R&D programmes.

Positioning Ranbaxy for Global Competition

As Dr Singh reviewed the changing panorama of Ranbaxy's domestic and global markets, he recognised that the years to come would fundamentally challenge his company and Indian business as a whole. Dr Singh called for Indian companies to rise to these challenges and reap the benefits of the opportunities they presented:

> This opportunity addresses our ability to respond to demanding international markets. It comprehensively challenges our methods of production, delivery, servicing, quality management and pricing. It raises demands on us to create a highly productive workplace, to innovate, to leverage technology, to network with a variety of institutions, organisations and people, and to compete successfully on

time. The adeptness with which we respond will alone ensure survival and growth.

In 1993, Ranbaxy's senior management underwent a strategic planning exercise—Vision 2003. At the end of this process, the company had clearly defined medium- and longer-term goals that would provide a framework for growth into the new millennium. By the year 2003 Ranbaxy aimed to achieve two milestones outlined in the company's 'vision statement': $1 bn in revenues and the development of one new therapeutic chemical molecule. The longer-term development of the company would be guided by the principles enshrined in the company's mission statement: 'to become an international, research-based pharmaceutical company'.

The mission statement posed significant challenges at all levels of the company and required that Ranbaxy radically change its business. At the most fundamental level, the company would have to redefine its product offerings and the markets it served. This new focus would in turn demand radical changes in the company's organisation and culture as well as the development of a range of new capabilities. It remained to be seen whether Ranbaxy could succeed in this ambitious venture.

Changing the Product and Market Focus

During the early 1990s Ranbaxy began to adjust its product mix, gradually replacing low-margin bulk pharmaceuticals with higher-margin formulations. This transition was the first step up a value curve (see Appendix 6) in which intermediates occupied the lowest margin position (2 to 12 per cent), rising through conventional generics (12 to 20 per cent), value-added/branded generics (30 to 40 per cent), new drug delivery systems or NDDS (45 to 60 per cent) and culminating in proprietary molecules or NDDR (60 to 80 per cent). By 2003 Ranbaxy's management hoped to generate 50 per cent of revenues from research-based products. Bulk chemicals would primarily be used for captive consumption.

Ranbaxy also aimed to be the No. 1 pharmaceutical company in the Indian market by 2003, commanding an 8 to 10 per cent market share, almost double of the share it commanded in 1997. This domestic business would provide 30 per cent of the company's total revenues. The overseas business would be supported by a significant presence in the US and UK as well as operations in Europe,

Russia and China. The company's revenues and international scope would place it among the top five generic companies in the world.

Ranbaxy had traditionally marketed branded generics but was becoming increasingly involved in non-branded generic markets. Success in each market depended on very different strategies. Ranbaxy's key branded generic markets included India, Russia and China. In these markets, the company sold branded products direct to GPs. This approach invariably required a large direct sales force, and demanded a high degree of marketing effort to build brand awareness. Over many years Ranbaxy had developed a broad portfolio of successful brands in the domestic Indian market. As Russia and China were relatively new markets, Ranbaxy focussed on marketing a few key products in these countries.

The UK and US were the non-branded generic markets in which essentially identical products competed for market share on the basis of price. Generic companies operating in these markets, such as Norton Healthcare in the UK, typically offered a very wide range of generic drugs. On entering these markets, Ranbaxy aimed to match this product breadth. The major barrier to realising this strategy had been to surpass regulatory hurdles. The company had met with considerable success in the UK, gaining approval for many products from the MCA, but had run into difficulties in the US. By 1996, Ranbaxy had been present in the US market since 1994 but had yet to successfully bring a product to market. To redress this problem, Ranbaxy dramatically increased the number of ANDAs filed. From 1995 to 1996 the US operation had filed two ANDAs. The subsequent two-year period saw the number of applications increase first to four and then to fourteen per year.

Internationalising the Business

In April 1993, worldwide business operations were regrouped into four regions, with four regional headquarters located in New Delhi, London, Hong Kong and Raleigh (North Carolina). Regions were operated as profit centres, reporting directly to Brar in Delhi.

Ranbaxy had established specific guidelines about the nature of its involvement in overseas markets. Traditionally, the company had sold bulk chemicals to foreign purchasers and had no direct presence abroad. A move 'up the value curve' to formulated products had created the need for increased market responsiveness, which demanded a local presence in foreign markets. In structuring foreign ventures, Ranbaxy focussed on controlling the entire value chain to maximise margins. The company had made an acquisition in the US with the purchase of Ohm Labs, a generic formulation company with an exemplary FDA approval record.

Ranbaxy's Worldwide Business

Region		*% 1997 Turnover*
Region I	Middle East	9.3
	India	46.2
Region II	CIS and Western Europe	20.7
Region III	China, Southeast Asia	15.9
Region IV	USA, Central/South America	7.9

Regional managers were generally given a large degree of autonomy; however, Indian management reserved the right to require overseas subsidiaries to market 'global brands'. Global brands were usually backward integrated with bulk chemicals produced in India. Regions were not required to pay development costs for these products but retained responsibility for meeting regulatory requirements at the local level.

Although Ranbaxy preferred 100 per cent equity participation, many foreign ventures were made possible through joint ventures and alliances. The company's highest profile partnership had been a series of joint venture arrangements with Eli Lilly, a US research-based pharmaceutical company. Under the terms of the agreement the companies set up equal participation joint ventures in India and the US. Lilly's interest in Ranbaxy originated in the latter's ability to devise a new process for manufacturing cefaclor, Lilly's best-selling antibiotic. Ranbaxy's process and low-cost manufacturing capability offered Lilly a means of competing in the newly genericised cefaclor market. In return, Lilly would help Ranbaxy access the US market.

Upgrading R&D

The second key element of the vision statement required that Ranbaxy develop a new therapeutic molecule with a total revenue potential of $400–500 mn beyond 2003. Dr Singh emphasised the need for developing a proprietary therapeutic molecule, even though the generic industry was attractive in its own right.

'We look at the development of a NCE ('new chemical entity')as a challenge, a stretch for the organisation. It upgrades the organisation. Why do we say that NCEs are only the preserve of the US and Europe? There is a market in generics; however, the real money will come in research. The example of the US generics industry is telling. It is highly cyclical and is volume- and cost-driven. That is not the kind of business we want to be in over the longer term.'

Other senior managers expanded on the importance of research for Ranbaxy within the context of the changing Indian business environment.

> Foreign pharmaceutical companies will at the end of the day, want to have their own presence in the Indian market. I grant you that the order of the day today is collaboration, not confrontation. But increasingly we will become vulnerable. We will have to give more than we get. We are buying time. We are also making investments internationally. In order to make these investments viable, we must also feed them new products.

The development of a new chemical molecule represented a very ambitious target for the company. Ranbaxy possessed an applied R&D capability which had traditionally focussed on process development for bulk chemical manufacture as well as on new dosage forms for formulated products. A new basic research capability would have to be built from the ground up to support the company's audacious objective. Given the very high costs of bringing a new drug to market, it seemed implausible that a small generics company could compete with the likes of Merck in R&D spending. Dr Singh commented on this apparent anomaly: 'I don't accept that it costs $300 mn to discover a new drug. We don't have that kind of money. We can factor that down by 4 if not 5. Spending $100 mn over a ten-year time period seems feasible.'

Although Indian scientists were paid less than their international counterparts, this was not seen as a sustainable source of cost advantage. Wages of highly skilled professionals were expected to rise to international levels within a few years. The real cost advantage of doing research in the Indian environment came from significantly lower ancillary costs. Administrative personnel, indigenous machinery and the low cost of running clinical trials all contributed to a significant overall cost advantage in R&D.

Ranbaxy also hoped to leverage its strengths in anti-infectives, focussing much of the new research effort in this area. As the Indian economy developed, it was anticipated that chronic illnesses would become more common. In anticipation of this trend, and with a view to the huge markets for these products that existed in the developed countries, Ranbaxy also targeted anti-cancer and cardiovascular drugs.

In 1997, Ranbaxy spent $12.6 mn on R&D, equivalent to 3.7 per cent of total revenues. This expenditure was planned to increase to $67 mn, or 6 per cent of turnover, by 2003. The increased R&D budget would be channelled into both traditional applied research and new drug development. The greatest increases would be seen in new drug development programmes.

The R&D expenditure programme had already enabled the development of a significant R&D capability. In 1994, the company opened a world class R&D facility in Gurgaon, India. Ranbaxy also hired an increasing number of foreign trained scientists. The investment in these facilities and staff had generated great pride throughout the organisation. One manager commented that realising an NCE had become 'the call of the company'. When asked if he thought the development of an NCE was possible, a senior US manager explained that this was not the relevant question. Instead, all that was required was that 'Ranbaxy's employees must have a dogmatic belief in the abilities of their scientists.'

Gurgaon developed the capability to rapidly perform bio-equivalence studies, giving the company critical speed in bringing novel dosage forms to market. The facility also co-ordinated clinical trials of new drugs for foreign ethical manufacturers. There was great interest in this capability, as ethical companies could screen drugs in India before doing vastly more expensive full-scale clinical trials in developed markets. Ranbaxy also agreed to in-license new molecules developed by Japanese pharmaceutical companies. In-licensing of molecules would allow Ranbaxy to perform full-scale clinical trials in India and to eventually market new drugs. These activities would provide the company with valuable experience and serve as a foundation for the development of their own NCE. Ranbaxy recognised that it would be prohibitively expensive to perform similar trials and marketing operations in the developed markets. Instead, the company proposed to rely on alliances and other partnerships to bring its own molecules to these markets.

Management Challenges

Upgrading the Organisation

As Ranbaxy's business continued to evolve, new demands were placed on organisational resources and capabilities. The company's management was involved in a continual battle to upgrade the organisation to meet the challenges of the new business environment.

A trend towards more complex and geographically diverse operations had made communication within the company more difficult. The regional reporting structure was created in response to these realities and to enable decentralised decision-making. Communication across the company was encouraged through the formation of numerous committees (see Appendix 7). Dr Singh emphasised the growing importance of a flatter organisational structure based on teamwork:

> We are moving away from a paradigm where we could achieve substantial gains based on the performance of individuals, departments or even companies working alone. In the case of Ranbaxy, it was possible in the past when we were smaller. Now, our operations are too far-flung and complex to rely on individual expertise in isolation. Increasingly the modern world depends on networking to deliver. Cross-functional teams (CFTs) are essentially about cutting functional boundaries and working together to leverage the combined knowledge of the operatives—they typify teamwork that will be central to success in the information age. Ranbaxy is a veritable minefield of opportunity to form these networks and to build and nurture such interdependence.

Although the necessity for a new way of working was clear, the company's legacy of a hierarchical, top-down management style proved hard to shake off. This was especially the case as the old ways of working had in many ways underpinned Ranbaxy's success. Some managers remained reluctant to change their attitudes and found it hard to delegate. As one senior manager commented: 'Before, I had to tell them what they had to do . . . now they bring me their proposals and I tell them how to do it right.' It had often been the case that CFT's found their decisions being overlooked. In one instance, a CFT decision which set transfer prices was overruled by senior management without any explanation. As it transpired, the figure proposed by senior management was correct. A catch-22 situation had emerged: until employees felt that they had truly been granted decision-making responsibility and had received adequate training, they would not feel able to assume the responsibility demanded of them. Moves by senior management to encourage delegation had been met with scepticism. Employees consistently complained that management was 'not walking their talk'. As one recent MBA graduate commented, 'The role of middle management is basically to carry out orders. Even if middle management come up with innovative ideas, they have to make a very hard sell to somebody above them.'

At the same time, senior managers of the company found it hard to delegate responsibility and accountability till they had the confidence that those they delegated to had both the competence and the commitment to take the company forward. At the heart of their hesitance was a profound loyalty to the company and a great deal of pride in how they had struggled to grow from a small pharmaceutical distributor into one of the most admired companies in India. They could not conceive of any action that would jeopardise the company's position and reputation. Ranbaxy was their life and they found it hard to trust anyone else with their legacy.

Age Spread Amongst Middle to Top Managers

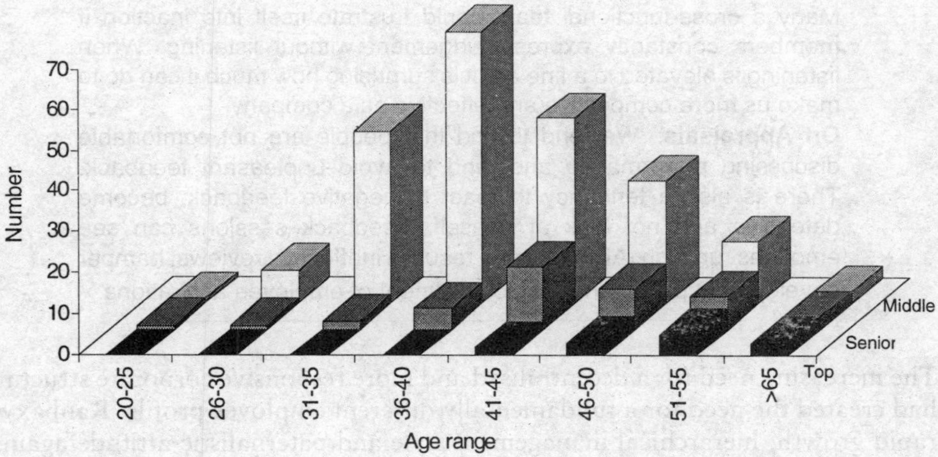

Ranbaxy's hierarchical tradition had also hampered efforts to improve internal communications. The company's attempt to introduce email was a case in point. Many top managers resisted this change and continued to dictate their emails to their personal assistants! Some insisted on having their full designation added to their email IDs—making it impossible to standardise addresses. As one manager commented, 'The biggest bottlenecks come from people not letting go of their power. Sometimes power derives from the position.'

The need for real change had become urgent. Frustration in the lower ranks at the lack of opportunities had caused many ambitious employees to leave. Almost 30 per cent of MBAs recently hired left the company in 1996–97. Dr Singh commented on the company's difficulties in retaining high performers: 'We are recruiting well and take on good people. Somehow our environment does not allow them to remain good and they become sub-optimised. We recruited the best—we now need to ensure they remain the best.'

Dr Singh recognised the need to fundamentally transform the corporate environment to encourage creativity, delegation and empowerment. Employees needed to be encouraged to take risks without the fear of reprisals should they fail. By learning how to listen and appraise, he encouraged his employees to take positive steps to redress these problems.

On Listening: 'While it is good to be confident of one's professional abilities, a precondition for productive team work is effective listening. Many a cross-functional team could frustrate itself into inaction if members constantly express judgement without listening. When listening is elevated to a fine art, it is surprising how much it can do to make us more competitive and effective as a company.'

On Appraisals: 'We tend to find that people are not comfortable discussing performance and tend to avoid unpleasant feedback. There is also a tendency to react to negative feedback, become defensive and not look at oneself. Feedback sessions can see emotions run high. All these may result in ineffective reviews, hamper development plans, and restrict fulfilment of employee aspirations.'

The increasing need for a decentralised and more responsive corporate structure had created the need for a fundamentally different employee profile. Ranbaxy's rapid growth, hierarchical management style and paternalistic attitude against layoffs had left the company with a bulging group of middle-aged middle management many of whom lacked the skills as well as the attitudes the company needed to pursue its ambitious vision. As the company continued to expand its presence overseas and develop a world class R&D capability, the availability of highly qualified personnel became a key constraint. Although the liberalisation of the Indian economy had made the country a more attractive place to work for many non-resident Indians, many key positions remained unfilled. As a senior manager of R&D commented:

> It is tough to motivate people to come to India. The top three positions are still vacant and the breadth of experience is lacking to do research. The company has become international in terms of dollars but not in terms of culture. People are still expected to conform to decisions made by top management but there is an awareness that things should be done differently.

The legacy of a hierarchical culture had also fostered a reliance on informal control and co-ordination mechanisms. As Ranbaxy's business became increasingly complex, a need for a more formal and professional style emerged. Senior managers cited two recent business problems which could be attributed to a lack of formal procedures. The first concerned a misunderstanding within the Eli Lilly joint venture. After conducting careful preliminary studies, Eli Lilly had proposed a three-year timetable for a joint project. A senior Ranbaxy manager overruled this timetable at the last minute, claiming on a hunch that it would take half that time. The project subsequently ran into significant delays.

A second business setback that was attributed to a lack of formal communication and control systems was Ranbaxy's initial unsuccessful submission of a cefaclor ANDA in the US. Ranbaxy had been confident that it could bulk manufacture cefaclor (based on its considerable Indian experience) and that it could get the required FDA approval (with the assistance of Eli Lilly). The company had been dubious about its ability to formulate a product for the US market, and had correspondingly focussed great efforts in this area at Ohm Labs. Communication and control problems subsequently hindered both the manufacture of the bulk drug in India and the ANDA submission in the US. Ironically, the formulation process, which had been identified as the major source of uncertainty in the venture, was faultless. The alliance's purported strengths became weaknesses and its weakness became a strength. The cefaclor ANDA subsequently failed to pass the FDA approval process, setting Ranbaxy back by four years in the US, at an estimated cost of $7.8 mn in lost revenues.

The moves towards a more complex international business environment also highlighted inadequacies in the company's support functions. It was felt that in-house legal and financial skills were not able to keep pace with the rapid international expansion. The legal demands of complex international joint ventures and alliances as well as the requirement of raising capital on international markets was straining Ranbaxy's existing capabilities to the limit.

Knowledge of international patent law would also increasingly be required as the company began to realise results from the NCE research programme. In 1997, this capability was completely lacking. Other areas of concern included the human resource function and lack of adequate technical support in the areas of quality, environment and occupational health.

Performance Improvement

In March 1997, analysts awarded Ranbaxy's stock a premium valuation but cautioned that this status was not supported by a reasonable return on capital. The company's ROCE was not projected to exceed its cost of capital until after 1998. Ranbaxy had also seen its ROCE slip from a healthy 41 per cent in March 1994 to 18 per cent in March 1996—less than the average return on the Indian stock market. The company had concentrated on the growth of its top line since the enunciation of its revenue target in 1993. Yet, in 1997, it was clear that the vision of an international research-based pharmaceutical company could not be

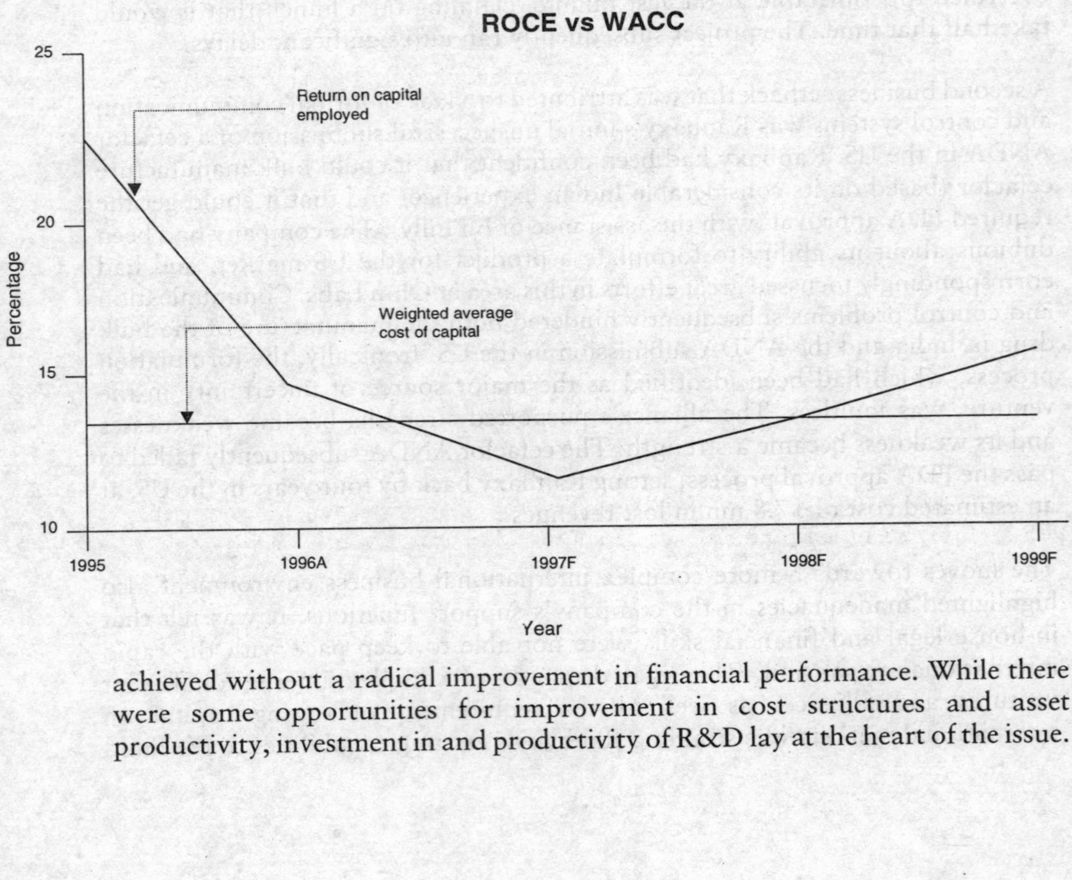

achieved without a radical improvement in financial performance. While there were some opportunities for improvement in cost structures and asset productivity, investment in and productivity of R&D lay at the heart of the issue.

Should the company really be trying to develop a new molecule? Should it concentrate its R&D efforts instead on improving its generic capabilities and drug delivery systems? Vision, strategy, financial performance and organisational arrangements are inextricably inter-related: to make its vision a reality, the company had to fundamentally question each of the other elements that would collectively shape its future.

APPENDIX 1

Ranbaxy and the Indian Pharmaceutical Industry

Phase	Year	*Industry*	Year	*Ranbaxy*
PHASE 1 (The Beginning)			1937	Ranbaxy founded in Amritsar for distributing Vitamin A and anti-tuberculosis drugs
	1950s	MNCs import bulk drugs and self-formulations		
	1954	Indian government intervenes in the industry to restrict import and promote self reliance		
	1958	Soviet Union recommends that India set up units to manufacture: • Antibiotics • Synthetic drugs • Vitamins • Surgical and medical equipment	1958	Joint venture with Italian pharmaceutical company Lepatit to engage in pharmaceutical manufacture in India
			1961	First manufacturing plant in Okhla
			1967	Dr Parvinder Singh (son of one of the founders) joins Ranbaxy and injects new technology and quality standards
			1969	Reverse engineered Calmpose (Valium) and Roscillin (an antibiotic)
PHASE II (Restrictive Policy)	1970	Process Patent Act introduced		
			1971	Commissions bulk drugs plant at Mohali in Punjab Commissions multipurpose chemical plant at Mohali
			1973	• Roscillin becomes the largest selling anti-bacterial in India • Cepahlexin (brand name Spirodex) introduced in India to become very successful anti-infective
	1975	FERA limits foreign holdings in Indian companies to 40 per cent	1975	Begins exports to Malaysia, Thailand, Sri Lanka, Middle East and Singapore
	1976	MNCs are required to produce 20 per cent of the bulk drugs in India		Commissioning of formulations plant at Dewas (India)

Appendix 1 contd. . .

		Industry		*Ranbaxy*
			1978	R&D achieves first indigenous technology for manufacture of Doxycycline
	1979	Drug and Price Control Order (DPCO) introduced		Commissioning of formulations plant at Dewas (India)
			1983	Joint venture in Malaysia to manufacture and distribute formulations
			1984	Novel process for bulk manufacture of Ranitidine (Zantac)
			1985	The Ranbaxy Research Foundation established
			1987	Commissioning of basic drug manufacturing facility in Taonsa (India), making Ranbaxy the largest manufacturer in India of antibiotics
PHASE III (Opening up of the Indian market)				Major internationalisation steps in:
			1992	Hong Kong office established to market to China
			1993	Moscow office established to market to CIS
	1994	DPCO relaxed (number of drugs under price control drops from 142 to 73) • FERA relaxed • MNCs not forced to manufacture bulk drugs • Government to recognise product patents by year 2005	1994	Opens offices in London and Raleigh R&D facility opened in Gurgaon with 250 scientists
	1995	MNC interest in India steps up • Glaxo PLC increases stake in Glaxo India from 40 to 51 per cent. Burroughs Wellcome's stake increases from 32 to 51 per cent. • Hoechst AG and Ciba Geigy apply to set up 100 per cent owned subsidiaries • MNCs begin to sell unrelated businesses in India	1995	Joint venture with Eli Lilly Opens offices in Poland, Vietnam and South Africa

APPENDIX 2

Export Growth

(Rs million)

	1986	1993	1994	1995	1996
Sales	939	4607	5934	7122	8766
Exports	107	1408	2225	3019	4121
Domestic	829	3199	3709	4103	4645
Gross Profits	38	465	797	1486	1829
Exchange rate	12.24	28.95	31.37	31.39	34.50

APPENDIX 3

New Product Development

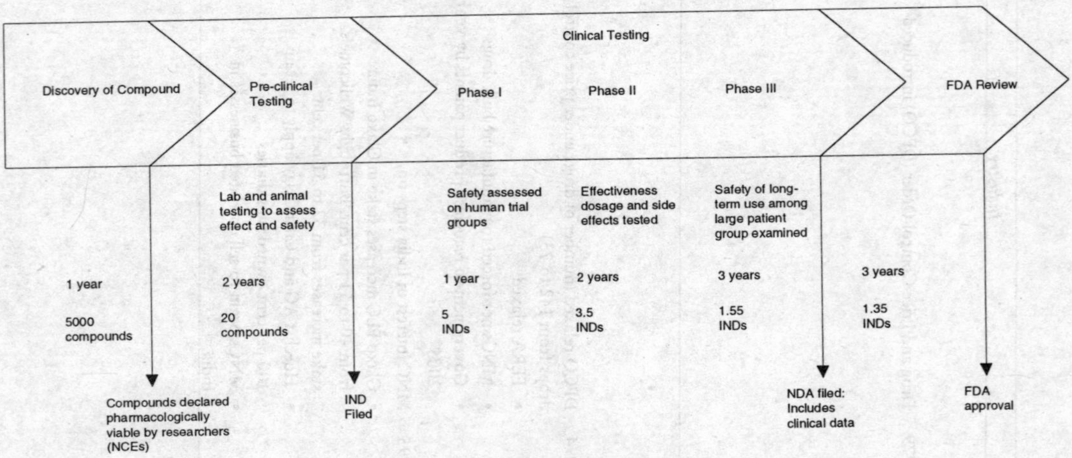

* Average quantity required at each stage to yield one FDA-approved prescription pharmaceutical at end of process

APPENDIX 4

Strategies Followed by Ethical Manufacturers

Consolidator	Research Powerhouse	Focussed Innovator	Disease Manager (Forward Integrated)
• Gain synergies through M&A • Core competence in integration • Exploit scale: R&D, global sales Glaxo Wellcome	• Emphasis R&D spending for differentiated new products • Develop scale in technologies and leverage across broad set of therapeutic areas Merck, Pfizer	• Build niche franchises • Active in/our licensing to maintain focus and leverage competencies • Gain competitive R&D mass in limited number of areas Melan, Elan	• Differentiate substitutable products through value-added services • Forward integrate • Develop superior information processing capability • Build alliances with IT and health care delivery companies

Lifecycle Manager	Sales & Marketing Org.	Virtual Company	Cost Leader
• Build franchise in generics/OTC • Develop expertise in 'pull-through' marketing • Acquire expertise build alliances in new formulations/delivery systemss SKB, Glaxo	• Invest in broad sales and marketing coverage • Actively seek licence to supplement portfolio in key categories. • Aim to be marketing partner of choice to product innovators Johnson & Johnson	• Disaggregate value chain • Regional sales and marketing alliance • Obtain local sales force coverage and capabilities • Focus only on core value-adding competencies Outsource others	• Relatively lower R&D spends • Outsource manufacturing • Rationalise detailing force to focus on formulary position • Other better pricing on substitutable products

APPENDIX 5

Strategies Followed by Generics Manufacturers

Fast Mover

- Move fast and buy-in during post-patent expiration 'window of opportunity'

▼

- Higher sales and marketing costs
- Higher R&D costs

One-stop Shop

- Offer wide range of products to capture contracts with purchasers with broad product needs (HMOs)

▼

- Higher complexity leading to higher manufacturing costs

Brand Developer

- Aggressive sales and marketing, heavy trade promotion to establish access to distribution channels

▼

- Higher sales and marketing costs

Niche Innovator

- Offer difficult-to-manufacture products to capture higher margin niche products segment

▼

- Higher manufacturing costs
- Higher R&D costs

Contract Manufacturer

- Be the lowest cost player by running lean on all costs to capture greatest volume

▼

- Operate on thin margins and high volumes

APPENDIX 6

The Value Curve

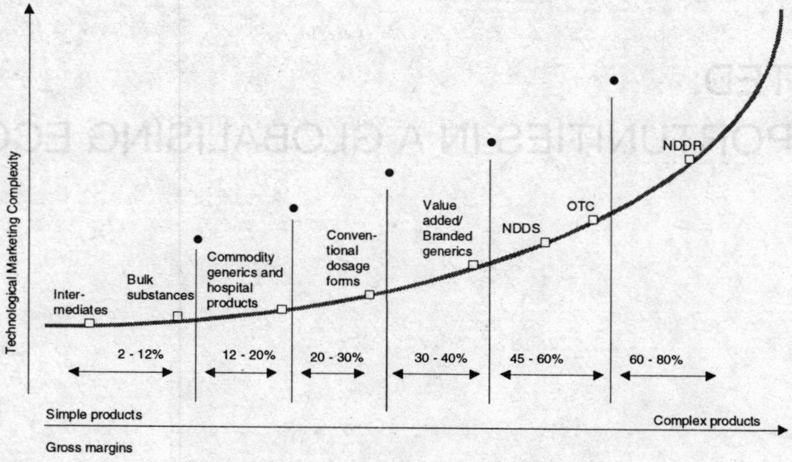

APPENDIX 7

Ranbaxy Committees

- *Ad-hoc Cross-functional Teams* (CFTs): CFTs were task forces which met on a needs basis to resolve problems. The teams were made up of representatives from R&D, pharmaceutical, chemical and engineering functions.
- *Product Review Committee* (PRC): Consisted of clinical, manufacturing and regulatory staff. Met once a month to discuss product development. A steering committee resolved any differences that arose in the PRCs. The agenda for the PRCs was formalised as a Product Initiation Form (PIF). PIFs were submitted by various regions and had been a major contributor to resolving misunderstandings between marketing and manufacturing regarding customer requirements.
- *Pharmaceutical Business Committee* (PBC): The PBC was an operational body (i.e., not policy making) whose remit was to discuss global and regional products and equipment. Typically, PBC meetings lasted for three days. A final day was reserved for inclusion of the Management Committee to resolve major issues.
- *Management Committee* (MC): The MC met as issues arose. The MC included Brar, Dr Singh and all the functional heads.

C A S E 8

NIIT LIMITED: NEW OPPORTUNITIES IN A GLOBALISING ECONOMY

NIIT had grown from a start-up in 1981 to a Rs 12.3 bn firm in 2000 employing 4,900 people worldwide mainly on the back of its strength and expertise in the area of software education and training, and software development. Beginning in 1991, the firm had also become increasingly global in its outlook and operations with 52 per cent of its revenues coming from outside India in 1999–2000. In 2000, NIIT was a global software training company and ranked the fourth largest software provider for global markets from India. It had operations in USA, UK, Australia, Bahrain, Belgium, France, Germany, Hongkong, India, Indonesia, Japan, Malaysia, Netherlands, New Zealand, Singapore, Sweden, Thailand and Yemen.

NIIT was a leader in information technology education in India with audiences ranging from 5- to 60-year olds. NIIT's market share estimates in India in the software education and training market varied from 38 per cent to 45 per cent.[1]

This case was written by Arvind Sahay, Professor at the London Business School. The author is grateful to NIIT Ltd for their help and support in writing the case. This case was first registered by the London Business School in 2000.

1. Neethi Agarwal, 'NIIT Rides High Overseas Tide', *The Economic Times*, 23 April 1998.

Aptech, the nearest competitor in India in the software education and training market, had a market share of 30 per cent. Education delivery was through classrooms, educational multimedia and the Internet. Alumnus population was over 1 million with student population at 320,000. Appendix 1 shows the financials of NIIT from 1992 through 1999. NIIT set itself an ambitious target of reaching the Rs 100 bn revenue mark in the next six years by 2006 (from the present Rs 12 bn), an eight-fold increase in sales from the revenues achieved in 1999–2000.

Financial Performance for the Last Five Fiscal Years

(US$ million)

	1998–99	*1997–98*	*1996–97*	*1995–96*	*1994–95*
Global revenues	243	179	119	78	46
Net revenues	161	127	90	64	42
Profits before taxes	42	31	20	14	10
Earnings per share ($)	1.02	0.77	0.49	0.34	0.23

Source: NIIT website.

History of NIIT

NIIT was founded on 2 December 1981 by Rajendra Pawar, Vijay Thadani and P. Rajendran as a provider of software education—it trained people to use and write software. In 1982, when NIIT began operations, it offered career courses for students with the target audience in the age group 15–25. In 1983, NIIT began offering corporate training courses which extended the age group of the target audience theoretically to 60 (in practice, the upper age limit went into the late forties at that time). NIIT's LEDA family club programme and C-Plan for schools extended the lower age limit to 5 years. NIIT was thus in a position where it catered to the needs of people from 5 to 60 years of age. It had three main business areas—software education and training, knowledge solutions and software development. The software development area included customer specific consulting contracts, systems integration, testing, etc., in a variety of functional areas.

Despite an intense focus on customers and technologies, NIIT had always considered itself to be in the 'people' business. As Pawar said: 'People are our most important resource'. That the top management paid more than just lip service to this approach was borne out by the fact that NIIT was considered to be among the best places to work in India. It was also borne out by the relatively low employee turnover in an industry sector that is notorious for employee turnover. NIIT operated at Level 5 of the Capability Maturity Model (CMM) developed by the Software Engineering Institute at Carnegie Mellon University for software firms.[2]

NIIT is People

- We have positive regard for each one of us.
- We will foster career building by creating opportunities that demand learning, thinking and innovation from each one of us.
- We expect each of us to contribute to the process of organisation building and thus derive pride, loyalty and emotional ownership.
- We recognise the necessity of making mistakes and risk-taking when it contributes to the learning, innovation and growth of each one of us.

The various businesses of NIIT are synergistic with one another. NIIT's R&D division is shared by both the software development business and the computer education business. Systems integration and software consulting brings NIIT's teams into close contact with the latest development in IT and these teams, cooperating with the R&D division, translate their knowledge into courses for NIIT's training wing. In response, NIIT's training division churns out people equipped with the latest in IT, which gives NIIT's software development the most critical resource in the international software market—skilled software personnel. NIIT considers this model to be analogous to a teaching hospital where (medical) knowledge is created, disseminated and used; and where people to whom knowledge is disseminated in turn create more knowledge for use in the hospital and elsewhere.

2. Maturity in CMM represents an organisation's ability to improve the knowledge and skills of its workforce and align performance with the organisation's business objectives. The maturity model has five levels which represent five different cultures. At level one is an organisation which does not have a common culture. And at level five is a company which is focussed on continued improvement and which requires significant changes in the way organisations manage people. To reach level five, a company has to take the management of processes and people very seriously. If there is a culture of commitment at the management level, it goes on to give the dedicated workforce that the company really needs.

Revenue Breakdown by Subsidiary

	Sales/Revenue		*Profit Before Taxes*	
	1998–99	*1997–98*	*1998–99*	*1997–98*
NIIT Ltd (Rs)	5836 mn	4586 mn	1519 mn	1134 mn
NIS SPARTA Ltd (Rs)	187 mn	141 mn	4 mn*	3 mn
NIIT GIS Ltd (Rs)	141 mn	91 mn	26 mn*	21 mn
NIIT USA Inc. (Rs)	60 mn	23 mn	850 mn*	600 K
PT NIIT Indonesia (Rupiah)	2805 mn	7838 mn**	62 mn	169 mn**
NIIT Asia-Pacific Pte. Ltd (S$)	19 mn	21 mn**	990 K	990 K**

* Figures for fifteen months ended 30 September 1999.
** Figures for fifteen months ended 30 September 1998.

Software Solutions Business

The software solutions business provided on-site and off-shore software development for client firms as well as on-site software consultancy and systems integration solutions. It was natural for NIIT to enter software development when it was training exactly the kind of people that was/is required by the industry. Some of these graduates were hired by NIIT on the completion of their computer training skills. And, as it did in training, NIIT moved up the value chain in software too. It started off with off-shore development, entered the on-site development market and then started offering consultancy. NIIT's latest effort in this field was systems integration to business customers. The business of software development itself involved a very high degree of interaction with customers. If NIIT did not understand what the customer's requirements were, it could not deliver a good product. It was not only a question of understanding the client's requirements but also understanding the client's processes in order to deliver optimal systems integration solutions that brought together an IT-enabled set of various business processes.

In providing software solutions to its customers, NIIT pursued alliances with major software providers like Microsoft, Oracle, Sybase, etc., to be able to develop the best solutions. Partly as an outcome of the relatively low employee turnover especially at the client interface level, NIIT frequently had a better feel for its client's businesses related to the software solutions it provided. For example, in a project that NIIT did for British Airways, the project manager from BA changed over the course of the project—and it was NIIT that had the institutional knowledge of the project.

> Rajendran opined: 'Often, we are able to provide our client firms with a better picture of how their systems have evolved over the past three to five years and why they have changed as they have. Of course, this happens only after the relationship has developed to a certain point. This knowledge helps us provide our customers with the optimum solution and move up the value chain as we increase our understanding of our client's business. It is also a key instrument of repeat business.'

NIIT's experience in education and training with individuals and firms led to the creation of NetVarsity, an on-line learning facility. In turn, the experience of creating and managing NIIT's NetVarsity helped NIIT win a major contract on a large software development project from University Tun Abdul Razak (UNITAR) for development of the First Virtual University in Malaysia. NIIT was also short-listed for the 'Smart Schools' project of the Malaysian government. In 1997, NIIT was awarded MSC status in the Malaysian Multimedia Super Corridor, making it the only company from India to be given this status among the first twenty companies.

North America is a major market for the software solutions business. For the twelve-month period to October 2000, the software solutions business grew overall by 69 per cent over the previous year—with the total number of customers at 247. Forty-five per cent of the revenues from this business came from on-site activities and 55 per cent from off-shore activities in India. The average on-site rate was US$ 79.6 per hour compared to US$ 25.4 per hour in India. These rates were expected to increase at annual rates of about 5 per cent, though the meltdown of the dotcom sector during 2000 decreased the upward pressure to an extent. Eighty per cent of customers are repeat customers with multi-year contracts. All contracts have built-in escalation of costs with personnel clauses to protect against losses. With the implementation of a reorganisation in 2000, the software solutions business consisted of five business units (US, Europe, Japan, Asia-Pacific and India) and one financial services vertical unit that worked across all geographical areas.

Knowledge Solutions Business

Computers and software familiarity were becoming norms across the world.

Therefore, the relevance of computer training in the future was being questioned. And NIIT was aware of this. Consider its knowledge solutions division, which was started as the educational multimedia business in 1992, with forty-five people. It was growing exponentially—in terms of employee count, revenue percentage and year-on-year growth. Estimates suggested that in the coming years, educational multimedia was likely to grow by 70 per cent, software by 50–60 per cent while the education and training business by a 'low' 30 to 35 per cent.[3] Schools, colleges, institutions and companies were looking for more and more educational multimedia products. NIIT had already developed educational multimedia packages for a variety of companies including IBM, Microsoft, Computer Associates, Hewlett Packard and Arthur Anderson. Such business orders gave NIIT the confidence to go the whole hog in this area. To Pawar, educational multimedia was the manifestation of one of the underlying strengths of NIIT, 'that of the ability to look at new product development at the interfaces of different businesses. Educational multimedia is a natural offshoot at the interface of education/training and software development'.[4] By the year 2000, educational multimedia had morphed into the Knowledge Solutions Business encompassing educational multimedia and all other products and services related to creating knowledge and learning.[5]

NIIT's software business was growing faster than the training business. This was largely a market function. The software business serviced global markets that were faced with a shortage of software professionals and earnings were boosted by the dollar multiple while the training business primarily generated its revenues from the Indian and other Asian markets. 'With virtually no competition in India and a not-so-difficult overseas market, we hope to carve a niche in this segment in India and abroad', said CEO Vijay Thadani.[6] In addition, NIIT was setting up its training and education business in Europe and the Americas.

The question was: Will the training market vanish altogether? The answer: Probably no. But it would certainly undergo a radical shift. The course content and students' profile would have to be changed. 'Corporate training and working professionals wanting to upgrade their skills will form a major chunk of our students', predicted Thadani. This is because 'the changes in the

3. Case writer estimates.
4. Personal interview, 2 September 1998.
5. Rajendra Pawar, via email, March 2001.
6. Malini Goyal, 'Okay, Kids, Log On to Your Homework', *The Economic Times*, 10 September 1998.

environment will be so fast that learning will no longer be in chunks, but a continuous process', he added. Of course, the nature of demand from the customer would vary in different markets.

NIIT had set up what is perhaps the world's largest educational multimedia development facility with over 500 trained instructional design team personnel. It had already developed over 190 educational multimedia software titles under NIIT's own brand names, Vista, Vista Multimedia and HyperLearn. These included subjects like Oracle, Sybase, Informix, C, C++, Object Oriented Programming, Lotus Notes, PowerBuilder, Delphi, Developer/2000, Visual C++, GUI Design, UNIX, AIX and HP-UX, and Client Server Computing.

NIIT's own educational multimedia products had a customer base of over several thousand users worldwide including Boeing, McDonell Douglas, Bank of America, Cargill, Wal-Mart, Rolls-Royce, British Telecom, Arthur Andersen, and the University of Wales. NIIT's expertise in electronic commerce enhanced its reach to include global customers and opened up new marketing avenues. These customers could pay electronically for accessing NIIT's computer-based training and Internet-based training products at NIIT's commercial sites, viz., the NIIT CBT Store and NIIT NetVarsity.

Education and Training Business

When NIIT initially began operations in 1981, it faced a dilemma. While the founders foresaw a huge potential market for computer education and training in the Indian market, they were not sure what the actual demand for particular training concepts would be like. Part of the problem lay in awareness levels about the benefits and costs of computer education and training. Another issue was the middle-class Indian mind-set where only medicine, engineering and the civil services were considered as 'real' careers. No one quite knew what a future job would be like after paying a handsome sum to get trained in COBOL or BASIC or other computer programming languages. Initial market research showed consumer resistance to both the product concept and the prices that NIIT expected from its customers.

By 1988, however, NIIT was well entrenched in the computer software education market in India—it was the leader with a strong reputation. In the initial years, the focus on quality and control meant that all training centres were wholly-owned by NIIT. As its reputation grew, NIIT began to be approached by entrepreneurs who wanted to become NIIT franchisees. NIIT evolved a franchising model that preserved its control and protected its brand image.

Of the 1,979 training institutes (facilities) in (India and overseas), 87 per cent were franchised.[7] The franchising operation contributed revenues in the form of royalty, technical know-how fees, sale of courseware and other training material, lease rentals and other miscellaneous receipts. The non-exclusive, non-transferable franchise agreement made the franchisee responsible for local marketing including advertising, providing facilities and conducting classes. All faculty of the franchisee were selected and trained by NIIT and all personnel employed at the franchises were first screened by NIIT.

Franchisees were expected to have at least a 70 per cent student capacity hour utilisation by the end of the third year of operations. NIIT defined operational details like room size, size of tables, number of PCs per student and the transparencies that were to be used for various modules. Faculty at the different centres came back to the NIIT School for between two and fifteen days for training every year. Territory technical managers got independent feedback about franchise operations. The franchise contracts were normally for three years. NIIT's franchisees were chosen very carefully and significant weightage was given to their commitment to the venture (against the ability to just invest). NIIT also had orientation programmes for franchisees to enable them to understand NIIT's core and its processes. For a consumer product company, this would translate into putting a dedicated and understanding distribution network in place.

Franchisees were graded on performance such as student satisfaction, capacity utilisation and profitability. 'Mirror image partners' were franchisees that had access to NIIT material during development and provided inputs to shaping the material. In the initial days, the faculty on NIIT's education and training programme were also software developers. From 1986, the firm started to recruit software developers separately. Personnel with the aptitude and skills were then routed from software development to training and back according to requirements. Over the eleven years to 2000, only 4 per cent of the franchisees broke their relationship with NIIT—largely due to personal issues relating to the franchisee.[8]

7. Of the 1,979 centres that provided software training to individual customers (students)—preparing them for jobs in the IT sector—105 were outside India spread across twenty-seven countries.
8. Rajendra Pawar, Personal communication via email, March 2001.

NIIT's association with the world's top software developer firms like Microsoft and its reservoir of trainers gave it a head start in the training business over smaller players. For example, on 25 June 1998, the day Microsoft released Windows 98 commercially, NIIT graduated 1,400 people trained in Windows 98. However, a concern remained. 'The previous generation had a lot to learn in terms of basic computer literacy but future generations will not', said Chief Operating Officer P. Rajendran.

The way a mature training market—like the US—behaves is expected to provide useful pointers for the future. The $16 bn training market in the US is a highly fragmented and specialised one. There, people learn on a continuous basis and with professionals wanting to upgrade their skills. NIIT learnt about the US market through first-hand experience. It was planning to enter the training business there. This would be a step further in spreading its international network on the training front. (Today, out of the total 650 NIIT institutes that deliver software education and training, only twenty are located abroad, most in Southeast Asia and China.) It would also complete the third leg of the tripod in its business model at the international level.

Beginning in 1991, NIIT started to expand outside India as the Indian economy became more open to the rest of the world.

Pawar opined: 'Being in a business that is software related, it was no longer possible to just sit in India. This would have limited our growth prospects and made us a niche player in worldwide terms. To serve better our customers, especially those who are outside India, we have to understand the markets they operate in. We need to become an insider in those markets as well. Being in close touch with software developments around the world enables us to offer the state-of-the-art in our education and training business as well.'

NIIT was also planning to enter the education and training market in Europe. Towards this end, it had posted a member of its board of directors permanently in the UK. The UK market for software education and training also tends to be fragmented. Recent market research indicated that one set of target consumers—for a 'degree course length' software education product—were not very aware of vendors of basic software training firms (see Appendix 2). While many of these consumers would have liked to do such a course to switch careers and to improve job prospects—as they saw IT as a booming sector—they were concerned about the price and the schedule of classes that they would have to juggle around their present full-time jobs. Gopal Chakravarthy, the resident director in Europe, wondered what other factors were relevant in estimating the demand for various educational product concepts and technologies. Another question that needed quick answers was the issue of demand creation. What was the state of the market—did NIIT need to estimate demand or to create demand? If latent demand existed, then what were likely to be the most fruitful avenues for demand creation?

For the education and training business, the directors had responsibility for specific geographical areas—Rajendran for India, Pawar for China, Chakravarthy for Europe, Thadani for North America and Thakur for Japan. It was the responsibility of each geographic director to understand the customers and the markets in that area. At the same time, as functions and employees moved to different locations in the world, top management was also following its customers. Not coincidentally, global expansion was also seen as a useful input in facing the challenge of retaining skilled personnel.

NIIT Educational Product Line

Education and training was done for individuals and for companies. NIIT's educational product line used a combination of continuous customer feedback and developments in technology that permitted enhanced product offerings. For NIIT, customer focus was the ability to deliver value and quality to the customer in the best possible way.

NIIT's approach to delivering computer education to children in the age group 6 to 14 was a case in point of delivering education in the best possible way. Children cannot be made to travel all over the city to attend classes. NIIT launched the LEDA (Learning through Exploration, Discovery and Adventure) family clubs in 1996 in major cities to tackle the network problem for kids. The LEDA family clubs (LFC) also offered the bonus of a 'home' environment where kids and their parents could be comfortable. Each LFC was a multimedia learning centre typically equipped with multimedia computers and guidance available from a trained instructor.

These clubs' main task was to teach academic subjects to children. This was done mainly with the help of multimedia. The higher level of interactivity (in playing with the models) made learning fun for children. The academic subjects available on CD-ROM were based on the Central Board of Secondary Education curriculum, which was an accepted and recognised standard in India. The multimedia content was developed in-house at NIIT.

Another example of tailoring 'best way of delivery' was the GNIIT course. The GNIIT programme of studies was rapidly becoming more popular among students pursuing graduation in a non-vocational area (see Appendix 2). The basic idea was that while students were pursuing a three-year degree course after their 10+2 (equivalents: high school in the US; A-levels or GCSEs in the UK), they could simultaneously do a graduation course in computer software by pacing themselves over four years. At the end of four years, students were the US/UK equivalent of a BS/MSc or the Indian four-year engineering degree and had the skills to be readily employed in a field that promised to absorb as many skilled professionals as producers like NIIT could turn out. Over time, NIIT hoped that it would be able to award university degrees to students that took products like GNIIT.

The GNIIT course cost Rs 76,000 over four years. In the professional practice part of the course, students were paid Rs 3,500 per month. Among 17- to 24-year olds in Mumbai and Delhi, a survey showed that NIIT had an unprompted recall of 83 per cent and a prompted recall level of 96 per cent, while the GNIIT programme had a recall level of 72 per cent. Up to a third of the students were placed in firms in North America and Europe on completing the course.

Another development in its GNIIT course reflected on its commitment to its customers and its customers' customers: NIIT offered Quality Management as an integral part of its GNIIT programme which enabled GNIIT students to achieve zero defect/error free results. The course contained several modules such as quality management concepts, quality management tools, ISO 9000 for software and SEI-CMM software quality assurance. Many of the franchisees had already qualified for the ISO 9000 series awards and NIIT continued to drive to maintain and increase its focus on quality. A study of publicly traded firms using data over a five-year period between 1993 and 1998 suggested that quality award winners had significantly higher market values and return on assets than other firms.

The GNIIT course included an internship programme which equipped the student with on-the-job experience. In most cases, this internship provided the edge to the student while looking for placement. NIIT had also taken the needs of the advanced IT professional into account and had launched a higher level course, ANIIT. The students were taught concepts such as systems integration, systems development and project management in the first semester. This placed ANIIT students at a higher level than GNIIT students: the course prepared students for a role that was more managerial and supervisory in nature than a usual software engineer's role. NIIT also offered a doctoral level programme, FNIIT, for very advanced developers.

In the education and training arena, NIIT's career package was a standard format of semesters consisting of modules further divided into sessions that had specific learning objectives. This gave NIIT two distinct advantages: first, consistency, in terms of the pace of learning and in terms of content; and second, flexibility. The flexibility aspect was very important: the latest development in a particular module may necessitate a change in only a few sessions in the module and any change in technology would require the recomposition of a single module rather than the whole course. If a major revamp was expected, the module could be shifted to a later part of the semester and the students could continue with another module.

Increasingly, the professional practice part of the GNIIT curriculum was an integral part of the product design process for organisational clients requiring software solutions. By the time students entered the professional practice part of the curriculum, they had the necessary skills to develop software solutions. NIIT offered the students the chance to work on live projects such as government informatics projects for provincial governments in India. The projects could be done at a fraction of the cost of employing experienced personnel and the states/provinces got state-of-the-art information infrastructure.

For existing IT professionals who couldn't spare the time for the ANIIT course and who wanted new concepts and a skills package, NIIT offered the Microsoft Authorised Technical Education Centre (ATEC) and also 120 of its own courses. These provided IT professionals with new concepts and inputs on the latest application development tools. For policy makers—the people who dictate company policy on terms of technology, infrastructure and investment—NIIT offered a series of seminars called the Foresight Seminars where international experts in a specified field were invited to talk. These seminars were curtain-raisers for technologies that were being developed and would be available for application in the future. This series reduced the time lapse between international developments and awareness in India. A similar curtain-raiser series was Infotalks, the difference being, Infotalks was geared for anyone from CEO to CIO to children.

NIIT's Automated Learning Centre for executives was a case in point for a different delivery system. Senior executives needed computer skills, but had a very tight schedule that may not allow them to come in for regular training slots. NIIT used what was called the 'doctor-patient' model for a course for senior executives. NIIT launched an Automated Learning Centre (ALC) which removed constraints in terms of time for senior executives. The ALC was a product offering that was woven into the social life of busy executives. The student had complete control over the offering and managed the product to suit his needs. The student had the freedom to pace his learning and learn what he wanted, when he wanted. He only had to fix up an appointment with his mentor and walk into the ALC (hence the reference to the doctor-patient model). The tutor then created a 'study path' for the student. The study path would list the technology inputs and the personal tutoring sessions. Technology inputs included computer-based training and video instructions.

NIIT offered a wide array of services and solutions, and IT training for organisations, with a high degree of flexibility to suit specific needs (see Appendix 3). Many of the courses designed for delivery to individuals were tailored and delivered on demand to corporate customers. In 1998, NIIT had more than 150,000 students enrolled in its various courses at any given point in time.

Product Design

NIIT had always laid great emphasis on research and development in order to come up with innovative methods of training as well as developing systems and software. Its R&D centres in New Delhi and Singapore were involved in basic research, technology forecasting, technology support, product and process localisation and identifying new product development needs in the area of cognitive technologies. R&D was headed by Sugata Mitra who was responsible for assessing new technologies for deployment and developing the scenarios for deployment. The deployment could be in education and training for individuals or corporates or in the development of software solutions for corporate clients. A sample technology for evaluation and use may, for example, have been Macromedia's Flash that enabled animation on Web graphics for improved presentation.

To stay on the cutting edge of technology, NIIT set up Centres of Competence in multimedia, net-centric computing, software R&D and manufacturing solutions to imbibe the best in these technologies in order to build intrinsic capability to deliver solutions and create products around them for customers worldwide. These centres drew on the technology deployment and selection decisions of the R&D cell. Quality was almost an obsession in the firm.

Rajendran opined: 'We are extremely quality conscious. Quality consciousness is both a deeply held intrinsic value within the firm and a requirement of our business model. The top leadership of this firm practically evangelises quality as an intrinsic value across all businesses. Our business model demands it because, at least in India, the education and training business functions primarily through franchising. Without proper quality controls, the NIIT brand will loose value.'

In a fast-moving industry, NIIT couldn't afford to be early or late. There have been cases where a product has been launched too early in the market and has lost. The market has to be prepared to accept the product. Therefore, technology identification and deployment processes had to be tailored for each market and its stage of evolution.

For example, consider NIIT's NetVarsity, which was based on a conventional university model and offered a similar ambience, allowing the student to assess the knowledge he/she had acquired from the online service. But the biggest bonus was that students would be eligible for certification for their education at NetVarsity. NIIT also offered placement assistance to the students of the varsity through its global placement databank on the Net. What was interesting about NetVarsity was that the Internet itself was a new phenomenon for people in India with about a million people having online access in 1998. In contrast, 70 million adults in the USA were online and had the potential to directly use online educational services. Which technologies should NIIT deploy on its NetVarsity site in order to deliver tailored content to different areas in the world? Which markets were ready for which technologies? How did NIIT estimate online demand?

Like its other businesses, NIIT moved forward in value addition in software development by moving into systems integration. Earlier, NIIT had tie-ups with certain companies in each aspect of systems integration—for hardware, software, networking, etc. It was a paradigm which went: 'We have all this ready. This is the problem. Now find the solution'. Now NIIT had no vendor bias and looked backwards from the solution. The paradigm became: 'This is the problem. Find the solution. Now, what all do we need?' This meant that NIIT had to shake up its existing relationships. For instance, NIIT was earlier a champion for Sybase. Now, if the client's system requirements needed something different, like Oracle, NIIT would provide Oracle to the client.

In putting together a solution for the client, NIIT usually employed teams that were quasi-permanent in nature. Team members rotated in and out over a period of time. Sufficient gaps were allowed to ensure that institutional memory which was important for the project, and in the longer term for client relationship management, was maintained and developed.

NIIT's employees were, without exception, put through an induction and orientation programme that clearly delivered NIIT's mission and values and ways of operation to the recruits. This function helped NIIT in inculcating the spirit of quality in its recruits. The work culture at NIIT was that of interdependence through cross-functional task forces and virtual teams for different projects. This brought together the best the company had for each assignment (the implication being the customer was best served). The company also had ongoing personal effectiveness programmes. According to Rajendran, membership of the Managing Director's Quality Club, a non-pecuniary annual award where previous members 'mentored' new entrants to the club, was one of the highest accolades within the firm. NIIT had 3,171 'NIIT-ians' on its rolls as on 30 September 1997, including 888 and 488 software and educational multimedia professionals respectively. NIIT's education and training activity engaged over 1,300 professionals as at the end of that year.

There were concerns about taking the education and training business global. The manner in which people learn in different countries tends to be quite different. In the US, students are much more apt to learn by doing something themselves; in India and China software education and training requires a higher level of lectures. Language usage was also a key point. English tends to get used differently in the US, UK and India. In China, entire curricula have to be translated into Chinese and the delivery is in Chinese. For the educational and training business, therefore, product development for each of the markets has had to be tailored accordingly. In effect, there has to be some level of cultural customisation. Tailoring educational products requires personnel who are conversant with the markets for which the product is being tailored. Across the world, the spread of long-distance learning was creating new challenges and opportunities for the education and training division.

At its board meeting in September 1998, NIIT decided to acquire an American software firm as part of its drive to get closer to its customers in the software development business and to gain a foothold in the education and training business in the Americas. The acquisition would increase the software development and marketing capabilities of NIIT and would enable it to leap-frog the normal lead time required to be considered an insider in the North American market. Appendix 4 shows the various subsidiaries of NIIT Ltd around the world.

Competition

In India, the main competitor in the education and training business was Aptech that had about 30 per cent of the organised market. Worldwide, Aptech had a network of over 600 centres spread over India, Nepal, UAE, Qatar, Oman, Bahrain, Malaysia and Kenya. Aptech moved into online software education and training in 1996. In 1997, Aptech grossed revenues of Rs 2 bn with 92 per cent of revenues coming from software education and training activities.

Aptech had also started offering courseware over the Internet from other subject areas in association with the University of British Columbia. Aptech had an agreement with the Indira Gandhi National Open University (IGNOU) in India to offer a Certificate in Computing (CIC) to students in the Middle East; the tie-up enabled both institutions to provide high-quality education and Indian-accredited qualifications to students outside India. The focus of the course was on computer applications. Through the partnership, the entry level course for the Certificate in Computing would be made available in the Middle East for those wishing to build a career in computer science. IGNOU was considered a centre for excellence in distance education by the Commonwealth of Learning. It had over 30,000 students and sixty-three academic programmes which included degrees, diplomas and certificate programmes.

In 1998, Aptech announced a tie-up with the UK-based Tack Training International to provide practical corporate training in India. Tack was a closely-held, global training company with operations in as many as thirty-five countries and eighteen languages. Tack's client list included Microsoft, Unilever, British Airways, Hewlett Packard, Shell, Motorola, British Telecom, ABB, DuPont and American Express.[9] According to the head of Tack: 'There's an

9. *The Economic Times*, 1 September 1998.

increasing awareness among companies to transform their business into a globally competitive company. Corporate India has woken up to the need for business process re-engineering to sustain the competitive edge, but the training of professionals has so far been ignored. No restructuring can work unless the people involved are trained to adapt to change. Tack will help them do just that.'

In the UK, the market for computer education and training was largely in-house or of the company outsourced variety. Firms hired university graduates from non-vocational courses into their IT departments. They then trained these graduates in-house and/or upgraded their skills though in-house training. Some firms hired software firms for skill upgradation. However, as of 1998, there did not appear to be a course like GNIIT on offer in the UK.

The largest player in the US in the education and training business was IBM with the division grossing $440 mn. A typical product profile from the IBM education division for Lotus Notes training is given in Appendix 5. Most firms were niche players—if one was strong on live training, another was good at technology or Internet-based training. Senior vice president and board member, Chakravarthy, viewed UK and the rest of Europe as a potentially fast growth new market for the education and training business.

Conclusion

From its start-up beginnings in 1982, NIIT had come a long way. Its rapid expansion in the previous few years was raising numerous questions for the management, in the education and training business in particular and more generally for the company as well. Which were the enabling technologies that NIIT needed to employ and how did it identify and deploy the correct technologies in appropriate businesses? In particular, for the education and training business, which products should NIIT pursue for consumers in the UK, Continental Europe, Japan and USA? How would NIIT estimate and/or create demand for the products/technologies in the education and training business in particular and more generally across all businesses in the global markets that it was aspiring to become a major player in? Identifying and pursuing optimal alternatives was important for future growth and profitability at NIIT.

APPENDIX 1

Financials at a Glance, 1992–93 to 1998–99

(Rs million)

Revenues and Profitability (For the year)	*1992-93*	*1993-94*	*1994-95*	*1995-96*	*1996-97*	*1997-98*	*1998-99*	*1999-2000*
Global turnover (NIIT and subsidiaries)	627	931	1670	2832	4307	6484	8800	12370
Revenues from operations of NIIT Ltd	627	931	1524	2305	3273	4586	5836	7499
Operating expenses	406	603	999	1549	2170	3020	3835	–
Interest and finance expenses	36	51	75	149	218	138	46	–
Depreciation	26	47	104	103	161	294	436	354
Profit before taxes (NIIT Ltd)	159	230	346	504	724	1134	1519	2448
Profit after taxes	135	215	336	480	679	1084	1428	2242
Equity dividends	34	52	58	84	90	97	129	–
Earnings per share (Rs)*	5.25	8.33	8.36	12.37	17.52	28.02	36.95	–
Operating margin (%)	35.25	35.23	34.45	32.80	33.70	34.15	34.29	–
CAGR (last five years), gross revenues (%)	48	79	70	52	50	35	–	–
Profits before tax/revenues (%)	25.36	24.70	22.70	21.87	22.12	24.73	26.03	–
Revenues/Person month (Rs. '000)	38	50	69	79	99	115	124	–
Net profits/Person month (Rs. '000)	8	12	15	17	20	27	30	–
Return on capital employed (%)	25.71	27.53	25.42	20.17	21.27	28.51	34.49	–
Equity dividend (%)	25	30	30	32.50	35	37.50	40.00	–

Appendix 1 contd...

Assets and Liabilities (As at 30 Sept.)	*1993*	*1994*	*1995*	*1996*	*1997*	*1998*	*1999*	*2000*
Sources of Funds								
Equity capital	170	172	257	257	257	257	386	–
Preference capital	0	0	80	110	70	70	0	–
Reserves and surplus	293	464	659	1039	1615	2601	3757	–
Loan funds	73	155	334	981	1256	872	1	–
Total	536	791	1330	2387	3198	3800	4144	–
Application of Funds								
Gross block (incl. capital work-in-progress)	295	472	845	1247	1725	1900	2115	–
Net block	221	353	623	923	1373	1270	1114	–
Investments	17	28	32	217	329	572	572	–
Current assets	413	628	1004	1745	2273	2545	3327	–
Current liabilities	126	228	337	505	783	592	873	–
Net current assets	287	400	667	1240	1490	1953	2454	–
Deferred expenditure	11	10	8	7	6	5	4	–
Total	536	791	1330	2387	3198	3800	4144	–
Debt-equity ratio	0.16	0.24	0.36	0.76	0.67	0.31	0.00	–
Current ratio	3.28	2.75	2.98	3.46	2.90	4.30	3.81	–
Fixed asset turnover (Times)	2.13	1.97	2.10	1.98	2.09	2.65	2.80	–
Total asset turnover (Times)	1.19	1.19	1.15	0.97	1.03	1.21	1.41	–
Receivable days	141	107	141	127	110	88	79	70
Share price as on 30 Sept. (BSE) (Rs)	52.03	173.42	165	241.50	615.75	1367	107	–
Market capitalisation (Rs mn)	894	2979	4252	6222	15866	35145	109188	–

* Based on current equity.

Source: NIIT website.

APPENDIX 2

Structure of NIIT's Programme of Studies

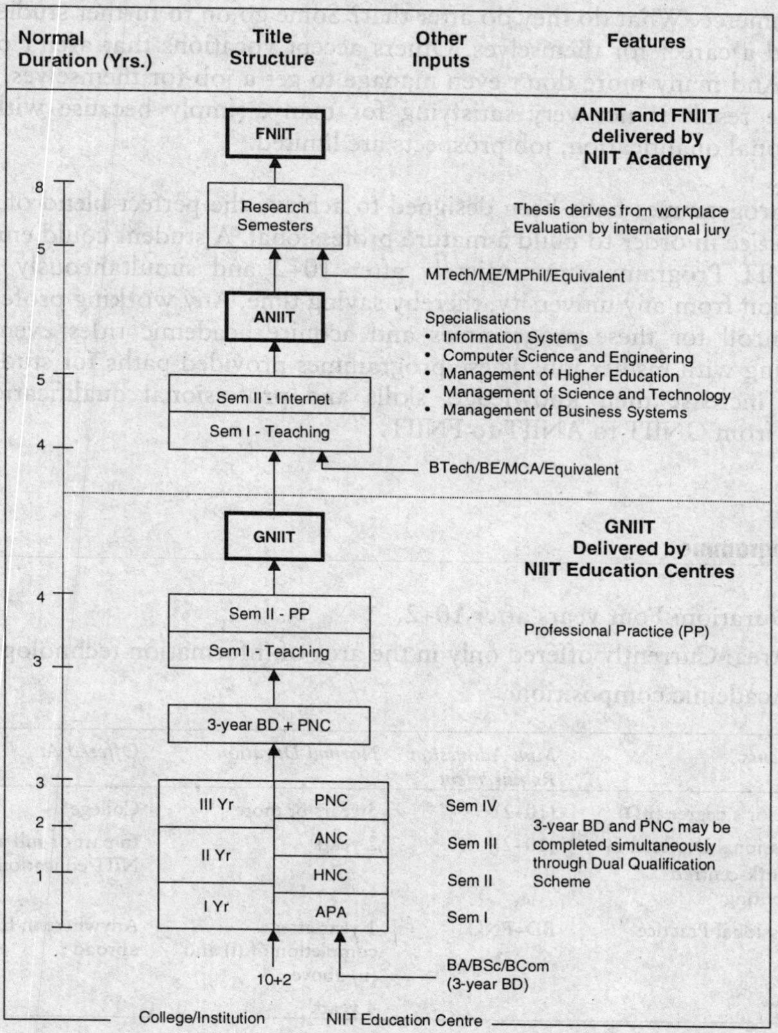

Abbreviations:
PNC: Professional Diploma in Network-centred Computing
ANC: Advanced Diploma in Network-centred Marketing
HCN: Honours Diploma in Network-centred Computing
APA: Advanced Certificate in PC Applications

The GNIIT Programme of Studies

Every year in India hundreds of thousands of students graduate in science, arts and commerce. What do they do after that? Some go on to further studies until they find a career for themselves. Others accept vocations that aren't of their choice. And many more don't even manage to get a job for themselves. Either way, the result is not very satisfying for many, simply because without a professional qualification, job prospects are limited.

NIIT's programmes have been designed to achieve the perfect blend of theory and practice in order to build a mature professional. A student could enroll for the GNIIT Programme immediately after 10+2 and simultaneously pursue graduation from any university, thereby saving time. Any working professional could enroll for these programmes and acquire academic titles even while continuing with his/her job. These programmes provided paths for students to steadily increase their knowledge, skills and professional qualifications by moving from GNIIT to ANIIT to FNIIT.

Details of the Programme

- Duration: Four years after 10+2.
- Area: Currently offered only in the area of information technology.
- Academic composition:

Components	*Min. Admission Requirement*	*Normal Duration*	*Offered At*
i) Bachelor's degree (BD)	(10+2)	3 years or more	College
ii) Professional Diploma in Network-centred computing	(10+2)	2 years	In part or full at any NIIT education centre
iii) Professional Practice™ (PP)	BD+PNC	1 year after completion of (i) and (ii) above	Anywhere in India or abroad
GNIIT		4 years	

A Bachelor's Degree (BD) for the purpose of admission to GNNIT means any degree, of minimum duration of three years after 10+2, awarded by any college or university.

Professional Diploma in Network-centred Computing (PNC) was a four semester programme offered at many NIIT education centres. A student taking admission in any of NIIT's education centres could pursue some or all semesters of the PNC programme depending on availability. Students had the option to migrate to a centre offering the complete four semesters in order to finish their PNC programme.

Professional Practice™ (PP) consisted of two courses, PP I and PP II, each of one semester duration. Professional Practice was conducted in an organisation. A student undergoing Professional Practice was a full-time employee/stipendee. The Professional Practice curriculum was derived from the day-to-day professional work of the student. The education process of Professional Practice did not interfere with normal work. The syllabus for Professional Practice was jointly derived in consultation with the industry.

A student had to complete a BD and PNC before being eligible for Professional Practice. Successful completion of Professional Practice lead to the GNIIT title.

Educational Process: PP I aimed to convert a student employee's everyday work into assignments, which would probe the strength of the student's basic concepts as well as test his/her ability to apply them in real-life situations. This course terminated with a semester report.

PP II required a student to demonstrate a higher level of capability of computer applications in his/her work environment and be aware of the latest developments in the IT industry. This course terminated with a semester report.

Teaching and Evaluation: A student was given training through ongoing professional activities to apply the basic concepts/skills in real-life situations. In the conduct of Professional Practice, NIIT as well as the host organisation (where PP was being carried out) provided valuable experiential inputs.

Evaluation was done by NIIT on a continuous basis. Evaluation instruments consisted of weekly interactions, assignments, seminars, term papers/project reports, viva, etc. Evaluation measured students' attributes which did not surface in a classroom situation. These would invariably focus on students' ability to function in a professional work environment and included personality traits.

Illustrative List of Evaluation Criteria

Professional Attributes	*Personality Attributes*
• Professional awareness	• Initiative
• Job clarity	• Creativity
• Ability to learn and adapt	• Interpersonal relations
• Work attitude and efficiency	• Sense of responsibility
• Analytical skills	• Adherence to deadlines
• Ability to apply concepts/skills	

Grading: NIIT, jointly with the immediate reporting officer of the student/employee, evaluated his/her performance. It was expressed in terms of a letter grade.

Delivery System: Fundamentally, it was derived from the well-known Off-campus Learning Process. However, it was purely of a correspondence type.

NIIT established proper linkages throughout the semester in order to ensure academic standards and performance. The interaction included periodic visits by NIIT to the organisation where a student/employee was pursuing Professional Practice.

ACE Credit Recommendations: The American Council on Education established College Credit Recommendations for NIIT's Professional Practice Programme, enabling NIIT-ians to seek credits in more than 1,100 American colleges and universities.

NIIT's ISO 9001 Certification: NIIT received ISO 9001 for Design and Delivery of Computer Training, with the associated services of Student Appraisal, Transcription and Certification, and Placement Assistance.

Semester 1: 26 Weeks

Semester End Profile: Power User on Networked PCs

This semester covered the following topics:

Computer Concepts
Disk Operation Systems

- MS DOS

Local Area Networks
Networking Essentials
Graphical User Interface

- Windows 95
- Windows NT

Office Automation–Office 95

- Word 7.0
- Access 7.0
- Excel 7.0
- Powerpoint 7.0

Introduction of Office 97
Application Development
Multimedia
Internet

- Browsing the Internet using Microsoft Internet Explorer
- Certain HTML pages
- Storing Web pages on a web server (Internet information server)
- Web publishing using Microsoft Front Page

Electronic Mail
Concepts and Tools of Quality Management

- Absolutes of quality
- Customer focus
- Problem-solving tools
- Case studies
- Individual corrective actions

Emerging Trends
Information Search and Analysis Skills (ISAS) Project

- MS-Access
- Presentation using PowerPoint

Seminar

Semester II: 26 weeks

Semester End Profile: Object-oriented DBMS Programmer on a Multi-user Environment

This semester covered the following topics:

Multi-user Operating Systems

- UNIX fundamentals
- UNIX shell programming

Programming Logic and Techniques
Object-oriented Programming using C++
RDBMS-Sybase SQL Server
Client-Server Computing using SQL Server and DB-Library
Software Engineering
SEI

- Capability Maturity Model (CMM)
- Maturity levels
- Key process areas and goals
- Measurement and analysis

ISO

- ISO and quality
- Procedures and standards

Information Search and Analysis Skills (ISAS) Emerging Trends Project

- Client-server computing and object-oriented programming
- Application of SEI and ISO concepts

Seminar

Semester III: 26 weeks
Semester End Profile: Object-oriented Application Developer on Networked Environment

This semester covered the following topics:

Visual Programming

- Visual C++ integrated development environment
- 32-bit Windows programming using Win32 API (Windows SDK)
- Object-oriented programming using Microsoft Foundation Classes (MFC)

Network Operating System

- Windows NT

Internet working using TCP/IP
Internet Information Server (IIS)

- Setting up an Intranet using a web server like IIS
- Storing and browsing HTML pages from IIS

Information Search and Analysis Skills (ISAS) Emerging Trends Project

- Visual C++ Programming using MFC
- Application of SEI and ISO concepts

Seminar

Semester IV: 26 weeks

Semester End Profile: Network Centred Software Engineer

This semester covered the following topics:

Internet Programming

- VJ++

Client-Server Front End Application

- Visual Basic

Personal Quality Management

- Dealing with personal habits
- Identifying areas of improvement including time management and planning
- Tools for measuring improvement

Software Quality Assurance

Windows Operating System and Services Architecture

- Windows Architecture and Use Interface
- OLE
- ODBC
- MAPI, TAPI and LSAPI fundamentals

Emerging Trends

Information Search and Analysis Skills (ISAS) Project

- Client-server computing concepts with Visual Basic as client and SQL Server as server
- Application of SEI and ISO concepts

Seminar

Source: Company documents.

APPENDIX 3

Corporate Training Products and Services

- Customised training for organisations
- Standardised training and assessment

Customised Training Solutions for Organisations:

- Development of comprehensive IT training
- Corporate training programmes
- Technology-based training (TBT) package
- Corporate Learning Centres
- Project-based training

Standardised Training and Assessment

- Executive training centres
- Automated learning centres
- Microsoft authorised technical education centres
- Authorised prometric testing centres

Range of Curricula Available

Operating Systems

- Unix
- Microsoft Windows NT
- Novell Netware
- Microsoft Windows 95
- MS-DOS, Microsoft Windows 3.1

Networking and Communications

- Concepts
- Microsoft TCP/IP
- Microsoft Internet Information Server
- Microsoft Exchange
- Microsoft-Systems Management Server
- Microsoft Windows OS & Services
- Architecture
- Lotus Notes

Client-Server and RDBMS

- Concepts
- Oracle
- Sybase
- Microsoft SQL Server
- DB2

Application Development and Object-oriented Tools

- C, C++
- Microsoft Visual C++ (MFC)
- PowerBuilder
- Microsoft Visual Basic
- CICS

Software Engineering IS Management

- Structured Systems Analysis and Design
- Object-oriented Analysis and Design
- IS Planning, Managing IT
- Executive Information Systems
- Software Project Management

Desktop Computing

- Basic
- Internet
- MS-DOS
- Microsoft Windows 3.1
- Microsoft Windows 95
- Microsoft Fox Pro
- Microsoft Word
- Microsoft Excel
- Microsoft Powerpoint
- Lotus 1-2-3
- Lotus WordPro
- Lotus Freelance
- Microsoft Access
- Microsoft Mail
- cc-Mail

APPENDIX 4

Subsidiaries and Investment

NIIT had subsidiaries in USA, Japan, Asia-Pacific, Europe and India. The subsidiaries and the purpose of their establishment were:

Subsidiaries	*To Address*
Wholly-owned Overseas	
NIIT Inc. USA	Training and software opportunities in USA, Canada and Latin America
NIIT Asia-Pacific Pte. Ltd, Singapore	Training and software opportunities in Singapore and Malaysia
HCL Asia-Pacific Pte. Ltd, Singapore	Training and software opportunities in Hong Kong, Thailand, Philippines, Australia and New Zealand
HCL Japan KK, Japan	Training and software opportunities in Japan
PT NIIT Indonesia, Indonesia	Training and software opportunities in Indonesia
NIIT Europe Ltd, United Kindgom	Training and software opportunities in Europe and the Middle East
Subsidiaries in India	
NIIT GIS Ltd	Joint venture with ESRI Inc, USA, to offer systems integration and software and training opportunities in the field of Geographic Information Systems in India and overseas
NIS SPARTA Ltd	Sales training in India and overseas
NIIT Finance Ltd	Financial solutions for NIIT products and services to NIIT customers, partners and NIIT-ians

NIIT's equity investments in these subsidiaries was specified in Schedule 6 of the Balance Sheet as on 30 September 1997. In addition in 1997, NIIT entered into joint venture agreements for taking IT education and training to China and for addressing software and systems integration opportunities in Japan through strategic tie-ups with strong partners. These ventures commenced full-scale operations in 1997–98. Accounts of NIIT's subsidiaries had not been merged with the parent company accounts for 1996–97 since Indian accounting standards did not permit consolidation of subsidiary accounts.

APPENDIX 5

IBM Education and Training Division: Product Profile

Title: OS/400 Integration of Lotus Notes (S6090)

Duration: Three days

Level: Intermediate

Type of Class: Hands-on labs (public or private classes available)

Tuition: $1,200 (US). Please call IBM TEACH at 1-800-426-8322 for current price information.

Course Description: This course teaches you how to install, configure and manage Lotus Notes on the AS/400. You will learn through lectures and extensive machine exercises to reinforce lecture topics.

Who Should Take This Course: System administrators who will be installing and configuring Lotus Notes on the AS/400 system.

What You Are Taught: After completing this course, you should be able to:

- Plan for OS/400 Integration of Lotus Notes hardware and software.
- Install and configure Lotus Notes on the AS/400.
- Install Lotus Notes server code on the IBM Integrated PC Server for AS/400.
- Install Lotus Notes code on a PC user workstation (OS/2 or Windows).
- Manage the IBM Integrated PC Server for AS/400 and Notes server storage spaces.
- Manage Notes users from the AS/400.
- Configure and manage the directory shadowing function.
- Configure and manage the DB2/400 integration function.
- Backup and restore.
- Server storage spaces and network server storage spaces.
- Individual Notes databases and documents.

Prerequisites: Before taking this course, you should have AS/400 skills in security, database, backup and restore, and TCP/IP. You should have PC skills in Microsoft Windows or OS/2 knowledge and hands-on experience. To successfully complete this course you must have training and experience as a Lotus Notes user. You can develop the AS/400 skills by taking:

- AS/400 System Administration and Control (S6019)
- AS/400 Internet Access and TCP/IP (S6092)

Enrollment Dates and Locations:

Start Date	*Course Number*	*Location*
29/09/97	S6090 JBI3	Atlanta, GA
27/10/97	S6090 JB13	Atlanta, GA
28/10/97	S6090 JAL9	Minneapolis, MN

Source: http://iws.as400.ibm.com/lotus_notes/notes400_16.htm

CSIR: PROFITING FROM R&D

Founded in 1942, the Indian Council for Scientific and Industrial Research (CSIR) comprises forty laboratories spread across the country. In 1997, CSIR employed 25,000 people, including 5,500 qualified scientists, working in a wide range of disciplines.

During the five decades CSIR had been in existence, its contribution was often judged to be worthwhile but lacklustre. On 1 January 1996, R.A. Mashelkar, the director general, and his colleagues proposed a new vision for improving performance and taking the CSIR labs into the 21st century. Encapsulated in a CSIR Vision 2001 document, this involved changes on several fronts—diminishing the reliance of CSIR on government grants while continuing to serve Indian society at large, bringing about a greater commercial orientation, earning foreign exchange by doing work for international companies, and revitalising an organisation that had got used to functioning as a 'government department'.

This case was written by Professor Vijay K. Jolly. The author wishes to acknowledge the generous help rendered by several CSIR staff members in the preparation of this case. The case was first registered by the International Institute for Management Development (IMD), Lusanne, Switzerland, in 1998. Not to be used or reproduced without written permission directly from IMD.

Although progress after the announcement of the vision had been encouraging, its implementation was not expected to be easy. To be successful, CSIR needed to come to grips with a wide range of challenges the vision would inevitably throw its way and to institute the changes required to overcome them. In doing so, it needed to recognise developments taking place both within India and abroad since the mid-1990s.

CSIR's Mission When Founded

At the time of CSIR's foundation in 1942, there was virtually no research infrastructure in India outside a handful of universities. It was natural, therefore, that CSIR's mission was a broad one, covering the many activities necessary to get scientific and industrial research started within the country. The mission included the following main elements:

- Promotion, guidance and co-ordination of scientific and industrial research in India.
- Establishment or development of institutions and assistance to departments of existing institutions for study of problems concerning particular industries.
- Establishment and award of research fellowships and grants for students.
- Utilisation of the results of research conducted under the CSIR for the development of industries in the country.
- Establishment, maintenance and management of laboratories, institutes and organisations to further scientific and industrial research.
- Collection and dissemination of information in regard to research and industry.
- Publication of scientific papers and journals.

The nature of CSIR's labs and the order in which they were set up (see Appendix 1) reflected the broad scope of activities with which the organisation was entrusted. CSIR needed to build basic capabilities in key scientific disciplines, which explains the early establishment of the National Physical Laboratory and the National Chemical Laboratory. At the same time, it needed to apply science and technology to tackle industrial problems, especially those relating to basic human needs. The setting up of the Central Fuel Research Institute, the Central Food Technological Research Institute, the Central Building Research Institute and the Central Drug Research Institute were in line with this second objective.

Organisationally, CSIR was set up as an independent society, with India's prime minister as president (see Appendix 2). This was in recognition of both its scientific vocation as well as its social mission. The governing body, to which the director general reported, was composed of eminent persons drawn from the country's scientific and political elite as well as from industry. As for the labs themselves, they were vested with a great deal of autonomy from the beginning. They typically set their own research agenda, using their own research councils for the purpose.

CSIR's director general traditionally played a dual role. In addition to being the head of the CSIR organisation, he was simultaneously the director general of scientific and industrial research, reporting to the minister of science and technology. In the latter capacity, he had responsibility for several nation-wide activities, such as technology promotion, the formulation of government R&D incentives policies, and the promotion of private in-house R&D. He was also head of the National Research and Development Corporation which, until 1988, was responsible for licensing all government-owned technologies, including those generated by CSIR.

CSIR Within India's R&D Landscape

For a variety of historical reasons, the government has been the principal supporter of research in India. Between 1947 and 1996 it invested over US$ 50 bn in setting up about 120 university institutes of technology and over 100 national laboratories. Even in 1996, it accounted for 80 per cent of the $2.2 bn spent on R&D in the country. Of CSIR's total budget of $190 mn that year, the government provided $125 mn by way of grants; the remaining $65 mn was earned by CSIR through contract research and royalties, some of it from government-owned companies and agencies.

Appendix 3 illustrates the overall organisation of R&D in India and CSIR's role within it. Private company R&D aside, there were three main categories of actors involved: government laboratories attached to individual ministries (and departments), the CSIR labs, and the Department of Science and Technology. Ministerial labs (see Appendix 4) were a complement to the various public (government-owned) enterprises that were organised by sector and grouped under their respective ministries. The most important among these were the defence and space labs, which together accounted for over 50 per cent of the government's expenditure on R&D. While some of these labs came directly under their ministries, others were organised as councils to signal their somewhat more independent status. The most important among the latter were the Council for Medical Research (which operated over thirty laboratories), under the Ministry of Health and Family Welfare, and the Council for Agricultural Research (whose annual budget matched that of the CSIR), under the Ministry of Agriculture. The distinguishing character of these labs was that they were mandated to advance the programmes of their concerned ministries, coming up with commercially viable technologies and even getting involved in the downstream phases of commercialisation—developing market-ready products, scaling-up production processes and, in some cases, engaging in production.

Compared to them, CSIR labs could not engage in downstream commercialisation activities. However, they could perform research for third parties and license their technologies to commercial enterprises within India or abroad.

As for the Department of Science and Technology, its mission consisted of monitoring and promoting science and technology overall. It made periodic surveys, identified gaps in the nation's research infrastructure, and formulated policies for encouraging R&D nation-wide, including inside private companies. Through its Science and Engineering Research Council (similar to the National Science Foundation in the US), it funded university research projects to the tune of $3 mn a year. It also administered various special programmes, such as the Technology Development Fund, which was used for funding industrial technology projects using the tax charged to Indian private companies on their royalty payments to companies abroad.

Until the late 1970s, roughly half the government's expenditure on R&D was channelled through science and technology agencies and half through various ministerial agencies. Since then, the share of the latter has become progressively larger, especially when including the R&D state-owned financial institutions have started funding.

Responding to National Priorities

Despite its independent status, CSIR had from the beginning been influenced by government policies, partly because of its link to the prime minister and partly because the government was its main source of funds.

The way in which these policies had a direct impact on its work, however, evolved over time. In the beginning, the emphasis was mainly on building an indigenous capability in science and technology. This got translated into a hands-off, indulgent attitude on the part of political leaders, allowing the labs to set their own research agendas. The emphasis was on creating a scientific culture in India, a desire enshrined in the constitution (adopted in 1950) which stated: 'It shall be the duty of every citizen of India to develop scientific temper, humanism and sprit of inquiry and reform.'

The country's First Five-Year Plan (1951–55) also endorsed this capability-building orientation. It was only with the Second Five-Year Plan (1956–60) onwards that a need was expressed to closely align the work of scientists in national laboratories to national development efforts. By then, Indian economic policy had become hostage to two sets of beliefs: one, that socio-economic benefits should reach a wide cross-section of the population as quickly as possible, and two, that scarce resources (notably capital and foreign exchange) should be allocated in a planned fashion to achieve self-sufficiency and balanced growth. These beliefs resulted in a highly interventionist stance on the part of the government, involving the setting up of a large number of government-owned companies, as well as directing what private companies were and were not allowed to do. The government, in other words, became the principal entrepreneur, competence builder and resource allocator in the Indian economy.

Between the late 1950s and early 1970s, CSIR responded to these economic policies in three main ways. In pursuit of the goal of self-sufficiency, it first concentrated on reverse engineering technologies and products available abroad. The aim was to build indigenous capabilities in them and to disseminate them cheaply to Indian industry. Thus, with no patents allowed on pharmaceutical products, the Central Drug Research Institute (CDRI) concentrated on copying basic drugs that were either off-patent or protected by 'product' patents abroad, developing its own process technology for each drug. The latter technology was then licensed to various Indian pharmaceutical companies, thereby creating a flourishing drug industry and drug prices which were among the lowest in the world.

This reverse engineering was done in parallel with attempts at finding cost-effective solutions to problems inherent in the Indian situation of that time—finding cheap building materials, techniques to reduce food wastage, substitutes for scarce wood, etc. A third leg consisted in developing technologies that relied on indigenous resources, such as coal and medicinal plants.

This phase in CSIR's development was also accompanied by the setting up of some regional research laboratories with multi-disciplinary capabilities. While intended to serve a region's needs, these laboratories developed some region-specific specialisations over time, based on the unique needs or resources of the region concerned. A large number of technology transfer and extension units were also established to bring scientific capabilities, such as testing and problem solving, closer to the user community throughout India.

By the early 1970s, national priorities had changed somewhat, calling for special emphasis to be placed on employment creation and improving the country's balance of payments situation. The consequence was a further broadening of CSIR's mission to include work on minimising imports and promotion of exports, pursuing projects of short duration so as to enable early transfer to production, developing labour-intensive technologies to alleviate unemployment and developing village and small-scale technologies to benefit the rural community.

These new demands did not replace those placed on CSIR in earlier years. They simply added to them, causing the organisation to continuously expand its range of research programmes over time. There were even occasions when certain labs were called upon to contribute to the nation's defence efforts, despite the fact that the Ministry of Defence had its own research infrastructure.

The variety of these demands inevitably led to a dilution in CSIR's focus and a lack of attention to basic research by the early 1980s. The Sixth Plan (1980–85), unfortunately, did little to address the question of focus. Instead, it kept most of the earlier expressed priorities in place while adding a new emphasis on modernising the research infrastructure and doing basic research to achieve international competitiveness.

CSIR's Achievements

Despite its relatively meagre budget by international standards and having to conform to a wide range of national priorities, many of which were not easily translatable into concrete R&D projects, and despite its having to function within India's bureaucratic milieu, CSIR succeeded in building up an enviable set of competencies and developing some useful technologies.

With regard to competencies, CSIR labs developed into fairly self-contained institutions, conducting everything from basic to applied research and, if needed, scaling-up their technologies to a pre-commercial stage. The Central Drug Research Institute (CDRI), for example, had one of the most complete drug R&D infrastructures under one roof of any institute, or even company for that matter, in the world. Its sixteen departments ranged from medicinal chemistry all the way to pharmacology, clinical trials and process development; with 500 rhesus monkeys and thousands of small animals, it had the largest animal testing facility in Asia. It was also well endowed with the latest scientific instruments, housing one of the Indian government's Regional Sophisticated Instrumentation Centres (RSICs) on its premises.

More generally, the laboratories under the CSIR umbrella constituted a unique resource for conducting industrial research. The diverse set of disciplines they covered offered an opportunity to work on many complex technologies. For example, CSIR was among the best positioned organisations in the world to work on fuel cells, which many saw as a major technology whose commercialisation was imminent. It could combine the expertise of the Electrochemical Research Institute (for overall cell design), National Chemical Laboratory (for catalysts), Glass and Ceramic Research Institute (for membranes), as well as others for fabrication, testing etc. The same applied to a number of environmental and system technologies that required assembling together a range of R&D capabilities.

As for the technological breakthroughs CSIR had been able to achieve over its fifty-year existence, these need to be seen in light of the country's resource constraints and the sheer variety of programmes with which the organisation was entrusted. Even so, a representative sample of what it achieved includes:

- The design and development of an all-composite two-seater trainer aircraft.
- Novel and cost-effective processes for over thirty drugs, including AZT (anti-AIDS), Acyclovir (anti-viral) and Metoprolol (cardiovascular), plus several new herbal formulations, including a learning and memory enhancer. It also developed the country's first major new-to-the-world drug molecule, Centchroman. The latter was first developed as a once-a-week female contraceptive but has since been found effective as a

therapeutic for diseases such as breast cancer and osteoporosis. For the latter purpose, it has recently been licensed to a Seattle-based company, Zympgenetics (a subsidiary of NOVO Nordisk) for conducting phase-II clinical trials and is expected to be CDRI's first international product.

- A number of basic research discoveries in biotechnology which have potential applications in the treatment and/or diagnosis of cholera, leishmania, malaria and tuberculosis.
- The development of a range of new catalysts (both zeolite and non-zeolite) for the petrochemical and chemical industries, making India one of the few countries self-sufficient in this important area.
- Several technologies in areas such as computational fluid dynamics, drug delivery, leather processing, geophysical mapping, environmental monitoring and beneficiation, electronics components and instruments, coal mining and utilisation, and food processing and post-harvest technology.

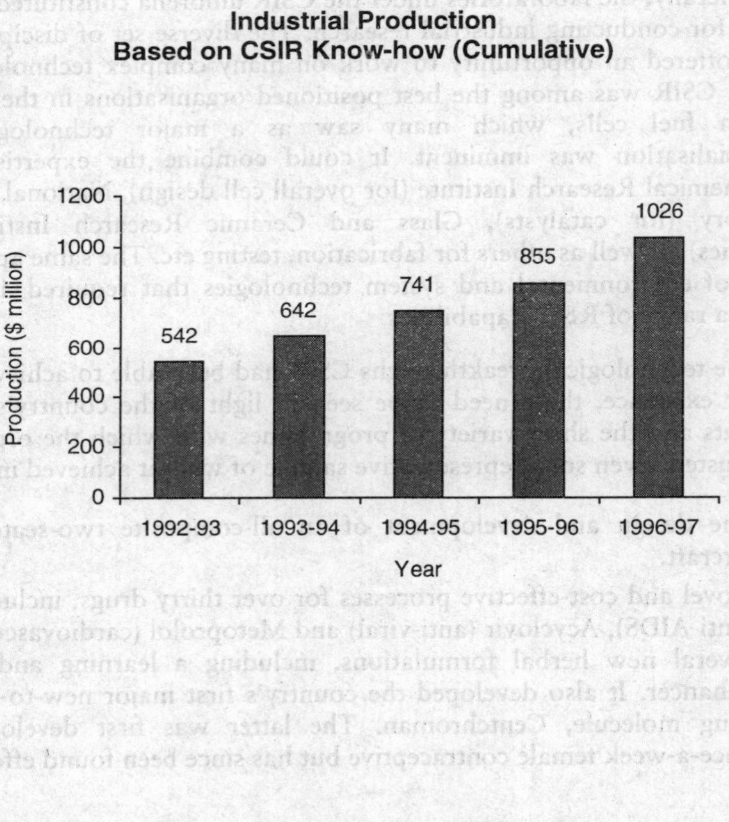

In terms of overall economic impact, CSIR technologies had generated roughly $3 bn of industrial turnover in India, productivity savings of $220 mn, and rural employment generation of 8 million man days between 1992 and 1997 alone. During this period, it executed 800 technology license agreements, made 250 new technologies (those developed since 1992) available for licensing, filed 920 patents in India and 120 abroad, and rendered technical assistance to about 4,000 entrepreneurs in India.

New Industrial Production to be Catalised (Incremental)

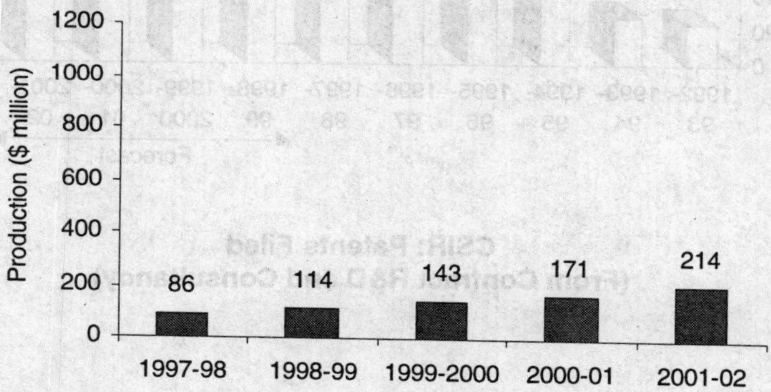

These achievements aside, some claim that CSIR's biggest contribution has been in the promotion of a science and technology culture within India and the development of new scientific talent. Apart from being one of the most 'open' institutes in the country, permitting anyone interested to visit, within limits, CSIR has complemented the role of universities by training budding scientists. In the beginning, the training of fresh graduates was to meet its own manpower requirements. With the growing need for such postgraduate training, CSIR introduced a fellowship programme, giving virtually anyone with a first class bachelor's or master's degree an opportunity to work in a CSIR lab towards a PhD. Successful candidates could then be eligible for a post-doc position at CSIR, ensuring a scientist a ten to thirteen year career in research after graduation.

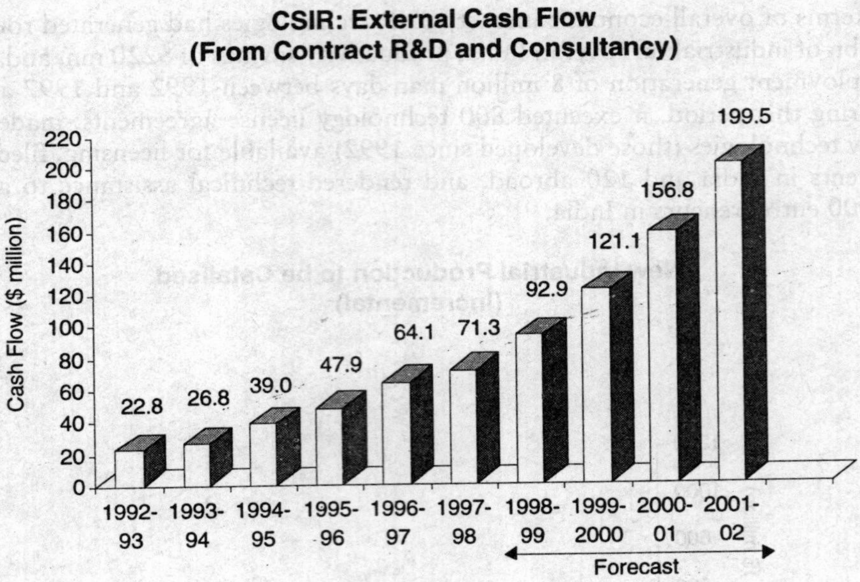
CSIR: External Cash Flow
(From Contract R&D and Consultancy)
Cash Flow ($ million)
220
200
180
160
140
120
100
80
60
40
20
0
22.8
26.8
39.0
47.9
64.1
71.3
92.9
121.1
156.8
199.5
1992-93
1993-94
1994-95
1995-96
1996-97
1997-98
1998-99
1999-2000
2000-01
2001-02
Forecast

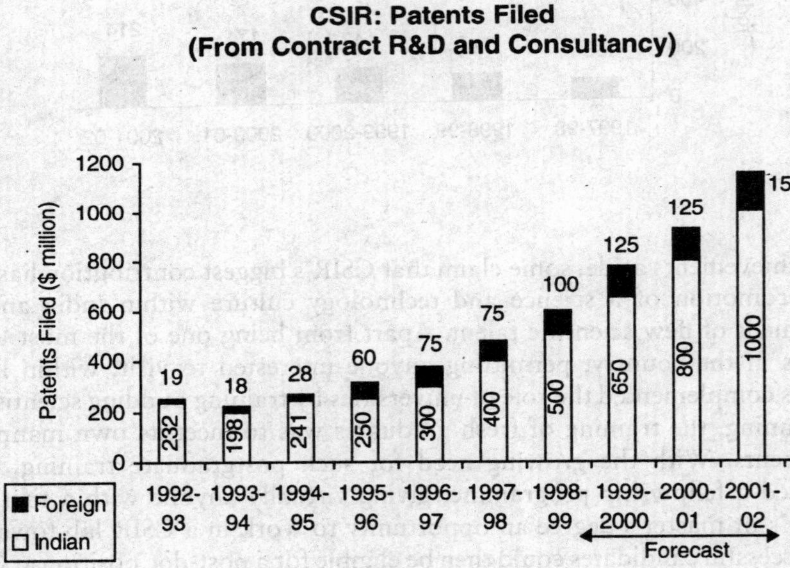
CSIR: Patents Filed
(From Contract R&D and Consultancy)
Patents Filed ($ million)
1200
1000
800
600
400
200
0
19
18
28
60
75
75
100
125
125
150
232
198
241
250
300
400
500
650
800
1000
1992-93
1993-94
1994-95
1995-96
1996-97
1997-98
1998-99
1999-2000
2000-01
2001-02
Foreign
Indian
Forecast

This fellowship programme was supplemented by some forty bilateral exchange programmes with thirty-two countries for exchanging scientific information, visits by scientists, and the use of each other's equipment and facilities. It also invited 100 PhD students from developing countries each year to work in CSIR labs, in addition to the eighty to 100 scientists who were provided training under various United Nations schemes.

Areas for Improvement: Findings of the 1986 Review Committee

These contributions notwithstanding, CSIR had often been criticised for not doing enough, given the resources devoted to it by the government. The criticisms of the last committee set up to review its performance in 1986 were particularly scathing:

> In the perception of some, the CSIR system appears to be unwieldy, if not grotesque, and gives the impression of unplanned growth as also of unfinished work. There are vast variations in the calibre of scientists in different laboratories, which does not always conform to standards of excellence. There is no clear sense of direction. The major failure, perhaps, is its inability to transform scientific results in the laboratory into technologies for industrial production. What is more, there has been a tendency to reinvent the wheel by placing disproportionate emphasis in terms of work on known products and known processes.[1]

The Review Committee did not really challenge the mission CSIR had been entrusted with at its foundation and many of its recommendations were of a procedural nature. Even so, its critiques suggested directions for the way CSIR ought to be managed as the country's economic ideology changed. Among the key findings of the Committee were:

- A lack of focus and direction, partly on account of CSIR's multiplicity of objectives.
- Sub-optimal scale of operations (lack of critical size) owing to the relatively small amount of resources devoted compared to other government labs and the large number of different projects being undertaken.
- Lack of interaction between CSIR and its actual or potential users (including both public and private companies, as well as with other government labs and universities in India).

1. Report of the CSIR Review Committee, December 1986, p. 2.

- The presence of a 'government culture' in spite of CSIR's independent status.
- Lack of a unified set of objectives among labs, which fostered the pursuit of individual recognition rather than successes based on teamwork.
- A disproportionate emphasis on basic research at the expense of applied research, with the former also not up to international standards of excellence.

The Committee was also of the opinion that CSIR could nevertheless play a useful role given India's stage of development. With universities and private companies still too ill-equipped to conduct major research projects, CSIR would remain, for a long time to come, the principal vehicle for exploring scientific frontiers and high-impact technologies.

Getting to CSIR Vision 2001

The 1986 Review Committee's recommendations were, however, overtaken by subsequent events. Starting in the early 1980s, a fundamental rethinking of the economic ideology the country had espoused for the previous thirty years had begun to take place. While the early set of policies had indeed succeeded in making the country self-sufficient in a number of areas, notably food production and defence, many within and outside the government felt a change was needed for the years ahead. To a large extent, this was spurred by the success neighbouring Asian countries were enjoying as a result of a more liberal and outward-looking set of economic policies.

A major push for change occurred in 1991, when a new government headed by P.V. Narasimha Rao took over. Noting that the feeble attempts at economic liberalisation made over the previous decade had had very little impact, the Rao government called for a dramatic break with the past. Rather than a controlled and inward-looking economy, with an emphasis on self-sufficiency and resource conservation, the government wanted market forces to drive economic development. This meant deregulating the internal market, encouraging foreign investment (both direct and portfolio), encouraging exports and achieving macro-economic balance. If all this meant a diminished role for the government in finance and industry, the government would concentrate instead on more social functions such as education, health and national security.

This new thinking also marked a watershed in how CSIR perceived its future role. While recognising its obligation to contribute to Indian society, it needed to become more productive and economically viable on its own. Rather than just absorb and adapt foreign technologies to the Indian environment, it had to become an equal player in the global marketplace for new technologies.

The need for CSIR to change had begun to be felt by the late 1980s at CSIR headquarters. The debate on what could and should be done was led by A.P. Mitra and S.K. Joshi, the director generals at that time, and H.R. Bhojwani, the head of R&D planning and business development who had earlier served as secretary to the 1986 Review Committee. Some laboratories had also taken initiatives in this direction. Among the latter was the National Chemical Laboratory (NCL), which Mashelkar joined as director in June 1989.

> He recalled: 'In addressing the NCL staff on joining, I spoke of NCL becoming an International Chemical Laboratory Ltd. The "Ltd" was used to signify figuratively the change required: from a "government-type" culture to a corporate one. "International" referred to two things: networking with foreign companies and researchers and ambition to export, rather than just import, technology, making India into a global R&D platform.'

Two months after the new industrial policy was announced in 1991, NCL ruthlessly cut all the projects that would not survive in a liberal economic environment.

The process NCL had started gradually began to give direction to CSIR as a whole. With the realisation that CSIR had to become more self-financing, CSIR set up a committee in 1992 to examine how the entire organisation could become more market oriented. Mashelkar was appointed chairman of this committee.

The Mashelkar Committee submitted its report, entitled 'Creating an Enabling Environment for Commercialisation of CSIR Knowledge-base', in January 1993. Among its key recommendations were:

- Set up a dedicated marketing group at each laboratory and at CSIR headquarters, which would be involved in the selection and planning of in-house and externally funded projects (while CSIR headquarters would be responsible for creating an awareness of overall capabilities and assisting in specific negotiations, particularly in the marketing of inter-laboratory capabilities, the lab marketing groups would be responsible for identifying marketable research projects and the formulation of proposals and contracts).

- Engage specialised professionals on a commission basis or as consultants for marketing laboratory technologies.
- Permit CSIR to invest in the equity of a company in lieu of payments for intellectual property.
- Permit CSIR staff to serve as directors on the boards of private companies.
- Establish commercial arms (subsidiaries) of laboratories.
- Make funds, including foreign exchange, available expressly for marketing purposes.
- Provide incentives, such as recognition, distribution of a share of royalties and fees, and sabbaticals in marketing-related institutions for the staff.

Also envisaged, virtually for the first time, was the formation of consortia with other R&D agencies, design and engineering consultants and financial institutions for packaging technologies for sale.

Although only a few of these recommendations were adopted, partly for legal or fiscal reasons having to do with CSIR's statutes and partly out of inertia, they provided a road map for what could be done. What they did serve to do was to constitute an agenda for Mashelkar himself when he was later appointed as director general of CSIR in June 1995. He became convinced that CSIR could prosper in the coming new liberalised environment the government was working towards, not by retrenching and rationalising, but by expanding its role to encompass both its traditional mission of serving as India's primary source of public technological expertise as well as a source of commercially valuable technologies that both Indian and foreign companies would pay for.

As Mashelkar put it: 'We had survived all these years because industry was not doing any R&D. Yet, R&D should be an industrial responsibility. Would CSIR then be needed and relevant by, say, 2020? In order to make ourselves relevant, we had to change. This change meant several things: financial autonomy and the managerial freedom that goes with it, but above all customer confidence, since no one comes and pays you unless you can deliver.'

These ideas got elaborated in a new vision for CSIR for the year 2001 published in January 1996. Its main elements were for CSIR to become:

- A model organisation for scientific industrial research and a path-setter in the shifting paradigm of self-financing R&D.
- A global R&D platform providing competitive R&D and high quality science-based technical services the world over.
- A vital source of science and technology for national societal missions which combine technology with a human face.

Accompanying this Vision was a set of goals for the year 2001 that represented no less than quantum leap in terms of what CSIR had traditionally been doing. These goals involved:

- A move towards the path of self-financing by generating over $200 mn from external sources, as opposed to $40 mn in 1994–95, of which at least 50 per cent would be from industrial customers (up from 15 per cent in 1994–95).
- Develop at least ten exclusive and globally competitive technologies in niche areas.
- Hold a patent bank of 500 foreign patents (up from fifty).
- Realise 10 per cent of operational expenditure from intellectual property licensing (up from <1 per cent).
- Derive annual earnings of $40 mn from overseas R&D work and services (up from <$2 mn).

Recognising the need for the staff to buy into these changes, a draft version of the Vision and the accompanying goals were first discussed at a day-long meeting of the forty lab directors in September 1995. The directors were then asked to take the draft with them, make as many copies as they wished, and discuss its contents with their own staff.

As Mashelkar explained: 'We had forty labs dispersed all over the country, which had never worked together with a common goal. I felt we needed a common mission and common goals. CSIR had never had quantified goals: we needed quantification in order to create internal pressures. The Vision, moreover, had to cover all the enabling things—human resource development, intellectual property rights, MIS, etc. By getting the draft widely circulated and discussed, I hoped to get all 25,000 employees of CSIR as stakeholders. Today, some people may still be skeptical, or disagree on certain points, but they feel a sense of ownership nevertheless.'

A new system of performance evaluation was also introduced to mobilise efforts around these goals (see Appendix 5). Each lab was to be evaluated according to a scoring system based on the external funds raised, contribution to industrial and social development (such as how much industrial production in the country was catalysed by its technologies), acquisition of new knowledge (so as not to dry out the pipeline of ideas) and the quality of R&D management (developing new talent, use of MIS, accreditation, etc.).

The intention was to preserve the autonomy the labs traditionally enjoyed within CSIR. However, the freedom an individual lab was given was to be in proportion to its level of self-financing. Labs that did well could keep their income as a reserve fund to be operated at the discretion of the director. He could use it to set up a marketing group or depute scientists abroad on business promotion.

The Issues Ahead

The fact that the new goals CSIR had set for itself were realistic was borne out of the recent experience of one of its labs: The National Chemical Laboratory (NCL). In 1989, NCL had no US patents. By 1997, it had thirty. It had no foreign clients in 1989. By 1997, it had over a dozen US and European companies who accounted for over 80 per cent of its external funding. Even so, there were several issues CSIR needed to confront as it went about its transformation.

One set concerned the competitive environment it faced. A number of countries with publicly funded research organisations had already, or were about to, announce similar initiatives. The hitherto exclusively government-focussed national labs in the US were already allowed, and indeed encouraged, to engage in collaborative research with private companies, including foreign-owned ones. The US government was even willing to share in the cost of such projects, anywhere between 20 per cent and 80 per cent, depending on the company and technology involved. The Frauenhofer Institute in Germany, which traditionally supported German industry, especially small and medium-sized companies lacking their own R&D infrastructure, was also looking for more clients outside Germany and contemplating setting up satellite organisations in the US and Singapore. The active debate on bringing about a commercial orientation at government-owned labs in the UK was tending towards privatisation even of these labs. In Australia, the Commonwealth Scientific Industrial Research Organisation (CSIRO) had been broken into a number of independent institutes with clear missions and targets for cost sharing with the private sector. New Zealand's Department of Scientific and Industrial Research was also restructured in 1992 and had been replaced by ten Crown-owned research institutes which were registered as independent companies under the Companies Act, with the freedom to enter into joint ventures with the private sector, borrow money on the open market for development, sell their intellectual property to the highest bidder, etc. Waiting in the wings were the 100-odd labs belonging to the Chinese Academy of Science as well as a number of research organisations in Japan and throughout Southeast Asia.

Fortunately for CSIR, Indian companies were under pressure to introduce world-beating technologies as a result of liberalisation and the opening of the Indian economy, thereby creating a local pull for the technologies and services it had to offer. Previously, CDRI had to approach Indian pharmaceutical companies after developing a particular drug and its manufacturing process. Now, these companies were eager to collaborate with CDRI from the concept stage and pay for the entire development. Apart from bringing money, this new approach ensured that there was a taker for CDRI-developed technology from the beginning. However, in order to benefit from the potential the local market offered, CSIR needed to develop strategies suited to companies that had never had to take R&D seriously until now.

A second set of issues concerned the nature of CSIR labs and their historical role. As one research manager put it: 'We have always been torn between our national mission of working on problems unique to India and doing good science to come up with internationally needed technologies in a competitive way. I don't think this is adequately addressed in our Vision 2001. The Vision expects us to strike a balance between the two, but how should one do that?'

A case in point was the work CDRI did. Previously, it received its charter of research mainly from the Ministry of Health and Family Welfare. This had translated into a more or less permanent focus on two areas: the control of parasitic diseases, such as malaria, filaria, diahreal diseases and lishmaniasis, and on family planning. Now it was targeting the CNS/CVS area, which promised much greater international market potential. But should that really be its mission?

Related to this was the choice between long-term basic research and applied research. As expected, some were worried that CSIR would assume a short-term development (not research) orientation, sacrificing good science. Mashelkar had the following to say on this point:

> Science will continue to be the rock-bed on which CSIR is built. There is no high technology without high science. Today at the National Chemical Laboratory, for example, we have 250 people working on their PhDs at universities. The topics we take up are not 'commercial' topics; they are topics, which throw more light on a commercial problem, building an enabling technology for addressing it creatively and deeply. If someone is working on new catalysts using molecular dynamics and simulations, why should he choose a problem some eminent professor abroad has been working on for fifteen years? He can look at the problem we are looking at, and see if he can bring greater depth to that. Instead of 'publish or perish', our new slogan is 'patent, publish and prosper'. Last year, we had two articles in *Nature* and one in *Science*. All three were based on inventions on which patents were applied for before publishing.

Last but by no means least important, was the change that needed to take place at the level of the individual scientist. As Jayant Narlikar, a leading Indian astronomer, put it:

> Our system in national labs or universities discourages initiative, innovation or inspiration. It is geared to the progress of the average scientist . . . as a society, we are uncomfortable with excellence.[2]

In order to create an environment congenial for scientific research, CSIR had done away with hierarchy amongst its scientific cadre in 1964. Instead of having junior and senior scientific officers, assistant and deputy directors, and the like, it had re-designated everyone as scientists with grades (A to F) signifying salary levels. It had also instituted a time-bound promotion scheme, involving five-year reviews with personal advancement linked to time of service rather than to vacancies. This egalitarianism was reinforced by strong unionisation among all levels of employees and a work culture that protected individual rights rather than rewarding merit or aligning people's effort to organisational priorities.

This egalitarianism continued to influence the way labs got managed. As one research manager put it:

> In India, you cannot touch anybody; you can't hurt human feelings. Democracy here is often equated with equal personal rights. If I ask someone who has been working on a certain problem for thirty years to

2. K.S. Jayaraman, 'Independence but No Nobel Winners for India Since Then', *Nature*, Vol. 388, 14 August 1997, p. 613.

stop his work and do something different, he will react strongly. All I can do is to say that if he is so attached to the problem, he can continue working on it, but that I will not assign any priority to it.

The CSIR policy with regard to giving monetary rewards to scientists based on the successful commercialisation of their research has had a checkered history. The principle itself was enshrined in CSIR's founding resolution of 1942. However, the first concrete policy was established only in 1961, under which 40 per cent of the amount of royalty and premiums earned was to be earmarked as 'researchers' share' and distributed to the staff. This was modified from time to time, and by the mid-1970s, the incentive formula was as follows:

		Share
(a)	Innovators	35%
(b)	Members of team	35%
(c)	Others providing inputs directly associated with the project	15%
(d)	Common lab pool and welfare fund	15%

Note: (a) and (b) were combined to 70 per cent where it was not possible to distinguish between the two categories.

This policy, however, came under criticism because of the jealously and preference for profit-oriented industrial projects it created among the staff. Apart from the difficulty of determining the exact credit to be given to all those involved in a particular project, it also created a climate of secrecy wherein scientists tended to keep high-value ideas to themselves until projects were well advanced. As a result, this incentive policy was abandoned in 1977, with the researcher share credited to a centrally-operated CSIR welfare fund. It was only in April 1994, after a gap of seventeen years, that the incentive scheme was re-instituted in the hope that it would motivate scientists to do commercially valuable work.

Even so, what type of motivation and reward policy to implement remains an open issue. Any effective resolution needs to consider all the other things CSIR management must do to make Vision 2001 a success.

APPENDIX 1

CSIR Establishments

1944	Indian Institute of Chemical Technology (IICT), Hyderabad
1946	Central Fuel Research Institute (CFRI), Dhanbad
1950	Central Food Technological Research Institute (CFTRI), Mysore
1950	Central Glass and Ceramic Research Institute (CGCRI), Calcutta
1950	National Chemical Laboratory (NCL), Pune
1950	National Physical Laboratory (NPL), Delhi
1950	National Metallurgical Laboratory (NML), Jamshedpur
1951	Central Building Research Institute (CBRI), Roorkee
1951	Central Drug Research Institute (CDRI), Lucknow
1951*	Publications and Information Directorate (PID), Delhi
1952	Central Road Research Institute (CRRI), Delhi
1952*	Indian National Scientific Documentation Centre (INSDOC), Delhi
1953	Central Electrochemical Research Institute (CECRI), Karaikudi
1953	Central Electronics Engineering Research Institute (CEERI), Pilani
1953	Central Leather Research Institute (CLRI), Madras
1953	National Botanical Research Institute (NBRI), Lucknow
1954	Central Salt and Marine Chemicals Research Institute (CSMCRI), Bhavnagar
1956	Central Mining Research Institute (CMRI), Dhanbad
1956**	Indian Institute of Chemical Biology (IICB), Calcutta
1957	Regional Research Laboratory (RRL, JM), Jammu-Tawi
1958	Central Mechanical Engineering Research Institute (CMERI), Durgapur
1958	National Environmental Engineering Research Institute (NEERI), Nagpur
1959	Central Institute of Medical and Aromatic Plants (CIMAP), Lucknow
1959	Central Scientific Instruments Organisation (CSIO), Chandigarh
1959	National Aerospace Laboratories (NAL), Bangalore
1960	Indian Institute of Petroleum (IIP), Dehradun
1961	National Geophysical Research Institute (NGRI), Hyderabad
1961	Regional Research Laboratory (RRL, JT), Jorhat
1964	Regional Research Laboratory (RRL, BHU), Bhubaneswar
1965	Industrial Toxicology Research Centre (ITRC), Lucknow
1965	Structural Engineering Research Centre (SERC, G), Ghaziabad
1965	Structural Engineering Research Centre (SERC, M), Madras
1966	National Institute of Oceanography (NIO), Goa
1966	Centre for Biochemical Technology (CBT), Delhi
1977	Centre for Cellular and Molecular Biology (CCMB), Hyderabad
1978	Regional Research Laboratory (RRL, TVM), Thiruvananthapuram
1981*	National Institute of Science, Technology and Development Studies (NISTADS), Delhi
1981	Regional Research Laboratory (RRL, BHO), Bhopal
1983	CSIR Palampur Complex (CSIR, PLX), Palampur
1984	Institute of Microbial Technology (IMT), Chandigarh

* Non-laboratories.

** Est. 1935, taken over by CSIR in 1956.

Source: CSIR, 1996.

APPENDIX 2

Organisational Structure

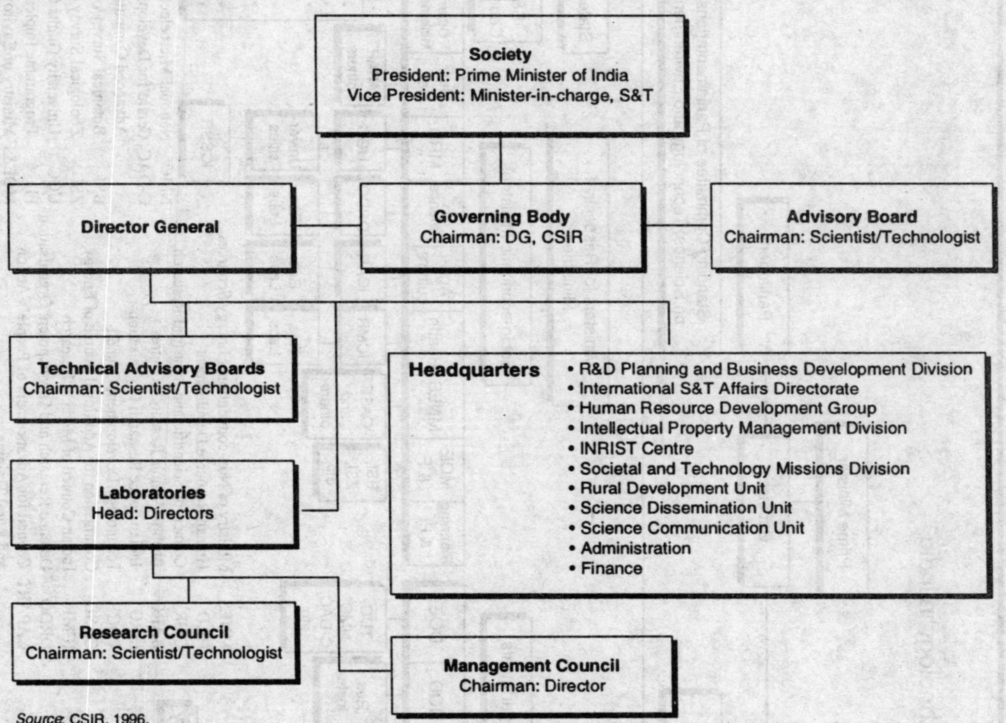

Source: CSIR, 1996.

APPENDIX 3

Organisation of Science and Technology in India

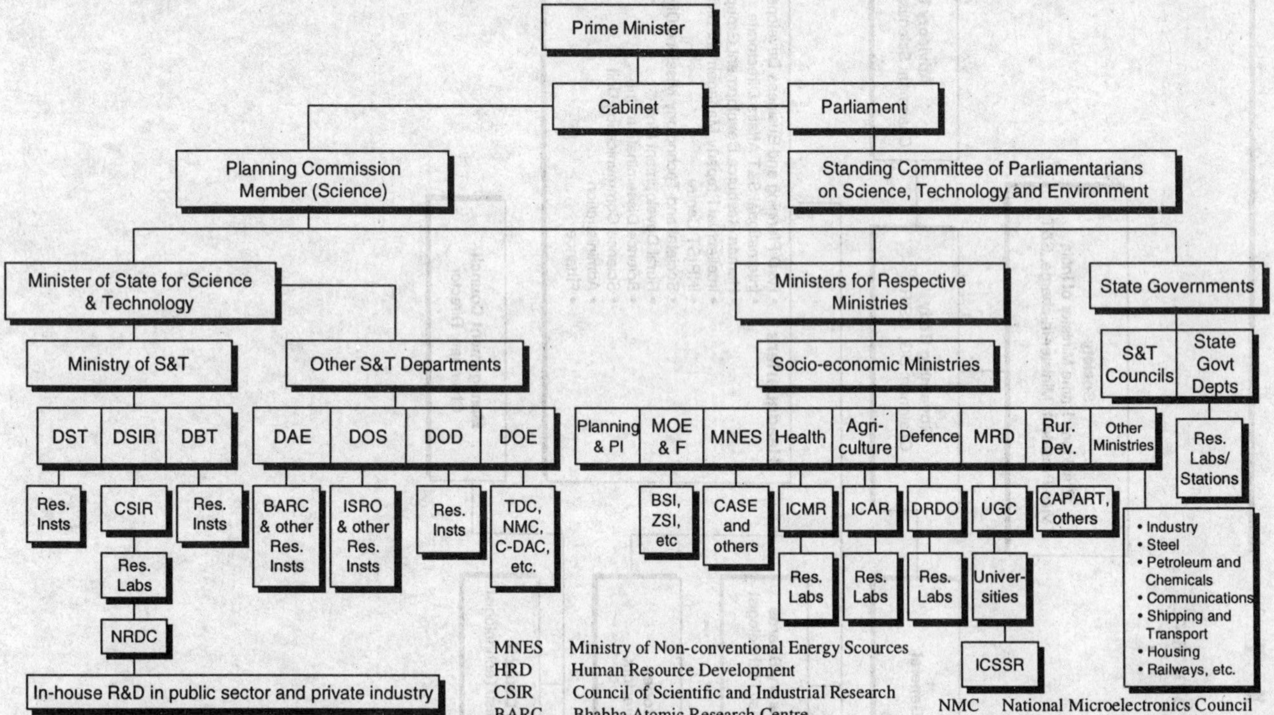

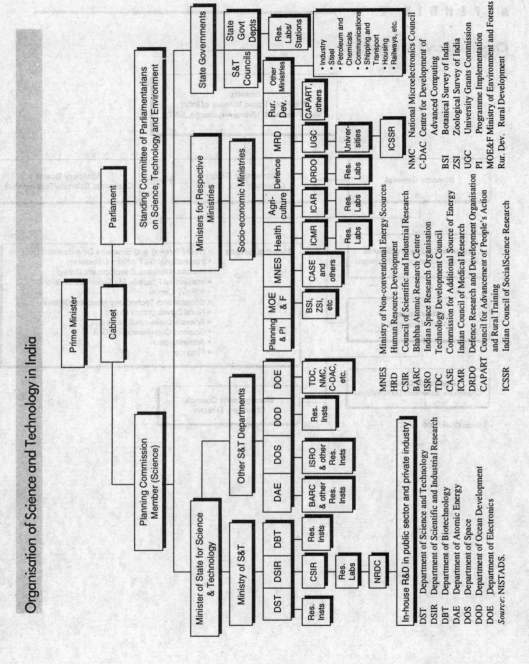

DST Department of Science and Technology
DSIR Department of Scientific and Industrial Research
DBT Department of Biotechnology
DAE Department of Atomic Energy
DOS Department of Space
DOD Department of Ocean Development
DOE Department of Electronics

Source: NISTADS.

MNES Ministry of Non-conventional Energy Scources
HRD Human Resource Development
CSIR Council of Scientific and Industrial Research
BARC Bhabha Atomic Research Centre
ISRO Indian Space Research Organisation
TDC Technology Development Council
CASE Commission for Additional Source of Energy
ICMR Indian Council of Medical Research
DRDO Defence Research and Development Organisation
CAPART Council for Advancement of People's Action and Rural Training
ICSSR Indian Council of SocialScience Research

NMC National Microelectronics Council
C-DAC Centre for Development of Advanced Computing
BSI Botanical Survey of India
ZSI Zoological Survey of India
UGC University Grants Commission
PI Programme Implementation
MOE&F Ministry of Environment and Forests
Rur. Dev. Rural Development

APPENDIX 4

Main R&D Policy Departments and Ministries in India

Department/Ministry	*Salient Policy Aspects*
Department of Science & Technology (DST)	National R&D issues, entrepreneurship, technology forecasting, international affairs, frontier areas, IPR awareness, co-ordination.
Department of Biotechnology (DBT)	Bio-technology human resource development, R&D, technology development, manufacturing, R&D infrastructure, safety regulations and international cooperation.
Department of Scientific and Industrial Research (DSIR)	Industrial R&D, technology development, transfer and exports, company level R&D and foreign collaborations, IPR, S&T information.
Council for Scientific and Industrial Research (CSIR)	Scientific industrial R&D policies for its chain of laboratories, including international affairs.
Department of Electronics (DOE)	Development of electronics related technologies and infrastructure, human resource development, informatics and software.
Department of Ocean Development (DOD)	Ocean policy, marine resource survey and utilisation, R&D, pollution, law of the sea and international treaties.
Department of Atomic Energy (DAE)	Matters relating to atomic energy, technology spin-offs, international affairs.
Department of Space (DOS)	Space sciences, technology and applications and industrial spin-offs, international affairs.
Ministry of Agriculture	Agriculture research, education (including animal sciences and fisheries), technology development and extension, regulations regarding introduction and exploration of plants and animals, IPR, international cooperation.
Ministry of Health and Family Welfare	Biomedical research, including communicable and non-communicable diseases, indigenous systems of medicine, regulations.

Appendix 4 contd . . .

Department/Ministry	*Salient Policy Aspects*
Ministry of Non-conventional Energy Sources (MNES)	Renewable energy sources R&D, technology development, transfer and exports, manufacturing, market development, utilisation, energy conservation, human resource development, international cooperation.
Other Ministries (e.g., telecommunication, industry, chemicals, power, surface transport)	Respective R&D units, public sector companies, foreign technology agreements, conservation and efficiency, trade and investments, productivity, cleaner technologies.
Department of Economic Affairs (DEA)	Economic affairs, administer the inflow of foreign funds.
Ministry of External Affairs (MEA)	Matters relating to foreign affairs.

Source: NISTADS.

APPENDIX 5

Evaluating the Performance of Individual Laboratories

Activity	*Weightage*	*Performance Grading*				*Overall Marks*
		Growth Rates			*Grading*	
		1995-96	*1996-97*	*1997-98*		
A: Self-financing Position						
• External Cash Flow (ECF) Generation						
Total ECF						
ECF from industry						
ECF from foreign sources						
• Commercial Rupee						
• Lab Reserve						
Generation						
Utilisation						
B: Contribution to Economy and Society						
S&T Inputs/Assistance for :						
• Catalysing New Industrial Production						
• Realising Productivity Gains						
• Employment Generation						
• Enhancing Value of Local Resources						
• Improvement in Quality of Life						
• National Issues/Causes						
• Others						
C: Contribution to New Knowledge						
• Papers in Top Refereed Journals						
• Patents Filing						
India						
Foreign						
• Other IPR						

Appendix 5 contd . . .

Activity		*Performance Grading*				*Overall Marks*
	Weightage	*Growth Rates*			*Grading*	
		1995-96	*1996-97*	*1997-98*		
• New Know-how for Marketing						
• New R&D Avenues/Areas Initiated						
• National/International Recognition						
D: R&D Management						
• Human Resource Management Initiatives						
Training of staff						
New recruitment (Group IV)						
Empowerment						
Grievance redressal						
• Quality Systems Initiatives						
• Restructuring and Change Management						
• Networking and Alliances						
Inter-laboratory						
Others (Mention)						
• Business Development Initiatives						
New markets/customers explored						
Customer satisfaction/rapport built up						
Others						
• Financial Management						
Economy measures						
Optimisation of resources						
Investment/portfolio management						
• Image and Visibility						
Stakeholders (Govt, CAG, Parliamentarians)						
Perceptions						
Media appreciation						
Total Grading						

Grading: Above target, A+=120%; On target, A=100%; 20% below target, B=80%; 30% below target, C=60%; more than 35% below target, D=40%

Source: CSIR, 1997.

CASE 10

BPL: GLOBAL COMPETITION AND GUERILLA WARFARE ON LOCAL TERRITORY

The economic liberalisation introduced in 1991 in India sparked widespread anxiety amongst many Indian businesses that domestic enterprises would be marginalised by the entry of multinational corporations. Nine years hence, if anything, large Indian local enterprises (LEs) have continued to flourish. It is argued in this study that the success of LEs centres around their ability to adapt their structures to match their institutional context, notwithstanding the serious upheavals that marked the entry of multinational enterprises.

In developing countries, due to the presence of highly fragmented markets, and underdeveloped related and supporting industries, incumbents within an industry need to perform a variety of functions. The markets themselves are not linked, and communication directed at one market does not necessarily spill over to other markets. There may be many market failures in co-ordinating

This case was written by Dr Pradeep Kanta Ray, Lecturer in International Business, School of International Business, University of New South Wales, Sydney. The author is grateful to the management and staff of BPL who provided untiring and invaluable assistance in data collection. The case was written in 2000.

investment decisions within any industry for several reasons: missing information, capital market deficiencies, economies of scale, interdependent investments in vertically related activities, externalities in skill creation and learning, and multiple linkages. Due to these market imperfections, transaction costs increase. MNCs therefore find the Indian industrial terrain rough, not having factored in differences in institutional infrastructure between their home and host environments. With the increase in the level of complexity and ambiguity in the local environment, the need for transforming internal governance and the importance of local knowledge increases, which requires greater subsidiary autonomy. Problems in communicating with customers when local infrastructure is weak and unpredictable government behaviour arising out of a volatile political environment can frustrate the operations of any MNC. Hence, firms need to adapt their strategies to fit their institutional context—a country's product, capital and labour markets and its regulatory systems.

Ironically, too many companies underestimate their home base advantage (and importance) in a market as big as India. The ability to understand the Indian customer and the Indian political environment, and how to operate locally can determine competitive advantage—within and beyond India. Distinctive choices about products, service and organisation can determine competitive strategy. Companies such as Godrej and Britannia have had years of serving consumers in a market where affordability is central to growth, and where pack sizes, price points and distribution structures are all different. Multinationals are grappling with similar issues across the globe. Yet those same international companies are burdened with huge embedded infrastructures, huge legacies and huge biases in the local environments they operate in.

The Development of the CTV Industry

Colour television transmission was introduced in India in 1982. The industry grew rapidly in the mid-1980s with a large number of manufacturers and assemblers of imported kits operating in a fragmented market.[1] Under recessionary conditions in the electronics sector during 1989–92, the CTV industry experienced an annual sales decline of 10 per cent over four years, until its partial recovery in 1993.[2] During this period, a partial shakeout of the

1. *Capital Market*, 15-28 August, 1994, p. 12
2. BPL Ltd, Prospectus, 1994.

inefficient players in the industry was followed by the emergence of leading local brands—BPL, Onida, Videocon and Optonica.[3]

In 1997, CTVs in India retailed at twice the price of CTVs in China and Taiwan.[4] The high prices for colour televisions put them out of reach of the great majority of consumers.[5] Whereas in 1995, China turned over around 20 million units per annum, in 1997 India's total production was only 2.02 million sets.[6] The low penetration of thirty-three sets per 1000 compared to China's 200 per 1000 was partly the result of steep rates of excise duty and entry taxes which comprised about 55 per cent of the cost of a CTV set.[7]

Installed Capacity and Actual Production, 1990–95

('000)

Company	*Capacity*		*Production*	
	1990–91	*1994–95*	*1990–91*	*1994–95*
Videocon	1100	NA	NA	970
BPL	320	750	633	525
Philips	100	200	22	146
MIRC	NA	652	31	156
Monica	102	102	NA	NA
Onida	20	100	NA	39
Kalyani Sharp	50	150	29	120
Weston	300	300	53	94
Solidaire	NA	400	112	77

Source: ORG.

With the bundling of components into integrated circuits, the minimum economic scale of CTV operations had increased to 1 million units in the developed world.[8] LEs in India produced well below minimum economic scales by a factor of 20:100 as compared to global producers, which resulted in higher

3. *Capital Market*, 15–28 August 1994, p. 12.
4. *Business Standard,* 12 February 1997, 24 February 1997.
5. According to the Consumer Electronics Manufacturers Association (CETMA) Annual Report, 1996.
6. CETMA Report, 1997.
7. BPL Ltd, Prospectus, 1994.
8. *Capital Market,* 15–28 August 1994, p. 12.

costs of raw materials and components.[9] In turn, this was further compounded by chronic under-utilisation of installed capacity.[10] In this context, multinational companies were therefore hesitant to commit investments in creating capacities within the country, for they could not obtain economies of scale without market development and expansion.[11]

However, the industry concentration ratio was on the increase, which led to large firms gaining market share at the expense of smaller ones, and increase in their capacity utilisation. Whereas in 1989, the top five competitors accounted for around 50 per cent of the market, by 1994 they had increased their share to 70 per cent.[12] Until 1994–95, the MNCs' share of the market was around 12 per cent. Between April 1996 and March 1997, MNCs accounted for 27.5 per cent share of the volume of 1.79 million units. By 1997, MNCs had increased their cumulative market share to around 35 per cent, out of which Akai's share comprised around 12 per cent.[13] Henceforward, Akai became the only MNC to position itself in the price conscious (economy) segment of the market in contrast to other MNCs who focussed on the top end. Aside from forcing market share losses of the big three players—BPL, Videocon and Onida—Akai also cornered the share of smaller competitors who have since exited the industry.

The Need for Linkages, Economies of Scale and Scope

During the 1990s, MNCs were expanding their global output incrementally through their 'screw-driver assembly' operations in India.[14] Because of demand constraints, MNCs undertook a greater component of production outside the country.[15] Their lack of in-depth manufacturing in India was also partially due to

9. Report on the Indian Telecommunications Industry, C-DoT, New Delhi, 1994, p. 145.
10. Report on the Indian Telecommunications Industry, C-DoT, New Delhi, 1994, p. 141.
11. *Capital Market,* 15–28 August 1994, p. 12.
12. BPL Ltd, Prospectus, 1994.
13. *The Economic Times,* 13–19 August 1997.
14. Up to 1991, the Government of India was avowedly against any screw-driver assembly type manufacturing in India in rhetoric, but could not enforce the practice of in-depth manufacturing, especially in new technologies which were often borrowed from the MNCs.
15. S. Vausdevan, Dy General Manager Marketing, BPL Ltd, Interview Transcript, March 1995.

Market Shares of CTV Manufacturers

Company	*1989–90*	*1990–91*	*1991 92*	*1992 93*	*1993 94*	*1994 95*	*1995–96*	*1997 (Mar–Oct)*
BPL	14	16	17	20	23	22	23	21
Videocon	16	21	23	24	20	23	26	22
Onida	14	17	17	18	17	19	11	9
Optonica	4	4	5	5	5.5	6	3	–
Crown	6	5	4	4	4.5	NA	3	–
Texla	2	3	2	3	3.7	NA	3	–
Beltek	NA	NA	NA	NA	–	NA	1	–
Shivaki	NA	NA	NA	NA	–	NA	1	–
Uptron	NA	NA	NA	NA	–	NA	1	–
Salora	NA	NA	NA	NA	–	NA	0	–
EC	NA	2	NA	NA	–	2	0	–
Weston	NA	4	NA	NA	–	2	0	–
Others	34	27	24	18	14	NA	5	–
Total Indian	90	92	92	92	88	NA	72	52
Philips	3	4	4	5	7.9	7	11	8
Sony	4	3	3	2	2.7	NA	3	3
Akai	–	–	–	–	–	–	5	13
Samsung	–	–	–	–	–	–	4	5
Panasonic	–	–	–	–	–	–	3	2
Thomson	–	–	–	–	–	–	2	2
Grundig	–	–	–	–	–	–	1	–
Daewoo	–	–	–	–	–	–	–	1
LG	–	–	–	–	–	–	0	1
Others	3	2	1	1	1.4	–	0	–
Total foreign	10	8	8	8	12	–	28	35

Sources: Columns 2-6: Francis Kanoi Market Research.
Column 7: Centre for Monitoring Indian Economy.
Columns 8: ORG-MARG.
Column 9: BPL-ORG.

the relative unavailability of critical components.[16] Furthermore, the third industrial revolution due to microelectronics enabled developed countries to substitute labour by capital to an unprecedented extent and sustain their competitiveness.[17] In this way, plants manufacturing mature products were no longer relocating as the boundaries between labour-intensive and capital-intensive industries were becoming increasingly blurred.[18]

The commitment to in-depth manufacturing meant costly investment that increased overhead expenses. Late MNC entrants suffered a disadvantage to first movers, especially in an inflationary economy, where cost of land, materials and construction were forever on the increase.[19] Many MNCs attempted 'dis-integration' by subcontracting services to other companies and selling off parts of their businesses to suppliers who become 'co-makers'. Under such a strategy, the chassis, the picture tube and the back cover entered as parts of the MNC's 'screw-driver assembly' plant.[20] Unlike local enterprises, vertical and horizontal multi-plant integration was largely absent within MNCs in India. This was often due to their stand-alone ownership structures as opposed to group structures in LEs. Finally, the rapid introduction of new products and obsolescing of existing product lines had the effect of engendering shallow types of plants, with little chance of developing competencies in component technology at the local level.

In contrast, certain large LEs in consumer electronics invested in-depth manufacturing to obtain cost benefits through transfer pricing and lower tax incidence. Their wider product range served as better ammunition to resist incoming MNCs.[21] These LEs were integrated in components up to plastics, injection moulding and picture tubes.[22] Their group structures and multi-plant integration provided economies of scale and scope, much like the strategies

16. Report on the Indian Telecommunications Industry, C-DoT, New Delhi, 1994, p. 141.
17. Dorner, 1991.
18. Ernst, 1991.
19. See Porter, Ghemawat and Srinivasan, 'Report on Developing Competitive Advantage in India', Confederation of Indian Industry, New Delhi, 1994.
20. Senior Development Manager, R&D, Philips India Ltd, Interview Transcript, November 1997.
21. A. Rajaram, Company Secretary, BPL Ltd, Interview Transcript, March 1995.
22. Senior Development Manager R&D, Philips India Ltd, Interview Transcript, Calcutta, November 1997.

pursued by some of India's largest conglomerates like Telco which combined production of passenger cars with production of vans, utility trucks and small buses.[23] In electronics and telecommunications, the drivers for vertical integration were supply uncertainties of imported components, lack of local suppliers of precision services and other industrial and service infrastructure, unreliable and limited communication facilities, government mismanagement of customs, and shortages of power.[24] These problems usually pushed the local firm to create internal markets, in order to rise above uncertainties in supply.

The Need for a Broadband Positioning

Within the CTV industry, 20 per cent of the buyers constituted the 'top end', consisting of seekers of brand image, state-of-the-art technology, status and contemporary designs.[25] Around 30 per cent comprised the 'functionalist segment' who sought feature-price benefits.[26] The remaining 50 per cent comprised the 'economy segment' which looked for low prices and basic features.[27] Traditionally, the differentiated LEs like BPL and Videocon had market shares across all three discrete market segments utilising their large range of products.[28] On the other hand, *de novo* MNCs sought relatively unfilled positions within the industry, which consisted of buyers who preferred global brand names. This strategy was usually described in the industry as the 'top-down approach'.[29] A less common strategy employed by MNCs was the 'bottom-up approach'. In 1998, Akai became the No.1 MNC and cornered 12–14 per cent of the market through its entry into the lowest price segment with inexpensive products made in China. Concurrently, 'top-down' MNCs like Sony, Panasonic, Thomson and Samsung forced market share losses from LEs like Onida.[30] However, the largest market in India was for the 20" CTV, in which

23. D'Costa (1997).
24. M. Porter, P. Ghemawat and S. Rangan, 'Developing Competitive Advantage in India', Report prepared for Confederation of Indian Industry, New Delhi, 1994.
25. BPL, 'Role of Pricing', A Position Paper, December 1997.
26. *Ibid.*
27. BPL, Internal Documents, Bangalore, January 1997. See also Drishti, 1997.
28. S. Vasudevan, Dy General Manager Marketing, BPL Ltd, Interview Transcript, March 1995.
29. BPL, 'Role of Pricing', A Position Paper, December 1997.
30. *The Economic Times,* 13–19 August 1997.

the top-down MNCs were not yet dominant. This implied that MNCs were targeting less than 20 per cent of the total market.[31] *De novo* MNCs like Panasonic, Thomson, Samsung and Grundig had a narrower range of CTV models in the market with higher price brackets than incumbents like Philips.

Retail Audit of Street Prices of CTV Models, March 1997

(Rupees)

MNCs	*Sony*	*Philips*	*Akai*	*Panasonic*	*Samsung*	*Goldstar*	*Grundig*	*Thomson*
	13877	11007	10960	12649	11288	10593	11946	12283
	13988	11240	17445	16060	15821	15984	16296	16099
	20282	15032	17582	18279	16448	16257	18511	21242
	22366	15445	18678	18968	21250	19897	20369	48209
	23213	17758	21205	54756	56131	43364	28786	
	33868	27223	22060				37766	
	60888	27274	42631					
		48063						
LEs	*BPL*	*Videocon*	*Onida*	*Texla*	*Uptron*	*Crown*	*Optonica*	*Salora*
	10749	9093	15123	9514	8674	10052	11743	11019
	14443	10257	15546	12359	11146	13669	15656	14619
	14595	10835	16565	12781	11446	14523	16608	14685
	15015	13304	19008	13584	12738	16206	18423	16365
	16572	13943	25470			22274	24791	
	16668	14053	44502			31892	52500	
	17028	14988						
	17460	16370						
	17481	16699						
	18509	20663						
	19805	24919						
	20698	30395						
	25047							
	25133							
	42090							

Source: ORG-MARG Retail Audit Data, April 1006–March 1997.

The television industry was also characterised by high advertising and sales promotion intensity among both local and multinational firms. BPL was the

31. *Capital Market*, 15–28 August 1994, p. 16.

most advertising efficient (vis-à-vis market shares) compared to all other players.[32]

Advertising Expenditures of Major MNCs and LEs in CTVs, 1997–98

(Rs million)

	BPL	*Videocon*	*Onida*	*Philips*	*Akai*	*Sony*	*Panasonic*	*Samsung*
Apr.–Sep.	37.9	54.72	48.92	24.06	87.89	14.84	10.58	25.63
Market Share	21.1	22.3	8.8	8.3	12.9	2.9	2.4	5.1
Mean	38.07							
St. Dev.	25.4							

Source: Complied by author.

By 1995–96 BPL was producing 700,000 to 800,000 sets in a year. If one were to take publicity and advertising as a percentage of turnover arising from this sale, the amount involved was substantial. For instance, with a turnover of Rs 7 bn from TVs alone, it was spending 5 per cent on advertising which totalled Rs 350 mn. For a smaller manufacturer who had just entered the industry, it was impossible to compete in advertising. Even for companies like Sony, whose turnover was not more than Rs 500 mn in 1995, the amount of Rs 350 mn was huge.

LEs aimed for further market *expansion* in the non-metro markets (B and C towns) where they had already gained first-mover advantages over the last decade-and-a-half. In these segments, LEs possessed intimate knowledge of locale-specific business practices and commanded an enduring brand loyalty. In contrast, MNCs' brand goodwill was derived in the sophisticated niches in the metros and mini-metros, which had been exposed to world-class brands through global spillovers in advertising.[33] Hence, buyers in the non-metro areas were unlikely prospects for the relatively unknown Sony or National brand name, since they had been exposed to local brands like BPL, Onida, Videocon, etc.[34]

The overall positioning of MNCs vis-à-vis LEs in final markets engendered

32. S. Vasudevan, Dy General Manager Marketing, BPL Ltd, Interview Transcript, March 1995.
33. *Capital Market,* 15–28 August 1994, p. 16.
34. *Ibid.*

different forms of linkages within a host environment. Since LEs targeted both urban and rural markets, it was possible to undertake greater value added production in India through economics of scope whereas MNCs which targeted only the metropolitan markets could not undertake a similar strategy. In the late 1990s, Philips along with Sony took the outsourcing route.[35] Furthermore, due to a limited segmentation strategy they often suffered a large build up of inventories, as experienced by Philips.[36]

The Need for Unbundling and Reverse Engineering

Market dynamics also influence innovations in product and process technology, since firms base their decisions of undertaking R&D upon the linkages they create in downstream activities. In the CTV industry, conventional technology draws heavily on upstream technologies in microprocessors, semi-conductors and displays.[37] In this mature industry, any new development is within the same technological trajectory of the initial innovation. Manufacturing involves testing of components, assembly into modules and assembly into final products.[38] Since MNCs in India are usually involved only in the final assembly, they cannot undertake process modifications. Almost invariably, most R&D expenses appearing in the balance sheets of MNCs are the laboratory expenses concerned with the fit of indigenous componentry with global designs. In contrast, since certain large LEs manufacture most basic components, they are able to undertake significant product and process modifications using their location-specific advantage to engineer cost competitive as well as differentiated products. The unbundled nature of technology facilitates reverse engineering as the common method of entering the business.

Witness now the path of development of one of the biggest companies in the CTV industry, namely BPL, to understand how the organisation carved out a defensible position within this highly competitive industry.

35. *Business World*, 1–15 April 1997 and *Business India*, 7–20 April 1997.
36. *Ibid*.
37. That is excluding HDTV and other forms of advanced technology emulating display media as of present.
38. MIRC Electronics Ltd, Prospectus, November 1992.

Consumer Electronics Industry Summary

(Rs crore)*

Consumer Electronics	*91/03*	*92/03*	*93/03*	*94/03*	*95/03*
Profit and Loss					
Sales	2110.48	3102.85	3269.09	3737.34	1259.64
Other income	16.56	47.43	24.1	20.68	6.62
Raw materials, stores and energy	1462.36	2087.75	2296.48	2570.09	830.14
Wages and salaries	93.97	123.7	148.63	158.3	87.3
PBDIT	190.36	359.21	327.45	405.8	138.79
PAT	80.69	129.06	80.71	198.04	45.39
PAT, net of non-recurring transactions	78.39	113.2	74.2	168.51	34.69
Net export	-195.22	-238.08	-226.17	-281.71	-84.1

* 1 crore = 10 million.

BPL Limited

BPL, the parent company of the group, was incorporated in 1963, in technical collaboration with BPL (Instruments) Ltd of UK. Intensive in-house development and technical tie-ups with international brand leaders like Sanyo of Japan widened the product range and made BPL a force to reckon with in the Indian electronics industry. In 1982, after colour transmission was introduced in the country, the company diversified into the field of consumer electronics, televisions and VCRs. As a joint venture between BPL and Sanyo of Japan, BPL-Sanyo was incorporated in 1983 to manufacture a range of video cassette recorders and video cassette players. It also manufactured the video deck mechanism and other critical components in its plant located at Bangalore. Electronic Research Limited, a member of the BPL group, was established in 1972 for the manufacture of electronic components. With time, the product line widened to include a range of critical components for televisions such as deflection yokes, flyback transformers and electronic tuners. Established in 1982, BPL-Sanyo Technologies became another group company engaged in the manufacture of a wide range of state-of-the-art radio cassette recorders, both for the domestic and the international markets. The company manufactured most of the critical components in-house, including audio deck mechanisms. It had two factories—one at Palakkad and another at Bangalore, which was an export oriented unit. These products subsequently established market leadership and were referred to as standard products by consumers throughout the country for their quality and reliability. In 1996, among the top fifty electronics companies of India in terms of sales and profitability respectively, BPL occupied the top fifth and second positions with annual sales of Rs 8.38 bn and profits of Rs 483.9 mn.[39] In BPL's basket of products, related risk diversification was lower wherein BPL offered washing machines, vacuum cleaners, microwave ovens, and a whole host of products which complemented its strategy.

What explains BPL's meteoric rise to industrial dominance? How was BPL able to organise its seemingly discrete businesses into a single coherent structure to gain competitive advantage? Let us now take a look at some of the organisational aspects of BPL that contributed to this success.

Organisational Structure

BPL's *symbolic* goals aim to respond to India's environmental context 'through the utilisation of appropriate technologies, manufacturing disciplines and marketing to give their customers the best value for their money.'[40] Spanning the institutional, managerial and technical levels, the parent company, BPL Ltd, controls a third of the turnover of the BPL group, and exercises managerial control through a central organisation. The group companies are independent in terms of assets and management, but the chairman and his family members have a stake in all member organisations under the group, whose directors are common.[41] In terms of co-ordination, BPL's apex body, called the management select committee, looks after the strategic (institutional) aspects, namely, 'new projects, areas of growth, performance of each organisation and inter-organisational transfers of people'.[42] Within BPL's fully integrated set up, linkages between the companies in terms of intermediate goods, transfer pricing, or any other problem is sorted out by this committee.[43] This obtains not only cost benefits but also a wider product range which serves as better ammunition to incoming models of MNCs. The organisational chart reveals a fully integrated functional structure. The vertical span of controls reveals that the group companies are organised through the family membership of the board of

39. CMIE, 'Top 50 Electronics Companies: The Indian Corporate Sector', April 1996.
40. BPL, Annual Report 1996–97, p. 1.
41. A.R. Rajaram, Company Secretary, BPL Ltd, Interview Transcript, March 1995.
42. BPL Ltd, Internal Documents.
43. A.R. Rajaram, Company Secretary, BPL Ltd, Interview Transcript, March 1995

directors as inter-dependent divisions, and are not dissociated from the corporate office.

Marketing and Distribution Reach

For the year ended March 1994, the organisation exported 48,000 CTVs valued at Rs 2.7 bn to European countries where BPL CTVs were rated as one of the finest by authoritative sources. In that year, it out-performed several Korean, Japanese and European brands while it was recognised as the sixth most recognised brand name in the country.[44]

CTV Sales

Size	*1993–94* (%)	*1994–95 (%)*
14"	12.3	15
20"	43.7	40.7
21"	31.4	23.6
FHR 21"	12.5	20.8
25"	0.08	0.12
Total	244945	310295

BPL's wide product line has a product leader at each price point for all three segments of the market.[45] It competed across several industry segments simultaneously using a broadband integrated strategy.[46] It deployed twenty-four CTV models spread over a wide spectrum of prices and competed neck-to-neck with the MNCs on product parity at the upper end, and had major shares in the middle and lower end that comprised 80 per cent of the market.[47] Competing aggressively across the functionalist and economy segments had the effect of breaking the barrier of affordability since price was a major factor.[48] BPL is of the opinion that penetration pricing strategies are relevant for developing economies

44. *Capital Market*, 15–28 August 1994, p. 20. Also BPL Ltd, Annual Report, 1997, p. 15.
45. S. Vasudevan, Dy General Manager Marketing, BPL Ltd, Interview Transcript, March 1995.
46. *Ibid.*
47. BPL Ltd, Annual Report, 1996–97, p. 7.
48. S. Vasudevan, Dy General Manager Marketing, BPL Ltd, Interview Transcript, March 1995.

while differentiation-based strategies are more relevant for the upper end markets in India.[49] Drawing on its functionalities of features and reliability, its competing models matched new product launches by MNCs in India, with advertising campaigns delineating feature-to-feature comparisons, negating the 'sting' from the MNC's launch.[50]

In 1995, BPL launched the new top dome CTV—a month ahead of the launch by National and became the first in India to launch this feature.[51] Through its first-mover advantages, BPL also blockaded the media in terms of taking the best sponsored programmes.[52]

BPL's Segment-wise CTV Sales

Segment	*1996–97 Industry Sales*	*BPL Sales*	*% of Total Industry Sales*	*% of BPL's Total Sales*
14"	280800	74753	27	14
20"	704800	181437	26	34
21"	750200	224060	30	43
25"	48800	44623	91	8
29"	6200	2151	35	0.4
Total		527024		
	1997–98 Industry Sales	*BPL Sales*	*% of Total Industry Sales*	*% of BPL's Total Sales*
14"	222400	48534	22	12
20"	540300	163232	30	39
21"	585700	169794	29	41
25"	40400	31049	77	7
29"	32500	4124	13	1
Total		416733		

Source: BPL internal documents.

49. BPL, 'Role of Pricing', A Position Paper, December 1997.
50. BPL Annual Report 1997, p. 7. Also S. Vasudevan, Dy General Manager Marketing, BPL Ltd, Interview Transcript, March 1995.
51. *Business Standard*, 8 October 1994. Also BPL Ltd, Annual Report 1997, p. 7 and S. Vasudevan, Dy General Manager Marketing, BPL Ltd, Interview Transcript, March 1995.
52. Being one of the first movers in CTVs, BPL has retained the sponsorship of programmes which afford the highest reach in television channels in India. S. Vasudevan, Dy General Manager Marketing, BPL Ltd, Interview Transcript, March 1995.

Interestingly, the competition for CTV sales is in the 'bazaar' rather than in sophisticated shopping malls.[53] Technological leadership—a durable strategy for Sony and National—was not practicable for BPL. BPL therefore had to find uniqueness in commercials, advertising intensity, advertising quality, USP positions and pre-empting positions such as media blockading. A competitor's advantage lay mainly in its distribution infrastructure and responsiveness.[54] BPL's network of 3,500 dealers, 7,000 shops and 198 exclusive showrooms and service outlets in any city or town with a population of more than 50,000 virtually represented every district of the country.[55] In addition, BPL used its own transportation system to ensure faster delivery whereas most others relied on contracts with transporters.[56] For late entrants, the cost of entry into the dealer's network was prohibitive. Whereas MNCs were paying between Rs 25,000 and 60,000 to buy a widow sign, as first movers, BPL's entry into the dealers network was far more cost effective.[57] Also giving the right model at the right time avoided the necessity for the dealer to keep his money blocked in unsold inventories.[58]

Distribution Network in Philips and BPL

	1994	*1995*	*1996*	*1997*
Philips' Network of Distributors and Service Centres				
Distributors	1000	900	900	1000
Service centres	–	109	115	124
BPL's Network of Distributors and Service Centres				
Distributors	–	3500	3500	3500
Service centres	–	400	450	600

Source: Philips Ltd, Internal documents, and BPL Ltd, Internal documents.

Strategic Infrastructure

The colour television manufacturing facility in BPL was vertically integrated

53. A.R. Rajaram, Company Secretary, BPL Ltd, Interview Transcript, March 1995.
54. BPL Ltd, Annual Report 1997, p. 9.
55. BPL Ltd, Annual Report 1997, p. 15.
56. A.R. Rajaram, Company Secretary, BPL Ltd, Interview Transcript, March 1995.
57. S. Vasudevan, Dy General Manager Marketing, BPL Ltd, Interview Transcript, March 1995.
58. BPL Ltd, Annual Report, 1996–97, p. 7.

where group companies made components like tuners, deflection yokes, fly-back transformers and plastic cabinets.[59] In 1996, it acquired the picture tube plant of Uptron, an erstwhile public sector company, thereby enabling BPL to control 90 per cent of the CTV components within the firm.[60] Group structures utilised the strategy of related diversification and multi-plant integration where interchangeable intermediate products manufactured a larger array of CTVs as well as consumer electronics products spread over audio-video systems, white goods and communication equipment. This gave BPL a better visibility in the market place, and spread not only advertising costs but also costs of downstream vertical integration.[61]

> Observed a senior manager in BPL: 'BPL as a group is very vertically integrated. We have strengths in manufacturing of key components like tuners, yokes and fly-back transformers, which are very critical components in CTV manufacturing. We also have excellent competence in sophisticated tool rooms and excellent moulding facilities and techniques of making dies and tools. We are actually bringing state-of-the-art manufacturing technology in automation in terms of manufacturing sophisticated dies and tools locally for India and for very complex designs which get into various CTV and audio products packaging, which are normally imported by most of the manufacturers.'

BPL's integrated production infrastructure was complemented by generation of its own power, transport and logistics, whereby 80 per cent of BPL's power was generated in-house to overcome uncertainties in power supply from utility providers.[62] This commitment to in-house manufacturing of a number of engineered items arose from the finding that successful global CTV companies manufactured all critical components in-house and kept a strict check on cost and quality in what was visibly a small margin business.[63] Most importantly, BPL was not constrained by the limitations of its vendors and was therefore able to accelerate product innovation through its research and applied engineering.[64]

59. BPL Ltd, 'Television 2000'.
60. BPL Ltd, Annual Report 1997, p. 24.
61. S. Vasudevan, Dy. General Manager Marketing, BPL Ltd, Interview Transcript, , March 1995.
62. A.R. Rajaram, Company Secretary, BPL Ltd, Interview Transcript, March 1995.
63. BPL Ltd, Annual Report 1997.
64. *Ibid.*

Interestingly, in the initial stages of BPL's operations, market demand was not sufficient for suppliers to take up production. It was then somewhat risky to invest heavily towards in-house component production that however paid off ultimately in terms of both quality and cost.[65]

> Observed their senior manager of quality assurance: 'Our strategy is that, for something critical we should not be overly dependent on the outside. A few years back, volumes were not enough for outside people to take up supply of some components. In those days our production (of CTVs) was also low. So it was a real gamble to invest so much in in-house facilities for componentry. But it has paid off and we are much better off today, having now obtained the volumes of scale.'

Vertical Integration, Import Intensity and Outsourcing in the Big Three Industry Players

	98/03	*97/03*	*96/03*	*95/03*
Gross value added/Sales				
BPL	19.18	19.19	17.87	18.17
Onida	13.05	13.83	13.45	14.37
Philips India	14.98	14.61	12.87	16.91
Import raw materials/Sales				
BPL	0.62	0.57	0.63	0.69
Onida	12.59	13.89	19.15	14.32
Philips India	8.07	6.4	7.8	6.06
Purchased finished goods/Sales				
BPL	0	0	0	0
Onida	40.72	27.81	29.44	21.32
Philips India	45.43	43.26	44.3	37.96

Nearly 65 per cent of all the industry's domestic production in components was controlled by BPL.[66] The benefits of integration was lowering of costs through higher volumes to reach economies of scale.[67] As of 1997, BPL's indigenisation

65. BPL Ltd, 'Television 2000'. Also V.B. Dominic Salvio, DGM Production, BPL Ltd, Interview Transcript, March 1995.

66. BPL Ltd, 'Television 2000'.

67. *Ibid.*

stood at 76 per cent of the bill of materials.[68] Also, BPL's 600 service centres allowed high levels of downstream vertical integration.[69]

Technology Development: Learning Through Transfers of Know-how

Television technology was new to India even as late as in the 1980s. In making of televisions, the basic work in R&D is not required. Most of the time, market requirements come as add-on features. Therefore, R&D concentrates mainly on extra features.[70] As BPL had no experience in manufacturing TVs, in 1982 BPL's Madras factory was fully set-up with the help of Sanyo.[71] Sanyo complemented hands-on training with technical documents and capital equipment. Following an initial push, BPL learned how to improve its production and raise efficiencies of its processes.[72] Since 1991, BPL has produced four chassis designs, with the most recent chassis having 30 per cent fewer components than the first one—and with superior features.[73]

In the subsequent years, BPL's research spending in quantum and as a percentage of the turnover increased from Rs 47.40 mn (1.05 per cent of turnover) in 1992–93 to Rs 80 mn (1.39 per cent of turnover) in 1993–94 and finally to Rs 105 mn (1.50 per cent of turnover) in 1994–95.[74] R&D efforts were directed towards development of new product and process technologies, improvement of product performance and quality, and reduction in costs, with a view to retaining market leadership.[75] Several new products were developed, including designs for single-chip chassis for almost all transmission systems in the world. In addition, BPL's R&D initiated work with Indian academic institutions on digital TV design.[76] In this connection, BPL's R&D office remarked: 'We have been awarded by the government for having the best in-house R&D. This work is

68. BPL Ltd, Annual Report 1997, p. 38.
69. BPL Ltd, Internal Reports, 1997.
70. For instance customers may ask for higher sound or super-woofer. And it becomes very easy to work on those small areas than from scratch to finish.
71. P.S. Thyagaraja, Sr Manager R&D, BPL Ltd, Interview Transcript, March 1995.
72. BPL Ltd, 'Television 2000'.
73. BPL Ltd, Annual Report 1997, p. 21. Also P.S. Thyagaraja, Sr Manager R&D, BPL Ltd, Interview Transcript, March 1995.
74. BPL Ltd, 'Television 2000'.
75. BPL Ltd, 'Technology and Process', Prospectus, 1994.
76. This includes large screen televisions, LCD projectors, infra red headphones, multi-system CTVs. etc. BPL Ltd, Annual Report 1997, p. 11.

recognised both nationally as well internationally. The designs made by us are meant for safety, simplicity of design, and best budget TVs.'

R&D and Foreign Royalty Paid as a Percentage of Sales

	98/03	97/03	96/03	95/03
R&D capital/Sales				
BPL	1.02	1.68	0	0
Philips India	0.05	0.12	0.05	0.17
Import royalty/Sales				
BPL	0	0	0	0
Philips India	0.26	0.14	0.48	0.22

Source: CMIE.

At present, the organisation's R&D unit for development of televisions does such things as layout, prototype development, testing, evaluation and pre-production. For export orders, BPL gets requirements for tele-text facilities or scan circuits which require R&D to make add-on circuits. There are altogether about forty personnel—nineteen in electronics and eighteen to nineteen in mechanical engineering. For new product development R&D gets inputs from two sources. First, from domestic market requirements whereby marketing managers determine the types of model and features required. The second is from their collaborators Sanyo, who provide these features. While most of the time they get the design from Sanyo, R&D also works on its own.

The Challenges Mastered

This case study has revealed that because of its institutional embeddedness, BPL is able to take accurate decisions regarding serving markets vis-à-vis MNCs, whose financial and investment decision making are centralised in their parent organisations.[77] In BPL, group structures provide the necessary linkages while the entrepreneurs involved are charismatic leaders, often personally attached and extremely vigorous in their retaliation.[78] This works strongly in favour of

77. R. Mishra, CEO, Monica Electronics Ltd, Interview Transcript, January 1995.
78. Alok Gupta, General Manager, Philips India, Interview Transcript, November 1997. Gupta explains: 'If the Nambiars (BPL) wanted to retaliate in the market, they can do it tomorrow but Philips almost definitely will not be able to do it tomorrow or worse still may not be able to do it at all. If rivalry were to lead a price war, Sony may take six months to decide whether they will retaliate or not.'

domestic brands, because, if consumer preference spaces are not filled by international brands, local consumers will favour local brands.[79] In the ultimate analysis, the ability of firms to adapt to local conditions is critical in consumer electronics where local adaptations can be in dissonance with global objectives. The higher export performance of BPL appears to suggest that BPL has performed well in the development of FSAs by drawing on the local context as a platform to building its international strategy.

BPL competes across the range of top-end, functional and economy segments. Its large range of products purports to pre-empt segments for the incoming MNC who is likely to employ a sequence of moves towards other industry segments. BPL's strategy of positioning itself in the minds of 'rational' buyers who seek *functional* features sets it apart from others who compete in segments where the end-users tend to make cognitive evaluations based on the safe haven of MNC brand names.

Moreover, BPL's vertically integrated group structure attains economies of scale and scope through its multi-plant linkages. This is achieved by offering a wider range of CTV models and consumer electronics products across the fragmented markets in India. BPL has historically undertaken proliferation of markets because of severe restrictions on output growth imposed by the MRTP regime in the past and due to the fragmented nature of markets. Its investment in plants and infrastructure signals its *commitment* to long-term competitive advantage building as opposed to responding to the quirks of the environmental context. BPL observes that the key to competitive advantage lies in control over supply, quality, prices of inputs and autonomy, i.e., the flexibility to configure the intermediate market by internalising the same within the firm. Firms which do not have this commitment are bound by the technological trajectory and spatial generation of knowledge (know-why) from without. This leads to lower flexibility and adaptability. The second advantage is in control over the volatility of the environment. This can be especially advantageous when the task environment is blighted by large discontinuities, fluctuations and volatility. For instance, volatility of exchange rates can hamper the smooth functioning of intermediate markets of the firm. Global shortages of components and ripples in global logistics can hamper the delivery of components and create severe shocks. Such circumstances point to the importance of vertical integration as opposed to outsourcing.

79. Alok Gupta, General Manager, Philips India, Interview Transcript, November 1997.

While BPL acquired initial know-how from foreign suppliers, its impetus towards reverse engineering was critical in providing the much needed ingredients for product differentiation and cost competitiveness. The dynamics of R&D behaviour of international and national firms thus reveal the influence of institutional autonomy determining the extent of innovation activity taking place within the firm and without. Finally, BPL's ability to utilise the national environment as a platform for outbound international trade has been the vital ingredient in the development of core competencies.

Summary and Conclusion

The *World Investment Report* (1997) reportedly found evidence that foreign enterprises tend to confine themselves to the upper end of the market and fumble when they cannot adequately anticipate the trends or competition in such narrow markets. A related issue is that since they are unwilling to serve the rural and lower income urban markets, the destruction of domestic markets may leave such markets unserved.

On the other hand, many local enterprises in India, despite environmental volatilities, appear to hold on to their competitive positions. These usually large enterprises rally with increasing pressures of competition by drawing on 1) the ability to meticulously nurture and regulate links with the government, 2) the ability to horizontally and vertically diversify their manufacturing base over a larger span of products, and 3) the ability to market, distribute and service their products nationally.

Moreover, governments in most emerging markets operate very differently from those of their Western counterparts. Despite the dismantling of the old 'license raj' in India, the government still requires the private sector to get permission to engage in a range of activities such as pricing of products and importing of raw materials. Large diversified business groups are known for their ability to manage bureaucratic relations at levels all the way down to the village council.

Hence, although a focussed differentiation strategy may enable a few activities to be performed well, firms in emerging markets must take responsibility for a wide range of functions in order to reduce market failures that get in the way of doing business effectively. Often, it calls for the ability to compete in multiple segments of the industry in order to draw on the synergies that obtain. The multiplicity of advantages that can emerge from diversified business groups include multi-market power to support a less rivalrous interaction to leveraging technology, brand names and distribution systems to achieve synergies, and mitigation of policy distortions through group structures.

Thus the combined dynamics of structural market asymmetries and regulatory frameworks pose a fairly unique challenge to the smooth functioning of foreign and domestic enterprises in India. There is a need for a fundamental rethinking of every element in the conventional business models, which incorporate major differences in the ways products are developed and distributed. So as to emerge with a coherent organisational profile and distill a set of clear competitive responses, organisations in India need to look closely at two major aggregations of aspirations of stakeholders in India: those of developmental and transformational needs. The case study leaves one in little doubt that the success of BPL has centred principally around its keen perception of the aspirations of its stakeholders and its ability to serve them effectively.

CASE 11

ISPAT INTERNATIONAL N.V.: SPINNING STEEL INTO GOLD

The dominoes are starting to fail in the US steel industry, and a little-known Indian businessman has just toppled the biggest one .... In agreeing Tuesday to pay roughly $1.43 billion for Chicago-based Inland Steel Co.—one of the oldest, proudest integrated steel companies in the US—Mr Mittal most certainly will upset the staid American industry, and he could usher in a new era of steel consolidation...[Mittal] is swiftly emerging as the Andrew Carnegie of the global steel industry.

Wall Street Journal, 18 March 1998

In less than a decade, the LNM Group which owned Ispat International N.V. had grown from a wire rod manufacturer with a single plant in Indonesia to the

This case was written by Donald Sull, Assistant Professor of Strategy and International Management, London Business School with the aid of Takayuki Sugata and Jorge Cabera, MBA class of 1998, London Business School, and Martin Escobari, MBA class of 1998, Harvard Business School. The authors are grateful to Ispat International N.V. for their help and support in writing the case. The case was first registered by the London Business School in 1999.

fourth largest steel producer by volume in the world.[1] Between 1992 and 1997, Ispat International increased sales at an average annual rate of 45 per cent, in an industry that was growing at 1 per cent annually (see Appendix 1). Founded by an Indian, Lakshmi N. Mittal, incorporated in the Netherlands and with a corporate office in London, Ispat sold steel in over sixty countries around the world and was considered by many industry experts as the only truly global steel company. The rest of the global steel industry, in contrast, consisted of a large number of players with production located in a single country. With 1997 revenues of $2.2 bn and earnings before interest, tax and depreciation of $406 mn, Ispat was the global leader in producing Direct Reduced Iron (DRI) as well as one of the largest exporters of steel slabs and the biggest producer of wire rod. Lakshmi Mittal, the founder, chairman and sole shareholder of the LNM group, owned 80 per cent of Ispat International stock—a stake valued at approximately $3 bn in 1997, which earned him a place among *Forbes* magazine's Global Power Elite.

The LNM Group Annual Steel Production, 1991–98

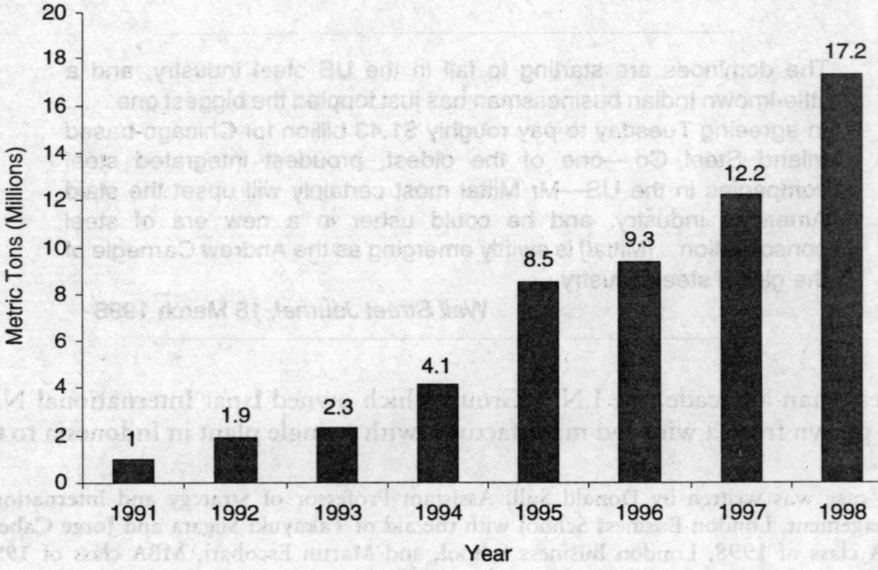

1. Including capacity of Inland as well as Ispat Indo and Ispat Karmet, both wholly-owned subsidiaries of the LNM group which controlled 97 per cent of Ispat International voting stock.

Much of Ispat's growth was driven by a series of acquisitions, with Ispat or its corporate parent the LNM group acquiring steel factories in Mexico, Canada, Trinidad, Germany, Ireland, Kazakhstan and the United States between 1992 and 1998. Most of these acquisitions followed a similar pattern. As governments around the world privatised their steel industries, Ispat negotiated favourable prices to acquire under-performing factories from government owners. Most of the acquired plants used DRI as raw material and melted steel in an electric arc furnace, and Ispat leveraged its expertise in these technologies to dramatically cut costs and increase volume at the acquired factories. The Inland acquisition, however, marked a departure from this formula. The business press, including the *Wall Street Journal* and *Financial Times*, lauded Mittal for initiating the consolidation of the global steel industry, which was highly fragmented in 1997 with the largest producer Nippon Steel accounting for only 3.3 per cent of global shipments. Some equity analysts, however, questioned whether Ispat could successfully turn around Inland, which did not rely on electric arc or DRI technology. Despite these concerns, Lakshmi Mittal believed that Ispat would become the world's most successful and profitable steel producer in ten years.

Ispat International N.V. Acquisition History, 1989–98

Company Acquired	*Location*	*Year Acquired*	*Acquisition Price (US$ million)*	*Required Capital Spending (US$ million)*	*Additional Capital Spending (US$ million)*
CIL	Trinidad	1989	Lease	–	–
Imexsa	Mexico	1992	220	50	300
Sidbec-Dosco	Canada	1994	186	73	–
CIL	Trinidad	1994	70	74	–
IHSW	Germany	1995	45	21	50
Irish Ispat	Ireland	1996	51	34	–
Thyssen Units	Germany	1997	88	–	–
Inland Steel	USA	1998	1430	–	–

Source: Ispat International documents.

Ispat Means Steel

Mohan L. Mittal, Lakshmi's father, founded the Ispat group (Ispat means steel in Hindi) in Calcutta in the 1950s to trade scrap metals. He expanded into steel production and overseas trade in the 1970s and by 1997 had made Ispat the ninth largest business group in India measured by sales. After graduating from St Xavier's College in 1970, Lakshmi joined his father's company at the age of 19, where he helped start a new steel mill in Calcutta and oversaw Ispat's export business in Southeast Asia. In 1976, Mohan acquired land to build a steel factory in Indonesia, but then changed his mind, and sent the 26-year-old Lakshmi to sell the land earmarked for the new mill. Upon arrival in Indonesia, however, Lakshmi observed that the Indonesian economy appeared poised for explosive growth, and successfully convinced his father to build a 'mini-mill'. A mini-mill was a small-scale steel factory that melted scrap metal in an electric furnace rather than producing virgin steel from iron ore, coke and limestone.

Lakshmi Mittal (hereafter referred to as Mittal) remained in Indonesia to design and build the new factory and to run the Indonesian business—Ispat Indo. Although electric arc furnace technology produced low-cost steel, Mittal was reluctant to rely on scrap metal as a raw material. He believed that Ispat Indo's success as a low-cost producer hinged on a reliable supply of low-cost, high-quality raw materials, and predicted that steel scrap supplies would tighten and prices grow increasingly volatile as more producers adopted electric arc furnace technology. Mittal also recognised that impurities in scrap degraded the finished steel and limited the level of steel quality achievable from scrap. To avoid reliance on scrap, Mittal evaluated alternative raw materials and eventually opted for DRI, a scrap substitute made directly from iron ore. In the 1970s, the novel DRI process for reducing iron ore to metallic iron produced a scrap substitute that varied widely in quality and was difficult to use in the electric arc furnace. Mittal grasped DRI's long-term potential as a scrap substitute, however, and believed that DRI quality would improve with time. In 1976, Ispat Indo broke ground to build a factory to produce 65,000 tons of steel rods per year using DRI and electric arc technology.

Ispat Indo's pioneering combination of DRI and electric arc furnace technology—which Mittal dubbed 'an integrated mini-mill'—produced steel at consistently low cost and high quality and fuelled the company's ten-fold growth in production in the following decade. Mittal was not content with his success in Indonesia, however, and by the early 1980s actively sought acquisitions that would enable him to achieve his ambition of creating the world's first global steel producer. Mittal's first opportunity for global expansion presented itself in 1988 when the Government of Trinidad invited Ispat to bid for Iscott, a state-owned DRI facility. Ispat Indo sourced DRI from the factory, which the Government of Trinidad had built in 1981 at a cost of $460 mn, and Ispat management was familiar with the plant's problems. By 1988, however, the facility was running at only one-quarter of its rated capacity and had lost an average of $1 mn per week since 1982. Teams of American and German consultants had both failed to improve the plant's operations, and the government invited three companies to bid for the facility.

Company Overview

- Six state-of-the-art, low cost steelmaking operations in Mexico, Trinidad, Canada, Germany and Ireland make Ispat International the world's only truly global steel company.
- Ispat International is the fastest growing steel company in the world.
- Global leadership in the integrated mini-mill process makes Ispat International one of the lowest cost producers of high quality steel products in the world.
- Ispat International combines a balanced flat and long product portfolio with world leadership in the production of high quality slabs and wire rods.
- Steel production has grown approximately twenty-five fold between 1989 and 1997, as annual sales increased to $2.2 bn and steel shipments reached 7.2 million tons.

Although he was well acquainted with Iscott's problems, Mittal was attracted by the technology and recent vintage of the Trinidad plant. Lacking the funds to buy the assets outright, Mittal proposed to lease the plant for ten years paying $11 mn per year and retaining the option to buy the facility in the fifth year at a price set by an independent appraiser. When the newly formed Caribbean Ispat Limited (CIL) assumed control in April 1989, losses at the DRI facility had grown to $7 mn per week. Mittal assembled a team of fifty-five managers and DRI experts from around the world and rapidly invested $10 mn in the first three months to remove production bottlenecks and improve quality. Production doubled in the first three months and CIL earned a small profit after paying leasing fees in its first year of operation. CIL secured financing from the World Bank's International Finance Corporation to increase capacity by 50 per cent and later exercised its option to buy the plant for $70 mn.

The Trinidad acquisition set the pattern that Ispat would follow in subsequent deals of negotiating a low acquisition price for modern mini-mills that had been badly managed by government owners. Between 1992 and 1997, Ispat went on to acquire plants from the provincial government of Quebec, the city of Hamburg, and the national governments of Mexico, Ireland and Kazakhstan. In addition to negotiating a low acquisition price, Ispat managers structured the deals to minimise their initial investment and risks. The Mexican government, for example, provided most of the financing for the Sicartsa acquisition and Ispat secured favourable financing from the World Bank to underwrite capital expenditures in Trinidad and Kazakhstan. In most deals, Ispat convinced government sellers to assume pension and environmental liabilities while Ispat acquired the tax loss carry forwards from historical losses. After negotiating a low price and favourable terms, Ispat managers rapidly improved the acquired plant's operations by applying their expertise in DRI technology. Ispat invested heavily to remove bottlenecks in the acquired plants and improve quality. After buying Karmet from the Kazakh government for $420 mn, for example, the LNM group committed to investing an additional $500 mn. Finally, Ispat managers transferred management practices from their existing plants, such as daily reports, daily meetings and incentive plans, to the newly acquired factories. In August 1997, Ispat International N.V., a member of the LNM group, listed its stock on the New York and Amsterdam Stock Exchanges.

Ispat improved the profitability of all the factories it acquired, although the level of improvement varied by plant (see Appendix 2). Most of the plants Ispat acquired were considered beyond redemption, and the governments only resorted to selling the factories after outside managers and consultants had failed to turn the operations around. A team of managers and technical experts from America's largest steel company USX, for example, failed to stem the losses of the Karmet plant in Kazakhstan. Outside observers initially doubted that little-known Ispat could succeed where industry leaders had failed.

Jai K. Saraf, finance director for Ispat International, recalled: 'When we acquired Imexsa from the Mexican government, no one in the world thought we could make it work. All the lenders were skeptical. In hindsight, after we made it work, then it looks like a great deal, but at the time nobody believed we could do it.'

Ispat turned the acquired plants around with few changes in the workforce. After acquiring Hamburger Stahlwerke, for example, Ispat brought in only five expatriate managers in a business with 653 employees. In Canada, Ispat left the entire management team at Sidebec Dosco in place. The acquisition and turn around of Ispat Mexicana S.A. De C.V. (Imexsa) illustrates Ispat's approach.

Ispat Mexicana

In the early 1980s, the Mexican government decided to build a new steel mill—Sicartsa II—adjacent to its existing Sicartsa facility located in Lázaro Cárdenas. The Mexican government invested $2.2 bn in a state-of-the-art facility, which included a pelletiser plant to produce iron pellets from ore, the first DRI plant in the world using HYL (III) technology, electric arc furnaces, casters to roll molten steel into flat slabs and a mill to convert these slabs into plates to produce pipes for the then-booming oil industry. Before the factory was completed, however, the end of the oil boom coincided with a faltering economy which forced Mexico to devalue the peso. The government curtailed investment in the planned pelletiser plant, which forced Sicartsa management to source high cost iron pellets on the open market. The government also abandoned the planned plate mill, forcing the plant to sell steel slabs—an intermediate product—rather than finished steel plates. Three years after opening, the plant operated well below its capacity of 2 million tons per year and incurred significant operating losses. Mexican government officials publicly blamed the management and employees of the factory for the losses, and decided to privatise both Sicartsa factories in 1991.

Due Diligence and Bid

Based on Ispat's turnaround in Trinidad, the Mexican government invited Ispat to join two other steel companies in bidding for Sicartsa. Mittal sent a due diligence team consisting of twenty managers representing all line and staff functions chosen from Ispat's Trinidad and Indonesian plants and instructed them to develop plans to turnaround the plant. Mittal also explained that some members of the due diligence team would have an opportunity to work in the Mexican plant if Ispat acquired the facility. The team spent several months in Mexico gathering data and meeting with managers, employees, labour unions and government officials. The team's due diligence revealed a factory plagued with technical problems, running at 20 per cent capacity, producing low quality slabs and manned by a dispirited workforce. The Ispat team was impressed, however, by the recent vintage of the assets and the enthusiastic workforce with an average age of 27 years and the large number of highly qualified engineers. The team recommended bidding for the plant and developed a turnaround plan.

Ispat proposed acquiring all the Sicartsa II factory's assets and liabilities, excluding contingent environmental liabilities. Ispat also bid for 50 per cent equity stakes in several of the businesses that supported the Sicartsa II plant, including PMT (a producer of welded pipe), Peña Colorada (which provided the factory with iron pellets), and Sersiin (which managed the deep water port facilities and distributed electricity). Ispat proposed a total consideration of $220 mn, consisting of $25 mn in cash and $195 mn in ten-year bonds (at 15 per cent interest) issued by the Mexican government and secured by a warrant for 49 per cent of Imexsa (not Ispat) equity. Ispat's bid outlined the company's five-year plan for improving Sicartsa's operations and included a commitment to invest an additional $350 mn to complete the plant's abandoned plate mill, with a $50 mn penalty if the company failed to follow through on its promised capital spending. Ispat's proposal also included a clause capping the number of employees it would lay off at 100, of the 1,050 workers. Impressed by the business plan, the Mexican government selected Ispat's bid, which was 60 per cent higher than the second bidder (the third company bid $1). Ten members of the due diligence team remained in Mexico to run various departments, including Dr Johannes Sittard, the former head of Iscott, who served as the managing director of Imexsa from 1991 to 1993.

Stopping the Bleeding

Ispat took control of Imexsa on 1 January 1992 in the midst of a global recession in the steel industry, and had to briefly shut down the furnaces because there were no orders for the steel and no place to store the finished slabs. Despite the shut-down, Imexsa laid off only seventy employees—thirty fewer than the agreed-upon limit—and ultimately hired an additional 270 employees.

> Mittal recalled his first steps at Imexsa: 'In Mexico we did what we do with every business . . . we sat down with the management of the acquired company to discuss various options for improvement and we developed the business plan. We sat down with each of the departments to understand their problems and viewpoints and gave our input based on international experience and our due diligence. Together we set very aggressive targets because we don't benchmark companies based on local standards, but on international standards. If the management of the acquired company is willing to commit to these targets, they stay. If they have any problems following our business plan and vision, they go. The Imexsa managers stayed.'

Production Planning Manager Oscar Vasquez recalled his first meeting with Mittal:

> In our first meeting, we presented two alternative production plans, one for 600,000 tons—it was conservative and based on our past experience—and another plan for 1.2 million tons. Mr Mittal saw both and said, 'Forget the small plan, just let me know what you need to implement the second plan.' We expressed concern that we might not find a market for the additional slabs, but he said, 'You will have the volume because I'm going to take care of that for you.'

Mittal used Ispat Indo's sales network to identify Asian customers for Imexsa's slabs, including a contract for 400,000 tons per year with a Taiwanese steel manufacturer. Although these orders provided low margins, they allowed Imexsa to increase capacity utilisation while improving quality to win more profitable business. Imexsa also reduced costs by switching to suppliers willing to match the lowest costs provided at Ispat's Trinidad and Indonesian plants.

Upon acquiring the plant, Saraf recalled, Ispat managers focussed on quickly developing 'cost consciousness and discipline' among the Imexsa management team. Managing Director Sittard instituted a daily meeting of the heads of each department in the plant, which began after the day shift ended at 5.00 p.m., and generally ran until 9.00 or 10.00 at night. The team evaluated the previous day's cost, volume, productivity and quality performance, discussed the current day's results, and agreed on detailed targets by department for the following day. Director of Purchasing, Om Mandhana, described the purpose of the daily meeting: 'The idea of the daily meeting was to cut red tape. You got together all of the people involved to talk through any issues, and as a means of co-ordinating and resolving day-to-day problems. The idea was to take a decision then and there rather than refer to committees.'

Raul Torres, director of the melt shop, recalled his first impressions of the daily meetings:

> Before Ispat bought the plant, the boss just told us how we should do things, but the daily meetings were nothing like that. Dr Sittard asked a lot of detailed technical questions to force us to think through problems to their root causes. If we were consuming too much steel in the electric arc furnaces, for instance, Dr Sittard would ask: 'Why are you consuming this amount of steel? Is there leakage? Why do you have this amount of leakage? Are you losing steel in the slag? How do you plan to improve this? Is that the cheapest way in the world? Who does this best in the world? Can we adopt their technology?' We had open and sometimes heated discussions, but once we agreed what the right thing

> to do was it was easy to get Dr Sittard's approval and any resources you needed to make it happen. But you had to commit to improvements—how much you are going to achieve and by when, and the entire team monitored how you did against the promised target. And Dr Sittard always asked for higher targets—he always kept the pressure on us to increase volume and quality and cut costs.

Imexsa's existing cost accounting system reported only aggregate production costs on a monthly basis and was first available three weeks after the previous month ended. Led by Saraf, Imexsa's accounting department began collecting detailed volume, cost, quality and productivity data for each step in the production process on a daily basis. Initially, Imexsa's accountants collected the data themselves every day and analysed it by hand. To monitor raw material usage, for example, the accountants asked warehouse workers to track the volume of materials leaving the store room each day.

When Narendra Chaudhary joined Ispat Mexicana as the director of maintenance he found the maintenance team dispirited and reluctant to act. 'Over time, the plant had become exceedingly dependent on external consultants, although internally we had a large number of highly trained engineers, and this dependence was highly demotivating and demoralising for the internal team. When I asked a member of the Imexsa team what to do in a given situation, the stock reply was, "We haven't received a recommendation from the consultants yet". When I asked what their opinion was, they were very shy. Even after extensive analysis they were still paralysed and conducted more analysis and consultation with the external consultants rather than acting.'

Chaudhary attributed the team's inaction to a lack of confidence and took steps to remedy the situation. As Chaudhary said:

> The root cause was lack of confidence, and coming in I needed to create confidence among the maintenance engineers. A few months after joining, I dismissed all the external consultants and worked with the team to institute a meeting in which the maintenance team analysed problems and came to decisions without outside advice. I deliberately did not impose my own opinion or recommendations, even if I had seen this problem before. Instead I asked, 'What is *your* analysis? Why do *you* think this occurred? What do *you* think should be done?' I remember one superintendent said, 'What if I try this and it fails?' and I said, 'So what if the machine is repaired and fails again? The sky will not fall down'. In the past he would have been criticised publicly for any

> failure, so he was afraid to try anything . . . . Today it never crosses anyone's mind to call external consultants—now our engineers are the experts in the Mexican steel industry.

Continuous Improvement

In 1992—the first year under Ispat ownership—Imexsa increased shipments from 528,000 short tons to 929,000 tons, decreased the cash cost per ton produced from $253 to $178, and earned a small profit. Under the leadership of Malay Mukherjee, Imexsa increased annual steel shipments from 929,000 tons to over 3 million tons between 1992 and 1998, and improved productivity from 2.62 to 0.97 man hours per ton (see Appendix 3). Antonio Gonzales, the pelletising plant supervisor, observed, 'There is no feeling of having finished the turn around . . . we keep resetting the targets, and now we are aiming for 4 million tons per year—that's double our rated capacity.' When Mukherjee left to run Ispat Karmet in 1997, M.R.R. Nair joined Imexsa as managing director from the Steel Authority of India, the seventh largest steel company in the world, where he had served as chairman and CEO and had received the Best CEO Award in India. Nair cited four mechanisms for maintaining constant improvement at Imexsa—daily meetings and reports, quality programmes, global integration and stretch goals.

Daily Meeting and Daily Report: The daily meeting, now held each morning for one or two hours, continued to play a pivotal role at Imexsa. A typical meeting (in March 1998) was attended by representatives from each of the departments, most of whom wore the khaki Imexsa uniform. A few of the managers, however, wore red Imexsa jackets awarded to recognise achievement of ambitious goals, such as increasing one of the DRI facility's production nearly 50 per cent above its rated capacity. On several occasions during the meeting, participants jokingly asked whether their targets were ambitious enough to earn a jacket. M.R.R. Nair guided the meeting with a series of questions, inquiring about the results of previous experiments to improve performance, asking what level of performance was budgeted for the following month, and probing why targets were not higher. Nair left the room for extended periods on two occasions during the meeting, but the discussion continued with the members of the different departments discussing targets and experiments among themselves. The participants frequently referred to the daily report which provided detailed data on cost, productivity, volume and quality for each of the departments.

Quality Programmes: In 1998, Imexsa used standard quality tools, such as ISO methods, to describe existing processes. Imexsa's quality efforts won numerous international awards. In 1996, Ispat Mexicana and Caribbean Ispat received ISO's prestigious Company Wide Recognition Award for quality, a distinction shared by only twenty companies in the world. More importantly, Imexsa's quality initiatives had helped the company upgrade its products to serve more demanding customers. Imexsa enhanced its product mix from 97 per cent low grade steel sold into construction applications in 1992 to 47 per cent of slabs sold for demanding automotive and coated plate applications in 1997. Despite Imexsa's success, Quality Director Rafael Mendoza wanted more. 'Traditional quality programmes such as ISO 9000 provide excellent statistical tools for documenting your current processes, but they are not as useful in accelerating continuous improvement. For this we introduced benchmarking, Top 10s and internal agreements.'

In benchmarking operating processes, quality team members looked at best practices within the Ispat network and the steel industry as a whole, and also identified and studied related processes at global leaders such as Ericsson and General Electric. When Imexsa management wanted to improve cafeteria service during the busy lunch hour, for example, a quality team studied the restaurant in a busy soccer stadium renowned for serving large quantities of excellent food quickly during half-time. Imexsa would only work with customers and technology suppliers who agreed to openly share information on new technological developments and applications, and in turn agreed to open their plants for benchmarking. Mendoza was not worried that Imexsa would surrender competitive advantage by allowing other companies to benchmark the plant. 'In the steel industry these days, all companies have access to good ideas through customers, suppliers and consultants. The difference is who can implement them successfully.'

In the Top 10 programme, each department identified projects to either cut costs or improve quality, quantified each project's financial impact (in US dollars per year), and rank-ordered the projects from one to ten based on their bottom-line impact. Each project was assigned to a project owner charged with selecting a multi-disciplinary team to quantify the benefits of the project, develop an action plan and monitor progress against agreed process milestones. In Mendoza's view, the Top 10 programme introduced a consistent discipline in translating proposed projects into financial results and allowed each department to prioritise its own projects for improvement.

In 1996, Imexsa initiated a systematic programme for making internal service agreements between Imexsa's departments and monitoring service delivery levels against these agreements. The heads of departments receiving a service would meet once a year with each internal supplier to articulate their key requirements and agree on targets and concrete measures of service delivery. Before agreeing to target service levels, a service provider could request any prerequisites necessary to guarantee delivery. The maintenance department might agree to provide preventive maintenance on time, for instance, providing they were notified at least one week in advance of the scheduled down-time. The head of the department providing the service was responsible for monitoring performance on a daily basis, and reporting to the head of the internal customer on a monthly basis, who would sign off on the performance evaluation. If a service provider repeatedly failed to meet goals, the failure would be elevated for discussion in the daily meeting, but this had occurred only once in the programme's first two years.

In 1998, Imexsa had 140 internal service agreements across twenty-eight production and service departments and sub-departments in the plant. Seventy per cent of the agreements fulfilled 100 per cent of the requirements, 11 per cent of the agreements met between 95 to 99 per cent, with the remainder fulfilling less than 95 per cent. These internal agreements yielded significant improvements in operations. The manager of maintenance described how the agreements improved his relationships with the internal traffic department responsible for providing machinery such as cranes and trucks within the plant: 'I used to order equipment two days before a scheduled job, call three to four times each day to check on the status of the necessary equipment, and still receive the wrong equipment three hours late. Initially, I hesitated to meet with the head of internal traffic to discuss agreements, because we had argued so often in the past. When we met, I was amazed to learn that he had no idea how much it cost us when the vehicles were late for a job. We discussed the main measures for our contract—the number and type of equipment and on-time delivery and agreed on our targets for delivery. Since we've had the agreements, the right equipment always arrives on time, and instead of me calling internal traffic, they call me to make sure the equipment has arrived. They monitor how they're doing daily and report to me monthly. If there is a problem, I talk it over with the department head outside of work over a beer . . . and he pays.'

Knowledge Integration Programme: The Knowledge Integration Programme (KIP) was an Ispat corporate initiative designed by Mittal to 'keep stirring the whole organisation'. A few representatives from each operating and staff function (twelve in total) at each Ispat plant would meet twice each year. These

KIP meetings lasted two to four days and rotated among the plants in the Ispat network. Prior to the meeting, department heads would send their suggestions for discussion topics to Ispat International in London, where the agenda was set and then distributed to each of the participants in advance. During the meeting, the participants would review their performance against targets including major accomplishments and disappointments, discuss common technical problems, update each other on developments in their plant and commit to future targets. The participants also communicated between KIP meetings. As Torres described: 'If I have a question, I don't have to wait until the next KIP meeting. I can make a phone call or send an email to Canada or Trinidad. I probably exchange at least one email every week with them.'

Annual Target Setting Process: Each department in Imexsa committed to annual targets for production volume, productivity and costs, and presented its plan for achieving these goals. P.S. Venkataramanan, Imexsa's marketing manger, described the planning process:

> In each of the departments, we set our own targets and decide how we will achieve them. When our business plan is completed, we present what we are going to achieve and how to Imexsa's top management, who ask a *lot* of questions to become sure that our assessment of the situation is complete, our reasoning is correct, and our plan is coherent and not guided by emotions.'

Nair believed these questions played a critical role in the planning process:

> In discussing business plans, I believe managers should ask the departments what they plan to do and how, rather than telling them. It is never useful to be prescriptive in telling people what they should do. Learning by doing is the best teacher. Even if you disagree with a plan, it is best to let them follow their own path. Based on our own experience we could say, 'It would be better done this way'. This might work once or twice, but after that people lose the desire to constantly improve. In my experience, if people are given freedom, freedom within limits, most of the decisions they take are responsible. It is when they are under too much control that they make mistakes.

Commercial Director R.R. Mehta agreed that Imexsa's top managers abstained from setting targets for the departments, but argued that they did place constant pressure to increase targets. 'When the areas present their targets for the year, we have a healthy discussion. The managers ask a lot of questions about the targets, but they never give orders or exert excessive force. Instead they say, "You achieved this level last year, why can't you do it again? They can achieve this level at another factory, what prevents you from doing the same? What do you need from us to achieve such targets—investment, time, expertise?" If there are mitigating circumstances, these are discussed and taken into account. After this discussion, the areas commit to a target, and they are usually very stretched targets. But they feel that it is truly *their* target—it was not coerced from above and they have whatever resources they need to achieve it.'

Raul Torres agreed with Mehta's assessment. 'I feel the need to constantly improve performance every day, but it's not forced on me by management. I'm not fighting against somebody else's budgets—I agreed to the goal, and the best way to reach a goal is not with a big gun to your head. I set stretch goals because I want Imexsa to win. At first, I wanted Imexsa to be the best steel plant in Lázaro Cárdenas, then the best steel plant in Mexico, but now I ask "Why can't we be the best steel plant in the world?" We always wanted to be the best, but we couldn't because the old management put up too many limitations.'

Imexsa's Challenges Going Forward

Nair believed that Imexsa had made significant progress, but was not complacent about the future. 'Steel is a cyclical industry, and a number of good years can be followed by a number of bad years, and we have prepared for any downturn when things were going well. Two things we religiously follow are moving upstream to higher quality steel and continuously reducing our costs . . . . When things are going well, as they are at Imexsa, people can become complacent and the system can decline. We could create a crisis to instill momentum, but crisis is an effective tool only when it is sparingly used; crisis after crisis destroys a company. Maybe we need a crisis once every three or four years—that is the time it takes for a successful group to become complacent. My biggest challenge is to get excitement from the people. Even with the best equipment and technology, if people don't have fire in their bellies, Imexsa won't succeed. Our job is to keep the excited gleam in our people's eyes. That is our job.'

Ispat International

Ispat International had several formal and informal means to encourage communication among the CEOs of the operating subsidiaries and between the CEOs of the business and corporate top management. In April and November of each year, CEOs of each Ispat company would meet as a group at one of Ispat's subsidiaries for seven days.

> As Mittal described: 'During the November meeting we discuss the business plan for the following year. Every company has to present a very detailed business plan—for actions, productivity, costs, products, marketing, capital expenditures, number of employees, safety and everything—which all the CEOs discuss and then approve jointly. In April we discuss the performance of the company and evaluate the performance of every unit . . . . We study all the companies' performances and we identify the major variances of the group.'

Nair described these meetings: 'If you sit through a meeting with Mittal, he speaks the least. You will find that even if he does express an opinion, many of us share opposing views and everyone expresses and debates their opinions. Most times the group comes to a decision. But if after discussion we don't agree, Mittal comes up with the final decision and that's it. You can't have license for people continuing to hold different views endlessly. That is just a mess in any organisation.'

In addition to the semi-annual meetings, the CEOs of Ispat businesses sat on the board of directors of their sister companies. Nair, for example, was a director of Ispat's Canadian company and would attend its board meetings and review its operating plans. Ispat headquarter staff also prepared daily, monthly and quarterly reports on each factory's production, productivity, shipment and variance against targets, and these reports were circulated among the CEOs of the operating subsidiaries. These formal mechanisms were complemented by informal communications. According to Nair: 'Many large organisations tend to get bureaucratic but in Ispat communication is very informal and frequent. Part of it is structured, like the KIPs and part of it is unstructured—I often speak with Mittal on weekends—and ideas get shaped and followed through at meetings . . . . And top management is accessible to everyone. My marketing chief can pick up the phone and talk to Mittal if he needs to talk to him. Nothing waits, nothing has to wait.'

> Mittal believed that Ispat's ability to attract and retain entrepreneurs was crucial to its success. 'Our management philosophy is very simple—that every manager of the company is an entrepreneur. He has to take risks and responsibility for the profits. We delegate a lot of responsibilities and they work like entrepreneurs.'

Nair elaborated on the ideal entrepreneur in Ispat and underscored Mittal's role in developing these managers:

> Entrepreneurial leadership requires the ability to make changes all the time—to see an opportunity, identify the change that is required, take risks yourself and get other people to take risks to move in that same direction. Mittal sets an example for all our managers. He sees opportunities that others miss; for instance, people thought that buying the plant in Kazakhstan would be Ispat's Waterloo, but he bought that plant and Ispat has made the deal work through hard work. Mittal also chooses his leaders well, and in the occasional cases where they have not delivered, he has asked them to leave quickly.

The Inland Acquisition

On 16 July 1998, Ispat International completed its acquisition of Inland Steel, the sixth largest steelmaker in USA, with capacity of 6 million tons per year. Ispat planned to increase Inland's shipments by 1 million tons per year, save approximately $120 mn annually through global purchasing synergies and implement the operating practices the company had in place at its other plants. Some analysts questioned whether Ispat could apply its winning formula to an integrated US steelmaker like Inland. Like the rest of the steel industry, Ispat faced fresh challenges triggered by the Asian economic crisis. As demand for steel in Southeast Asia collapsed, steelmakers diverted their shipments to other markets, depressing steel prices around the world. Mittal was confident, however, that Ispat would make the acquisition pay off and by December 1998 Ispat was realising cost savings faster than projected at Ispat Inland.

APPENDIX 1

Ispat International Financial Highlights, 1992–97

(US$ million)

	1992	*1993*	*1994*	*1995*	*1996*	*1997*
Net sales	342	427	782	1925	1859	2190
EBITDA	7	34	160	474	336	406
Total assets	2292	2479	3073	3650	4394	5242

Quarter-on-Quarter Growth, 1997

(US$ million)

	Q1	*Q2*	*Q3*	*Q4*
Net sales	473	513	533	671
Gross profit	87	114	121	161
EBITDA	74	94	104	134
EBITDA margin (%)	15.6	18.3	19.5	20.0

Note: Financials for Ispat International only, and exclude Ispat Indo and Ispat Karmet held by LNM group.
Source: Ispat International Annual Report, 1997.

APPENDIX 2

Turnaround History of Selected Plants Acquired by Ispat

	Year Acquired	*Steel Shipments (Millions of Tons)*		*Cash Production Cost (US$ per ton)*		*Labour Productivity (Tons per Employee)*	
		Year Prior to Acquisition	*1998*	*Year Prior to Acquisition*	*1997*	*Year Prior to Acquisition*	*1997*
CIL	1989	395	802	233	190	400	899
Imexsa	1992	528	3408	253	167	418	2214
Ispat Sidbec	1994	1294	1509	317	301	560	891
Ispat Germany	1995	936	2338	280	249	1248	1505

Note: Ispat Germany includes IHSW, ISRG and IWHG for the fourth quarter of 1997 and the full year 1998.
Source: Ispat International Annual Report, 1997.

APPENDIX 3

Imexsa Financial and Operating Performance, 1992–97

	1992	1993	1994	1995	1996	1997
Operational data						
Steel shipments ('000 tons)	528	929	1389	2388	2536	3066
Labour productivity (man hours per ton)	2.62	1.88	1.45	1.13	1.11	0.97
Financial data						
Net sales (million US$)	187	266	403	827	743	860
EBITDS (million US$)	3	20	103	270	184	207
EBITDA margin (%)	1.6	7.5	25.6	32.6	24.8	24.1
Breakdown of sales by region (%)						
USA	14	34	76	51	61	–
Mexico	0	0	15	19	22	–
Asia	62	66	10	18	15	–
Europe	24	0	0	13	2	–
Total	100	100	100	100	100	
Breakdown of sales by value added (%)	0	–	–	–	–	11
Highest (e.g., exposed auto parts, sour gas)	3	–	–	–	–	36
High (e.g., non-exposed auto, tin plate, galvanised)	63	–	–	–	–	42
Medium (e.g., appliances, drums, furniture)	34	–	–	–	–	11
Low (e.g., structural steel for construction)	100	–	–	–	–	100

Source: Imexsa documents.

APPENDIX 4

Ispat International Summary Financial Data, 1993–97

	Years Ended December 31				
	1993	1994	1995	1996	1997
	(In Millions of Dollars, Except Per Share Data)				
Statement of income data					
Amounts in accordance with IAS					
Net sales ($)	427	782	1925	1859	2190
Cost of sales (exclusive of depreciation)	346	580	1.379	1458	1707
Gross profits (before deducting depreciation)	81	202	546	401	483
Gross margin	19.0%	25.8%	28.4%	21.6%	22.1%
Depreciation	38	56	110	116	152
Selling, general and administrative expenses	47	42	72	65	76
Deferred assess written off	–	–	–	–	20
Operating income (loss)	(4)	104	364	220	235
Operating margin	-0.9%	13.3%	18.9%	11.8%	10.7%
Other income (expense)–net	(22)	7	(2)	8	4
Financing costs					
Net interest expenses	(33)	(35)	(75)	(48)	(62)
Net gain (loss) from foreign exchange and monetary position	21	(167)	(89)	102	59
Amortizarion of negative goodwill	352	368	409	415	64
Income before taxes	314	277	607	697	300
Net income	314	275	620	677	289
Earnings pet common share	2.83	2.48	5.59	6.10	2.46
Amounts in accordance with US GAAP					
Operating income	–	–	$337	$268	$337
Depreciation	–	–	46	49	55
Net income	–	–	83	234	236
Basic and diluted earnings per common share	–	–	0.75	2.11	2.02
Balance sheet data					
Amounts in accordance with IAS					
Cash and cash equivalent	167	55	70	310	790

Appendix 4 contd . . .

	Years Ended December 31				
	1993	*1994*	*1995*	*1996*	*1997*
	(In Millions of Dollars, Except Per Share Data)				
Property, plant and equipment	1836	2290	2557	3068	3199
Total assets	2479	3073	3650	4394	5242
Notes payable to bank and current portion of long-term debt	332	325	383	368	431
Subordinated note payable to controlling shareholder	256	256	236	142	0
Long-term debt	248	524	716	967	1104
Negative goodwill	1063	910	530	173	134
Shareholders' equity	442	743	1310	2334	2970
Amounts in accordances with US GAAP					
Total assets	–	–	–	1955	2882
Long-term debt	–	–	–	878	1104
Shareholders' equity	–	–	–	59	662
Other data:					
EBITDA (IAS)	–	–	$474	$336	$406
EBITDA (US GAAP)	–	–	383	317	392
Total production of DRI (thousand tons)	2077	3042	4557	5030	5765
Total production of liquid steel (thousand tons)	2057	3209	5800	6404	7775
Total shipments of steel products (thousand tons)	1922	2932	5373	5931	7256

Note: Financials for Ispat International only, and exclude Ispat Indo and Ispat Karmet held by LNM group.

Source: Ispat International, Annual Report 1997.

CASE 12

NICHOLAS PIRAMAL LIMITED: INTEGRATING DIVERSITY

There is a story from the ancient Indian epic, the *Mahabharata*, which Ajay Piramal often quotes. An archery contest is on and the target is a fish spinning from a branch of a leafy tree. Difficult as that is, the contest is made harder by the fact that contestants are not allowed to see the fish but only its image in a bowl of oil placed at their feet. When Arjun, the main character in the epic, succeeds in piercing the fish, people crowd round him, asking, 'How did you do it? How did you see the fish?' Arjun replies, 'The fish? No, I did not see a fish. I saw only the pupil of an eye and that is what I focussed on.'

'Focus' is what makes Piramal recount the story so many times. 'If you keep your eye on your objective, success will follow.'

Ajay Piramal is chairman of Piramal Enterprises, one of India's top forty business

This case was written by Harsh Piramal, Breno Machado, MBA students at the London Business School, Gita Piramal, business historian and Sumantra Ghoshal, Robert P. Baumann Professor of Strategic Leadership at the London Business School. The authors are grateful to Nicholas Piramal Ltd for their help and support in writing this case. The case was first registered by the London Business School in 2000.

houses, with interests largely in pharmaceuticals, textiles and retailing, but also having a presence in engineering (ferrites, auto components and tools), glass and, most recently, information technology. In 2000, the group consisted of twenty-six companies (including joint ventures), with aggregate revenues of about Rs 20 bn. The fastest growing company—and the most profitable—was Nicholas Piramal, a pharmaceutical firm (earlier known as Nicholas Laboratories) (see Appendix 1).

Pharmaceuticals was a relatively new business for this third generation group, founded in 1933 by Piramal's grandfather. Until 1987, most of the group's revenues had come from the textiles business, and Morarjee Mills was India's oldest surviving composite textile mill. However, strikes and government policies had increased the uncertainties for the organised segment of the textile industry. And the development of the textile industry in China had changed the competitive environment, driving prices down and reducing margins dramatically. Piramal felt it was time to diversify into a sunrise industry to safeguard the long-term survival of the group. The business had to have major long-term growth potential with effective entry barriers, be it through technology, investment, marketing, distribution or patents. This was not to imply that the group would exit its existing businesses: the group also needed to develop and implement a strategy to ensure healthy and strong long-term growth for all of them (see Appendix 2).

While mulling over this issue and poring over industry reports, Piramal was offered the opportunity to acquire Nicholas Laboratories, a pharmaceutical company. In 1984, the group had acquired a small glass company, Gujarat Glass, which supplied bottles and vials to the pharmaceutical industry, but this was the sum limit of the group's exposure to this business. While Piramal was not certain that Nicholas Laboratories met his key objective, viz, a business with 'a major long-term growth potential with effective entry barriers, be it through technology, investment, marketing, distribution or patents', he was sanguine that he would be able to turn it around. After all, the group's genesis and growth had been through the acquisition route. Over the years, it had turned around no less than four companies. Nicholas Laboratories had an impressive product portfolio, including Aspro, the popular OTC headache remedy. It owned some valuable real estate. And he could afford the price.

The success of its first foray into the pharma sector encouraged the Piramal group to acquire a second pharma company, and then a third, and then a fourth, and so on—until share prices plummeted. Analysts became concerned that the companies were being used for profit transfers. For example, they were worried that Nicholas Laboratories, as it was known then (where the Piramal group held 45 per cent of the equity) could outsource to Piramal Healthcare, formerly Roche India (where it held a 74 per cent stake) at a favourable transfer price. In 1998, Piramal announced the merger of all the three pharmaceutical companies in the group. He also announced that all future investments by the group in the pharmaceutical sector would henceforth be routed through Nicholas Piramal. Share prices promptly soared and, with it, confidence in the management.

However, the merger announcement brought to the fore several issues:

1. If Nicholas Piramal were to absorb every best practice, process and standard of the three companies, it could submerge under the weight of this gold plating. So what should be kept and what should go?
2. The pharma sector was doing well and the outlook was bright. Nicholas Piramal was well on its way to becoming one of India's five biggest pharma companies. But eventually the country would run out of reasonably priced, mismanaged, poor-performing companies to buy. The merger offered an opportunity to build for the future, to move from purely acquisitive growth to organic growth. So what should be the strategy? What competencies needed to be built into Nicholas Piramal?
3. Piramal Enterprises was a professionally run group. But waiting in the wings was a new crop of young Piramals who hoped to find managerial berths in the group companies. What should be their role in Nicholas Piramal?

The Logic of Acquisitions

The Acquisition of Nicholas Laboratories, 1988

Aspro Nicholas, Nicholas Laboratories' parent company, wanted to quit India for several reasons. Nicholas was performing poorly and could not find its way through the Indian bureaucracy to get approval to launch new drugs. It also had problems dealing with its strongly unionised workforce. Before Piramal came on the scene, another potential buyer, Reckitt and Coleman India, a pharmaceutical company, had walked away. In its due diligence it discovered that the excise tax department had slapped a substantial liability on Nicholas Laboratories and that the amount of warranties outstanding against Nicholas Laboratories was higher than the asking price. The deal collapsed. Piramal however was undeterred, and in June 1988 the government cleared the group's application to purchase an initial 24.5 per cent of Nicholas Laboratories' equity for Rs 16.4 mn. Shortly thereafter, the company's name was changed from Nicholas Laboratories to Nicholas Piramal India Limited (NPIL).

Within six months of the takeover in December 1988, Piramal brought in Chandrakant M. Hattangadi as the company's new managing director. Hattangadi had worked for Parke-Davis India as chairman and managing director. He had also worked at Pfizer, both in India and the Philippines. He had earned a strong reputation in the Indian pharmaceutical industry by virtue of being president of the Organisation of Pharmaceutical Producers of India (OPPI)—the industry association supported by MNCs and the larger Indian pharma companies—during the critical 1987–88 period when the industry was negotiating with the government for a liberal policy.

The first step was to identify clear objectives, and three emerged:

- To be amongst the top five fastest growing companies in the pharmaceutical industry in India in order to achieve 'critical mass'.
- To raise profitability to the upper quartile of the industry.
- To form strategic alliances with the best multinational pharmaceutical groups so as to have access to new molecules in the post-GATT/IPR era.

To meet these objectives, substantial investments would have to be made in both manufacturing and distribution. 'It occurred to us that these would be the two assets that multinational companies would value the most when looking for a local partner in India and these capabilities would also improve the company's sales, market share and profitability', said Hattangadi.

New Plant at Pithampur: Nicholas had two plants, at Deonar and Ambernath, both small and considerably outdated. It commissioned a new manufacturing plant in Pithampur in central India. The plant cost approximately Rs 100 mn and began operations in 1991. It was further expanded in December 1996, bringing investment up to approximately Rs 250 mn. The plant was built to comply with USFDA standards to allow Nicholas to access the enormous American generics market, but more importantly to increase its credibility with potential partners so that Nicholas could attract post-GATT product licensing agreements. Its central location facilitated efficient distribution and its modern manufacturing technologies allowed substantial improvement in productivity and cost savings, although its capacity was well above current needs. For example, Pithampur could make eye drops at a 41 per cent cost saving over the Deonar plant. 'At my old company, it took me six years to get an approval for a relatively minor investment from the parent company. At Nicholas, I was taken aback by the speed of decision making. I think this is what makes family entrepreneurship so different', said Hattangadi.

Cost Savings at Pithampur, 1994

Dosage Form	*% Cost Savings vis-à-vis Deonar*
Eye drops	41
Tablets	7
Liquids	5
Capsules	10

Source: Company reports.

Manufacturing Cost Comparison

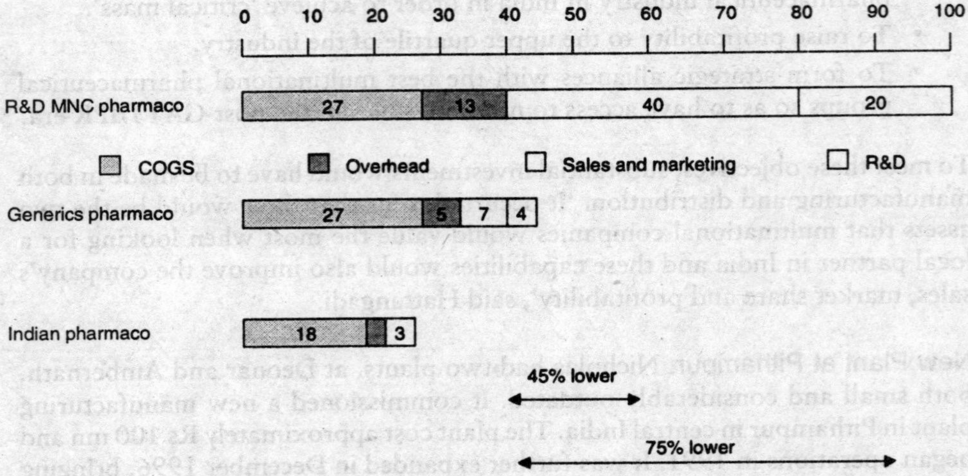

Source: McKinsey Quarterly Report, 1996

Sales and Marketing: The new management made considerable investments in the sales, marketing and distribution network. The field force increased from

191 sales reps in 1990 to 482 in 1995. The number of C&F agents jumped, making available sixteen warehouses widely spread across the country. The number of distributors also jumped from 587 in 1990 to 1,400 in 1993. This enabled Nicholas to reach out to more doctors. Its doctor coverage doubled from almost 74,000 in 1990 to 130,000 in 1993.

Investments in Marketing and Distribution

	1990	*1991*	*1992*	*1993*	*1995*
Field force	191	263	319	450	482
Distributor network	587	814	1083	1400	1662
Doctor coverage	74000	82000	89000	130000	–

Source: Company reports.

Marketing/Distribution Chain

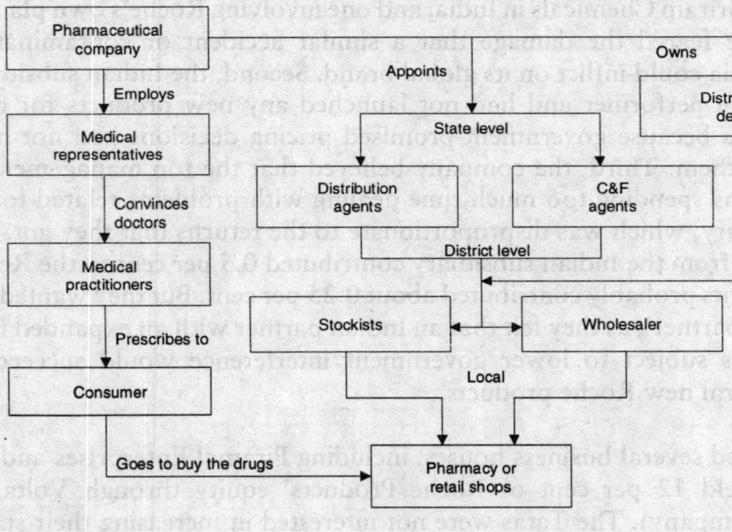

Product Portfolio: In order to minimise the effect of stringent governmental price control on the company's profitability—one of the reasons why Aspro Nicholas had decided to exit the Indian market—Nicholas reviewed its product mix, launching twelve new products outside price control. In 1993, new products contributed 29 per cent of the group's turnover. In contrast, new products represented only 3 per cent of 1989 sales.

Company vis-à-vis Industry, 1993

	Nicholas	*Industry*
Ratio of controlled to decontrolled products	51:49	76:24
Material cost sales (%)	48	56.8
Employee cost sales (%)	10.4	12.4

Source: Company reports.

The Acquisition of Roche Products (India) Ltd, 1993

In April 1993, F. Hoffman–La Roche, the Swiss pharmaceutical multinational, sent a team to India to seek potential buyers for Roche Products (India). There were several reasons for this. First, Roche was anxious about operating a chemical plant in India. Three serious accidents had occurred involving Union Carbide and Shriram Chemicals in India, and one involving Roche's own plant in Europe. Roche feared the damage that a similar accident or contamination problem in India could inflict on its global brand. Second, the Indian subsidiary was a mediocre performer and had not launched any new products for over seventeen years because government-promised pricing decisions had not been favourable to them. Third, the company believed that the top management in Switzerland was spending too much time dealing with problems related to the Indian subsidiary, which was disproportionate to the returns that they got. For example, sales from the Indian subsidiary contributed 0.5 per cent to the Roche group and profits probably contributed about 0.25 per cent. But they wanted the buyer to be a 'partner', as they felt that an Indian partner with an expanded field force who was subject to lower government interference would succeed in launching several new Roche products.

The team visited several business houses, including Piramal Enterprises and the Tatas (who held 12 per cent of Roche Products' equity through Voltas, a distribution company). The Tatas were not interested in increasing their stake, but for the Piramal group the timing was just right. Four years after the Nicholas takeover, the company had been turned around and the group was hungry for growth and an opportunity to strengthen its position in the Indian pharma market. As Piramal said, 'Look at it from our side. We had no R&D and no access to new products or technology. We knew that with GATT rules being introduced sometime in the future, we would need access to new products. Also, size matters—we needed critical mass to leverage on marketing and distribution as well as to increase the utilisation of the Pithampur plant.'

The acquisition would enable Piramal to:

- Access Roche's new, post-GATT products.
- Be the sole manufacturer of Vitamin A in India (of significant importance in human and animal nutrition, prevention of blindness and reduction in child mortality).
- Combine synergies between Roche and Nicholas in products, field force and manufacturing.

Yet, the first meeting, attended by Hattangadi, Mahesh Gupta (the group's CFO) and Piramal with Dr Ruede and a few others from the Roche team, was inconclusive. 'We were not clear about what they wanted. Frankly, I thought that they were there for an alliance. However, they did not seem to be stating their intentions clearly at the meeting and it broke off inconclusively', said Piramal.

As he reflected on the meeting, Piramal got the sense that Roche was looking for something more than an alliance. Therefore, he pushed very hard for a one-to-one meeting with Dr Ruede at Roche's headquarters in Basle, Switzerland. They met in May 1993. Piramal recalls, 'The key was to get into his mind. This meeting was crucial in the whole process because it allowed me to understand their true intentions. The meeting also made clear to me the kind of acquirer that Roche was looking for.'

To Piramal, it seemed that Roche were actually looking for a company who would be more like a partner rather than a simple acquirer. They did not want to lose the brand image that they had built in India because they felt it might be useful to them in future. So, the partner had to be able to implement a successful turnaround of the company. Besides, they did not want their partner to compete against Roche in the international arena via exports of generic products. They also wanted a company with a strong sales and distribution network in India that would give a boost to new product launches and royalty revenues. 'As the meeting ended, I asked Dr Ruede for another follow-up meeting but he insisted that we first put in a bid', Piramal recalled.

As Piramal returned to Bombay, all these issues were playing heavily on his mind. Within the group, opinion was mixed about the proposal. Several did not agree with the proposed acquisition. They questioned the wisdom of buying a multinational company subsidiary that had been making thin profits and had not introduced a new product for years. They did not see it adding value to Nicholas. Nonetheless, they started preparing for the next meeting with Roche. Said Piramal, 'We did an evaluation of our product portfolios to make sure that there was no major clash. We also focussed heavily on the fit between Roche and Nicholas. In this way, we avoided having the bid as the central issue of our proposal—I did not want to commit to a particular number.'

Before the next round of negotiations, Piramal invited the managing director of Roche Products (India), Jean-Jacques Vorsanger, to visit Nicholas' newly built, state-of-the-art plant at Pithampur. This helped convey a very positive note to Basle about the group's commitment to the pharmaceutical business. In its proposal, the Piramal group ensured that Roche's requirements were met.

Commented Piramal: 'We did have several advantages vis-à-vis our rivals. First, Roche was already associated with Nicholas in Europe. Second, we had had a very good track record in the four years since we had taken over Nicholas. Third, we did not export generics because we already had an agreement with Nicholas which restricted us from doing so. This conveyed to Roche that we fulfilled our commitments to our partners and would not compete with them internationally. Fourth, I struck up a good rapport with Dr Ruede. And finally, we moved really fast, which showed our commitment to completing the deal.'

On 3 November 1993, Piramal Enterprises (not Nicholas Piramal) took over the entire 74 per cent equity of Roche in Roche Products for Rs 320 mn. After the acquisition, the company retained the right to manufacture and distribute all existing Roche products under the Roche brand name. Furthermore, it was given the right of first refusal for all new Roche patented pharmaceutical, OTC, vitamins and feed supplement products to be sold in India. This would allow Roche Products to access F. Hoffman–La Roche's powerful pipeline in pharma, biotech, genetic engineering, bulk drugs, vitamins and fine chemicals. There was also a distribution agreement for Roche products. However, this agreement would remain valid only until 2003, when Piramal confidently expected to extend it based on the successful results that Roche would have carved from the partnership.

The company's name was changed from Roche Products to Piramal Healthcare. It was not merged into Nicholas Piramal because 'it would have diverted management attention from business to administrative issues. Furthermore, relationship with labour unions is a very sensitive issue in India. Therefore, the management did not want to risk affecting the whole group with the potential adverse reaction that might arise from the planned shutting down of some of Roche Products' plants', explained Piramal. The turnaround strategy was to:

- Make a smooth transition from distributor to C&F arrangements.
- Focus on reduction of working capital.
- Improve cash generation.
- Impose stricter control on costs and headcount.
- Launch new Roche products.
- Optimise utilisation and return on assets.

Rationalisation: Roche Products had two plants and 679 employees. A voluntary retirement scheme (VRS) was implemented at both plants. As the average age and skill of the workforce differed in both plants, the VRS had a different implementation strategy and impact on each plant. In Tardeo, there was a massive adherence to the scheme and the workforce was reduced from 282 to virtually nil. In Thane, which was a more complex plant that produced vitamins and employed younger and more skilled workers, management rejected most of the employees' applications and they continued to work there.

Roche Products Turnaround: The VRS Proposal

Location	*Total Employees**	*VRS Applied*	*VRS Accepted*	*Transfers*	*Balance#*
Tardeo plant	282	276	261	-21	Nil
Tardeo office	69	64	59	(-1+1)	10
Thane plant	328	156	33	21	316
Total	679	496	353	–	326

* 31 March. # 1 April 1996.
Source: Company reports.

Roche Products Turnaround: Impact of VRS

(Rs million)

Head	*FY96*	*FY97*	*Saving*
Staff expenses			
Factory	60.8	5.9	54.9
HO	21.7	8.2	13.5
Total	82.5	14.1	68.4
Power/Fuel/Cons/Stores	10.7	0.8	9.9
Depreciation	5.2	5.2	–
Rates and taxes	3.9	3.3	0.6
Repairs/maintenance	4.1	0.5	3.6
Travelling	3.3	2.8	0.5
Contract manufacturing expenses	1.4	31.9	-30.5
Insurance	1.0	0.4	0.6
Others	22.7	9.4	13.3
Total	134.8	68.4	66.4

This calculation factored 10 per cent estimated cost for inflation.
Source: Company reports.

The Tardeo plant, which occupied expensive real estate in central Bombay, was shut down and production transferred to the Pithampur plant. Costs had to be brought down. Personnel expenses and material costs at Nicholas Piramal, for example, were 49.9 per cent. At Roche it was 67.6 per cent. Combining Roche and Nicholas cultures was not an easy process but was facilitated by the fact that the Pithampur plant was young and benefited a lot from Roche's experienced managers and workforce who were transferred there. The top management was sensitive to the potential conflicts that could arise and made sure that the tone of the relationships between existing employees and the new arrivals was one of knowledge transference and co-operation, instead of antagonism and rivalry. According to Piramal: 'We found out that many of Roche's problems were basic. For example, we reduced inventory substantially by marketing the products more aggressively, secured price increases for some price-controlled products, changed the product mix so that it focussed more on non-price-controlled drugs and severed our distribution agreement with Voltas which was adding more cost than benefit. Also, we changed the compensation system, giving higher salary increments to good performers. In summary, we did not try anything fancy—we only applied our fundamental management sense to running the business.'

Senior Management: 'Those managers who could not take up the challenge that we presented for them ended up leaving the company subsequently', Piramal noted wryly. These included the marketing, manufacturing and distribution managers. The managing director, an expatriate, and three other senior executives had left earlier to return to F. Hoffman–La Roche. Nonetheless, Piramal stressed: 'I do not believe in going into companies and making radical changes. I prefer the soft approach.'

Strengthening Partnerships: Under the former Roche management, no new products had been introduced for seventeen years. After the takeover, the company introduced sixteen new products over the next four years. Profits quadrupled. F. Hoffman–La Roche also earned four times as much as it had earlier.

Roche Products Profit Performance

(Rs million)

	Roche Management			*Piramal Management*		
	*FY90**	*FY91*	*FY92*	*FY93*	*FY94**	*FY95*
PBT	16.00	5.20	5.50	37.30	68.50	143.20
PAT	11.00	3.00	1.90	15.60	67.60	143.20

* Annualised.
Source: Company reports.

F. Hoffman–La Roche Income from Roche Products

(Rs million)

	Roche Management			*Piramal Management*	
	FY92	*FY93*	*FY94*	*FY95*	*FY96*
Dividend+Purchases from FHLR, Basle	13.7	27.0	23.9	68.4	106.0

Source: Company reports.

The Acquisition of Sumitra Pharmaceuticals and Chemicals, 1995

After Roche, Piramal started looking for other companies to acquire, particularly one in the bulk drugs sector. The logic behind this was that the group could vertically integrate and have control over its raw material source. Moreover, exports of bulk drugs and intermediates had shown accelerated growth. If the group could acquire a USFDA approved chemicals plant, it could tap the large US generic formulation market. One such company, Sumitra Pharmaceuticals and Chemicals Limited in Hyderabad, became available in 1995. The logic of acquisition was simple: through Sumitra, Nicholas Piramal could get a captive facility, large capacities, existing customers, proven technologies and manufacturing facility, a ready pool of technical and R&D staff, and was capable of being upgraded to obtain FDA certification.

Within weeks, Nicholas Piramal had acquired Sumitra's bulk drugs division (not the company). The deal was paid for with Nicholas Piramal stock without any cash outlay.

'In retrospect, this was a badly-timed move', said Piramal. 'The bulk drug market slumped due to severe price competition from countries like China as well as an increase in domestic supply. Add to this the low yields and poor Good Manufacturing Practices and you do not have a very comforting scenario . . . . The problem was as much with culture as it was with the performance of the company. In fact, they were intimately linked to each other.'

The bulk drugs division continued to be the sore point in Nicholas Piramal's overall performance. A couple of years after its acquisition, Sumitra was spun off as a subsidiary to enable an MNC partnership. It was hoped that the new company would be able to benefit from proprietary technology and access global markets through the MNC partner. An MoU was signed in 1998. After struggling for three years, the business was finally disinvested in 1999.

The Acquisition of Boehringer Mannheim India Ltd, 1997

Meanwhile, another opportunity arose for Piramal to acquire a prestigious prize: Boehringer Mannheim India (BM), the Indian subsidiary of Boehringer Mannheim AG of Germany. The then managing director of BM India, Peter Stenson, was a friend of Piramal's wife. At a dinner party one night in May 1996, Stenson proposed to Piramal that BM India and Nicholas Piramal jointly promote Recormon, a biotechnology product to be launched by Boehringer Mannheim AG around the world.

From BM's point of view, Nicholas Piramal was an attractive *partner* because of its state-of-the-art Pithampur plant and its large field force. BM itself at the time was not doing too well. Its sales had remained flat for several years, it was making losses and had not launched a single new product in over a decade.

From Nicholas Piramal's point of view, BM was an attractive *acquisition* because of its similarity with Roche Products. Neither could deal with the bureaucracy, both were severely under-performing in the market, and both had not launched a new product in years. 'So, at the next meeting that we had with the Boehringer India management, I proposed the idea that they sell out their stake and form a strategic alliance with us, just like Roche. As with the Roche case, we did a lot of work before-hand. We built a strong case for them as to why they should sell out in India, we pointed out their problems and how similar they were to Roche, and finally we pointed out our track record with Roche India so far, which was excellent. They seemed to see the logic of our argument, and I had the feeling that they would come round to our point of view', said Piramal.

In the meanwhile, tragedy struck BM India. On 12 September 1996, two patients died after consuming Comsat Forte, a vitamin manufactured by BM India. As a result of this incident, several directors were issued arrest warrants. The BM management, both in India and Germany, panicked. Stenson fled the country. Carlos Chavez was appointed to take his place, but he also fled the country fearing arrest. The Asia Pacific head, Dieter Dormann, was then appointed to oversee the operations of BM India, but he refused to do so from within India.

Piramal seized the opportunity. 'BM was deeply concerned about the worldwide repercussions of this incident. I knew that in their own minds, they had now decided to exit from their business in India. The tragedy that occurred simply accelerated the decision in their own minds', said Piramal. Within hours of receiving a call one night from Dormann, Piramal was on a flight to Germany.

'I proposed that BM India be merged with Nicholas Piramal. Not only would this have prevented Nicholas Piramal from invoking the takeover code, but it would also reassure the government and consumer groups that a reputed Indian company was dealing with the situation. This would limit the damage done to BM's name and the paranoia that had emerged against using its products. However, I did attach one condition: that Nicholas Piramal would agree to take over the civil liabilities arising from any damage claims from the Comsat incident, but would not take on any criminal liabilities. They were more than willing to agree to this.'

Back in Bombay, Piramal and his team thrashed out the final details. By October 1996, the deal was sealed. 'Once again, preparation was the key and speed was of the essence. The speed convinced the management in both Germany and India of our commitment to see the deal through. Our knowledge about the scenario and our experience and track record in dealing with multinationals gave us an edge. Also, Roche and Boehringer Mannheim have traditionally shared close ties, so I'm sure that Roche also gave us a glowing recommendation which no doubt helped make up their minds. Needless to say, there were several other players, very powerful players, in the race to acquire the company once news got around that it was for sale. But due to all these reasons, we were the only ones really in the race by this time.'

Nicholas Piramal was clear about the rationale for the acquisition. It would get guaranteed access to all BM Germany's research products for launch in India. These would be in the areas of pharmaceutical products, diagnostics (instruments, kits and chemicals) as well as biotechnology. The merger would add Rs 1000 mn to Nicholas' top line and it was believed that BM would be capable of adding a very good bottom line from the next financial year. The increase in Nicholas' equity would be a minimal Rs 17 mn. The 300-strong BM field force when added to Nicholas' 450 would make the combined field force of 750 one of the largest in the country, and this figure would rise to more than 1,200 if one added Roche Products' representatives. The merger would also add new lines of business: BM's diagnostics and patient care divisions. BM Diagnostics was already the No. 1 player in India and BM Germany was the second largest worldwide.

Unlike the earlier acquisitions, BM was immediately merged with Nicholas Piramal. On taking stock of the situation, the Nicholas management felt that 'the company was in pretty much the same state that Roche and Nicholas were when we took over—the basics were quite good, but the people had not been stretched enough—they were pretty relaxed and needed to be given a bit of a push.' At this time, Piramal had also begun thinking of inducting fresh leadership into the company.

Boehringer Turnaround

(Rs million)

	Before *1995–96*	*During* *1996–97*	*After* *1997–98*
Headcount*			
Factories	525	289	111
Marketing	421	415	407
Head office	110	93	76
Total	1056	797	594
Staff costs	153	114	85
Net sales	848	761	868
Operating profit	28	2	166

* No. of people.
Source: Company reports.

To start with, 'Francis Pinto was inducted into the organisation as a consultant in January 1996 as a kind of test period prior to his appointment as CEO. Now, along with the merger, we also announced his appointment as CEO of Nicholas Piramal. However, I insisted that Hattangadi continue as managing director because he was great to have at the head of the company. He had been responsible for drawing out the long-term strategic plan for our pharma business; under his leadership he had brought about the turnaround of Nicholas as well as Roche Products Ltd. He had also successfully formed our first JVs with Allergan and Scholl in 1995 and had initiated discussions with Boots and Reckitt and Coleman. Most important of all, I thought his hands-on experience of running a successful pharma business in India would be synergistic with Dr Pinto's experience abroad. Besides, my selection of Dr Pinto was also in a way influenced by Hattangadi's recommendation in favour of Dr Pinto as both had known each other for quite a few years. It was Hattangadi's opinion that, in view of the WTO and IPR, his successor should be someone with global pharma experience—I agreed whole-heartedly. I was therefore more than confident that there would be synergy and harmony during transition and no conflict of any kind. Fortunately, my confidence was not misplaced.'

Integrating Diversity

Rationale for One Company

In the months following the BM acquisition, analyst scepticism grew at the prospect of having three health care companies controlled by one group. Analysts speculated that the companies would ultimately be used as tools for profit transfer. For example, Nicholas Piramal manufactured for Roche Products. Analysts believed that profits could be transferred from Nicholas Piramal (in which the Piramal family had a 45 per cent stake) to Roche Products (in which the Piramal family had a 74 per cent stake) through favourable transfer pricing.

'We took a real beating in those few months. Nicholas' market capitalisation fell from about Rs 5 bn in October 1996 to Rs 4.1 bn in six months. Having said that, it was always our intention to merge all three companies into a single entity. We were waiting for BM to recover from its poor position and also waiting to see if any liabilities would arise from the Comsat Forte incident', said Mahesh Gupta, CFO.

Finally, in April 1997, the three companies announced a triple merger—and share prices promptly rose. Since that time, Nicholas Piramal's market capitalisation has grown by over 30 per cent CAGR.

Board of Directors: After the triple merger, Piramal re-constituted the board of directors as a step in the drive towards professionalisation. He convinced some friends and family members to resign and also brought in top bureaucrats and managers from across the country. He also inducted several Nicholas Piramal managers on the board (a practice that was not common in India at the time) to align the interests of employees and shareholders.

Creating a high quality board in India was difficult, partly because no one could be on more than twenty company boards, but also because directors' remuneration was limited by law to Rs 2,000 per meeting. Nicholas Piramal used commissions as a percentage of the company's net profit to enhance the compensation package and to motivate outside directors to put in their full effort to help Nicholas Piramal enhance its performance. The number of board meetings was also increased to ensure seriousness. The board met about six times a year and all members had access to essential information such as annual operating plans, budgets, long-term plans, quarterly results, information about investments, alliances and acquisitions, labour-related issues, environmental liabilities and legal processes.

Top Management: The top management team at the 'new' Nicholas Piramal had a number of new faces. Apart from Ajay Piramal and his wife Swati, CFO Gupta and COO Vijay Shah were from group companies; MD Hattangadi and Jagdish Saigal came from Nicholas Laboratories. But the rest were head-hunted from outside and had no links with either Nicholas, Roche or BM, or indeed with other group companies. Each brought a different and unique set of experiences and perspectives enabling a new identity to emerge from their interactions with each other.

The Integration Process: Once the legal and stock market formalities were through, it was time to come to grips with the nitty-gritty job of integrating the companies. Each company shared some common ground: each had an MNC background, was in the same industry, and had demonstrated lacklustre performance for more or less the same reasons—low investment and interest from the parent company in India and the Indian market, low morale and interest among managers and workers in the company and its future, low profitability because of a product mix tilted towards price-controlled products and overcapitalised plants. At the same time, there were significant differences in operating styles, culture and organisation.

To truly merge the companies, the first step obviously was a major overhaul and rationalisation of manufacturing facilities, the product mix, and the marketing and distribution infrastructure. Equally important, however, was the issue of how to integrate people so that even though they came from different backgrounds, they would all understand what was required of them in the new entity, approve of the changes and then stretch themselves to fit in. A third important step was upgrading processes. Taking the best from each company and cobbling them together was not an option. It was entirely possible that by taking the best processes from each company, the new entity would become completely unviable.

It was important therefore to become something more and yet different, one that would be in tune with the 21st century. There had to be a 'new' Nicholas Piramal which was radically different from the old one. The new Nicholas Piramal had to have a fresh identity of its own, with a vision and goals which everyone in the erstwhile companies could identify with. None of these critical steps took place in isolation, nor were they definitively discussed at any given moment of time. As in all business decisions, what seemed important got done first.

Operational Rationalisation

The most urgent need following the merger was operational rationalisation. The plants, the products, sales, marketing and distribution needed immediate action. Many workers were given the 'golden handshake' and plants shut down. Instead of three head offices, there was just the one. The distribution network and marketing organisation were re-jigged apart from the rationalisation of the product portfolio.

'These mergers were unique in that we took people into confidence before the mergers took place. After that, Piramal and Hattangadi planned the integration and how the intellectual capital would be used and valued. This charged every manager in each company', said Ramesh Balgi, vice president, corporate HR, who was part of the team that implemented the integration.

Manufacturing Integration: 'In manufacturing, we did what was need based at the time', said Pinto. Nine plants were reduced to five and the headcount went down from 2,631 to 1,950 with a saving in excess of Rs 100 mn per annum. Products were re-aligned to make the remaining plants stronger. BM's Thane (Kolshet) plant, for example, was shut down at a cost of between Rs 70 and 80 mn and its production transferred to Nicholas' Pithampur plant. Meanwhile, production at BM's Mahad plant was immediately upgraded to Pithampur standards and within two years, Mahad followed Pithampur's best practices.

Plant Rationalisation

Plants/Locations	*Company*	*Workforce*	
		Before	*The 'New' Nicholas Piramal*
Pithampur	Nicholas	502	513
Deonar	Nicholas	320	323
Tardeo	Roche	315	Closed 1995
Thane	BM	152	Closed 1998
Thane-Balkum	Roche	398	386
Thane-Kolshet	BM	80	Closed
Mahad	BM	90	94
Hyderabad	Sumitra	752	634
Ambernath	Nicholas	22	Closed
Total		2631	1950

Source: Company reports.

How was the rationalisation carried out, especially given the fact that there were three unions involved in the process? The Nicholas union was a Marxist union based in Calcutta. Roche Products had a standard MNC union. BM had only half its employees unionised. The half who were not unionised were called professional service officers (PSO). According to Pinto, 'Firstly, we modified the jobs in the plants and then we accelerated the VRS.' The closure of BM's Thane plant skilfully applied the hard-earned lessons learnt during the closure of Roche's Tardeo plant. 'We also did an exercise comparing the salaries till retirement of a worker at BM and at Nicholas Piramal. To their credit, all employees understood, they accommodated and they changed.'

Balgi added: 'When we announced the VRS at the BM plant at Thane, we had actually "broken the coconut" for the bulk plant. But the Thane plant had problems. We gave the workers the option of either taking a VRS or continuing to run the plant. It was an open and frank discussion between the union and the new management. Over 150 workers took the VRS. We let go of 144. The benefits that the employees got were something they could never have imagined. For some, this process took place within a year of joining the plant. Each of the 144 people who left met Dr Pinto and me and thanked us for taking care of them. After that, all production went to Pithampur. It resulted in confidence levels rising.'

The new Nicholas Piramal still had eight unions. There were five manufacturing unions, one at each remaining plant. Here again, half the workforce was non-unionised. This was done by expanding non-unionised jobs. There were also three unions in the field force were a legacy of the old unions; but half the field force was non-unionised.

Marketing Rationalisation: The field forces of the three companies were re-focussed, re-trained and regionalised. Over 100 representatives were asked to take accelerated retirement, but overall this area saw the least redundancies. Some were transferred to joint ventures with Boots, Allergen and others. Still, with more than 1,600 representatives on its payroll, the new Nicholas Piramal had one of the largest field forces in the country. This field force was expected to reach out to and maintain contact with 200,000 doctors across India.

The field force structure was also changed. It used to have four levels: national sales manager, the zonal manager, the regional manager and the field manager. The new structure was much flatter with eighteen state business managers (SBMs) who looked after their states like entrepreneurs. Also, Nicholas Piramal, Roche Products and BM all had separate offices all over India. Post-1997, there were just eighteen state offices and one head office—a new one located inside the Morarjee Mills complex in central Bombay.

Staff Field Force Strength

Before		The 'New' Nicholas Piramal	
NPIL	400	Multi-speciality	730
BM	410	Extra care	230*
Roche	210	Diagnostics	130*
OTC	80	Patient care	30
		Biotech	40*
		OTC	170*
Total	1100	Total	1600

Source: Company reports.

The field force was also separated into newly created divisions formed along customer lines. 'What used to happen was that two reps were going to the same doctor, which was producing negative results. We quickly basketed products so that the doctor would not be bothered by more reps than was necessary', said Balgi. The strategic business unit (SBU) concept was introduced at this time. In terms of marketing rationalisation, the management divided the field force into five 'specialities' or business units. In each case, the manager with the best knowledge of those products was selected to head the unit:

- Multi-speciality division: Roche head.
- Extra care division: BM head.
- Patient care division: BM head.
- Diagnostic division: BM head.
- Biotech division: Nicholas head.

The 'New' Nicholas Piramal and The OTC Market

Year	*Sales (Rs mn)*	*Strategies*
FY97	140	Revitalise Saridon, Aspro, Rennie
FY98	220	Acquire Lacto Calamine, Burnol
FY99	2500	Strategic alliance: Reckitt, Scholl, Boots, others
FY2000	3500	Complete transitions and new products

Source: Company reports.

With 730 people, the multi-speciality division was the largest and the most unionised with field forces drawn from all three companies, each with its own salary structure which had to be brought in line with the salary structure of Nicholas Piramal. For example, at BM, salaries were higher but there was also a bigger differential between grades than at Nicholas Piramal or Roche Products. In September 1997, the management began harmonising salaries. Settlements due from October 1996 were taken up to June 2001.

'We were able to achieve this harmonisation relatively easily. What made the difference in this process was the high comfort level: every SBU head could run independently. There was more freedom than before. There was also a high level of confidence. No one felt threatened in their jobs. Otherwise every level would have been shaky. In fact the Roche Products head of the multi-speciality division was later promoted to be Nicholas Piramal's point person for all Nicholas Piramal alliances and JVs. A Nicholas Piramal manager took over from him', said Balgi.

Divisional Productivity

Division	*1997–98**	*1998–99**	*% Change*
Multi-speciality	3.89	5.12	32
Extra care	2.42	2.76	14
Patient care	5.40	6.20	15
Diagnostics	2.60	2.87	10
Biotech	2.80	4.06	45
Total	3.38	4.32	28

* Rs million per representative
Source: Company reports.

Distribution Rationalisation: This was completed with a supply chain focus. The number of C&F agents was brought down from sixty-four to twenty while wholesalers increased from 1,800 to 2,500. The new Nicholas Piramal was engaged in cutting back the number of wholesalers to 2,000. In the new Nicholas Piramal, 100 vendors supplied to the five plants and the production went to twenty C&F agents who passed on goods to 2,000 distributors who in turn supplied 100,000 pharmacies. Meanwhile, another chain led to 5,000 hospitals. Nicholas Piramal estimated that approximately 200 million people were consuming Nicholas Piramal products.

Financial Rationalisation: The three companies were generating different types of reports. This was because each company was on a different platform. In the new Nicholas Piramal, all finance was under one CFO. At Roche Products, it was easy because the French managing director simply retired. In BM, nobody wanted the MD's job after the Comsat Forte incident and the finance head was MD for some time. He was then transferred to HR & Admin. under Leonard d'Costa. Everyone else shifted from their scattered offices to the new Nicholas Piramal head office at the Morarjee Mills complex in central Bombay. 'This was very important, otherwise the other integration would not have been feasible. Our staff strength has reduced by almost 30 per cent over time since the merger. Web-based ERP will further reduce that', said Gupta, who spent 80 per cent of his time at Nicholas Piramal and the balance for the group. Nicholas was reimbursed for group services rendered by him.

Overall, it took a little more than two years for the operational rationalisation to be completed. As Balgi pointed out: 'We are one of the few companies in India where the entire process of integration has taken place. We started in September 1997 for all three companies, when we started physically moving three sets of people, and the process was more or less completed by December 1999 though we are still trying to get to grips with developing a new culture.'

Two-way Movement of People

Transfers: Between 1997 and 1999, there were a spate of transfers, with people being moved out of their companies into new positions at Nicholas Piramal. Gupta explained: 'People would have preferred to stay in their own pre-merger silos, but we broke this structure and consolidated and transferred people keeping in mind the company's needs and their strengths. For example, in treasury, the BM person was stronger; in sales accounts, the Roche manager was stronger; and in general ledger and MIS, the Nicholas person was stronger. So the head of each function was from those companies but below him, his team was brought together from all companies. People moved into these new groups, and their strengths and cultures were integrated.'

A similar exercise was undertaken for all jobs. At every level, the best person was selected, irrespective of the company he or she had been in earlier. At the same time, an effort was made to redesign jobs so that all the three people working at that level in their company were given equal importance in the new Nicholas Piramal. The HR function, for example, was divided into three parts, with all three HR heads being given equal importance: HR (Marketing) was Balgi from BM, HR (Training and Development) was given to Mendonca (who returned to the merged entity after having worked previously at the group), and HR (Manufacturing) was given to Dhanawade from Nicholas.

'The company might have lost out a little bit in terms of money in the short term, but the image of the company grew, both within and outside. The image rubbed off on joint ventures and helped us in getting the alliance partners we needed', said Balgi. BM's IT head became the IT head of the new Nicholas Piramal. Nicholas Piramal's IR and legal head became president of this function for the entire company. Manufacturing was headed by Jagdish Saigal (originally from Nicholas Piramal), who was the most experienced in this field. He was senior and so was instantly acceptable. A quick assessment was made and taken care of at the third and fourth levels. 'The acceptability of the choices was not a problem because Dr Pinto, who was totally new in the company himself, was perceived by employees as an unbiased and fair person', said d'Costa.

Redesigning Work: 'We eliminated top levels of management without firing many people', said Pinto. 'In many cases, a person's job underwent a major overhaul. The BM finance manager, for example, was very good in taxation. After the changes, he looked after taxation for the entire Piramal Enterprises group. His role and job content was enlarged.' In another case, there was Baseen, a promising rep from the field force without a role to play. 'Baseen lost 5 kg, knew nothing about computers and learnt from scratch, and offered to look after one of the learning centres that we were planning to build. Today, he is one of the stars in our Delhi office', said Pinto.

In April 1999, the state business manager (SBM) concept was introduced. Majority of the eighteen SBMs had been formerly working as regional managers. However, three junior managers were given the opportunity to be SBMs. 'So, the situation and feeling was created that wherever you may be, you can rise quickly through the organisation if you perform', said one middle level manager. Nonetheless, it was a traumatic period for everyone. As Gupta pointed out: 'We looked at our employee strength, we rationalised plants and cut overheads. As people reduce and integration takes place, people feel less important. Also, as the whole group was growing fast, some normal attrition was there, but then we also had a pool of ready people.'

Upgrading Processes

The process of integrating diversity was used as an opportunity to benchmark processes in each of the companies and the best was accepted as the new standard. During the evaluation exercise, at times entirely new processes evolved which were better than the earlier ones, making for a stronger company.

Manufacturing Processes: The gain in productivity at the plant was 30 per cent and increased by 10 per cent every year. The Pithampur plant was commissioned in 1992. It was of international standard and made tablets. Mahad, also of international standard, concentrated on capsules and liquid. There were several advantages of making these plants conform to international standards:

- The prestige and confidence of producing world-class products under common Good Manufacturing Practices (GMP) standards.
- Improved flow of processes.
- The ease and readiness with which MNCs and strategic alliance partners gave contract manufacture of their products to the units.

Accounting Processes: 'We use our systems to spread the Return on Capital Employed (ROCE) "mantra" all over the organisation. Nowadays, all business units have real-time access to information such as the contribution of each product line to the results of the company, including ROCE calculations. This information is very important as their remuneration is linked to it. And making it available instantaneously has a powerful motivational impact on the senior and middle management levels', said Gupta.

IT and Knowledge Management: 'Meetings are not enough to achieve control and share knowledge. It is essential to have the right systems in place. We have invested heavily in IT lately to use it more effectively as a tool for internal governance and decision making. We have connected all business units and functions with Lotus Notes and we are using VSAT to overcome limitations in the Indian telecommunications infrastructure. As a result of our efforts, we must be one of the few Indian pharma companies to have a homogenous IT infrastructure. Some of our rivals, for example, run on three different systems. The IT systems are complemented by and integrated with the management systems. It is fundamental for us to develop best management practices in every sphere if we want to succeed in the WTO era', said Piramal.

He added: 'Regarding knowledge sharing, we have implemented a knowledge management system that will serve as a knowledge database for the company with instant access to all units and functions. We will use it fundamentally to share successful stories in the most effective and quick way inside the group. We also think there is a motivational aspect in this initiative, as people will get empowered by seeing their successful stories being shared in the company. It will be a powerful way to recognise their contribution.'

Best Practices Programmes: As part of its policy to imbibe best management practices, the company has developed several internal programmes, such as:

- ISO 9000, 5S and Kaizen quality programmes.
- WOW: Winners of the World (a benchmarking programme).
- RAP: Rapid Action Projects (small cross-functional teams involved in specific projects. A tool to generate quick wins and motivate the workforce).
- SMART: Simple, Motivated, Accountable, Responsive, Thoroughly professional.
- TACS: Total and Absolute Compliance with Standards.

These programmes not only improved the quality of the final products and the efficiency and safety of the processes (essential to achieve USFDA approval), they also made the organisation more responsive by improving employees' motivation and commitment.

Audit Committee: Besides external governance, Nicholas Piramal was also trying to create appropriate internal controls. Said Gupta: 'In India, several companies get their audits done by local companies, some of whom have the habit of overlooking numbers that don't tally. This has resulted in a loss of credibility with investors, in general, for Indian audit firms. Since corporate governance and transparency are fundamental to retaining shareholder confidence, we retained PriceWaterhouseCoopers, who are internationally reputed, as our external statutory auditors and formed a committee made up of non-executive directors, so that the process was totally transparent. In my view, such things add to your credibility as a company'.

Piramal also proposed the creation of an audit committee, made up of only non-executive board members specialising in financial and legal disciplines, to monitor the activities undertaken by the company. In addition, the company created an active internal audit department overseen by PWC that reported directly to the board.

Changing Behaviour

Changing Guidelines: Changing the behaviour of people is very difficult, therefore it is easier to change culture. Each of the erstwhile organisations had its own culture. MNCs pay their people more and expect certain dress codes. Nicholas was formerly a branch of Schering, so an MNC culture existed in it. It was driven from the top, and there were rules and regulations to follow. However, it was not as professional in that reps did not wear ties, etc, Roche had a Swiss culture. It was hierarchical and also driven from the top. Here, there were even more rules and regulations to follow. Reps were meant to dress in a certain way when going to see the doctor. In Roche (and BM), if a rep did not wear a tie, he felt like he had no clothes on! BM had a German culture. It was more decentralised than the other two. It was similar to Roche in that it also had an MNC culture where reps had to follow dress codes, etc., but their pattern of making calls to the doctor was very different since they sold diagnostics also. Now we had to set an example for them. In the first two years after the merger, we made them wear suits. Now we are gradually making them more informal', said Pinto.

'In Nicholas, in fact in all three companies, the bottom line was pretty average. We implemented change without changing people. For example, the change in Roche was immediate. They used to take four to five months to close audited accounts. We achieved the same in seventeen days. Of course, when we told them this, they said it was not possible. I said, "Don't tell me what is not possible; tell me what you need to make it possible". And in April 1998, at the end of the financial year, we made sure that performers were rewarded. And we delivered exactly what was promised', said Gupta.

The career of Rajiv Nangia is perhaps the best example of the impact the changed environment had on managers' behaviours. A middle-level manager from Delhi, Nangia was a regional manager who was promoted to SBM. 'He did not know how to read a balance sheet, but now he does. He runs his office like a business. He is measured on entrepreneurship and people. Earlier, he would maybe have been classified as a '5 on 10', but now he is a great performer. Delhi grew by 52 per cent in 1999-2000. Another example is Assam. Assam used to feel very isolated from the rest of the country and the company. Now, they are growing at 10 per cent', said Pinto.

7Σ Project: The 7Σ project was the most important of the change programmes introduced at the new Nicholas Piramal. According to Pinto, Σ is a symbol for 'togetherness, unity'. It was strongly linked to the remuneration policy for senior management (it started with about forty managers and within two years covered about 100). Each of the seven aspects of the framework (Action, Strategy, People, Entrepreneurship, Customers, Technology and Systems) had its own weight in the managers' remuneration package. The strongest weightage (almost 50 per cent) was given to entrepreneurship.

Pinto also remarked, 'I can't stress enough the importance of entrepreneurship for us. We Indians like to talk a lot, but you need to focus peoples' energy into action. Therefore, we have linked the compensation policy with the 7Σ framework. All managers have to fill the 7Σ form monthly for their individual performance appraisals. One important aspect of this framework is that it was not imposed on the management team. It was thoroughly discussed and the version that exists today is a result of consensus among the entire team. So they are strongly committed to it.'

Piramal said: 'One of our main challenges is to keep the entrepreneurship flame alive throughout the company. Therefore, we are trying to give as much autonomy, authority and responsibility as possible to the business units. We know that we may reach a tough situation in the future, when the business units become larger and we need to find the balance between autonomy and integration. But so far we have managed to reconcile both needs without any problem. We balance autonomy with control by holding regular meetings with the business and function heads. We have a matrix structure, with the business units sharing functional resources such as R&D, manufacturing, distribution and marketing. Regular meetings at both the business unit and functional levels help us keep track of what is happening as well as induce knowledge sharing across the company and its joint venture subsidiaries. The programme has helped improve standards through the company. It was also a blend of finesse and training that has made the integration as smooth as it has been.'

When the Best is Not Always Wise: Said Balgi, 'When it comes to compensation packages, we could not take the best from each company. For example, the retirement ages at Nicholas Piramal, BM and PHL were 58, 60 and 60 respectively. Also, we could not give the best in terms of salary at every level. So we came up with a new structure altogether for management.'

Salaries were 12–15 per cent below industry levels. 'We felt that this could lead to sub-performance', said Balgi. Therefore, a new pay-for-performance scheme was introduced for the top 100 managers in Nicholas Piramal. It had a fixed component to compensate for inflation and a second component to recognise entrepreneurship through the measurement of ROCE, sales and profits, formalised through the Σ7 programme.

Creating A New Identity

Investor Relations: 'We realise the importance of being respected and admired by investors. This is fundamental if we want to have access to capital markets, both locally and internationally. To this end, we have created the part-time position of vice president, investor relations. He organises quarterly meetings that involve Dr Pinto, Mahesh Gupta, CFO, myself and more than 100 investors. We also care about providing investors (and the board) with relevant and timely information', said Piramal.

'We have started providing a US GAAP version of our accounts. As far as I know, we will be the first Indian pharmaceutical company to do so. We will also improve the quality and transparency of our annual reports. The entire management team agrees that Indian accounting principles are not transparent enough if we wish to go international or list on a foreign exchange. Also, they are not adequate enough to account for alliances and acquisitions, which are an important aspect of our strategy. We believe that these moves will make us more investment-friendly to Indian and international investors. The Confederation of Indian Industry (CII) has developed a thorough and progressive corporate governance code that is also helping us improve the quality of the information we provide to the public', said Piramal.

Corporate Governance: Piramal also laid stress on the issue of corporate governance. 'We have made it a point to make all important announcements public. For example, I have committed that all PEL's interests in the pharmaceutical sector will be handled through Nicholas Piramal. I have also committed that we will not use the cash generated in the pharmaceutical business to invest in other group companies. If we have cash lying in our bank account for more than three years without any attractive investment (which means an ROCE of at least 25 per cent), we will distribute it as dividends. I have also committed that we will not go into capital-intensive projects. We do not plan to become overloaded with assets. That was the logic that drove the spin-off of Gujarat Glass.'

'You may think that these announcements constrain our managerial flexibility', he continued, 'but I believe that they are very important because they force us to be disciplined and bind us to some key principles, which I don't believe will change in the short or medium term. They also give confidence to investors and other stakeholders—everybody prefers to play the game when they clearly know and understand the rules. Good corporate governance ensures that investors will feel comfortable to invest in you, partners will feel comfortable to develop alliances with you, and employees will feel comfortable and motivated to perform for the company.'

'Another move we made was to sell 9.9 per cent of the company's equity to EM Warburg Pincus, which is a US private equity fund and one of the largest in the world. They are a highly regarded investor, specialise in the health care industry, and by getting them on board we will improve our credibility in the eyes of investors and other stakeholders. They also have a long-term perspective, and this is the kind of investor that we want. We have given them a place on the board of directors—this once again forces more governance on the company and forces more discipline on our managers. Also, given our international expansion aspirations, we believe they will be a valuable source of funds and expertise in the future.'

Building a Common Goal and Vision

At Nicholas Piramal, long-term planning for the future meant taking into consideration:

- Accelerated long-term growth potential of the pharma market in India.
- Implications of the post-GATT period on the Indian pharma industry.
- Anticipated gradual changes in the geographical expansion of the domestic market and the differential product portfolio needs of urban vs. rural areas.
- Potential of India as a global source for world-class pharma products at low cost.

In terms of a business strategy to capture this potential business, Nicholas Piramal felt that it had to:

- Become the most admired health care company in India with world-class management capability, with sales in excess of Rs 10 bn and profits above Rs 1.5 bn.

- Develop a powerful new product pipeline.
- Build a state-of-the-art medical marketing programme in India with a strong market share in the selected categories of biotech, nutrition, diagnostics, gastro-intestinal, CVS/diabetes, infectious diseases, OTC and select-speciality niches.
- Build three independent, profitable, stand-alone businesses in pharma, bulk drug and flaconnage (glass).
- Boost shareholder value by improving quality of earnings.
- Fulfill trusteeship obligation to customers, employees, shareholders and society.

The question was, how does one become the most admired company? What should be the benchmark? Eventually, it was decided that Nicholas Piramal would set its new value statement as the standard for measuring performance.

Nicholas Piramal's Value Statement

In our pursuit of excellence and growth, we shall act as Trustees for our Customers, Employees, Shareholders and Society by:

- Continually enhancing value for our customers with quality products and services to meet their changing needs.
- Empowering our employees, encouraging innovation and entrepreneurship in an environment which makes work fun.
- Steadily building wealth for our shareholders.
- Contributing to the well-being of society and the environment.

We shall make innovation and change a way of life at all times and conduct ourselves with honesty, fairness and trust in God.

Underneath the fuzzy value statement was a hard, clear action plan which called for a focus on disease segments and new products. Twenty new products were to be launched over the next two years.

Results of the Strategy

Growth

Nicholas Piramal became one of India's fastest-growing companies. Sales increased twenty-six-fold in the ten years (CAGR 40 per cent) since the group acquired Nicholas Laboratories in 1988, or nine-fold (CAGR 33 per cent) if the period 1988-96 before the triple merger occurred is considered. From 1988 to 1997, the company climbed up the sales charts, going from the forty-eighth to the fifth position. Profitability also increased significantly: seventy-three-fold between 1988 and 1998 (CAGR 53 per cent), or thirty-eight-fold between 1988 and 1996 (CAGR 58 per cent), considering only the pre-triple merger period. Nicholas Piramal's market capitalisation increased from Rs 66 mn in 1988 to about Rs 13 bn in September 1999 (CAGR 58 per cent).

Piramal Enterprises: For the Piramal group as a whole, the diversification into pharmaceuticals had fulfilled the group objective of reducing dependence on the Mumbai-based textile industry.

Interconnect 99: In December 1998, there was a group-wide meeting called Interconnect 99. The purpose of this meeting was to exchange ideas between group companies, for each of them to put forward their future strategies, and for top management to communicate the vision and discuss the values of the group as a whole (as had been discussed in preceding months by the top twenty-five or thirty managers in the group). The event lasted for two days and involved more than 300 people, including middle managers and top executives of the entire group.

The other businesses also benefited from the abilities developed in the pharmaceuticals arm of the group, such as the ability to deal with the unionised labour force, and expertise in developing and managing alliances and joint ventures. 'We have disseminated the culture of alliances in the whole group. Morarjee Mills has recently floated two joint ventures. In the hard ferrite business, we have formed an alliance with TDK of Japan. So, our experience with Nicholas has really helped the group as a whole', opined Piramal.

The Family: 'When I think of investors, I don't forget that the family also has to be considered. A big question on my mind today is the role of the family in the future. And given our large stake in the business, it is very important to assure that we play the right role in the company. My view is that we must be interested in building "wealth" instead of "control". That is the best way to align our interests with the interests of all other stakeholders. And we will only be involved in management if we can add value to the company. I do believe that if you have a shareholder who also has management capability, this is a powerful advantage because it makes it easier to align the interests of management and shareholders. Still, I have not fully resolved this question in my mind yet.'

'Finally, regarding my own role in the group', explained Piramal, 'I feel that I have undergone a transition from business development to people development. Initially, my main role was to drive the acquisitions we made. Then, I got involved with the forming of alliances; but now that the team has became so good at doing all these things, I do not have to involve myself in the details anymore. As time goes by, and as we become larger and more dispersed over countries, I feel that my role will evolve to one of providing the right values and overall strategic direction for the company, and to challenge, develop and motivate the employees.'

As the company looked forward to a bright future in the 21st century, the present was reassuring. Good strategies, world-class plants and the new emphasis on performance had resulted in the company entering a fast growth track. Integrating diversity had worked well because growth had ensured space for everyone.

But as the environment becomes more competitive and the forces of globalisation impact the Indian pharmaceutical industry, new challenges will present themselves to both the Piramal family and the team of professionals running the company. In which areas will they have to change? What should be the path ahead to safeguard and ensure Nicholas Piramal's long-term survival?

APPENDIX 1

Piramal Group Revenues by Sector, 1987–88 and 1999–2000

(Rs million)

Company	Business	Sales FY88	Sales FY00
Nicholas Piramal	Pharmaceuticals	–	4860
Alliances and subsidiaries	Pharmaceuticals, OTC	–	4850
Gujarat Glass (Subsidiary)	Glass	104	2250
Morarjee and JVs	Textiles	1098	3400
Miranda Tools and JVs	Machine tools	89	300
PMP	Auto components	71	220
GP Electronics	Ferrites	22	120
Piramal Holdings, Piramal Retail, etc.	Mall management, retail, entertainment	–	625
Others	IT	120	15
Total (Approx.)		1504	16640

Source: Company reports.

Nicholas Piramal: Sales Growth

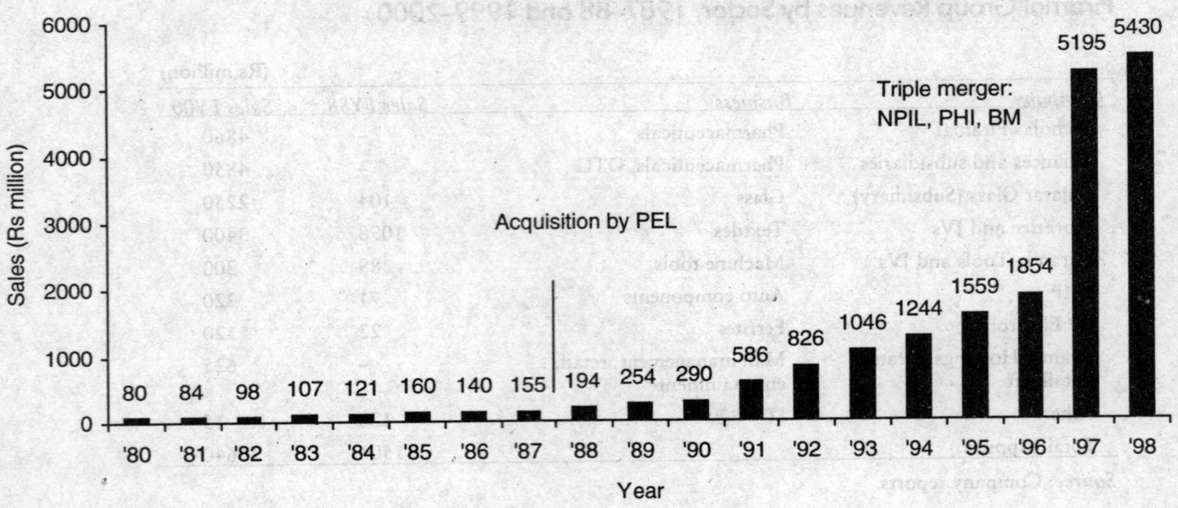

Nicholas Piramal: Profit after Tax

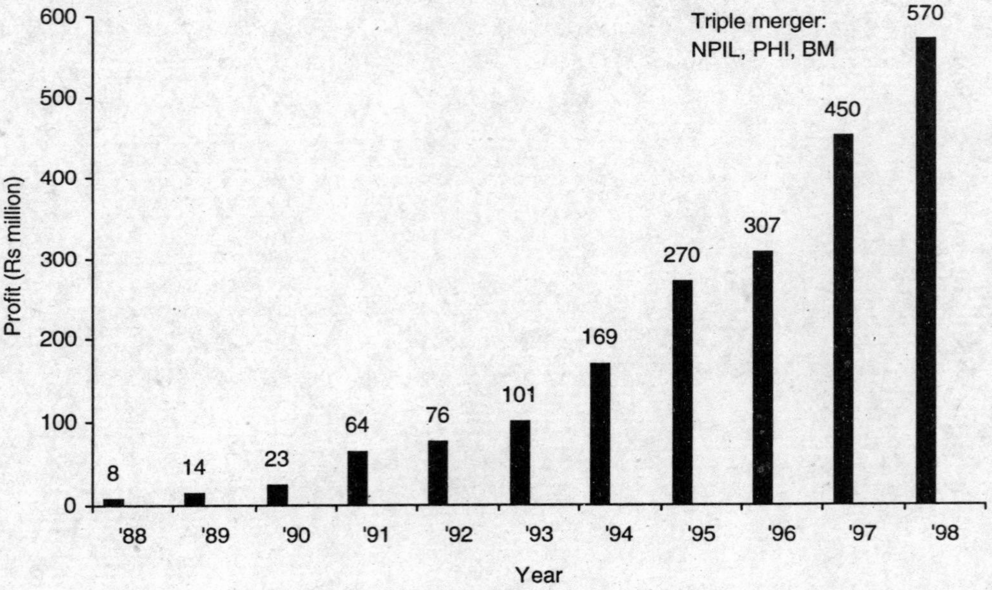

APPENDIX 2

Piramal Group Strategy Ladder

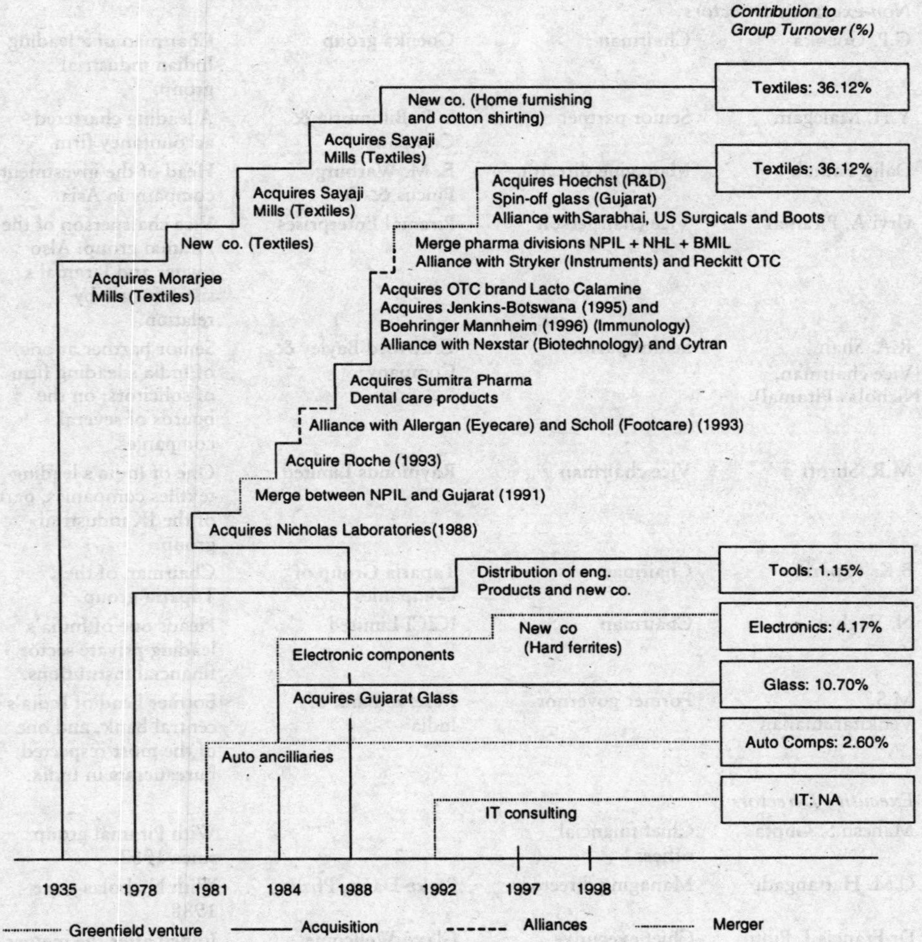

Contribution to Group Turnover (%)
Textiles: 36.12%
Textiles: 36.12%
New co. (Home furnishing and cotton shirting)
Acquires Sayaji Mills (Textiles)
Acquires Sayaji Mills (Textiles)
New co. (Textiles)
Acquires Morarjee Mills (Textiles)
Acquires Hoechst (R&D)
Spin-off glass (Gujarat)
Alliance withSarabhai, US Surgicals and Boots
Merge pharma divisions NPIL + NHL + BMIL
Alliance with Stryker (Instruments) and Reckitt OTC
Acquires OTC brand Lacto Calamine
Acquires Jenkins-Botswana (1995) and
Boehringer Mannheim (1996) (Immunology)
Alliance with Nexstar (Biotechnology) and Cytran
Acquires Sumitra Pharma
Dental care products
Alliance with Allergan (Eyecare) and Scholl (Footcare) (1993)
Acquire Roche (1993)
Merge between NPIL and Gujarat (1991)
Acquires Nicholas Laboratories(1988)
Distribution of eng. Products and new co.
Tools: 1.15%
New co (Hard ferrites)
Electronics: 4.17%
Electronic components
Acquires Gujarat Glass
Glass: 10.70%
Auto Comps: 2.60%
Auto ancilliaries
IT consulting
IT: NA
1935
1978
1981
1984
1988
1992
1997
1998
Greenfield venture
Acquisition
Alliances
Merger

Source: Business Today, 7 January 1998, and company reports.

APPENDIX 3

Nicholas Piramal Board of Directors, 2000

Non-executive Directors			
G.P. Goenka	Chairman	Goenka group	Chairman of a leading Indian industrial group.
Y.H. Malegam	Senior partner	S. B. Billimoria & Company	A leading chartered accountancy firm.
Dalip Pathak	Managing director	E. M. Warburg Pincus & Co.	Head of the investment company in Asia.
Urvi A. Piramal	Vice chairperson	Piramal Enterprises	Vice chairperson of the Piramal group. Also owner and Piramal's sister-in-law by relation.
R.A. Shah (Vice chairman, Nicholas Piramal)	Senior partner	Crawford Bayley & Company	Senior partner at one of India's leading firm of solicitors; on the boards of several companies.
M.R. Shroff	Vice chairman	Raymonds Limited	One of India's leading textiles companies, part of the JK industrial group.
B.K. Taparia	Chairman	Taparia Group of Companies	Chairman of the Taparia group.
N. Vaghul	Chairman	ICICI Limited	Heads one of India's leading private sector financial institutions.
M.S. Venkitaramanan	Former governor	Reserve Bank of India	Former head of India's central bank, and one of the most respected bureaucrats in India.
Executive Directors			
Mahesh S. Gupta	Chief financial officer		With Piramal group since 1982.
C.M. Hattangadi	Managing director	Parke-Davis, Pfizer	With Nicholas since 1988.
Dr Francis J. Pinto	Chief executive officer	Glaxo Wellcome, Pfizer	Joined after the merger in April 1997.
Ajay G. Piramal	Chairman	Family	
Dr Swati A. Piramal	Chief scientific officer	Family	
Vijay Shah	Chief operating officer	Gujarat Glass	Moved to Nicholas Piramal after the merger.

APPENDIX 4

Nicholas Piramal Top Management Team, 2000

Ajay Piramal	Chairman	Family
C. M. Hattangadi	Managing director	With Nicholas since 1988
Francis Pinto	Chief executive officer	Glaxo Wellcome (New)
Swati Piramal	Chief scientific officer	Family
Vijay Shah	Chief pperating officer	Gujarat Glass (New)
Mahesh Gupta	Chief financial officer	With Piramal group since 1982
Leonard d'Costa	President, HRD	Taj Group of Hotels (New)
Rustom Bharucha	President, IR and legal	Glaxo India (New)
Jagdish Saigal	Exec. Dir. (Vitamins and bulk)	With Nicholas since 1983
Harish Chawla	Chief information officer	From IBM (India), joined 1999

CASE 13

WIPRO CORPORATION: BALANCING THE FUTURE

Azim H. Premji returned from Stanford University in 1967, abandoning his engineering studies, to take charge of the family business that was left rudderless due to the sudden demise of his father. Over the next twenty-seven years, Premji transformed the Rs 70 mn cooking and baking fats company—Western India Vegetable Products Limited—into the Rs 7.24 bn diversified Wipro Corporation that, in 1994, was one of the top 100 publicly held companies in India. Apart from being the market leader in the traditional cooking fats business, the company held the No. 2 position in India in the information technology and medical systems businesses, and the No.3 slot in the precision engineered hydraulic products business (see Appendix 1). Over the preceding ten years, the company's sales and profit after tax had grown at an annual compounded rate of 26 per cent and 25 per cent respectively, and its net worth had recorded a compounded annual growth rate of 22 per cent. Over the same period, capital

This case was written by J. Ramachandran, Professor at the Indian Institute of Management, Banaglore and Sumantra Ghoshal, Robert P. Baumann Professor of Strategic Leadership at the London Business School. The authors are grateful to Wipro Corporation for their help and support in writing this case. This case was first registered by the London Business School in 1997.

appreciation and dividends had yielded an average 62 per cent compounded annual return to the company's shareholders, who also had the satisfaction of seeing their company being widely cited as a model of the 'ethical corporation'.

In 1994, however, the company was in the midst of what Premji described as a 'paradigm shift' in its environment. Radical changes in the government's economic policies and the resulting large scale entry of multinational companies in India had led to competition that was not only much more fierce but also qualitatively different from the past. As a result Wipro was confronting a situation where it had to make some hard choices or else risk hitting the dividers on the road.

Perhaps the most fundamental choice was about the very basic identity of the company. Even though Premji disliked the label of a conglomerate, Wipro was essentially a combination of a number of very different businesses. Unrelated diversification had proved to be an effective means to growth in a regulated environment. However, regulatory and other barriers that had prevented large global companies from operating directly in India, and had partly facilitated Wipro's successes, were being rapidly dismantled. As a consequence, Wipro, to stay competitive, needed to support each of its businesses with significant financial and managerial investments against competitors with the world's best technologies and brands as well as deep pockets and commitments. Should Wipro sustain all the businesses through such investments? Or should it focus on a relatively few businesses and build a more homogeneous portfolio? Should it, through such a process, aim to become a very different company than what it was in 1994?

A similar review was necessary of the company's basic management approach. What should be the roles and responsibilities of the teams managing each of the businesses? How should the corporate management, including Premji himself, add value? Historically, the corporate–division relationship in Wipro followed neither a holding company philosophy nor that of a typical integrated industrial company. Should the somewhat ambiguous but highly flexible relationship that had been so effective in the past be continued in the future? Or did it need adaptation—perhaps some more clarity and formalisation—given the increasing size and complexity of the company and of the businesses themselves?

Wipro in 1994

In 1994, Wipro Corporation's activities spanned vanaspati, toilet soaps, toiletries, hydraulic cylinders, computer hardware and software, lighting, financial services, medical systems, diagnostic systems and leather exports. While the various activities were structured into five distinct legal entities, Wipro Corporation, for the purposes of management control, was split into eight separate 'mini companies', each with its own separate 'equity' (see Appendix 2). These were Wipro Consumer Products, Wipro Lighting, Wipro Fluid Power, Wipro Financial Services, two businesses in the field of information technology—Wipro Infotech and Wipro Systems—and finally the two health care related businesses—Wipro GE and Wipro Biomed. While Wipro had international tie-ups in many of its activities, only Wipro GE, its medical systems business, was a financial joint venture between Wipro and the US giant General Electric (GE).

Wipro Consumer Products

The Rs 2 bn Wipro Consumer Products (WCP) was, for long, the largest 'company' in Wipro Corporation's portfolio. However, following three flat years in turnover, it yielded this position to Wipro Infotech in 1993 (see Appendix 3). It manufactured and marketed the traditional vanaspati products, fatty acid and glycerine, toilet soaps, toiletries and leather products for the export market.

In 1994, WCP produced vanaspati at three plants spread over the western and southern parts of India, the markets it operated in. The industry was segmented along geographical lines due to high transportation costs. All the players operated in specific geographic pockets. The company's 'Camel' and 'Black Bird' brands, which served the needs of commercial users like biscuit manufacturers and bakeries, were the market leaders in the institutional segment; and its flagship brand 'Sunflower' had recorded gains in market share, despite increased competition, in the consumer segment.

The market for vanaspati, which constituted 15 per cent of the edible cooking medium market in India, was fiercely competitive and margins were wafer thin. P.S. Pai, president, WCP, said: 'On the one hand we confront fierce competition from small unorganised players among whom tax evasion is rampant and on the other we are faced with a government policy which provides 9 per cent advantage to a new entrant in a 4 per cent margin business!'

Favourable government policy had led to large-scale entry and in 1994 the industry was riddled with excess capacity. Further, prices of the major raw material—edible oil—fluctuated on a daily basis. As a consequence, the vanaspati business had become what Pai described as a 'commodity trade' business. 'Today even the consumer segment has become price dependent. Vanaspati is a low margin–low value addition business. Material cost control is the key. Both input prices and output prices fluctuate on a daily basis. Every Monday morning I sit along with my vice presidents in-charge of buying and sales—all of us have been with Wipro for over fifteen years now—and take positions for the week. Our practice for over two decades, when Premji first introduced it, has been to take weekly positions and not daily positions. That it works is reflected in our bottom line.'

Vanaspati operations contributed to over half of the WCP turnover in 1993-94. However, its share in WCP turnover has been coming down over the years due to growth in other WCP activities, especially its toilet soap business. In 1993-94, the toilet soaps business contributed Rs 60.04 mn to WCP's turnover.

While WCP had earlier entered the toilet soap market through 'Bubbles', a special soap for children, and had also established a distinct niche through Wipro Shikakai, a special hair care soap containing soap nut extract, its real success in that business followed the 1985 launch of Santoor, a soap based on a turmeric-sandalwood combination, a traditional Indian recipe for beauty and skin care. Pai explained: 'Swastik, which had been the leader in hair care soaps, was dying due to internal troubles. We seized the opportunity and entered that segment with Wipro Shikakai. Similarly when Mysore Sales International—whose Mysore Sandal brand was the market leader in the sandalwood segment—was experiencing management trouble, we sensed an opportunity and launched Santoor.'

In 1994, despite the dominance of the Indian toilet soap market by Hindustan Lever, and P&G–Godrej, the local joint venture of the US giant Proctor and Gamble, Wipro's 'ethnic' brands held their own. Their success was both due to their sharp focus on distinct niches and the absence of competition from the toilet majors in these niches.

Pai said: 'Our strategy in the toilet soaps business is to operate below the radar zones of the giants. They know about it and respect us for it.'

While scanning for 'below the radar zone' opportunities, the WCP team, in 1990, identified an opportunity in the baby care products market, long dominated by the local subsidiary of the US multinational Johnson and Johnson (J&J). The Wipro team not only found J&J products to be high priced, but also that the retail channels were extremely dissatisfied with the service they received from J&J. They sought to leverage both—Wipro's reputation for quality and the strong links they had built up with the retail channel—and launched the Wipro Baby Soft range of products, with price as the principal benefit to the consumer. With substantial advertising support in the launch year, the Baby Soft range quickly garnered 18 per cent share of the market.

The Baby Soft range, however, could not gain any further share as J&J reacted strongly. J&J stepped up its ad spends significantly and launched a number of strong promotion schemes for the channel. WCP went on the defensive as the Baby Soft range was not contributing to the bottom line. It streamlined and reoriented its advertising budget and, in 1994, the company planned to use direct marketing in a major way for generating volumes and to use mass media to primarily create reassurance about the product.

The launch of Baby Soft also signalled WCP's entry into the toiletries market with talcum powder, a segment dominated by another Unilever subsidiary in India, Ponds. In 1993-94, Wipro Baby Soft talcum powder and Santoor beauty talc together had 2.6 per cent share of the talc market and contributed Rs 37.5 mn to WCP's turnover.

'High fashion' shoe uppers was another product in WCP's portfolio. This export market-oriented business generated a turnover of over Rs 70 mn, bulk of which stemmed from sales to a single customer, viz., Clarks of UK. The returns from this business had improved following devaluation and partial convertibility of the Indian rupee.

In 1994, Pai and his team were in the middle of preparing a ten-year perspective plan for WCP. Not only were they targeting to regain their lost leadership position in Wipro Corporation's portfolio, they were seeking to increase market share in all product categories significantly. Pai said: 'We are aiming for 10 per cent of both the edible fats market and the Indian toilet soap market at the end of ten-years.[1] It is a ten-year investment now. The days of three-year payback

1. The edible fats market, included, apart from vanaspati, edible refined oils. The edible refined oil market was yet another competitive market, with a multitude of players including WCP rival in the vanaspati market Lipton. The other major players were ITC—a

period are over. We need to invest in building brands. The competition, especially from MNCs, is severe and returns not easy to come by despite our strong distribution strength.'

Wipro Fluid Power

Wipro Fluid Power (WFP), in 1994, was a Rs 2 bn operation. The company was the market leader in hydraulic cylinders and its customers included all major earth-moving and construction equipment manufacturers in India viz., TELCO, Escorts JCB and Bharat Earth Movers Limited. WFP's product range included hydraulic truck tipping systems, pumps, valves, and custom-built hydraulic systems. It manufactured hydraulic tipping systems with technical know-how from Nencki, Ag., Switzerland. It also had a strategic alliance with Eaton Corporation, USA, for marketing their steering systems, hydrostatic transmissions and other hydraulic elements in the Indian market.

Wipro entered the hydraulics market in 1973. M.S.Rao, president, WFP, who has been with WFP right from inception said, 'Hydraulics seemed a good niche market to get into, requiring just the kind of investments we could afford with our size of business at that time.' Premji added: 'It was a high growth market and the competition was weak. We were confident that by focussing on the right segments we could generate significant returns.'

At the time of its entry, Wipro did not have any in-house capability for the manufacture of hydraulic cylinders. Nevertheless, it decided not to take on any foreign collaborator for the manufacture of cylinders as it wanted to avoid getting locked into rigid foreign specifications. A small research and development team was set up to design and develop the cylinders. Market acceptance of the product developed in-house was difficult to come by. The resistance was high, not the least of which was due to Wipro's then image of a vanaspati company. However, due to the good quality and design and superior performance of its products, WFP improved its market position and in 1994 was the fastest-growing and best-known manufacturer of hydraulic cylinders. Between 1990 and 1994, the company's turnover, despite recessionary trends in some of the end user market segments like machine tools and hydraulic cranes, had nearly trebled with an even better performance on the profitability front. Premji attributes the sustained improvement in WFP's market position to

---

Rs 40 bn diversified company and one of the largest private sector companies in India with presence in cigarettes, hotels, and printing and packaging, and the government co-operative National Dairy Development Board, the current market leader in the edible oils market.

Wipro's strong belief in R&D and customer service.

> 'We have invested considerably in R&D facilities and have established expertise in offering design solutions to meet customer-specific requirements and are able to absorb and adopt proven and recognised designs. As a consequence, our relationship with our major customers is very strong. Some time back when we had a strike in our manufacturing facility, our customers were willing to wait for our product.'

In 1994, WFP was being positioned to act as one of the spearheads of Wipro's plans to become a global operation. Premji said, 'We are targeting to be global players in the hydraulic cylinders business as we are highly cost and design competitive.' WFP had begun its export thrust in 1991 with the export of 500 cylinders to Sweden. Since then it has been exporting this product to other countries in Europe and Japan. The company was investing Rs 150 mn over the next three years to widen its product range and improve its presence in international markets.

Wipro Infotech

In 1994, the Rs3.2 bn Wipro Infotech (WIL) was the second largest information technology company in India. Its product offerings included PCs, minis, superminis, engineering workstations, mini supercomputers, on-line transaction processing mainframes, laser and dot matrix printers and software products and services addressed to specific customer needs. In 1994, WIL received for the fourth consecutive year the Government of India Department of Electronics Award for Excellence in Electronics. The company had been a recipient of a number of other awards, including the National R&D Award for Electronics. The Wipro PC was the only PC in India to have been awarded the Department of Electronics Certificate of Quality. Independent computer and business journals routinely rated WIL as the best on various parameters, including professional management and customer trust.

Wipro's entry into the computing industry was spurred by the exit of IBM from India in 1977. At that time Premji was seeking to further diversify Wipro's product portfolio and the Indian computer industry, in the absence of a global major like IBM, seemed to offer a good opportunity for Wipro to pursue. Premji expected the demand for computers for commercial applications to grow rapidly and zeroed in on the minicomputer as the appropriate product as it provided the benefits of a mainframe computer, viz., a multi-user environment without being as expensive.

While identification of minicomputers as the appropriate product was relatively easy, it was not easy to access the technology. This was the era of proprietary technology and minicomputer pioneer, Digital Equipment Corporation (DEC), controlled the technology. WIL ruled out the option of approaching DEC for technology as it did not expect the American company to be interested in a partner with no lineage in computing (or electronics) and located in 'far away' India. Further, the company assessed that even if DEC were interested, it would be merely interested in providing Wipro with 'kits' for assembly and would not part with the technology. It, therefore, decided to develop its own minicomputer using Intel's 8086 chip. The choice was largely dictated by the non-proprietary nature of the Intel chip, the availability of other support chips (for input-output operations and memory) for the 8086 and by Intel's plans to develop advanced and faster microprocessors (the subsequent 80286/386/486, etc.). To save time and cost, WIL opted to source the operating software and internal circuitry from a small firm in the US called Sentinel, and a yet-to-be-fully developed database management software from Tominy, another small firm located near Sentinel's office in California.

It took WIL about a year to sort out all the design and software related issues and develop a marketable product. In 1981, WIL unveiled the Wipro Series 86 at the annual computing fair of the Computer Society of India.

The Wipro Series 86 was an instantaneous hit and WIL quickly emerged as the market leader in minicomputers, a position it held in 1994. The company kept pace with the technological changes in the global computing industry largely on the strength of its close relationship with Intel, supported by its own in-house R&D. It had access to Intel's newest offerings six months before their commercial release by Intel. This enabled WIL to offer products in the Indian market which incorporated the latest Intel technology almost at the same time when products incorporating this technology were available in global markets.

WIL also exploited the other changes in the global industry to enhance its product range in the Indian market. The opening up of the PC market, following IBM's radical decision to throw open the technology for PCs to other manufacturers, provided WIL with an opportunity to enter the PC segment. WIL's entry, however, was delayed (HCL, the market leader, launched its PC much ahead of WIL) as it did not have the licence to manufacture PCs. It had to wait for a change in government policy in this regard.

The company, with a view to absorbing the new technology, opted to manufacture PCs by importing components instead of opting for the then popular 'kit' approach, which essentially involved importing PCs in completely knocked down form and assembling them and marketing them. Within a year of the launch of the Wipro Genius range of PCs, WIL became the second largest (after HCL) PC vendor in India.

In 1988, WIL entered into an alliance with Sun Microsystems, USA, for the manufacture and marketing of Sun workstations and quickly became the leader in the workstation market in India. Ashok Soota, president, WIL, said: 'It was the first relationship we actively sought. The workstation market was growing rapidly and we decided to enter it. Sun was the obvious choice as it was the leader.[2] Sun, however, was reluctant to allow us to manufacture, as they did not want to invest their time. I told them we did not want any Sun personnel in India, we just needed the documentation and training for three or four of our people. They finally agreed. Within three weeks of receipt of the first shipment from Sun we were rolling out Sun products from our manufacturing facility. They visited us one year later to audit our facilities. After that visit, they agreed to our exporting to the Russian market from here.'

Following its success in the workstation market, WIL wanted to grow faster than the rest of the industry. Soota explained, 'The only way to do so was to expand the existing segments we were operating in and to enter new segments and become a broad line player.'

To become a broad line player, WIL embarked on a strategy of entering into technological and/or marketing tie-ups with international companies. It entered into a technology tie-up with Seiko-Epson of Japan for the manufacture of dot matrix printers and emerged as one of the leading players in the market for printers (No. 2 in 1994). In addition, it also marketed Epson's laser printers. It entered the mainframe market segment through an alliance with Tandem Computers, USA, for marketing their on-line transaction processing systems for mission critical applications, and with Convex Computers for marketing their superminis in India. And in 1993, the company entered into a strategic alliance with Apple to market the Macintosh range of computers in the Indian market.

2. Apollo (later acquired by HP) was the other major player in workstations and had a tie-up with HCL.

WIL also entered the export market for both hardware and software. It exported its own PCs and the products it manufactured on the Sun platform and undertook software development projects for its partners, Tandem and Sun.

The first part of the 1990s saw a sea change in the computing industry in India. Virtually all the global majors entered the market, either directly or through joint ventures. Digital Equipment, which had a joint venture with its erstwhile distributor, Hinditron, and Fujitsu, which had a presence through the ICL subsidiary in India, ICIM, were joined by Hewlett Packard, which acquired a 26 per cent stake in HCL, the market leader in India, and IBM, which re-entered by setting up a joint venture with Tata, the largest industrial house in India, as its partner (see Appendix 4). WIL, however, stayed away from any overall alliance with a single company. Soota explained: 'The last thing I want to do is surrender my independence. Because of our demonstrated capabilities, we are the first choice for most new entrants. We have the largest and the best dealer and after sales service network in the country. Our Wipro brand equity is high. It is synonymous with quality and integrity. We are also known and respected for the way in which we manage our relationships with foreign partners. In fact, IBM, as we discovered later, had been looking at us as potential joint venture partners. When they had come to meet us they did not tell us they were exploring a joint venture. Instead they told us they were exploring sourcing opportunities from India. We were cool and full of macho feeling then. We don't regret it. I believe we can be competitive without a joint venture. We are in a position to offer the best technology solution to the customers in India and not be tied down to a single technology solution because of our wide ranging alliances.'

In 1993, WIL won the largest single order in Indian computing industry history from the Bombay Stock Exchange (BSE), the leading stock exchange in India. The order, for the second phase of the computerisation of the BSE, was for Rs 380 mn. Umesh Bajaj, vice president, Transactions Solutions Division, said, 'We won the order as we offered the Tandem product. Tandem was ideally suited for the solution they were seeking in that phase.' WIL had won the order for the first phase of the computerisation as well. It had, for that phase, offered a Sun machine-based solution. Soota said, 'We won both the orders because we could offer the product most suited for the solution the customer was seeking.'

However, WIL's strategy of offering the 'best technology solution' was increasingly being rendered difficult by technological and other developments in the global computing industry. The accelerated shift towards open systems, the emergence of networking environments and the rapid growth in client server computing were blurring the lines differentiating the various product market segments globally and in India. As a consequence, companies who were once in distinct market niches had begun to compete with one another. Sun, for example, sought to grow beyond the workstation market and pursued the market for commercial applications aggressively. As a part of this effort it targeted the financial services industry, a niche occupied by Tandem. Both now competed in this market segment worldwide. This had a direct impact on WIL. Sun, following the loss of the BSE order, and with a view to increasing its share of the Indian financial services market, appointed ICIM as a value added re-seller of its products in this market segment in India. ICIM was fairly strong in this segment in India.[3] Additionally, Fujitsu, which had a stake in ICIM (through ICL UK) was the largest worldwide OEM vendor for Sun.

The rapid technological changes also resulted in most computer firms entering into a complex web of alliances, including alliances with their competitors. In some cases this involved acquisition of an equity stake. For example, HP, which had a joint venture with HCL, WIL's major competitor in the Indian market, acquired an equity stake in Convex, with whom WIL had a tie-up for its supermini range of computers.

WIL, thus, was increasingly being forced to cope with the conflict arising out of its multiple alliances and interests. Not only was there an overlap between its representation of Tandem and Sun in the Indian market, it also faced an overlap between its own indigenously developed line of products which were addressing the commercial applications market in India, and the Sun line of products, as Sun increasingly sought a greater share of the commercial applications market. In response, WIL restructured its organisation. It carved itself into nine business divisions (see Appendix 5), each with its own marketing and sales staff, distribution channels, and finance and human resources departments. Each division was set up around its distinct product lines. For example, the Network Systems division was created around the Sun Platform and Sun solutions, the Business Solutions Division was responsible for WIL's indigenously developed line, and the Transactions Solutions Division was responsible for the Tandem and Convex lines. Each of these divisions was allowed, and indeed expected, to compete with the others freely in the marketplace.

3. Sun's tie-up with WIL did not preclude it from appointing other representatives. It had earlier appointed PCL—one of the fastest growing companies in the Indian computing industry—to sell its systems, even though it had a tie-up with WIL at that time. However, the arrangement did not last as PCL failed to make much headway in the market.

A.V. Sridhar, chief executive, Network Systems Division, said: 'We work as a company within the company. Earlier on, our field sales force was not clear whether to quote WIL's Synergy Line or the Sun line to a client. Now, we compete independently. This year we increased our sales of the Sun line substantially by addressing the commercial applications market. In a number of cases we competed head-on with the Business Solutions Division. For example, for the second phase of the BSE order, we competed with the Transactions Solution Division.'

Soota added, 'Our greatest challenge today is to manage the multiple interests. It is quite demanding. So far it has worked well. Though I must add that Sun was not too happy about losing the BSE order to Wipro–Tandem. But that is part of the game. Ultimately, it is a function of how we grow each of the lines.'

In addition to growing the existing product lines, WIL was seeking to further leverage its strong R&D capabilities. In 1994, the company renamed its R&D as Global R&D wing and was in the process of expanding the number of its 'India Development Centres'. Conceived in 1993, these centres provided high level support in developing advanced products for a few select clients. It had already set up three such centres in association with Tandem, Sun and NCR respectively and was planning to set up two more in association with Chorus of France and Ungermann Bass of Germany. Dr Sridhar Mitta, executive vice president (technical) said: 'In 1990, we had to make a choice: we either closed down our R&D, as most other competitors had done, or went global. I felt if we created an international environment here, we could be global providers of technology, services and products. We identified our core competencies as hardware design, operating systems and networking technology. We decided to stick to them and work with a few select customers whom we chose with great care. We also made sure that we did not add more than two customers per year. Our strategy paid off. In 1994, we earned a revenue of Rs 210 mn.'

Soota was also pursuing opportunities for growing WIL beyond the computer industry. The increasing integration between computers and telecommunication was opening up new horizons for WIL. Soota was targeting the emerging market—estimated to be in excess of Rs 4 bn by 1996-97—for value added telecom services. The company had already entered into tie-ups with Nokia for installation, service and maintenance of cellular networks, and with British Telecom for other value added telecom services.[4]

4. Nokia had a tie-up with HCL for marketing its pagers.

Wipro Systems

In 1994, Wipro Systems was one of the star performers in the Wipro Corporation's portfolio, having achieved a growth of over 70 per cent in its revenues. The Rs 440 mn business was the fifth largest software operation in India in 1994 and was primarily in the business of exporting software, including both provision of professional on-site services to overseas clients and undertaking offshore (in India) software development projects for its international clientele (see Appendix 6). In addition, it operated in the domestic market, where, apart from developing customised and standard software packages, it marketed imported software products.

Wipro Systems commenced operations in the early 1980s to tap the growing demand for software. In the initial years, it focussed on developing packaged products on the PC platform for both the domestic and international markets. While its Instaplan, a project management software package, was successful (selling over 40,000 copies in the US market), all others failed. Most of the other products, which were essentially look-alikes of international products such as Lotus 1-2-3, performed poorly even in the domestic market where pirated versions of the international products were available at rock-bottom prices.

Up to 1988-89, the business was in the red. In 1989-90, following a change in the CEO, it turned the corner by making a profit of Rs 3 mn on a turnover of Rs 29 mn. The turnaround was achieved largely by selling imported software products, principally products of Ashton Tate, in the domestic market.

In 1990, following yet another change in CEO, Wipro Systems changed its focus once again. This time it focussed on providing on-site professional services—disparagingly referred to as 'body shopping'—to overseas clients. Until this time, it had steadfastly refused to enter the market for these services, though most software houses in India earned a bulk of their revenues by providing these services. Wipro Systems' entry into this market had a substantial impact on its performance. Turnover increased by over Rs 80 mn in 1991-92 and profits nearly doubled. And for the first time since its operations began, its cumulative profit performance was positive.

Following the turnaround, the then CEO set about expanding the company's hardware facilities and invested Rs 80 mn in acquiring an IBM ES/9000 mainframe. The company also sought to re-enter the domestic packaged software products market and started developing a new accounting software package called Compact.

In 1992, yet another CEO was associated. While the earlier CEOs had been recruited from outside, V. Chandrasekaran, the new CEO, was an 'insider'. Prior to assuming this position, he was vice president in charge of customer services at Wipro Infotech. Chandrasekaran said: 'While I was an insider in the sense that I was from the Wipro group, I was still an outsider here, because over the years an iron curtain had been erected between Wipro Systems and Wipro Infotech. Ironically, Wipro Systems at that time considered Wipro Infotech its major competitor and not Tata Consultancy Services, the market leader.'

Soota, who took over as vice chairman of Wipro Systems at the same time, added: 'To break down the walls, we did contemplate merging the two, as Wipro Infotech also had a strong presence in software development. We, however, decided against it as we felt that the merger could result in Wipro Systems losing IBM and HP as its customers. Wipro Infotech competed against these two in the hardware market.'

Following the changes in leadership, Wipro Systems reviewed its focus. Chandrasekaran said: 'We looked at the market opportunity differently. We were essentially a "services" company. Our strength was our highly talented pool of engineers. We wanted to leverage this strength fully so we targeted the market for offshore software development projects. We decided to focus on a few large accounts and penetrate these accounts deeply and increase our share of software projects from these companies. We then set about looking for customers who would be interested in building a long-term relationship and who would over time consider us an extension of themselves. At that time GE was looking for out-sourcing software from India. We bid for GE's business. They evaluated us, along with others, before awarding any business to us. Here we leveraged Wipro Infotech's standing in the marketplace.'

This strategy of focussing on a few large accounts paid off handsomely. In 1994 over half its software export revenues came from a few clients like GE, USA, Bell Northern Research, Canada, Sequent Computer Systems, USA, etc. By 1994, it had established three software development centres (SDCs) in Bangalore—a fourth was on the anvil—dedicated to servicing the software needs of individual clients. The largest of them, the GE-SDC, had a core group of 140 software engineers who exclusively handled software development, conversion and maintenance assignments for major GE businesses in the US and Far East.[5] In addition, it had a person positioned in GE, USA, as an account manager, whose

5. The other two were the Bell Northern Research SDC and the Sequent Computer Systems SDC.

cost was borne by GE as it felt that having such a person improved the service significantly. Chandrasekaran said: 'We intend to replicate this strategy by taking on a few more major clients and becoming their extension to achieve software exports of a $100 million by year 2000. We will continue to operate in the on-site services market but would increasingly move towards offshore projects.[6] This is rendered even more essential with the new visa restrictions imposed by the US government, which makes obtaining visas for on-site service providers a cumbersome and difficult process.'

In 1993-94, Wipro Systems achieved a turnover of Rs 437 mn. Software exports accounted for Rs 300 mn (in 1992-93 they accounted for Rs 171 mn) or 69 per cent of the total revenue. Of the Rs 130 mn revenue from the domestic market, Rs 40 mn came from consultancy service and the rest from sale of imported software products in the domestic market. The business had agency/distribution tie-ups with Borland, SPSS, WordPerfect, Novell, etc. Besides distributing Borland products within the country, it was authorised to duplicate, market and service Borland products in India, Sri Lanka and Nepal. Its own products, however, continued to fare poorly. It withdrew Compact, the accounting package targeted at large businesses, from the market as it realised that large corporate customers preferred customised accounting software.

In 1994, Wipro Systems' profits were at an all-time high of Rs 43.8 mn. This was in spite of the company having to bear the heavy interest and depreciation charges arising from its Rs 80 mn investment in the IBM ES/9000 mainframe, which had failed to pull in adequate revenue. Software projects on the IBM mainframe were hard to come by, as the market had shifted to client-server computing, following explosive growth in computer networks. Chandrasekaran said, 'We should have foreseen this. But the dominating personality of the earlier CEO caused a breakdown in our otherwise rigorous planning process.' Premji, however, did not agree. 'We had no reason to doubt his judgement. After all he had delivered results.'

Wipro Systems had, in 1993, reorganised its staff around technology and marketing functions. The technology function, headed by a former vice president (R&D) at Wipro Infotech, was split into groups around hardware platforms like VAX, IBM and Tandem, and around market segments like telecom, systems software, etc. The overseas marketing function was reorganised along territorial lines. Eight overseas offices were opened in the US (which accounted for over 90

6. In 1994, 32 per cent of the software export revenues came from offshore software development and the target for 1995 was to increase this share to 55 per cent.

per cent of the export revenues). Additionally, an office was opened in the UK, and a consultant appointed for France. It also entered into arrangement with Epson Malaysia, an 80 per cent Epson owned joint venture there, for achieving entry into the Southeast Asian markets.

> Chandrasekaran said: 'We have moved away from being a 'personality' led organisation, to a more decentralised and systems driven organisation. A "personality" led organisation cannot tap the huge market opportunity lying out there. While one can feel happy at growing at rates better than Indian industry, we need to realise that even the largest software company in India has only a micro-cent share.'

In 1994, Wipro Systems was aiming to be one of the top three software operations in India by the year 2000. Soota said: 'The key issue of course is holding on to talented people. The burgeoning growth of software exports industry has attracted the attention of every major industrial house and almost all of them are planning to enter this industry. Further, all major computer companies (IBM, etc.), who were earlier customers, are setting up or expanding their operations in India. We are one of the prime targets for their recruitment managers.'

Wipro GE

In 1994, with a turnover of nearly Rs 600 mn, Wipro GE (WGE) was the second largest player in the medical systems market in India (see Appendix 7). The Rs 5 bn Indian medical equipment market comprised both imaging systems and therapy instruments, with the former constituting 60 per cent of the market. WGE's product offerings were mainly in this segment. Apart from marketing the products it manufactured—CT scanners, ultrasound systems and Image Intensifiers for X-ray systems—the company marketed and supported the whole range of GE's value added medical systems in India. The company also marketed X-ray equipment manufactured by another local GE joint venture: Elpro International Limited.

In the late1980s, Wipro had identified, as part of its regular opportunity scanning exercise, medical electronics as an area to diversify into. Despite its relatively low potential for growth in terms of turnover, the medical equipment market seemed to offer a good opportunity because of its very high profit potential. Wipro entered this market in 1988 by representing Beckman Instruments, USA. It, however, was keen to go beyond being a distributor of medical equipment of overseas companies and set up local manufacturing facilities.

At the time Wipro was seeking to expand its presence, GE was looking for tie-ups to shore up its presence in India. It had an agency tie-up with IGE, which marketed its medical equipment, including the low end X-ray systems manufactured by its local joint venture, Elpro. After considering over forty prospective partners, GE narrowed its choice down to two: Wipro and its arch rival in the computer industry, HCL. Vivek Paul, president, Wipro GE, who was part of the original GE negotiating team for the joint venture said: 'We looked at Wipro because it was a trusted name. But it was not Wipro's manufacturing or service capability which swung the deal, though they were of great importance, especially Wipro's capability to manage and more importantly grow businesses with high technology content. It was the compatibility between our values and Wipro's values that critically influenced the choice. Both demand very high standards of performance and integrity and both believe in being competitive without compromising on integrity.'

Prasanna, who was then corporate vice president at Wipro Corporation, took over as president of the joint venture with Vivek Paul as the marketing director. The company started its operations by taking over the marketing activities of IGE. Local manufacture began in early 1992. Girish Gaur, formerly vice president operations at WGE and currently corporate vice president, human resources, at Wipro Corporation, said:

> We laid down for ourselves three milestones when we acquired the land for manufacturing facility in April 1991. One was that the plant would be operational in a year's time. We commenced assembly operations in February 1992. The second milestone was to reverse, at least partially, the flow of components by becoming a world class plant by March 1993. Within the first full year of operation we achieved 60 per cent indigenisation on the ultrasound scanners. What's more we received orders for Rs 20 mn worth of components from GE Japan. We also shipped locally manufactured ultrasound scanners to Samsung Medical Systems, South Korea. The third milestone was to develop a new product for the global market by March 1994. We have already developed the prototype of a compact portable ultrasound scanner, designed by our product development team, for the global markets, which would be marketed worldwide as a GE product.

The local manufacture enabled it to offer superior support to customers—a key advantage in the highly competitive medical equipment market. All the global players were operating in India either through their own subsidiaries, as was the case with Siemens, Germany (the world leader) and Philips, Holland, or through Indian representatives as was the case with Toshiba (Indchem), Hitachi (Blue Star), Picker (HCL subsidiary, Network) and Shimadzu (Toshniwal). Vivek Paul said: 'We are successful, despite the tariff benefit afforded to imported systems, because we are committed to offering the Indian medical fraternity something more than just the world's best technology. We offer them total solutions.[7] This includes project feasibility analysis, site planning, marketing support, applications training and the luminary programme.[8] We are keen to build a strong domestic market base. This is crucial for our plan of becoming an important regional sourcing centre for GE to fructify. The larger we become in the domestic market, greater the chances of becoming a global sourcing centre.'

WGE's plans to become a global sourcing centre received a fillip in 1993 when, following changes in government policy, GE increased its equity stake in the company to a majority 51 per cent. Wipro agreed to GE raising its stake on the understanding that it would use WGE as a global sourcing point for ultrasound equipment, subject to the local joint venture meeting GE's quality standards. The two partners also made an agreement that GE's medical software development will be done at Wipro GE. In 1993, WGE exported medical and information services software worth US$ 1.1 mn to GE.

Wipro Biomed

Wipro Biomed was formed in 1988 to lead Wipro Corporation's foray into health care. It began by marketing and servicing bio research and diagnostic systems from Beckman Instruments, USA. The company started expanding its activities in 1992-93 with a view to becoming a 'single comprehensive source' for bio research and diagnostic instruments. According to Vinod Wahi, chief executive of Wipro Biomed: 'We were anyway meeting the same customer, in the research institutes, in the universities and in the R&D establishments of pharmaceutical companies with our Beckman products. We thought why not leverage this and become a single comprehensive source to these customers.'

7. Imports of complete systems were exempt from any customs duty while Wipro GE incurred a 15.5 per cent customs levy on the import of its raw materials and a 5.5 per cent excise levy on its finished product.
8. Under this programme the world's leading physicians and researchers come and interact with their Indian counterparts on the latest achievements in medical imaging.

In 1994, the company was representing, beyond Beckman, Becton Dickinson, Bio-Rad Labs and Serono Diagnostics. It also had an Application Laboratory at Delhi which provided on-line tailor-made solutions to specific customer application needs.

Following Wipro GE's successful entry into hospitals with their radiology and imaging systems, Wipro Biomed targeted the hospital segment. The company tied up with PPG Hellige of Germany, a pioneer in the field of cardiology equipment having launched the world's first portable electrocardiograph in 1929, to market their cardiology and patient monitoring systems in India. 'We realised that we would be able to leverage our corporate reputation for quality and service—apart from Wipro GE, Wipro Infotech had a presence as it was selling computers to hospitals—and build a strong presence in this segment', Wahi explained.

Wipro Biomed, however, had its own sales team and operated independently of Wipro GE. 'We do participate in their bid for turnkey projects. We, however, do not differentiate between Wipro GE and Siemens or others. We are keen on increasing our market share. Wipro GE too is not obliged to buy the products of the companies we represent', Wahi said.

In 1993, Wipro Biomed entered the analytical instruments market by representing Hewlett Packard (HP), USA, a world leader in test and analytical instruments, for a select range of products. 'HP was keen on our representing their entire range. We, however, could not as some of them clashed with Beckman. We now represent them in products which are complementary', explained Wahi.

In 1994, the Rs 135 mn Wipro Biomed was making a foray into manufacturing. It extended its Beckman collaboration into a manufacturing one and was setting up a plant to manufacture diagnostic reagent kits with know-how from the American company.

Wipro Financial Services

In 1994, Wipro Financial Services (WFS) recorded the best performance in Wipro Corporation's portfolio. It had generated revenues totalling Rs 461 mn (up from Rs 21 mn in the previous year) and a post-tax profit of Rs 362 mn (previous year Rs 10 mn). According to S.R. Gopalan, president WFS, the spectacular performance was due to the clear focus the company had since its inception in 1992. He said:

> We focussed on asset and trade financing for 'high tech' products like computers, medical systems, telecom systems, energy systems and one or two other specialised areas. We did not aim to be everything to everyone. We leveraged our expertise and intimate knowledge of these areas: both of the technology, especially the obsolescence factor, and the needs and profiles of the customers for these hi-tech products. We put this expertise to use in tailoring products and services to meet the individual needs of the customers. For example, we have a scheme under which we extend financing facilities to customers for the purchase of the Solar Photovoltaic Water Pumping System manufactured by Tata BP Solar India Limited. In terms of customers we targeted mid-range companies, who often do not have smooth access to the banking system like large companies do.

The activities of WFS included leasing, equipment finance and advisory services. It extended medium- to long-term finance to companies for the purchase of capital equipment. The advisory services included advice on ways to raise funds in the debt market and working capital facilities, and assessment of companies for takeover. Contrary to the prevailing practice amongst most financial services companies in India (see Appendix 8), the company did not operate in the consumer finance segment. Asked why WFS did not participate in this segment, Gopalan said: 'This activity is manpower intensive and people are the scarcest resource today. Prompt customer service is the key to success in financial services. Otherwise, why would a customer opt for a relatively high cost source like us and not go to a bank which is cheaper. We are a lean outfit. All our employees are what we call "generalised specialists". The executive in charge of resource mobilisation, for example, is trained to, in the absence of the marketing executive, put together a financial package for a customer. Entering consumer finance would imply expanding our manpower base. We do not want to do that. We want to remain a lean outfit. For example, I do not have a personal secretary. I use the pool support. We also do not have a switchboard operator. When the phone rings, any one of us picks it up. I usually wait for it to ring a couple of times. If nobody picks it up, I do. This is not because we can't afford a switchboard operator. We don't feel the need for one.'

Wipro had contemplated diversifying into financial services in the mid-1980s, when the industry experienced a boom. Most industrial houses in India entered this industry at that time as did a number of 'fly-by-night' operators. However, following the advice of consultants it had employed, the company decided against this proposal. Gopalan said: 'We finally entered it in 1992, largely due to the impetus provided by the reforms in the financial sector. On hindsight we should have entered the industry much earlier.'

In 1994, the business was intensely competitive. The industry had undergone massive transformation following the government's decision to throw the financial sector open for participation by both domestic and international companies. Almost all the leading global players—Goldman Sachs, Jardine Fleming, Alliance Capital, Merrill Lynch, Peregrine, GE Capital, James Capel—had set up base in India either directly or through joint ventures or tie-ups ('association' arrangements) with Indian finance companies. The erstwhile development financial institutions too were rapidly evolving into full-fledged financial 'services' companies. ICICI, a leading financial institution, for example, had tied up with JP Morgan and had started a separate investment banking joint venture.

Access to funds, especially low cost funds, was critical to success in the industry. Financial services companies were allowed to raise debt funds to the order of ten times the shareholders' funds. In order to leverage this facility, Wipro Corporation, after the initial success of WFS, hiked its investment in WFS equity to Rs 50 mn, up from the initial Rs 7.5 mn. WFS was in the process of mobilising additional debt funds. Gopalan said, 'Securing additional credit lines from banks and financial institutions is not very difficult for us because of our corporate reputation.'

In 1994, WFS was planning to grow aggressively. It was not averse to a tie-up with an international player, including setting up of a joint venture. Gopalan said, 'We expect the partner not only to provide expertise in some areas in financial services like operating in foreign exchange markets, but also facilitate access to low cost funds from international financial markets.'

Wipro Lighting

Lighting was a major new diversification for Wipro. Premji explained: 'We enter businesses where competition is either weak or indifferent and where we can leverage our "management" capability. The lighting business offered good margins, provided the business was well managed. We found that despite the presence of major players like Philips India (the Indian subsidiary of the Dutch multinational) and Crompton Greaves, who have over the years invested in building their brands, the lighting market was a semi-commodity market and that distribution held the key. We had access to the retail channel through Wipro Consumer Products and importantly a distinctive competence in dealer management.'

In the first phase of diversification, Wipro Lighting (WL) invested Rs 400 mn in setting up its manufacturing facilities. WL's product range consisted of incandescent and fluorescent lamps and a full range of luminaires for industrial and office lighting, street lighting, flood lighting and special lighting systems for varied applications. In addition, WL sourced products from other lighting companies—a practice common to the lighting business in India.

WL launched its Wipro brand of lighting products in the southern and western markets of India in 1992-93. In its first full year of operation, 1993-94, WL achieved a turnover of Rs 220 mn. It, however, failed to generate profits. WL's expectations that it would be able to leverage access to the retail channel through Wipro Consumer Products and achieve a strong presence in the market place was only partially realised. Over 60 per cent of lighting products were purchased from electrical outlets—a channel not accessed by WCP. Further, WL confronted strong competition in the marketplace, especially from MNCs. The economic reform programme had not only attracted new MNC entry—GE, Wipro's joint venture partner in Wipro GE, acquired an equity stake in the local company Apar and had put in a bid to acquire a stake in the ailing Mysore Lamps—it had also resulted in Philips Holland, the parent company of the market leader Philips India, evincing greater interest in the operations of its local subsidiary.[9] The MNC parent had raised its equity stake in the subsidiary to a controlling 51 per cent and had started transferring state-of-the-art technology to the local subsidiary.

These developments led to Wipro Lighting rolling back its plans to go national. 'It took us some time to understand this business. I think we set ourselves rather unrealistic targets', Premji said.

Holding the Corporation Together

Premji described Wipro as a diversified *integrated* corporation. Integration was achieved through a set of shared beliefs and leadership values, and through

9. Wipro Lighting too had bid for acquiring a stake in Mysore Lamps, one of the oldest manufacturers of lighting products in India.

people and through management processes.

Integration through Shared Beliefs and Leadership Values

Premji had, in 1973, 'much before it became fashionable to do so', articulated a set of beliefs, which since then have governed the management of Wipro.

Wipro Beliefs

1. Respect for the individual. People are our greatest asset.
2. Achieve and maintain a position of leadership in each of the businesses we are in.
3. Pursue all tasks to accomplish them in a superior manner.
4. Govern individual and company relationships with the highest standards of conduct and integrity.
5. Be close to the customer in action, example and spirit, and ensure superior quality products and services.
6. Measure our effectiveness by the long-term profits we achieve for our enterprise.

Premji, commenting on the Wipro Beliefs said:

> Our beliefs are mutually compatible and supportive of one another. All of them have equal priority and need for constant practice. Our goals, objectives, policies and actions flow from our beliefs. Conceptually, our Beliefs are at the top of the pyramid. From them flow our five year goals, three year/annual objectives for the corporation and business units, departmental objectives and individual objectives. To meet the challenges of the future we are prepared to change everything about ourselves except our Beliefs, as they alone guide, govern and bind us together as an organisation. It is essential that we consciously internalise our Beliefs and be fanatical about consistently practising them. It we fail to honour our Beliefs, we will lose credibility, not only as individuals, but also as an organisation.
>
> At Wipro we walk the talk. For example, we are not flexible about boosting our sales by securing orders the non-Wipro way. If any deal requires practices that compromise our integrity, we will not do it. We have blacklisted a number of customers who seek paying or accepting favours while entering into business deals. I do not think by adopting

> this stance we are losing market share. The business heads are expected to achieve their targets—despite lack of flexibility over issues of integrity. I expect them to factor this inflexibility in while setting targets. Ultimately I believe any customer seeks good technology, good after sales service and a competitive price. We offer all of them. We will not compromise on these three critical factors. We can therefore afford to be inflexible on the integrity issue.

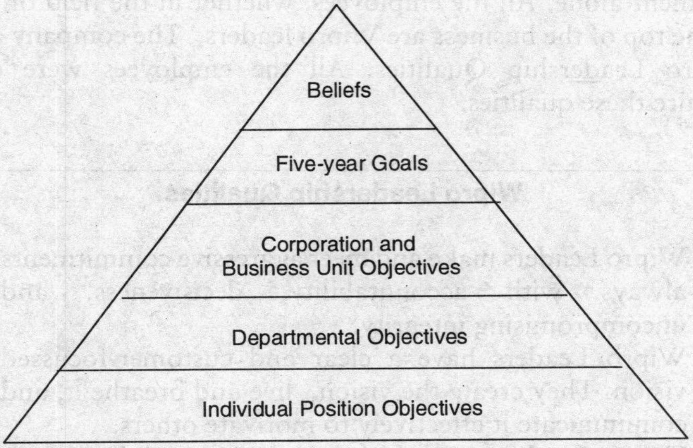

Almost every year Wipro issued thirty to forty notices to employees who were suspected to be short on the integrity front. And if any inappropriate behaviour was proved, the employee was sacked—regardless of his or her position. 'Recently, in 1993, we dismissed the employee union leader at Wipro Fluid Power, when we discovered that he had falsified his travelling expenses. Following the dismissal we had a strike at Wipro Fluid Power. We preferred facing a strike, even though the market was just coming out of recession and customers were waiting for delivery. We preferred to explain to the customers the principled stand we took', Premji added.

The Wipro Beliefs have not undergone any change since they were first articulated, save for the addition, in 1982, of a sixth belief—'Being Close to the Customer'. In 1992, a proposal for dropping the belief 'Measure our Effectiveness by the Long-term Profits We Achieve for Our Enterprise' was once again made (it had earlier been contemplated in 1989). It was argued that enough emphasis had been built into the organisation on profits and that it did not merit inclusion in Wipro Beliefs and that it would be appropriate to incorporate it as part of the Five-year Goals. However, the Belief was retained.

Wipro believed that leadership played a critical role in embedding a value-based culture that was in consonance with the Wipro Beliefs. Pai said, 'I lead by example. My staff see me operating without a personal secretary and yet, they know, I have all the information at my fingertips. Therefore, when I exhort my team to save on costs, I am credible.' Girish Gaur added, 'At Wipro the prerogative of and the responsibility for providing leadership is not that of the top management alone. All the employees, whether in the field or on the shop floor or at the top of the business are Wipro leaders.' The company articulated a set of Wipro Leadership Qualities. All the employees were expected to possess/acquire these qualities.

Wipro Leadership Qualities

1. Wipro Leaders make and meet aggressive commitments always with accountability, decisiveness, and uncompromising integrity.
2. Wipro Leaders have a clear and customer-focussed vision. They create the vision, live and breathe it, and communicate it effectively to motivate others.
3. Wipro Leaders are able to energise and invigorate others and have a high-energy approach themselves.
4. Wipro Leaders are self-confident.
5. Wipro Leaders exhibit ownership in thought and action—and value this in other members of the team.
6. Wipro Leaders are committed to excellence through quality, speed, simplicity and elimination of unnecessary bureaucracy.
7. Wipro Leaders develop star performers yet build teams: they consider their people as cherished assets, whose individual and team commitment is crucial for organisational success.

Integration through People

Though closely held—Premji's family held over 75 per cent of the equity—Wipro had a strong and powerful top-management team of professionals. 'One of Premji's outstanding abilities has been to repeatedly recognise, develop and support highly talented executives', said Soota. Almost every one of Wipro's businesses had been built around and in turn built by the people who were heading them. The turnover at the top had been negligible and the long tenure of people with the corporation was a strong integrating force.

Wipro believed in employing the best people and investing in them. It recruited from leading educational institutions in India by participating in their campus placement programmes and built its management from within, save for specialised or strategic requirements. According to Gopalan, president of WFS and formerly chief financial officer at WIL, 'For very new business we enter, the internal person is given a shot at it, and only if someone internal is not available or suitable, someone from outside is taken.' However, Wipro did not have a strong record of rotating people across businesses. Often the business unit heads were reluctant to release talented people, as each business was considered fairly specialised and distinctive. 'We have not felt the need for it so far, the growth in each of our businesses has provided exciting career growth opportunities for the employees. This however is changing to some extent now with the movement of people from Infotech to Systems, etc.', said Girish Gaur.

The culture at Wipro was an open and sharing one. Gopalan said, 'I am psychologically incapable of coping with intrigue. I am very uncomfortable operating in environments which are full of politics and where decisions are not taken on grounds of merit. At Wipro, we have independence of work. I do what is essential for the business and do not worry about it. If I am fired, I am very sure that if I were sitting in the decision maker's chair—Premji in this case—I too would arrive at the same decision. I can get fired only for unethical behaviour or non-performance. Not for any other reason.' Soota added, 'We discuss even our "dirty linen" in the open. Sometimes I think we are much too open.'

Discussion on managerial values, business plans, strategies and policies was encouraged. Every year, after the annual planning exercise was completed in March, Premji travelled across the country to the offices of the various businesses and addressed the employees to communicate and share the plan with them and invite their suggestions. While Premji shared the plans for the corporation as a whole, the respective business unit heads shared the plans for the business to which the employees belonged. 'This reduces dependence on control mechanisms, and improves individual commitment to goals and adoption of sound methods', Premji said.

Wipro was the first company in India to introduce an employee stock ownership programme. The Wipro Equity Linked Reward Programme (WELRP) was a novel one. Each Wipro business, regardless of its legal status, had its own separate internal 'equity' and 'net worth'. Part of the compensation of the employees entitled to participate in the WELRP programme was linked to growth in the 'net worth' of that particular business. In 1994, the eligibility to participate in WELRP had been pushed down to the middle levels of the management hierarchy.

Integration through Management Processes

Each of Wipro's businesses enjoyed a wide latitude and operated quite independently. However, approved corporate-wide policies were inviolable, regardless of the circumstances the individual businesses might find themselves in. Premji said, 'Each business exists for the enhancement and betterment of the whole corporation.'

> Asked whether it would be right to describe him as a hands-off manager, Premji said: 'Yes and no. I spend a lot of time with my people, asking the right kind of questions to find out what is happening in our various businesses. I may not be an operations man. But then, neither am I merely an investor-chairman.'

Chandrasekaran said, 'Premji is a details man. Although he allows us tremendous freedom, he knows exactly what is happening where.'

The Wipro corporate office played an important role in ensuring the 'betterment of the Corporation as a whole'. Certain powers and responsibilities were reserved for the Wipro corporate office. These were:

- *Setting* beliefs, goals and basic policies, certain plan drivers and other standards of measurements.
- *Approving* plans and budgets appointments at middle management and above, employee salary structures, benefits and incentive plans, appointment of advertising agencies, interaction with the government on key policy issues, charity and other contributions.
- *Responsibility for* selecting statutory auditors and counsel, corporate audit across the corporation.

The corporate office held the overall responsibility for the corporation's finance, human resources, corporate planning and business development and government and legal affairs functions. While each of the businesses independently carried out these functions, the heads of these functions at the individual businesses had a dotted line relationship with the corporate functional heads.

The annual planning exercise was the key operational management process by which integration was sought to be achieved. Each business prepared its own business plans for the year. Wahi said, 'In addition to our open culture, one of our strengths is our very strong planning and review culture. We document not only our plans but also have a rigorous system of preparing minutes of our review meetings. We have monthly reviews with the chairman and quarterly reviews with the CEC (Corporate Executive Council).' According to Chandrasekaran, however, the documentation often exceeded what was necessary or desirable. 'We generate too much paper. We need to reduce it. We need to appreciate that there is no perfect plan. We need to change it as we go along. Excessive details kill the spirit. Increasingly I find ourselves moving away from being a presentation-discussion oriented company to a paper document oriented company.'

Each business was required to define its key result objectives for the year. The number of variables for which the objectives were required to be defined was restricted to six. In 1994, the corporate office defined four of the variables, with the definition of the other two being left to the discretion of the individual businesses with only a stipulation that the variables defined by them be measurable. Two of the variables defined by the corporate office were Speed and Customer Satisfaction and were to be valid for the next five years. Each business was expected to reduce all current cycle times by 20 per cent each year and increase by 5 points each year the percentage of customers who rated Wipro 'overall' a 5 and 4 in a 1-to-5 point scale. The other two variables stipulated by the corporate office for which the individual businesses had to define their objectives were Financial and Employee Morale. The measurement criteria for the Employee Morale objective was through an annual Employee Perception Survey, attrition rates and internal growth. The individual business financial objectives were to necessarily cover objectives on:

- Sales, sales growth and market share.
- Profit before tax.
- Profit after tax.

- Cash flow.
- Return on average equity.
- Return on capital employed.

The corporate office also informed the individual businesses of the norms for approval of investments. In 1994, these were 29 per cent return on average equity and a minimum 22 per cent return on capital employed. All investment proposals had to meet these criteria for approval. Only in exceptional cases, where the proposal came from the newer businesses and the considerations were strategic, proposals which did not meet these criteria got approved. Additionally, a debt equity norm was specified. Gowrishankar said, 'We specify the debt equity norm as each business unit organises its own debt funds. We believe in adhering to strict self-imposed norms. At WFS, for instance, we maintain debt to equity ratio at 6:1 even though the company is entitled to go up to 10:1.'

Pai said, 'We are in many ways a strongly decentralised operation. I am not dependent on the corporate office. In fact I keep them at arms length. However, I must admit we are much too finance dominated.' Endorsing this view, Gopalan said, 'The plan, once approved, gives me the target and the authority but it also freezes my opportunity.'

The annual plans were approved by the CEC comprising Premji, the presidents of the various businesses, and the corporate heads of finance and human resources. The CEC was the apex policy making body at Wipro. Apart from articulating the vision for Wipro Corporation as a whole, it was the final arbiter of policies in Wipro. While the corporate office monitored the performance of the individual businesses on a monthly basis, the CEC met every quarter to assess, comprehensively, the performance of the individual businesses and the corporation as a whole. The CEC also approved of extra plan corporate initiatives (strategic thrusts) and other corporate-wide programmes. 'The CEC enables the chairman to manage the diversity', Gopalan said.

In 1994, apart from the CEC, there were two other councils which were fora for discussing common issues across the various businesses and to initiate and implement corporation-wide strategic thrusts. These were the Wipro Finance Council (FC) and the Wipro Human Resource Council (HRC). The formation of two other councils—the Materials Council, which would focus on supplier management, and the Marketing Council, which would focus on the marketing dimension—was being debated by the CEC.

The FC was headed by the corporate vice president (finance) and had the chief financial officers of all the businesses as members. In 1994, the FC embarked on an extra plan initiative of achieving a corporate-wide savings/earnings to the tune of Rs 25 mn through adoption of superior financial practices in the corporation. The HRC was headed by the corporate vice president (human resources) and had the chiefs of the human resource function in all the businesses as members. In 1994, the HRC was the prime driver of the PRIDE programme which aimed at bringing about a mindset change within the various businesses. Girish Gaur, the chief of the HR council explained, 'PRIDE—which stands for Productivity improvements, a Responsive organisation, and Involved people, by Driving change and Empowering them—is a method of problem resolution. It involved setting up of cross-functional teams, each comprising five to seven members, who were then given the mandate to find solutions to specific problems.' In 1994, twenty-nine cross-functional teams were functioning at Wipro and the number was expected to go up to 130. Premji said, 'We need to shock people to rethink the business. A business-as-usual attitude will not succeed in the drastically changing environment.'

Balancing the Future: Challenges in 1994

The fundamental challenge confronting Wipro in 1994 was *how* to sustain its growth in the changed environment. The competition it confronted was severe. And the competitors in most of its businesses were multinationals, who not only had immense financial power but could also leverage their global product and marketing technologies.

Balancing the Portfolio

In the past, Wipro, as a part of its growth strategy, had sought international tie-ups in businesses where partners brought technology, access to global markets and process know-how while Wipro brought access to local markets, management capability and in most cases an existing presence. In the changed policy environment, MNCs sought a greater involvement in the businesses in the form of both higher equity stakes and greater say in the management. The challenge Wipro faced was two fold: (1) *how* to achieve the right balance in its portfolio between financial joint ventures and those which were independent of such financial partnerships, and (2) *how* to ensure that Wipro continued to bring value to the table on an ongoing basis to be an equal partner.

Premji said: 'When GE sought to increase its stake in Wipro GE, we debated their acquisition of the majority stake over an eight month period. It was a tough emotional decision. GE is a 51 per cent mindset company. I had to go beyond myself as a majority owner of Wipro and put the employees ahead. We did drive a hard bargain. We got an equal representation on the board and also finalised the norms for transfer pricing—always a thorny issue in a joint venture. We also made an agreement that while GE's medical software development will be done at Wipro GE, the information services software projects will be carried out by Wipro Systems. I am, however, aware that they would increasingly want to be in the driving seat. In future, our focus would be on setting financial targets for Wipro GE and leveraging the learning the association with GE provides us in our other businesses, including transferring their best practices.'

Vivek Paul, who continued to be a member of the CEC even after the change, said: 'Some things have definitely changed. We are in transition. We have started using the Delhi office of GE for our government liaison work. Further, the GE planning exercise is carried out two months before the Wipro planning exercise. So, today we are juggling two sets of numbers as the definition of the financial year varies. Additionally, there are three different sets of demands being made on me. While Wipro wants to maximise contribution, the GE Medical Systems Division headquarters wants to maximise top line and the GE international division wants Wipro GE to become a low cost base of operation.'

Following the GE acquisition of a majority stake in Wipro GE, the CEC decided that it would derive 75 per cent of its profit after tax, as a Corporation, from businesses in which Wipro controlled the destiny and was not subordinate to financial joint venture partners. 'This has been a difficult decision, particularly when, as a Corporation, we are uniquely positioned to attract and have joint ventures with leading companies in each of the six businesses we are in', said Premji.

The CEC took two more policy decisions:

1. It would take on joint venture partners *only* in products where product success was critically dependent on having a technological edge and it could not access the required technology otherwise. For example, in the health care business it planned to operate in the joint venture mode

and/or represent world leaders in the specific product market segments. Similarly, the relationship with Nokia was expected to evolve into a 50:50 joint venture.

2. It would not enter into financial partnerships where the company had a strong brand franchise, and/or where it was on top of world class technology and/or where it had a cost edge. Further, in businesses where it could develop technology on its own or *cafeteria shop* technologies from medium-size European, American and Asian companies, it would not take on joint venture partners and would retain its independence. Soota said, 'As we search more in this area, we are amazed how much high quality technology is available today with medium-size companies.'

The adoption of these policies implied that the company would continue to operate independently or through technology licensing arrangements in its information technology business. However, in a sudden turnabout in late 1994, the company signed a memorandum of understanding with Acer, Taiwan, the tenth largest PC company in the world, to set up a joint venture to manufacture and market jointly branded PCs. The tie-up also envisaged setting up of a design centre for software and hardware services. Asked about the turnabout, Soota said, 'Currently the market is dominated by local brands, but one must acknowledge the strengths and pull of MNC brands. One has seen it in other industries and one cannot take it lightly. At the same time there is no need to be overawed.' Premji added, 'The trick is to know when to take partners and when not to take partners and generate enough self-confidence and not be naive or macho. We need to balance our control and growth needs.'

Balancing Growth

Wipro aspired to be among the top-ten most admired corporations in India. The key attributes identified for this reputation were:

- Quality of management.
- Quality of products and/or services.
- Innovations.
- Growth in net worth.
- Financial soundness.
- Ability to attract, develop and retain talented people.
- Use of its assets and exports.

Wipro planned to periodically commission independent polls to evaluate its performance on these criteria.

Additionally, it aspired to be among the top ten industrial groups in India in terms of profits after tax by the year 2002-2003. The financial targets articulated in the Wipro ten-year vision were sales of Rs 100 bn, profits before tax of Rs 5 bn and profits after tax of Rs 3 bn. The vision also envisaged 20 per cent of the sales coming from exports and overseas presence, with marketing presence in fifty countries.

Wipro was seeking to realise this vision without adding more industries to its portfolio. Premji said, 'I am not looking to add greater diversity. We are essentially looking at related businesses.' While admitting the need to contain the diversity, Gopalan said, 'We also need to re-examine our portfolio and our growth strategy. We have a large number of relatively small-sized businesses operating in relatively small-sized markets. We today cut off the option of contemplating a Rs 5 bn project.'

The vision identified resource mobilisation as the critical factor which would impact the achievement of the objectives. Premji said, 'Our current shareholding pattern allows more than enough latitude to dilute ownership, if necessary, without losing operational and management control. But we need to maximise internal resource generation. Consequently, profit after tax and cash flow were adopted as the two key plan drivers.'

As a part of its efforts to realise the vision, the planning process was modified to build in a 'commitment to commitments' mindset. In the past, actual performance invariably fell short of plan targets. From 1994, commitments made in the plan were treated as sacrosanct. Actual performance was required to be within 5 per cent of the plan target. 'At GE this is strictly followed. The business units *had* to achieve their plans. We need this kind of American toughness built into our management processes', said Girish Gaur. 'The plan commitments have to be taken seriously. Without it, resource planning becomes very difficult', said Gowrishankar. Not all the business unit heads were in full agreement with the adoption of the Commitment to Commitment policy. According to Vivek Paul, 'GE itself is rethinking its policy.' Pai said, 'I believe in setting ourselves high targets and attempting to achieve them. It does not matter if we end up achieving only 80 per cent of it. What is more important is to aim high. Why not let each business unit head decide what is more appropriate?' Premji, however, did not agree. 'It is a question of mindset. I do not think stretched targets cannot be specified under the new dispensation.'

Balancing Management

The issue of balance between integration and independence was being debated within Wipro. As described by Soota, 'Today, only our values are common. Otherwise we are almost six different companies, with every business unit head focussing only on their respective businesses. We need to achieve greater integration.' However, this sharp focus on one's 'own' business had its advantages. As Soota admitted, 'Most of us are heavily involved in managing our own business. That has been our model so far and has worked well. We run our businesses as proprietors. I do not go beyond into the Wipro Corporation-level issues. That is largely the domain of Premji and the corporate office. They do get heavily involved in a start-up business like lighting, which requires financial support and nurturing. For established businesses like WIL, they get involved only if I need help. Otherwise we operate quite independently except for participating in the CEC. Apart from Premji, who is our strongest integrating force, it is our shared values which integrates us.'

However, according to Gopalan, 'We value common threads too much today. We seek too much order. We must increasingly learn to live with unintegrated diversity and with ambiguity. I would prefer CEC to be a driver of growth rather than being a policy making body. I do not think we are today tapping fully the capability of the Wipro top management'. Another senior manager echoed this view. 'Take the issue of employee remuneration. We try to balance the compensation of our employees across the various businesses. We need to appreciate the fact that the competition we confront is very different in different businesses.'

Retention of talented people was a common problem confronted by all the Wipro businesses. The strategy of most new entrants, especially MNCs, was to raid well managed Indian companies for talent. Wipro was one of the prime targets.

Premji said: 'Beyond competition in the product markets, retention of talented people is the biggest challenge confronting us at Wipro. I personally believe that the new environment provides much more opportunities to grow and prosper. The key, however, lies in holding on to talented people. Our biggest strength has been our people; our management capability. We need to sustain it.'

APPENDIX 1

Estimated Market Size and Shares

(Rs million)

	Estimated Market Size 1993	Wipro Sales 1993
Information Technology:	33228	2238
Wipro Infotech	8848	257
Wipro Systems	–	–
Total	–	2495
Wipro Consumer Products		
Vanaspati	33300	1091
Toilet soaps	19433	875
Toiletries	2132	135
Leather products	7500	72
Total	62365	2193
Health Care		
Wipro-GE	3269	589
Wipro BioMed	3158	121
Total	6427	710
Wipro Fluid Power	1768	262
Wipro Lighting	9585	37
Grand total	122213	5697

Note: Wipro Financial Services is excluded from above.
Source: Company documents.

APPENDIX 2

Wipro Corporation: Organisational Set-up

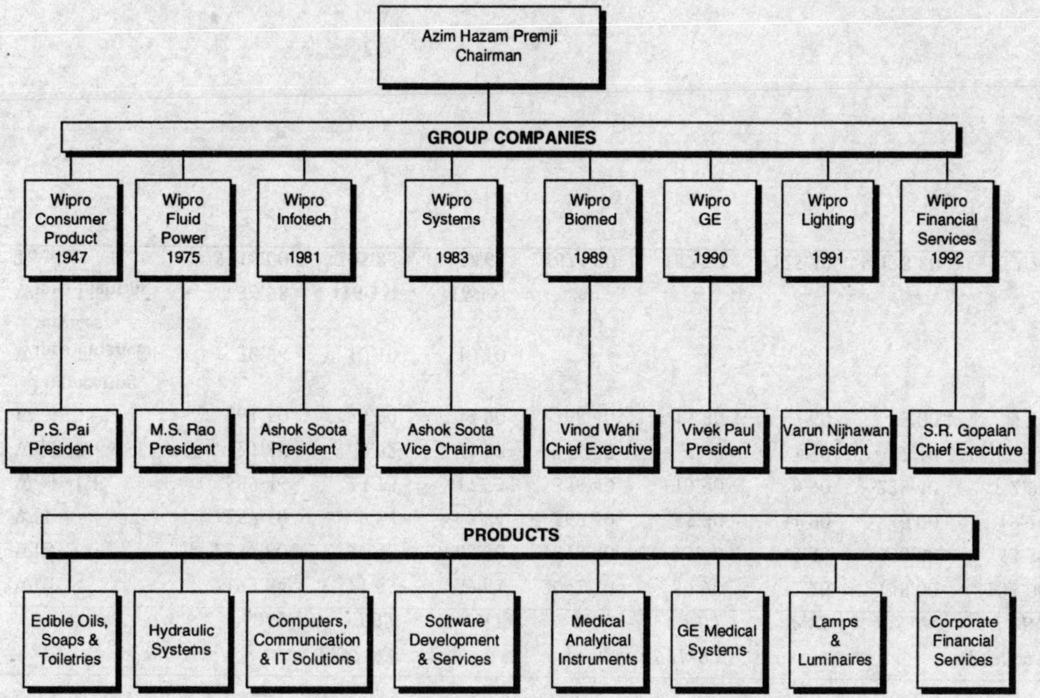

APPENDIX 3

Wipro Corporation Portfolio: Turnover and Profits

	1992–93			1991–92			1990–91		
	Sales	*PBT*	*PAT*	*Sales*	*PBT*	*PAT*	*Sales*	*PBT*	*PAT*
WCP	2193.84	71.95	39.61	2042.30	59.90	32.20	2148.00	103.00	75.00
WIL	2237.60	97.40	68.90	1818.80	75.00	45.50	1550.00	53.30	28.60
WSL	257.50	9.84	9.84	169.40	35.30	31.90	60.00	19.20	18.90
Wipro GE	589.46	23.73	17.73	356.40	13.90	8.90	228.40	2.90	0.90
Wipro Biomed	121.86	8.92	4.87	51.30	4.40	1.80	32.10	(3.60)	(3.60)
Wipro Engineering	261.50	23.90	13.90	168.40	15.80	7.60	98.00	9.60	3.10
Wipro Financial Services	20.96	10.10	10.10	–	–	–	–	–	–
Wipro Lighting	36.98	(16.15)	(16.15)	–	–	–	–	–	–
Total	5715.00	205.83	157.62	4624.90	187.70	125.30	4178.80	157.70	105.00

APPENDIX 4

Vanaspati Industry Production, 1992–93

	(in tons)
West Zone	
Wipro	36293
Other leading producers	
MP Oil Federation	21137
Madhusudhan Industries	20071
Aswin Vanaspati	16025
IVP Limited	10631
Dipak Veg.	10252
Godrej Foods	9362
West zone total	199692
South Zone	
Wipro	4427
Other leading producers	
Lipton	7409
A.P. Agarwal Industries	14115
South zone total	42170
East Zone	
Wipro	–
Other leading producers	
Kusum Products	18199
HLL (associate of Lipton)	9499
Ipinit Vanaspati	7418
East zone total	47261
North Zone	
Wipro	–
Other leading producers	
Lipton	24623
United Vanaspati	15683
North zone total	104349
All India	393472

Source: Vanaspati Manufacturers' Association of India.

APPENDIX 5

Wipro Infotech Limited

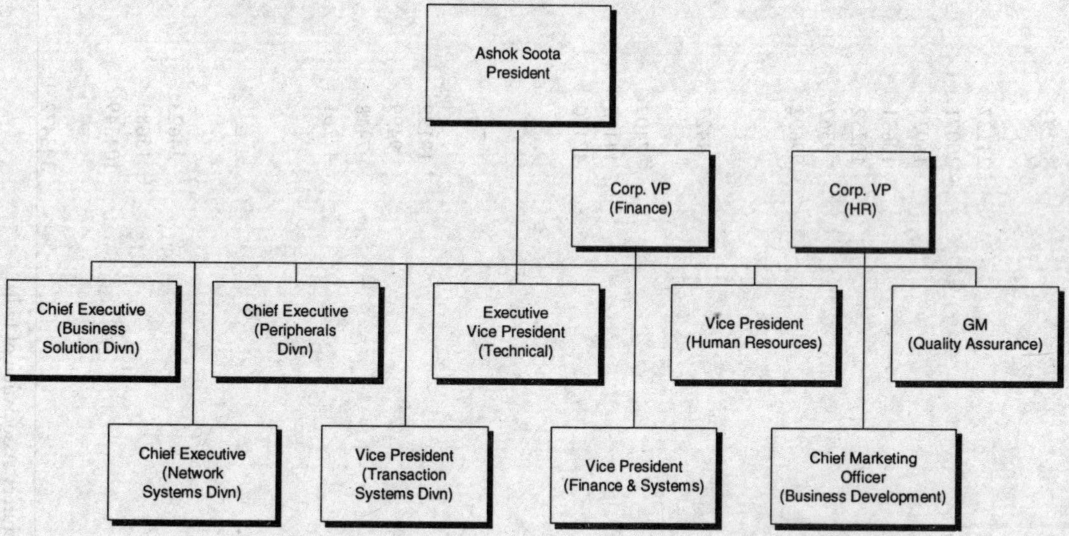

APPENDIX 6

Foreign Partners of Major Players in the Computer Industry, 1993

Company	Sales (Rs million)	Profit (Loss) (Rs million)	Foreign Partner	Sales ($ billion)	Profit (Loss) ($ billion)
HCL-HP	2490	(30)	Hewlett-Packard	16.4	0.55
Wipro Infotech	2230	689	Sun Microsystems	3.62	0.17
ICIM	1220	135	Fujitsu	27.9	(0.26)
Digital Equipment	1110	(50)	DEC	14.03	(2.79)
Tata Unisys Ltd	910	10.36	Unisys	8.42	0.36
Modi Olivetti Ltd	520	(30)	Olivetti	6.5	(0.53)
PSI	180	958	Bull	5.7	(0.89)

Notes: 1. Except Wipro Infotech, all other foreign players had a direct or an indirect equity stake in the Indian operations.
2. In addition to the above, IBM entered in 1972 with a equal 50:50 joint venture with the Tata group.
Source: *Business Today*, 7-21 August, 1993, p. 68.

APPENDIX 7

Major Players in 1993

(Rs million)

	Export Software	Domestic Software
Tata Consultancy Services	1754.00	410.00
Tata Unisys Ltd	560.00	134.00
Digital Equipment (India) Ltd	317.80	–
CitiCorp	209.40	77.70
Wipro Systems Ltd	172.00	80.80
CMC Ltd	–	269.90
Onward Computer Technologies	–	94.40
Top 15 players' share (%)	63.5	37.3

Source: National Association of Software and Service Companies.

APPENDIX 8

Medical Systems Market Share, 1992-93

Company	*Share (%)*
Siemens	32
Wipro GE	28
Phillips	10
Hitachi	4
Picker/Network	4
Toshiba	1
Shimadzu	1
Others	15
Refurbished	5

Source: Company estimates.

APPENDIX 9

Major Private Sector Players in Financial Services

(Rs million)

	Gross Income	*Profit After Tax*	*Net Worth*	*Business Focus*
1. Kotak Mahindra	775	260	670	Trade financing, capital markets operation, lease, vehicle finance (cars)
2. Sundaram Finance	1500	200	910	Vehicle finance (trucks), lease
3. Apple Industries	500	165	700	Lease, trade finance, vehicle finance (cars)
4. Lloyds Finance	320	145	700	Trade finance, lease
5. 20th Century Finance	725	135	560	Asset finance, merchant banking
6. Ashok Leyland Finance	510	93	250	Vehicle finance (trucks)
7. ITC Classic	570	75	575	Lease, trade finance, merchant banking
8. Tata Finance	490	70	525	Lease, trade finance

Source: Company estimates.

STUDDS ACCESSORIES LIMITED: PANGS OF GLOBALISATION

Every successful company faces this dilemma at some point. Having established a profitable business on one's home turf, there's always the temptation to expand into other markets. But should one go it alone, or with a partner? How should one choose a partner? And how does management and control work in a joint venture? Keen to internationalise their helmet making company, Madhu Khurana and his brother Ravi were taken aback by the range of challenges which came up.

After months of highs and lows, by February 1995, Madhu Khurana, the managing director of Studds Accessories Ltd, was considering breaking off Studds' joint venture agreement with Nolan of Italy. The Studds-Nolan joint venture was Studds' first equity venture with a foreign partner and the preliminary negotiations for this venture had been completed six months earlier. However, as the two parties worked to finalise the agreement, they had reached an impasse. Tension and distrust marked the current negotiations. Khurana,

This case was written by Jaideep Anand, Professor at the University of Michigan and Andrew Delios, research student at the University of Western Ontario. The authors are grateful to the Studds group for their help and support in writing the case. This case was written in 2000.

while anxious to have a foreign partner for access to world markets, was concerned about several problems which had arisen since the joint venture was initiated. He had serious doubts about the long-term viability of the venture. Strategically, the joint venture had appeared to be a good decision, combining Studds' low cost, quality manufacturing capabilities with Nolan's international marketing expertise, reputation and reach. However, after early implementation problems, the joint venture was dissolved and Studds elected to approach world markets alone. What happened?

The Studds Group

Gadgets India, the first company in the Studds group, was formed by two brothers, Ravi and Madhu Khurana, in 1969. Trained as engineers, the brothers started a manufacturing unit in a garage, making moulded engineering items on a custom basis for the automotive, textile and white goods industries. In 1973, a helmet manufacturing process was developed in-house with the first sale occurring in 1974. The helmet line was marketed right from its inception under the brand name 'Studds'.

Studds' development of indigenous technology contrasted with the way in which other companies grew in the regulated environment of India in the 1970s and 1980s. Most large Indian companies formed equity and non-equity alliances to access and acquire foreign technology.

In the mid-1970s, helmet usage was not popular in India. Consequently, early sales were low and grew slowly. Two competitors existed in this embryonic market: Steelbird, who sold high-priced helmets, and Concorde, a low-end manufacturer of cheap, industrial helmets. Studds competed in both ends, producing a premium helmet priced 10 per cent lower than Steelbird's, as well as lower quality helmets for more price-conscious consumers. Studds quickly secured a leading position in both the high and low ends of the nascent helmet market. The brand became synonymous with helmets in India, and its market leadership was virtually uncontested through the remainder of the 1970s and into the first half of the 1980s.

The Organisation

In 1994, the Studds organisation consisted of Gadgets India and Studds Accessories. Studds Accessories Pvt Ltd was formed in 1984 and it took over the marketing function from Gadgets India. Thus, Studds Accessories conducted all marketing activities, while Gadgets India performed all manufacturing for Studds. By 1990, Studds Accessories had established a dealership network that penetrated most areas of the vast and widely dispersed Indian market. This network consisted of 800 dealers.

Both companies were family-owned and controlled, with equity split equally between the families of the brothers, Ravi and Madhu Khurana. Gadgets India remained a partnership, while Studds Accessories was a public limited company, wholly-owned by the two Khurana families, friends and relatives.

Gadgets India manufactured its entire range of products in compliance with the relevant national or regional standards. It employed 380 people, of which sixty were supervisory staff, 145 were skilled labour and 175 were semi-skilled or unskilled labour. The main manufacturing facility was located in Faridabad, India, and could produce 370,000 two-wheeler helmets per year when operated at capacity. In 1994, 320,000 helmets were manufactured.

Gadgets India was led by Ravi Khurana, the group chairman. A general manager reported to Ravi Khurana and the division of responsibility and control was along functional lines, with six managers reporting directly to the general manager. Studds Accessories was organised in a similar fashion. Madhu Khurana, the managing director, had a general manager and four functional managers reported to him. Twenty-five people were employed in Studds Accessories which had an advertising budget of Rs 200,000 (in mid-1994, US$ 1 equaled Rs 30.77).

Managers, responsible for a specific functional area, did not interact very much with their peers in other functions. Where responsibilities overlapped and conflict developed, resolution was sought through discussion with either Ravi or Madhu Khurana. Managers were reluctant to assume responsibility for decisions, and the general managers were reluctant to release such responsibility to the managers. Consequently, both Ravi and Madhu Khurana were intimately involved in the day-to-day operations of their companies.

Union Relations

Employees of Studds were heavily unionised. Unions were active and vocal in India and possessed considerable bargaining power because of the Indian government's 'no fire' policy. Under the terms of this policy, once an employee had been hired, the company was obligated to employ this individual for the lifetime of the company or employee. Dismissals were rare and were often accompanied by a considerable payoff.

Union activities sporadically disrupted activities outside the Faridabad plant and consumed senior management time. Studds helmets were distributed throughout India by road and deliveries were subject to interruptions based on the relations of the trucker's union with the trucking companies. Additionally, in 1994, a strike by dockworkers at the Bombay port delayed a recent shipment of Studds helmets to the North American market.

The strength of the union made changes in the manufacturing process difficult. In 1992, an injection-moulding machine was purchased. This machine was to be used for the manufacture of plastic moulded-helmets for the lower-end segment of the market. Injection moulding was a capital-intensive process, utilising less labour than that used in the production of fibreglass helmets, a premium product. However, unions resisted the implementation of this process, and the injection-moulding machine remained idle, inhibiting expansion of Studds helmets in the growing lower-end market segment.

Products

Approximately 70 per cent of the revenues for the Studds group came from helmet sales to the two-wheeler market. Studds marketed helmets in both the lower and premium segments of the market, though lower-end models were priced higher than inexpensive locally-made brands. Studds produced both open-face and full-face helmets. Open-face models ranged from Rs 280 to Rs 650, and full-face models were priced between Rs 400 and Rs 650. The most expensive helmet in the Studds line was priced at Rs 1,200; however, sales of this model were small. Aerostar's models ranged in price from Rs 100 to Rs 500.

Studds produced seven models in the full-face design and five models in the open-face design. As each model was produced in several colour schemes, over 120 designs and colours of two-wheeler helmets were produced. Both full-face and open-face designs had achieved ISI, ECE22.03 DOT, CSI, SNELL and ANSI certification. Among a similar range of products, Aerostar had only received ISI certification for two models.

Studds also produced helmets for other user groups. Sales of sports helmets, used in cycling, canoeing, horse-riding, skating and skateboarding, accounted for the remaining 30 per cent of revenues. All helmets in this line were manufactured to meet ANSI-Z–90 (a US standard) specifications. Studds' adherence to stringent international quality control laws had enabled its bicycle helmets to receive quality approvals from the US, Canada, Mexico, and all of Western Europe. Receiving Canadian (CSA) approval was an important benchmark, as companies from only nine nations worldwide had achieved it.

Market Share

From its inception in the early 1970s, the helmet market in India had grown to an annual size of nearly 1 million helmets in the 1990s. In 1992, Studds was the market leader and held a 36 per cent share. Aerostar, with a 12 per cent share, was in second place. Aerostar, which entered the market in the 1980s, competed directly against Studds' premium product line. Adopting a strategy similar to that used by Studds against Steelbird, Aerostar priced its premium product 10 per cent less than Studds' and undercut Studds' prices at the low-end of the market as well. Steelbird, with a 5 per cent share, was the third key player. Vega, which sold about 10,000 helmets per year, led a host of more than ninety other manufacturers who divided the remaining portion of the market amongst them. Helmets from these small manufacturers were low-end models, generally sold in low-end retail outlets.

A few of these smaller manufacturers infringed on Studds' brand name. These small manufacturers made helmets identical in appearance to the Studds line but at much lower cost. The copies bore the Studds name and could not be distinguished from genuine Studds helmets. Copies retailed for Rs 170, while Studds' cost of manufacture was greater than Rs 210. Trademark infringement was illegal under Indian law; however, when Studds had prosecuted violators of its trademark in the past, the penalty was not too high.

Geographically, Studds' sales were concentrated in the northern states of India. However, this was misleading, as wholesalers were concentrated in North India, and helmets sold to these firms were distributed to all regions of India. Thus, Studds helmets were actually used across India. Though Studds helmets were popular across India, Studds' market share in individual markets varied dramatically. For instance, in New Delhi, Studds had a market share of approximately 10 per cent; and in Bombay, Studds commanded 75 to 80 per cent of the market.

Regions within India had the authority to create their own helmet laws. As a result, helmet use was mandatory in some regions and optional in others. Helmet laws were enacted and retracted frequently, as local governments changed. In 1994, only three cities, Delhi, Calcutta and Bangalore (with an aggregate population of approximately 30 million people, or 1/30 of India's population) had made helmet use compulsory. These three urban areas accounted for a large fraction of the two-wheeler market.

Studds enjoyed its largest market share in regions that had optional helmet use. Motorcycle and scooter riders, who were safety conscious, were willing to pay for a premium product, such as a Studds helmet. Other helmets were perceived not to offer the safety or style desired by voluntary wearers of helmets. In regions in which the rider was forced by law to wear a helmet, the sole criterion for helmet purchase was price. Safety, style and brand name were not important factors in these consumers' minds. As a result, Studds' largest market share was in regions in which helmet use was optional.

Consequently, Studds was not an advocate of compulsory helmet use. While Studds would gain a few sales should helmet use become mandatory across India, its market share would be eroded. The large increase in sales would be absorbed by low price, unbranded helmet lines. The long-term trend in India was towards the mandatory use of helmets, especially as national concern for health and safety increased.

Currently one in five two-wheeler drivers wore a helmet voluntarily. Passengers seldom wore helmets. Even in regions in which helmet use was mandatory, only the driver was required to wear a helmet. Passengers were permitted to travel without helmet, and at times, the number of riders on a two-wheeler reached four or five, as a motorcycle or scooter often served as a family's main mode of transportation.

Stimulus for Change

By the mid-1990s, both Madhu and Ravi Khurana were restless for change. They were losing market share and margins were getting squeezed by lower end competition. The company's growth rate had slowed down, though export sales were good. More importantly, there was a new feeling of optimism in the air generated by macro-economic developments. The Khuranas began to consider expanding their export efforts by entering into a partnership with an international player.

The 1990s Liberalisation Process

Between 1991 and 1996, India underwent a major resurgence. Policy reforms, designed by Manmohan Singh, the finance minister, and implemented by the Narasimha Rao government in July 1991, created a feeling of widespread optimism in the country. Despite initial high inflation and a February 1992 stock market scandal, early indications were that the economy had responded positively to economic liberalisation. GDP growth increased from less than 1 per cent in 1991–92 to a projected 5 per cent in 1994–95, and 6 per cent in subsequent years.

The dollar value of imports and exports grew by 25 per cent in this same period, while foreign direct investment tripled. In addition, numerous multinationals had established a presence in India by 1994. Many markets were opened to foreign competitors under the new policy guidelines. Automatic approval existed for the markets in which Studds competed and in the transportation markets from which the demand for Studds' products was derived. The middle class, the main purchasers of motorcycles and scooters, was expected to reach 300 million people by the turn of the century.

Infrastructure was an area of developmental concern. While India possessed an extensive network of railways and roads (there was 1.97 million km of roads of which less than half were paved), the road network was still insufficient for the number of vehicles on the roads. Traffic tie-ups were frequent, and travel by road was complicated by the wide variance in modes of transportation. Motorised trucks, cars and two-wheelers shared the nation's highways and urban roads with pedestrians and animal-drawn vehicles. On-time delivery of goods was hampered by road congestion.

Other conditions in India hindered firm efficiency. For example, government approvals were required at several stages in a joint venture set-up. Investment (both capital goods and monetary) by foreign partners in a joint venture had to be approved by the secretary for industrial approvals of the Department of Industrial Development, Ministry of Industries. Joint venture agreements had to be approved by the Reserve Bank of India (the central bank) and permission was required from the Reserve Bank to issue shares to the foreign joint venture participant.

Other regulations governed the remittance of royalties and dividends, and the repatriation of capital. Furthermore, land purchases for industrial use often had an unaccountable component. This informal aspect to the economy was, at times, a reality in doing business in India. While conditions such as these impeded the conduct of business in India, an overall optimism, reinforced by several years of strong economic growth, prevailed.

Declining Market Share

The domestic market for helmets, a derived demand from two-wheeler usage, grew steadily through the early 1990s, from less than 200,000 units in 1985 to over 650,000 in 1995; the number of competitors rose in tandem. However, in recent years, Studds' domestic sales had been fairly stagnant. As a result, their market share had declined from its 36 per cent level in 1992 to 30 per cent in 1994.

Export Potential

In 1994, exports accounted for 20 per cent of Studds' sales. Studds had exports to thirty-five countries in several regions of the world. Its greatest presence was in South America, followed by Southeast Asia. Based on large populations and increasing two-wheeler usage, tremendous potential existed in developing country markets. However, as Studds was still new to international markets, a market focus had not been determined.

Studds' Export Markets

Country	*% of Exports*
South America	38.20
Southeast Asia	19.60
North America	15.90
Europe	15.10
Middle East	7.90
Africa	3.30

The Studds group was the only Indian helmet manufacturer selling in international markets. It began to consider foreign markets in 1990 because of a slack in the domestic market and a substantial growth in international markets. In 1991, when Studds decided to go international, the company elected to attend, with the assistance of the India Trade Promotion Organisation (ITPO), the IFMA Cologne Motor Show at Milan. The show provided a high-profile presence for Studds, as it was the premier trade show for motorcycle, and motorcycle-related products.

In subsequent years, Studds tried to distance its display from other Indian manufacturers and ITPO, as other Indian products did not enjoy as good a reputation internationally. Studds helmets were equivalent in quality to leading international manufacturers, and following the initial order from Mauritius, the helmets penetrated world markets rapidly and aggressively. From 1991–92 to 1993–94, export sales quadrupled.

Most of the sales were under its brand name. The exceptions were Canada, where Studds helmets were sold under the CKX brand to snowmobile riders, and in Sri Lanka. In Germany, helmets for the lower end of the market maintained the Studds brand name; but helmets for the upper end of the market were built on order and custom-branded. The company did not spend money on marketing and advertising in any of its international markets. International sales were too low to fund such expenditures. Larger companies such as Arai, however, were actively involved in developing and maintaining their brands.

All of Studds' international contacts were made through trade shows where it contacted distributors who would move the helmets to local retailers. Four or five distributors were sufficient to cover a region the size of the United States. The principal competitors for Studds in most markets were companies from Taiwan and South Korea. Other India-based competition was non-existent and Studds held a considerable cost advantage over its foreign competitors. Studds, operating with a 15 to 20 per cent margin, sold open-face helmets for Rs 280–650 and full-face helmets for Rs 400–650; and its South Korean competitors, the next lowest-priced producers, sold full-face models for Rs 1,550–1700. Labour costs, particularly in fibreglass models, accounted for Studds' cost advantage. Studds' cost advantage once prompted a South Korean firm to offer Studds a subcontract on a North American order.

Moreover, Studd's testing facilities ensured that its helmets conformed to standards and specifications required of safety-related products in various countries and regions. Had these helmets not been manufactured to these standards, they could not have been legally sold in the relevant regional market. Despite these major advantages, two key issues faced Studds before it could become a world player:

1. Studds did not have an internationally recognised brand name. Major helmet manufacturers regularly advertised in specialty magazines aimed at car and motorcycle enthusiasts, and had their helmets worn or brands displayed at motorcycle and car competitions.

2. Studds had still to secure international distribution channels. Specialty shops and mail order firms were the two most common ways in which consumers bought helmets.

Studds had limited financial and managerial resources to develop its brand name and to secure international distributors. Its annual advertising expenditure was Rs 200,000 or about $7,000.

The Global Market

At a general level, the two-wheeler markets in developed and developing economies had a number of interesting differences. The variation in these markets had important implications for Studds as consumer preferences and the requirements for success differed. The following table underscores the issues identified by the Studds management team.

The Two-wheeler Market: Developed vs. Developing Economies

Market	*Characteristic*	*Implication*
Developed economies	Higher incomes	Two-wheeler is a sports vehicle Lower usage of mopeds and scooters, move to increased bicycle usage Greater average individual expenditure on vehicle and accessories Less price-sensitivity, more concern with brand
Developed economies	Colder climates	Less usage annually Two-wheeler cannot be used as primary vehicle for full duration of year Smaller proportion of population uses two-wheelers Users may be wealthier segment of population, greater concern with brand names
Developing economies	Lower incomes	Two-wheelers are primary vehicle Higher usage of mopeds and scooters Lower expenditures on vehicle and accessories Greater price sensitivity Less concern with brand name
Developing economies	Warmer climates	Greater usage annually Two-wheeler can be used all year round Larger proportion of population uses two-wheelers All segments of population use two-wheelers, less concern with brand names

Two important trends emerged from this. Consumers in developed economies were more brand-conscious and less price-sensitive, and the greatest potential for growth in demand for two-wheelers was in countries classified as developing economies. Combining the higher incidence of (per capita) usage in developing economies with the large populations in this region demonstrated the tremendous potential for two-wheeler usage and related helmet demand in the countries of this region.

In this context, while export sales growth had been impressive, Studds helmets were still a small component of total world sales. The global market for motorcycle and bicycle helmets was estimated by Madhu Khurana to be approximately Rs 20 bn and for sports helmets Rs 10 bn. Studds covered all three segments, with the strongest sales for motorcycle and bicycle helmets in the British and South American markets. Studds had identified Canada as a promising future market for bicycle helmets. It was expected that helmets would be made compulsory for all bicyclists by the mid-1990s, creating a demand for 2 million helmets. Studds intended to garner 5 per cent of this market.

In international markets, firms from Italy and Japan were strongest, and they competed primarily in developed country markets. Italian companies held a 55 to 60 per cent share in international markets and the two main Japanese firms a 15 to 20 per cent share. Companies from Taiwan held a 5 to 7 per cent share. The remainder was accounted for by a variety of firms from, for example, South Korea and India (Studds).

The Studds Nolan Joint Venture

By early 1994, the Studds management had decided to expand capacity in helmets and motorcycle accessories. To be competitive in international markets, Studds' management felt that the new facilities built in this expansion must incorporate the most modern manufacturing technology. For this reason and the desire to access world markets, Studds decided to partner with one of the world's market leaders.

During March 1994, Studds identified the top ten helmet manufacturers in the world. Each of these manufacturers received a letter from Studds stating its intention to expand capacity and offering the opportunity for a joint venture. Serious responses were received from three companies, two from Italian companies and one from a German company.

A Comparison between Nolan, Bieffe and Fimez

	Nolan		*Fimez*		*Bieffe*	
	1991	*1992*	*1991*	*1992*	*1991*	*1992*
Sales	23	27	11	13	20	21
Net income	1.0	0.8	0.1	(0.1)	0.2	0.1
Cash flow	2.6	2.7	0.5	0.4	0.8	0.3
Number of personnel	184	169	NA	NA	84	84
Debt vs. Banks	6.8	6.3	1.7	3.3.	7.2	6.7
Investments	1.1	1.4	0.7	0.8	0.2	(0.3)

Note: All monetary figures in US$ million.
Source: Company documents.

Representatives from both Italian companies visited Studds in May 1994 and discussed, in depth, the possibility of a joint venture. In July 1994, a team of managers from Studds visited the two Italian manufacturers—Bieffe and Nolan—and on the basis of its market leadership position and well-defined policies selected Nolan as their joint venture partner (see Appendix 1 for a description of Nolan). The planned Studds Nolan joint venture was Studds' first equity venture with a foreign partner.

Letter of Intent

The Studds group and the Nolan group of Italy signed a Letter of Intent on 27 July 1994, thereby agreeing to establish a helmet-manufacturing unit in Faridabad, India (see Appendix 2 for a summary of the Letter of Intent). Under the terms of the agreement, which were valid until September 1994, Studds Accessories was converted from a closely held to a widely held public limited company. The two groups had equal equity participation, with new manufacturing activities added to the existing trading activities of Studds accessories. The name of the existing company was changed to Studds Nolan Ltd.

While both partners had equal ownership (Rs 10 mn) in the venture, each possessed only a 20 per cent share. The remaining 60 per cent was to be issued to the public. At the time of the agreement, the current paid-up capital of Studds Accessories was Rs 2 mn. Rs 8 mn more was soon contributed to bring the holdings of Studds to the requisite Rs 10 mn. Nolan invested Rs 10 mn in the form of cash and moulds. The total equity of the venture was US$ 1,625,000.

The Joint Venture Agreement

In September 1994, representatives from Nolan visited Studds in India for a second time to work out a final joint venture agreement. During these meetings tension began to enter the relationship. Nolan's Indian attorney inserted new clauses into the legal agreements for the joint venture, which were not included in the original Letter of Intent. Still keen to proceed with the joint venture, Nolan gave Studds the option of framing the basic terms of the final joint venture agreement. The attorney for Studds framed a new agreement, which was handed over to Nolan in November 1994.

At this point, both parties became very cautious about the legal aspects of the agreement. The intervention by attorneys led to increased concern with the exact wording of the legal agreement. Both parties wanted to be sure that the agreement would fairly lay out the exact conditions under which the joint venture would be operated.

Implementation

Studds' managers began to implement certain aspects of the agreement in late 1994. The first task was the land purchase. The total cost of the land exceeded the budgeted Rs 7.2 mn. The additional expenditure for the land was related to the informal economy in India. Some of the disbursements made by Studds were necessary to secure the land but were to parties that could not issue a receipt. Nolan became concerned about these payments, and felt that Studds was not being completely honest in accounting for these expenditures. Other expenditures, too, had unaccountable components. Consequently, Nolan's managers expressed a desire to get more closely involved in the day-to-day operations, contrary to earlier agreements.

In the new agreements put forth by each partner, both sides were in agreement in their treatment of technology transfer, the location and set-up of the venture, methods of payment, and the transfer of moulds and dies. However, some divergence emerged concerning the management and administration of the venture. The two sides could not resolve what were to be day-to-day concerns and what were to be long-term issues.

Nolan's proposal listed fifteen decisions that required the approval of the board of directors. Many of the decisions were related to strategic concerns; however, others related to operational issues and expenditures. Specifically, real estate property and machines exceeding Rs 2 mn in value could not be bought or sold without prior approval of the board of directors. Studds' proposal contained no such provision, though both proposals stated that all day-to-day operating expenses of the joint venture might be incurred by a director or official of the company, provided the expenditure fell within the approved budgets and guidelines.

The February 1995 Meeting

In February 1995, Studds' management team visited Nolan in Italy to resolve concerns about the operation of the venture and to finalise the joint venture agreement. Neither partner felt confident about the other, and much of the discussion concerned the legal jurisdiction for the joint venture agreement. Studds insisted on India but Nolan was firm on London or Paris as the place for adjudication.

The meetings continued for three days, and the remaining faith that the parties had in each other continued to deteriorate. Both Nolan and Studds began to feel that the joint venture could not be salvaged. They began considering breaking off the existing agreement.

Signs of Discord

Eager for quick wins, the speed at which the two partners had earlier signed the letter of intent meant there was little time to develop relationships at a personal level. Generally, strong relationships between owners and senior managers facilitate and ease a joint venture through the inevitable periods in which partners have disagreements. And in a joint venture to which both partners have committed a significant portion of their assets, there is likely be a strong concern with control over the venture. In the Studds Nolan relationship, while the two parent companies agreed about the strategic direction of the joint venture, they could not resolve operational issues. Appendix 2 illustrates the level of detail to which Studds and Nolan were concerned with the operation of the venture.

In their proposal for the final joint venture agreement, Nolan's managers instituted a number of new provisions which would provide them with greater control over decisions made on a daily basis. However, their lack of familiarity with local operating conditions did not make their participation in the operations of the venture particularly valuable. Once Nolan's technology had been transferred to the manufacturing facility in Faridabad, the venture's interests could possibly be better served by leveraging Nolan's marketing strengths and using Studds' local knowledge to operate the plant efficiently and effectively.

Without informal control mechanisms, a series of formal mechanisms were developed to control this venture. However, these mechanisms did not allow operating managers to take decisions in a quick and timely way and impeded the operation of the venture. Thus, when Studds' managers could not account for all of their expenditures, though they were entirely legitimate expenses in the context of the business environment, Nolan's management reacted adversely and believed that their partner may be cheating them. The result of this reaction was to seek more formal controls (e.g., carefully worded legal agreements, setting points of adjudication, more control over the board of directors, and less discretion and latitude for operating managers).

Both Nolan and Studds were small firms, and neither had had experience in partnering with other firms. The venture represented a fair portion of their assets. Because they were single business enterprises, the venture's failure or success would have a larger impact on the parent firms than would be the case with larger corporations. This increased the desire for control in both firms.

Strategic Choice for Nolan

As the Nolan management team reassessed its choice of Studds as an international partner, they summarised the pros and cons from their point of view as follows:

- *Cost leadership*. Studds' cost leadership, which was virtually uncontested among non-India based production, was an important consideration.
- *Market leadership*. There was no doubt that Studds was the top performing Indian firm.
- *Small size*. Rapid decision making was possible but financial and managerial resources were limited.
- *Autocratic management style*. The general manager made almost all the decisions, there was no delegation, and this was combined with a reluctance to release control.
- *Operations were at capacity*. A new plant would have to be built to serve new markets.
- *Labour relations*. The Indian employees were heavily unionised and

management could not hire and fire employees freely. Also, it was difficult to implement new technologies. From the perspective of a joint venture partner, the potential for strikes and other forms of disruptions decreased the attractiveness of Studds. Studds was most vulnerable at the source of its strength.

- *Brand*. Nolan had an added motivation for maintaining control. Its biggest asset was its brand name and helmet design capabilities. The lack of international property rights protection in India was an area of concern. Studds' experience with brand name infringement illustrated the reality of this risk. A second brand-related risk existed for Nolan outside of India. A negative country of origin effect could lead consumers in other countries to question the quality of Nolan's helmets produced in India. In the first MoU, the two partners had agreed on a combination of the two brand names. The new hybrid brand, Studds Nolan, typified many of the problems with the venture. Combining brand names reflected the pride of the firms and their desire to assume a dominant position.

Strategic Options for Studds

From Studds' point of view, breaking off the Nolan joint venture would delay Studds in its efforts to become a global leader in helmet manufacturing. However, Bieffe and other helmet manufacturers remained as potential partners for Studds should the agreement be terminated. Studds could also take other courses of action.

The expectations of Studds' management from the partnership with Nolan included providing Studds with new technology, an internationally recognised brand name and access to distributor channels in Europe and North America. Until then, the majority of Studds' export sales had been to Latin America and Southeast Asia, while 91 per cent of Nolan's sales in 1993 were to European and North American consumers.

But was the desire to penetrate developed markets the only option? What about the developing economy markets? Here Studds would require a lower cost product and access to consumers. Product it had, all that would be needed was to develop distribution channels to these regions. Consumers in developing economies desire a simple helmet which provides adequate protection and conforms to local standards and laws. Price and availability are the key considerations in these individuals' choice and Studds' products appeared more suited to this segment than to the demands of consumers in developed countries.

Studds did not require Nolan nor any other partner with a strong brand name if it chose to grow domestically and in developing country markets. The advantage which came with complementary resources in developed markets was not as strong an advantage in developing country markets. Studds could go it alone or choose to form a non-equity alliance with an international distributor. If Studds became successful in penetrating these markets over time, as the bi-wheeler market matured, the Studds name could become a strong brand in itself.

In moving to international markets, Studds had attempted to supplement its manufacturing strengths with marketing-related strengths and new technology. Strategically, the joint venture appeared to be a good decision, combining Studds' low cost, good quality manufacturing capabilities with Nolan's international marketing expertise, reputation and reach. But, the decision to partner was made quickly and it did not appear likely that Studds' objectives would be met under the current partnership. Ravi and Madhu Khurana met with their senior associates to review and discuss the options available to the company:

Four possible options were identified and then they went on to discuss the pros and cons of each option:

1. Reconcile with Nolan.
2. Select a new foreign partner.
3. Go international alone.
4. Concentrate on domestic markets.

Studds' Decision Tree

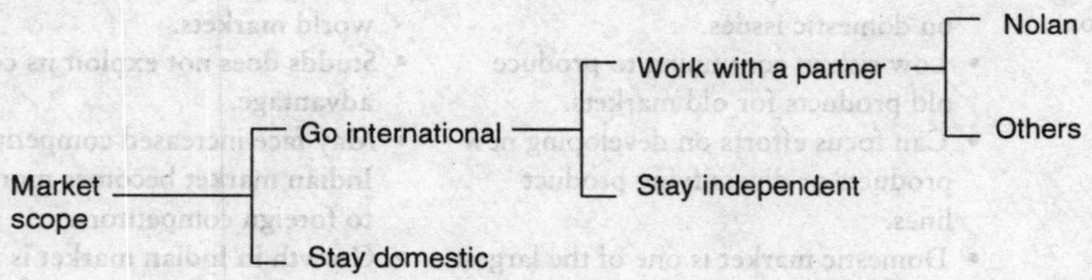

Options Available

Option	*Pros*	*Cons*
Reconcile with Nolan	• Preserves ideal partnership. • Provides Studds with access to world markets and to current technologies. • Allows Studds to move immediately to world markets. • Restricts a leading competitor from competing against Studds and its own domestic market.	• Studds' managers become constrained in their operations in India if issue of control not resolved. • Potential remains for future conflict, in the event of lingering distrust. • Joint venture remains at risk. • May not be able to implement new technology because of labour unrest.
Select a new partner	• Allows Studds to develop a new relationship. • Can learn from mistakes made with Nolan in setting up new partnership. • Two or three other firms were interested in partnering with Studds. • Removes Studds from an existing acrimonious relationship.	• Studds loses access to world markets, at least temporarily. • Management time and effort as well as dollar cost of setting up relationship lost. • Studds' credibility as a partner damaged. • Same problems may arise again. No guarantee that new partner will be better than the last.
Go at international markets alone	• Export growth has been very rapid to date; exports may continue to grow as fast as Studds can expand production. • Studds develops new capabilities in serving international markets alone. • Studds has an absolute cost advantage that can be exploited in world markets.	• Studds' internationalisation slowed. • Management time and effort as well as dollar cost of setting up relationship lost. • Studds' credibility as a partner damaged. • Studds does not have resources to advertise in international markets. • May not be able to establish a brand name, relegated to low cost/low end competitor.
Remain focussed on domestic market.	• Studds management can concentrate on domestic issues. • Low risk in continuing to produce old products for old markets. • Can focus efforts on developing new products or diversifying product lines. • Domestic market is one of the largest and fastest growing in the world.	• Management preference is to enter world markets. • Studds does not exploit its cost advantage. • May face increased competition, as Indian market becomes more open to foreign competitors. • Growth in Indian market is in lower end segments. • Miss opportunities in world markets.

What Happened

The meetings in Italy concluded with the joint venture's dissolution. The partners could not resolve their lack of confidence and trust in each other. The news of the Studds Nolan break-up spread rapidly throughout the industry. During April 1995, Bieffe Helmets contacted Studds about the possibility of a joint venture. However, Studds' management had become much more cautious and had realised the difficulties as well as the risks of offering equity to foreign partners. Differences in work cultures were identified as one of the reasons why Studds did not want to form a joint venture with another Italian company.

Studds tried to secure a non-equity arrangement—a technology transfer—with Bieffe, but Bieffe was unwilling to transfer any technology without acquiring a permanent stake in the new business. Studds concluded that its current capabilities and lower production costs were sufficient for competing internationally, and the scope of its business was being expanded. Although there was no indication of the geographical scope of internationalisation, Studds' goal remained global market leadership.

APPENDIX 1

Nolan's Company Profile

The companies that formed the Nolan group produced protective helmets for motorcyclists, bicyclists and other sports enthusiasts. Nolan, formed in the 1970s, began as a supplier of motorcycle and car accessories to a large multinational. In twenty years of operations, competitive pricing, high technical performance and consistent quality characterised the company's products. Substantial innovations and product developments had improved the aesthetic appearance and performance of the helmets, while consistently respecting regulations and standards that governed safety products.

Nolan's marketing strengths had grown with its technical expertise. Nolan's trademark had increased in importance in principal markets, and was one of the most well recognised across the world. A network of loyal distributors contributed to Nolan's success. The dealers comprising this network specialised in sales in this market and adjusted their sales tactics to Nolan's product line changes. Recently, a new line of Nolan products had been developed, but had not yet reached the market. These new items were designed to increase protection to the face and had excellent mechanical and optical qualities.

Investment supporting continued renovation and improvements in the product lines came to US$ 1.53 mn in 1993. For 1994, investment was projected to exceed US$ 1.75 mn. These investments, which accounted for 6.4 per cent of gross revenues, were for renovations in machinery and products alone. A further 3.6 per cent of sales was dedicated to ongoing product design and research.

Nolan's 1993 sales were divided between several markets. Exports were larger than domestic sales.

Nolan's products were marketed domestically and abroad using a common advertising strategy. Nolan used standard industry promotional vehicles such as advertising in specialty magazines and sponsorship of race car drivers and motorcycle riders. However, the company preferred to concentrate on the commercial end in its marketing strategy. It helped retailers display, promote and demonstrate its products to the customer. Thus, the company's advertising was less aggressive than its competitors, since Nolan preferred to provide good service to its dealers and customers rather than pay for other, more glamorous, forms of advertising.

Nolan's Financial Performance

(US$ million)

	1993 (Actual)	1994 (Projected)
Turnover	26.408	30.761
Cost of sales	16.584	19.187
Gross profit	9.824	11.574
Less depreciation	1.539	2.137
Less other operating expenses	5.465	6.322
Operating expenses before interest	2.819	3.115
Net interest	(1.261)	(847)
Extraordinary items	(0.265)	(233)
Profit before taxes	1.294	2.035
Taxes	(0.515)	(1.018)
Accelerated depreciation	(0.285)	0
Net profit	493	1.017

Source: Company documents.

Summary of Nolan's Sales

	Sales (US$ million)	% of Total Helmet Sales
Subdivision of sales		
Helmets	24.521	–
Optical area (Visors)	1.555	–
Subdivision of helmet sales		
Domestic		
Italy	4.832	19.71
Exports	19.689	80.29
Subdivision of export sales		
Europe	15.051	61.38
North America	2.487	10.14
Other countries	2.151	8.77
Total (55 countries)	19.689	–

Source: Company documents.

APPENDIX 2

The Studds Nolan Letter of Intent

The factory of the venture was to be located in Faridabad, Haryana, about 6 to 7 km from the present offices of Studds. The existing offices and sales staff of Studds Accessories were to be used for marketing activities. In the joint venture agreement, land for the factory building and measuring $6000m^3$ was to be purchased by February 1995. The land price was estimated to be Rs $1000/m^2$. With duties, brokerage fees and other set-up costs, the total cost to the company for the land was estimated to be Rs 7.2 mn.

Machinery and Equipment

Machinery	600 ton injection moulding machine	Rs 7.00 million
	400 ton injection moulding machine	Rs 5.50 million
	180 ton injection moulding machine	Rs 2.00 million
	Assembly equipment	Rs 14.50 million
	Maintenance equipment	Rs 0.50 million
	Sales tax	Rs 1.20 million
	Installation expenses	Rs 1.95 million
Total machinery and equipment costs		Rs 18.15 million
Moulds and Dies	Moulds and dies imported	Rs 3.00 million
	Customs duty (25%)	Rs 0.75 million
	Freight, insurance, etc.	Rs 0.40 million
Total moulds and dies		Rs 4.15 million
Generators and Vehicles	1 no. generator set 500 KVA	Rs 2.00 million
	1 no. generator set 250 KVA	Rs 1.20 million
	Vehicles	Rs 1.00 million
Total generators and vehicles		Rs 4.20 million
Factory workers (annual costs)	Skilled labour (40 @ Rs 3,500/month)	Rs 1.680 million
	Unskilled labour (30 @ Rs 2,700/month)	Rs 0.972 million
	Total labour	Rs 2.652 million
	Add: 35% (other associated labour costs)	Rs 0.928 million
Total annual labour cost		Rs 3.580 million

Construction on the factory building was to begin in March 1995, following purchase of the land and receipt of approval from the relevant authorities. The factory building was proposed to consist of 25,000 square feet, at a cost of Rs 6.25 mn. Machinery installation was to occur in November and production would start in December 1995. The commercial launch date for Studds Nolan helmets was to be January 1996. The figures in this agreement were considered realistic given Studds managers' familiarity with local operating conditions.

Management of the Joint Venture

A board of directors, which numbered five including the chairman, controlled Studds Nolan Limited. The chairman was from the Studds group and Nolan and Studds both appointed two other directors. The chairman and one director of the Studds group were the working directors and took care of day-to-day operations of the company.

The board of directors would meet quarterly to review the performance of the company. The Nolan directors would be reimbursed for travel to and from India for two of their trips each year. Employees, both skilled and unskilled, were locally available; thus all managers and factory staff were from India. The organisation was structured in a form similar to that of Studds Accessories.

Studds Nolan Organisational Structure

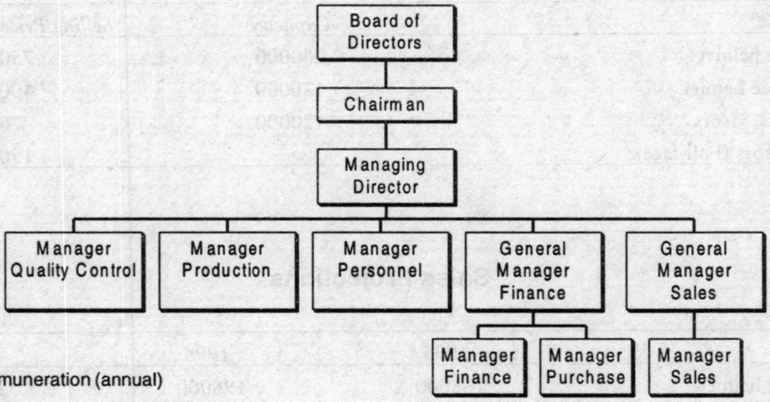

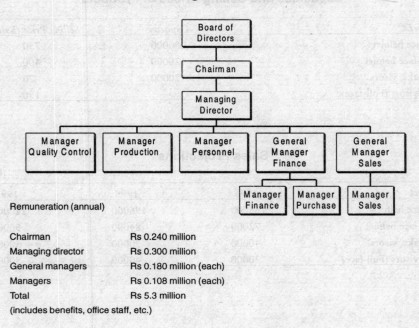

Remuneration (annual)

Chairman	Rs 0.240 million
Managing director	Rs 0.300 million
General managers	Rs 0.180 million (each)
Managers	Rs 0.108 million (each)
Total	Rs 5.3 million

(includes benefits, office staff, etc.)

Projections

Several detailed projections were made concerning production, prices, sales and revenues. Capacity estimates were based on a three-shift operating schedule, during which both full-face and open-face helmets were to be produced. Full-face helmets had greater market value and margins than open-face helmets; thus more of these would be produced.

While close to 400,000 helmets could be produced at capacity, sales were estimated to be less than this amount during the first few years of operations, though early sales would exceed the break-even quantity of 92,000 helmets. Helmets would be sold under the Studds Nolan brand name. If sales grew as projected in a market survey, 75 per cent of capacity would be utilised in 1998, the third year of the factory's operation. Most raw materials for production could be sourced locally, though anti-glare visors for the full-face helmets would be procured from Nolan or Korean suppliers depending on the price offered. The venture was expected to be profitable in its first year of operation.

Capacities and Selling Prices of Products

Product	*Capacity*	*Selling Price (Rs/unit)*
Full-face helmet	280000	750
Open-face helmet	120000	400
Sunpeaks, visors	120000	70
Spare visors (Full-face)	–	190

Sales Projections

(Units)

Product	*1995*	*1996*	*1997*
Full-face helmet	168000	196000	210000
Open-face helmet	72000	84000	90000
Sunpeaks, visors	40000	50000	50000
Spare visors (Full-face)	30000	40000	50000

Pro forma Income Statement

(Rs million)

	1995	*1996*	*1997*
Sales	163300	191700	206500
Cost of sales	112900	132640	143400
Gross profit	50400	59060	63100
Depreciation	3381	3381	3381
Operating expenses	23800	27785	31137
Operating profit	23219	27894	28582
Interest	5425	5600	5200
Profit before tax	17794	22294	23382
Taxation	4046	6230	7106
Net profit	13748	16064	16276
Dividend	9400	9400	9400
Profit for general reserve	4348	6664	6876
Return on capital	27%	29%	27%

Part 3
Revitalising People, Organisations and Relationships

RASHTRIYA ISPAT NIGAM LIMITED: STEELY CHALLENGES

It was 6:00 pm on 8 July 1996, and a frown crossed and settled on his otherwise pleasant countenance. Fifty-seven-year old Jatinder Mehra, chairman of the public sector steel giant Rashtriya Ispat Nigam Limited, had just returned after a week to Vizag from Delhi. As was his wont on such occasions, he had asked his directors to come in and see him. The news was not at all good. Thirty-seven months ago he had taken over a sinking ship, only to see it go from strength to strength. From losses to operational profits, cash profits, higher cash profits and towards net profits; from morale that had touched its nadir to a point where employees' enthusiasm was matched only by their CMD's optimism; he had seen it all, participated in it, led from the front. The discussion with his directors lasted for only thirty minutes, but underlined one important problem. The first quarter production report was on his table, and as he thumbed through it purposefully, he couldn't lay his finger on just what had caused the dip in that quarter's performance. True, the months of April and May were never the best as

This case was written by Sudeep Mitra and Himanshu Tambe, COSMODE, with the help of R.P. Shrivastava, RINL, and under the overall supervision of Dr Dharni P. Sinha, COSMODE (Consortium For Strategic Management and Organisation Development). The authors are grateful to Rashtriya Ispat Nigam Ltd for their help and support.

March was always the most stressful month. By June, production had always picked up. But not this time. Various thoughts came to his mind, vignettes from an eventful career. 'You can never tell what would work this time', he almost said aloud. 'You need to reinvent solutions', he thought, 'to problems that manifest themselves in new forms.'

Background and History

Visakha ukku, andhralu hakku— 'A steel plant at Vizag is Andhra's right'—was the slogan adopted by those clamouring for a steel plant to be put up in Visakhapatnam. Speaking on the resolution put forth by the state legislative assembly that demanded an integrated steel plant (ISP) to be set up at Vizag, the then chief minister of Andhra Pradesh Brahmananda Reddy said, 'I would not be surprised if the Andhras were to lose their patience.' The agitation took a violent turn in the Circar districts of Visakhapatnam, Srikakulam and East Godavari districts, with the police opening fire, killing seventeen and wounding sixty-four in the process.

Replying to a question arising out of a statement made by the steel minister on 4 November 1967, Prime Minister Indira Gandhi said, 'We do not have resources for a fifth steel plant anywhere now'. However, later she did a volte face, and on 17 April 1970, she announced the government's decision to set up an integrated steel plant. A site near Balacheruvu creek was chosen in view of its topography, greater land availability and proximity to the port. The site was formally inaugurated by Indira Gandhi on 20 January 1971 (see Appendix 1 for chronology of major events).

Why then, did it take twenty years for the first 'heat' of steel to be produced at RINL? The plant started operating over four years after its scheduled commissioning date and cost Rs 46.52 bn more than its original estimate. However, the Vizag Steel Plant is not the only large Integrated Steel Plant (ISP) where project management plans have gone awry. Expansion projects at SAIL's Bhilai and Bokaro plants were delayed by seventy-three and 131 months respectively; their costs also surpassed their original estimates by over Rs 10 bn.

M.N. Dastur & Company (Dasturco) had prepared the feasibility report for the project, based on a capacity of 2 million metric tonnes (MMT) of ingot steel as early as February 1972. However, based on cost-capacity economics, it emerged that a plant that produced 3 MMT of liquid steel would be best placed to optimise investments and costs. Dasturco was then asked to prepare a detailed project report (DPR), which it submitted in October 1977. An understanding between India and the USSR on economic and technical cooperation was signed between the two governments on 12 June 1979. With this, Vizag was to become the third ISP after Bhilai and Bokaro that was built with Soviet assistance, and Steel Authority of India's fifth ISP. Dasturco engineers worked together with GIPROMEZ, the USSR state institute that designed steel plants, to prepare a comprehensive revised detailed project report (CRDPR); this was submitted on 30 November 1980. At this stage, the plant was designed to produce 3.4 MMT of hot metal, 3.4 MMT of liquid steel, 2.983 MMT of saleable steel, projected to cost Rs 22.56 bn and take an estimated six years to commission, with the first stage of 1 MMT estimated to take four years.

'Inadequate and inconsistent flow of funds', according to B.N. Rath, the then director (construction), 'delayed the project'. The funds, which came in bits and pieces, were inadequate even to acquire the land, leave alone go in for construction. By then the cost of the project had spiralled upwards to Rs 38.97 bn and SAIL, which was seeking funds for expansion and modernisation of its existing plants, decided to abandon this project. This paved the way for the formation on 18 February 1982 of a new corporate entity, Rashtriya Ispat Nigam Limited (RINL), that would own the Vizag Steel Plant (VSP), India's latest ISP in the public sector. The ISP concept involved substantial backward integration—into mining of coal, iron ore (RINL doesn't have these mines), limestone, dolomite, etc., coke production, running of power plants, oxygen making plants, operating workshops, laboratories for quality control, and more. With the release of funds finally coming through, construction work began for the project in April 1982.

Even after this, there was no steady flow of funds (see Appendix 2). During 1982 through 1984, RINL had at the helm as many as three managing directors : V Subramaniam, K.V.B. Pantulu and K.R. Sangameshvaram. 'Faced with what seemed to be another white elephant at its hands, the government seriously considered the option of abandoning the project and cutting its losses', said R.J. Darjee. This meant the cancellation or holding in abeyance orders for equipment that had already been placed. Not only did this slow down the progress made on construction, it also attracted penal provisions and escalation clauses as part of contractual obligations.

The fourth MD, who was designated chairman-cum-managing director (CMD), D.R. Ahuja, served between 1984 and 1990. After a three-year stint as managing director of the Indian Iron & Steel Company (IISCO), he served as managing director of SAIL's Bokaro Plant, and thereafter assumed office as CMD of RINL on 10 October 1984. He decided not to let RINL run the way other steel plants did—with bloated (direct) manpower; instead, he engaged a substantial number of contract labour. While a hospital was put up in Vizag, external parties were invited to set up schools, transportation was subcontracted out and later dropped, food supplies for guest houses too were outsourced. His handling of rehabilitation of displaced persons ensured that the plant, unlike other steel plants in India, was unencumbered with excessive manpower. He also believed that a team of young, first generation industrial workers who had no prior experience in the steel industry would be more adaptive to the new technology, and, therefore, be more productive in delivering the goods.

By December 1987 the project cost had spiralled upwards to Rs 68.50 bn. It was at this stage that Ahuja suggested to the government the 'rationalised plant concept' which would reduce time and cost overruns and take the project to its logical conclusion. This involved reduction of liquid steel making capacity from 3.4 million tonnes to 3 million tonnes by setting up of one instead of the two steel melt shops (SMS) envisaged earlier, and uprating capacity of the residual SMS. Convinced that it made more sense to go ahead than to abandon the project, the government retracted its earlier stand and decided to give the go-ahead to RINL.

The uprating of capacities coupled with the reduction of project costs by Rs15.00 bn breathed life into the project. This, however, also meant achieving a labour productivity of 231 tonnes per man year—twice the existing Indian productivity standard and closer to Brazil (204), Canada (272) and Japan (323). By 1988, fund flow had stabilised. Within a period of three years, the first heat of steel was poured on 6 September 1990 with the commissioning of Convertor-A.

By 1991, momentous changes swept across the global political and economic landscape. The cold war had come to an end and socialism had come to be regarded as a quirk in economic theory, something that was impractical. Things had come to such a pass in India that foreign exchange reserves were available to cover barely two weeks' imports. It is under such circumstances that India approached the World Bank for exceptional financing. The World Bank responded with its standard Structural Adjustment Programme, which made economic liberalisation a sine qua non.

Thus, it is by a quirk of fate that this steel plant whose seeds were sown in the pre-liberalised economic era was left to survive and grow in the liberalised environment. As budgetary support to PSUs was of low priority, RINL never received the kind of state protection that SAIL plants received in the past. The financial charges, viz, interest and depreciation, added an additional burden of about Rs 3,600 per tonne of steel at 100 per cent capacity utilisation. The market price of saleable steel ranged between Rs 8,000 to 10,000 per tonne in 1992–93, whereas RINL's average cost inclusive of financial charges for the year worked out to over Rs 13,000 per tonne. This meant that every tonne of steel produced by the organisation had a negative contribution to its profitability! The organisation approached the government in 1989 with a plan to restructure its finances, but the proposal gathered dust.

By 1990, B.N. Rath had taken over as CMD. To avoid being saddled with surplus construction manpower at the end of the project and in view of the resource constraints, RINL decided to forgo the 'turnkey' concept of implementation. The entire project was managed by a core group of 180-odd construction engineers, who even stationed themselves at various factories in the erstwhile-USSR to expedite imports and monitor their despatches to meet construction schedules. It is during Rath's tenure in June 1992 that Stage II commissioning was undertaken, after which the plant was rated to produce 3 million tonnes (see Appendix 3). In June 1993, J. Mehra, director (operations), took over as CMD.

At the latest count, the project is estimated to have cost Rs 85.29 bn, i.e., a cost overrun of Rs 46.32 bn and a time overrun of fifty-four months. Of the total overrun, only Rs 3.13 bn was due to an increase in the scope of the project concept; the balance Rs 43.19 bn was caused due to an uneven flow of funds. According to Darjee, 'We have had to repay the Russians at the exchange rate of Rs 35 to a rouble because of the agreement, whereas the dollar rate of the rouble is abysmally low.' Escalation clauses contributed to Rs 17.22 bn, exchange rate variations to Rs 8.12 bn, added duties/taxes to Rs 2.97 bn, and financial charges including interest to Rs 14.88 bn.

Strategy for Survival

'When I assumed office as CMD', said Mehra, 'there were three areas that needed most of top management's time and attention.... The need for changing the mindset of employees (which was rooted in the past), restructuring the company's finances (to offset the adverse impact of the heavy financial charges), and the need to achieve rated capacities quickly and reduce costs.'

Time was of the essence, so these initiatives were taken up simultaneously.

Mindset Change

The inordinate delay in commissioning the project, the massive cost overrun, the government's near decision to abandon the project, all taken together had lowered the morale of RINLs 17,000-odd executives and workmen. Incredulity over the plant's viability began with executives, percolated down to workmen and began to permeate the public at large. Would the plant be commissioned? On completion, would it operate at full capacity? Would it ever make profits? Doubts such as these assailed workmen and executives alike.

An organisation survey commissioned by RINL in 1993 revealed the following perceptions among the workforce:

- *RINL can never achieve its rated capacity*: According to several executives, 'a similar converter shop having three converters of 133 cubic metres (at Bhilai) was rated at 1.5 MMT, and it was therefore considered unrealistic and perhaps, unfair, that this plant was rated at 3 MMT'. Uprating of the BF and SMS capacities may have saved the project and the organisation, but was considered impractical and, therefore, unachievable.
- *RINL has unusually low manpower*: Other steel plants in the country with comparable capacity, whether in the public sector or private, had over 40,000 and in some cases 60,000 employees, while Vizag Steel had only 13,500 employees at the works. As realisation dawned that the uprated capacities were to be achieved by a comparatively slim workforce, the productivity gap between the Indian average of under 100 tonnes per man year and the targeted 231 tonnes per man year appeared to be daunting and insurmountable.
- *RINL can never make profits*: Merchant bankers who were called in to financially restructure RINL, in their report submitted in 1992, commented, 'based on 1991 fourth-quarter steel prices, RINL can achieve cash breakeven at 170 per cent utilisation and breakeven at 290 per cent utilisation of capacity.'

> 'After all, how does a mindset get hardened?' asked Mehra. 'The mindset is a function of the environment in which you operate. On realising this, I started sending teams of executives and workmen abroad to study technological processes and work practices in world class steel plants in Korea, Japan and the USA, so that they would understand just how world class productivity standards could be achieved. The idea was to imbibe best practices from these organisations and transfer learnings back home. I deliberately prevented them from visiting Indian steel plants so that they could learn to uphold international norms and benchmarks, undeterred by what was the best in the country.'

The learning process was followed by presentations made by these teams to their colleagues back home in groups, followed by question-answer sessions and intense discussions. It took RINL about a year to internalise these learnings and remove mental blocks regarding the rated capacity of the plants. According to T. Ramamurthy, director (personnel), 'the process of mindset change was reinforced by systems change in the form of an innovative incentive and reward package that was designed to boost productivity levels'. The incentive schemes were linked to both production and techno-economic factors. Non-executives as well as executives were eligible for incentives, though the schemes differed. The group-based reward scheme was linked to shift production in the SMS and not to daily production, to bolster production in all shifts. They were made operative only if production rose for three consecutive days and not just for one day, so that production could be hiked on an ongoing rather than an ad hoc basis. This emphasised teamwork and improved employee morale, while fostering healthy inter-brigade competition. All this was achieved while keeping manpower costs to below 10 per cent of revenue.

Cost Management and Financial Restructuring

The financial charges of about Rs 7 bn on depreciation and Rs 4.5 bn on interest, detracted Rs 11.50 bn per annum from the bottom line. These translated to about Rs 3,600 per tonne, to be recovered at full capacity utilisation. They also called for sustained operations at 100 per cent capacity, so as to achieve net profits by 1996–97.

To address this issue, the company adopted a two-pronged approach: cost reduction combined with revenue maximisation on the one hand, and financial restructuring on the other. According to P. Doki, director (commercial), 'These two considerations required us to pare down operating costs to the bone while improving realisations to achieve profits at realistic levels of capacity utilisation. We achieved this by institutionalising budgeting, controlling inventory levels, eliminating wasteful practices, and by monitoring costs on a daily basis.'

A series of workshops were conducted to improve cost awareness across the company and to build a culture of cost consciousness. Within a short time of its commissioning in July 1992, the plant had achieved several landmarks in steel production techno-economics in the country. For instance, productivity levels improved from117 tonnes per man year in 1993–94, to 156 in 1994–95, and 183 in 1995–96. As a result, its conversion processing cost of liquid steel was the lowest in the country and competitive with global majors.

After liberalisation, in 1992, the government agreed in principle to restructure RINL's asset-liability structure. This came into effect in August 1993. As a result, 50 per cent of the outstanding government loans of Rs 23.69 bn as on 31 March 1992 were converted to equity capital, and the balance 50 per cent was converted into 7 per cent non-cumulative redeemable preference shares, to be redeemed after ten years. Further, the Rs 7.91 bn interest liability was converted into an interest-free loan for seven years. All loans drawn after 1 August 1993 were to be converted into 7 per cent non-redeemable preference shares payable after ten years, and penal interest payable on defaults on payment of principal and interest up to 31 March 1992 were waived. Redemption was to be done over a five-year period beginning from 2005–06 in a phased manner. This was the largest relief ever given by the Indian government to a PSU.

The relief was granted on two conditions: that RINL would achieve the rated capacity of liquid steel of 3 MMT by 1996–97 and that it would make net profits by 1997–98. 'Though the government agreed to convert into preference shares loans given after August 1993, only Rs 3.23 bn that it had given us in 1992–93 was treated as such', said C. Siva Prasad, joint general manager (corporate finance). 'The balance Rs 5.43 bn given to us as non-plan funds between 1993 to 1996 was treated as loans, attracting interest of over Rs 800 mn per annum.'

The company had massive share capital of Rs 64.94 bn, including Rs 48.90 bn of equity and Rs 16.04 bn of preference shares. The massive capital base made it difficult to finance expansions through issue of fresh capital. 'Had it managed to convert the outstanding loans into interest-free loans instead of equity, it might have been a different picture altogether', opined a merchant banker. With its net loss of Rs 1.8 bn for the year 1995-96, the accumulated losses up to 31 March 1996 was as much as Rs 31.70 bn.

Though the government did not agree to all the suggestions made by RINL, this gave the company much needed breathing space, in the process bringing down the interest burden to about Rs 2.75 bn and helping RINL to improve its liquidity position (see Appendices 4 and 5). Consequent to restructuring, the company's financial charges were less of a drain on the bottom line.

Comparative Costs

(Rs per tonne)

Year	*RINL*		*SAIL*		*TISCO*	
	WC	*TC*	*WC*	*TC*	*WC*	*TC*
1992–93	7731	13013	9404	11138	8498	10264
1993–94	7555	12185	10543	12105	9245	11105
1994–95	6552	10641	12122	13662	9640	11674
1995–96 (Estimated)	7112	10671	12350	13947	11362	13625

WC: Works cost. TC: Total cost (= WC + financial charges).

According to R.C. Jha, director (operations), 'Reaching targeted productivity norms quickly was central to our strategy for achieving financial viability.' The work culture in RINL is quite unlike most other PSUs; there is a business and profit orientation, according to executives. Some of the measures adopted since inception like abolition of overtime for workmen, use of overlapping shifts to ensure continuity in operations during changeover, and the latest—a messengerless office—were innovations in the Indian steel industry.

In 1992–93, RINL made an operating loss of Rs 310 mn. One hundred per cent continuous casting in the SMS was introduced for the first time in India. Requirement of balancing facilities, time taken for technology absorption and lack of experienced manpower led to slow pick up in production from the SMS, which became a bottleneck. Contraction in SMS output not only throttled production in downstream units; its offtake also imposed an upper limit on how much hot metal the BF could produce. The rationalised concept, which had acted as a life jacket for the sinking company, created such and other problems. Another vexatious issue was the optimisation of space and layouts which had been planned and partly implemented with the earlier DPR in mind, but actually used with the rationalised DPR concept.

The workshops on 'changing mindsets' threw up the approach of demonstrating success in select areas by achieving production targets and reducing operating costs. With reference to the SMS, one upstream unit (BF) and one downstream unit (WRM) were chosen to demonstrate success with a view to boost employee morale.

The two blast furnaces were designed to produce 3.4 MMT of hot metal, of which 2.815 MMT was to be utilised by the SMS and the balance 0.585 MMT was to be converted to pig iron for sale in the open market. Though the SMS offtake was lower than envisaged, it was decided that the BFs would be allowed to raise their output phasewise to achieve rated capacities, and the residual hot metal that was left after supplying the SMS would be converted into pig iron and sold in the open market. While the help of SAIL was taken in BF-I, in-house engineering expertise was used to commission BF-II. This led to a soaring of confidence among executives and workmen, many of whom were new recruits. Quality improvement in cast house refractories, enhanced equipment availability and utilisation, particularly in the pig casting machines, skill development among employees by arranging for plant visits abroad, and on-site skill transfer by reputed international agencies helped in production build up from below 1.4 MMT in 1991–92, to 2.37 MMT (1993–94) and to 3.21 MMT in 1995–96. The level of capacity utilisation of 95 per cent achieved in 1995–96 included a 'last quarter' level of 102 per cent.

The WRM was chosen because wire rods were RINL's premium products. The WRM has state-of-the art technology and high levels of automation. Mastering skills in operating these high-speed mills was the most challenging technological exercise undertaken at the plant. This was achieved through focussing on operations and maintenance of automated devices on a continuous basis, and by evolving and rigorously implementing standard operating practices (SOPs) and standard maintenance practices (SMPs) in critical areas. Besides, deputing employees on plant visits abroad and transferring skills back home helped to broaden perspectives, and providing on-site assistance by international agencies helped to master intricate skills. In November 1994, the WRM received the ISO 9002 certification.

The SMS requires the highest levels of managerial co-ordination between the converters and the continuous casting machines, and also takes a comparatively longer time to provide stabilised output. The poor performance of this shop not only affected RINL's operations and profitability, it also affected employee morale. The increase in heats per day, the parameter that measures the overall productivity of the SMS, limped from an average of 21 per day (1992–93) to 25 (1993–94). This was variously attributed to deliberate bypassing of automated controls during commissioning, structural inadequacy that resulted in poor co-ordination, and an inconducive work environment.

It is against this background that Mehra decided to invite, in 1994, Voest Alpine, an Austrian company specialising in steel technology which also operated its own steel plants, to review RNIL's operations and to make recommendations that could be used to step up productivity at the SMS. Based on the recommendations and internal discussions that followed, several steps were taken, including re-engineering of work processes, provision of balancing facilities in select areas, and increasing the capacity of the steel ladle to handle 20 tonnes more of liquid steel than its nameplate level. 'Voest Alpine's intervention has definitely contributed to improving production at the SMS', acknowledged Dr J.K. Bagchi, secretary, Ministry of Steel.

Existing systems were also improved, e.g., refractory management systems to increase ladle and convert lining lives, and developing and implementing SOPs and SMPs in critical areas. Innovative incentive and reward schemes were adopted to improve productivity levels and achieve rated capacities. 'We were the first in India to try 100 per cent argon rinsing from the bottom and to use gunnited tundishes rather than bricks. It took us two years from 1993 to streamline productivity and to achieve 15 per cent reduction in costs', said H.S. Sethi, general manager (operations), who as DGM (SMS) had spearheaded the change at the SMS. By March 1995, productivity had increased to an annual average of 33 heats per day, and by March 1996, this had risen to an average of 41 heats per day. Liquid steel production increased by 43 per cent in 1994–95 and by 23 per cent in 1995–96. The capacity utilisation increased to 79 per cent in 1995–96, with the last quarter recording 90 per cent utilisation. This demolished the myth that SMS capacities were overrated.

Productivity

Parameter	*1992–93*	*1993–94*	*1994–95*	*1995–96*
Liquid steel (MMT)	1.05	1.36	1.94	2.38
Heats (MT)	7603	9123	12207	14926
Heats per day	20.8	25.0	33.4	40.8
Productivity (Tonnes/ man year)	110	117	156	183

Strategy for Growth

By June 1993, Mehra was of the opinion that while his three-pronged consolidation strategy might make RINL viable, it would not make it a growing and vibrant company. 'After all, what has been the bane of this company?' he asked. 'The financial charges. This left us with two options to attack this issue. One was to swap our existing high-cost funds with low-cost funds. We thought this and even toyed with the idea of sourcing low-cost overseas funds. But these appeared impractical in the face of unfavourable (capital) market conditions.'

The only other way was to raise the productivity of capital, by adding to the existing capacity so that the plant could realise its full potential. The plant had the space and allied infrastructure that would allow it to expand upto 10 MMT. The investment per tonne for a greenfield plant worked out to Rs 30,000 per tonne, but for an existing plant, it would have been far less. 'It would cost us about Rs 9.84 bn to add 1 MMT', said Mehra. 'Further, it would contribute to top line as well as bottom line growth.'

Bottom line growth was very much on Mehra's mind in those days. He was aware that the company, strapped for cash as it was, would not be able to invest in expansion or diversification, either related or unrelated. He started toying with the idea of creating a portfolio of businesses that would supplement steelmaking. These businesses 'should help in achieving faster growth, and throw up higher returns with relatively modest investments.'

Mehra also believed that RINL needed a structure that would help in putting the corporate strategy on ground. He decided to call in external consultants to reorganise the company in a way that would not only ensure current survival, but also pave the way for future growth. In RINL's case, the order of priorities was to first survive and then grow.

> 'We decided to grow. In order to survive too, one needs to grow', said Mehra.

In a series of half-day meetings designed to understand the perceptions and perspectives of executives on their company and also to bounce ideas based on recent strategies of global steel majors, the consultants met over 350 executives across levels. 'While speaking to them, we were faced with a mindset that believed that RINL could never make it', recounted the leader of the consulting team. 'But on probing further, we were flooded with suggestions—forestry and horticulture, slag-based cement, fly ash-based building materials, a port, international trading, power plant, auxiliary shops that are capable of building a steel mill every year . . . . Suddenly, the ideas came in thick and fast.' RINL emerged as an entity that was much larger than the Visakhaptanam Steel Plant.

While reflecting on the operating structure, the consultants made a startling observation: 'Even though they had the lowest manpower in Indian Steel Industry, there were too many levels of hierarchy' (see Appendix 6). This caused diffused accountability, dilution of responsibility, overlapping roles and obsessive concern with hierarchy. Five reconfigured levels were arrived at by combining levels that performed similar nature of work. For example, E1, E2 and E3 were clubbed as E123 which was the level of a shift-in-charge responsible for operations in his shift, achievement of targets, maintenance of machinery and adherence to technology parameters. The other levels were redesignated to E45, E67, E89 and D1. The recommendations highlighted the following:

1. Restructuring was based on activities and business processes, not functions.
2. Operations and maintenance were integrated at the shop floor (section) operating levels.
3. The shift manager became the centre of performance accountability.

The consultants visualised RINL as a conglomerate which would consolidate the core business of steel making, divisionalise support businesses and diversify into new businesses. After generating a series of options, the structural choice emphasised sharpened multiple centres of accountability. The recommendations involved the creation of five Strategic Business Groups (SBGs)—Steel Division, Coke Ovens & Coal Chemicals Division (CCCD), Project Engineering & Consultancy Services (PECS) Division, Marketing Division and New Business Division—each headed by an executive director (see Appendix 7). The corporate office would comprise only three functional directorates, viz., finance, human resources and commercial. It would be lean and be responsible for policy making, profit planning and monitoring and decentralisation of all functions. It was also suggested that the CMD's secretariat be entrusted with the responsibility for strategic planning, corporate communications and interface management.

Consolidation of Core Business

In words of a senior official representing its stakeholder, 'The success factors that are critical to RINL's survival and growth are operations, finance and managing people.'

Operations: Vizag Steel Plant was the most sophisticated ISP in India. It was also the first ISP to be sited at a port. 'As with other modern plants, we decided to go in for what we had then considered a judicious mix of proven, i.e., state-of-the-art, and promising but as yet unproven technology', said S.N. Sarna, chief (quality assurance and technology development). 'But, we were governed by the technology transfer agreement that accompanied the 450 million long-term rouble agreement. This created problems for us. The SMS was held up because the Russians did not have billet casting technology; this had to be sourced from Skoda, a Czech firm.'

'By the time the DPR was rationalised in 1986–87, construction had gone too far ahead till the BF stage to reverse anything, leaving only the SMS and the mills. Accordingly, we dropped one SMS and uprated the capacity of the residual SMS from 1.15 MMT to 3 MMT, the WRM from 0.6 MMT to 0.85 MMT, LMMM from 1.57 MMT to 1.875 MMT, and MMSM from 0.7 MMT to 0.875 MMT. The Russians were reluctant to uprate the capacity of the SMS to beyond 2.5 MMT, but we argued and debated and managed to uprate the plant in line with international productivity norms.' Some of the problems that were faced in SMS and MMSM were because of the technological decisions that had to be made then. For instance, the layout of the continuous casting shop placed constraints on material flow and crane utilisation on the one hand, and an unusually high burden on the gas cutting machines on the other. It was also widely believed that the level of automation in the SMS was inadequate.

Even with the levels of automation available, instances of operating practices being violated were plenty, leading to bypassing of automated controls in favour of manual ones. This was partly attributed to inadequate training and concern for meeting deadlines. Though productivity and production increased steadily, it was accompanied by an increased number of breakdowns, causing work slippages and increased downtime.

The major minerals required for steelmaking (see Appendix 8), viz., iron ore and coal, needed to be externally sourced because RINL did not have captive sources of supply. 'The DPR suggested use of 80 per cent indigenous and 20 per cent imported coking coal, but we had to reverse the ratio as coking coal of suitable quality was not available indigenously', said C.D. Mathew, DGM (materials). Coking coal contributed as much as 33 per cent of the materials cost. 'We are planning to join hands with SAIL with a view to increasing our negotiating leverage on account of the substantial purchases made by both of us. This hopefully should drive down prices of coking coal.'

The organisation was also trying to increase the size of the vessels used so that the coal could be transferred to smaller vessels which could be berthed in the port. This was expected to drive down prices by $2 per tonne on the staggering quantity of 3 million tonnes, resulting in savings of $6 million or about Rs 200 mn. However, using the Capesize vessels would involve almost trebling the load to be handled at an already overcrowded port. 'At times, we have had to request SAIL to grant us preferential berthing to avoid demurrages', explained a materials executive. Efforts were on to convince the port authority to increase berthing capacity on the one hand, and increase discharging capacity by modifying the layout of the discharge area.

The advantage of being close to the port was a myth. Though the rail-head adjacent to the port was only 25 km away from the steel plant, the railway charged its minimum distance freight, i.e., for 75 km (100 km from 1996–97). The volumes were enormous, making it impossible to move them by road. RINL approached the Railway authorities to charge tariff related to actual distance. RINL also started encashing on its port-based location by importing materials that were available locally, wherever imports were cheaper, e.g., aluminum.

'The other material requirements were on account of spares and consumables', said Mathew. 'From an inventory level of Rs 6.5 bn in 1993, we have managed to contain inventories to only about Rs 4.5 bn in 1996, through a combination of methods including utilisation, substitution, and exchange and disposal.' The cost control strategy forced inventories to be slashed to lower levels. 'We are also negotiating with suppliers of high value materials like ferro-silicon to convert material supplied by us on a preferential basis, and charge conversion costs.' About 200 SSIs supplying various inputs required by RINL had been supported by the company, of which about 100 were functional. The registered list of vendors was evaluated every year under a vendor evaluation system, based on criteria such as regularity of supply, quality, cost, after sales service, and business integrity.

RINL had managed to remain forex neutral by continually increasing exports against its various and growing imports. But with focus shifting to the domestic market, this could become difficult in future.

Marketing: RINL first embarked on an export trust and avoided a head-on confrontation with SAIL and TISCO, who had a wider product mix. 'Though this was done at the cost of realisations', said S.K. Dutta, the then executive director (commercial), 'we wanted to command respect internationally for the quality of our products. Our port-based location helped us become the largest exporter of iron and steel products in India. We also wanted to communicate to our global customers that we were in for the long haul.' The major products exported were pig iron to discerning markets such as Japan and wire rods to the USA. The high level of exports also had a positive impact on the morale of its employees. Within four years of commencing operations, the SMS and all the finishing mills along with the finished products were certified under ISO 9002.

Once Vizag Steel started receiving international recognition, Indian consumers found it difficult to ignore them. 'The policy environment had changed, making it uneconomical for them to sell in the large North Indian market. Therefore, they decided to concentrate on the southern and western markets', said Ashok Basu, former Jt. Secy, Ministry of Steel and ex-chairman of the joint plant committee.

'The changing environment in the country and the perseverance of our sales and marketing team helped us gain a solid footing in the markets in which we operated', said Dutta. As did the slow responsiveness of its competitors, who were still learning what it took to retain customers. 'The steel marketing mindset in those days was a hangover of the licence raj. Consumers queued up outside our offices to pick up whatever quantities could be allotted to them,' said the sales manager of a competing steel company.

A variety of innovative measures including quarterly contracts for large customers, loyalty bonus for repeat purchasers, delivery at doorstep, etc., helped RINL make inroads into these markets. As it could not match discounts offered by SAIL and TISCO, RINL sought to compete not on price but on service. 'By focussing on superior service through timely availability of products and their responsive delivery, we found that we were able to market our products', said Dutta. Customer counselling cells were set up to assist customers in working out detailed specifications, arrive at optimal tonnage needed, and to ensure just-in-time delivery schedules. With time, quarterly contracts were replaced by annual contracts, and memorandums of understanding were signed with large customers for sale of merchant pig iron and wire rods.

However, the views of smaller customers tell a different story: 'Though product quality of RINL is undoubtedly superior, service and documentation procedures are unsystematic and bureaucratic. It takes a day for issuance of the DO, even thereafter the material is not available. The only reason we persist with them is that they believe in building relationships and help at times of crisis.'

Sales turnover grew by 19 per cent in 1994–95 to Rs 22.66 bn. Domestic sales grew by 43 per cent in volume and 62 per cent in value terms, showing improved realisation. RINL's South India share grew to 42 per cent and all-India share to 22 per cent. 'While we do not benchmark ourselves against RINL, we recognise their strengths in pig iron and wire rods, as well as their dominance in the southern markets', said Arvind Pande, vice chairman of SAIL.

Appendix 9 shows the realisations earned by RINL over the years, and its relative market share vis-à-vis Indian steel companies. Appendix 10 shows RINL's profitability vis-à-vis global steel companies. 'In future, RINL's marketing decisions will take into consideration the trade-offs involved between four factors, viz., products, markets, price, and volume of offtake, with a view to maximising profitability—whether for the domestic or the export markets', said Dutta.

A fair share of RINL's marketing success and the reason for its positive public image was due to its high profile corporate communications campaign. A sustained campaign directed at both the external and internal public began with the environment friendly theme, emphasising its superiority vis-à-vis competitors from cradle to grave. They planned to spend as much as 10 per cent of their multi-crore budget for 1996–97 on internal communication such as the in-house journal, safety campaigns, etc. Of the balance, about half was being spent on reinforcing the company's image through television and national magazines, whereas the other half was being spent on emphasising product strengths in national and South Indian dailies, technical magazines and financial magazines.

RINL's products were typically 'longs' and 'structurals' that found applications in the construction, railways and infrastructure sectors. However, it was through manufacture and sale of flats that SAIL and TISCO had notched up high profits recently.

Finance: 'Because of the high cost of bank borrowings, profits made by the company have not eased the short-term financial situation', said A. Chatterjee, director (finance). 'The quality of current assets, however, is posing liquidity problems'. RINL offered a credit period of thirty days, as against SAIL and TISCO, who could afford to offer up to forty-five to sixty days' credit. However, he expected the liquidity position to improve soon. 'With our focus now shifting from the export to the domestic market, we expect better contribution from our products as exports contribute an average of 10 per cent gross on the margin vis-à-vis 20 per cent on domestic sales. Moreover, by opting for a 75 per cent spot marketing vs. a 25 per cent credit marketing mix, we would be able to improve on our liquidity considerably', he said.

RINL's loan portfolio included Rs 13.88 bn of secured loans, Rs 24.43 bn of unsecured loans and Rs 760 mn of deferred credit from suppliers. Non-government lenders included UTI, GIC and subsidiaries, PSUs and foreign banks. Chatterjee kept the cost of funds down by a careful mix of institutional and foreign bank financing. 'We have selectively opted for rollover of some of our high-cost loans', said Chatterjee. 'While this will hike up interest costs, it will not have any impact on cash flows', said Siva Prasad.

The bottom line tells its own story rather vividly—from operating profits in 1993–94 to gross profits in 1994–95 and 1995–96. Moreover, the gross margins of RINL, SAIL and TISCO were all comparable at 17 per cent in 1994–95. In 1995–96, RINL's gross margins were 20 per cent as against TISCO's 19 per cent.

RINL's Top Line and Bottom Line

(Rupees crore)*

Parameter	*1993–94*	*1994–95*	*1995–96*
Income	1747	2458	3206
Operating profit	115	419	644
Gross profit	(231)	53	238
Net profit	(559)	(348)	(181)

*1 crore = 10 million.

Despite the improvement in bottom line performance, concern for costs permeated the company across all levels. 'Further downsizing would be required if RINL is to become cost competitive in the long run', was the view of senior officials of the Ministry of Finance. 'Perhaps the only way RINL can emerge out of its debt trap is through a comprehensive restructuring of its finances—one that looks not only at present costs, but also takes into account projects in the pipeline. This calls for portfolio planning', said another official.

Organisational Processes: 'The development of a strong union leadership is considered a prerequisite to RINL's success', said Panchanan Chaudhuri, addl. GM (industrial relations), who was also handling the corporate communications portfolio. Workshops for union leaders were conducted to widen their horizons. Initiatives on 'quality of work and quality of life' were carried out. Suggestion schemes carrying cash incentives were instituted. All these interventions enthused executives and workmen and motivated them to deliver their best. The labour productivity at RINL was the highest in the Indian steel industry.

Day-to-day issues were discussed and sorted out through shop floor cooperation committees. The plant level cooperation committee sorted out workmen related issues on a monthly basis. As many as sixty participative committees were functioning, which provided fora for workers' participation in management. The most notable of these was the corporate business information forum, a multi-lateral forum in which the organisation's monthly performance was shared and the logic of various strategic initiatives was discussed. The directors in charge of operations and personnel, general managers, general secretaries of the officers' association and employee unions were in attendance in this forum, which was used for generating ideas as well.

The annual performance planning (APP) process was streamlined by abandoning the previous system that involved joint budget preparation by the divisional head and the finance department, and introducing a system that required every division to make presentations on their annual budget in a forum where divisional heads (DGMs), general managers, executive directors, directors and the CMD were present. This clarified the plans by bringing in an activity focus and then translating it into financials. 'Though we dreamed it initially, it brought in tremendous discipline and led to focussed effort on part of everyone. No one wanted to do a less than excellent job.' This not only provided a forum for sharing information; it made divisional managers sensitive to other divisions' activities. The planning process for the financial year beginning in April commenced in January that year. The results for each quarter were reviewed by the same executives, and steps were taken to monitor the implementation.

The last two years had seen the departure of several of its best and brightest at levels ranging from deputy general manager to executive director; executives who were clearly identified for assuming higher responsibilities. 'While we are not averse to losing manpower, it is the kind of manpower that we are losing that is posing problems', said Ramamurthy. 'Retaining major challenge', said Mehra, 'but given the kind of salaries being offered in the private sector, it is rather difficult.' Recently, an external consultant was commissioned to develop a systematic career development and succession planning method which provided a framework for identifying and carefully grooming a successor in a 'drop-dead' and 'back-stop' situation. In a novel endeavour, role profiles for sixty-seven middle and senior management positions were developed; simultaneously psychological testing was used to understand the personality attributes of close to 100 executives. This had been put into a computerised database to generate options for decision making.

In an effort to understand employee perceptions, the HR department conducted employee satisfaction surveys on a regular basis. 'The first such survey was conducted by a consultant in 1993 as part of the restructuring process. 'Since then, we have been doing similar surveys on a regular basis. They have resulted in various initiatives like team-building across all middle levels, the corporate business information forum, and even a top management retreat', opined Y. Manohar, assistant general manager (HRD). Organisation research was also systematically used by senior executives to gain an understanding of specific shopfloor situations. Recently, the department conducted a series of workshops on 'Reaching Rated Capacity' for the blast furnace, steel melt shop, LMMM and MMSM. The findings were later used as the basis for designing workshops by the same title. HRD climate surveys in various production shops were a regular fixture.

The company maintained a computerised database on personnel aspects of all employees. An executive information system (EIS) was developed in collaboration with a South Korean firm and implemented for the corporate office. This was a user-friendly, highly intensive system that placed information on all important areas of the company's status on a real-time basis at the fingertips of the corporate management.

Faced with resistance from within, Mehra decided to implement the restructuring recommendations in a gradual and phased manner. 'Creation of all five SBGs simultaneously, it was felt, might lead to excess manpower requirement in the functional areas within the SBGs', he said. 'Further, we would have had to establish transfer prices for common services, and set procedures governing interactions between two SBGs, SBG-Corporate, etc. It was a bureaucratic maze.' Out of the five SBGs, it was decided to create two of them at the first instance. 'The success-demonstration effect in non-core areas would help managers appreciate the difference caused and cause them to actually seek similar interventions in the core area of steelmaking.'

Divisionalisation of Support Businesses

Project and Engineering Consultancy Services (PECS) SBG: The SBG had its origins in the projects and design and engineering department of the steel plant. This group of 273 engineers who were instrumental in the erection and commissioning of the steel plant were now faced with a tapering work load. The birth of the SBG could not have come at a more appropriate time.

The PECS SBG was formed with the objective of providing project technology, design and engineering, construction and project management services, both to the steel plant and to the outside market which saw liberalisation. The opening up of infrastructure sectors like steel, power, hydrocarbons, petroleum, roads, ports, etc., saw a host of private and foreign players entering India. In Visakhapatnam itself, APIIC projected Rs 170 bn worth of investment, including the Jindal Refinery, Essar Gujarat's pelletisation plant and the port-based thermal power plant. PECS, it was felt, was well placed to capitalise on this growing opportunity. It would operate as an independent profit centered unit of RINL, providing services to the steel plant on a first charge basis.

The structure was based on the work flow, from basic design to commissioning, focussing on accountable socio-technical units while keeping in mind distinct areas of continuity of operations. The role of the corporate office in the changed scenario was quite different—limited to policy formulation, review and appraisal; leaving day-to-day functioning of the SBG in the hands of the SBG chief and his unit board. The SBG now focussed on business rather than on functions, and managed all its business affairs relating to business development, procurement, finance and personnel. By focussing on profits rather than the product or project alone, the SBG was like a 'company' within the company.

The consultants recommended the adoption of a business plan and a document of delegation of powers as integrative mechanisms that would help the SBG understand its operating boundaries. The business plan included a project-wise, month-wise activity plan, a revenue plan, a manpower utilisation plan as also a project-wise profit plan, cash flow plan, investment plan, proforma profit and loss statements and balance sheet. As part of the SBG-level business planning, transfer prices for various services offered were also determined in consultation with internal customers. Accounting for project-wise profitability helped to balance internal and external priorities.

The SBG had booked orders worth over Rs 300 mn in 1995–96. However, all transactions were being controlled by corporate finance and financial autonomy remained largely on paper. 'We are using advances paid by external clients to mobilise for the various projects at hand. About eighty people are placed in the field', said a senior manager. 'We are hamstrung by the lack of seed money for working on projects. Another disadvantage is the relatively high age-mix—the SBG is top heavy'. Fortunately, this translated into a competitive advantage in the marketplace. 'We are able to place DGMs as project managers in all our projects, whereas our competitors are represented by relatively junior executives.'

Coke and Coal Chemicals Division (CCCD) SBG: Coke oven gas is a valuable by-product produced in the process of manufacturing metallurgical coke. When processed further, it provides a wide variety of chemicals including coal tar, benzol and sulphates, which are inputs to the dyestuff, explosive and chemicals industry. Spinning it off as a separate SBG made eminent sense in view of the restructuring criteria, since it had an external interface and enhanced profitability at relatively low incremental investment. Prior to restructuring, the consultants were told, 'this SBG had the potential of generating profits worth Rs 200 mn on a turnover of Rs 120 mn, as against the steel plant which made losses on a Rs 25 bn turnover.' Further, it was capable of spawning off units that provided for value addition.

The SBG saw the light of day as late as November 1995, almost a year after its conceptualisation. Intricate linkages for raw materials and pooled services with other production units needed to be resolved. Unresolved transfer pricing formulae, stemming from inadequate systems for measuring and metering consumption of common services, were presented as the ostensible reason for delays.

When the change management team met and brainstormed for hours along with the consulting team, solutions to these vexatious issues emerged. It was decided to ensure uninterrupted supply of coke to the steel plant on a first charge basis, at a transfer price that reflected actual raw material cost in addition to the operating costs and allocatable overheads. Further, MOUs with internal supplier and customer departments were entered into, assuring timely response at a mutually decided transfer price. It was decided that marketing would transfer the erstwhile team looking after by-product marketing, while materials, finance and personnel would identify executives to join the unit board team of the CCCD SBG.

The role of the corporate vis-à-vis the SBG was another thorny issue to be resolved. After much debate, it was concluded that procurement of coking coal would continue to be a corporate materials subject, while the SBG would play a role in deciding delivery schedules and supplier selection. Executive establishment matters and cash management continued with corporate personnel. All internal transactions between the corporate and the SBG were considered as book entries, while external sale realisation, and materials purchases (except coal) were being managed by SBG finance. 'Yet, appraisal of functional executives such as us who were transferred to the SBG continued with their departments, with whom they only had a dotted line relationship', bemoaned a CCCD executive.

CCCD achieved the focus that it was expected to usher in. 'The SBG head spends more time in meeting customers and bringing in new business', said Mehra. The SBG was concentrating on technical selling that was required to be done, as opposed to the selling of steel. As long as it had remained within corporate marketing, this focus was missing. Operations also received more focus. The SBG doubled production of ammonium sulphate fertiliser and benzol products in the first quarter of 1996–97. 'Realisations and collection efficiency has also increased', said the GM of the SBG.

Expansion and Related Diversification

The general plant layout had been developed to allow for smooth and uninterrupted operation of 10 MMT per annum. RINL had planned to raise its liquid steel capacity to 4 MMT by 2000 AD. This would have been possible through the usage of 100 per cent imported coal, adoption of new technology, and addition of new facilities—all of which would have entailed an investment of Rs 9.84 bn at 1995–96 prices. 'We're planning to meet 70 per cent of this requirement through internal accruals and the balance from market borrowings', said Chatterjee. The thrust of this expansion would be on complementing the existing product mix by adding a thin slab caster that would manufacture flat products, which find application in the white goods industry. The project had an attractive IRR of 24 per cent per se, and 12 per cent if combined with the present plant.

Diversification into New Businesses: In order to take advantage of the positive contribution made by every potential business opportunity, RINL was leveraging its resources and capitalising on its port-based location. In order to circumvent the investment requirements, it was forming a host of alliances which required it to provide only facilities, expertise or material resources. Some of these included the setting up a finger jetty at its captive beach at Gangavaram, a joint venture with SAIL and Kudremukh Iron Ore Co. Ltd to float a shipping venture, setting up of a 2 million tonne slag cement plant by a cement company in the private sector, and five mini cement plants, which would ensure continuous offtake of slag and limestone from its captive mines at Jaggayapetta. Besides, it was setting up units for conversion of billets into bar products, wire rods, and structurals of up to 300,000 tonnes per annum capacity; entering into a strategic alliance to optimally utilise fly ash waste by manufacturing building materials; planning a strategic alliance with Essar Gujarat to source iron ore fines in slurry form; expand power generation capacity through JVs with other Vizag-based companies like HPC, BHPV, HZL and Cormandel Fertilisers; alliances with housing finance companies like HDFC and HUDCO for housing construction; and exploiting tidal energy for power generation.

While some of these projects crystallised, others were still on the drawing board. These businesses were being championed by a department within the PECS SBG, and Mehra was closely monitoring their implementation. These businesses would be contributing to the bottom-line without entailing any substantial requirement of funds. For instance, the slag cement plant would ensure that RINL was compensated for its slag as well as the limestone. It would not only lead to disposal of three 300,000 tonnes of slag per annum (600,000 from the third operational year), it would translate into benefits of about Rs 70 mn per annum for the first two years and about Rs 150 mn from the third year onwards. Capital intensive projects such as the power plants were to be spun off into independent units, largely on the strength of the superior performance of the existing power plant.

Other strategic initiatives for diversification that were planned included the creation of an in-house travel agency which would cater to the public on a commercial basis; a subsidiary to diversify into airline operations; and commercial plantations of teak, cashew, mango, jackfruit and neem. Additionally, plans were afoot to set up an advertising agency which would cater to in-house requirements and the needs of other organisations as well.

In continuation of earlier efforts, the following structural changes were planned:

1. Operating as a conglomerate of five SBGs—PECS, CCCD, steel, marketing, new business.
2. Implement, in steps, restructuring of the other three SBGs.
3. Reduction in number of levels from the (existing) eight to four, with a view to increasing role clarity and accountability at each level.

Leadership

'He (Ahuja) never once raised his voice and yet commanded the respect of all his people', commented a middle-level manager. 'He was, however, not quite accessible to people down the line and preferred to retain his exclusivity', said another. Ahuja's vision of building a high performing PSU led him to build an organisation unencumbered with bloated manpower. He streamlined operations through use of overlapping shifts. His efforts to make RINL competitive ensured that while peripheral development was taken up in earnest, demands for operating jobs from the local people were not acceded to, beyond the stipulated norm. It is also due to his determination that RINL was alive and growing today. However, according to a senior executive, 'Ahuja left the organisation as a result of misunderstandings with officials in the steel ministry.'

Rath's elevation to the top job was prompted by the need for the organisation to quickly commission the project. Rath, the then director (construction), 'was very much a team player who listened to everyone's suggestions before deciding on important issues. He could carry people, and he had excellent boundary management skills—especially where it concerned the steel ministry, the state government, and the local administration', opined a middle manager.

Views about Mehra were also many and varied. 'It is his vision that has given RINL its successes and the confidence to invest in the future, that too under adverse conditions', said a senior bureaucrat in the steel ministry. The results speak for themselves. When Mehra joined, morale was low and no one knew whether production targets would ever be met. 'We have not only set ambitious targets, but consistently surpassed them. In 1993, engineers in the SMS talked about achieving a maximum of 15 heats. By the year end, we had achieved an annual average of 20 heats! Next year, they talked of a maximum of 25 heats. Again, we achieved an annual average of 30 heats. We never thought that this plant would ever achieve rated capacity. Now, we know that we will surpass it.' Profit targets were set and achieved systematically. From achieving its first ever (operating) profits in 1993–94, RINL achieved cash profits in 1994–95, and quadrupled cash profits in 1995–96. 'Though we have committed to making net profits by 1997-98, we shall achieve these by 1996-97', quipped an enthusiastic junior manager, on being asked when RINL would be in the black.

After taking over as CMD in 1993, Mehra first tried to strengthen the top management team by recruiting his directors in charge of operations, finance, personnel and commercial. He also brought in a few committed and responsible executives at the DGM level with whom he had worked either at Rourkela or Durgapur. 'I joined RINL because I had worked with Mehra at Rourkela', said a deputy general manager. 'I knew before joining that it meant giving up a relaxed job and taking on a challenge—that of building an organisation from scratch. But Mehra's dynamic leadership and his belief in not yielding to adversity, has succeeded in getting the best out of colleagues.'

Mehra was the quintessential workaholic—'he works for an average of over sixteen hours in a day, and over 100 hours in a week'. 'Whether on the shopfloor or during presentations in the corporate office, he is extremely demanding', opined a director, 'making life miserable if you don't measure up to his exacting standards. He pushes relentlessly until you deliver.' But what probably carries the day is that 'you realise that he harbours no grudge or bears no malice. He doesn't have favourites either.' But, his method of getting to the root of the problem, 'his style of reaching directly to the level at which the information is available by circumventing formal hierarchy, makes it difficult for us', said a middle manager.

Mehra spent a lot of time in meeting and convincing people about operational matters. 'His persuasive style is at times a deterrent', opined a senior manager, 'because you tend to agree with him as he sounds so convincing. But later, you're not sure whether you could carry it through.' The same went for those who didn't open up at meetings. 'Mehra convinces people who may not agree but don't say so. As a result, they agree to do something, but not everybody implements it', said he.

'It is this constant setting of stretch goals that are higher than what may be achievable that motivates executives towards superior performance. His energetic demeanour permeates down the line, and this has created a performance-enhancing culture in RINL. History is replete with examples of how only leaders who are both driven and driving, are able to make a difference in adverse situations under complex environments.'

However, not everyone agreed with this point of view. 'Are we giving our people an opportunity to develop, or are we breathing down their necks? It is perhaps time for us to consolidate our gains and institutionalise systems, so that we can ensure continuity along with change. Otherwise, we shall continue to depend on individuals for times to come.'

Having almost reached RINL's nameplate capacity, and having launched two of the SBGs, Mehra decided that it was perhaps the right time to push for further growth. With this in mind, an external consultant was invited to facilitate the Vision for RINL in the 21st century, through three exploratory workshops conducted for the purpose. This was articulated as:

> RINL shall be a self-supporting, growing company with continuous improvement in productivity, quality, and customer satisfaction.

The core values that supported the Vision were:

- Commitment.
- Customer satisfaction.
- Continuous improvement.
- Concern for the environment.

Future Concerns

'This is the year of reckoning, the year in which the promise made to the Government of India would have to be kept . . . Liquid steel production of 3 MMT, labour productivity of 231 tonnes per man year, and above all generating net profit (latest) by 1997–98.' Before calling it a day on 8 July Mehra went over the problems one by one. Institutionalising maintenance practices, achieving higher productivity through process re-engineering, retaining key executives, implementing automation and IT applications in key areas, etc. were all short-term concerns.

For one who had managed to balance long-term concerns with short-term ones with rare panache, Mehra, in the twilight of his career, wanted to be well placed to hand over a vibrant, growing and profitable organisation to his successor. But some issues still troubled him. 'The plan for expansion was contingent upon the union government's willingness to defer repayments. How could RINL grow its steel making capacity from 4 MMT to 6 MMT and beyond to 10 MMT so as to achieve its potential? The core, support and new businesses have so much potential.' He wished he had a way out.

APPENDIX 1

Chronology of Major Events in History of RINL

Date	*Event*
October 1996	Steel plant agitation turns violent in Vizag, Vijaywada, Hyderabad.
April 1970	Union government announces plan to set up Vizag Steel Plant.
January 1971	Prime Minister Indira Gandhi inaugurates site.
February 1972	M.N. Dastur submits feasibility report for 2 MMT plant.
October 1977	M.N. Dastur submits detailed project report (DPR) for 3 MMT plant.
June 1979	India, USSR sign pact on techno-economic co-operation to set up VSP.
November 1980	M.N. Dastur–Gipromez team submits revised DPR for 3.4 MMT plant.
February 1982	RINL incorporated owing to SAIL's withdrawal.
April 1982	Construction commences at Vizag.
1985–86	Union government's plan to drop Vizag gains momentum.
1987	Rationalised concept mooted; one SMS dropped.
1989	Proposal for finance restructuring placed before union government.
March 1991	Commisioning of Stage I.
July 1991	India launches economic liberalisation.
July 1992	Commissioning of Stage II.
August 1993	Union government agrees to RINL's financial restructuring.
October 1993	Flash strike at factory gate.
March 1994	Maiden operating profits.
November 1994	WRM receives ISO 9002 certification.
March 1995	Maiden cash profits.
April 1995	Project engineering and consultancy services (PECS) SBU launched.
November 1995	Coke oven and coal chemicals (CCCD) SBU launched.

APPENDIX 2

Resource Position

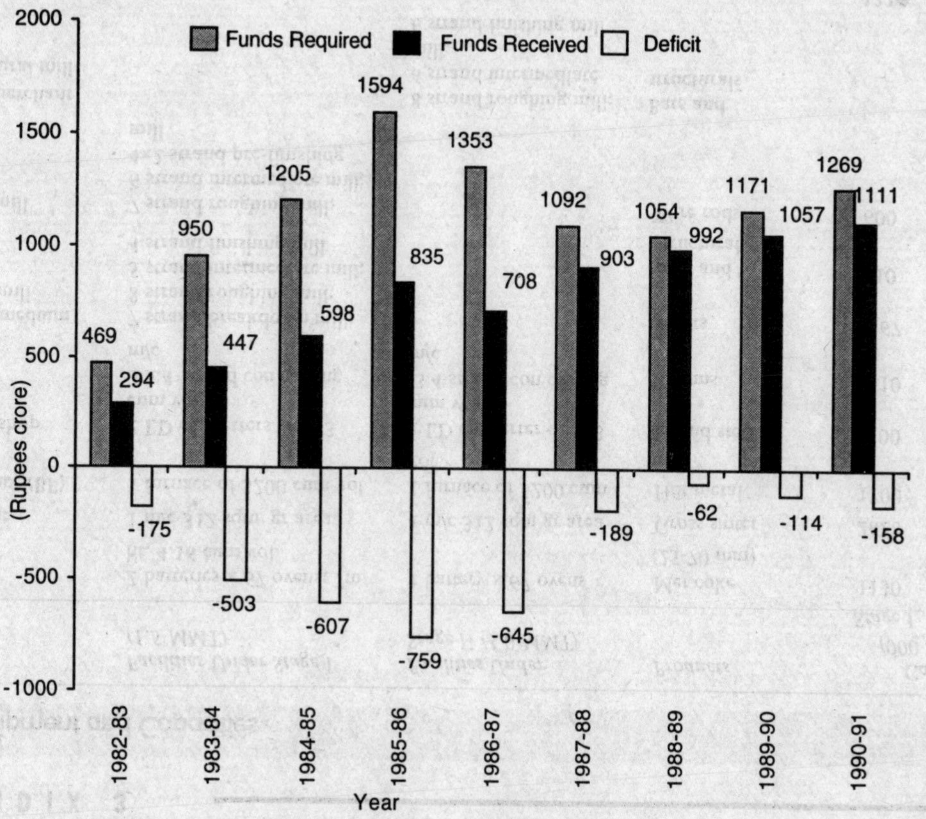

APPENDIX 3

Major Equipment and Capacities

Unit	*Facilities Under Stage I (1.5 MMT)*	*Facilities Under Stage II (3.0 MMT)*	*Products*	*Capacity (000 Tonnes)*	
				Stage I	*Stage II*
Coke oven	2 batteries x 67 ovens; 7m ht, 4.16 cum vol.	1 battery x 67 ovens	Met coke (25-70 mm)	1130	2261
Sinter plant	1 m/c 312 sqm gr area	1 m/c 312 sqm gr area	Gross sinter	2628	5256
Blast furnace (BF)	1 furnace of 3200 cum vol	1 furnace of 3200 cum vol	Hot metal	1700	3400
Steel melt shop (SMS)	2 LD converters of 133 cum vol;	1 LD converter of 133 cum vol;	Liquid steel	1500	3000
	3 x 4-strand con casting m/c	3 4-strand con casting m/c	Blooms	1410	2820
Light and medium merchant mill (LMMM)	7 strand breakdown mill; 8 strand roughing mill; 5 strand intermediate mill; 4 strand finishing mill		Billets	1367	1857
			Bars and structurals	710	710
Wire rod mill (WRM)	7 strand roughing mill; 6 strand intermediate mill; 4x2 strand pre-finishing mill		Wire rods	600	850
Medium merchant and structural mill (MMSM)		8 strand roughing mill; 6 strand intermediate mill; 6 strand finishing mill	Bars and structurals	–	850
Saleable steel				1326	2656

APPENDIX 4

Balance Sheet (as on 31st March)

(Rupees crore)*

	1990–91	1991-92	1992-93	1993-94	1994-95	1995-96
Sources of funds						
Shareholders' funds	3505.84	3505.84	6170.57	6527.54	6527.53	6527.54
Loan funds	3924.44	5476.28	3494.61	3473.68	3734.56	3830.60
Deferred capital	119.74	158.14	168.74	139.71	107.37	76.64
Total	7550.03	9140.28	9833.92	10140.93	10369.47	10434.78
Application of funds						
Fixed assets (Net)	3472.22	4326.85	5130.73	5961.07	6541.91	6214.22
Capital w-i-p	3546.17	3058.62	2101.90	1081.28	178.87	218.04
C A loans, advances	671.01	967.94	1219.84	1121.44	1487.95	1686.91
Less: C L and provisions	641.62	725.13	691.86	659.57	837.92	893.44
Net current assets	29.38	242.80	527.98	461.88	650.03	793.47
Misc. expenses	24.70	47.51	40.52	31.27	28.94	39.39
P & L account	477.55	1464.48	2032.77	2605.43	2969.71	3169.66
Total	7550.03	9140.28	9833.92	10140.93	10369.47	10434.78

* 1 core = 10 million.

APPENDIX 5

Income Expenditure Account

(Rupees crore)*

	1990–91	1991–92	1992–93	1993–94	1994–95	1995–96
Income						
Sales	245.15	772.44	118.84	1751.04	2208.57	3038.57
Internal consumption	30.71	9.75	108.20	106.63	10.11	1.26
Other income	31.48	82.06	267.11	(-)110.81	239.78	165.81
Total	307.33	864.25	–	1746.86	2458.46	3205.64
Expenditure						
Raw material consumption	275.27	402.93	680.17	875.40	1083.46	1402.82
Consumption of trial run production	0.93	42.53	68.00	4.60	–	–
Employees' remuneration	29.13	53.76	76.52	102.50	128.46	154.66
Stores and spares	36.61	109.26	174.66	165.02	209.27	261.16
Power and fuel	41.92	61.49	97.13	83.85	66.82	82.33
Repairs	29.03	32.66	66.88	60.12	43.92	43.12
Contributions	13.05	44.65	20.32	23.91	33.22	0.39
Freight	28.77	85.59	121.69	101.01	120.57	138.64
Excise duty	20.80	58.18	96.95	95.50	212.88	256.15
Others	27.05	79.12	115.69	129.57	151.06	231.95
Interest	192.13	436.81	275.12	346.44	365.82	406.58
Depreciation	197.23	411.18	329.21	328.53	401.35	419.31
Total	791.93	1818.17	2122.63	2316.44	2816.85	3397.12
Less inter A/C adjst	7.04	9.42	7.70	10.46	10.62	10.64
Net expenditure	784.89	1808.75	2114.93	2305.98	2806.23	3386.47
Loss for year	477.55	944.50	554.79	559.12	347.76	180.83
Prior period adjst	–	42.43	13.50	13.53	16.52	19.11
	477.55	986.93	568.29	572.66	364.28	199.94
Loss of last year B/F	–	477.55	1464.48	2032.78	2605.43	2969.71
Loss carried to B/S	477.55	1464.48	2032.78	2605.43	2969.71	3169.66

* 1 crore = 10 million.

APPENDIX 6

Organisation Structure Prior to Restructuring

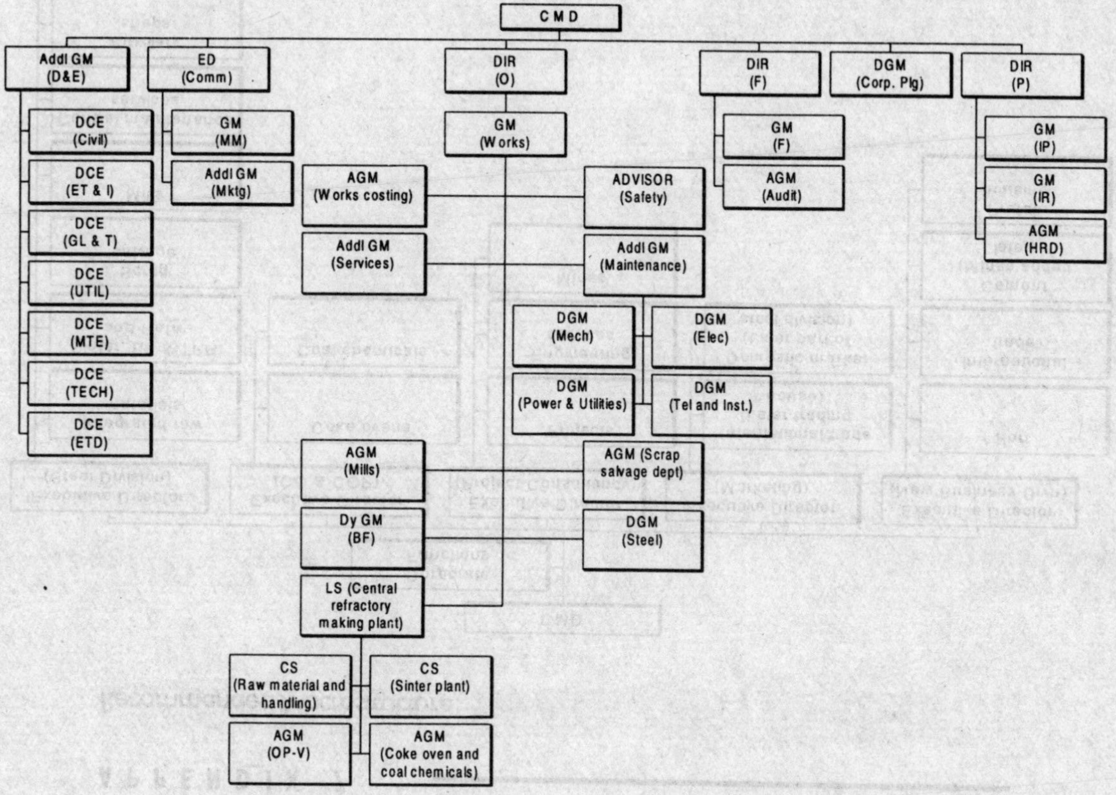

APPENDIX 7

Recommended Macrostructure

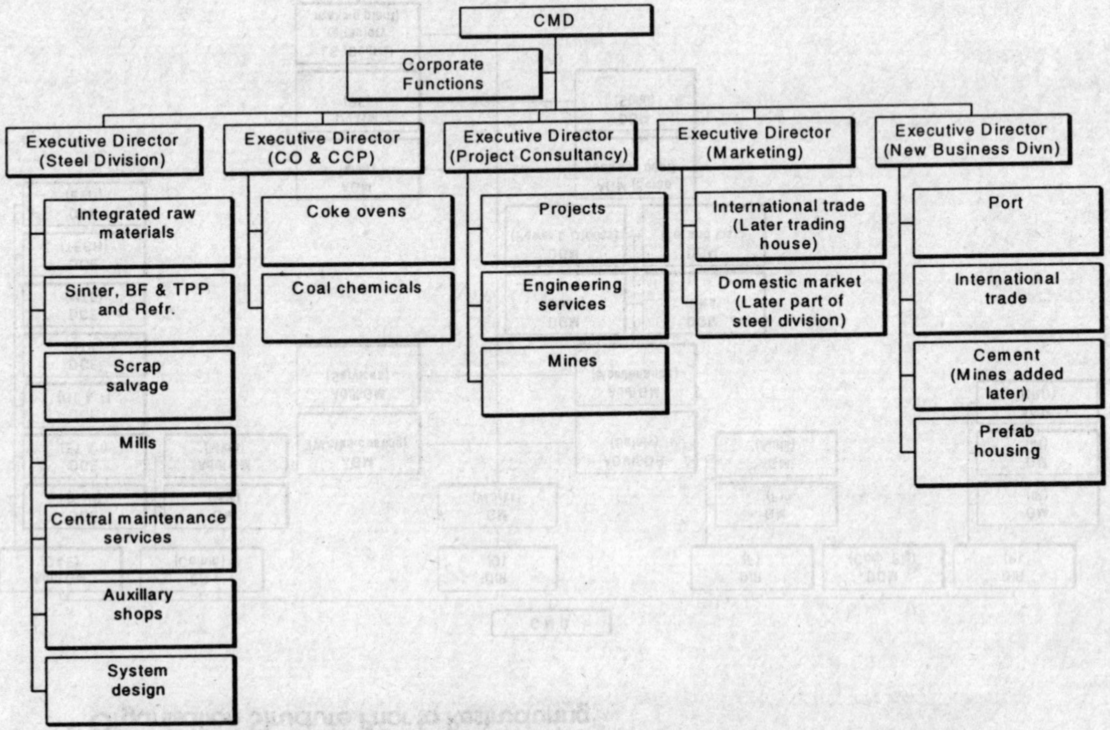
CMD
Corporate Functions
Executive Director (Steel Division)
Integrated raw materials
Sinter, BF & TPP and Refr.
Scrap salvage
Mills
Central maintenance services
Auxillary shops
System design
Executive Director (CO & CCP)
Coke ovens
Coal chemicals
Executive Director (Project Consultancy)
Projects
Engineering services
Mines
Executive Director (Marketing)
International trade (Later trading house)
Domestic market (Later part of steel division)
Executive Director (New Business Divn)
Port
International trade
Cement (Mines added later)
Prefab housing

APPENDIX 8

Major Raw Materials: Sources and Quantities

Raw Material	*Source*	*Annual Requirement (MMT)*
Iron ore		
Lumps	Bailadilla (MP)	1.544
Fines	Kirandul	3.770
Limestone		
BF grade	Jaggayyapeta (AP)	0.323
SMS grade	Imported from Dubai	0.633
Dolomite		
BF grade	Birmitrapur (Orissa)	0.524
SMS grade	Matharam (AP)	0.138
Manganese ore	Chipurupalli (AP)	0.068
Coal		
Medium coking coal	Swang, Kargil, Gidi, Kathara	1.027
Imported coking coal	Imported from Australia	2.669
Boiler coal	Singareni (AP)	1.610

APPENDIX 9

Realisations and Gross Margins

Parameter Year	Volume (MMT)		Turnover (Rs crore)		Realisation (Rs/MT)		Gross Margin (Rs crore)	
	Dom.	Exp.	Dom.	Exp.	Dom.	Exp.	Rs	MT
1992–93	1.28	0.28	972	212	7586	7584	(31)	—
1993–94	1.31	1.00	1215	535	9287	5347	114	494
1994–95	1.50	0.77	1755	453	11733	5918	416	1840
1995–96	1.79	1.02	2331	707	13004	6911	637	2261

MT: Metric tonne. MMT: Million metric tonne.

Market Shares of Major Players in India

(Figures in %)

Product	SAIL	IISCO	RINL	TISCO	Secondary Producers
Pig iron	18 (26)	18 (19)	12 (18)	0 (0)	52 (37)
Semis	22 (18)	0 (1)	10 (10)	4 (7)	64 (64)
Bars and rods	14 (15)	1 (1)	10 (7)	7 (6)	68 (70)
Structurals	27 (32)	9 (9)	8 (4)	8 (7)	48 (48)
Total steel	19 (19)	2 (2)	10 (8)	6 (7)	63 (64)
Finished steel	18 (19)	3 (3)	10 (7)	7 (7)	63 (65)

Note: Unbracketed figures are data for 1995–96; bracketed ones for 1994–95.

APPENDIX 10

Profitability of Major Steel Companies in the World, 1994–95

Company	*Ebdit/Sales*	*EBIT/Sales*	*ROI*	*Net Profit/Capital Employed*
India				
RINL	18	0.08	–	5
TISCO	17	11.5	–	4.5
SAIL	17	13.5	–	10.3
Japan (Average)	13	10	13	–
Nippon Steel	11	9	16	–
Kawasaki Steel	14.5	12	15	–
Europe (Average)	3	2	3	–
Eregli Demir	20	14.5	24	–
Hoogovens	9	0.5	0.3	–
Rautaruuki	2	14	13.5	–
Thyssen	4.5	(1)	(3)	–
British Steel	3	(2)	(2)	–
USA (Average)	8	9	9	–
Bethlehem Steel	5	(1)	(2)	–
Nucor	14	8	14	–

CASE 16

HINDUSTAN LEVER LIMITED: THE SPIRIT OF ENTREPRENEURSHIP IN THE BIG–SMALL COMPANY

> In spite of being at the most successful stage of its life so far, India's mightiest marketing super power, Hindustan Lever, is determinedly plotting to immolate itself. And to rise, from the ashes, a Phoenix that's stronger, nimbler and more customer-driven than ever before.'
>
> —*Business Today*, 1999

When Keki Dadiseth became chairman of HLL in 1996, he inherited India's most

This case was written by Gita Piramal, business historian, Sudeep Budhiraja, Research Fellow, London Business School and Sumantra Ghoshal, Robert P. Baumann Professor of Strategic Leadership at the London Business School. It was written as part of a research programme supported by the Aditya V. Birla India Centre. The authors gratefully acknowledge the extraordinary co-operation and support of Hindustan Lever Ltd without which this case could not have been written. This case was first registered by the London Business School in 2000.

admired company. Three years later he unfolded Project Millennium, an ambitious plan to turn the FMCG giant into a clutch of entrepreneurial 'virtual' companies each with its own 'virtual CEO'.

Project Millennium's genesis lay in HLL's hunger for growth. In 1996, HLL represented about 5 per cent of Unilever's global sales turnover. Dadiseth's stretch target was for HLL to represent 10 per cent of the revenues and profits of Unilever by 2000–01. Within India, the economy, markets and the competitive environment were changing, and to keep ahead of the pack meant taking stock of the changes and doing business in different ways. Dadiseth began by identifying three key issues:

- 'How do I retain the aggressiveness and agility of a smaller company as we get much larger?'
- 'While we are a $2.5 bn corporation on revenues, in purchasing power parity terms, we are a $11.4 bn company. We must organise accordingly and allow the business heads to run their business under the overall supervision of the board. The issue is, how does one pass on experience without interfering?'
- 'How should HLL re-connect with the consumer so as to be absolutely sure we are delivering what the consumer expects?'

Hindustan Lever in 1998–99

Headquartered in Mumbai, HLL was the largest consumer products company in India and by far the largest Unilever operation in the Asia-Pacific region. Incorporated in 1956, the forty-three-year-old company had developed a wide portfolio of products (soaps, detergents, personal products, oral care, perfumes, food products and frozen desserts) enabling it to rack up gross sales of Rs 94.81 bn and net profits of Rs 8.37 bn in FY98. Cash rich and investor savvy, HLL was one of the bluest of the blue-chips on the Indian stock exchanges, making even the hottest IT and internet stocks bite the dust. Its distribution network was arguably one of the best and strongest with HLL products available at over 1 million retail outlets throughout India. Armed with over 124 brands (sold in over 1,022 different sizes/packs), HLL derived approximately 55 per cent of its total revenues from India's rural areas. Between 1998 and 1999, HLL introduced sixty-four product innovations (forty-four new launches and twenty re-launches) and over 50 per cent of growth during this period came from these launches. For running its seventeen businesses, the company employed 36,000 people and operated 100 factories besides dealing with 2,000 suppliers and associates.

In India, where a substantial chunk of the top 100 companies in the private sector were family owned and family run, HLL—owned 51 per cent by Unilever—stood for professional management at its best. Its board of directors comprised two genres of internal directors besides the chairman. The first set were the four heads of cross-business functions: legal, personnel, finance and exports. The second set were the heads of the four largest businesses: soaps and detergents, personal products, beverages and frozen foods. Soaps and detergents, and beverages between them contributed over 50 per cent of net sales.

HLL's Sales by Products

(Rs million)

Products	*1998**	*1997**
Soaps and detergents	35650	33600
Personal products	15260	8840
Beverages	17990	15440
Processed triglycerides, oils and vanaspati	6530	5420
Dairy products	790	870
Ice cream and frozen desserts	1550	1530
Canned and processed fruits and vegetables	1190	970
Branded staple foods	1600	1120
Speciality chemicals	2270	1560
Animal feeding stuffs	2780	2720
Others	9210	6130
Total	94820	78200

* Net of excise.
Source: HLL website, October 1999.

Below the board, HLL's management hierarchy was fashioned along functional lines. There were seven divisions and each consisted of a board with up to four executives, designated as the divisional vice-president and the general manager or marketing controller, reporting to the director in charge of the business. Under this elite were approximately 1,480 managers and 25,500 workers besides the 6,000 seasonal workers hired on HLL's tea and coffee plantations.

Corporate India accorded HLL's managers respect and envy in equal measure: respect for their ability to continuously outperform themselves; envy for meticulous systems which helped HLL's managers deliver world class results in a country lacking basic infrastructure in so many areas. Every year, HLL did better than the previous one. In over ten years, HLL's revenues and profitability had not dipped even once. The YoY ratios might flicker and lengthen, but in absolute terms, the HLL juggernaut lurched from strength to strength. Few companies, be they Indian or multinational, could boast of such performance.

HLL's Ten-year Growth Record

(Rs million)

	FY89	*FY90*	*FY91*	*FY92*	*FY93*	*FY94*	*FY95*	*FY96*	*FY97*	*FY98*
Sales*	10314	12340	15076	17570	20632	28265	33670	66001	78197	94818
PAT	538	587	802	955	1273	1900	2392	4127	5803	8374
EPS#	3.84	4.20	5.73	7.03	9.09	13.02	16.40	20.72	28.14	36.70

* Net of excise.
\# in Rs and adjusted for bonus.
Source: HLL's website, October 1999.

Comparison with Peers

Company	*Price (Rs)*	*P/BV*	*P/ CEPS*	*FV/ SALES*	*FV/ EBITDA*	*FV/ EBIT*	*ROE (%)*	*P/E Relative to ROE*	*P/E*
HLL	1.429	28.7	60.6	4.3	47.6	52.4	50.8	1.4	68.7
Nestlé	266	10.3	34.0	2.5	21.4	25.7	21.3	2.3	48.5
Britannia	360	8.0	26.5	1.0	23.8	31.2	21.3	1.8	37.3
Cadbury	270	5.2	19.0	1.7	12.2	15.1	19.2	1.4	27.2
P&G	823	8.9	35.0	3.6	24.8	29.5	19.7	2.3	45.3
Average	–	14.2	38.5	3.4	28.8	33.1	28.7	1.8	47.8

Source: ICICI Securities and Finance Co Ltd, Company report on HLL, 21 October 1997.

World-class managers producing world-class results inevitably translated into attractive market shares. Not surprisingly, HLL was the market leader in most of its businesses.

HLL's Market Shares

Segment	*HLL's Market Share (%)*
Fabric care	38
Personal care	65
Home care	25
Food	25

Source: ICICI Securities and Finance Co Ltd, Company report on HLL, 21 October 1997.

So what made HLL such an unusual company? Some of the usual factors were obviously present. A nimble ability to move with the times and develop new businesses. A hardy capacity for recharging old ones. Good HRD practices from top to bottom, i.e, a finely honed production line which steadily delivered managers from the careful recruitment of management trainees, to thoughtful training procedures, to the nurturing of fast-track talent, and ending in a plentiful supply of CEO material. But to these competencies, HLL added a few more. A bias for technology. And inspired teamwork.

Building for the Future

These factors came together particularly successfully after 1991. Prior to that India's strict monopolies legislation had straitjacketed HLL. Freed from constraints, HLL's entrepreneurial character asserted itself. 'Dr Ganguly was chairman at the time and we looked at all kinds of opportunities—software, petrochemicals, fertilisers. At the same time, Unilever allowed us to grow away from traditional businesses', said K. S. Srinivasmurty (head, strategic services). The parent company had mushroomed into over 400 operating companies and more than 1,200 brands, and was managed by twelve regional business group presidents who were displaying increasing autonomy.

Despite the temptations, HLL recognised the realistic constraints and felt the need to grow in its core businesses. The huge jump in sales between 1991 and 1996 from Rs 15 bn to Rs 66 bn under the chairmanship of S.M. Datta was due to a series of mergers and acquisitions, several of which were sister concerns. The unified HLL then began to flex its muscles. As mentioned earlier, between 1998–99, HLL energetically introduced eighty product innovations and over 50 per cent of growth during this period came from these launches.

Personal care and processed foods (tea, coffee, tomato-based products and ice cream) were identified as thrust areas for growth. A few years earlier, HLL had launched packaged salt and *atta* (wheat flour) under the Kissan Annapoorna brand name. It also commissioned a new facility for personal care products. For the future, HLL planned a capex of Rs 2 bn between 1998–2000 to develop cold storage chains to improve its ice cream and processed foods business. The manner in which HLL went about developing the ice cream and *atta* businesses provides an insight into the company, its strategic thinking processes and competencies.

Ice Cream

Unilever was a major world player in ice cream with the Walls brand but in India, HLL entered this business only in 1994, with the purchase of the 'Dollops' brand from Cadbury India. The acquisition was but the first step of a much larger game plan. Within the next year-and-a-half, HLL purchased Kwality's (from the four branches of the family who sold the Kwality brand of ice cream across the country), then Milkfood, Yankee Doodle, and Sub-Zero among others.

Through these purchases HLL acquired thirty ice cream factories across the country but virtually all were in bad shape with poor hygiene. Product quality was generally poor and most sales were in bricks or in cups. This was relevant as the ice cream market was split between parlour-based products (cups and bricks) and impulse buys (which were generally hand-held). The margins in impulse buys were higher and lent themselves more easily to branding.

One of the first things HLL did was to establish 'Kwality Walls' as the new house brand and all products were immediately brought under this single brand name. Next, the thirty factories were scrutinised on a range of factors. Only sixteen survived and HLL expected to further reduce the number to four high quality, well-located facilities. Once the clean up was complete, HLL introduced a number of sub-brands such as Feast, Cornetto and Snacks which were brought in from overseas with the assistance of Unilever's Ice Cream Category Team. Volume now shifted from parlour-based to impulse business. Impulse business was expected to touch 10 mn litres a year, representing about 40 per cent of volume but much higher on value.

This expectation was based on the fact that India consumed a total of 100 mn litres of ice cream at about 0.1 litre per capita. This compared unfavourably with 1.0 litre per capita for countries like Thailand, where ice cream was more visible and affordable. The comparison raised the issue of distribution channels and the high cost of establishing and maintaining a cold chain throughout the country. 'The biggest challenge was how to grow the market', recalled K. P. Ponnapa (director, ice cream and frozen products).

Looking at the data, HLL found that their branded push-carts in Delhi outsold retail stores 3:1 at 2,000 to 3,000 litres per push cart per annum (retail stores did an average of 700 to 800 litres per annum). Further, push cart sales were almost entirely impulse buys, whereas stores did 50 per cent impulse and 50 per cent bulk sales. Push carts were unmistakably more powerful. But the high cost of dry ice used to maintain a temperature of -50°C in a push cart put HLL's R&D team to work.

Within months, R&D developed liquid pouches which were both reusable and cheaper than dry ice. Moreover, the pouches maintained a temperature of -23°C which was safer for children (biting into an ice cream cooled to -50°C can be a painful experience). The R&D team also developed a smaller, more compact, push cart with a lower capital cost and a lower carrying capacity of 50 litres instead of the previous 300 litre push cart. The strategy was to engage push cart concessionaires, each responsible for managing twenty push carts, who would retain a 10 per cent margin. The push carts remained the property of HLL and were issued against a deposit to the concessionaires. Further research continued into the design of the push cart and HLL's engineers were looking at the possibility of using super-insulation materials to reduce the push cart's cost by two-thirds and of stabilising ice creams at -10°C to reduce energy costs. From the initial 400 push carts in Delhi, HLL by 1997 had 2,000 push carts.

These efforts resulted in a larger and more rewarding distribution system with comfortable gross margins even though more than 90 per cent of HLL's ice cream products sold for under Rs 10. The success prompted HLL's managers to explore the possibility of expanding the market by developing a frozen refreshment product priced at Rs 2-3 as a substitute for bottled beverages which sold at Rs 8-9 a bottle (Coca-Cola, Pepsi, etc.).

For the future, HLL expected a shakeout in the ice cream business with smaller players being eased out. Internally, HLL expected that Amul, which currently had a 5-6 per cent market share, would grow to about 20 per cent, that a new player, maybe Nestle, would capture another 20 per cent, leaving HLL with 60 per cent market share.

Popular Foods

Worldwide, food was one of Unilever's traditional lines of business along with soaps, detergents and personal products, besides accounting for about 50 per cent of its overall sales. Gradually, HLL began to see it as a major unaddressed opportunity in India.

The Indian foods market amounted to some Rs 3,200 bn with the single largest segment (40 per cent) being staples such as wheat, rice, sugar and salt. Other large segments were milk products, meats and edible fats. Historically, HLL's participation in foods was limited to Dalda in the vanaspati sub-segment of edible fats and through various brands in the processed foods segment which accounted for 6 per cent of the total market.

Datta observed in 1994 that salt represented 30-40 per cent of the formulation of detergents and suggested that HLL look at the possibility of packaging salt for consumers. Dadiseth then was director for detergents and seeing the opportunity, he took responsibility for developing it further and this activity was parked with the Wheel team. The company undertook a test market for salt and within six months added *atta* to the exercise.

Atta was identified after looking at all the major staple food categories against a set of criteria which included processing complexity, shelf life, etc. *Atta* was chosen over rice as its processing was complex allowing HLL to add value through its R&D strengths and also because it had a relatively short shelf life of two weeks and could leverage the vast distribution strengths of HLL. Also, both salt and *atta* were produced by a myriad of small suppliers and most of the volume was unbranded. Salt consumption was 6.5 million tons, but the two largest brands in the market (Captain Cook and Tata) accounted for only 400,000 tons or 6 per cent of total consumption. There was room for a new strong brand.

HLL began test marketing salt and later *atta*. Testing ran for a year for salt, and one-and-a-half years for *atta*. Once the tests were deemed successful, a new popular foods business was constituted with its own resources but continued to be parked within the detergent group. This seemed logical as the foods business was preoccupied with the new ice cream business, the merger of the tea companies and the absorption of the Kissan brands. Also, the distribution requirements of the popular foods business were more similar to detergents than to tea and other food products.

Having been in the business for a while, the popular foods team was clear that while staple food categories such as *atta*, rice, salt and spices differed, they all needed some core competencies and these were:

- A good understanding of consumers.
- Good procurement skills.
- Technology and processing expertise.
- High frequency distribution.

The focus was on strengthening these core areas. For instance, while developing the *atta* business, HLL conducted research which told them that while there were regional differences, consumers wanted soft chappatis both when fresh and after they got cold. Nutrition was another factor. HLL accessed bakery know-how in the Bangalore R&D centre and in the Bakeries Research Group in Rotterdam to develop the softest chappatis in India. This know-how was provided to four vendors who processed *atta* for HLL.

As a staple food, the product had to be price competitive. Market research showed that even a Rs 2 premium per kg for HLL's Kissan Annapoorna brand would be unaffordable. 'The housewife doesn't calculate the price of her time, and this was challenging when it cost Rs 1 per kg for packaging', recalled Gunender Kapur (general manager, popular foods). The only option was to maximise savings in the supply chain. HLL organised a wheat procurement network which allowed it to obtain more desirable strains of wheat at a lower cost. Farmers were asked to grow harder wheat as more molecules were then damaged in the milling process, which allowed greater water retention which in turn made softer chappatis. Kissan Annapoorna was positioned as a healthy choice with the best sensory benefit (soft chappatis) and as the only brand endorsed by ICCITD (an affiliate of the World Health Organisation). Further savings were garnered by cutting out depots and despatching direct to stockists from the factory.

For the future, HLL wanted to produce and sell specialised flour for puris, parathas, etc., and perhaps ready-to-cook chappatis, biscuits, pasta, etc. In 1998–99, popular foods was still a start-up business. Sales in FY98 were Rs 1.6 bn but HLL expected the figure to cross Rs 5 bn within five years. And Unilever was considering duplicating the Indian experience in Indonesia and Brazil. Meanwhile, local competition was heating up. UK's Pilsbury tied up with the Godrej group to introduce a similar product. The new venture was headed by a former HLL manager. USA's Cargill was also expected to jump into the fray.

Rebuilding the Old: Marketing

Any company with market leadership in several businesses or market segments has to accept stiff competition from multiple firms of varying levels of sophistication and size. Secondly, growth opportunities in India at the close of the century were highest in the lower price segments. Combined, this meant HLL had to 'take care that the manufacturing system operated at the lowest possible cost and that extra costs were ruthlessly stripped away', said Arun Adhikari (divisional vice president, marketing, detergents). In Europe, in the detergent business, relatively speaking there was a small difference between the top end of the market and the bottom end, say Rs 150 to Rs 100. In India, on the other hand, the top end could fetch Rs 600 while the bottom end could afford only Rs 100. And the bottom end accounted for 70 per cent of the market. Thus HLL had to have products to cater for the bottom end if it wanted to maintain its '51 per cent market share and direction, to build leadership and dominance so as to cover every segment'.

'Regional players have several advantages over HLL', explained Adhikari. 'There are some structural advantages. They don't have an expensive head office. They have lower geographical costs. Our transport costs can be up to Rs 1,000 a ton higher. They have a different mix of trade margins and lower levels of advertising and consumer support. And their profit expectations differ from ours. They want a gross margin of 6-10 per cent while we need at least 15-20 per cent. We use technology to bridge the difference.'

Adhikari provided the example of how HLL saved Rs 7 per ton on polypacks by printing in three colours on the front but a single colour on the back. Next HLL's R&D team re-examined the laminate structure and found a new polymer which would make better polypacks at a lower cost and with better printability. The exercise, which took three months, was initiated by the detergents division and spread to the tea division before being taken up by Unilever worldwide.

All in all, in 1998–99, HLL had embarked on a cost rationalisation programme to save Rs 1 bn per annum. It also planned to unlock Rs 5 bn from real estate to enhance its ROCE in the coming years. At the same time, HLL took a hard look at its existing businesses to see if there were new ways of operating them to get better returns.

Resuscitating a Brand

One of the businesses to get the makeover treatment was Dalda, one of India's oldest brands and one of the most robust. In 1996, *A&M* magazine in its popular annual independent ranking positioned Dalda at fifteenth place. This in itself was not remarkable, but becomes much more interesting when you learn that the brand had not been advertised for fifteen to twenty years.

The edible fats market in India consisted of four categories: filtered oils, refined oils, bakery fats and vanaspati (hydrogenated vegetable oils). Dalda, a vanaspati, was introduced in 1937 as a cheap substitute for pure ghee (cooking fat produced from milk fat). In 1989–99, the total vanaspati market was about 1 million tons/annum and it had remained static for ten years as vanaspati was now seen as heavy and difficult to digest. The market was split into branded products (both small and bulk packs) and unbranded bulk producers who accounted for some 70 per cent of the market. At 61,000 tons/annum, Dalda represented 22 per cent of the branded market by volume and about 28 per cent by value.

Dalda was the original cash cow within HLL which had funded the growth of the detergents business. It had been ignored for the past decade as its manufacture and sale was heavily regulated in various ways, making it uneconomic. As an important basic food product, vanaspati's composition was heavily regulated so there was no real differentiation in the formulation of the different brands. Another issue was that pre-1991, a 51 per cent owned FERA company had an obligation to export 10 per cent of its turnover. Also, the price of vanaspati was fixed by the government. This resulted in the Dalda business being shifted to Lipton in 1984, which at the time was a 40 per cent subsidiary.

Post-liberalisation, pricing controls were lifted and the subsidies provided by the government-sponsored 'Dhara' brand of refined oils through lower import duties ended. This made it possible for HLL management to take a fresh look at Dalda and they found they had a powerful brand, but low growth and poor financial performance. For sentimental reasons, a decision was taken to try and breathe some life into Dalda even though it clearly did not fit the mould of a high growth brand. Furthermore, fixed assets deployed were large, at 11 per cent of sales turnover.

As a first step, the production and supply chain was re-engineered. This resulted in the closure of one factory and in new agreements with seven third-party manufacturers. Working capital requirements were reduced by growing supplier finance from 4 per cent of sales in 1996 to a negative 3 per cent of sales in 1997. This along with better packaging and distribution resulted in improving the ROCE from 4 per cent in 1996 to 27 per cent in 1997, making it comparable to 25 per cent for detergents and 50 per cent for personal products.

Simultaneously, the Dalda business unit started working with the R&D team to develop modified versions of Dalda which would make it more acceptable to health-conscious customers and improve gross margins. This was expected to result in two new versions of Dalda. The first would flow from a process of 'interesterification' to produce a 'light' Dalda which was a yellow fat with a higher gross margin than the normal Dalda. The other was an effort to get closer to pure ghee in taste and texture and position it as a 'healthier ghee'.

With the application of HLL's time-tested brand management and enhancement skills, a staid brand like Dalda justified that it deserved to live.

Rebuilding the Old: Manufacturing

HLL's internal targets demanded the doubling of revenues and earnings every four years. This in turn required a continuous improvement in margins, which in turn required steady reduction in manufacturing costs, materials costs and financing costs.

Maximising Production

In the detergents business, HLL started out with two factories in pre-independence India. Over time, these factories were expanded and they produced the entire detergents supplied until 1985. HLL added ten factories between 1985 and 1992 to meet the growing demand. Another new factory was added in 1993 and with the three factories that came with the 1993 TOMCO acquisition, the number had risen to sixteen. In 1993, these sixteen factories produced 1 million tons of products and employed 9,500 people.

Post-liberalisation in 1991, HLL reconsidered its manufacturing requirements and revamped its existing network using linear programming models. The closures were done rationally with the best interest of the business in focus, but also on a humane basis. In J&K, HLL had a factory with a capacity of 40,000 tons per annum, whereas they required only 4,000 tons of product. After much deliberation, the plant was deemed unviable as the cost of bringing in raw materials and transporting out finished products added about Rs 1,200 per ton for a total overhead of Rs 2,400 per ton. Once the decision was made, management discussed the issue with the employees and the union and offered a fair VRS package. In addition, they re-trained employees in new professions such as bee-keeping, cycle repair, etc.

By 1999 there was a comprehensive review process in place and all factories were graded as follows:

A. Long-term future.
B. Medium-term future.
C. Slated for closure.

In retained factories, there was a clear focus on right-sizing the workforce and on improving manufacturing efficiency, which was benchmarked at a minimum of 90 per cent. This became a part of the negotiations at each wage settlement cycle and HLL increased incentive compensation by 10 to 15 per cent at each settlement in return for higher efficiencies.

Cutting Edge Technology

HLL had a manufacturing research cell which continuously looked at tweaking the process and modifying machines in an effort to improve yields. In addition there was a campaign to convert the manufacturing process to a continuous no-touch process. This resulted in a cleaner workplace where workers had more interesting jobs as well as more time. Change-overs in production had been reduced from 8 hours to 2.5 hours and were targeted for 1-1.50 hours by end-1998.

In the soap business, HLL's innovative spirit was represented by the fact that it was the only Unilever entity to use castor oil, neem oil and sal oil in the manufacture of fatty acids (an intermediate). Other manufacturers used a combination of coconut oil and palm oil. The HLL process split the oils into glycerine and black fatty acids. Extra distillation was needed to turn black fatty acids white. Sophisticated DFA (distilled fatty acids) plants had to be commissioned and were put up entirely by the internal engineering projects group.

Managing the Supply Chain

There was a continuous process of not only controlling costs, but reducing them. This strategy was partly due to a recognition of the vast opportunities for low cost products in India. But it was also a fallout of the 1980s when Nirma, a small Ahmedabad company, introduced a low-priced detergent and discovered a huge, entirely new and untapped market. Nirma was able to swiftly ramp up

production and grew to become one of the largest players in the market. HLL responded aggressively to Nirma with a new product and brand, Wheel. The experience raised the awareness of managing raw material costs much more aggressively. In 1989–90, the supply chain had been functionally managed and consisted of the following departments:

- Raw materials sourcing.
- Production planning.
- Distribution to the sales system.
- Finance.

These functions were integrated to create the commercial stream within HLL, which complemented manufacturing and marketing and was responsible for managing the entire supply chain. Post-1991, it became more feasible for HLL to outsource raw material supply instead of creating it within the company. Import duty at 120 to 140 per cent became higher than the 120 per cent excise duty, so locating and developing small-scale suppliers was seen as the only real option. This effort started in 1990 and by 1994 HLL had developed a network of thirty suppliers who supplied all the key raw materials required.

One of these suppliers started out as a small group of employees of HLL who wanted to go into business for themselves and who had a good technical person in the group. They left HLL to become a captive supplier to HLL's personal products business. When HLL wanted to grow their shampoo production from 1,000 to 25,000 tons, this supplier ramped up production from 25 to 1,500 tons per week of imports. From HLL's point of view, this was very much like a completely integrated supplier and there was a clear sense of a shared destiny. The group of ex-employees became personally wealthy and HLL had a raw material supply source at 50 per cent of the cost of global scale plants. Quality was world class and they started supplying to Unilever in China and Indonesia.

Another example was Essel Packaging, which was part of the Zee TV group. When Essel started working with HLL, demand was 250,000 tubes, but it confidently invested in a 16mn tubes plant. This was when HLL was just getting into toothpastes. HLL grew in due course and Essel became the second largest manufacturer of flexible tubes in the world.

The personal products business required a fair amount of silica, which was supplied by three to four companies. These suppliers were developed with technical support from HLL and they have established production capacity at a capital cost of Rs 55 mn per ton, a figure considerably lower than the international norm of Rs 800 mn per ton.

Another example of HLL's stress on continuous efficiency improvement lay in distribution. Traditionally, manufacturing supplied goods to HLL's fifty depots, from where sales and marketing took over and supplied goods to 3,200 stockists, who in turn supplied up to 1.5mn retailers. In the early 1990s, it used to take twenty-four to forty-two days to re-stock the fifty depots with the consequent cost of holding inventories, working capital requirements, etc. HLL's 100 manufacturing points (including thirty to forty outsourced suppliers) would supply goods to the depots using 600–700 trucks with an average distance of 900 km. Re-stocking was done on demand.

By 1998–99, all factories produced continuously and production was shipped out daily to four regional buffer points. The buffer points supplied the fifty depots, who in turn supplied the stockists. Data on the daily offtake from the fifty depots was sent at the end of each day to the four buffer points which determined the mix of products that should be shipped to each depot the next day. The four buffer points in turn communicated the next day's needs to the factories so that they could plan production. This process resulted in a dramatic drop in the re-stocking of the fifty depots to an average of a day, and a maximum two-day delivery. Inventory holdings collapsed, generating Rs 10 bn in extra cash for HLL.

All this was made possible through the use of a private satellite communications network, using a VSAT link provided by Hughes Escorts. 'We took the IT standards from Unilever but modified them for India', said S. Ravindranath (general manager, commercial detergents). At an initial outlay of Rs 110 mn and the cost of a twenty person people information technology group, the new process generated a very large return on investment. The next stop was for the network to be extended to the 3,200 stockists of HLL. This would further reduce costs and improve the reliability of supply to retailers and customers.

Negative Working Capital

Working capital management was another area that received attention within the supply chain. A by-product of excellent supplier relations was that HLL had been able to negotiate growing supplier credit facilities. This substantially reduced working capital requirements to the point where various businesses within the company operated on a negative working capital.

Right-sizing

Between 1996 and 1999, HLL had rationalised all the businesses acquired through mergers with Lipton, Brooke Bond, Pond's, Plantations, Lakmé and others. The company had exited from non-core businesses such as leather tanning, textiles, leather garments and catfish farming, to direct resources to the main growth businesses of the company.

People Power

The Indian affiliate's contribution to Unilever went beyond numbers. In 1998–99, there were sixty-eight Indian managers overseas in the Unilever system, several of them strategically placed. Acknowledging the value of this Indian input, Unilever's 1995 annual report stated, 'Our companies in India in particular are an important source of quality management, innovation and relevant business processes, not only for Asia but further afield.'

Within India, after supplying 197 CEOs to other companies and over 200 managers in other board-level positions, HLL had a very well-deserved reputation as an excellent recruiter and developer of people. Interestingly, Dadiseth, a UK-trained chartered accountant, was the first non-technical professional after four successive technocrats to head HLL. Predecessors Vasant Rajadhyaksha, T. Thomas, Ashok Ganguly and S.M. Datta were all technical men. Prakash Tandon, HLL's first Indian chairman, was also a chartered accountant but had worked in marketing. Thus, Dadiseth was the first person from the finance function to make it to the top job.

HLL had a reputation for producing 'tough' chairmen. After 1993, the company embarked on a process of decentralisation. 'The moment one interferes, accountability disappears', remarked Dadiseth. 'A lot of top management is about signals. It used to be that when someone is promoted, they would get a bunch of perks—which had to be approved by the chairman. But I said these are contractual. Because these affect the lives of people, this became a powerful signal.' At the same time, as Dadiseth wryly noted, 'Learning new tricks is easy. Unlearning them is very difficult.'

Merging Cultures

Experience makes a good teacher. Dadiseth had been a key player in the M&A team which had cobbled together the re-unification of the Unilever companies in India between 1991 and 1998.[1] Thus HLL by 1999 had become a strange hybrid. Having been promoted by Unilever, Brooke Bond, Pond's, Lipton and others obviously possessed core Unilever values and culture. At the same time, over a period of time, they had evolved their own, unique characteristics. The challenge after the mergers was to create a new HLL culture. 'To have harmonised would have been sub-optimal. We had to make something new and special', said A. Lahiri (director HR, corporate affairs and technology).

What were the core values and culture of the main companies according to various managers?

- *HLL*: Managers described HLL as a restless company, target driven, with everyone striving to outperform others. Responsibility for the bottom line was shared and everyone knew the numbers. HLL could translate objectives into targets which people could relate to at every level. It had a tradition of working in teams. Command and control rested at the board level with a network of leaders below. Specialists would step out of their spheres to work in a team.
- *Brooke Bond*: Had far more 'command and control' than HLL. Managers below the top would not know much beyond their own objectives, and had limited idea of what the company was trying to do. Individual responsibility was the norm. Robust in resources, people were extremely dependable and would deliver on the basis of what they were told. Managers were proud of their big brands.
- *Pond's*: Managers felt they were more entrepreneurial than HLL. Each felt they had they flexibility to achieve their targets. Recruitment and talent pool at the top level was as good as HLL.

The process of welding these cultures was still being tackled in 1999. At the same time, as the company pulled together, several jobs overlapped or became

1.	HLL	51 per cent equity held by Unilever
	Brooke Bond	40 per cent held by Unilever
	Lipton	40 per cent held by Unilever
	Pond's	57 per cent held by Unilever
	Quest	98 per cent held by Unilever
	Doom Dooma Tea	74 per cent held by Unilever
	Tea estates	74 per cent held by Unilever

redundant. There were too many managers at some levels and too few at others, producing new strains in the company. 'We had to drop the baggage of history', was how one manager euphemistically put it. Luckily there were many takers for HLL managers. Its famous recruitment process ensured that anyone leaving HLL would be quickly snapped up.

Producing World-class Managers

Management recruits to the company typically joined either as direct recruits (DR) or as management trainees (MT). DRs were those who were brought in through head-hunters to fill a specific position, or in some cases those who had applied having already had a few years of work experience. Even DRs were hired into the company in Grade 3 and, after an assessment, could rise to Grade 1 positions (the next level was that of a general manager as Senior Grade 1 and then a director).

The company rarely hired externally for senior positions as it had a rich pipeline of candidates and it was difficult for a person to be accepted if he/she had not been through the training process and been brought up in the company's culture. One example was a manager who joined directly as a branch manager after fourteen years in Metal Box and left HLL after five to six years. 'In HLL, if you understand the system, it appears logical and rational and very easy to put across your proposals. Otherwise it's seen as bureaucratic, slow and difficult', said Adhikari, who joined HLL as a management trainee in 1977.

Once recruited, a DR was put on a six-month probation and placed directly into a job. After the six month period, the DR went through a confirmation review with HR and the line director. While recruitment as a DR was considered less prestigious than coming in as a management trainee, it was a perfectly acceptable way of joining the company and roughly half the members of the present board of directors had joined as DRs.

The MT recruitment and training process was a major exercise. It started with campus interviews at all the major business schools, Indian Institutes of Technology and various elite colleges across the country. This process had been widened recently through regular visits by the R&D and HR directors to the USA as well as use of internet, video-conferencing and CD-ROMs in identifying suitable candidates.

The company preferred group discussions to one-on-one interviews to screen and shortlist candidates. These candidates then met at least two directors before a final offer was made. Once hired, trainees were paid a competitive stipend and provided accommodation in a chummery (a separate room in an apartment shared with other trainees) for the period of their training. The training programme was highly structured and provided exposure to various aspects of the company, including driving a push cart and selling for a month—a humbling experience which left managers with a strong sense of empathy for the sales force.

Non-MBAs went through a two-and-a-half week basic business course at IIM Ahmedabad. This was interspersed with stints in the field doing different functions. The field training started with shadowing (following and learning from) a sales officer for a week and then four weeks as a salesman. This was followed by a week at a branch office before being assigned a project for a month. The next stage was a six-week stay at the Integrated Rural Development Centre at Etah, where each trainee lived with a village elder (female trainees were accommodated in a guest house) and worked on projects such as building roads, developing smokeless cooking stoves, and negotiating with government offices for development assistance. This experience helped trainees understand the realities of rural life and assisted them in their careers while creating new products, delivery systems and so on.

Adhikari was in the first batch of MBAs to be put through HLL's famous Rural Development Programme. 'I can't say that the experience is pleasant but it gives a real sense of how 70 per cent of India lives. You also see what the government and other institutions are supposed to do; and the power available if you can access it. The programme gives a sense of reality which lasts for the rest of your life. It helps one understand salesmen and their challenges.'

Once the training was over, each trainee moved into a job and was given a subordinate charge (supervised) for a three-month period. This job was consistent with the stream to which he or she had been assigned, i.e., manufacturing, supply chain management or marketing and sales. This was the trainees' first opportunity to manage people and taught them the basics of leadership skills. A confirmation interview was held at the end of the subordinate charge with the HR director and the relevant line director and a decision taken on whether or not the trainee should join the ranks of HLL's management. Once accepted, managers received regular guidance from seniors on-the-job as well as nominations to attend relevant development programmes as part of the annual appraisal process. 'We offer careers, not jobs', was HLL's stated position.

Among the values inculcated in young managers during their initial years were integrity and ethics. This was considered very important within the company and HLL encouraged the reporting of colleagues, both junior and senior, if there was clear evidence of poor ethical practices. This reputation for a high ethical standard was responsible for several HLL managers becoming CEOs in other companies. Multinationals, who when first entering a new country wanted to ensure their own ethical standards were maintained, found that hiring an HLL executive was a good way of achieving this.

Recruitment of some of the better talent in the country combined with a robust training program and rotation through a range of jobs and product categories inevitably made HLL vulnerable to head-hunters. The attractiveness of HLL managers led to regular departures and while the company hired about forty trainees each year, it expected to lose about twenty in the first ten years and then another ten over the next five years. So only 25 per cent of new trainees were still there fifteen years after joining the company. HLL had adjusted to this reality and recognised that it did not have enough top jobs to meet the aspirations of all HLL managers. The appraisal process was open and enabled managers to know exactly where they stood so that they could make an informed decision on their future.

At the same time, HLL managers faced two drawbacks: the HLL way both functionalised them and accustomed them to a great deal of support from each other. Thus, they frequently found it difficult to operate as effectively outside the company as they were used to within HLL. Functionalisation was caused because people became general managers only by Senior Grade 1. Until then they had a lot of exposure and experience, but they remained in either manufacturing, supply chain management or marketing and sales. According to Adhikari, there were three kinds of support: from the peer group, from functions such as the legal division, and from senior managers who 'add rather than police'.

Discipline and Teamwork

As the ice cream and *atta* examples demonstrated, HLL had a tradition of quickly putting together teams. For Project Millennium, HLL picked twelve dedicated managers and thirty part-timers with Harish Manwani (director, personal products), 46, as the process-owner. As Dadiseth pointed out, 'The key concept here is when there is a huge problem and people sit down as a team to address it, we may not reach the solution, but the solution comes within sight.'

How did everyone come together time and again in such a predictable way in a company as large and as diverse as HLL? The process was driven by the concept of unified objectives which were established on a company-wide level (based on a bottom-up and top-down process) every five years through the process of strategic planning and through a recognition that complex, ambitious and difficult tasks can only be done by a team.

The Business Group Strategic Plan (BGSP) was a five-year plan and the responsibility of the business head for each business. The current planning cycle started in 1997 and would run to 2002. The BGSP was a consolidation of the plan for all the product categories within the business and this plan in turn reflected the plans for each brand. The BGSP defined a market share and revenue target and this drove the investment required to create sufficient capacity. The investment plan affected the manufacturing plan and the supply chain plan. The plan translated into a target for each year and this remained an estimate until the previous year when it was firmed up based on developments. Once firm, the annual target was broken up into quarterly and monthly numbers which had to be met. A failure in meeting the target in marketing and sales would work its way into the supply chain and manufacturing as a variance on inventories, lower capacity utilisation or some other anomaly. So, when there was a problem or a blip, everyone pulled together as a team to get back on track.

The five-year planning process served to set 'stretch' longer-term targets, which were almost always exceeded, facilitated long-term facilities planning and forced people to think beyond the immediate. The annual estimate was a rigorous process which involved serious discussions and negotiations before an agreement was reached on the annual objective.

Teamwork was a key requirement at HLL, and reward and remuneration followed a team's success. Selectors tried to identify appropriate skills in aspiring MTs and at each stage during their careers managers had both personal and team objectives. Teams were created regularly at the head office in Bombay to try and resolve significant problems and to transmit best practices throughout the company. These teams came together for a purpose, worked together to meet the purpose and once this was accomplished, were disbanded. There were at least fifty such teams at work within HLL at any point of time.

According to Lahiri, 'One of the greatest things about this company is that after the debate once a decision is taken, everyone falls in line and works in unison to achieve the corporate objective. This happens across the organisation and all the way down to the worker on the manufacturing line. Everything comes together.' Dadiseth put it more succinctly: 'Once they agree to a target, that is a contract.'

The Dancing Elephant

Clearly in 1998–99, HLL was in an outstanding position. Yet Dadiseth felt compelled to tamper with the sure-fire success formula. Why?

- *External Environment Issues*: Did he feel that HLL in its present avatar would not be able to cope with competitive factors, move with the time, not be a company of the future?
- *Internal Factors*: Did he feel that HLL in its present avatar did not have the financial, human and other resources to cope with the demands which would be made on the organisation in the future?
- *Parental Pressure*: Were new norms being set, new directions taken, at Unilever which HLL was expected to follow?

> According to Dadiseth, 'Project Millennium is a look into the future, to see what is required for high-growth performance, to internally live up to our ambitions, and to externally meet people's expectations.'
>
> —*Business Today,* 7 August 1999

The way Dadiseth saw it, there were two key areas of concern: growth and people.

Leveraging Growth

HLL's two main businessses—soaps and detergents, and beverages—contributed 56 per cent of net sales. But penetration levels were too deep to allow high growth in the future. 'We need to develop distinctive insights by understanding how on going economic and social change is affecting the business environment. We must also have the ability to foresee the future and prepare for it so that when the opportunities arise, they can be fully captured', said Dadiseth.[2]

2. 'Project Millennium', *Business Today,* 7 August 1999, p. 61.

On the growth issue, the way forward was to re-connect with the consumer and make absolutely sure the company was delivering what the consumer expected. The cleaning, care and hygiene of consumers and their houses was the business of HLL, but most senior managers at HLL didn't cook themselves or use a washing machine. The board was conscious of this and members had started using HLL products regularly. 'HLL had to be committed to using customer service to maintain a distinct competitive advantage.' Technology would be the tool to deliver this objective and Dadiseth wanted 'to bring back a much greater focus on technology'. At the same time, right-sizing the company at all levels was a key priority. 'We have to ensure that our overhead costs decline as a portion of revenues over time.'

According to Dadiseth, the customer was a greater worry than competition. The path to growth lay not in beating rivals but in managing customers—in getting them to move through the company's product portfolio, to use more of HLL's products and to find a need for the value-propositions that its brands offerred.

HLL's managers were encouraged to ask where new customers could come from. Did the 40 per cent of the population that was below 21 present a new marketing opportunity? If 70 per cent of the growth was coming from rural markets, how could the company cash in on that? As a result of this enforced quest for answers from all its 36,000 employees, every idea of the past was systematically challenged. For example, HLL had traditionally been a larger advertiser. In 1998, it had spent Rs 6690 mn. Even this was now contested, with some managers wondering whether to re-direct some of this spending on retailing.

The HLL of 1999 was an amalgam of six companies. Between 1993 and 1998, it had absorbed TOMCO, Lipton, Brooke Bond, Kissan, Lakmé and Kwality. Thus, inorganic growth accounted for 49 per cent of HLL's sales. Also the different businesses—especially the younger ones such as colour cosmetics, fragrances or foods—moved to rhythms different from those of the mature—and larger—markets of soaps, detergents and beverages. Their demands on HLL's capital and intellectual resources varied widely too. So HLL needed to ensure that different product categories set their own cadences.

Working closely with McKinsey to map its present and prospective businesses to the different levels of growth and profits that they could yield, HLL divided its portfolio into three time/value capsules—Horizons 1, 2 and 3.

Horizon	*Business Portfolio*	*Strategic Objective*
1	Mature business.	Profitable growth.
2	Business with growth possibilities where the company has already made a start.	Top line growth.
3	New business areas with either small or no markets at the moment but which could explode.	Development and learning.

Horizon One	*Horizon Two*	*Horizon Three*
Soaps and detergents	Personal products	Direct-to-home products
Beverages	Popular foods	Value added foods
Oils and dairy fats	Ice creams	Breads and biscuits
Speciality chemicals	Culinary products	
	Homecare products	
	New beverages	

Virtual CEOs

The people issue was even trickier than growth. There were too many bright people getting older by the day whose usefulness was not being adequately tapped or challenged. 'We've been able to shed workers but have a problem with moving out managers. Ideally we should lose upto 20 per cent of our managers in order to improve efficiency. There have to be changes in the personnel system', said Dadiseth. 'Twenty years ago, what were my aspirations? Today there is a huge difference. People are more willing to move to greener pastures. I am unhappy with the bonus system.' Aspirations of HLL's managers had changed with time and 'we have to be prepared to respond with high differentiation in compensation and fast-track careers for the high-fliers'.

Landing a job at HLL used to be the ultimate yuppie manager's dream but by 1998–99 was losing status. The slow journey to the top by even the fast-trackers–potential CEOs in HLL-speak—had made HLL a less-coveted employer than it used to be five years ago. For example, even the brightest trainee could at best expect to be a vice-president—two rungs below the CEO and one step below the board—by the age of forty. In any other MNC, he/she could well be the CEO. The benchmarks: the CEOs of Reebok, Corn Products and Kellogg India were in their early- to mid-forties. 'Managers are concerned about their career track slowing down as the organisation gets larger', said one director.[3] For example, during 1998–99, three HLL directors had moved on as CEOs to other large organisations: vice chairman R. Gopalkrishnan joined the Tata group in July 1998; director (speciality chemicals) Debu Bhattacharya joined the Aditya

3. 'Project Millennium', *Business Today*, 7 August 1999, p. 62.

Birla group in December 1998; and director (culinary products) Pranab Barua moved to Reckit & Coleman in March 1998.

Dadiseth was convinced that HLL needed a new business model where people would long to work. Could or should the key detergent business be split into five profit centres? Perhaps soaps could become one profit centre on its own. 'To win, we must continue to attract and excite the best talent in the country. Our people will be invested with unparalleled power to imagine, innovate and implement new ideas. Our business model will make Levers not just a great company but also a great employer'.[4]

Virtual CEOs

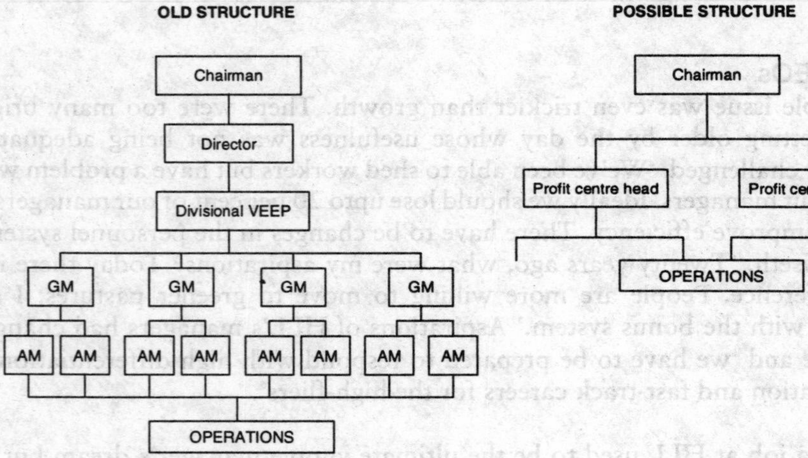

Source: *Business Today*, 7 August 1999, p. 63.

Project Millennium's single point radical solution was to decentralise and break up the company to create small, highly entrepreneurial businesses. This was a 180 about-turn from the man who had worked on the crack M&A team which had unified HLL between 1991 and 1998. Quite how the target of the big–small corporation could be achieved was not certain. One possible blueprint was presented to the HLL board when it met in Goa on 13 January 1999. To help

4. 'Project Millennium', *Business Today*, 7 August 1999, p. 62.

design the new organisation, HLL adopted a holistic, enterprise-wide approach. Hundreds of managers were interviewed, a twenty-page questionnaire was sent out to all employees and scores of workshops were conducted to involve, include and capture ideas and the thinking in every part of the organisation.

Project Millennium commuted HLL from status quo mode to revolution. Was it worth tampering with a proven, sure-fire success formula? Or was it change for change's sake? More importantly, would it work?

CASE 17

CENTRE FOR DEVELOPMENT OF TELEMATICS: SWITCHING ON THE TELECOM REVOLUTION IN INDIA

When Alexander Graham Bell introduced his ingenious telephone receiver at the Philadelphia Exposition in 1876, he could not have possibly imagined how widespread the usage of his discovery would be. The telephone's popularity created a need for complex switching systems (telephone exchanges), systems which are at the heart of today's telecommunications revolution. In India, the Centre for the Development of Telematics, better known as C-DoT, was founded in 1984 with the objective of discovering a cost-efficient way to deliver the benefits of telecommunications to as many of India's burgeoning population as possible.

The project as conceived by two men, Prime Minister Rajiv Gandhi and Sam Pitroda, a US-based technocrat of Indian origin, was wildly ambitious. In the late

This case was written by Dr Pradeep Kanta Ray, Lecturer in International Business, University of New South Wales, Sydney. The author acknowledges the support of the management and staff of C-DoT who provided untiring and invaluable assistance in data collection. The case was first registered by the School of International Business, University of New South Wales in 2000.

1980s, developing countries invested only 0.4 to 0.6 per cent of GNP in telecommunications, whereas Singapore invested 1.1 per cent and Malayasia 2.3 per cent. In 1994, nearly 90 per cent of world production of telecom equipment was located in OECD countries.[1] The five most advanced countries accounting for approximately one-tenth of the world's population had access to over 50 per cent of all telephones.[2] The entire continent of Africa with over 500 million people had less telephones than the city of Tokyo.[3]

Starting from scratch, C-DoT cherry-picked some of the most talented Indian engineers in the field to develop its own technology—technology which would be relevant to India and Indian conditions, which would be capital sensitive and labour intensive, which would be rugged and cheap. By 1994, around one-third of India's total switching capacity came to rely on C-DoT technology and by 1999, C-DoT had 40 per cent of the total lines installed in the country. This achievement has to be seen in the context of a rise in teledensity (lines per hundred inhabitants) which went up from 0.53 in 1989 to 2.2 in 1999 on a larger population base.

How was this impressive feat achieved and what challenges faced one of India's most controversial projects?

Indian Telecommunications Sector

After independence in 1947, the Government of India subsumed switching under the Department of Telecommunications (DoT) to address developmental objectives by means of a state monopoly. Due to inadequate financing and consequent lack of growth in switching capacity, the industry was characterised by excess demand throughout its history.[4] DoT suffered from capital and foreign currency shortages, many competing demands and the government's appropriation of operating surpluses to the detriment of investment in that sector.[5] Additional weaknesses included a faulty organisation structure and

1. A.J.M.—Roobeek, 'Te lecommunications: An Industry in Transition', in H.W. de Jong (ed.), *The Structure of European Industry*, 1988, Dordrecht, Kluwer Academic Publishers, pp 297–328.
2. *Telematics India*, October 1994.
3. *Telematics India*, May 1994.
4. *Business World*, 10–23 August 1994, p. 120.
5. *Ibid.*

government interference, which prevented DoT from operating as a commercial enterprise. Lack of autonomy, lack of incentives to reduce costs and increase customer service, non-competitive remuneration and lack of career opportunities were some of the more serious HRD policy inadequacies.

In 1948, the Indian Post and Telegraph Department purchased the Strowger Exchange (electro-mechanical switch) technology from a foreign vendor at a high price of Rs 11.2 mn and began local manufacturing. At the time of its purchase, the technology was already in the downward phase of its product life cycle.[6] Even after two decades of manufacturing, the Indian Telephone Industries (ITI) had not achieved defect-free manufacturing techniques, its rate of rejection being as high as 20 per cent in the early 1980s.[7]

The second major phase of technological change occurred when ITI decided to license and manufacture the Belgian Penta Conta Cross Bar exchange in the 1960s. This technology was not only unsuited to the needs of the economy but also much of the R&D that followed got bogged down in adapting this inappropriate technology.[8] Repeated import of technology before absorption of the previous generation of technology did not engender development of any significant skills required for duplicative or adaptive technological attainments.[9]

Eventually in 1982, the next phase of technological change was ushered in with the signing of technology collaboration agreements between Alcatel-CIT of France and ITI for the manufacture of E-10B digital switches. Alcatel entered India aided by the political backing of the French government, where the decision to adopt the technology was made by Indira Gandhi herself.[10] This agreement was supposedly a political one, concluded in return for French assistance in the purchase of defence equipment for India.[11] Thereafter, Alcatel's E-10B switch established an almost unchallenged position in the Indian market. The quality of exchanges as well as the success of indigenisation improved

6. S. Mani, 'Output Growth, Technology Behaviour and Employment: Indian Electronics Industry under Liberalisation', in A.K. Bagchi (ed.), *New Technology and the Workers Response: Microelectronics, Labour and Society,* New Delhi, Sage Publications.
7. *Ibid.*
8. *Telematics India,* October 1994.
9. S., Mani 'Output Growth, Technology Behaviour and Employment', in A.K. Bagchi (ed.) *New Technology and the Workers Response: Microelectronics, Labour and Society.*
10. *Telematics India,* September 1993, P. 7.
11. *Telematics, India*, October 1994, p. 46.

significantly through this agreement.[12] However, the cost per line, at around Rs 7,000, was quite high by world standards. Furthermore, despite the successful introduction and absorption of foreign technology from Alcatel, demand continued to outstrip supply.

In 1984 Indira Gandhi was assassinated and her son, Rajiv Gandhi, won the elections with an overwhelming majority in parliament. Declaring that India must move quickly into the 21st century, Rajiv Gandhi not only encouraged NRI (non-resident Indian) technocrats to return to India, but he also encouraged bureaucrats such as Abid Hussain in the Planning Commission to identify five specific projects which would leverage IT to improve living standards. C-DoT was one of the enterprises which emerged from this initiative.

An unexpected economic crisis in 1991 required the intervention of the International Monetary Fund, which deemed India should open up its economy and welcome foreign investment.[13] Even as these events transpired, the endemic problem of the telecommunications network continued, with demand for lines far outstripping supply. Widespread dissatisfaction with service and corruption prompted DoT to move to a deregulated structure. In order to grow faster it had to be able to raise more funds,[14] the most obvious source for which was foreign direct investment (FDI).

In July 1991, the New Industrial Policy permitted FDI in the telecommunications manufacturing industry for the first time, without the requirement of an industrial licence.[15] The Reserve Bank of India (RBI) permitted foreign equity participation of up to 51 per cent through automatic approval.[16] Shortly afterwards, DoT asked several multinational enterprises (MNEs) to supply 100,000 lines on a deferred payment basis.[17] In order to get access to foreign sources for funding of large telecom projects, the Government of India put telecommunications in the list of bilateral government negotiations.[18]

12. *Ibid.*
13. B. Datta, *Indian Planning at the Crossroads*, 1992, New Delhi, Oxford University Press.
14. *C&C*, March 1994, p. 100.
15. *Telematics India,* November 1995, p. 23. Also P. Balakrishna and M. Singh, 'Indian Telecom Market', *Northern Business Information*, June 1997, New York, McGraw Hill, p. 117.
16. P. Balakrishna and M. Singh, 'Indian Telecom Market,' *Northern Business Information*, June 1997, New York, McGraw Hill, p. 117.
17. *Telematics India*, September 1993, p. 7.
18. *Telematics India*, December 1991, p. 36.

A number of MNEs arranged to provide the much needed foreign exchange loans, including soft credit, for India. Most notable was Siemens, Germany, which offered DM 500 million to finance the import requirements of DoT.[19] To improve foreign exchange inflow, the German giant offered to buy additional software from the recently established Siemens software centre and promote export of Indian products through 'barter trades with the support of our group's worldwide connections'. It also limited the foreign exchange outflow by maximising the local content of exchanges through component purchases from Indian manufacture rs.[20] Similarly, Alcatel offered a loan of 528 million French francs for the production of the E 10-1000 family of switches and prepared a package offering 0.1 million lines on lease.[21]

These offers along with drastic reductions of import duties collapsed prices. Duties were virtually halved to a maximum of 85 per cent, bringing down the price per line of foreign switches from a pre-reform price of Rs 9000 to Rs 5036 (in 1991). By 1994, the price had further fallen to Rs 4674.[22] In 1997, the import tariff telecom equipment stood at 30 per cent as opposed to 40 per cent in 1996, while components attracted a duty of 20 per cent.[23] Ironcially, tariffs on components were higher than imports on whole equipment, which encouraged imports instead of local manufacturing.[24]

In order to improve the functioning of this strategic industry, under the New Telecom Policy 1994 the government deemed that the inflow of technology should bring forth full advantage of the emerging new technologies while at the same time ensuring the creation of competencies to meet national demand and compete globally.[25] The Government of India formulated specific strategic goals which included:

1. Availability of telephones on demand by 1997.
2. Provision of access to basic telephony covering all urban and rural areas.

19. *Indian Express*, 19 December 1991.

20. *Ibid*.

21. *C&C*, March 1994, pp 104-106.

22. *Telematics India*, July 1992 , p. 34 and May 1994, p. 26.

23. A.F. Ferguson & Co., 'Status Paper on Indian Telecommunication', 1997, Madras, Confederation of Indian Industry, p. 52.

24. *Ibid*., p. 139.

25. *National Telecom Policy 1994*, Appendix 4.1, 13 May 1994, Ministry of Communications.

3. Affordability to rural customers.
4. Creation of a major telecom manufacturing base in India.
5. Coverage of all 576,000 villages by 1997.
6. Defence and security of the country.

Despite these efforts, by 1996, the Indian telecommunications sector still had exceptionally low telephone density and a multiplicity of technological problems. The overall teledensity in 1996 was only 1.31 per 100 inhabitants.[26] The rural population, which accounted for over 75 per cent of the total population, had access to only 10 per cent of direct exchange lines (DELs). India's teledensity was also lower than those of many other developing countries in Asia like China (12.7), Pakistan (2) and Malaysia (13).

Comparative Availability of Telephone Lines in 1994

Country	*Total number of telephone lines*
USA	156.8
Japan	59.9
Germany	39.2
France	31.6
UK	28.4
China	27.2
Italy	24.5
Russia	24.1
Canada	16.8
Spain	17.7
Brazil	12.9
Turkey	12.2
India	9.8
Australia	8.6

C-DoT

When C-DoT first started, its mission was to develop India's own digital

26. Refers to 1996 figures. See R. Venkatesan, 'Socio-economic Impact of Rural Telecommunications Services', Working Paper No. 45, 1994, New Delhi, National Council for Applied Economic Research, pp. 5–11. See also 'The Great Telecom Windfall', *Telematics India*, July 1994, pp 26–32.

switching technology and its own 40,000 line digital switching equipment, which was to be upgraded to have full fledged ISDN capability. That mission was modified around 1989 and further modified when the transmission group of the TRC was merged into C-DoT and it covered both switching and transmission. Thereafter, C-DoT began the development of transmission products, wireless satellites as well as products in optical areas.

Initially, C-Dot was set up in 1984 with an outlay of Rs 350 mn. C-DoT's role entailed an intensive developmental effort towards creation of a technology suitable for a local context through its own R&D organisation, intensive local integration, and establishing a number of plants spread over many licensees with long production lengths. Up to March 1994, a total of Rs 4.5 bn ($150 million) was invested by manufacturers of equipment based on C-DoT designs, employing some 20,000 personnel.[27] By 1994, around one-third of the total switching capacity of the country came to rely on C-DoT technology and, by 1999, C-DoT had 40 per cent of total lines installed in the country.[28]

Through its location specific advantages (such as the abundance of well-qualified and cheap technical and software manpower), C-DoT spent only Rs 720 mn ($28 million) on developing technologies. This compared favourably with Alcatel and Siemens, which had spent $1 billion and $1.3 billion respectively.[29] C-DoT's modular exchanges optimised the use of electronic components and brought down the cost per line to Rs 3,400 as compared to Rs 7,000 in the previous period when India relied on Alcatel switches.[30] Through its vendor development policy, C-DoT was also able to build up an indigenous component industry that reduced foreign exchange outflow.[31]

The Beginning

Despite the odds in the field of digital switching, C-DoT successfully developed a switch from scratch—a switch not only isomorphic to the profile of India's unique environment but also independent of global technological trajectories.

27. *Ibid.*
28. *C&C*, October 1994, pp 69–90.
29. R. Venkatesan, 'Socio-economic Impact of Rural Telecommunications Services', Working Paper No. 45, 1994, New Delhi, National Council for Applied Economic Research, pp 5–11.
30. 'C-DoT – a Profile, January 1995.
31. *C&C*, October 1994, pp 69–90.

It had to, it had no other option. Its management was well aware that wholly internalised technology transfer under the form of foreign direct investment was a relatively less risky yet effective mechanism of accessing new technology. It could have imported foreign technologies 'fully packaged', where the process was commercially proven, and the parent provided the hard ware and the software, did the start-up, training and adaptation, and managed the operation and marketing. However, C-Dot preferred to move away from simple, assembly type production to developing its own innovative technologies.

As is well known, backward and forward linkages can constitute powerful mechanisms for stimulating (or retarding) industrial growth in developing economies. Geographical and cultural proximity to advanced users and a network of institutionalised (even if informal) user-producer relationships are an important source of diversity and of comparative advantage, as is the local supply of managerial and technical skills and the accumulated tacit knowledge.

Secondly, the incredibly fast pace of development in the global industry can go against the very grain of domestic confidence in developing a technology considered state-of-the-art in telecommunications. A strong entrepreneurial and scientific leadership was therefore necessary on the part of the local enterprise—along with firm governmental support to correct market failures in investment in this area. In this regard, the isomorphy of the switches developed by C-DoT and their modularity of design fulfilled a range of communications needs from rural to metropolitan applications and also corrected market failures in intermediate goods and knowledge through institution building.

C-DoT's early objective was to create a vision of what was to be done and then make it happen. This required not just of visionaries but also much greater emphasis on product development, product engineering and manufacturing besides building an extensive vendor base for telecom equipment.[32] Up to this period, management concerns were primarily related to consolidating the technology development process leading ultimately towards production and field operations. According to B.D. Pradhan, executive director, C-DoT: 'Local industry is going through an evolutionary process. When we are starting from

32. 'C-DoT did not want to invest in very expensive imported capital equipment and automation, especially testing and manufacturing equipment. The purpose was to create jobs for people. So that led C-DoT to develop its own functional testers instead of spending on very expensive testing equipment. Similarly the assembly lines was more manually oriented rather than automated' said K.B. Lall, director (switching) C-DoT, Interview Transcript, January 1995.

scratch, there is a need to look at the process in a particular way'.[33]

In achieving its goals, three aspects of design strategy were employed. First was a product strategy that entailed the commonality of hardware and software. The second was an equipment process technology strategy which entailed capital-sensitive and labour-intensive methods. For example, PC-based testing equipment was used instead of advanced electronic testing jigs, and it did not have a fully automated plant so that initial investment was low and more labour was used. The third strategy was to have an open, non-hierarchical and egalitarian organisational culture which would promote creativity.

Its engineers were specifically interested in developing relevant technologies for developing countries which were characterised by such contextual factors as extreme environmental conditions, high temperature, dust and humidity.[34] Manufacturing had to have a focus on simplicity of design, manufacture, operation and maintenance.[35] Emphasis was placed on low costs, rural applications, low power consumption, and minimisation of peripherals like air-conditioning and without the elaborate maintenance of a dust-free environment.[36] Hence, C-DoT switches did not offer any expensive 'frills' or cosmetic features.[37]

The way a switch was developed, produced and marketed by a manufacturer had important implications insofar as the features it provided to its customers, its suitability in use and the linkage effects it generated upon ancillary industries. Often, MNE-affiliates were more comfortable in focussing on developed country markets which demanded high quality products and where a premium for this knowledge advantage could be realised. However, increasing competition and the developmental costs of digital switches which had ballooned from a mere $50 million to about $0.5–$1 billion, put pressure on MNES to move out of their geographic area of operations to recover their costs of development. In this connection, a senior executive in Alcatel observed: 'The core strategy (in the subsidiary) cannot be any different because the core strategy is driven largely, in

33. *C&C*, Telecom cover story, October 1994.
34. *Ibid.*
35. C-DoT's manufacturing line showed manual assembly of cards instead of 'through hole techniques'.
36. C-DoT, Interview Transcript, New Delhi, January 1995.
37. As an example of their domain of competition which typically included the lower end of markets there are 100 or so MAXs installed in Vietnam, ten in Bangladesh and several more in Ethiopia, Mongolia, etc.

industries of this nature, by technology. And since technology emanates from the centre, automatically everyone has to follow. It is not that globally Alcatel is developing product A and I find the market for product B. We cannot make product B because the volume of production for the local market will not justify spending on R&D for product B in the Indian market.'

Moreover, many technologies were available only through FDI or were too complex for local capabilities, and had to be imported in internalised forms. In order to bear the risks, cost and expenses of locally absorbing very complex technologies, it would be necessary to promote large scale. Technological adaptation could be a legitimate goal of industrial policy, since the development of indigenous design and innovative capabilities has beneficial externalities This raises an additional point of debate concerning standardisation versus local adaptation.

Instead of standardising to suit all needs through one switch, which was us[illegible] cost-effective solution for MNEs, C-DoT simultaneously provided 'plain telephony' for rural areas and state-of-the-art exchanges in metropolitan cities. C-DoT's offerings were positioned to fit consumer preference spaces through a four-pronged product line strategy, which included its switching products: (1) PABX, (2) RAX, (3) MAX-L and (4) MAX-XL.[38]

Its field deployment of switching revealed that its product deployment in urban and rural areas was more balanced than those of MNEs, who competed mainly in the metropolitan cities.

Field Deployment of C-DoT and MNC Switches

	Rural (%)	*Urban (%)*
C-DoT	91	45
MNC	9	55

Source: C-DoT, January 1997.

C-DoT Under Fire

Five years into the project, promise had begun to translate into results. However, following the fall of the Rajiv Gandhi government in 1989, the new National Front administration, keen to distance itself from anyone close to the Congress

38. C-DoT, Internal Documents, New Delhi 1995.

party, requested Pitroda to resign.[39] Though C[illegible]oT had by this time been able to develop a family of digital switches, it c[illegible]e under increasing attack for its 'failure' to develop the large switch with[illegible]e specified time of three years.[40] The National Front also set up the Namb[illegible] Committee to investigate the affairs of C-DoT.[41] With C-DoT substan[illegible]y debilitated and struggling to regain credibility, an acrimonious de[illegible] flared up in the country with rival political parties accusing each other o[illegible]spiring against indigenous capabilities with the help of foreign interests.[42]

Meanwhile, in 199[illegible] National Front government fell. The new Congress administration u[illegible] Prime Minister Narasimha Rao and Finance Minister Mannohan Si[illegible] ushered in a slew of reforms aimed at liberalising and de-regulati[illegible] economy. In the switching equipment manufacturing sector, these mo[illegible] to a significant enhancement of capacity and a substantial increa[illegible] number of lines installed and the number of exchanges.

Key Indicators of the Indian Telephone Network

	1989	*1994*	*1996*	*1997*	*1999*
Operational performance					
DELs (MLN lines)	4.17	7	13.1	14.54	21.59
Teledensity	0.53	0.8	1.31	–	2.2
Switching					
Capacity (MLN lines)	–	–	14.6	17.74	26.05
Exchanges	13713	18000	21000	22212	24869
Satellite earth stations	–	–	191	235	439

Sources: 1. CMIE, Infrastructure in India, 1996.
2. Telecom Commission, Ministry of Communications, 1997.
3. Indian Telecommunications, DoT, 1999.

In 1989, India had only 4 million telephone lines with a telephone density of 0.5

39. *See* G.B. Meemansi, *C-DoT Story,* for a detailed account of the events that transpired during this time, the political interference and the numerous attempts to break up C-DoT by the Minister for Telecommunications, K.P. Unnikrishnan, allegedly with the backing of MNEs.
40. S. Mani, 'Output Growth, Technology Behaviour and Employment' in A.K. Bagchi (ed.), *New Technology and the Workers Response,* New Delhi, Sage Publications.
41. G.B. Meemansi, *The C-DoT Story: Quest, Inquest, Conquest,* 1993, New Delhi, Kedar Publications.
42. *C&C,* October 1994, p. 69. See also 'The Great Telecom Windfall', *Telematics India,* July 1994, pp 26–32.

per 100. After 1991, both teledensity and the number of Direct Exchange Lines (DELs) improved significantly. The number of exchanges increased from 13,717 in 1989 to 18,000 in 1994 and further to 25,000 in 1999. DELs increased from 4 million lines in 1989 to 7 million in 1994 and further to 21 million in 1999. The most remarkable improvement was in teledensity, which increased from 0.53 in 1989 to to 1.31 in 1996 and further to 2.2 in 1999.[43] Following increased domestic competition there was also a fall in equipment prices.

Decline in Equipment Prices, 1997

Equipment	*Reduction*
Large switching systems	50
Telephone instruments	50
Radio systems	65
Optical cable	43

Source: Telecom Equipment Manufacturer's Association.

Until 1991, DoT apportioned its orders for switches between C-DoT and Alcatel's licensees. In the 1994 tender, limitation of the size (configuration) of switches and the Busy Hour Call Attempt (BHCA) factor undermined C-DoT's bid. Thereafter, DoT determined that orders for large switches would be placed with MNEs until C-DoT switches could meet all DoT specifications. On the other hand, in line with the infant entrepreneur argument, DoT deemed that orders be placed with C-DoT exclusively for switches for smaller towns, semi-urban and rural areas.

Switching Requirements of DoT, 1992–97

(Million lines)

Equipment	*Requirement*
Small exchanges	8.431
Large exchanges	21.296
Trunk automatic exchanges	1.93
Total	31.657

Source: C-DoT.

Just as changes were taking place in equipment manufacturing capacity, the entry of MNEs also transformed market shares. In 1995–96, the ratio of market shares of MNE switches to C-DoT's indigenous switches was 3:1. This effected a

43. Background Paper - JBC 11.10.93

shake-out of many of C-DoT's licencees who could not buy materials on credit like their bigger counterparts in the industry.[44] Additionally, Remote Line Units (RLUs) of large exchanges of MNEs fed on C-DoT markets in small towns.[45] This reversed the earlier policy of confining MNE switches to metros and C-DoT switches to where the population was less than 0.5 million.

Market Shares of Telecom Equipment Suppliers, 1993–94 to 1996–97

('000 lines)

Company		*1993–94*	*1994–95*	*1995–96*	*1996–97*
Alcatel	ITI	60	300	301	–
	Modi	200	100	537.5	–
Siemens	SIL	110	260	217.5	–
	HTL	–	–	260	–
AT&T		–	150	165	–
Fujitsu		130	100	140	–
NEC		–	–	–	100
Ericsson		200	100	215	–
E-10B		383.5	418.7	610	566.1
Total MNE		1083.5	1428.7	2446	666.1
C-DoT		759.9	749.2	820.4	1043.5

Source: Northern Business Information, 1997.

Throughout the 1990s, a fierce debate raged over the efficacy and suitability of switches provided by MNEs vis-à-vis LEs. The proponents of foreign technology observed that the digital electronic switches offered by AT&T, Siemens, Ericsson, Fujitsu and Alcatel provided not only plain old telephony, but several advanced services.[46] Furthermore, they claimed that C-DoT's switches were inferior in features and facilities and were only capable of meeting the needs of low-density rural and semi-urban towns.[47] Admittedly, though C-DoT's exchanges were well proven in terms of reliability and features, prolonged delays in the provision of advanced features prevented it from getting orders for large switches, which permitted MNEs to gain a foothold in the Indian market.

44. *Telematics India*, May 1994, p. 29.
45. *Business India*, September 1994, p. 43.
46. The advanced features include CCITT (Common Channel Signalling System No. 7), Integrated Services Digital Network (ISDN), Asynchronous Transfer Mode (ATM), intelligent networks (IN), and higher Busy Hour Call Attempts (BHCA), etc. *Telematics India*, October 1994, p. 61
47. *Telematics India*, October 1996, pp 66–67.

The claims of better maintainability and price competitiveness of MNE switches vis-à-vis C-DoT's RAXs were, however, debatable. The latter has been proven to operate in conditions of extreme environmental perturbations, which gave it a locale-specific differentiation advantage in relation to buyer needs.[48] The servicing cost of switches based on foreign technology was higher than those of C-DoT switches, taking account of the fact that integral costs to the buyer included operating and maintaining costs for the switch's complete lifecycle. C-DoT's DELs priced at Rs 3,400 were significantly lower than the international price of US$ 200 per line at 1991 price levels.[49] According to C-DoT, MNEs deliberately undercut LEs in the 1994 tender by reducing the prices of their equipment and bearing up-front losses. At the same time, they raised prices of spares for after-sales maintenance. When the equipment failed, customers paid dearly to restore services.[50] C-DoT alleged, therefore, that MNEs resorted to up-front predatory pricing in the 1994 tender.

Price of Exchanges Quoted in DoT Tender Between 1994 and 1997

(Rupees)

Company	*1994*	*1996***	*1997**
Alcatel	4283	7298	6060
Siemens	4670	7349	6249
Ericsson	4670	7388	6188
Fujitsu	4912	7439	6188
NEC	—	7504	6288
ITI	5780	7550	5294
AT&T	5095	7851	6191
HTL	4569	7600	6343

* *Communications Today*, March–April, 1996.
** *Communications Today*, September–October, 1997.

Pitroda also worriedly predicted that with the influx of MNEs the roles of technical professionals would change from creative design and development to routine purchasing and procurement.[51] By 1995, the differentials in salary and

48. 'C-DoT: A Profile', January 1995; P. Balakrishna and M. Singh, 'Indian Telecom Market', *Northern Business Information*, June 1997, New York, McGraw Hill, p. 117.
49. R. Venkatesan, 'Socio-economic Impact of Rural Telecommunications Services', Working Paper No. 45, 1994, New Delhi, National Council for Applied Economic Research, pp 5–11.
50. C-DoT, Interview Transcript, New Delhi, February 1995.
51. S. Pitroda, 'Telecom Privatisation: Why and How', *Telematics India*, October 1994.

benefits paid to executives and engineers in MNEs and the consequent turnover of highly skilled personnel from C-DoT to MNEs was creating an environment of confrontation and frustrating local efforts.[52] Around this time, C-DoT's executive director commented: 'MNCs are trying to hurt us in every possible way. By luring our technocrats away with attractive salaries, they only want to remove us from the entire switching scene so that they have a free run'.[53]

C-DoT's products, however, still lacked the aesthetic appeal of those of the MNEs, who designed packaging around their home country context. To counter this, C-DoT asserted that its MAX switch was more cost-effective because material costs and direct labour costs in manufacturing were lower than those of MNEs. On the practical side, it highlighted the advantages of a much more cost-effective network, which increased DoT's profits. More importantly, the software cost in the switch, which was 75 per cent of the total cost of developing the switch, was lower because software engineers in India were paid only a fraction of the rates in the developed world. Training of people and documentation, which constituted about 25 per cent of the cost of equipment, was also lower since the cost of producing such documents is infinitesimally smaller than that in the developed world.[54]

By end 1994, C-DoT had nearly 3 million lines of switching equipment in the network, which accounted for nearly one-third of the total network of the country. This exposure gave C-DoT tremendous confidence in the whole development process, and a superior knowledge of not only the development aspects but also the operational aspects of the technology, and goodwill, insofar as the ground level subscribers responded to the local equipment. In addition, C-DoT had designed the equipment to cater to the country's specific requirements in comparison to other foreign products that were designed and built for different environments. C-DoT's new objective was, therefore, to see how they could exploit this advantage by:

1. Marketing their own products to other operators.
2. Getting DoT to appreciate that their alliance with C-DoT on the locally developed technology would give it an edge over its competitors.

Since the design of the switch was totally in C-DoT's own hands, it could provide

52. *Ibid.*

53. *Computers Today*, January 1995.

54. For example, this is what obtains in the US.

enhanced features in the hardware locally without referral to foreign entities. For example, when it came to the upgradation of the software of the switch, all the source codes were totally in local hands, and C-DoT could meet the upgradation requirements quite effectively. Also, when it came to adding value on the existing software, C-DoT possessed the capability to develop the value added service requirements on its own software platform. Moreover, all these advantages were available to DoT at very nominal costs, which was an important source of C-DoT's competitive advantage vis-à-vis other competitors in India.

As matters stood in 1995, on the one hand, India needed the high technology switches of MNEs to gain access to the electronic gateway of global commerce. On the other, it needed a strong developmental effort to link the rural areas into the mainstream Indian economic life. MNEs, using the universal laws of physics, chemistry, biology and other sciences provided an underlying unified technology that could, in principle, be applied anywhere with identical or similar results. Therefore, insofar as large global MNEs were able to sell their products and services worldwide and produce them in many different locations, they acted as very powerful agencies tending towards worldwide standardisation of technology and output.

The traits that distinguished C-DoT were its practice of in-depth manufacturing and multi-plant integration.[55] Since C-DoT's products were the outcome of a single R&D programme, substantial economies of scale in R&D had been achieved, while indigenisation of 70 per cent of the bill of materials had saved import tariffs and reduced total costs further. Also, C-DoT plants, operated by its licencees, were not fully automated, so that the initial investment for its licensees was low. More importantly, the switch had been developed on the foundation of an open-architecture, where growth to the switch in higher configurations was modular, i.e., the largest configuration utilised components of the smallest configuration.[56] Seventy-five per cent of the hardware in the largest MAX XL (which was a 40,000 line exchange) was similar to the RAX (500 line exchange). Commonality and hence economy of investment were the reasons why manufacturers were licensed on a step-by-step basis.

Furthermore, C-DoT's repairs were conducted at the component level whereas MNEs replaced sub-assemblies, i.e., en-bloc import and replacement of cards instead of repair.[57] The practice of replacing sub-assemblies instead of repairing

55. C-DoT, Interview Transcript, New Delhi, January 1995.

56. *Ibid.*

57. *Ibid.*

faults in the componentry led to discarding of cards, a custom that was not only foreign to the Indian context but also ecologically unsound and economically wasteful.[58] In 1995, their executive director observed: 'Whereas the philosophy today is that you throw away cards because of the new packaging technology and new manufacturing technology.... The costs that are associated with it specially in the West—they don't think its worthwhile trying to repair a card, so (they) throw it away and replace that card. I don't think we have reached that stage here in India.'

Thus, between its avowed goal of development and protection of the infant entrepreneur and the needs for transformational efficiencies, the national government appeared to have reached a 'compromise solution' by reserving smaller switches for C-DoT and large ones for MNEs. The real issue facing India, however, was the continuation of support to C-DoT in order to enable it to reach international competitiveness. This had to be weighed against the massive investments necessary to transform the Indian economy as a whole, which required the government to invite MNEs into the country.

Achievements of C-DoT

The major success of C-DoT was to build a reservoir of highly motivated and enthusiastic young and talented scientists for R&D activities in the field of digital switching systems (DSS).[59] A second achievement was self-confidence.

With economic liberalisation, C-DoT experienced overwhelmingly high-selling pressures and publicity expenditures from individual MNEs than what its licensees could expend together. In terms of direct canvassing of products, MNEs invariably managed to penetrate the higher echelons of decision makers in the ministry and canvass through influencers down the line. On the other hand, C-DoT inspired confidence bottom up, getting the field level operators of the switch to whet their approval in reiterating that the switch was suitable for their operations.[60]

To counter the MNEs' marketing clout, C-DoT guaranteed any Indian operator that existing investments would remain good and productive as all modifications/new developments on C-DoT products would be retrofitted so

58. *Ibid.*
59. *Telematics India*, October 1994, p. 61
60. C-DoT, Interview Transcript, New Delhi, January 1995.

that their network always remained state-of-the-art throughout the life of the equipment.[61] Moreover, the C-DoT range of switches were heat and dust resistant, and required low maintenance costs throughout their life cycle.[62] These features enabled C-DoT to successfully export switches to developing countries, viz., Nigeria, Nepal, Vietnam, Yemen and Bangladesh, where its products were hailed as very price competitive and ideally suited for the harsh climatic conditions.[63] In terms of location responsive features of the system, its user friendly service at the operator level enabled any operator with interactive help dialogue to set up the console without extensive assistance from the manufacturer—a feature that C-DoT highlighted as a distinct advantage for the user. In this connection, its project manager observed in 1998:

> Having our own indigenous R&D set-up here, we are much faster in understanding and solving, at low cost, the problems relating to the designing, augmenting, modifying and installing (the switch) on-site, whereas the foreign vendor has to refer the problem back to their home country. In fact if they have fly out for the customer, they will charge for it, whereas we can provide a cost-effective solution very quickly. As far as internal support is required we have established a round-the-clock set-up. They (customers) can call up and we can give a solution over the phone itself. That's our advantage.

C-DoT also played a strong developmental role in a country characterised by high income inequality, poverty, illiteracy, and a divide between urban and rural populations.[64] Often rapid evolution of technology leads to information asymmetries between buyers and sellers. As Pitroda observed:

> While developments in the telecom sector are critical in modernisation of India, successful privatisation has to take into account each country's own ecosystem as a process with a long range vision instead of piecemeal; an ongoing dialogue with stakeholders; high level of commitment; and new management and new work, re-engineering, and human resources. With privatisation it is possible that businesses may only focus on lucrative urban and corporate markets whereas universal service has been achieved in all advanced countries through

61. 'C-DoT Does Not Fear Competition', *Telematics India*, October 1996.
62. C-DoT, Interview Transcript, New Delhi, January 1995.
63. *C&C*, October 1994. Also *Telematics India*, April–June 1994.
64. R. Venkatesan, 'Socio-economic Impact of Rural Telecommunications Services', Working Paper No. 45, 1994, New Delhi, National Council for Applied Economic Research, pp 5–11.

cross-subsidies. Hence, a certain minimum level of local engineering development is essential to enable developing countries to choose the right technology from overseas and also build and keep in-country talent. This raises the importance of tailoring firm-specific objectives to the cultural, legal, political and economic conditions.[65]

C-DoT's progressive indigenisation, supported by strong backward integration through ancillary units, engendered powerful linkage effects in the country. The second effect of C-DoT's operation was its indirect effect, or the externalities it generated on local industrial structure, conduct and performance. Most of C-DoT's 4000 components were sourced from 372 local vendors.[66] The extent of indigenisation achieved was to the tune of 70 per cent of the bill of materials. By contrast MNEs procured components at the lowest possible price sources. On the other hand, the manufacturing of line cards in exchanges by MNEs provided some opportunities for the local manufacture of four or five components of the switch, such as cabinets, transformers, wires and cables, PCBs, and small plastic and metal parts.[67]

Since developing its first switches, C-DoT had licensed its technology to about thirty licensees. In so doing, the organisation had created a broad-based manufacturing base and facilitated the diffusion of technology, skills and knowledge. However, as a downside, the capacity utilisation of the licensees remained as low as 20 to 30 per cent.[68] These licensees competed in a small market, and none of them attained any economies of scale. Additional problems appeared in co-ordinating the efforts of these multiple licensees, whereby more time was wasted on training.

By 1994, 139,324 villages in India had been linked up through C-DoT's Rural Automatic Exchanges (RAX) under the 'RAX-a-day' programme.[69] Today, there is no rural area where C-DoT has not reached, In addition several configurations of Private Automatic Branch Exchanges (PABX) were being manufactured

65. S. Pitroda, 'Telecom Privatisation: Why and How', *Telematics India*, October 1994; A.F. Ferguson & Co., 'Status Paper on Indian Telecommunication', 1997, Madras, Confederation of Indian Industry, p. 93.
66. In RAXs the import content is 12 per cent only. In medium and higher capacity exchanges it is about 22 per.
67. *C&C*, Telecom cover story, October 1994.
68. *C&C*, Telecom News, April 1994. See also K.N. Gupta, 'C-DoT Does Not Fear Competition', *Telematics India*, October 1996.
69. *Telematics India*, July 1994.

across many plants throughout India.

Nevertheless, C-DoT's indigenous development of digital switching technology succeeded despite the high entry barriers in this technology intensive industry. Besides USA, France, Germany, Sweden, Japan and Korea no other country has been successful.[70] The C-DoT experiment was largely triumphant, not only in developing high technology digital switches for the Indian network but also fostering the linkages to externalise spillover effects from such an enterprise.

Challenges Ahead

As mentioned earlier, technological deepening can be a legitimate goal of industrial policy, since the development of indigenous design and innovative capabilities has many beneficial externalities. It is therefore worth considering a policy implication arising from the case study. According to some scholars, in emerging industries where local capabilities are weak, industrial policy should protect infant entrepreneurs until such moment that they are capable of taking on full global competition. However, one might argue that even as protection is afforded, a sound institutional infrastructure needs to be created before local firms can effectively respond to global competition. And since all firms, be they MNE-affiliates or LEs, are really dependent on the relevant institutions, the question of protection cannot extend across the board to all industries, ignoring the individual asymmetries that obtain both within and between each of the industries. Indeed, the relevant question to ask is whether the gap between LEs and MNEs in this high technology industry will narrow in the future. Given time, it will be interesting to see how the two rivals perform, and whether the enhanced country-specific competencies in software and engineering will enable LEs like C-DoT to compete on an equal footing with MNEs in telecommunications and other technology intensive industries.

And can C-DoT keep up with rapid changes in telecommunications technology? Developments in the use of point-to-multi-point radio for connecting customers with MNE switches (through remote line units) raised questions about the efficacy of C-DoT's 17,000 small rural exchanges.

70. *Telematics India*, October 1996, p. 69. See also S. Mani, 'Output Growth, Technology Behaviour and Employment', in A.K. Bagchi (ed.), *New Technology and the Workers Response*, New Delhi, Sage Publications.

And can C-DoT keep up with rapid changes in telecommunications technology? Developments in the use of point-to-multi-point radio for connecting customers with MNE switches (through remote line units) raised questions about the efficacy of C-DoT's 17,000 small rural exchanges. Proponents for foreign technology claim that downsized configurations, or remote line units of MNE switches may supplant C-DoT's RAXs through better maintainability and world class features at prices competitive to C-DoT's.[71] However, currently, C-DoT exchanges incorporated the most advanced features required by DoT.[72]

C-DoT's new mission objectives in 1997 included its stride towards becoming:

1. A premier telecom R&D institution.
2. A telecom software house.
3. A world leader in rural telephony.[73]

71. *Telematics India*, October 1996, pp 66–67.
72. 'Indian Telecommunications: Investment Opportunities, 1999', Department of Telecommunications, p. 24.
73. C-DoT Presentation Documents for the DoT, p. 53.

CASE 18

HERO HONDA MOTORS: A WEB OF RELATIONSHIPS

> Like the ancient Roman god, Janus, Hero Honda Motors was a strange being. Traditionally, Italian artists represent Janus with two faces, one looking forward and the other backward. This depiction symbolised Janus' awesome ability (he ruled over a golden period of Rome's history before being deified) to see the past and the future, and also focussed on his wisdom. For 'during the reign of Janus, people were perfectly honest, there was plenty and there was complete peace'.
>
> —*Penguin Dictionary of Classical Mythology, 1990*

India's largest motorcycle company equally had two faces. One aspect was the Gurgaon plant. New, modern, dust-free and bright, the plant looked the epitome

This case was written by Gita Piramal, business historian, Sudeep Budhiraja, Research Fellow, London Business School and Sumantra Ghoshal, Robert P. Baumann Professor of Strategic Leadership at the London Business School. It was written as part of a research programme supported by the Aditya V. Birla Centre. The authors gratefully acknowledge the extraordinary cooperation and support of Hero Honda Motors Ltd, without which this case could not have been written. The case was first registered by the London Business School in 2000.

of the factory of the future. Smart workers, intelligent supervisors, a benign management composed of two cultures all working together amicably to produce consumer-friendly bikes in a green environment.

Hero Honda Motors' head office represented the company's second aspect. Located in the heart of Delhi, the office was dark and cramped, stuffed with people jostling for elbow room. Indian family business culture sat uneasily with Japanese managers who wandered in and out of the office, looking a bit out of place. The pace was frantic, the office alive and buzzing.

If these comparisons appear somewhat superficial, one has to understand the critical third parallel between Janus and Hero Honda Motors. 'Perfect honesty', 'peace' and 'plenty' is what two parties look for when they come together to collaborate in a joint venture. The expectation is that by being honest with each other, both sides will bring something to the commercial table which will rake in profits for both. Unfortunately, far too often, the opposite happens. Few 50:50 partnerships actually work.

In the case of Hero Honda Motors, the unexpected happened. Two dissimilar business groups from radically different social and business cultures succeeded in making a partnership work. There were many strains in the collaboration—many moments of insecurity. The most significant was when Honda decided to work with the Shriram family to launch the Honda car. The next was when Honda decided to produce scooters in a 100 per cent Honda-owned facility, instead of leveraging the existing Hero Honda experience and adding scooter production to HHM.

Yet, overall, the partnership had been an outstanding success. Why? What did the Honda Motor Company and the Hero group do right which others could learn from?

The story goes deeper than the relationship between Honda and Hero. The Hero group demonstrated its sensitive understanding of the concept and needs of partnership not just with Honda but with all its collaborators—members of a large and growing family, dealers, vendors, and customers. Sure there were cases where ventures between the Hero group and its partners had soured (notably Puch and BMW), but the success stories greatly outnumbered the failures. What were the factors at work? Could they be identified, and could the Hero model be replicated? Every partnership, like the faces of Janus, has two sides. But Janus was also a person with wisdom and foresight. How can two partners achieve 'plenty' and 'peace'? Is 'complete honesty' enough?

The Hero Group

The Ludhiana-based Hero group was founded by the four Munjal brothers of whom Brijmohan Lall, while not the oldest, was the acknowledged leader, both within and outside the group. In 1994, *Business India* accorded him the prestigious Businessman of the Year award. Well-established makers of bicycles since the 1940s, in 1986 the Hero group entered the Guinness Book of World Records as the biggest bicycle maker in the world. Two of the group's companies, Hero Cycles and Gujarat Cycles, between them sold 2.03 million cycles that year. The second largest company was Huffy Corporation, USA, with 2 million units.

After China, India was the second largest cycle market in the world (8 million) and one of the most price competitive. The Hero group earned its leadership by making its bicycles sturdier than its rivals. The bike's steel frame permitted it to be loaded with 80 kg of cargo and two adults. The Munjals' belief in giving value for money was a sure-fire success formula. In 1998, the Hero group's aggregate cycle production nudged 4.5 million units. As its production expanded, competition shrank: the number of cycle producers in Ludhiana dropped from twelve to just two, and across India from 100 to four (Hero, Atlas, Tube Investments and Avon).

When Honda scanned Indian companies in the transport business, it noticed that Hero Cycles had one of the highest labour productivity rates in the world (even though it was not technology driven). Management had a tight focus on financial and raw material processes, enjoyed low employee turnover and had cordial industrial relations (the main plant had never had any stoppages except for a few days during Operation Bluestar).

Honda probably selected the Hero group for a variety of reasons, which included:

- Its engineering capability.
- The relevance and salience of the Hero brand.
- Its distribution network.

- Its commitment to quality (by Indian standards).
- Its know-how and experience in handling large volume production and distribution.

Honda Motor Company

Japan's most important two-wheeler company came to India in the mid-1980s when the Indian government cracked open the door to foreign investors. Initially, Honda flirted with Bajaj Auto, one of the world's top five two-wheeler companies (Indian regulations then did not permit foreign companies to set up shop on their own). When that failed, Honda shortlisted the Pune-based Firodia group and the Ludhiana-based Hero group as partners. Honda reportedly offered the first choice of vehicles to the Firodias. Given the scenario (in FY86, for example, of the total 2.66 million two-wheeler units sold, scooters accounted for 45 per cent, motorcycles for 30.5 per cent and mopeds for 24.5 per cent), the Firodias opted for a scooter collaboration. The Hero group got what was left—motorcycles.

If he was disappointed by the way Honda had limited his options, Brijmohan Lall hid it gracefully and philosophically—then and later. Others were not as diplomatic. 'We felt we got a raw deal', a Munjal burst out. 'Motorcycles were perceived then as unsafe machines. We had to work doubly hard to shake off that image.'

Apart from the joint ventures with the Firodias and the Hero group, Honda had two other tie-ups in India, both with the Delhi-based Shriram group. One was Shriram Honda Power equipment to make portable power generators, the other was the Honda Siel Car Company to make passenger cars.

Hero Honda Motors: The First Decade, 1984–94

Hero Honda Motors Ltd (HHM) was jointly promoted in January 1984 by Hero Cycles (Private) Ltd, world's largest manufacturer of cycles, and Japan's Honda Motor Company, world's largest manufacturer of motorcycles. The two promoters entered into a technical and financial collaboration in June 1984. HHM agreed to pay a lump sum amount as technical fee and a royalty on its products to Honda, but otherwise it was an equal partnership in that each contributed 26 per cent to HHM's equity. Of the remainder, the public was offered 22 per cent and others 26 per cent. The two partners brought different skills and capabilities to the table: Honda contributed technology and the Hero group contributed experienced local managers and a thorough knowledge of the Indian market. But could David and Goliath ever be equal partners?

Honda had four representatives as directors on the original twelve-member board, including the joint managing director, a whole-time director and two non-executive directors. There were four Munjals on the board: Brijmohan Lall (chairman and managing director), his son Raman Kant (managing director), Pawan Kant (whole-time director and second son of Brijmohan Lall) and Om Prakash (non-executive director and brother of Brijmohan Lall). After the untimely death of Raman Kant (who was widely credited within the group for the successful creation of HHM and for managing it on a day-to-day basis), Brijmohan Lall's brother Satyanand joined the board as a non-exeutive director. Of the remaining four directors, one was the nominee of a leading financial institution and three were professional Indian experts. Honda also had five senior executives for technical and quality related support. Other key functions such as plant heads, marketing, materials, finance and HRD were manned by Indians (see Appendix 1). Cheques were signed jointly.

The joint venture's first product, the CD 100, rolled off the conveyor belt in April 1985 at a plant at Dharuhera (Haryana). HHM started with just one model, a 100cc bike, which boasted the first 4-stroke engine in India. A memorable advertising slogan was used to promote it: 'Fill it, Shut it, Forget it'. Hero reliability, Honda quality, and the 4-stroke engine's fuel-efficiency combined to quickly establish the motorcycle's reputation and HHM grabbed a 50 per cent share of this market segment within a short period of time.

Until HHM came on the scene, TVS-Suzuki had enjoyed a monopoly of the 100cc market but other manufacturers weren't too far behind. By 1990 the segment was crowded with models offered by two others—Escorts Yamaha and Bajaj Kawasaki. Nonetheless, the Hero Honda bike sold 1 million units within a decade, a Honda record. But by 1994, a lack of capacity began to severely handicap HHM's growth. As production stagnated, HHM's market share dipped from a high of 54 per cent in FY93 to 43 per cent in FY96 (in the 100cc motorcycle segment) and from 33.6 per cent in 1992 to 27.5 per cent in FY97 (in the overall motorcycle market), though the company recovered ground over the next couple of years. A waiting list emerged.

Market Shares in the 100cc Motorcycle Segment

	1997–98		1998–99	
	Sales	%	*Sales*	%
Hero Honda Motors	407564	36.6	530533	38.8
Escorts	179452	16.1	188458	13.8
TVS-Suzuki	211667	19.0	264118	19.3
Bajaj Auto	314898	28.3	382631	28.0
Total	1113581	100	1365740	100

Source: Hero Honda Motors.

The buoyant sales, however, did not translate into profits for a long time. Customers' interest-free deposits became an important contributor to the bottom line. For instance, in FY86, HHM earned a net profit of Rs 11.5 mn. That year, deposits were Rs 430 mn. Deposits were lower the next year, a mere Rs 20.4 mn, and HHM recorded a Rs 310,000 loss. In FY88, deposits surged to Rs 34.4 mn and HHM was back in the black with a Rs 14.4 mn profit.

Hero Honda Motors: The Early Days

(Rs million)

	FY86	*FY87*	*FY88*	*FY89**	*FY90*
Sales (units)	63769	62488	96243	91870	96235
Sales (value)	492.1	695.1	1109.0	1044.8	1512.6
Raw material	340.3	536.8	821.2	788.8	1185.0
Interest	51.0	58.1	75.5	65.4	75.0
Gross profit	31.7	17.0	38.7	(13.9)	48.3
Depreciation	20.2	20.1	23.4	35.9	52.8
Net profit	11.5	(3.1)	14.4	(49.7)	(4.5)

* Nine months

The trouble was the rising yen. In 1984 when project reports were being prepared, the rupee–yen rate had been Rs 100 to Y 2100. By the time production was in full swing, the rupee had started depreciating. The yen climbed from Y 1350 per Rs 100 in June 1986 to Y 960 in December 1987 and Y 832 in December 1988. Indigenisation was on the cards but initially most of the bike was outsourced (96 per cent) and, of this, most components were imported. HHM's woes were compounded by the fact that the customs duty component kept rising in rupee terms. The rate remained the same but in effect the duty more than doubled as the yen rose. That all Indo-Japanese joint ventures were in the same boat was no consolation when HHM made a loss on every bike sold.

As production costs zoomed up, HHM pushed some of the costs on to consumers, but not everything could be passed on. The price of the CD 100 was hiked thirteen times between 1985 and 1990: from Rs 12,741 to Rs 22,669, a rise of 78 per cent. By comparison, scooter prices rose by 40 per cent during this period. As one HHM manager noted wryly at the time, 'Earlier, with little difference between our prices and scooter prices, we were playing with a bigger market share. Now half the scooter market is out of our reach.' A 150 cc Bajaj scooter was then available for Rs 11,000.

The tide turned after 1990. The rupee–yen rate stabilised, the beneficial effects of the indigenisation process kicked in, demand for its products was encouraging (petrol prices had hit the roof too and a HHM bike was very economical on fuel and delivered 80 km to a litre) and capacity utilisation was high. HHM's managers learnt to control their inventory better: from Rs 265 million in FY89, it came down to Rs 199 million in FY90 and Rs 120 million in FY91, while production and sales rose rapidly.

As Brijmohan Lall told *Business World* at the time: 'There are various factors involved in the turnaround but everything boils down to the increased margin per vehicle.'

—21 November 1990

HHM started earning Rs 1,000 on every bike sold. With a monthly production of around 10,000 units, this translated into a profit of Rs 10 mn a month. HHM's share price reflected renewed confidence in the company. Quoted at Rs 50 when it went public in 1985, HHM's price had plummeted to Rs 15 in 1989 but zoomed to Rs 95 in December 1990. HHM quickly became the largest company in the Hero group (see Appendix 2).

The Munjal Family

From the time the four Munjal brothers set up shop in Amritsar to sell bicycle parts in 1945 (see Appendix 3), they had stuck together. If the family stood united, it was largely due to impeccable equity planning and Brijmohan Lall's charisma and personal standards of fair play.

Talking to *Business India*, a manager of Tube Investments once said: 'They are both our customers for chains and tubes that go into Hero Cycles as well as our competitors in the bicycle business. The uniqueness about Brijmohan lies in the way he balances the two opposing roles.' The man himself, simply said, 'I look at myself as an advisor, as a support system. I won't call myself the brain behind the group. The group functions well through marvellous planning and execution. Advice is available to all key personnel.'

—19 December 1994

The original partnership understanding between the four brothers continued. Promoters' holdings in the various group companies were structured in such a way that each of the four families controlled 25 per cent each. Perhaps the reason why the Hero group stayed together when so many business houses splintered messily was because relationships were not taken for granted: succession planning and the need to balance equity between family members was constantly on top of the mind of the patriarchs.

According to Brijmohan Lall, 'We have always tried to give every incoming family scion a meaningful role to play in the group's growth.' He and his brothers meticulously worked on stability. Over the years, as new companies were launched, they ensured that all four branches of the family held equal stakes in the new ventures. Since the family stakes were identical, all got equal returns on their investments in the form of dividends or bonus shares. Moreover, to prevent a possible split, there were in-built systems. The companies were controlled through an intricate network of family-owned investment companies. And none of the four families could transfer its share to a third party.

In an attempt to further reduce tensions, elders kept young minds busily focussed on work rather than on one another. New companies or divisions were floated for every incoming blueblood—the 1980s witnessed sharp growth with seven new companies being promoted. It was no coincidence that this period saw a large influx of family members.

In the mid-1990s, the need for growth fed the group's bid for Scooters India, a tie-up with Austria's Steyr Puch to make mini-motorcycles, and a flirtation with

Germany's BMW to make expensive 650cc motorcycles as well as cars. Within the existing businesses, several new models of cycles were introduced both to meet the needs of the newly emerging leisure cycle market and to keep family members occupied. The 1990s also saw the opening of a cold rolling mill in Ludhiana which ensured the quality of the group's basic raw material—steel—as well as a reliable supply at reasonable prices. The mill's output went to all Hero group companies and other buyers as well.

Hence the Hero group was constantly exploring avenues for growth. The responsibility for managing prime companies or divisions depended on the member's competence rather than which branch of the family he came from. This was both an opportunity and a cause for future worry and insecurity. In 1998, there were twenty-one family members working in different businesses of the group, up from three in the 1950s. In the future, inevitable differences of opinion could upset the fine balance in the second and third generations.

There was no question that there would be stability while the first generation held the reins. Respect for elders, and particularly for Brijmohan Lall, kept the apple-cart moving without tipping over. But age was catching up with Brijmohan Lall, as well as his brothers. Their word was law. Would the status quo continue after the first generation had passed the baton?

Shared Destiny: Managing Vendors

The legend on one of HHM's many advertisements for its 100cc bike read: 'It is the Honda in it that makes it a Hero'. True. The fuel-efficient 4-stroke engine was the source of HHM's wild success. But over 190 components go into a motorcycle and, generally, Indo-Japanese motorcycle makers outsource more parts than non-Japanese or wholly Indian motorcycle makers.

Like most joint ventures, the Hero group's collaboration with Honda was governed by Indian government regulations which demanded a high degree of local sourcing of components. This process took place rapidly, 'faster than Honda would probably have preferred', acknowledged Pawan Kant Munjal. Within five years of start-up, indigenisation was 90 per cent, by 1996 it was 95 per cent (85 per cent by cost), a record for a Honda plant overseas. In terms of CKD value, whereas a bike had 65,000 yen worth of imported parts in 1985, this was down to 7,800 yen by 1994.

Outsourced Components, FY96

Company	%
Hero Honda	96
Kinetic Honda	93
TVS	92
Escorts	88
KEL	87
LML	62
Bajaj Auto	57

Source: Crisil, '2/3 Wheelers Sectorview', December 1996, p. 28.

The indigenisation process was aided by the nature of the Hero group, which provided reliable supplies of aluminium castings, wheel rims and other components to the joint venture. In 1998, 65 per cent of HHM's outsourced Indian components by volume were supplied by Hero group companies.

The degree of outsourcing and the pricing of components were key factors in the relationship between Honda and the Hero group. The supply of these components was important to fulfil Munjal family needs. Pricing balanced the profit each party earned from its partnership. At the same time, outsourcing affected the profitability of HHM, which was a publicly listed company, and raised issues of corporate governance. Therefore, achieving symmetry required delicate handling of several sensitive issues among three sets of interests.

The financial implications of HHM's outsourcing decisions on the Hero group's fortunes were enormous. In FY97, component manufacturing contributed 15 per cent to group sales of Rs 18.96 bn. Of course, not all orders came from HHM. The Hero group was a vendor not only to itself and HHM but to outside companies as well. But, it was no secret that the fortunes of at least six Hero group companies were intimately linked to HHM. And another twelve of HHM's 168 vendors were owned by family friends; many others were traditional suppliers to the Hero group, who had supported Raman Kant by setting up ancillary units when Hero Honda was created. When questioned, Brijmohan Lall's response was simple: 'I never wanted to march alone'.[1]

1. *Business India*, 19 December 1994, p. 57.

HHM's Key Vendors

Company	*Product*	*Management*
Munjal Showa	Shock absorbers	Yogesh Munjal
Sunbeam Castings	Aluminium castings	Ashok Munjal
Munjal Castings	Castings	Ashok Munjal
Hero Cycles	Wheel rims	Vijay Kumar Munjal
Rockman Cycles	Motorcycle chain	Suman Kant Munjal
AG Industries	Plastic processing	Geeta Anand

Munjal Showa, run by Yogesh Munjal, for instance, was specifically promoted in 1985 to supply shock absorbers to HHM. It was a joint venture between the Hero group and Japan's Showa Manufacturing Company, itself a Honda subsidiary. Roughly 50 per cent of Munjal Showa's business came from HHM. In FY97, Munjal Showa, a publicly listed firm, had an equity capital of Rs 80 mn and net worth of Rs 549 mn. The stock traded at Rs 303 and Rs 95 in the twelve-month period between March 1999 and March 2000.

Most companies avoid the practice of appointing family and friends as vendors because of the sensitivities involved. The Hero group, however looked upon this as a competitive advantage. Turning the relationship back-to-front, it pointed to the ensuing high degree of co-ordination between HHM and its suppliers. HHM had a tighter control on the cost and quality of components, as well as on the regularity and timeliness of supply, thereby minimising its inventory. Added Rakesh Duda: 'What's special about HHM is that so many of our vendors are family and friends who have been with us for decades. We have a good supply chain with technological support for vendors from Honda.'

Sunbeam Castings illustrates the relationship. Run by Ashok Munjal, one of Brijmohan Lall's many nephews, the plant was set up with Honda's help. 'It was a new component which was being made in India for the first time', recalled Ashok. 'At first Honda hesitated in allowing castings to be outsourced in India, then it changed its mind. Later, when new models came in, Honda participated fully in helping us develop the nine new dies which were needed. Resulting from its close relationships with suppliers, HHM can get all its supply of key components from a single source. Otherwise it would have had to go to three or four vendors. I want to be India's biggest die-caster, supplying not just to HHM but to everyone in the automobile industry.'

Little slack was permitted in the system. This was possible because of a shared philosophy. As Brijmohan Lall explained, 'When we started HHM, school friends from Ludhiana who shared the same philosophy became key suppliers.' Strict norms were established to maintain efficiency. Many of the Hero group's practices were similar to those of Honda, making for a close cultural fit. These measures included:

Proximity

Vendors had to be located near the mother plants. If there was one major factor in the Hero group's success, it was this, claimed the Munjals. And whenever they lost sight of this factor, they lost money. The Gujarat Cycles experience was a case in point. 'It was my own doing and the wrong choice of geographical area was my undoing', remembered Brijmohan Lall. Gujarat Cycles was an export project which sadly went awry. The greenfield plant was located away from Ludhiana and their normal vendor channels. 'Any composite industry has to have ancillaries close by. We tried to bring in ancillarisation but it didn't work as we were the only buyers.' Over 50 per cent of components were supplied by vendors based within 60 km of HHM's two plants.

Just-in-time

Just-in-time (JIT) inventory was another practice which had been the Hero group's way of doing business since the 1950s. 'JIT is a new word but for us it is a fifty-year-old compulsion. We were short of money', remembered Brijmohan. According to one vendor, 'Brijmohan always used to say that he wanted to provide the cheapest mode of transport for the poorest of the poor.' This was achievable only when the vendors' efficiency enabled Hero Cycles to operate at zero inventory levels. On a visit to the Hero Cycles plant, Arun Firodia, managing director of Kinetic Engineering and Kinetic Honda, saw that 'vendors would bring in the goods, they would be paid instantly and by the end of the day the finished product would roll out of the factory'.[2]

Technology and Quality

'Everything is specified. We have to follow the instructions on the drawings and the processes. The Japanese keep following up on this.' HHM assisted vendors in improving plant design layout and reducing costs. When HHM started, Honda sent out forty engineers, most of whom left once outsourcing had taken off and the Dharuhera plant had stabilised.

2. *Business India*, 19 December 1994, p. 57.

Loyalty

According to a HHM manager, the Munjals used special techniques to develop loyalty. 'The family is always friendly when a supplier comes and doesn't deny him anything. If he needs a car, they'll get one for him. They make him feel at home. And they listen to him. Payment is always on time. All terms are settled on logic, not sentiment. Pricing is transparent, and if full details are given to the company, they will not be exploited or misused. Suppliers are generally brought in by the Munjals and the personal loyalty is there, but loyalty is not enough. They make sure that vendors make money also.' 'We know the value of an established vendor because we came from this field ourselves', explained Brijmohan Lall.

Dealers: The Public Face of HHM

When HHM was promoted, overnight it was able to establish a strong distribution network spread across the country. All it had to do was to hand-pick its dealers from Hero Cycles' pool of over 4,000 dealers. Most of these dealers had been associated with the Hero Group for over two decades and had excellent track records. In FY98, HHM had 375 dealers which compared favourably with Bajaj Auto's 400, given the latter's wider product range, higher sales volume and the fact that it was a much older company.

HHM's Dealer Network, 2000

Zone	*No.*	*Service Points*	*Automated Workshops*
East	52	11	74
North	116	24	84
South	107	62	23
West	106	29	77
Total	381	126	258

Source: Hero Honda Motors Ltd.

In 1984, 65 per cent of HHM's dealers were former Hero group dealers. By 1998, this had come down to 50 per cent. When appointing dealers, HHM went for youth: the average age of dealers was 26–27. Infrastructure was another consideration. 'While other two-wheeler companies were content with 500 sq. ft of showroom space, we straightaway asked for 1,600 sq. ft', said V. Uppal, deputy general manager, sales. 'Honda was also surprised but we wanted the outlets to have an imposing identity.' A dealership-cum-service centre had to have an additional 1,500 sq. ft for the workshop, whereas other two-wheeler makers asked for just an extra 250 to 300 sq. ft.

HHM provided substantial inputs to its dealers such as workshop layouts and different kinds of support including various training programs. 'We taught them about profitability and to think about the future', claimed Uppal, 'That from their earnings, they should reinvest one-third into the business, spend one-third on future growth and enjoy the remaining one-third. And they have prospered with us.'

HHM worked on a cash basis and dealers made about Rs 1,500 per bike. This was higher than what Bajaj Auto offered, but necessary in order to compensate dealers for the lower volume of business. HHM understood that with increasing competition and greater variety of model offerings, dealers would have a greater role in influencing customers' purchase decisions. Gone were the days when Indian customers just wanted a two-wheeler and were satisfied if the dealer could give them one. Customers had also begun asking for service, both pre-sales and after-sales. HHM maintained about 150 authorised service centres. Most of these service centres were at dealerships.

HHM maintained close links with its dealers, links that went far beyond a business association. 'I know every dealer by name, his background, his family structure, his type of organisation. It is a bond', said Uppal. Traditionally the Hero Group had taken care to foster these bonds. 'In our group, whenever there is a happy event in the lives of any colleague or any dealer, an officer has to be there. But if there is any sadness in their lives, one family member must go', said Brijmohan Lall. The Hero culture was extended to HHM. In small towns, when a company official attended the wedding of a dealer's daughter, the act enhanced the latter's social standing. Being a HHM dealer had prestige associated with it—HHM bikes had a waiting list—even for senior police officers and other key officials. Dealers were flattered when they stopped by at their outlets. And if a dealer faced a financial crisis, HHM's head of sales was authorised to lend him up to Rs 300,000 without question.

Uppal recounted the story of one of their Pune dealers. 'He was one of our finest dealers but he invested in real estate and other activities. He became so overambitious that he could not even meet his family expenses. We didn't dump him. We gave him vehicles on credit. Still, he could not fulfil his obligations. But we knew he was a good guy. We kept supporting him and brought him back on track. He slowly returned the money. Any other company would have dumped him.'

It wasn't all milk and honey, however. There were checks and balances. Any dealer who dropped sales even for a month was checked out. By the head of sales himself, not a mere HHM junior officer or even the regional manager. And if a dealer flouted company norms or was found to have misappropriated funds, retribution was swift. 'After all, he is the public face of HHM. People deposit their money with him', said Uppal. Through frequent interaction with brokers and customers, HHM made it a point to keep tabs on dealers and would come to know of any infraction within days. HHM would investigate all complaints and, if sustained, dealers would have their dealerships taken away and even be taken to court. HHM also vetted their dealers' financial health through the latters' bank managers, and dealers learnt to accept this.

The Hero group had always looked upon its relationship with dealers as a generational one. The Munjal family business was born for perpetuity. It would always need dealers. Once again this philosophy was extended to HHM dealers, particularly from small towns and villages where traditional orthodoxies prevailed. They were encouraged to break out of their moulds. They were encouraged to send their children to good schools, to allow them to attend computer classes and eventually engineering colleges. HHM made no bones about its self-interest in this process. 'If we help them with their succession planning, we will deal with better business associates.'

This nurturing continued at the business level. Pawan Munjal would periodically take HHM's top fifty dealers to Honda's plant in Japan. During the ten-day trip, they were exposed to Honda technology, Honda showrooms and Honda dealerships. HHM believed that such trips gave dealers confidence and the motivation to invest in HHM. Honda paid for a part of the expenses. 'One of our dealers, a rustic sardar, was so moved by his Japan experience that after coming back, he put in carpets and even air-conditioned his showroom. While he was there, he always had a paper and pencil. He drew the stands and later he replicated a Honda showroom in Bhatinda', recalled an HHM manager.

HHM ran incentive schemes by which dealers could get free holidays in Europe with their wives. HHM paid half the cost of the holiday and helped organise tour details like hotel bookings, visas, foreign exchange and traveller's cheques—a valuable service for smaller dealers and those in rural areas—but dealers had to pay the other half. Typically such trips cost the company Rs 4 mn—money well spent according to senior managers.

Honda was easily able to relate to such business-level schemes, but despite being an Asian company, found it difficult to understand Munjal paternalism. Nonetheless the global giant tacitly acquiesced in its partner's whims.

The 1994 Negotiation

The original ten-year agreement between Hero Cycles and the Honda Motor Company expired in 1994 and was subsequently renewed for another ten years (2004). In between the relationship would undergo some phases of difference and synergy. 'But even in the toughest stages of decision making in our joint venture, there were no strains and crucial strategic issues were resolved in a very congenial approach', said a Munjal.

The Indian motorcycle market accelerated between 1993 and 1996 with a CAGR of 31 per cent. The Indo-Japanese segment saw the highest growth, moving from 6 per cent in 1984–85 to 66 per cent in 1995–96. Despite the high demand for its 100cc bike, HHM could not expand production because of the uncertainty surrounding the renewal of its agreement. Not only did HHM fail to capitalise on the buoyant demand for its products, but the time lag whittled away its market leadership.

Motorcycle Makers: Market Shares

	1990	*1991*	*1992*	*FY94*	*FY95*	*FY96*	*FY97*
HHM	24.5	30.2	33.6	32.1	28.2	28.4	27.5
Bajaj Auto	26.7	26.2	27.6	28.6	30.5	29.5	31.1
Escorts	33.4	28.6	26.0	24.5	24.5	23.2	22.2
TVS-Suzuki	7.2	8.3	7.7	11.3	13.4	15.5	16.8
Others	8.2	6.7	5.1	3.5	3.4	3.4	2.4

Note: Figures in percentages. 1990 and 1992 are calendar years. Remaining are financial years.
Source: AIAM.

By the time Honda and the Hero group arrived at a consensus, Bajaj Auto had stepped up its motorcycle production to overtake HHM (which, however, HHM regained in FY98). More importantly, the Pune giant seized HHM's USP by driving squarely on to the 4-stroke track through the launch of the KB 4S. The television commercial aired to promote the KB 4S pulled no punches. '*Kyon*, Hero?' asked a dashing young jacket-clad biker contemptuously after he had just braved a rough ride.

As Bajaj Auto was menacingly revving up its engine, HHM added extra features to its basic model, the CD 100, to widen its customer base. HHM had provided the Indian market with contemporary 4-stroke technology way ahead of competition, but it was now time to offer some variety. The Sleek was introduced in April 1989, the CD 100SS in November 1991, the Splendour in January 1994—but these were variations on an old theme. No new model came to HHM out of the Honda garage until the 1995 agreement had been sorted out. Brijmohan Lall felt this keenly. 'In a market place where other players have a variety of products to sell and you have only one product to live on, you cannot feed your dealers or consumers effectively and you start feeling helpless.'

Brijmohan Lall's frustration was shared by the entire group. Not content to sit idle, the Hero group scouted for opportunities outside the arrangement with Honda. In 1986 Pankaj Munjal met with Steyr Puch, an Austrian company owned by Daimler-Benz which wanted to get out of motorcycle manufacture. Pankaj bought designs for three models and four engines (one 65cc and three 50cc). From this was born Hero Motors. It took a while for the company to stabilise, but once it did, Hero Motors began exporting CKD packs to its dealers in Iran, Mauritius, Bangladesh, Egypt and Vietnam, besides feeding the Indian market. In 1993 Hero Motors began talks with BMW to produce 250cc motorcycles, talks which ultimately fizzled out. From Honda's point of view, the very fact that these talks took place was hardly a good portent.

What went wrong? Why did the relationship which had weathered so many ups and downs—the early days particularly had seen many teething troubles—sour? Why did the terms of the partnership suddenly feel onerous? Had the environment changed or the people? According to Pawan Kant Munjal, 'There was a small phase once, between 1993 and 1996, where we did not have a good relationship with one individual and we did suffer because of this failure. It was the basic nature of the person. He was difficult to get along with. Always making objections. The first reaction was always no. We had to keep trying to convince him, sometimes successfully, at other times not so successfully. And we suffered in getting a new model.'

Typically, Honda would send out an executive to India for a two- to three-year term, and at any given point of time, there would always be two senior Honda managers at HHM's Delhi head office. An internal board meeting was held with metronomic regularity every month, attended by the two Honda representatives, Brijmohan Lall and Pawan Kant. 'All kinds of decisions were taken at this informal meeting, but once they had been taken they had to be implemented by the next meeting', said Brijmohan Lall.

Within the Hero group, there was a strong feeling that they had given a lot to the partnership and that the Hero group had suffered because of that. The younger Munjals were vociferous on such issues, but Brijmohan Lall took a more statesmanlike attitude. 'For an alliance to work, one must control one's ambitions. It is no different here. Yes, we suffered in Majestic Auto because we gave the best to HHM—dealers, managers, our people, my sons. And yes, Honda's financial charges were heavy. But I don't get too upset by it because the success of HHM is a feather in my cap.'

'Every Japanese is a different person. The important thing is to understand Honda's philosophy. Before we started HHM, Honda asked me, can I climb the wall which is Rahul Bajaj. I said yes. Like him I want to be in both the scooter market and in motorcycles. Honda wants to be the number one in every market. So do we. That's what drives us. If one can attain and achieve shared objectives, then two partners do well.'

Once the 1994 agreement had been hammered out, however, HHM steadily expanded capacity and product range. Production at its Dharuhera plant sprinted from 150,000 units in FY94 to 350,000 in FY97. A state-of-the-art Rs 1650 million plant at Gurgaon was inaugurated with great ceremony on 26 February 1997 by Nobuhiko Kawamoto, Honda's president and CEO. Capable of producing half a million motorcycles, the plant started with 100,000 units, with plans to add 50,000 units annually to reach 300,000 units by 2001.

Production Trends

(Units)

1985–86	*1991–92*	*1993–94*	*1994–95*	*1995–96*	*1996–97*	*1997–98*	*1998–99*
43244	135260	147570	183490	262700	269477	407500	530533

Source: Hero Honda Motors Ltd.

A few days before the Gurgaon plant was inaugurated, HHM cheekily launched the Street in Pune, Bajaj Auto's hometown. The Street was a 100cc motorcycle version known as a step-thru in industry jargon. Its importance did not lie in the fact that HHM had finally introduced a new model but that the Street was based on Honda's global best-seller, the Honda Dream (which reportedly sold over 25 million worldwide). It marked Honda's willingness to share its latest technology with its Indian partner. Further proof of a fresh give-and-take attitude in the partnership lay in HHM's purchase orders. The agreement's aftermath saw the Munjal companies supplying more to HHM. For instance, Hero Cycles started supplying rims and in 1996 Rockman Cycles began making motorcycle chains.

A third aspect of the 1994 agreement was that HHM could now move into scooter manufacturing. This had been a long-standing desire of Brijmohan Lall, but the fly in the ointment was the fact that Honda simultaneously allowed the Firodia group to make motorcycles. Kinetic Honda promptly announced its intention to launch a 125cc motorcycle. Honda had made substantial concessions to the Hero group, but it equally injected a piquant situation in its own Indian operations and between its two partners. Brijmohan Lall put on a brave face. 'Honda is a very intelligent business conglomerate. They would not like to see a conflict of interest in the Indian market.'

The Munjal ambitions were dealt a second blow when Honda selected the Shriram group as its partner for a car project. 'Yes, I had a dream', said Brijmohan Lall ruefully, 'and I still have a dream. We had a long chat with Honda to make cars—they would have been only too happy to partner with us for the project—but somehow it didn't click. But my nephew Pankaj, through Hero Motors, is discussing a possible 50:50 joint venture with BMW.'

The only true consolation was that HHM was much more profitable than Kinetic Honda. HHM was India's 13th biggest wealth creator according to *Business Today* (22 February 2000), with a market cap Rs 22,606 mn (up 67 per cent over the previous year). Sales in FY99 were Rs 15,523 mn (up 30.2 per cent), with a PAT of Rs 1,214 mn. EVA was Rs 622 mn with a growth rate of 91.8 per cent.

The Mantra: Profitability

One of the nuggets in Brijmohan Lall's lexicon was 'profits have precedence over numbers'. Another was, 'there is always room for improvement'. These two maxims stood the industrialist from Punjab in very good stead. HHM constantly re-examined where it could cut costs, improve its productivity and add value to marketing. The result was efficient cash management, as displayed by its high liquidity and low debt equity, despite large expansion plans (see Appendix 4).

Aggressive pricing by Bajaj Auto and TVS Suzuki also played a role in galvanising HHM's management into reviewing its cost structure. As Brijmohan Lall said, 'We kept improving output and abilities to extract full value out of materials, men and machines, and to cut all superfluous expenditure.' Initially (i.e., 1984–1994), HHM had drawn on the Hero group's experience with low-cost vendor development to bring down its products' import content to less than a tenth of its value. But others too had done that by the mid-1990s. And were winning.

Two-wheelers: Cost Comparisons, FY96

Rs '000/Vehicle	*Hero Honda*	*TVS-Suzuki*	*Bajaj Auto*
Sales	27.49	15.04	17.55
Raw material consumed	20.67	10.50	9.56
Cost of goods sold	21.90	10.79	11.01
Gross margins	5.59	4.25	6.54
Personnel costs	1.17	0.57	1.33
Operating costs	25.22	13.34	17.32
Operating profit	2.20	1.71	3.55
Interest	0.26	0.12	0.08
Other income	0.35	0.11	1.67
Depreciation	0.47	0.22	0.57
PBT	1.82	1.48	4.57

Source: Morgan Stanley, 'Hero Honda Motors Ltd: Changing Gears', 6 May 1997.

For HHM, the challenge was to cut costs at the Dharuhera plant, inject cost consciousness into all its regular activities while simultaneously building manufacturing capacity at Gurgaon. This was no easy task. In 1994–95, for example, steel prices tripled and aluminium prices quadrupled. To reduce the impact of these price rises, HHM honed in on recycling scrap at the component manufacturing stage. Stoppages were also brought under a microscope, with impressive gains. At the Dharuhera plant, in FY93, for example, stoppages averaged 3,000 minutes of production time every month, nearly enough to make 2,200 vehicles. By FY97, interruption time had been scaled down to 70 minutes per month, thanks to a new information system. Inventory planning became a rigorous mathematical exercise worthy of a Cambridge don. 'You have to change attitudes and then bring in technology', explained Brijmohan Lall. 'We don't make purchase orders without studying the overall cost implications to vehicles.' This axiom translated into money.

HHM: Increasing Value

	FY90	*FY91*	*FY92*	*FY93*	*FY94*	*FY95*	*FY96*	*FY97*
Sales (units)	96235	120091	135260	128649	147570	183490	230084	269477
Value added* (Rs million)	284.2	506.6	569.2	589.0	707.4	910.7	1288.4	1819.4
Value added per employee # (Rs '000)	174	267	356	365	426	538	719	1032
Vehicle prod. per employee (Dharuhera)	58	71	76	70	77	95	113	132
Vehicle prod. per employee (Gurgaon)	0	0	0	0	0	0	0	20

Only regular employees of Dharuhera plant.

* Value added = Total sales + (difference between opening and closing of material and energy consumed).

Source: Company reports.

This was all on the operations side. Financial management was also overhauled to discover smart cash flow ideas. The time lag between collecting cash and paying it out was stretched. Creditors were now paid after sixty days while buyers had to pay up within ten. Good dealer relationships meant that HHM sometimes got all its money in advance (the norm was 40 per cent). In 1990, HHM managers celebrated when they were able to shave costs and earn Rs 1,000 per vehicle. By 1997, costs had been pared to the bone and each bike now earned Rs 1,500.

Some of the improvements in earnings came from lower royalty costs. Royalties as a percentage of net sales dropped steadily from 2.6 per cent in FY90 to 0.5 per cent in FY99. After 1995, HHM managed to persuade Honda to accept a mere Rs 200 per vehicle as royalty fees. And in the case of Street, HHM paid a one-time sum of US$ 1 mn to Honda, Japan, for the right to manufacture Street. This amount was to be written off over seven years. For future product launches, the royalty was based on 4 per cent of sales value. This was expected to increase HHM's technology sharing cost and it was agreed that the two partners would review this issue in 2004.

Royalty Costs as % of Net Sales

	FY90	*FY91*	*FY92*	*FY93*	*FY94*	*FY95*	*FY96*	*FY97*	*FY98*	*FY99*
Royalty/ Net sales	2.6	2.9	2.8	1.1	0.8	0.7	0.7	0.9	0.7	0.5

Source: Hero Honda Motor Ltd annual reports.

Even as cost-cutting was in full swing at the Dharuhera plant, HHM was spending money hand-over-fist at Gurgaon. HHM preferred not to tap the equity markets to raise the Rs 1,650 mn needed for the new plant. Instead Gurgaon was financed through foreign currency loans (Rs 950 mn in US dollars and yen), leasing finance (Rs 390 mn at 19 per cent per annum interest), institutional term loans (Rs 350 mn) and the balance from internal accruals.

HHM did not pay import duties on the plant and equipment, preferring to take on an obligation to export 132,000 motorcycles in eight years. This amounted to 16,500 bikes annually. In FY97, HHM exported 15,060 vehicles, mainly through Honda channels.

HHM: Export Performance

Year	*No. of Motorcycles*	*FOB (Rs mn)*
1995–96	11937	343.3
1996–97	15058	450.0
1997–98	18404	592.0
1998–99	11385	420.1

Source: Hero Honda Motors Ltd.

Competition and Market Share

Once the 1994 agreement had been hammered out, the way was clear for HHM to tackle competition head-on and recapture market share. Brijmohan Lall's target: 1 million vehicles per annum before turning twenty in 2005. At the same time, Brijmohan Lall refused to be drawn into a macho game of one-upmanship against Bajaj Auto. 'I get concerned if I don't maintain my profitability. I am willing to forsake some of my market share to maintain it', declared Munjal.

The name of the game in the future had to be the customer. Bigger engine bikes for the thrill-seeker. Rider comfort for the safety-seeker. Something for everyone, all the way from petite teeny-boppers to 100 kg leather-knuckled brutes. HHM had to find a new USP, for it no longer enjoyed its 4-stroke engine monopoly.

It began its attack sideways. The Street offered rider comfort. Women and trendy yuppies were the natural target. While commercials of the Yamaha RX 100 and TVS-Suzuki's 125cc Shogun reeked of testosterone, HHM's relaxed 'We Care' messages with images of clear skies shouted quietly. One spot showed a father jogging with his daughter in a park overflowing with greenery. To get the message across, HHM hiked its ad spend to Rs 157 mn in FY96, up from Rs 68 mn the previous year.

Keeping its fingers crossed, HHM set a sales target of 40,000 Streets in the first year. It was an ambitious target, notwithstanding the model's proven global success, given its premium pricing at Rs 34,000 and upwards. In India, Kinetic Honda's ZX with an electric start was Rs 39,000 or Rs 5,000 cheaper than the Street's self-start version. TVS-Suzuki's Scooty was Rs 25,000; that of Hero Motors' Winner Rs 29,000. But the Street's stiffest competition was Bajaj Auto's 80cc step-thru, the M-80, which had sold 150,000 units in 1995–96 and was priced at Rs 20,000 ex-showroom vis-à-vis Street at Rs 34,000. In the event, Street's sales targets had to be slashed by 40 per cent. Because of the high price, HHM had reduced the dealer margin on the Street, but this apparently was not a major factor.

HHM's Product Range

Launch	*Model*	*Positioning, Features*	*Sales (Units) (FY99)*	*Sales (% of Total)*
May 1985	CD 100	Fuel efficiency, economy. Businessman's bike	122457	23.1
Apr. 1989	Sleek	Style. Racy, streamlined fuselage, trendy colours. Youth segment.	2603	0.5
Nov. 1991	CD 100SS	Rural segment. To cater to the rough driving conditions, it had stronger suspension, greater ground clearance, wider tyres and an engine guard.	133468	25.2
Jan. 1994	Splendor	Combination of Sleek (good looks) and CD 100SS (ruggedness). Wide tyres. Fuel efficiency.	235705	44.4
Feb. 1997	Street	Driving ease, unisex appeal, fuel efficiency.	36300	6.8
Feb. 1999	CBZ	Larger 156cc engine delivering 12.8 Ps power through a 5-speed gear mechanism and with a Transient Power Fuel Control system. For the young at heart.	–	–
Total			530533	100

Rural Market

The appeal of HHM's products widened with the opening up of the rural market. In 1990, the urban to non-urban market split was 80:20. By 1997 it was 55:45. The motorcycle's larger wheels were more comfortable than a scooter's small tyres in rough terrain. That year two-thirds of HHM's sales came from semi-urban and rural dealers. Of its 430 dealers, 270 catered to this market. The company started feverishly expanding its network. 'We have exposed our rural customers to service standards which were until now confined to large cities', said a manager. Workshops were upgraded. Far-flung areas, which didn't justify service centres, were visited by service vans.

Growth

Gradually the lines between scooters, motorcycles and mopeds were blurring. Customers bought a two-wheeler not according to whether it was a scooter or a motorcycle or a moped but according to the balance between specific cost/features. Recognising this need, manufacturers introduced hybrids. The step-thru was a cross between a scooter and a motorcycle, and the scooterette a hybrid between a moped and a scooter. At the same time, price differentials became blurred. In 1998, some scooters could be more expensive than a motorcycle. Some mopeds or scooterettes were more expensive than a scooter. The consumers decided how much they wanted to pay and which features they wanted.

In this fluid scenario, Pawan Kant's views were firm. He wanted HHM to reach 1 million vehicles per annum by 2003—a figure a little more ambitious than his father's target of 1 million before turning twenty in 2005. 'We've done well so far, but after a certain life, we need to offer customers more even if the customer doesn't ask for it. If I want to get to 1 million, we need at least two brand new models and two or three major updates or model changes.'

However, he wasn't sure whether this target would be met. 'The timing of a launch is very critical. For new models, Honda has a certain rationale, a global plan. They are terribly busy, their R&D is busy for someone or the other. We don't get the latest, but even for an old model, many new things are needed. They need twelve to fifteen months to re-design for India. We have to slot ourselves in. We have to make payments, but this payment is not a strong enough inducement.'

Where Do We Go from Here?

Such uncertainties raised question marks about a hugely successful joint venture. What was the future?

Honda

From Honda's point of view, India was an attractive potential market. If unit prices were low, this did not mean it would always be so. Generally, the Indian consumer class was expanding and getting richer, making it worth Honda's while to wait for the country to grow up. Also, the Japanese giant had been in India for almost fifteen years now. It had become familiar with the country, its business practices and its market behaviour. It had a 'critical mass' (as one HHM manager put it) of Japanese managers back home who had been out to India. The question was: Why then should Honda continue to share its business and profits with the Hero group?

None of Honda's other three partnerships in India had been as successful as the tie-up with the Hero group. In July 1997 Honda had to hike its stake in the Rs 1,535 mn Shriram Honda from 33.33 per cent to 90 per cent at a cost of Rs 620 mn. In the case of Honda Siel Cars, in mid-1998, Honda had had to raise its stake in it to 90 per cent when financial constraints prevented its partner from maintaining its stake before a single car could roll out. Then in early 1998, Honda had had to sell off its 51 per cent stake in Kinetic Honda to the Firodia group for Rs 347.4 mn at Rs 45 a share.

The behind-the-scene events before the Kinetic Honda sale was concluded were an interesting pointer to Honda's dilemma in India.

- Honda was in an equal partnership in a financially and infrastructurally sound motorcycle company but had a majority stake in an ailing scooter one.
- If Honda wanted leadership in the Indian two-wheeler market, it perforce had to dominate the scooter market.
- Could this be done by reviving Kinetic Honda? But despite Honda's 51 per cent stake and management control, glitches with the Firodia group seemed to preclude profitable growth in scooters through Kinetic Honda.
- Should Honda infuse technology in HHM or Kinetic Honda?

Caught in a catch-22 like situation, Honda's India strategy became so confusing that the industry and media kept asking Honda's men in India why it was playing its partners against each other.

As the situation worsened, Honda tried to exploit the synergies between the two companies, e.g., use HHM's distribution network for Kinetic Honda; source Kinetic Honda's engine from HHM; reduce HHM's CD 100 surplus capacity at Dharuhera by allowing Kinetic Honda to export the CD 100. In these tripartite talks, HHM's attitude was pragmatic. As a HHM manager said at the time, 'Egos will have to be left home. The only thing that matters is the final bottom line.'

When these talks broke down, Honda floated the idea of merging the two companies. Nothing would have suited Pawan Munjal better. 'I had on a number of occasions offered to support Kinetic Honda, especially in the supply of critical components. And who is doing better? Honda at some time has to decide which basket in which to put its eggs in. We feel that if we were to manage Kinetic Honda, we would run it better.' The idea that Honda could bring its two partners together finally died when Honda walked out of Kinetic Honda.

Hero Group

The break-up of the Honda–Firodia tie-up naturally eased many Munjal insecurities but the key one remained. Without Honda technology, the biggest and most profitable company in the Hero orbit would be in trouble. Little transfer of technology had taken place and in-house development was virtually impossible because Honda had clearly announced upfront that it would have only three R&D centres worldwide and India was not one of them. As P.B. Menon said, 'We are dependent on Honda for both know-how and know-why.' Moreover, earlier, Honda had been content to leave marketing to the Munjals but, after the 1994 talks, had begun to take considerable interest in this area.

Hero group patriarchs were also bedevilled by the need to find new opportunities for a growing family. Earlier there were only four brothers. Now there were twenty-one working members. Each had to be given an independent profit centre, to be recognised as a breadwinner for his self-respect, for group respect and for respect in society.

> As Brijmohan Lall pointed out: 'In the end, what is respect? Best technology, large production, warm relationships, and good quality. This is what one works for.'

Simmering under these needs was the raw, unfulfilled ambition to dominate the two-wheeler market. In 1984, when talks first opened between the Hero group and Honda, a 100cc motorcycle taking on the scooter had been a genuine possibility. The cheapest Bajaj scooter was Rs 11,000, the CD 100 was supposed to be Rs 10,000. This picture dissolved into a mirage as the yen strengthened against the rupee and other factors forced motorcycle prices to reach double that of scooters. But HHM's ambition remained unquenched. 'We want to be present in all segments of the two-wheeler market in the coming years', declared Brijmohan Lall. In the early 1990s, the abortive bid for Scooters India, the establishment of Hero Motors' Ghaziabad plant, the talks with BMW—they all symbolised the group's latent hunger to be another Bajaj Auto. In the late 1990s, the Hero group initiated talks with US-based Briggs and Stratton for engines, and with an Italian company to make scooters.

Honda brought technology to the partnership but it was not as if the Hero group's contribution was insignificant. On the contrary, the Hero group had two areas of clear advantage.

- Its relationships with vendors and dealers.
- Its understanding of the Indian consumer, and particularly the rural market.

Were these contributions sufficient to ensure Honda coming in with current technology at all times? Sure Honda could learn all this but it would take time, a change in cultural mindset and a huge investment in managers. Was it worth breaking off with Munjals who, after all, were running the show well?

After much public deliberation and endless gossip, Honda decided to go its own way on manufacturing scooters in India. By going alone, Honda told the Indian industry that it considers India to be a very important long-term market. The questions this raised in the minds of observers were: What does this mean for the long-term future of Hero Honda Motors? Will the Munjal clan be able to ensure that HHM remains the only manufacturer of Honda motorcycles in India?

APPENDIX 2

Hero Group: FY98

(Rs million)

Companies	*Sales*
Publicly Listed Companies	
HHM*	11606.6
Gujarat Cycles	313.3
Hero Cycles	6160.0
Munjal Showa	1531.3
Majestic Automobiles	2600.7
Privately Held Companies	
Omax Autos	895.1
Highway Cycles	1242.0
Rockman Cycles	512.0
Munjal Castings	111.0
Munjal Gases	NA
Hero Motors**	–
Sunbeam Castings	800.0
Hero Exports	472.0
Hero Honda Finlease	NA
Hero Financial Services	NA
Total	26244.0

* Joint venture.
** Division of Majestic Motors.

APPENDIX 3

Growth of the Hero Group

Year Founded	*Company*	*Location*	*Ownership in 1988*	*Product*
1956	Hero Cycles	Ludhiana	100	Bicycles
1960	Rockman Cycle Industries	Ludhiana	100	Chains and bicycle hubs
1961	Munjal Gases			
1971	Highway Cycle Industries	Ludhiana	100	Freewheels and special machine tools
1978	Majestic Auto	Ludhiana	100	Mopeds and fitness equipment
1979	Hero Fibres#	Ludhiana	25	Spinning of textile fibre
1981	Munjal Castings	Ludhiana	100	Non-ferrous castings
1984	Hero Honda Motors	Delhi	26	Motorcycles
1985	Munjal Showa	Gurgaon	39	Shock absorbers
1987	Sunbeam Castings	Gurgaon	100	Non-ferrous castings
1988	Hero Cycles (Unit II)	Sahibabad	100	Bicycles
1988	Gujarat Cycles	Waghodia	25	Bicycles for export
1988	Hero Motors*	Ghaziabad	100	Mini-motorcycles
1990	Hero Cold Rolling Division	Ludhiana	100	Cold rolled steel
1991	Hero Honda Finlease	Delhi	65	Financing of motorcycles
1993	Hero Exports**	Ludhiana	100	Commodity exports
1993	Hero Financial Services	Delhi	100	Moped financing
1996	Rockman Cycles: Motorcycle chain division			Motorcycle chains

Sold to Oswal group in 1989.

* Division of Majestic Motors.

** Not as random a diversification as it appears. The Hero group wanted to import machinery to improve Hero Cycles' operations. The Indian government offered an incentive scheme by which machinery could be imported on payment of 15 per cent customs duty instead of 65 per cent as long as goods worth three to five times the value were exported within five years. To meet this obligation, the company exported steel strips, rice, garments, woollens, bicycles and components—anything and everything.

APPENDIX 4

Hero Honda Motors: Financial Highlights

(Rs million)

	1994–95	*1995–96*	*1996–97*	*1997–98*	*1998–99*
Sales (No.)	183650	230164	268931	407546	530545
Growth in sales (%)	24	25.3	16.8	51.5	30.2
Total income	4838	6421	7828	11561	15529
Growth in total income (%)	30.7	32.7	21.9	47.7	34.3
Profit before tax	295	419	651	1096	1728
Profit after tax	195	263	504	767	1214
Share capital	200	200	200	200	399
Reserve and surplus	563	762	1192	1870	2609
Total debt	442	541	1041	878	878
Net fixed asset	839	1020	1962	2153	3086
Total asset	1346	1640	2573	3087	4024
Market capitalisation	4490	5791	5,986	17448	34955
Economic value added	-5	16	174	324	622
Growth in EVA (%)	78.3	420	1000.1	86.8	91.8
Key Ratios:					
Long-term debt/Equity	0.4	0.3	0.6	0.4	0.3
OPBDITA*/Total operating income** (%)	8.3	8.4	11.3	12.6%	13.5%
Profit after tax/Total income (%)	4	4.1	6.5	6.6	7.8
Return on equity (%)	28.2	30.7	42.9	44.3	47.8
Return on capital employed (%)	27.5	32.1	35.0	41.5	50.7
EVA/Capital employed (%)	-0.4	1.1	8.2	11.5	17.5
Dividend per share (Rs)	3.0	3.2	3.5	4.0	6.3**
Dividend payout (%)	25.5	24.1	14.6	11.5	22.7
Earning per share (Rs)	9.8	13.3	25.3	38.4	60.8***
Free operating cash flow per share (Rs)	10.8	14.9	31.8	32.4	78.9***
Market value/Book value	5.9	6.1	4.5	8.6	11.9

*OPBDITA: Operating Profit Before Depreciation, Interest, Tax and Amortisation.

** On post-bonus equity.

*** On pre-bonus equity.

Source: Hero Honda Motors Ltd, 16th Annual Report, 1998–99.

APPENDIX 5

Manpower Status as on 20 October 2000

Grades	Locations HO & RO	HHD	HHG	Total
SM5	1	1	0	2
SM4	2	0	1	3
SM3	2	1	1	4
SM2	5	6	1	12
SM1	9	6	6	21
M4	9	5	5	19
M3	8	24	13	45
M2	25	48	19	92
M1	25	75	37	137
E3	44	84	65	193
E2	26	65	80	171
E1	16	52	53	121
S2	17	63	10	90
S1	22	96	10	128
ST3	11	49	11	71
ST2	8	18	37	63
ST1	5	17	50	72
C1	0	0	10	10
SS4	21	0	0	21
SS3*	13	67	0	80
SS2	1	0	0	1
SS1	12	0	4	16
MT	3	2	2	7
PGT	1	0	0	1
GET	5	11	15	31
JET	0	0	1	1
DET	0	2	4	6
Other trainees	0	2	29	31
Staff total	291	694	464	1449
Workers	0	1236	989	2225
Total	291	1930	1453	3674

* HD - SS1 - SS4

Part 4
Transforming Leadership Philosophy

HOUSING DEVELOPMENT FINANCE CORPORATION: THE EXTRAORDINARY–ORDINARY COMPANY

An extraordinary company, run for ordinary Indians by ordinary Indians—that was the Housing Development Finance Corporation (HDFC) in 1998. It is India's premier housing finance company and one of the most successful, most admired and most competitive institutions in the country.

The usual customer of HDFC was a very average person. In 1997, the average cost of a flat or house financed by the company was Rs 398,000 (about $10,000), and its size was a mere 76 sq. m, or about 800 sq. ft. The average size of a loan was Rs 199,000—roughly 50 per cent of the cost of the unit—with an average payback period of 11.21 years. This average 38-year-old customer had a monthly household income of Rs 10,800 (about $250)—neither the elite at the top of the pyramid in Indian society, nor the very poor at the bottom, but

This case was written by Sudeep Budhiraja, Research Fellow, London Business School, Gita Piramal, business historian and Sumantra Ghoshal, Robert P. Baumann Professor of Strategic Leadership at the London Business School. It was written as part of a research programme supported by the Aditya V. Birla India Centre. The authors gratefully acknowledge the extraordinary cooperation and support of HDFC, without which this case could not have been written. The case was first registered by the London Business School in 1998.

squarely in the middle. This average Indian, however, was an extraordinarily reliable borrower, as evidenced by the company having had to charge off a mere Rs 8 mn as bad debt since its inception, against a total loan disbursement of Rs 12.2 mn.

Equally ordinary were a vast majority of the 1 million depositors who provided the bulk of the funds that HDFC disbursed to its borrowers. Attracted by the company's courteous and efficient service—the investors received their Certificate of Deposit on the spot and the interest payments reached them exactly on the due date—they entrusted the company with their savings, eschewing potentially higher returns offered by many other institutions.

The employees of the company were of a very similar profile. The culture and hiring practices of HDFC discouraged 'stars'. As a matter of policy, the company did not recruit fresh MBAs from the top-rated schools—the favourite hunting ground for most financial services companies in India. Management recognised and accepted that they could be giving up an opportunity to hire the best raw material. But, in doing so, they were also avoiding the baggage that typically came along—prima donna antics, jealousies, and an aggressively competitive environment. HDFC hired people from the next-tier institutions who tended to have more subdued personalities and were able to work jointly with others. The management of HDFC had a firm belief that the efficiencies and synergy of harmonious team-based operations far outweighed the cost of ignoring the best intellectual horsepower. In turn, the top management of the company stressed its own ordinariness—avoiding the typical status symbols of their levels. Their salaries were low by industry standards, they drove ordinary cars, and sat in relatively small, cramped offices.

The only thing not ordinary about the company was its performance. In a poll conducted by *Euromoney* in 1998, HDFC was voted the most competitive company in India. For two years in a row, it was also ranked as the best-managed company in the country. Despite enjoying a dominant 58 per cent share of India's housing finance market, the company was continuing to grow at about 33 per cent per year—improving its share by about 3 per cent each year in a rapidly growing market. It had a very strong balance sheet, with a capital-to-risk-adjusted asset ratio of 20.8 per cent, against the norm of 8 per cent minimum set by India's National Housing Bank. As a result, it was the only AAA-rated financial services company in the country. Its financial and capital market performance were stellar (see Appendix 1) and it was consistently highlighted by the World Bank as a model private sector housing finance agency for developing nations.

But, perhaps, the company's greatest achievement of all lay in the enormous contribution it made to Indian society. It had pioneered the housing finance market and had, in essence, created the opportunity for middle-class Indians to own a home. At the same time, it had demonstrated that a wholesome business, meeting an important social need, could also be extremely profitable.

In 1998, however, both the environment in which HDFC operated and the company itself were in the midst of some profound changes. The Government of India had recognised the importance of the housing sector and had begun to create a legal and financial infrastructure to address the huge unmet housing need in the country. As a result, the housing finance market was becoming more crowded and more competitive. Beyond the spate of specialised housing finance companies, large commercial banks were entering the fray, attracted by the very success of HDFC. At the same time, rapid deregulation of the financial services industry had opened up a variety of new opportunities for HDFC and the company had entered a number of new businesses, typically in partnership with a major global player: for instance, with GE Capital in consumer finance, with Colliers Jardine Asia Pacific Ltd in property services, and with Natwest for retail and corporate banking. While all of these activities were a part of the HDFC Group, they were structured as separate companies, with HDFC representatives on their boards but with very different management styles, employee pay scales and organisational culture. Within HDFC itself, there was much talk about leveraging the company's 1.9 million customer relationships to become a financial services supermarket. Deepak Parekh, the company's much admired CEO, wanted to nurture the ambition of transforming the company into a universal bank.

Issues and Questions

- Why has HDFC been so successful and what lessons can be drawn from the company's outstanding performance since its inception?
- What are the key challenges facing HDFC over the next five years? What are the potential upsides and downsides? What must the company do to achieve the upside and avoid the downside?
- Should HDFC try to emerge as a universal bank? If not, why not? If it

should, how? What actions should it take to create the pathway for getting to that destination?

The Housing Market in India

With a population estimated at close to 950 million people, India was by far the second most populous country in the world. It created approximately 5 million new households each year and these were about evenly split between rural and urban India. The National Building Organisation looked at the housing shortage in India and came up with the following demand estimates.

Housing Demand Estimates

(in million)

	Rural			*Urban*			*Total*		
	1981	*1991*	*2001*	*1981*	*1991*	*2001*	*1981*	*1991*	*2001*
Households	94.1	113.5	137.0	30.7	47.1	72.2	124.8	160.6	209.2
Housing stock	88.7	106.2	127.8	28.8	42.6	64.8	117.5	148.8	192.6
Of which, unusable	10.9	13.6	16.3	4.3	5.9	8.1	15.2	19.2	24.4
Housing gap	16.3	20.6	25.5	7.0	10.4	15.5	23.3	31.0	41.0

While the inherent demand was large, in a poor and highly regulated country like India it did not necessarily translate into a market for equivalent numbers of ready housing. As a USAID report stated at the end of the 1980s, 'It is axiomatic that there is tremendous unmet demand for both housing and housing finance. More careful observers note, though, that effective demand may be much more limited, resulting from a variety of price and non-price reasons. In other words, if housing and housing finance were available in unlimited quantities at acceptable prices, the market would be huge. However, prices are high and non-price rationing devices are so effective that only a relative few are able to exercise their demand.'

In the early 1950s, newly independent India invested slightly over 3 per cent of GNP in building housing stock. By 1974–78, this had declined to just over 1.5 per cent. This contributed to a rising shortfall of housing stock. As housing was considered a non-productive sector, it received little if any government funding. This, combined with the absence of a formal housing finance sector, left individual buyers to fund purchases by using accumulated savings in combination with retirement and provident fund drawdowns. Very limited institutional support was available apart from some loans to existing customers from the public sector Life Insurance Corporation (LIC) against accumulated savings. This was despite the Reserve Bank of India going on record in 1976 with a recommendation that mortgage lending institutions be created.

All over the world, the housing finance industry operated with some basic minimum requirements before a loan could be disbursed. These included clear title, ability to provide some collateral, and a regular and verifiable source of income. Unfortunately, the poorer sections of Indian society could not meet at least two and perhaps all three of these requirements. Therefore, housing finance, as it concerned HDFC, was only relevant at the middle and upper ends of Indian society, who tended to be urban dwellers.

One of the factors that had inhibited the growth of housing stock in India was the very high stamp duties charged by local municipal authorities each time there was a change in ownership on a real estate title. The rates ranged all the way from 3 to 15 per cent of the value of the property and varied based on the level set by each state. The high stamp duty typically resulted in transactions being done at well below true market price, with the balance being paid in cash. This practice had contributed to a huge and growing black market and had kept professional developers out of the re-development market. The central government recognised the problem and encouraged various state governments to move towards a uniform and much lower stamp duty. Once lower stamp duties arrived along with a generally lower level of interest rates (the prime lending rate in India had been kept high by the large nationalised banks who used the large spreads to help fund the costs of non-performing loans and generally low productivity), securitisation of mortgages was expected to create more capacity for housing finance companies and also result in lower costs for borrowers.

Tenant protection laws and the Urban Land Ceiling Act (ULCA), products of India's socialist aspirations, historically had had the opposite effect of inhibiting construction and development of housing stock. The government had begun the slow process of chipping away at tenant protection laws, and its actions were expected to expand the urban housing market and, therefore, the market for housing finance.

Recognising the various price and non-price constraints on the housing market, HDFC estimated that the cumulative housing shortfall in India was of the order of 19 million homes, of which some 7 million were in urban India and the balance shortfall of 12 million was spread across rural India. New annual demand was about 4 million units and the addition to housing stock was about 3 million each year, resulting in a net incremental shortfall of about 1 million units each year, divided almost equally between rural and urban sectors.

HDFC: The Early Years

HDFC was the product of a dogged determination of one man—H.T. Parekh—who sensed a strong need for housing finance in India, and staked his professional reputation on building an institution that would meet this need. A finance professional with a degree in Banking and Finance from the London School of Economics, Parekh had spent some time with a brokerage firm in Bombay before joining ICICI (a leading Indian financial institution) in 1956, where he had risen to the position of executive chairman.

The problems of housing in India had made an early impact on Parekh and he had carefully tracked the role of the S&L's (Savings and Loans Associations) in the US and of their equivalent Building Societies in the UK. These were special purpose entities which specialised in raising funding to provide long-term loans through mortgages to prospective buyers. Clearly India had no equivalent and the commercial banking system had made no attempt to meet this very important social need. Right through his years as the chairman of ICICI, H.T. Parekh continued to talk to people about setting up a housing finance vehicle. The idea was not well received as the law did not provide for easy and smooth re-possession on payment defaults and there was a general perception that the losses would be very large.

Parekh persisted and in 1976, after his retirement from ICICI, put together an outline for a housing finance bank. He firmly believed that a well-motivated, professionally managed company would be able to identify and deal with 'good' borrowers who were keen savers and who would go to any length to stay current on a housing loan. Despite a lukewarm response, he pressed on, and HDFC was incorporated on 17 October 1977. With a less-than-enthusiastic response from the government and the banking sector, its equity capital was subscribed by the Indian business community (Rs 45 mn), an Indian public issue (Rs 40 mn), ICICI (Rs 5 mn), IFC, Washington (Rs 5 mn) and HRH The Aga Khan (Rs 5 mn).

The company was incorporated with a mandate to specialise in the area of providing housing finance to individuals, co-operative societies and the corporate sector. Its primary objective was to enhance the residential housing stock in the country by providing housing finance on a systematic and professional basis and to promote home ownership. Another key objective was to increase the flow of financial resources for housing through the integration of housing finance institutions with the domestic capital market.

HDFC's Founding Principles

- There was a major need for housing finance targeted at the household throughout the country.
- Performance in loan recoveries was a direct function of the credit creation process.
- Resource mobilisation was critical and therefore required an institutional structure which commanded confidence.
- Initially, a financial institution of this type would be required to mobilise wholesale resources and lend retail, implying a mortgage bank structure as opposed to a savings and loan type institution.
- It would be preferable to establish an all-India institution rather than one based on a regional concept.
- Managerial inputs would be critical to the nature of the institution conceived, especially to introduce and operate systems that minimised high transaction costs per loan in a retail financial activity. Recruitment of young talent would be necessary to infuse the institution with a set of operating practices not normally found in development banking.
- Success would require a lean and efficient organisation, capable of minimising transaction costs per loan, thus being able to survive on fairly thin spreads between the cost of funds and the lending rate. Most important would be a very strong customer orientation, not normally observed in this type of institution.
- The institution would be market-oriented, seeking funds and designing products that met with market preferences. Success depended on both sides of the balance sheet: resource mobilisation and mortgage lending.
- Finally, the institution should be structured in a manner which would combine both the public and private sectors, together with the involvement of the public at large.

Based on his experience, H.T. Parekh was very aware of the critical role that funding and the funding strategy would play in enabling HDFC to raise the resources required for longer-term mortgage lending. The basic options were a large well-organised retail deposit gathering activity or a focus on larger institutional/multilateral/government loans. He made an early choice to go with the latter option.

Parekh was able to lobby the government to have public sector financial institutions such as the LIC provide financing to HDFC. This, along with a US$ 4 million line of credit from a promoter (IFC) and government guarantees on long-term external funding from bilateral and multilateral financial institutions such as the World Bank, USAID and Kredinstalt für Wiederaufbau (KfW) set HDFC firmly on the road to its destination as the premier housing finance institution in India.

As a development finance institution (DFI), HDFC was also automatically entitled, under the Indian Income Tax Act, to appropriate 40 per cent of pre-tax profits into a tax-free Special Reserve Account, effectively reducing the tax burden. However, there was a proviso that the balance in the Special Reserve Account should not be greater than twice the paid-up capital (excluding reserves) of the company. This resulted in HDFC being overcapitalised relative to assets, as it kept diluting equity to primarily get the tax benefit and secondarily the free funding which further contributed to total income.

After a start in 1978 with a capital of Rs 100 mn and a US$ 4 million line of credit, HDFC had become a substantial financial entity by 1991. Total loans disbursed had reached a level of Rs 6.7 bn in 1990-91, with a profit after tax of Rs 298 mn.

At that time, the company was generating more than 90 per cent of its resources wholesale and lending funds to mostly individual borrowers. This happy situation was rocked by India's macro-economic problems of 1991, leading to a downgrading of the country's credit rating. At the same time, domestic interest rates moved up to support the currency and to control the growth of money supply. Faced with these environmental problems, the banking sector and other public sector financial institutions were not in a position to continue to support HDFC, leading to an immediate upward impact on HDFC's borrowing costs. This resulted in a major liquidity crunch within the company, which was compounded by its inability to pass on the cost of expensively raised local funds to its individual borrowers. As most houses were lived in and not rented and most borrowers were on a salary, they had virtually no ability to absorb a sudden increase in interest rates. If HDFC had re-priced loans upwards, that would have contributed to deteriorating non-performing loan numbers. So, senior management and the rest of the team were left with no option but to dramatically switch strategy and start focussing on raising funds from retail depositors. Done efficiently, this would certainly raise the average cost of funds, but the impact would be considerably lower than borrowing through the issuance of bonds at 16-17 per cent. The Reserve Bank of India had set the minimum lending rate at between 18 and 19 per cent, which further prompted HDFC to consider retail canvassing.

As the story goes, HDFC had built up so much goodwill and trust since 1978 by providing a good product with good service, that investors swarmed into its branches around the country and started funding the company to the tune of Rs 10 mn a day. This put HDFC on the path to developing a retail deposit clientele and the company reciprocated by providing excellent service to depositors. The investor, for example, was given his/her Certificate of Deposit on-the-spot and the interest warrant reached on the day it was due. In 1998, 54 per cent of HDFC's incremental borrowing requirements were met through small retail deposits.

> As Deepak Parekh, H.T. Parekh's successor of HDFC, once said: 'In one sense the economic crisis of 1991 was the best thing that happened to us because it created a brand new source of funds.'

Nurturing Competition

HDFC was essentially the solitary player in the formal housing market at the time of its formation. Its only competition was from national, state and local co-operatives, who were inefficient and poorly managed. These public sector entities served as administrative channels for directed and subsidised lending for low income housing. They depended on government allocations, financial institutions and commercial banks for funds. From the very beginning, HDFC looked at the creation of a business model which called for funds to be lent to creditworthy borrowers at market rates. This strategy, combined with a dedication to customer service and a commitment to increasing productivity, resulted in its outstanding success. Being the only serious player with no meaningful competition helped build HDFC's financial performance and its status in the market among borrowers, investors and the general public. HDFC management found they had an excellent business in a fast-growing market with very large unmet demand.

The Indian government also noticed the significant success of HDFC and started looking for ways to expand the availability of home loans. The National Housing Bank Act was voted in by the Indian parliament in 1987, and the National Housing Bank (NHB) was established by the government as a subsidiary of the Reserve Bank of India (RBI), charged with the responsibility for regulating, promoting and refinancing the housing finance sector.

With the creation of the NHB, the government had signalled its strong commitment to housing finance and its interest in seeing an expanded reach. It then worked with RBI and directed commercial banks to lend 1.5 per cent of all new deposits to this sector.

HDFC management welcomed the new governmental support to the sector and decided to take an active role in the creation of its own competitors. It worked with government or public sector entities to set up housing finance companies—with State Bank of India (SBI Home Finance), Canara Bank (Canfin Homes Ltd.), General Insurance Corporation (GIC Housing Finance) and the Gujarat state government (GRUH Finance). HDFC kept a significant equity position in each of these companies and supported the new companies on strategy and training, helping them to become stand-alone entities. Each of these companies operated independently in the market and competed for business with HDFC. A comparative summary of the main players in the housing finance market is given in Appendix 2. It's interesting to note that all the affiliates of HDFC were amongst the largest players in the market. LIC decided to go alone and set up its own captive housing finance company—LIC House Finance Ltd.

Over time, HDFC concentrated its efforts in western India, although it had offices all over the country. In 1998, 50 per cent of its business came from western India, 25 per cent from the North, 20 per cent from the South and 5 per cent from the East. The portfolio of SBI Home Finance was concentrated in the East and North-East, Canfin in the South and PNB Home Finance (a subsidiary of Punjab National Bank), a smaller competitor, concentrated its efforts in North India. LIC House Finance (HDFC's largest competitor) worked equally across all regions.

A somewhat older comparison of the leading housing finance companies is given in Appendix 3. The numbers go back to March 1993, but they do provide a basic understanding of the cost structure, funding strategy and relative profitability of the different companies. Appendix 4 provides a more recent comparison of the top two companies: HDFC and LIC Housing Finance.

Taken together as a group, the housing finance institutions were by far the largest lender to the housing sector. The working group on urban housing for the Ninth Five-Year Plan (1997-2002) estimated that the total investment required in housing during this period would be about Rs 1,500 bn or Rs 300 bn per year. It was estimated that the organised housing finance sector could fund no more than Rs 330 bn over the five-year period, or about one-fourth of the total required. This was expected to be sourced through Life Insurance Corporation of India (LIC) (Rs 45 bn), General Insurance Corporation of India (GIC) (Rs 10 bn), commercial banks (Rs 55 bn), housing finance institutions (Rs 150 bn), mortgage securitisation (Rs 25 bn) and others (Rs 45 bn).

While housing finance institutions remained the largest lender, the gap was narrowing, as insurance companies and commercial banks had started to recognise the opportunities available in housing finance, with higher yields and lower loss ratios on a portfolio secured by the underlying property.

HDFC by itself had already funded over Rs 50 bn in the first two years of the five-year period.

Market Share of Housing Finance Companies

	1994 (%)	*1997 (%)*
HDFC	49	58
LIC Finance	26	20
GIC Finance*	2	4
SBI Home Fin*	4	5
Can Fin *	5	3
Dewan Finance	5	2
Others	9	8

* HDFC affiliates.

In 1998, HDFC conducted its business with an infrastructure of forty-five branch offices across the country in addition to the Mumbai head office. The offices organised outreach programmes spread across eighty-four locations which enabled the company to sanction loans for properties in over 2,500 cities and towns. Outside India, HDFC opened its first international office in Dubai,

United Arab Emirates, to service non-resident Indians in their efforts to acquire residential properties in India.

In addition to its own staff, HDFC had a network of 42,000 part-time agents who generated retail deposits against a commission ranging from 0.5 per cent for one year deposits to 1.5 per cent for three years. About 15,000 of these agents were active and generated at least a few deposits each month. About 70 per cent of the agents also represented LIC who paid a much larger incentive fee of 35 per cent of first year and 10 per cent of subsequent premiums on endowment policies. HDFC had created a reputation for fairplay and quick disbursement of commissions, which allowed it to compete successfully for the agents' 'share-of-mind'.

Between 1994 and 1997, the company had grown at an average annual rate of 33 per cent, consistently enhancing its market share. Perhaps it could have grown even faster, but the management of HDFC firmly believed in the benefits of stability, continuity and robustness. Higher growth rates, they believed, would have exposed the company to possible lay-offs in a downturn and also the possibility of higher non-performing loans. In 1998, the approvals growth rate was 29 per cent while the disbursements growth rate was 31 per cent.

From Values to Action

The 1996-97 Annual Report of HDFC carried the following statement in its introduction:

> This year for the annual report, we have chosen to underline some key principles HDFC has adopted and maintained for nearly two decades of its existence. They constitute the 'core values' that we hold dear—values that are not subject to compromise and reinterpretation as the environment changes around us. They are immutable and true through time and circumstances . . . .
>
> Core values are the basis of a vision, they do not constitute it . . . . Visions can be wrong, hopelessly off the mark if they are not born from strong values . . . .
>
> Values without principles are hollow . . . . Principles form the immutable and unchangeable core of right action. HDFC from its very first day of operation has built a principle-centred organisation. By this we mean . . . an organisation that has been built on the basis of fairness, kindness, efficiency and effectiveness.

While assertions such as these are not unusual in corporate annual reports and publicity brochures, what set HDFC apart was that it had institutionalised a set of practices so as to live by the values and principles that had been articulated by its founder. At the heart of these practices lay the company's firm commitment to building long-term, mutually supportive relationships with all its key constituencies—its employees, investors, depositors, borrowers and regulators.

Corporate Values and Culture

- Above all, we value integrity, honesty of purpose and commitment to the interests of the organisation.
- To HDFC, business is not merely earning profits, but a way through which we provide essential and valuable services to society.
- 'Customer Service' is the key activity in our operations. This is reflected in our promptness and caring attitude towards our customers. A positive and personalised approach to our customer's needs is what we have always strived to attain.
- We adopt a 'Learning by Doing' philosophy which encourages decision making as well as learning from the process of doing. The philosophy demands feedback and a tolerance of constructive criticism.
- People are our most important resource. It is our intimate concern to continuously develop them.
- We appreciate good inter-personal relationships and supportive leadership, coupled with strong teamwork both within and between departments.
- We believe in smooth and effective communication to ensure better flow of information and understanding amongst employees at all levels. Every employee can meet any executive for airing personal grievances, giving suggestions or putting forth any creative idea. This 'open door' policy has resulted in a very open and informal culture.
- Our approach to discipline is reformative and not always penal. Employees are expected to adhere to rules and regulations as laid down from time to time.

Goals

- Develop close relationships with individual households and meet their needs with sensitivity and efficiency.
- Maintain image domestically as a premier housing finance institution and to spread it internationally.
- Nurture innovative spirit amongst employees.
- Maintain high degree of professional integrity.
- Provide consistently high returns to shareholders.
- Maintain growth through diversification—a financial supermarket.

Regulatory Relations

Meeting an important social need, rather than personal profit, was clearly the key motivator for H.T. Parekh in founding HDFC, and he firmly believed in the need for building a symbiotic relationship between the public and private sectors for achieving economic and social progress in India. His personal background as the chairman of the quasi-public sector ICICI had undoubtedly influenced his views. As a result, both he and his successor, Deepak Parekh, maintained very strong relationships with all related government agencies, and both of them consistently invested significant amounts of time and energy working on government projects and initiatives, not all of which were of direct commercial interest to the company they led.

At the same time, these relationships also helped the company achieve some significant regulatory successes. Some of these successes included:

- Commercial banks were required to on-lend 1.5 per cent of deposits to the housing finance sector.
- Initially, HDFC got the government to guarantee long-term foreign currency loans from the USAID, World Bank and other development-oriented lenders.
- The Malhotra Committee on reforms of the insurance industry (of which the HDFC chairman was a member) recommended private sector entrants into the insurance sector. HDFC was one of the companies expected to be approved for entering the business, and it had already established a strategic partnership with Standard Life of the UK to commence operations as soon as the new regulations were put in place.

Shareholder Relations

HDFC had about 130,000 shareholders and was described as a 'core holding' by several analysts who followed the company. The reason was simple: for years, it had been one of the star performers in the Mumbai stock exchange.

> As Deepak Parekh, Chairman HDFC, said in December 1996: 'I am merely a professional who happens to be at the helm of affairs of a corporation, which is rather atypical. HDFC has no single financial institution, or government, or multinational, or FII or family holding dominant ownership. Thus, I have always viewed my own role as that of a trustee, who is enjoined with the task of running a business enterprise.'

The company was managed by professionals on behalf of its various shareholders. Parekh and his team had a declared internal goal—minimum 20 per cent return on equity. They were very concerned about returns to shareholders and worked consistently on increasing the return on equity.

Throughout HDFC, there was a strong focus on productivity and the company was managed for performance. The management's philosophy was to outsource all non-value-adding functions. These included data entry, security, housekeeping, canteens, etc. They watched headcount growth very carefully and ensured that their own employees only worked on value-added activities intrinsic to the HDFC business proposition.

Customer Relations

> A house is the biggest and single most important asset that a family buys—and it is for life. So we have to be helpful.
>
> —Deepak Parekh

As described earlier, the average borrower at HDFC was a very average person, who would typically have to stand in queues to get anything done at another financial institution. Relating well to this average customer was seen by HDFC management as the key to the company's mission. Every employee of the company was trained in handling customers through a customer relations workshop. This workshop was customised for HDFC employees and was based on the material used by S&Ls. Key components of this workshop, which have been run regularly since 1980, were:

- How do you guide the process of an interview?
- How do you manage the communication process?
- How do you manage difficult customers?

Each branch provided real-life examples of difficult situations and these were used as learning opportunities during the workshop.

So, while the general attitude towards service was driven by senior management, who set an example and talked incessantly about the need to make customers feel appreciated and wanted (this was done through their regular visits to branch officers and at the head office), servicing techniques were taught through formal training sessions.

HDFC as a company was very well tuned into client perceptions and needs. It used agents and front-line staff to sense shifts in client behaviour. Simultaneously, it consistently looked for ways to improve on existing products and delivery systems. An important example of this is how the loan approval cycle time was progressively reduced from two to four weeks, to a point where the decision could be made and communicated across the table. Importantly, this was done in an environment wherein HDFC was the best service provider and much better than its nearest competitor.

Initially, all loan applications were finally reviewed and approved at the head office and, typically, it took four weeks to approve a loan. Clients were so happy to get the money that they did not worry too much about the delay. However, management felt that four weeks was too long and hired Dr V.S. Mahesh, a Professor of Service Management at the University of Buckingham, UK, to work with the company to start collapsing the cycle time.

This process was started in 1989 with a workshop attended by all branch managers in each region. It kicked off with an overview of service management and then proceeded to identify specific bottlenecks in HDFC's loan approval processes. Cross-functional groups were established to investigate each bottleneck and recommend solutions. A 'champion' was identified for the most vexing issues (20 per cent) and the participants agreed to develop a solution within a tight timeframe. At the end of the prescribed period, the various groups came back with their proposals and the company found how to reduce the cycle time from an average of four weeks to two to five days, once all the recommended changes were implemented.

The next stage came in 1994, when customers started noticing the two- to five-day cycle time and started seeing it as a delay. The company went back to the 1989 formula and ran another set of workshops. They found they had various unnecessary manual operations around the approval process and this resulted in needless delays. Non-essential items like manual filing were eliminated and a new set of standardised procedures were put on the computer. This called for a team of two people to prepare each application and another two to check and approve the loan. Once implemented, this resulted in the capability to approve applications across the table.

A commitment to customers was an all-encompassing theme at HDFC. Further evidence of this commitment can be found, for example, when loans were pre-paid: the company arranged to promptly return all original title documents to the borrower. There were no unnecessary delays similar to those the borrower would experience at almost any of its competitors. Also, while the documents were stored by HDFC, they were kept in a well-organised secure facility which ensured that they were safe, easy to locate, and not damaged by moisture or other elements. This practice was almost unique in the Indian finance industry.

Employee Relations

Between 1991 and 1997, HDFC had quadrupled its loan assets while increasing its employee count from 724 to 794. Despite a booming market for finance personnel, it had consistently enjoyed extremely low employee turnover and no senior manager had left the company in many years.

Why did people join HDFC and why did they stay? An informal survey among a wide cross-section of HDFC officers and staff yielded the following responses:

- An informal atmosphere. This was carefully cultivated by senior management, including the chairman, who frequently walked through the offices in shirtsleeves and willingly answered a ringing phone in an empty office (typically, he left a message for the person concerned). H. T. Parekh was credited with creating the informal atmosphere and Deepak Parekh for maintaining it.

- **A concern for people.** The company worked with an open-door policy. With virtually no staff turnover, everyone knew everyone else and they could walk into the office of the managing director, executive directors or a general manager (even the chairman if he was in) to raise their concerns and have them addressed. Tenure was given a lot of respect in the company. When HDFC Bank shares were being distributed at par to employees, the allocation formula was transparent to all, and while it recognised seniority in terms of position, equal weightage was given to tenure.
- **Large responsibilities.** HDFC was a merit-oriented organisation and it did not hire laterals (with very rare exceptions). There was a shared belief that lateral hires might not fit as well into the culture of the company. As the business was growing at over 25 per cent per annum, there were significant advancement opportunities for most employees. The company had a transparent performance appraisal process wherein employees were kept fully informed. For officers, the form consisted of six sections: (i) Self-assessment, (ii) Appraisal of overall performance, (iii) Appraisal of personal attributes, (iv) Objectives for the following year, (v) Comments by appraiser (includes commentary on self-appraisal as well as achievement of objectives and promotability), and (vi) Development and training needs focus. Each officer was aware of and involved in all the sections of the appraisal except (v).
- **Free sharing of information** through a regular and active communication programme. There were few status symbols accorded to senior managers. They drove fairly ordinary cars and were not particularly well paid by industry standards. So, there was no real 'we'–'they' distancing between the seniors and others. There were many internal communication organs and perhaps most important, the full-time directors made it a point to address all employees at the various locations of the company on a regular basis.
- **The people did not see themselves as employees or the company as an employer.** The company belonged to them as much as they belonged to the company. This was an extended family. Management had a no-firing policy except in cases of fraud/deception, etc. This sense of belonging and security resulted in a very high level of both loyalty and commitment. A simple illustrative example could be found in people's response to a major fire in the company's main office in Mumbai. The ground floor was gutted and it was impossible to serve customers in the office. So, while some employees sacrificed their personal time to re-group and re-equip the

office, others took the office to the pavement outside the building and handled customer enquiries on the roadside. Another indicator: there was no union at any location of the company.

- **Personal development**. Management had set-up a specialised housing finance training centre at Lonavala. All employees rotated through the training centre on a regular basis and had ample opportunities for personal development. In addition, the company reimbursed each employee for the cost of two professional qualifications. This process of training and development, along with a commitment to merit and a reluctance to hire laterals, created some unique opportunities. For example, the manager (deposits) in the head office had joined the company as a stenographer in 1981. In India, very few other companies would have offered this possibility.
- **No politics**. The 'no-star' policy of the company described earlier led to a very open environment, with very little overt politicking.

The Role of Leadership

In November 1996, Deepak Parekh, chairman of HDFC, was chosen as Businessman of the Year—the most visible and coveted recognition for corporate leadership in India. Explaining its choice, the selection committee highlighted the following accomplishments of Parekh:

- His all-pervasive influence both within HDFC and outside that had, over the years, not just earned the respect of colleagues and peers but also of decision makers in government, international institutions and foreign collaborators. It was no secret that his office had become the first port of call for many potential investors into the country who came to seek his guidance.
- His company both met a social need and was extremely profitable—vibrant proof that the two were not mutually exclusive.
- Though market leader by a wide margin, it continued to set standards in customer service adding to the tremendous bank of goodwill that it had built up.
- Leading an organisation that had come to be regarded as world class, this forward thinker represented the best side of Indian business.

Deepak Parekh studied Commerce at Sydneham College, Bombay, before qualifying as a chartered accountant from London. He returned to India and worked in a small business before joining Grindlays Bank in their Merchant Banking division. He then moved to Chase and rose to become Chase's representative for South Asia, before moving on to HDFC in 1978. Despite the much lower pay and uncertain prospects, he could not resist the vision and passion of H. T. Parekh, who also happened to be his uncle. Deepak Parekh joined HDFC as a deputy general manager and quickly became a key player with a sense of mission. He rose to become managing director of the company before succeeding H.T. Parekh as the chairman in 1994.

While the Businessman of the Year award merely confirmed it, Deepak Parekh had become a management icon in the country. Reputed to be addicted to people and a familiar face at a variety of high level forums in India, he was the classic networked executive. A member of the Advisory Board of Bankers Trust in New York and of the Capital International Group, he also served on the boards of twenty companies and social or educational institutions in India.

As an individual, Deepak Parekh had the reputation of being a delegator, on the one hand, who had the faith and the courage to empower people to an extent that was highly unusual in India, and a firm leader, on the other, who regularly stepped in to assume a hands-on role and expected his decisions to be unwaveringly followed. An excellent public speaker in constant demand in national and international seminar circuits, he served as a source of inspiration and a motivator for extraordinary efforts within the company. Under his leadership, HDFC entered a number of new activities by creating new joint venture companies, and it was his passion and charisma—like that of his uncle before him—that had attracted a number of high-profile executives to join as CEOs and senior managers in these ventures.

Strategically, Deepak Parekh enjoyed the reputation of being a visionary—someone who could see opportunities early so as to be able to get in before others and lead rather than compete in the business. He had driven the policy of collaborating with public sector banks, helping them create their own housing finance companies, instead of taking a competitive posture. He had also taken the lead in creating subsidiary companies in the infrastructure leasing business and in the credit rating business—well before others woke up to the opportunities.

Interestingly, through serendipity perhaps rather than design, HDFC had developed a 'two hat' system for the top job from the very beginning. H.T. Parekh was the visionary and statesman who created the company after he had

had a full career and retired as the executive chairman of ICICI. Once HDFC had been created, he concerned himself with the big picture. He was the external face of the company and represented HDFC to the press and to the regulators. Within the company, he was the father figure who created a caring culture—for both customers and employees. Deepak Parekh, on the other hand, was the businessman who was responsible for managing the company on a day-to-day basis and ensuring the quality of operating results.

Once H. T. Parekh stepped down as chairman, Deepak Parekh succeeded him as the visionary and statesman and anointed Deepak Satwalekar as the managing director. An HDFC veteran who had earlier worked for a short period with Citibank, Satwalekar together with his team of executive directors had taken over Deepak Parekh's earlier role of running the company on a day-to-day basis.

HDFC - Universal Bank of the Future?

'I will steer HDFC to become one of the largest financial supermarkets under one roof.'

—Deepak Parekh, 1992.

HDFC saw itself as a company with a customer base of 1.9 million people and plenty of opportunities. A wide cross-section of managers within the company shared a strong desire to reposition HDFC from a housing finance lender to a personal finance company. This aspiration was sufficiently widespread within the company to suggest that the decision had really been made and was actually under gradual implementation.

The company had already developed a number of affiliate companies in a wide range of related businesses. Most of them had been set up as strategic alliances with acknowledged leaders in their fields: Colliers Jardine Indian Property Services Ltd and Maruti Countrywide Auto Financial Services Ltd were two examples. Generally, the strategic partner had management control while HDFC benefited from learning the business, extracting synergies with its own activities, and enjoying outstanding returns on its financial investments in these alliances. In a few cases, such as the HDFC Bank and CRISIL, the companies were managed by trained professionals hired by HDFC from the market. Only in

Housing Finance

- GRUH Finance Limited (with International Finance Corporation, Washington, The Aga Khan Fund for Economic Development, Geneva, and with the support of the Government of Gujarat).
- SBI Home Finance Limited (with SBI Capital Markets, a subsidiary of State Bank of India).
- Can Fin Homes Limited (with Canara Bank, Unit Trust of India and Asian Development Bank).
- GIC Housing Finance Limited (with General Insurance Corporation).

Finance Services

- Infrastructure Leasing and Financial Services Limited (IL&FS) (with Central Bank of India and Unit Trust of India).
- The Credit Rating & Information Services of India Limited (the first rating agency in India, co-promoted with ICICI and others).
- Countrywide Consumer Financial Services Limited (joint venture with General Electric Capital Corporation, USA).
- HDFC Bank Limited (promoted in strategic alliance with Natwest Markets, UK).
- Maruti Countrywide Auto Financial Services Limited (with Maruti Udyog Ltd and GE Capital India Ltd).

Property Development and Management

- Colliers Jardine India Property Services Limited (co-promoted with IL&FS and Colliers Jardine Asia Pacific Ltd).
- HDFC Developers Ltd (a wholly-owned subsidiary of HDFC).

exceptional circumstances did HDFC send its own management talent to the new entities.

As a result, the cultures and norms that had been developed within these affiliate institutions were often very different from those of HDFC. HDFC Bank, for example, was much closer to Citibank—Aditya Puri, managing director, was a career Citibanker and had given up his job as Citi's country head in Malaysia to join HDFC Bank. His vision was to establish HDFC Bank as the first bank in

India that would bring together the people and product strengths of the better foreign banks and the advantages of a local bank. He built the new organisation with smart, highly self-confident and aggressive people, with the top team recruited entirely from the management ranks of foreign banks operating in India. In 1998, even though the organisation was just getting off the ground, Puri and his team had few doubts about the bank's eventual success. They were building a broad retail franchise, as well as strong relationships with selected blue-chip corporate clients. They adopted the very latest technology—HDFC Bank was designed to be almost paperless—together with management processes aimed at fast decision making and implementation. The market appeared to reflect the enormous self-confidence of HDFC Bank's management—indeed, it has been recognised by *Asiamoney* in its 1998 report as one of the best-managed companies in India, along with its parent, HDFC.

Despite the enormous differences in technology, decision-making processes, people, leadership style and culture, Aditya Puri acknowledged the possibility that HDFC and HDFC Bank might one day come together. It was Deepak Parekh's vision and passion that had persuaded him to give up his career in Citicorp and return to India, and he had great respect for Parekh as the founder of HDFC Bank and as a strategist. So, he was comfortable to leave the decision about the future relationship between the parent and the offspring to Parekh, while focussing his own energies in building HDFC Bank as a premier institution in the country.

The story at Countrywide, however, was very different. It was a GE company. It had recruited ambitious, smart and aggressive professionals and it operated with GE policies and procedures. It too was a highly successful company, and there was a great deal of gratitude in Countrywide for all the support that HDFC extended to it in the start-up phase (Countrywide worked out of HDFC offices for the first two years). In 1998, however, it saw itself unambiguously as a part of GE Capital, and employees of Countrywide saw their own future within GE's global network. Increasingly, they had begun to view HDFC as a future competitor in financing durable goods. From HDFC's perspective, it was a matter of some regret: as Deepak Satwalekar said, 'We should never have given a 50 per cent share to GE Capital. They told us it was important for them for accounting purposes, so that they could consolidate the financials of Countrywide in their global accounts . . . . But, we have learnt.'

In 1998, almost all of HDFC's affiliates were doing well, improving their capabilities and their customer bases aggressively. But each was very different, with very different kinds of people, very different compensation strategies and very different leadership styles. To realise Deepak Parekh's ambition of developing a financial supermarket, one day it would become necessary to mould these diverse offsprings together with the parent. Could that be done? Should that be done? If so, when should the process begin, and how?

APPENDIX 1

HDFC: Key Financial Indicators

Indicator	*FY93*	*FY94*	*FY95*	*FY96*	*FY97*
EPS growth (fully diluted) (%)	-20	41	26	12	26
Return on avg. equity (%)	21.6	25.5	21.3	16.5	15.8
Return on avg. assets (%)	1.9	2.8	3.1	3.3	3.4
Equity to assets (%)	9.7	12.3	16.5	22.9	20.3
Loan growth (%)	20	20	22	27	20
Market price per share (Rs)	1230	2800	2050	3240	2750
NPL/Total loans (%)	0.86	0.90	0.69	0.57	0.52
Provisions/NPL (%)	147	151	174	186	237
Profit/Employee (Rs lakh)	8	14	19	25	31
Debt/Equity (Ratio)	9.30	7.10	5.10	3.50	4.10
PER (X)	15	25	14	20	14
Price/Book value (X)	2.6	5.2	2.4	2.7	2.0
Dividend yield (%)	2.0	1.0	1.6	1.1	1.6

APPENDIX 2

Particulars of Housing Finance Companies in the Approved List (as on 31 March 1998)

(Rs crore)*

Name of Housing Finance Co.	*Paid-up Capital*	*Net Own Funds*	*Deposits*	*Loans O/S*	*Sanctions 1997–98*	*Disburse-ment 1997-98*	*No. of branches*
HDFC Ltd	119.11	1777.24	8148.45	6944.07	3251.27	2753.61	41
LIC Housing Finance Ltd	74.99	404.86	2978.78	3077.40	872.54	802.10	75
GIC Housing Finance Ltd	17.97	78.90	400.38	402.66	159.38	130.48	16
Can Fin Homes Ltd	20.49	68.22	575.34	583.43	138.67	137.18	36
Dewan Housing Finance Ltd	28.01	59.90	435.97	444.46	110.70	102.79	29
SBI Home Finance Ltd	15.00	26.87	542.57	335.91	89.39	88.77	24
GRUH Finance Ltd	13.25	29.42	286.36	264.83	106.95	89.29	24
Global Housing Finance Ltd	22.52	25.25	8.03	25.88	8.72	8.35	5
PNB Housing Finance Ltd	10.00	29.28	156.49	115.60	60.49	50.78	13
Ind Bank Housing Ltd	10.00	15.34	217.08	149.26	30.76	25.82	13
Peerless Abasan Finance Ltd	11.00	14.91	38.95	29.18	8.30	8.55	5
Cent Bank Housing Finance Ltd	10.00	14.16	75.48	79.83	25.33	24.73	13
BOB Housing Finance Ltd	7.60	16.65	101.56	109.21	51.43	44.80	24
AB Home Finance Ltd	9.00	14.38	117.87	111.26	44.49	34.90	16
Vysya Bank Housing Ltd	4.50	13.72	120.12	106.23	45.41	40.29	13
Hometrust Housing Finance Ltd	10.00	12.46	61.97	59.74	37.03	31.89	9
Vijay Homes Loans Ltd	7.42	8.40	24.71	25.93	8.05	8.07	16

Appendix 2 contd. . .

Name of Housing Finance Co.	*Paid-up Capital*	*Net Own Funds*	*Deposits*	*Loans O/S*	*Sanctions 1997–98*	*Disburse-ment 1997-98*	*No. of branches*
GLFL Housing Finance Ltd	8.25	11.51	80.16	80.96	34.50	28.80	8
Vijayabank Housing Finance Ltd	6.00	7.07	15.83	20.21	14.75	13.75	10
Parshrawanath Housing Finance Ltd	3.00	3.16	9.05	12.51	0.02	0.02	3
Livewell Housing Finance Ltd	5.00	4.53	14.94	18.16	7.65	7.42	4
Saya Housing Finance Ltd	3.00	3.00	1.02	2.80	0.02	0.02	6
Orissa Rural Housing Dev. Ltd	7.25	9.48	40.90	30.92	27.22	17.82	1
Weizmann Homes	4.25	16.33	17.42	27.20	16.47	15.02	10
Mercantile Housing Finance Ltd	10.00	10.74	2.36	7.54	10.46	7.44	4

* 1 crore = 10 million.

APPENDIX 3

Comparison of Major Finance Companies, March 1993

(Rs crore)*

	Year Est.	Bran-ches	Empl-oyees	Annual Distb.	Cumm. Distb.	Units	Loans Out	Total Assets	Sh. Funds	Borrow-ings	Depo-sits	PBT	PAT	Debt/ Eq.	Admn. Cost/ Loans Out	ROTA
LIC Fin	1989	60	694	476	874	135642	852	946	56	889	–	18.8	13.5	15.8	0.76	1.42
Can Fin	1987	26	220	59	347	52347	281	355	36	154	165	534	5.3	8.9	1.17	1.50
Dewan	1984	16	273	77	162	28008	155	154	11	105	38	2.2	1.9	13.1	1.97	1.26
SBI Home	1988	12	59	40	96	30274	86	117	18	32	67	3.6	2.5	5.4	1.59	2.10
GIC	1989	4	60	33	42	13121	45	64	7	57	–	2.1	1.5	7.8	2.26	2.27
GRUH	1986	10	47	15	46	6268	39	47	6	38	2	0.8	0.6	6.4	3.20	1.37
HDFC	1977	26	728	720	3594	719458	2652	3363	326	2009	1029	73.1	55.6	9.3	0.83	1.65
Total/ Avg.	–	154	2081	1419	5162	958118	4020	5047	461	3284	1302	106.0	80.9	9.5	1.68	1.65

* 1 crore = 10 million.

APPENDIX 4

Peer Comparison, 1997

Indicator	*HDFC*	*LICHF*
Interest rate spread (%)	1.73	1.90
Return on avg. equity (%)	19.8	20.0
Return on avg. assets (%)	3.2	2.3
Loan growth (%)	20.4	22.1
Equity/Assets (%)	18.5	11.4
NPL/Total loans (%)	0.5	4.6
Price/Earnings	15.4	6.0
Per two year EPS growth (98E)	0.55	0.23
Price/Book value	2.3	1.1
Dividend field (%)	1.4	4.0
Market cap./Avg. assets (%)	47.5	13.5

INFOSYS TECHNOLOGIES LIMITED: GOING GLOBAL

> 'Between 1996-1997, Infosys almost doubled its turnover from Rs 1.4 bn to Rs 2.6 bn, while net profit grew from 370 mn to 600 mn. Market capitalisation during this period soared by over 300 per cent from Rs 7.31 bn to Rs 29.63 bn. What is more, Infosys has come to be viewed as a role model across the Indian industry in terms of corporate transparency, enhancement of stakeholder value and global benchmarking. It is expected to be the first Indian company to have its shares listed on an American stock exchange.
>
> —*The Economic Times*, 3 September 1998

'Business at its Best: The Economic Times Awards for Corporate Excellence' are announced. Company of the Year: Infosys Technologies Limited.

This case was written by Kavita Abraham, PhD student, London Business School and Sumantra Ghoshal, Robert P. Baumann Professor of Strategic Leadership at the London Business School. It was written as part of a research programme supported by the Aditya V. Birla India Centre. The authors are grateful to Infosys Technologies Ltd for their help and support. The case was first registered by the London Business School in 2000.

A week before the awards were announced N.R. Narayana Murthy, chairman and managing director of Infosys, gathered his staff around him for an open meeting from the boardroom, which would be transmitted across the entire organisation over the intercom. There had been some murmurs in the company about potential changes in the top management structure. The new direction for Infosys had been debated, discussed and articulated throughout the firm for nearly a year. 'Infosys is Going Global' was a clear and concise strategy. Infosys was not trying to be an Indian multinational, nor was Infosys going to continue to play in the commodities market. Infosys was going to create a brand and move up the value chain from a cost-based model of selling to a value-based model of selling.

All that remained was to establish what changes, if any, were necessary in the top management structure. Who would drive this new endeavour? What would happen to their leader of the past twenty years? What roles would the original six founders take on? Who would be the new face of Infosys? Who would be the heart and mind behind the vision?

The boardroom was overflowing with people and the rest had gathered around the nearest microphones within the company. Narayana Murthy walked in, in his quiet and unobtrusive manner, and the room fell to a hushed silence. 'Twenty years ago when I thought of starting this company . . .,' began Narayana Murthy. Speaking of his company, he described where the company had begun, what the expectations of the founders has been, and how, due to the human capital that they had managed to secure and the liberalisation policy of the Indian government over the preceding seven years, Infosys had in every way surpassed original expectations (see Appendix 1 for consolidated financial summary).

Looking forward, Narayana Murthy noted that Infosys was on the verge of entering a new game. This challenge that the organisation had set for itself—of becoming a truly global company—had no precedence in the Indian software industry. There was no role model to follow. This new venture of Infosys Technologies would have different requirements of the organisation as a whole and of its top management. The restructuring of the top management group would involve two main movements. Narayana Murthy was going to stand down from the post of CEO. The new CEO would be Nandan Nilekani. Nilekani had been with the Infosys group since the founding of the organisation. With youth on his side, long experience and in-depth knowledge of the fabric of the company and a personal 'hands-on' approach, Nilekani would be the ideal person to guide Infosys through this transition.

Narayana Murthy went on to explain his new role in the organisation. He felt that the strategy of globalisation required at least one 'full time person' who would be available to sit down, think and plan for the future of the company; someone who could think long term and see the big picture without having the immediate pressures of targets, productivity measures and quality standards to be met. He planned to take on that role.

The Evolution of Infosys

Infosys was the product of one man's vision. An employee of Patni Computers Ltd in Pune, India, Narayana Murthy saw the enormous price differential between the pay for software engineering in India versus those in overseas markets such as the United States. The gap was so wide that even exporting manpower for on-site developments left a wide profit margin. The seeds of an entrepreneurial idea were sown. In his heart a die-hard socialist with strong leanings to the Left, Narayana Murthy, during his university years, had realised that the distribution of wealth must, almost without exception, be preceded by the creation of wealth. Thus, armed with his political identity, this business opportunity and six colleagues from Patni computers, he set about fulfilling his intention—to create a hundred 'Rupee millionaires' in India via the creation of an ethical business firm based on a highly competent and skilled workforce in the area of software development technology.

Infosys was set up in 1981 with a capital of Rs 10,000. When the company first went public in 1993 the stocks were offered at Rs 95. In 1998, after several 1:1 bonuses, the share price of Infosys was around Rs 2,610. Initial investors had multiplied their investment capital nearly eighty times in five years while Infosys had grown to become a leading player in the software services industry.

The First Phase: Body Shopping

When Infosys was founded it comprised seven employees—the original founders. The business model was entrepreneurial and flexible. The customers were mostly located in the United States. The entire process of software development was carried out at the client site. The employees of Infosys would go to the customer site and plan, prepare, develop and implement the system and train organisation members on-site. Only on project completion could the manpower resources be re-allocated to the next project. The profits of the organisation came from the price differential between the cost of software developers in the US versus the cost of employing, training and deploying equally qualified software engineers from India. The margin was large. For example, in the early 1980s, wages in Bangalore were one-tenth to one-fifteenth of those in California and the supply of English-speaking, trained software engineers was abundant in India, with 100,000 engineering graduates being produced annually in the country.

Infosys' core competency lay in its ability to leverage low cost manpower to create a product or service which had a demand in foreign markets where a local company had to spend a lot more to create the product or service in-house. This fundamental business logic remained as valid in 1998 as it had fifteen years earlier: the overall cost of software development in India was still less than 50 per cent of the cost in the United States.

The Second Phase: Offshore Software Development Centres (OSDCs)

Soon the Indian market was flooded with competitors also cashing in on the low wage environment. Infosys held its ground and position by markedly improving along the corporate skill dimensions of technical excellence and customer responsiveness.

As the business and the clientele grew, Infosys developed a new business model. It created an Offshore Software Development Centre (OSDC) in Bangalore, adjacent to its corporate office, where most of the actual software development work could be carried out. In essence, the OSDC functioned as an extension of the customers' information systems departments. Bringing work back from the client site enabled economies of both scale and skill, maximising internal learning of individual software engineers while keeping costs low. The physical separation also allowed for increased productivity through 24-hour operations.

Infosys set up a marketing office in the US and offices in London and around Europe. Most of Infosys' customers were located overseas, and activities such as marketing and customer servicing were carried out in the country of the customer. Most of the company's business followed the main stages of this process line. When a potential customer was identified in the overseas markets, it was approached by a business development manager (BDM) with the backing of the marketing division, which was located in the Infosys headquarters in Bangalore. Most contracts at this phase were finalised on the basis of estimated hourly rates.

In this phase, the company was internally focussed on building infrastructure and developing its skill base. Various support functions were created to aid operations, including a rigorous in-house training centre along with a compulsory training course which all new recruits had to undertake on joining Infosys. Over time, this training process became extensive and rigorous enough for a senior manager in a major American IT company to describe it as the 'equivalent to a full bachelor's training in computer software development at any of the top schools in the US'.

Infosys in 1998

Between 1993 and 1998, Infosys achieved a compounded annual sales growth of 65 per cent. By 1998, Infosys had grown in size from its original seven members to an employee base of 3,167 people. This number was rapidly expanding with Narayana Murthy leading the call for 'growth, growth, growth'. An overwhelming majority of Infosys' customers was still overseas. The business was directed and supported from its corporate headquarters in the Electronics City located just outside Bangalore. This centre also provided backend support for both marketing and sales plus the bulk of the software development. Infosys' marketing division, although supported from Bangalore, functioned from the US. There were a number of marketing personnel scattered over the UK and Continental Europe as well.

Below the top management team, the organisation was structured into eight departments (see Appendix 2). The eight Strategic Business Units (SBUs) were guided by two deputy managing directors, Nandan M. Nilekani and S. Gopalakrishnan. The SBUs were divided along the parameter of domain specific knowledge and skill development. Areas of development included financial services, engineering, etc. However, the movement of personnel, knowledge and information across the SBUs was fairly fluid, resulting in the actual structure (within the two operational arms) being closer to a matrix form. A competitive internal market had developed providing a forum for peer recognition of excellence and skill development. Project managers had free access to the skilled pool of software engineers and could interview anyone who appeared to have the right skills package for their team. Project managers had to then negotiate with each other to try and create the most effective teams for their proposed projects.

The other eight departments provided support functions to the board, to the company and to operations. An intranet 'Body of Knowledge' project launched by the education and research department provides an illustration of this support

Revenues by Geographical Segment

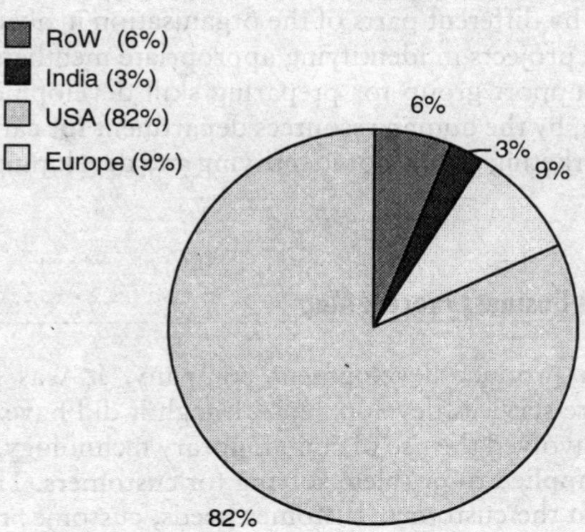

Revenues by Business Segment

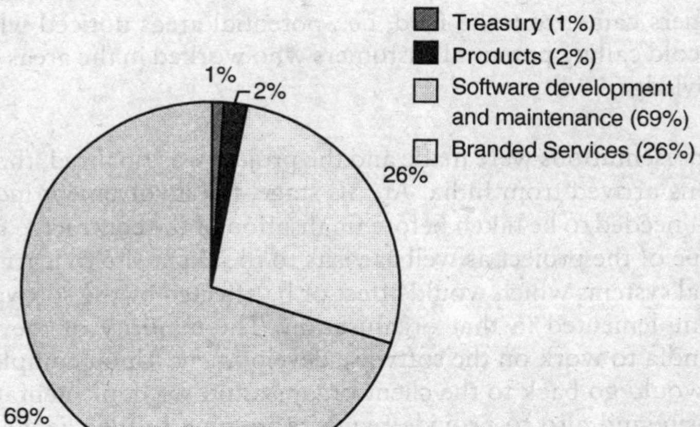

role. This project was designed to assist in the co-ordination of skills, resources, information, domain knowledge and process insights across all SBUs. Project teams were required to input any information learned on the job which might be relevant to future work of the company such as new skill developments, more efficient methodology and even potential sites for new projects. This information could then be used by different parts of the organisation in a variety of ways: by managers of future projects in identifying appropriate members for their teams, by the education support group for preparing skill development plans for the whole organisation, by the human resources department for career tracking, and by the sales and marketing groups for identifying and developing new customers.

Infosys Marketing Model and Business Process Map

Infosys was not a product development company. It was primarily in the business of software services development (though it did have a few products). Software services involved the use of contemporary technology, tools, principles and methodology applied to problem solving for customers. The entire focus in the business was on the customer, customer needs, customer requirements and solutions based on existing customer systems.

Marketing within Infosys was based on a relationship model with a strong emphasis on building long-term partnerships wherever possible. Information about customers came from the field, i.e., potential areas noticed while on the job, or from cold calling potential customers who worked in the areas of Infosys' domain knowledge.

Once initial presentations were made and the project was finalised, the first team of Infosyscions arrived from India. At this stage, the involvement included any decisions that needed to be taken before finalisation of the contract, e.g., delivery date and scope of the project as well as visits to the client site to learn about the organisational systems which would affect or be affected by the software project soon to be implemented in that organisation. The majority of the team then returned to India to work on the software development. Upon completion, part of the team would go back to the client organisation for implementation of the software on-site and also to provide requisite training to the client's operating personnel. Due to the immense level of travelling and transfer of knowledge that such a business process required, leading edge technology was not sufficient for being competitive—a high level of process discipline was also required (see Appendix 3).

> 'Success in this field is dependent on use of tools, methodologies, process orientation and discipline. Here processes are to be obeyed and followed in a disciplined manner. Bright and innovative people are used to "elevate" the process through innovation within the architecture of certain fixed processes.'
>
> —Nandan Nilekani

Infosys Quality Measures

Infosys had achieved two very demanding benchmarks in the arena of software quality standards.

- It was an ISO 9001 company. This certification was a rigorous, independently validated process. This universally recognised symbol of quality helped Infosys, a relatively small overseas software company, gain credibility and legitimacy with international clients.
- It had achieved the Carnegie Mellon University Software Engineering Institute Capability Maturity Model (SEI CMM), Level 4. There were only twenty-four companies in the world with such standards of proficiency in software design and development. Achieving CMM Level 4 signalled powerfully to the market that Infosys was positioning itself not as a low cost offshore alternative to leading American software developers, but rather as a high quality player in the global software development market, competing with the best in technical and managerial competency.

Embodying the Indian Middle Class

> 'We are a group of middle-class people with middle-class values who started this organisation to reflect these values. These are honesty, transparency and the highest ethical standards.'

In late May 1998, senior executives from the New York Stock Exchange and NASDAQ travelled to India to scout for listing prospects. Very high on their agenda was a visit to Infosys Technologies. 'I am after companies like Infosys. It is an American company in India', said Patrick Sutch, NASDAQ Asia-Pacific head. And herein lay perhaps one of the most unique features of the company—while it was very American in some aspects of its operation, it was very Indian in its heart and soul. Indeed, this symbiosis of the East and West was manifest both in the company's physical infrastructure and in its organisational processes and culture. As a middle manager of the company emphasised, Infosys not only had American process discipline but also an 'Indian middle-class' heart. The atmosphere around the company was unique, deliberately and carefully created by its leadership, to be 'just as it was in college'.

The company's head office and software development centre were located on five acres just outside Bangalore in the new Electronics City. The requirements to be on the Infosyscion team (once you had made it through the very rigorous selection procedure) were simple: forty-five hours of work a week. That was it. The perks and benefits of being on the team, besides the sheer pride of being a member of one of the hottest software development groups in the country, were numerous.

For an outsider, walking into Infosys was an interesting, if somewhat unsettling, experience. Unsettling because Infosys was a combination of many elements which ordinarily could not be combined. On the one hand, no visitor could overlook the fact that this was one of the most successful companies in India in terms of sheer growth, development, rising market capitalisation, shrewd management and sharp business acumen, having left most of India's software developers far behind as it graduated to the international league in terms of quality, performance and competitiveness. At the same time, one could not but notice that there was something strangely different in the fabric of the company. Something very humane.

The reception area led to a bridge over a little stream, running through a landscaped garden. The bridge led to the canteen, a little kiosk which sold cool drinks and snacks, and the basketball court. Almost all through the day, individuals or groups could be seen either deeply involved in some heated debate about the project on which the team was working or simply lying on the grass and having the quintessential '*chai*-break' (tea-break). Coffee and tea drinking was an essential feature of the daily life in Infosys, spilling over from the cultures of the engineering institutes where most Infosyscions spent their college years. Beverage stations were located on each floor and dispensed almost 2,400 cups of tea and coffee a day. One of the most important and highly awaited members of the community was the '*chaiwalla*' (tea boy) who travelled through the halls every few hours offering tea and coffee.

> 'The campus like workplace is certainly critical as the company mostly recruits freshers from engineering colleges and IITs. This environment helps in the transition from a semi-campus to a productive environment.'
>
> —S. Goparaju, project manager

As in college, except for scheduled meetings (the equivalent of classes), there was no fixed timing for anything. Infosyscions could work hours that suited them just as they could play in the hours that suited them. The 'campus' had basketball, volleyball and tennis courts, and people could be found playing these games at any time of the day. For the less competitive, there was a health club and for the more sedentary, the sauna. Artists could display their creations in the 'Galerie de Art Infosys' while internet junkies could spend their breaks at the cybercafe on the internet or the equally interesting intranet.

Inside the buildings, the office space was divided into large cubicle areas which were occupied by about three to six individuals normally working in the same department or project. The ceilings were high and each cubicle was bright and airy, so as to create an attractive work environment.

Like a space station of electronic activity, Infosys came alive at about 7 a.m., with the arrival of the first of many buses transporting Infosyscions from their homes in Bangalore city, located about 20 km away. All employees travelled in these buses. Breakfast, lunch, tea and dinner were served in the canteen where everybody—from directors to the tea boys—had their meals. Dormitories were available in the office for people to stay overnight if they got held up over a project deadline, or they needed to communicate with their US- or Europe-based operations over a telelink after 11 p.m., when the last bus left for the city.

Embodied within this physical architecture in which coconut trees—the symbol of rural South India—co-existed with cybercafes, the management ethic of the company reflected the same curious mix. No company in India had demonstrated greater aggressiveness in the market and greater willingness to take risks—by committing huge resources in building the OSDC, for example. Yet, in its financial structure, Infosys was ultra-conservative. Like all traditional middle-class Indians, Infosys abhorred debts. In strict financial terms, the company's balance sheet was sub-optimal. It could have clearly improved its return on equity through higher gearing. 'We take operating risks, and counterbalance it by avoiding financial risks', was the response of Mohandas

Pai, Infosys' CFO. Its considerable cash reserves were deployed in completely secure but low return deposits, contrary to the practices of most Indian companies who routinely used cash to make money in the lucrative market of inter-company loans. Its accounting practices reflected the same conservatism—expensing as much as possible each year and avoiding capitalisation by accepting lower annual profits.

In terms of behaviour, Infosys encouraged debate and challenge but not impoliteness or unpleasantness. 'You can be critical, but not discourteous', said Narayana Murthy. Modesty was a key value—with Narayana Murthy and his top management colleagues setting visible examples. While being enormously wealthy because of the steep appreciation of their equity holdings in the company, they all dressed modestly, drove ordinary cars and avoided all status symbols. Narayana Murthy, for example, travelled economy class on domestic flights (completely unthinkable not just for top managers but even for senior managers in Indian companies), and only recently had changed to a modest, domestically-made Opel Astra which he parked in the office parking lot wherever a slot was available. Typically, that was not a problem, however, since he was among the first to arrive at work. 'The others travel by bus, I have a private car. So, if I work like them, I must reach office before them', was his explanation.

Attracting and Retaining Human Capital

According to Narayana Murthy, the success of Infosys was due, above all else, to its ability to attract, develop and retain outstanding human capital. Given the nature of its business and its aspirations, Infosys had to compete on the strength of its people. This meant that its employees had to be experts, often the very best, in their technical abilities and in their domain knowledge related to their customer's businesses. To this end, Infosys invested heavily in recruitment, training and development to constantly upgrade the knowledge and skills of its people.

But, such expertise was also highly marketable in India. Domestic competitors were forever on the lookout to hire the best Infosyscions away, often offering them significantly higher levels of remuneration and rewards. Not having made the investments Infosys had made in the development of these people, it made economic sense for competitors to offer such pay rises. Consequently, Infosys constantly faced a dilemma: if they tried to keep people by matching competing offers, not only would they get no returns on their investments to upgrade employees' human capital, they would also have vitiated the internal environment and would have created a context that bred individual mercenaries rather than committed organisational members. But, if they did not match the offers, they were likely to lose their very best people.

In recent years, the problem had become even more acute because of an influx of prestigious multinational companies setting up their own software units in India. Beyond higher wages, these companies could also offer international career opportunities. And, inevitably, Infosyscions were their first targets.

Despite this constant threat of losing existing people and stiff competition in hiring new graduates, Infosys had done outstandingly well in both attracting and retaining its employees. The reason lay in the kind of people it attracted, and the organisational processes and cultures within which these people worked.

As a left over of the country's colonial legacy, public school English and sharp dressing were highly valued in corporate India. These were also the kind of people foreign companies found most attractive. As a result, middle-class men and women, brought up in traditional, conservative homes, found it difficult to join the elite league, despite their often superior academic records, technical skills and ingrained capacity for hard work. These were precisely the people that Infosys targetted and who found the middle-class values of Infosys so satisfying that they did not leave even when they were offered other attractive opportunities.

In the campus recruitment processes in the best technical and management institutions in India, competition for talent was fierce, with most companies trying to woo the top rankers with the highest salary offers. Infosys never offered the highest salaries in the market. It never went for the 'stars'—the most competitive graduates who survive all forms of competition, thrive on them, and typically leave as soon as the conditions are not entirely to their liking. In fact, its interview processes were designed to eliminate individuals who were overly aggressive or brash. Instead, Infosys relied on a written test to identify individuals with a high degree of technical competence and what the company called 'learnability'—willingness and ability to quickly learn new skills and grasp new materials—and an interview process to ferret out those who did not fit into Infosys' middle-class values. As a result, it recruited individuals who were modest, often to the point of shyness, and who had a deep respect and hunger for knowledge—which the company saw as the key to personal progress.

Immediately after joining Infosys, all professional recruits had to undertake a three-month-long training course. Designed to create a standard starting point of technical skills, this intensive course had a boot camp-like schedule and any student emerging successfully from this training developed technical skills equivalent to a graduate in the United States with a Bachelor's degree in Information Systems.

Beyond technical training, this course was also designed to serve as an intense process of socialisation into the values and culture of Infosys. For example, till the recent past, Narayana Murthy himself would be one of the first faculty members the new recruits would confront. And he would teach a very technical class, emphasising a core value of the company—that it was a company in which technical skills were highly valued. Even the CEO, despite being almost wholly involved in managing the company, still kept himself continuously updated in the latest technical developments in the field. Beyond this initial training, Infosyscions received regular training inputs, intermingled with their job assignments.

The Marvel of Stock Options

There is no doubt that the personal charisma of Narayana Murthy was a key reason why people did not leave Infosys. Undoubtedly one of the most visible and celebrated business leaders in the country externally, he was also an embodiment of the soul of the company internally—admired, held in a bit of awe, but, above all else, loved by almost all employees. Beyond his personal appeal, the norms and values of the company appealed to those who were carefully chosen because they shared them. But, beyond the social and emotional appeal, Infosys had also pioneered a system which ensured that employees had a full share of the fortunes of the firm. Modest and hard working as they were, Infosyscions were not poor.

In fact, by Indian standards, Infosys employees were very rich. That is because, in India, Infosys pioneered employee stock options. As the $1,000 investment in a company started in Narayana Murthy's apartment ballooned into a $70 mn company with a market capitalisation of nearly $962 mn, these stock options made a very large number of Infosyscions not merely rupee millionaires—Murthy's original dream—but millionaires many times over.

This was an innovation shaped by a dream. Indian regulations did not allow allocation of stocks to employees at below market rates. Yet, one of the founding premises of Infosys was to create wealth and to distribute it among those who helped create it. To overcome regulatory barriers, Infosys created a special trust at the time of going public and allocated a large part of its equity to this trust at the original issue price. It was out of this equity pool that stock options were granted to employees. With the stock appreciating by over 140 per cent annually, and by a staggering 270 per cent over 1997 alone, not only did these options fulfill Narayana Murthy's socialist dreams, they also became a major instrument for the company to attract and retain the best local talent.

The Challenge of Going Global

Despite the spectacular progress in the 1990s, it was clear to the Infosys management that business-as-usual was not a viable option. This was because of the three key challenges confronting the company—commoditisation, cost and competition.

> 'There is the legendary trend in the software industry within India to commoditise all its business. The only discriminant in a commodity business is price. It is extrarordinary.'
>
> —Nandan Nilekani

It wasn't only in the software business that commoditisation was a permanent threat. The same phenomenon was at work in a variety of other export-oriented industries such as textiles, garments, engineering and so on. Western buyers typically viewed India as a source of low cost, standardised products and services. In the software industry, body shopping epitomised this commodity approach—with people as the ultimate commodity. As little garages and back rooms were converted into outfits for recruiting, training and exporting young software professionals cheaply, the market was labeled more and more as a source of commodity offering, with an ever-growing pressure on price and, therefore, on margins. To do business internationally, this was an inherent liability of Indianness.

At the same time, costs were constantly rising. In India, salaries constituted 30 per cent of the revenue of software companies. And, salaries were rising annually by about 25 per cent, increasing costs by about 7.5 per cent every year. Travel and related direct expenses constituted another 10 to 12 per cent of revenues.

This figure too was going up by about 10 per cent annually, contributing another 2 per cent to annual cost increases.

What this meant was that a company's margins inevitably declined sharply unless per capita revenues went up to offset the cost increase. Besides, just offsetting the cost increase was not good enough; to invest in the physical and technological infrastructure necessary to keep up with the rapidly changing business, a company had to constantly increase its margins simply to retain its place.

Finally, intense competition was perhaps the most critical of these three challenges. 'The industry as a whole is teaching the customers how to negotiate', said Nilekani. 'It is destroying itself.' He offered an example. In 1995, a major American disk drive manufacturer had almost finalised a contract with Infosys based on a working rate of $18 per hour for work to be done in the OSDC. All negotiations were through and the representatives from the company had come down to India to do a final facility check. On their visit, they explored other software developers, with the knowledge and help of Infosys, as a general investigation of the standards of the industry and so forth. One of Infosys' main competitors made them an offer of $9 per hour for the work—exactly half of Infosys' offer. The company representatives returned to Infosys with the deal in hand. In these circumstances Infosys offered a 10 per cent discount but could not offer any further price reductions as that would be a negative signal about Infosys: if they could do the job at $9 per hour, why were they offering $18 in the first place? As a result, the American company shifted its business to the competitor.

The strategy of globalisation was Infosys' response to the pressures of commoditisation, costs and competition. The only way to protect and enhance margins was to move up the value curve. Globalisation was seen by the company as the essential requirement for doing this and for staying ahead of the commoditisation envelope.

Value-based Selling: The New Buzzword at Infosys

In essence, Infosys competed in two market segments. One segment was based on a cost-plus selling model where the main competitors were other Indian software companies. The main characteristics of this segment were a customer with an RFP which was filled up to specification. The number of hours were quoted, together with costs, expenses, salaries and profit margins. This calculation led to a fixed price which was presented to the customer. In 1998, this cost-plus segment accounted for a significant majority of Infosys' total revenues.

The remaining revenues came from a value-based model. Here the main competitors were foreign-based, such as Cambridge Technology Partners, Andersen Consulting, and Sapient and Keane. In this segment, prices depended on the value that the customer derived from the project. 'Because of the value that a customer perceives in the product, they are willing to pay on that basis. There is negligible negotiation based on the actual specifics of inputs from Infosys in terms of hours or manpower. Infosys has articulated that it must have a 20 per cent margin of profitability after tax for the next five years. To meet this, the model of selling must move from cost-based to value-based', said Nandan Nilekani.

To achieve this move up the value curve, Infosys was focussing on two key tasks:

- The creation of international brand equity, and
- The localisation of its organisation at the customer interface.

Creating Brand Equity

To move to a value-based model, creation of brand equity was the key. Within India, Infosys had a very high brand equity, both as a supplier and as an employer. To develop a similar brand equity in foreign markets was the challenge. Access to and recognition in the niche within which the chief information officers gathered their information in these markets was, therefore, of great importance.

A listing on NASDAQ was the first step the company took to respond to this challenge. The enhanced prestige of a US listing was an attempt to potentially provide a degree of increased comfort to Infosys customers and prospective employees in the global market. The US$ Employee Stock Offer Plan (ESOP) helped attract and retain high quality, customer-interface staff in the talent-competitive markets of the US, Europe and the Far East. This listing also helped provide additional financial resources to part-fund marketing and brand creation efforts. Infosys also intended to maintain its historical growth rates over the next few years, and needed the financial resources to create new technical and physical infrastructure.

The second aspect was the creation of high quality branded services which would result in high productivity for customers. Four such services had already been developed: In 2000 (essentially to support Y2K projects), Internet Consulting, Re-engineering, and Maintenance.

Finally, perhaps the most powerful way of building global brand equity lay in developing domain-specific knowledge. Infosys was focussing its attention on providing services to a few industries in an attempt to become specialists in industry-specific technologies and applications. Financial services, health care, telecommunications and engineering had been selected as the focal industries and the company was attempting to develop new clientele from these industries so as to expand its domain knowledge and expertise. As companies like EDS, Andersen Consulting and others had shown, project size and value inevitably increased when a software services supplier developed such domain-specific reputation.

> 'Infosys must have a clear value proposition. If three to five years from now, when there is a $25 mn project, if the CIO were to ask his or her next in command whether the company had received the Infosys proposal, then I would feel that we have arrived.'
>
> —Narayana Murthy

Localising the Face of Infosys

One of the main challenges facing Infosys in the global market was a paucity of location-wise domain knowledge within the home countries of its customers, together with lack of know-how in customer relation matters. To succeed globally, the company had to develop insider positions within the networks of business relationships in each key international market. Twenty per cent of the business effort needed to be near the customer, e.g., requirement definition, presentation, sign off, installation, etc. Proximity Development Centres (PDC) represented the company's proposed solution to this challenge. It was intended that PDCs would be staffed predominantly by local people in an attempt to provide an image of a local company. The first PDCs were scheduled to be opened in early 1999 in Fremont and Boston, consisting of people who were local, acclimatised physically and socially, who had a high awareness of the local culture and could build relationships easily.

As the front end centres developed and created more business, the development of new back end centres in various cost effective regions of the world was envisioned. In the long-term strategy of becoming totally global, the opportunity to create back end centres at more viable cost locations such as Brazil, Mexico and Costa Rica were being looked into.

A nagging question remained, however: Could Infosys retain its 'Indian middle-class values' while becoming a global company? Could it find people around the world who would cherish these values? 'Our core values are honesty, courtesy, transparency and fairness to all stakeholders. There is nothing uniquely Indian or middle class about these values', said a Infosyscion. 'They are universal values of a majority of people working for our customers and of those who can be our employees.' But, was this realistic? Was it possible that to be successful as a global company, Infosys had to first stop being what had made it so successful till this stage of its evolution?

APPENDIX 1

A Historical Perspective

(Rs lakh)

Particulars for the year	*1981–82*	*1993–94*	*1994–95*	*1995–96*	*1996–97*	*1997–98*	*1998–99*
Revenue	11.63	3008.47	5770.43	9341.34	14380.77	26036.57	51273.83
Operating profit (PBIDT)	–	970.71	1985.97	3395.36	5005.78	8861.15	19174.84
Interest	–	4.64	–	–	61.09	–	–
Depreciation	–	80.88	459.53	863.42	1051.64	2274.82	3589.30
Provision for taxation	–	76	194.00	431.00	524.97	550.00	2294.00
Profit after tax from ordinary activities	3.78	809.19	1332.44	2100.94	3368.06	6036.33	13291.54
Dividend	–	117.32	231.39	362.93	399.23	702.92	1210.76
Return on average net worth (%)	96.88	39.61	29.71	29.53	34.96	42.24	54.16
Return on average capital employed (PBIT/average capital employed) (%)	96.88	43.14	31.79	33.12	40.16	46.09	63.51
As at end of the year							
Share capital	0.1	335.11	725.88	725.88	725.88	1601.74	3306.96
Reserves and surplus	3.78	2535.00	5519.92	7257.94	10557.63	15693.99	54136.16
Loan funds	–	–	633.91	426.06	–	–	–
Gross block	0.02	827.38	2532.01	4685.75	7129.16	10513.91	16892.38
Capital investment	0.02	712.71	2523.05	1555.49	2731.04	3440.97	7167.92
Net current assets	6.27	1394.34	3246.95	4117.17	5419.85	9722.64	47296.04
Debt-equity ratio	–	–	0.1	0.05	–	–	–
Market capitalisation	–	19101.50	34842.00	35597.10	73104.17	296342.23	967280.00
Per share data							
Earnings from ordinary activities (Rs)**	377.77	2.45	4.03	6.35	10.18	18.25	40.19
Dividend per share (Rs)	–	3.5	4.5	5	5.5	6	7.5
Book value (Rs)**	383.1	9	19	24	34	52	174

Note: The above figures are based on Indian GAAP.

* 1 lakh = 100,000.

** On a fully diluted basis and adjusted for bonus issue of 1:1 during 1994–95, 1997–98 and 1998–99.

APPENDIX 3

Distribution of Work Between OSDC (Back End) and Client Site (Front End) in a Typical Project Cycle

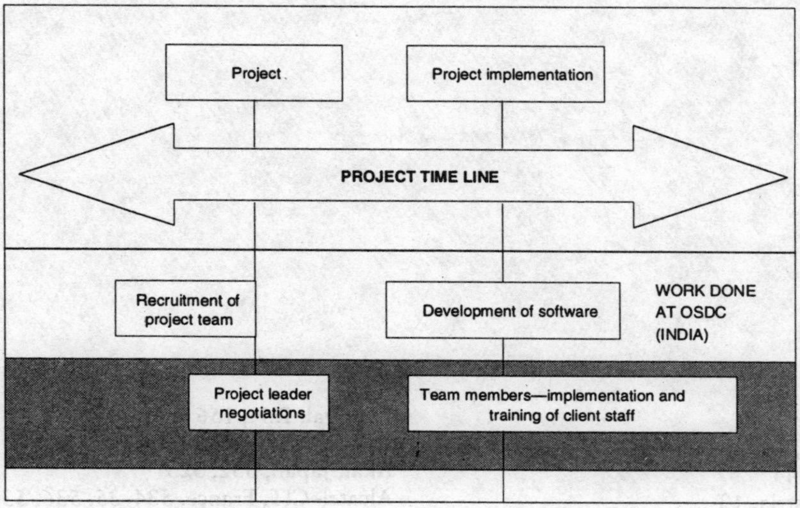

INDEX